REDRESS

REDRESS

Ireland's Institutions and Transitional Justice

edited by

KATHERINE O'DONNELL,
MAEVE O'ROURKE AND JAMES M. SMITH

UNIVERSITY COLLEGE DUBLIN PRESS
PREAS CHOLÁISTE OLLSCOILE BHAILE ÁTHA CLIATH
2022

First published 2022
by University College Dublin Press
UCD Humanities Institute, Room H103,
Belfield,
Dublin 4

www.ucdpress.ie

ISBN 978-1-910820-89-6 pb

CIP data available from the British Library

Typeset in Dublin by Gough Typesetting Limited, Dublin
Text design by Lyn Davies
Cover Image © Alison Lowry
Printed in Scotland on acid-free paper by Bell & Bain Ltd,
303 Burnfield Road, Thornliebank, Glasgow G46 7UQ

Contents

Contents

Acknowledgements

This edited collection emerged initially from a two-day international conference entitled 'Towards Transitional Justice: Recognition, Truth-telling, and Institutional Abuse in Ireland,' held at Boston College on 1–2 November 2018. A double special issue of *Éire-Ireland: An Interdisciplinary Journal of Irish Studies* [55:1–2, (Spring/Summer 2020)] including fourteen essays by participants at the conference followed thereafter. Thirteen of those essays are reprinted in this volume, together with seven new essays, also by participants at the conference, as well as four long-form journalism essays addressing related content brought together and reprinted side-by-side for the first time. We thank all our contributors for their patience and support throughout.

The financial support of Boston College, and in particular the Institute for the Liberal Arts, the Office of the Provost, the Dean of the Morrissey College of Arts and Sciences, and the Irish Studies Program, was generous and absolutely necessary in underwriting the conference. We also acknowledge the Consul General of Ireland in Boston and Ireland's Department of Children and Youth Affairs for supporting the conference, and in particular the latter for funding the attendance of four representatives from the survivor-based Collaborative Forum.

We are also grateful to the Board of the Irish American Cultural Institute for allowing us to reprint the essays that previously appeared in *Éire-Ireland* and to Dr Vera Kreilkamp and Dr Nicholas Wolf, the journal's co-editors, for their assistance with the earlier publication. Likewise, we would like to thank the following publications for granting permission to reprint material in this volume: *Human Rights Quarterly*, *The Irish Examiner*, *The London Review of Books*, *The New York Times* and *The New York Review of Books*.

For editorial assistance, we are pleased to acknowledge the work of Emily Lyons (Boston College) and Dr Colleen Taylor (University of Notre Dame).

Many thanks are due to Alison Lowry for granting permission to use her art from the exhibition *(A)Dressing Our Hidden Truths* as the image for our book cover and to Dr Audrey Whitty and the National Museum of Ireland for supporting and facilitating that process.

Ours is a large book and we want to acknowledge the subvention support received from the Boston College Morrissey College of Arts and Sciences and The National University of Ireland that enabled this publication.

Finally, we thank Noelle Moran and Conor Graham at UCD Press and all the team who worked so hard on the production of this volume. We would also like to thank the dozens of peer reviewers who generously gave their expertise to read and advise on individual chapters, and the reviewers from UCD Press.

The Editors are donating all royalties in the name of survivors and all those affected by Ireland's carceral institutions and family separation to the charity Empowering People in Care (EPIC).

Katherine O'Donnell, Maeve O'Rourke and James M. Smith
March 2022

Editors' Introduction
REDRESS: Ireland's Institutions and Transitional Justice[1]

Katherine O'Donnell, Maeve O'Rourke and James M. Smith

You had the church's representative, you had the solicitor and a barrister, and then you had the judge and a psychiatrist. It was adversarial, and you felt like you were on your own… The church had said that it was a fantasy what had happened to me – that I was sexually abused in that institution – and I had to relive it. So, in a way, having to relive it, it's a bit like, you know, you're put on an operating table and you are cut open and you're left there to fester.
—Mary Lodato, *Redress: Breaking the Silence*[2]

These records are an invaluable tool to assist Survivors establish their identity and family reunification… I think it's important that survivors' families should have access to this information as it can help them understand how their childhood impacted their lives…
—Carmel McDonnell Byrne, Submission to the Joint Education Committee regarding the Retention of Records Bill 2019[3]

These precious records should be treated as a treasure and a gift. We must learn from the past mistakes we made in our society and help to lay safeguards that we will need to protect the children of the state into the future. We should not be afraid to face the past. If we lock away for seventy-five years the very information that could be vital to our present and future generations… we cannot deal with the present and future in an informed manner.
—Tom Cronin, Submission to the Joint Education Committee regarding the Retention of Records Bill 2019[4]

In my position, you're very dependent on the state to see you right, but it feels like all Ireland is doing is abusing us again… they haven't booked anyone or brought anyone to justice. It doesn't surprise me that they have never prosecuted the nuns. There is still this ideology—they're nuns, and Christian Brothers, we're Magdalenes or Industrial School children… The Government doesn't want to offend the Church. The Government is persecuting us and violating us still, by bowing to the people who did this to us.

—Elizabeth Coppin, Witness Statement
to the UN Committee Against Torture[5]

REDRESS: Ireland's Institutions and Transitional Justice explores the ways in which Ireland – North and South – treats individuals and families who suffered in the twentieth-century 'architecture of containment.'[6] This collection of international and multi-disciplinary essays engages with that architecture – a legislative, bureaucratic and judicial apparatus supporting an array of interdependent institutions including Magdalene Laundries,[7] Mother and Baby Homes, County Homes/Workhouses, industrial and reformatory schools and the nation's closed and secretive adoption system – used to confine women and children across both jurisdictions.[8] Far from being historical, these structures, which gave rise to widespread and systematic abuses in the past, continue as a political arrangement that exerts power over survivors, adopted people and generations of relatives, and over the remains and memories of the dead. As we mark the centenary of both jurisdictions on this island, this collection examines the States' so-called 'redress' schemes and the investigations and statements of apology that accompanied them over the past two decades. Rather than focusing solely on one investigation or report, *REDRESS* considers how a transitional justice approach might assist those personally affected, policy makers, the public, and academics to evaluate the complex ways in which both the Republic and Northern Ireland (and other states in a comparative context) have responded to their histories of institutional provision and family separation, and to the legacy of continuing harms attending such provision. Ultimately, we ask what constitutes justice and, moreover, how might democracy evolve if survivors' experiences and expertise were allowed to lead?

Seamus Heaney notes that dictionaries record multiple meanings for the word 'Redress.' His interest lies not only in redress as '[r]eparation of, satisfaction or compensation for, a wrong sustained or the loss resulting from this,' but also in exploring an obsolete use of the word: 'To set (a person or a thing) upright again; to raise again to an erect position. Also fig. to set up again, restore, re-establish.'[9] Heaney spoke about poetry's capacity to act as a form of 'redress' that is 'an upright, resistant, and self-bracing entity within the general flux and flex of language.'[10] Like Heaney, the authors gathered in this collection are motivated by the understanding that their intellectual work is in service to a programme of cultural and political realignment, reaffirming the ideals of equality enshrined in the 1916 proclamation of the Irish Republic, or indeed in any egalitarian democracy. Responding to dominant narratives coming from established powers in Ireland, these essays provide a more robust knowledge of our recent past and a better understanding of our present, in order to imagine and facilitate a more inclusive future.

Both the idea for this collection and the majority of the essays originated in a conference, 'Towards Transitional Justice: Recognition, Truth-telling, and Institutional Abuse in Ireland,' which we organised at Boston College (BC) in early November 2018.[11] Over two days scholars, policy makers, survivors, people affected by adoption, artists and advocates came together to consider the nature of both the Republic and Northern Ireland's responses to Magdalene Laundries, County Homes/Workhouses, Mother and Baby Homes, child residential institutions, child foster care and the closed, secret and coercive adoption system. As academics and members of the Justice for Magdalenes Research (JFMR)[12] advocacy group, for the past decade the editors of this collection have endeavoured to place the motto of survivors, 'nothing about us, without us,' at the centre of our research and activism regarding the class, race, disability and gender-based abuses so evident in Irish carceral institutions. We have attempted always to ensure that our work is led by survivors' experiences, perspectives and critique, and we have consciously continued such practice in putting this collection together. Reflecting this commitment, the first essay in this book gathers testimony from eight survivors – Mary Harney, Mari Steed, Caitríona Palmer, Terri Harrison, Rosemary Adaser, Conrad Bryan, Susan Lohan and Connie Roberts, residents of Ireland, the United Kingdom and the United States – who participated in a round-table discussion at the conference in Boston. Essays by Patricia Lundy, Laura McAtackney and Caitríona Palmer, among others, also foreground survivors' voices and survivor testimony is featured in a number of long-form journalism essays brought together and reprinted in this collection for the first time.

Over the past 20-plus years the Irish State has initiated a plethora of inquiries into twentieth century institutional and gender-based abuses, leading to the publication of a series of lengthy final reports, including the Commission to Inquire into Child Abuse (*Ryan Report*, 2009), the Inter-Departmental Committee to establish the facts of State interaction with the Magdalen Laundries (*McAleese Report*, 2013), the Symphysiotomy Inquiry (*Harding Clark Report*, 2016), and most recently the Commission of Investigation into Mother and Baby Homes and Certain Related Matters (*MBHCOI Final Report*, 2020). Released to the public in January 2021, the latter Report addresses the experiences of the 56,000 unmarried mothers and 57,000 children it estimates spent time in the fourteen institutions and four sample County Homes under investigation. The Report contends that some 9,000 children, or 15% of those in the institutions examined, died while in the State's care.[13] The Commission failed to identify burial locations for a large proportion of these children, however, and its Report contains no recommendations to Government regarding the need to find and identify missing relatives.[14] The Report concludes that '[t]he costs involved would probably be prohibitive' and '[i]n cases where the mothers were in the homes when the child died, it is possible that they knew the burial arrangements or would have been told if they asked.'[15] The Report asserts, moreover, that 'there is no evidence' to suggest that 'women were forced to enter mother and baby homes' and 'very little evidence' to support claims that 'children were forcibly taken from their mothers.'[16] Survivors have roundly criticised the Commission's findings,[17] the manner in which their testimony was taken (without a transcript being made or provided, and without notice of the Commission's decision to destroy all audio recordings),[18] the Commission's clear disregard of testimony provided by hundreds of people to the Confidential Committee,[19] and the Commission's refusal throughout its work to provide survivors and adopted people with their own personal data or records concerning deceased relatives.[20] The Commission's findings were reflected in the Government's proposal for a 'Mother and Baby Institutions Payment Scheme' published in November 2021.[21] Among other things, the proposed scheme does not recognise the harm of forced or unlawful family separation, per se, in that it excludes any person institutionalised for less than six months before being separated from their mother, it does not offer payment for forced labour in thirteen of the fourteen Mother and Baby institutions examined, and it fails entirely to recognise abuse of children who were 'boarded out' and the forced and otherwise unlawful family separation perpetrated in settings beyond the institutions investigated by the Commission. Ultimately, the Irish High Court declared on 17 December 2021 that eight survivors, including Philomena Lee and Mary Harney, were denied fair procedures by the Commission, specifically the right to comment on draft findings and that some of the Commission's findings did not accurately reflect the survivors' evidence. The government deposited a copy of the High Court declaration in the Oireachtas Library alongside the Commission's Final Report and also posted a list of the impugned paragraphs alongside the Commission's Report online.[22] Along with those directly affected, academics and cultural commentators too are now offering increasingly critical analyses of the nearly 3,000-page Report, early examples of which are signalled in this collection in the contributions of Maeve O'Rourke, James Gallen, and Máiréad Enright and Sinéad Ring.[23]

This collection, however, underlines a much larger point: namely that the aforementioned inquiries have frequently hampered or excluded other avenues of accountability that should ordinarily be available in the democratic state. Sequestering documents and testimony that are crucial sources of evidence, these investigations have largely operated in private. They have failed to use constitutional or human rights law as a framework of analysis, or as a guide to ensuring procedural fairness for all. Survivors and relatives of the deceased, and frequently also the police, have been prohibited from accessing the inquiries' archives. The Director of Public Prosecutions brought charges against one person only in relation to the contents of the *Ryan Report*.[24] Neither the Magdalene Laundries nor the Mother and Baby Homes have been the subject of criminal cases. Survivors' access to the civil courts has been stymied by myriad procedural barriers and a lack of access to relevant evidence and to affordable legal aid. The State has made conditional offers of financial redress to survivors in exchange for their silence and/or their agreement not to pursue wrongdoers in court.[25] The State, furthermore, still denies adopted people statutory entitlements to their own identity and early life and adoption files. The essays in the section entitled 'Irish State (In)Justice,' notably by Colin Smith and April Duff, as well as by O'Rourke, Enright and Ring, and Gallen lay bare these substantive deficits in contemporary state practice.

Northern Ireland's Historical Institutional Abuse Inquiry (*Hart Report*, 2017) similarly denied many child abuse survivors legal representation, access to records or an opportunity to submit questions for the Chair to ask of witnesses – in direct contrast to the alleged wrongdoers' entitlements. Patricia Lundy's essay in the section entitled 'Children in State Care' details these and further causes of re-traumatisation, while Gordon Lynch's chapter towards the end of the book exposes flaws in the Hart inquiry's historical analysis. An opportunity to learn from previous practice North and South, to adopt human-rights-compliant investigative practices and to establish a more accurate history, now arises with the recent publication of an academic research report on Mother and Baby Homes and Magdalene Laundries in Northern Ireland[26] and the Northern Ireland Executive's subsequent appointment of an independent Truth Recovery Design Panel to co-design with survivors and relatives the framework for a state investigation into Magdalene Laundry, Mother and Baby, and Workhouse institutions.[27] As of November 2021, the Executive Office has taken responsibility for implementing all of the recommendations of this independent process, beginning with the establishment of a survivors' and relatives' Forum to influence and monitor, among other measures: the progression of records preservation and access legislation, the establishment of an Independent Panel of investigation and statutory Public Inquiry, and the administration of a wide-ranging redress process.[28] Notably, the academic research report by Leanne McCormick and Sean O'Connell found significant cross-border movement of women and children, including the adoption in the Republic of Ireland of children born in Northern Irish institutions and the detention in Northern Ireland's Magdalene Laundries of girls and women ordinarily resident in the Republic.[29] This suggests an urgent need for additional comparative study of cross-border, inter- and intra-national traffic of formerly institutionalised women and children and of the obstacles they and their families continue to face in the pursuit of justice.

This collection addresses the question of what these state practices mean for those most directly affected and for our proclaimed democracy. We believe that the concept of transitional justice can contribute to redressing these deficits. The United Nations defines transitional justice as 'the full range of processes and mechanisms associated with a society's attempts to come to terms with a legacy of large-scale past abuses, in order to ensure accountability, serve justice and achieve reconciliation.'[30] Scholars frequently describe a transitional justice approach as comprising four principles or pillars: namely, truth-telling, accountability, redress and reparation, and guarantees of non-recurrence.[31] Operating simultaneously, these four elements are said to provide a holistic method of responding to large-scale and widespread injustice.[32] The transitional justice approach has been deployed in numerous countries seeking to move from a situation of mass violence and human rights violations (engendered, for example, by civil war, apartheid or violent insurgency) to the establishment of robust democratic institutions and processes.[33] Significant academic attention has been paid to the potential of transitional justice measures in Northern Ireland as a way to come to terms with the impacts of the three-decades-long Troubles.[34] More recently, and with great relevance to the subject matter of this volume, transitional justice scholarship has started to consider how the model could be applied to systematic institutional abuse and injustice in settled democracies: for example, the removal of indigenous children from their families in Canada and Australia, or the forced migration of children from the United Kingdom to both aforementioned jurisdictions, and these children's further mistreatment in residential institutions.[35] Essays by Gordon Lynch, Rosemary Nagy and Shurlee Swain offer the opportunity to learn from international comparisons and the inter- and intra-national dimensions of state responses to historic institutional abuse.

We are conscious, however, of the real danger that the language of transitional justice may be co-opted by the state to justify offering a 'specialised,' selective and limited justice model that in fact stymies accountability by denying access to established 'democratic' institutions such as the courts, the coroners' system, academic research and cultural and artistic expression and participation. Essays by James Gallen, Fionnuala Ní Aoláin and Ruth Rubio Marín in the section entitled 'Transitional Justice: Opportunities, Limits' explore both the potential and the pitfalls of employing the principles of transitional justice as a guiding practice with which to evaluate state institutional responses.

With the pros and cons of this method in mind, the BC conference focused on a series of questions: What, if anything, might the concept of transitional justice offer with regard to Ireland's history of institutional and adoption-related abuse? Can it act as a lens to help us better understand this abuse and its legacy, including the state's (non-)responses to survivors' needs and demands? Is it an avenue by which alternative framings and responses to the past could be designed? Asking these questions provoked a series of further ones, such as: What is it that Ireland still needs to learn about its treatment of women, children and others marginalised by poverty, sexism, racism, ageism and ableism both in the past and in the present? What do the methods with which Ireland has attempted to deal with its past tell us about the state's current approach to power, dependency and incarceration? What are the implications of recent state-sponsored investigations into institutional abuse for contemporary Irish society, including children in foster care, young adults leaving state residential care settings, older people in nursing homes, psychiatric patients, people in Direct Provision, and those in prison? What can Ireland learn from transitional justice responses to similar recent histories and contemporary problems in other jurisdictions? Do transitional justice processes have the potential to assist Ireland in building a more impactful human rights infrastructure, thereby helping to guarantee non-recurrence of previous failures? The essays in this collection consider these questions from different perspectives, disciplines and methodologies.

A key aspiration in advancing this collection was to set an innovative agenda for Irish Studies by proposing that academics studying Ireland (both North and South) could benefit from using the framework of transitional justice as an evaluative lens to understand and address not just the suffering caused by colonial sectarian conflict but also the violence and civil liberties violations wrought by post/colonial theocratic regimes. In using the slashed term 'post/colonial,' we refer to the differing experiences of colonial settlements on either side of the Irish border whereby the Irish Free State, later the Republic of Ireland, won independence from the United Kingdom a hundred years ago and the six counties of Northern Ireland currently operate under a peace settlement that is facing new challenges as the UK negotiates life outside the EU. Widespread across both jurisdictions, systems of institutional confinement and forced family separation functioned for most of the twentieth century imposing social control over tens of thousands of vulnerable citizens, approximately 1% of the Republic's population in 1950 according to one study.[36] And, as examined in essays by Paul Michael Garrett, Mary Burke and Claire

McGettrick, codes of silence, secrecy and shaming related to social reproduction in general, and female sexuality in particular, also persist today.

As the 'Decade of Centenaries' draws to a close in 2022, there will be a focus on the violence of the War of Independence, Civil War and Partition.[37] These centenaries offer an opportunity to reflect on the other systematic forms of violence and abuse that have marked our island and cultures during the past 100 years. The essays in this book – representing diverse and interdisciplinary academic fields, including law, international human rights, sociology, philosophy and ethics, literature, history, performance studies, social work, archaeology, anthropology and heritage studies, journalism and creative writing – consider whether the principles of transitional justice might guide both the Republic of Ireland and Northern Ireland through a transition, from societies traumatised by violent conflict and severe social oppression to more stable societies that embrace diversity and address socio-economic disadvantage.[38] The essays that follow also consider whether practices implied in the concept of transitional justice hold the potential to mobilise a shift away from pervasive gendered, class and racial injustice, and a history rooted in the privatisation of educational, health and social welfare services and their administration by the Roman Catholic Church in particular. Contributions by McGettrick, Palmer and Lundy, among others, examine whether transitional justice can provide a route to the dignified treatment of survivors, and the generations of their families that continue to suffer the effects of our abusive past.

Two final questions informed our approach to the conference and this book. First, how do we as academics engage with the voices of institutional abuse survivors; in other words, how might our scholarship be guided by their testimony? Many essays in this book affirm survivors' truth. In addition to the compilation of survivor testimony, we include a selection of long-form journalism by prominent writers, including Dan Barry, Anne Enright, Conall Ó Fátharta and Clair Wills. Their crucial interventions foregrounded survivors' voices and in doing so drew international media attention that helped bring informed public pressure to counter what Katherine O'Donnell in her essay defines as the belligerent ignorance of the Irish establishment. Our decision to begin this collection with the 'Truth-Telling' section is meant to ensure that readers recall survivors' experiences as they engage with the later essays. Second, what are the roles that the humanities and social sciences might play in imagining a flourishing Ireland and facilitating its emergence? Transitional justice has generally been considered the work of legal and political scholars and centres for the study of human rights. With these essays, we seek to set a fresh agenda for the field of Irish Studies that, in addition to law and politics, would bring studies in the humanities (e.g. Mary Burke, Laura McAtackney, Katherine O'Donnell, Emilie Pine et al., James M. Smith), social sciences (e.g. Paul Michael Garrett, Patricia Lundy, Claire McGettrick) and the creative arts (e.g. Emer O'Toole, Caitríona Palmer, Connie Roberts) into conversation around a new set of coordinates. In particular, 'truth-telling' and 'guarantees of non-recurrence' connect to the work of many colleagues in the wider Irish Studies community whose scholarship focuses on the role of testimony-gathering, story-telling, life-writing, oral history, access to records, archival research and curation, genealogy, survivor culture, memorialisation, heritage, curriculum design, education and digital scholarship. We also see a pedagogical imperative in transitional justice that has the potential to reinvigorate the work we do in our respective classrooms. Teaching students about Ireland's treatment of the socially marginalised combats contemporary complacency and creates a bulwark that, we hope, will help ensure non-recurrence of such harms in the future.[39] In rooting our pedagogies in new interdisciplinary approaches orientated toward social justice for all we will continue to offer dynamic rationales for the value of a liberal arts education.[40]

To return to Seamus Heaney's consideration of poetry's potential to enact redress, we consider that academic activism meets a similar challenge and opportunity:

> to place a counter-reality in the scales – a reality which may be only imagined but which nevertheless has weight because it is imagined within the gravitational pull of the actual and can therefore hold its own and balance out against the historical situation.[41]

Like poetry, scholarly work is too often dismissed as ineffectual in the push towards progressive change. This collection of essays presents 'a glimpsed alternative, a revelation of potential that is denied or constantly threatened by circumstances.'[42] We hope that the alternatives proffered might present new imaginative standards for our democracy in the twenty-first century.

TRUTH-TELLING

One

Testimony

Mary Harney, Mari Steed, Caitríona Palmer,
Terri Harrison, Rosemary Adaser, Conrad Bryan,
Susan Lohan and Connie Roberts[1]

What follows are excerpts from a public roundtable discussion among individuals with experience of Ireland's institutional and gender-based abuses and moderator James M. Smith at the international conference entitled Towards Transitional Justice: Recognition, Truth-Telling and Institutional Abuse in Ireland, held on 2 November 2018 at Boston College.[2]

All of the discussants have previously written and spoken publicly about their experiences, and all have provided the editors with their consent to publish their contributions to the roundtable. The participants were Mary Harney, Maine resident and civil-rights activist, painter and educator; Mari Steed, Virginia resident, co-founder of Adoption Rights Alliance and executive committee member of Justice for Magdalenes Research (JFMR); Caitríona Palmer, Washington, DC, resident, journalist and author; Terri Harrison, Dublin resident, musician and community organiser; Rosemary Adaser, London resident, activist and founder and CEO of the Association of Mixed Race Irish (AMRI); Conrad Bryan, London resident, activist and member of the AMRI; Susan Lohan, Dublin resident and co-founder of Adoption Rights Alliance; and Connie Roberts, New York resident, poet and lecturer at Hofstra University.

Terri, Rosemary, Conrad, Mary and Susan were, at the time of the conference, members of the Collaborative Forum for Former Residents of Mother and Baby Homes and Related Institutions established by Ireland's Department of Children and Youth Affairs in 2018. The Government published the Collaborative Forum's summary recommendations on 16

April 2019, although it declined to publish the forum's report in full. Readers will note references to the Collaborative Forum in the text below.

The audience for this discussion included not just the conference participants and attendees but also survivors and other members of the public who watched via live stream on the FJMR Facebook group page and engaged in their own conversation in response over Facebook and Twitter.

I. Mary Harney

My name is Mary Harney. I am the proud daughter of Margaret 'Peggy' Harney. I was born in Bessborough in 1949. My mother and I stayed together in the Mother and Baby Home for two and a half years. When I was born, I apparently almost died, and I was put into what was known as the 'dying room.' But my bawling and my crying and my gurgling apparently kept me going until the morning, and I was handed to my mother the next day.

My mother chose to do some of the most menial tasks within the institution like sluicing out the babies' napkins (in America you call them 'diapers') so that she could sneak in to see me and pick me up, because women were not allowed free access to their children at any time of the day.

I suffered whooping cough and measles while I was there, and therefore I was not eligible to be trafficked to America. Those were communicable diseases, and in getting children to America, they had to be free of such prior conditions. A bit like America today, really. My mother was given a half an hour's notice to get me ready to have me taken from her. She and the other women used to knit for their children. And she had made me a little – I guess you could call it – a coat-type thing and a little bonnet. And when she got me dressed, she put me in those clothes. She walked me down to the nun who took me from her, and basically that was the last time my mother was ever supposed to see me. Within half an hour of being taken away from her, the nun came back and threw the little knitted clothes back at my mother and said, 'She won't be needing those where she's going.'

I was illegally fostered by an elderly couple who knew nothing at all about children, and they took me to a house in Cork that was terrifying in its tininess. I had been in an institution, a Mother and Baby institution, and now I was in a small house. I was put into a wooden bed that had above it, on the side wall that I could see quite clearly, a picture of St Michael the Archangel with his trident shoving the snakes back into hell. It had a flickering light in front. This is one of my very early memories. It flickered at night and I could see the flames coming out of the snakes. The nightmares and the terror – of just being locked in that room alone – are still with me today.

Because of their neglect, and also because I was probably suffering from malnutrition, a neighbour called the authorities and I was taken from the foster parents in 1954. I was brought to the courthouse in Cork, and the judge sentenced me to twelve and a half years in the Good Shepherd Industrial School at Sunday's Well in Cork City. I was taken to the industrial school where the doors were locked as soon as I was put in. My childhood there was years of intermittent abuse, but severe in many cases. We were deprived of food if we disobeyed rules. We were always deprived of water; we had no free access to water. We were beaten and we were abused sexually, emotionally and physically. I bear some physical scars, but for many years I bore the mental and emotional scars of my time there.

It was there that I learned how to begin to resist. When I refused to lean down and tie my shoes and when I got severe beatings, I would not cry. It was there that I learned that I am Mary Harney. I am not Number 54. I am not 'pig.' I am not 'smelly pig.'

I am Mary Harney, the proud daughter of a mother that I traced on my own when I was 17 years old. I traced my mother with threats. Not with questions, not with gentleness, but with threats that I would publish my story in a newspaper called *The News of the World,* which is equivalent to your *Enquirer* [in the United States]. Within two weeks of sending that letter, I had – I still have it today – a tiny letter, two pages, telling me my mother's married name, that I had two half-sisters, and my mother's address.

Without any Freedom of Information Act, without any GDPR or whatever they call it in the United States, I found my mother with the help of a Catholic priest who was a good person and a magnificent support for me. He brought us together. It was one of the biggest shocks of my life. I had dreamed of a mother that was Greta Garbo and Betty Davis mixed together, holding a long cigarette. What I got was a small, fat Irish woman with two children running around and a long streak of misery for a stepfather.

Without any counselling, without any support, it is very hard for mothers and children to reunite. I could not put a bond of 17 years back in place. Neither could she. We had a 31-year relationship, and I loved my mother, but it was the same as if I loved someone else's mother. There was something missing. There was no closeness. My mother did not hug very much. I wanted to, but I realised that she needed to and could not. My journey through 'recovery,' as I call it.

I am not a survivor. I am a small, yet mighty, resisting worker for justice. And I have spent 50 years finding that out.

I buried my mother in 2013 or 2014. Sorry, Mammy, I can't remember. But I honoured my mother, I respected my mother, I loved my mother. She is my hero for what she went through as a mother. For that I will always be grateful. I dedicated my Master's thesis at NUI Galway – I wrote about the Irish industrial schools and forced labour – to my mother and all the women who went through such things.

I have a tote box, a plastic tote box, at home filled with redacted information and redacted letters. I have found that my personal truth-telling has been a part of my pathway to healing and recovery, but forgiveness has not yet come for me. I'm working on it. I sometimes feel that I am truth-telling to a government that does not listen and that speaks – as one of our very famous men here in America says – 'fake' all the time. I think someone talked about it this morning, this fake shame and fake explanations of 'we are going to do so much to move this along.' It's fake because there is no action.

I want to see action because we are telling our truths and the government is not telling us the truth about our identity. That, I think, is where there is a big gap in this truth-telling exercise. We, the people who have been through it, are telling our truths at last. The government is hiding behind the Freedom of Information Act, all sorts of personal-privacy legislation, and the adoption bill. They are all being created to impede access, if you like – to enable the government to once again abdicate its responsibility to its children and women by denying us the knowledge of who we are.

I serve on the memorialisation subcommittee of the Collaborative Forum. As Mari so aptly puts it, we don't need any more statues for pigeons to shit on. We do need memorials. And one of the first things I believe we must do is identify the dead and give the dead names, so that we can memorialise the children and the mothers that died in these institutions before we do anything else. One other legacy, which comes out of Holocaust studies, is that we must teach children the history of this dark chapter in Ireland and keep that memory alive so that it never happens again. So those are two of the numerous issues our committee is working on, but it is a very hard task, and we are just fighting at the edges of it.

II. Mari Steed

I was born Mary Terese Fitzpatrick at the Bessborough Mother and Baby Home in Cork in 1960, and I and 2,000-plus children were trafficked from Ireland to the United States for the specific purpose of adoption by American couples. I landed in Philadelphia and grew up there. At 17 I fell pregnant in my senior year in high school. I was forced to give my own daughter up for adoption – even as late as 1978.

I reunited with my daughter in 1997 and also embarked on a search for my own mother. I did find her, but not until I learned a lot about my own history, my own background, as well as her background. I was fairly well armed, but it was work largely done on my own. There was no giving of information by the Sacred Heart nuns in Cork or any other bodies or authorities in Ireland. I just had to call and write my way through countless letters and do my own research. What I learned about my mother is that she had also been born out of wedlock in 1933 in Wexford. She came up through the Good Shepherd's Industrial School, St Dominic's, in Waterford. From there she was shifted to the Good Shepherd's Magdalene Laundry at Sunday's Well in Cork, where she spent ten years in the sewing room doing absolutely beautiful work. I saw examples of some of the work, which she had kept with her. So they got their money's worth out of my mother.

At age 26 she was released by the sisters to a job opportunity at Our Lady's Hospital in Dublin. It was her first experience out from under the washboards of the nuns, and as so many survivors can attest, they came out of the system very vulnerable, with absolutely no life skills or understanding of sexuality. She promptly fell pregnant with me, whereupon she immediately was sent back down to Cork, to the Mother and Baby Home at Bessborough, where she gave birth to me. Our mothers actually stayed with us, which was the practice if you were not a private fee-paying patient in these Mother and Baby Homes. She, of course, could not afford it, so again she was put to work sewing for the nuns, and had to stay there until I was sent for adoption at 18 months. During that time she breastfed me, she sang to me. She would slip away into the nursery at night and sing me lullabies that I still retain in my head to this day.

I found her in 2001, living in the United Kingdom. She had made a life for herself and she had done quite well, I think, by a lot of our standards based upon the damage inflicted on people. I think moving to England – and we see this with other women – it freed her to be a bit more herself, to escape the shame and stigma. If she remained in Ireland, I dread to think what kind of life she might have led.

So a lot of that obviously has informed my work. It's sort of the perfect storm of the convergence of carceral institutions in Ireland.

I was also part of the 1960–61 Burroughs Wellcome vaccine trials in Bessborough, conducted without my mother's consent. She was still there when this happened, still legally my parent.

So, of course, I have heaps of documents and information that I've amassed over the years to, sort of, prove my provenance and to provide what information is needed for my mother and her family. We are a living legacy of that system, and we are testament to the fact that this is generational. It does go on. It has lasting reverberations. I think this whole truth-telling notion, especially as it's promoted by the Irish government...,

I do commend the efforts to move forward with the Collaborative Forum with that purpose in mind, to truth-tell. But I am keenly aware that we cannot truthfully tell our story without knowing our story. The linchpin to that is access to information.

For those of us that have come out of these institutional settings, knowing our story is the one thing we lack, that we are denied, and that we continue to be obstructed on. So I think that's what we have to move forward on. Without that access to information – be it to mothers, be it to children – we cannot really get to the truth-telling process.

One of the interesting obstacles that we face is an inconsistency in the level of access. Having the advantage of U.S. citizenship, one of the 'perks' I enjoy is an immigration file that I can access under freedom of information. So I can FOI my immigration file and get a full copy of my original Irish birth certificate, which is something denied to my companions in Ireland. So that is a problem as well: the inconsistencies between the layers of the adoption legacy.

The world is changing so radically, from DNA advances to websites like *Ancestry.com*. They are becoming an invaluable tool. We are finding Irish children showing up on flight manifests coming into the United States. They may have travelled on what were known as American family passports. So you really only had to have 'mother' and 'father,' and they could list anybody they wanted. The other piece of that puzzle was military families and military transports. Nobody was watching these military planes that were going out of Limerick, out of Foynes, or the United Kingdom. Nobody's going to question a major or a captain coming in with a bonny baby in his arms, and they were flying into military bases here in the United States, to bases here in Massachusetts, Westover Air Force Base, and to McGuire in New Jersey. Flights were chock-a-block with children, and not just from Ireland. That was in the wake of World War II, which might explain why the Irish babies were not questioned or why people turned a blind eye to it. From Americans' perspective they were rescuing war orphans.

We also are finding naturalisation petitions online through *Ancestry.com* going back as far as the 1940s and very early 1950s. An American parent would present themselves to a federal court in their jurisdiction, be it Pennsylvania, New York or wherever. They present the child. They may not have all the necessary documents that you would think should be required, like the visa from Ireland and some sort of certification saying you have been vetted as a prospective adoptive parent. But they have got enough information because it's major so-and-so, or from a wealthy family. They present themselves to a federal courthouse saying, 'I have adopted this Irish child; I have taken them into my home; I would like to have them naturalised as a citizen.' And it was just never questioned. That is how parents were able to get the child into school and take on a new name. Then the process gets finalised by the parents going to their local family court and getting an adoption decree in that state. And again people didn't just question it back then. It was horrible.

III. Caitríona Palmer

I was born in April 1972 to an unmarried mother in Ireland and placed for adoption through the state-licensed St Patrick's Guild agency. Unlike Mary, I was with my mother for only two days before I was taken – quickly baptised on the way and taken – to St Patrick's Infant Hospital, Temple Hill, in Blackrock. I was adopted by Liam and Mary Palmer, my beloved parents. I grew up in an incredibly happy home. I was adored by my parents and siblings and given every privilege and opportunity I could have ever asked for. But in spite of all that privilege and opportunity and love, I grew up haunted by the loss of my mother and upset by a feeling of incompleteness, of discombobulation, of dislocation that I could never fully understand. I was the good adoptee, a really good girl. I did very well at school.

I tried to make my parents very proud, but I still didn't feel like myself. In 1999, when I was 27 years old, I searched for my natural mother – my biological mother – which is something I never thought I would do. I found her quickly and we were reunited. She was overjoyed, just so thrilled to have me back in her life. It seemed like the fairy-tale was complete until she told me she had never actually told anyone about me or my existence and that moving forward our relationship would have to be a secret. I had just found her and didn't want to lose her, so I agreed to the terms of our relationship. I thought naïvely that in a week or a month or a year she would tell her husband or her children about me. But that week turned into a year, into five years, ten years, fifteen years. And now, 20 years later, as far as I know I'm still a secret in her life.

I am a journalist, and so as a journalist I was intrigued by my own story, and I wanted to investigate why this remarkable woman, this sophisticated woman in the new secular Ireland of the post–Celtic Tiger era could not come out and say, 'I had a child and here is that child.' And so, without knowing that I was embarking on a book project, I began to write and investigate the facts of my own life, which led to my memoir called *An Affair with My Mother*, which was published in March 2016.

I'm aware that it's a very provocative title – *An Affair with My Mother* – but there was no other way for me to describe the clandestine affair that I was conducting with my mother. Meeting in hotels across Dublin, hiding out from her family. And that's really the story. It's a story of love and redemption but also of pain. I wrote the story to explain that you can grow up in a happy home and be adopted, yet feel haunted by grief. And I also wanted to tell the story of my biological mother, who is broken by my mere existence. She has lived a bifurcated, haunted life, and I wanted to exonerate her publicly.

For me it is very simple: everyone has a basic human right to know where they come from. It is 2018, and we need to address Ireland's closed, secret adoption system. I would like to have access to my adoption files, to my own birth certificate. I know who my natural mother is, and my father, and yet I am still denied those official documents. We have ushered in extraordinary social change in Ireland in the past few decades, and yet this remains one intractable, closed, dark chapter. I have been so moved and so impressed by everything that's coming out of this conference, but for me, as the adoptee here, I would really like access – a statutory access – to our information.

IV. Terri Harrison

Look at this stage filled with beautiful, wonderful people. Our adult children inherit the ripple effects of their pariah mother – because that's the only word I can think of. We have no rights whatsoever. We are not mentioned in any literature. We do not come under any umbrella of any platform because we were the girls locked up in what they describe as the 'Mother and Baby Homes.' There were no homes in our country. I won't agree to that. And these beautiful people here on the stage today give me hope for my son – 45 years of age now – who I got to have six weeks with, my beautiful, beautiful son. Then he was taken; he was abducted.

I have talked to all the legal people: there is no statute of limitations for kidnapping, to my knowledge. In 2002 I attempted to bring the Irish state to court on the grounds of the kidnapping of my son, and my case was turned down on the basis of the statute of limitations. I had hope, a long time ago, and hope sometimes fades. One of the speakers talked about the importance of listening. I have to say to the women, please put your fingers down your throat and vomit up the part of you that feels that shame. It doesn't belong to you. It belongs to our country. The shame is not yours. That is the first thing. And the second thing I wanted to tell you all, and especially the adult children: every woman that I have encountered suffers from acute guilt, including myself, that we didn't kill the bitches who hurt us. That we didn't kill them on behalf of our children. And that's the guilt we are living with today.

The abandonment and the rejection of our entire society fell upon our children. And it hurts me greatly to hear the speakers talk about that void inside of them. If they only knew, if they really only knew. I wish I had a tape recording of what I heard in the institutions. The screams and the cries were terrible. And you'd say, 'Oh God, they've taken another one.' And you knew you could be next.

During the visit of the Pope to Ireland [in summer 2018], many survivors spoke at a protest on O'Connell Street about the longing they feel to be Irish again. I will never be Irish until all of this is resolved. I'm not a Catholic, I'm not a Protestant, I have no religious affiliation. My father was an atheist and my mother was a Catholic. I have met with so many ministers over the years. So many promises, and then they leave office, and then we get a new one, and it just goes on, and on, and on. I want to address the young people, the people of tomorrow in my country and in your country. I hope that I live to see a day where I can say simply, 'I am an Irish woman.' Nothing else. It doesn't matter. The rest is irrelevant.

For Ireland today this whole conference is remarkable. It's astounding. It's a privilege for me to be sitting here today, and it's thanks to Katherine Zappone who funded representatives from the Collaborative Forum. I couldn't afford this trip. I also represent hundreds of women at the Christine Buckley Centre on Jervis Street in Dublin. I have been helping to run support groups since 1991. The Christine Buckley Centre gave us women a home. There is nothing visible about the women that I represent. We are faceless, nameless and voiceless. But not anymore. Now we have a place on the platform. I can speak for Terri Harrison, and I have permission to speak for the many, many women who come through the Christine Buckley Centre doors for support and ask me, 'Why? Why won't they believe us, Terri?'

How do you answer that question? Because I do not have the answer. Like the question I asked yesterday: 'Who gave them permission to treat us like criminals?' For picking life. The miracle of precious life. There is one thing I just want to make clear to everybody. There is us mothers and there is our children, and in between there was the establishment. Everything that happened, happened *to* us, not *by* us. We did not come along and say, 'Don't give our children our information.' Every human being has a right to the origins of their family and their identity.

Please know that every woman in the institutions was told the exact same thing: if I ever attempted to find my son, I would be arrested by the gardaí. Every woman was told that.

V. Rosemary Adaser

My name is Rosemary Adaser and I am the founder and CEO of the

Association of Mixed Race Irish. I know for the Americans here, the fact that I am sitting here and saying I am Irish might come as a bit of a shock, but that's alright, we get that in Ireland, we get it wherever we go.

I wanted to pick up on the question, 'What does Ireland mean to you?' What I think Ireland means to me is the exploitation of difference. I think that, speaking from within my community, we have committed two crimes. The biggest crime was that we were born to African men. That was the biggest crime. I met my mother when I was 36 years old, and she told me that I needed to understand her decision to abandon me because she had broken the code. She had mated with a member of the slave race. And that one statement has peppered my life throughout Ireland and its industrial schools. I have a love-hate relationship with Ireland, I think it is fair to say. I have a history. I have been in a lot of homes as a baby. I was in industrial schools as a child. I was indentured. I actually have the file, and on the document it has a form called 'indenture,' and I was indentured to a couple in their sixties. On my file it actually says, 'Come to the institution and pick the child up who most accommodates your lifestyle.'

My welfare was not part of the equation at all. I think it is really important that in our discussion about the system of abuse that ran throughout Ireland, we acknowledge that the welfare of the child was never a factor. And it did not matter whether you were a person of colour or a beautiful, bonny child like Caitríona, a couple of days old, or a baby whisked off to America. Your welfare was never a factor in the deliberations. There are more checks and balances in picking a dog from a pound than there is with the treatment and care of children in Ireland.

Moving slightly forward to what all this means to me: I think there are two things that I have picked up. One is that the process is even more important than the outcome, speaking to the redress schemes offered by the state. What redress meant for industrial-school survivors was blood money – and in exchange for this blood money we'll give you a gagging order so you can no longer tell your stories. That blood money carried with it a lifetime sacrifice of silence. So I think the process is absolutely critical.

The other thing I wanted to say about this conference that really struck me is the history of inter-institutional connections. We never really discussed this whole separation: 'Oh, you were adopted, you were in industrial schools, you are a natural mother, you're this or that.' And actually, it's all a history of connections and interdependency, and I really, really want the Collaborative Forum to finally link all those dots, and together with these amazing ladies and men, come together with one voice and say, 'Enough really is enough. Ireland, get your shit together.'

In denying access to information, the state claims it is protecting the rights of mothers. No way. We do not have access to our own records. Once again the state is deflecting blame onto the mothers, onto the children. Again, this is about making those linkages between the various agencies. Mums do not have access to these records either.

VI. Conrad Bryan

My name is Conrad Bryan, and this is the first time I have been in the United States of America, and I really want to thank Katherine Zappone for allowing me the opportunity to come here. This is the land of Martin Luther King – my hero. There is a quotation of his that is actually quite appropriate for me personally today: 'Darkness cannot drive out darkness. Only light can do that. Hate cannot drive out hate. Only love can do that.' That quote is meaningful to me on this day when talking about truth-telling and questioning 'What is this light?' and 'Whose truth is it?'

There is truth that many of us [children who grew up in institutions] held. There is truth that families held, where mothers have not told their children that they had a child out of wedlock. There is truth at a state level, as we heard today, where it refuses to give information out to people. And there is a truth denied by the Catholic Church. I would like some answers particularly from the church. I'd like to see them speak out, to answer simple questions like, 'Why did they stop allowing adoptions of coloured children, mixed-race children?'

I found a letter in the archives of the Department of Foreign Affairs where there was a discussion of making black babies available for adoption, and the response was, 'We can guarantee that we have no problem with children of colour here in Ireland. We can guarantee that we won't send children of colour to America.' So I need answers to questions like that. It is remarkable that the Protestant adoption agencies were inundated with people looking for mixed-race children. Why weren't we offered up to Protestant adoption agencies? The discrimination is on so many levels, and I'd love to know the truth about why I was not adopted. I have my father stating that the only reason I wasn't adopted is because I was coloured. The evidence is in the file, and I have only recently started to investigate as a result of my work with Rosemary and the Association of Mixed Race Irish. There is truth on many levels I want to know.

Hate cannot drive out hate. I think that Dublin needs to recognise that we need to move on from hate and contempt and actually listen to us and listen to what we have to say because we are the truth-tellers.

VII. Susan Lohan

My name is Susan Lohan and I am the co-founder of Adoption Rights

Alliance, together with Claire McGettrick who is speaking here today. In the early 1990s, myself, Claire and Angela Murphy over there [in Ireland], and Mari Steed here [in the United States] were all members of an earlier group called Adoption Ireland. So it is quite untrue for the Irish government to say that they are only slowly becoming aware of these issues that we have been discussing over the past two days. We have presented paper after paper after paper. We have met every single minister for children.

The government's great big idea in 2001 was to propose an adoption bill that contained a brand-new crime. Perhaps half of the people in this room could never, ever be convicted of it because you are not adopted. The crime was contacting your natural parents without their express prior permission, and it was punishable by up to five years in prison and a fine of £5,000. That was 2001.

Unfortunately, in today's Department of Children there is the same continuing mantra. There is an adoption bill going through parliament now, and people are being promised 'extracts' compiled from documents in our personal files as constructed by social workers. So they are going to allow the state to write its own version of our story. And we would have to sign a legally binding undertaking in order to gain access to even a small amount of information, and we can be challenged in court.

We talk about Ireland's closed, secret adoption industry, but we are actually talking about facts that are hidden only from the actual subjects within that industry. In the majority of cases, especially for adoptees leaving Ireland, all of our births were properly registered and they were registered publicly. So if I know my name at birth, I can walk into the General Register Office, go down the list, find my birth and request the birth certificate. Of course, our name at birth is the one piece of information we do not possess. So that is where the secrecy comes in.

The only entity in Ireland who can link the original identity and the adoptive identity is the Adoption Board, now called the Adoption Authority. But I think there has been deliberate misinterpretation of the 1952 Adoption Act, which says that only the Adoption Board shall have access to the index linking these two identities. At the time, that stipulation was put in place so as to prevent public curiosity or public scrutiny. I do not believe it was ever intended to keep the linkages secret from the people who were the subject of those adoptions, and I would really like to see greater legal scrutiny of some of those provisions.

In response to the question, 'What does it mean to be Irish?' I think we are very self-serving in recent legal advances we have made. I think it has been very easy to bring in gender-recognition bills, marriage equality – perhaps less so was Repeal the Eighth. These are items which will not cost the Irish exchequer anything, and they make us look good on the world stage, but please do not be fooled by that.

I think what actually happened to our mothers amounted to a sort of ethnic cleansing, as they were the women who were deemed not to be following the rules of the bureaucratic state. They were not decidedly different, but their politics were, and their class. Even when Terri talks about being kidnapped from England, I would describe that as an extraordinary-rendition flight. We have really propagated massive human-rights abuses against our people.

VIII. Connie Roberts

I am one of 15 children, and we all went through the industrial-school system. Like Mary, I spent twelve and a half years in my particular industrial school, and I am here 35 years in the United States. I teach at Hofstra University in New York.

Regarding the industrial schools, I think the Irish government has taken steps toward transitional justice in many ways, with the introduction of the Commission to Inquire into Child Abuse, the *Ryan Report*, the Residential Institutions Redress Board and Caranua. All welcome steps, all important steps, all needed. But as I said yesterday to a few people, like a fellow institutional inmate, 'You know "please, sir, we want more?"' It is not a question of 'may we have some more?' asked with a begging bowl in hand. 'May we have some more?' No. We want more. We need more. Truth-telling in a more comprehensive way.

Even today – I never met Mary before, but we both went through the industrial schools. We have different stories, different truths, but it all needs to be told. You cannot throw reports at us, commissions of investigation at us, and money at us and say, 'That's done and dusted. That's industrial schools taken care of. Now, let's get on to Mother and Baby Homes. Out of the way, that is history.' You cannot, it is not good enough. And I am so happy that there is this type of a forum to bring that to the floor and say, 'We are not done here yet.' This is part of Irish history. It is staying in Irish history, and we need to keep telling the truth.

Earlier this year I met Irish writer Eileen Casey in Dublin, and she was putting together an anthology to celebrate the fiftieth anniversary of the Irish poet Patrick Kavanagh. She gathered a group of poets and asked each of us to pick a poem of Kavanagh's and write a response to it. I didn't want to pick one of the more popular poems like 'Canal Bank Walk' or 'Stony Grey Soil of Monaghan,' so it was his poem 'My People' that resonated with me. Patrick Kavanagh is talking about the rural farmers up in County Monaghan, and I started thinking about my people. Kavanagh's poem is written in a question-and-answer format between the poet and a stranger. As any writers in the room know, you always gather things in your back pocket and say, 'I'll write about that at some stage down the road.'

In 2017, living in New York, I read this article in *The Irish Times* in which Mary Higgins, then director of the Caranua fund, made disparaging and hurtful remarks about those of us who grew up in child-residential institutions in Ireland. I was giving her the benefit of the doubt and said sometimes journalists get it wrong. But then I went online to RTÉ to listen to the Joe Duffy radio program, where she reinforced what she said. And I thought to myself, 'Oh my God, how could you?' I just shook my head and I put it in my back pocket and said, 'I am going to write about that at some future opportunity.' I am not here to crucify Mary Higgins, but the day she sat down for that interview with *The Irish Times*, she checked her compassion at the door. To have someone representing the Irish state in an official capacity talk about survivors as 'damaged people' and then allude to 'criminality' – to bring all that into the interview as well. Words matter. She could have talked about the resilience of us survivors – you see it up here on this stage and in the audience, the resilience. She could have talked about how difficult it is to go before Caranua and the Redress Board. But she didn't, she chose to talk about 'damaged people' and 'these' people.

This poem articulates where I'm coming from. But I am an optimistic person, so there is also a note of hope at the end of the poem. There is a reference to the winter storm in 2014 in the United Kingdom and Ireland, where things that were buried came to the surface – re-emerged, so to speak. And I talk about this bridge, in the spirit of this conference where we are building bridges and healing together. There is a time for anger and there is a time for love.

Anyway, I think most of you would know about the independent body Caranua, but it was established in 2012 by the Irish government to manage the €110 million pledged by the religious congregations to enhance the lives of survivors of institutional child abuse. Caranua is the Irish word for 'new friend.'

My People

After Patrick Kavanagh's 'My People'
&
In response to Caranua CEO Mary Higgins's remarks in The Irish Times *and on RTÉ's* Liveline, *20 March 2017*

Stranger: Tell me about these people,
these damaged people.

Is it true that the hole in
them cannot be filled,
that the damage is so
deep it doesn't matter
what anybody does,
it's never going to be enough
to satisfy them, make them feel
cared for, loved, honoured?

Poet: I'll tell you about my people.
They are the bravest people I know.
For 50, 60, 70 years, their bones
have carried the stones of their past.
Their bodies have kept the score. And more.
So, every now and again, they buckle
from the belt of ago.
Can you blame them for wanting
wrongs righted?

Stranger: Ah, now, my new friend,
fair is fair,
don't these people's grievances
suit a narrative,
of the big, bad State
of the big, bad religious?

Poet: O, stranger,
it takes a storm
to raise a
sunken forest,
for the shin-high, petrified
pine stumps to emerge.
It's the winter squall that gifts
the red deer antlers,
the black-mud horse skull
and the wattled walkway.

— *Connie Roberts*

Two

Antigone in Galway: Anne Enright on the Dishonoured Dead[1]

Anne Enright

In September the Irish government held a state funeral for the exhumed remains of Thomas Kent, a rebel and a patriot who was executed in 1916 and buried in the yard of what is now Cork Prison, at the rear of Collins Barracks, once the Victoria Barracks. His coffin was first removed to the garrison church, where thousands of people – including Dr John Buckley, the bishop of Cork and Ross – filed past to pay their respects. The funeral echoed the reinterment of Roger Casement – thrown in a lime pit in Pentonville Prison in 1916 and repatriated in 1965 – when Eamon de Valera got out of his sickbed to attend and a million people lined the route. Thomas Kent was buried in the family plot at Castlelyons and the Taoiseach, Enda Kenny, gave the graveside oration. 'Today,' he said, 'we take him from the political Potter's Field to lay him with all honour among "his own".' Although the land in which he had lain is now, technically speaking, Irish, the prison yard still held the taint of Britishness, the memory of his dishonour.

'Potter's Field' is not a term much used in Ireland, though we have many traditional burial plots for strangers. These are marked 'Cillíní' on Ordnance Survey maps. Sometimes translated as 'children's graveyard,' the sites contain the graves of unbaptised infants, but also of women who died in childbirth, 'changeling' children, suicides, executed criminals and the insane (infanticides were typically disposed of without burial). Some are situated on sacred sites and in ancestral burial grounds that existed before the shift to the churchyard in early medieval Ireland. These earlier graves served a territorial function: they are found near the boundaries of ancient kingdoms, and by the water's edge. Cillíní are often situated between one place and another, at the limits of things. After the Second Vatican Council, in the 1960s, allowed burial rites for the unbaptised, the Cillíní, along with the idea of limbo, fell out of use.

Some of those I visited in Connemara command a mighty view. One lies beside a path known as Mámméan (the Pass of the Birds) that pilgrims still use on the way to the well of St Patrick. Individual graves are built up with large stones, for the length of the body beneath, and there are no crosses to be seen. The bodies of infants were buried by a father or an uncle, often at night. The scant ritual and the isolation of the setting is offset by the beauty that surrounds it: the place feels both abandoned and sacred. Which is not to say that the women whose babies were so buried did not resent the lack of a marker, or feel the loneliness of the spot (if, indeed, they were told where it was). It was a great difficulty to have someone close to you, buried apart. Irish graveyards are, above all, family places. 'Would you like to be buried with my people?' is not a marriage proposal you might hear in another country, even as a joke.

Emigration split families, and this may have made the need to gather together stronger for those who remained, even after death. In a country of the dispossessed, it is also tempting to see the grave plot as a treasured piece of land. But the drama of the Irish graveyard was not about ownership, and only partly about honour (in the Traveller community, to step on a grave is still an indelible insult). Irish ghost stories tell of graveyards actually rejecting those who do not belong – by which is meant Protestants. The ground itself might refuse, and yield their bodies up, or if they did stay put, the wall could jump over them in the night, to put the Protestants on the other side. Whole churchyards went wandering in order to leave them behind, and these ideas of purity and aversion persist in the undisturbed Irish earth, even into modern times.

When Enda Kenny praised the nieces who'd lobbied for the reinterment of Thomas Kent – 'These three women have tended the flame of his memory' – he was speaking from the heart of the Irish rhetorical tradition. Under the censorship of British rule, the graveside was a rare opportunity for political speech, and it was a woman's role not just to mourn and love, but also to remember the revolutionary martyr. The job of remembering was also a work of silence: 'O breathe not his name!' was the song by Thomas Moore, the name being that of the patriot Robert Emmet, executed after leading the 1803 rebellion, who asked that his epitaph remain unwritten until his country had taken its place among the nations of the earth. High speech and silence, this was the patriotic way, and no silence more urgent than that of the graveyard. And so we get the great speech by Patrick Pearse, eight months before the 1916 Rising: 'the fools, the fools, the fools! – they have left us our Fenian dead, and while Ireland holds these graves, Ireland unfree shall never be at peace.'

★

It is tempting to see *Antigone* as a play not just about the mourning female voice, or about kinship and the law, but about the political use of the body after death. Creon, the ruler of Thebes, dishonours the body of his nephew to serve as a warning to other potential enemies of the state. One brother, Eteocles, has been buried 'in accordance with justice and law,' the other, Polynices, 'is to lie unwept and unburied' – this according to their sister Antigone, who has already decided at the play's opening to ignore Creon's edict and bury the corpse. And so she does. When asked to deny the crime, she says, in Anne Carson's 2012 translation of Sophocles: 'I did the deed I do not deny it.' She does not seek to justify her actions within the terms of Creon's law: she negates the law by handing it back to him, intact – 'If you call that law.'

Antigone later says she is being punished for 'an act of perfect piety,' but that act is also perfectly wordless in the play. The speeches she makes to her sister Ismene and to Creon are before and after the fact. She is a woman who breaks an unjust law. We can ask if she does this from inside or outside the legal or linguistic system of the play, or of the state, but it is good to bear in mind that Antigone does not bury her brother with words, but with dust.

Her appeal, when she makes it, is not to Creon but to a higher order of justice, 'the unwritten unfaltering unshakeable ordinances of the gods.' Antigone looks into her heart, you might think, and towards the heavens, while Creon looks around him to the business of government. But this system collapses before the end of the play into something more simple and self-enclosed. 'The dead do not belong to you,' Tiresias tells Creon, 'nor to the gods above.' There are moments – and death (or more properly decay) is one of them – that belong neither to sacred nor to secular law, but to themselves. Antigone has known this all along: 'Death needs to have Death's laws obeyed.' Carson doesn't use the word 'ghost.' The idea that Polynices has some residual agency or voice creeps into other translations, but not into this one. The body remains a body – 'rawflesh' for dogs and birds – not a human presence. It is only when Antigone herself goes to die that she calls her brother's name.

★

'They say a grave never settles,' Catherine Corless remarked as we walked the convent wall in Tuam, where she suspected adult remains might lie. I looked at the ground and I could believe it; the shadow of vegetation that grew more lush formed an oblong, seven feet by five. This was beyond the little plot where locals say babies from the town's Mother and Baby Home were buried. A small grotto in the corner is tended by the residents of the housing estate that was built on the site in the early 1970s. Corless was doing a local history project and, intrigued by the unmarked burial plot, went to the Bon Secours sisters to ask for records. These had been passed on to the county council in Galway they said. The county council told her they were passed on to the Health Board, the Health Board said it only had 'individual records,' which she would not be allowed to see. She then went to the Births, Marriages and Deaths Registration office in Galway to get, at her own expense, the death certificates of 796 babies and children who died in the Mother and Baby Home in Tuam between 1925 and 1961. The location of their bodies is unrecorded. They have not yet been found.

In 1975 local boys had told of seeing the small bones of children in some kind of tank, under a broken concrete top. There was a strong response from the media when Corless said that this might be a disused septic tank that is marked on the map as lying under this spot. There was much rifling through the statistics and records; yes, the death rate among illegitimate children was up to five times that of those born within marriage, but institutions are great places for disease to spread, and what about measles? In fact, Corless was accusing no one of murder and, besides, the story was not new. There had been a brief report in a local paper two years earlier, and no one had seemed to care. It was the word 'septic' that did it; the association with sewage, the implication that the bodies were not just carelessly buried, or even discarded, but treated like 'filth.' After the words 'septic tank' appeared in the world's press Corless found herself besieged by journalists. She was misquoted, then called a liar for things she hadn't said. With all that shame flying around, it needed a place to stick and clearly it was her fault, whatever it was – sewage tanks, babies, all that dead history, Ireland's reputation abroad.

Maps, photocopies, ledgers and certificates littered the kitchen table. Over the course of an hour, two people rang Corless's mobile, looking for female relatives who may have been in the Tuam Mother and Baby Home. They might already have asked the nuns and the county council and the Health Board, but even babies born in the home do not have the statutory right to see their records, because of the secrecy clauses signed by the mothers who, willingly or not, gave them up for adoption. The information they do find may have been falsified at the time. Great desperation leads people to local historians like Corless. She told me about a man she helped, who was born in the home 70 years before. He had led a full life, with six children of his own – but one of them was disabled and he thought this was a punishment of some kind. When he found his mother's grave, he brought flowers to it, and wept. He just wanted to meet her, he said, and tell her that it was all right.

When I asked Corless why she had brought the problem of the missing dead to light, she said: 'It was the little ones themselves crying out to me.' Her interest in historical research began when she tried to trace her origins after the death of her own mother. There was 'some load there, some secret.' Her grandmother had entered a second relationship with a Protestant man, her mother was fostered out and never went back home. Corless managed to trace an aunt and when she made contact, decades after these events, the woman said: 'We have nothing here for you now.'

It did not take many women to run the Mother and Baby Home – four or five nuns, Corless said, for up to 100 pregnant and nursing women, and their children, who might be taken away for adoption at any time. They had nowhere else to go, clearly, but they must also have been very compliant. What were they like? Fear kept them quiet, Corless said, the threat of being sent to the asylum or the laundry. 'That,' according to Julia, a long-term resident, 'is how the argument was settled.'

Dr Coughlan was GP for the Galway Magdalene Laundry from 1981 to 1984. 'The Residents were a delightful and happy group of ladies,' he says, 'each lady presented as a unique individual, with a unique personality, well able to ask relevant questions and to express her opinion and, above all, ready and willing to gossip, to tease and be teased and to joke.'

And perhaps it is true. Irish women are often nice.

When the Bon Secours nuns left Tuam for good, they exhumed the remains of their dead sisters – 12 in all – and took them with them to their new home in Knock. The controversy Corless started about the 796 missing bodies has provoked a commission of inquiry into the Mother and Baby Homes in Ireland, led by Judge Yvonne Murphy. A few weeks ago a geophysical survey was taken of the ground using penetrating radar and magnetometry. Corless is confident that the remains of an untold number of children will be found there. But if they are not found – and that is also possible – there will be much fuss and distraction from the fact that no one knows where the bodies of 796 children have gone.

*

The living can be disbelieved, dismissed, but the dead do not lie. We turn in death from witness to evidence, and this evidence is indelible, because it is mute. It started in 1993, when the Sisters of Our Lady of Charity of Refuge sold off a portion of their land to a developer in order to cover recent losses on the stock exchange. As part of the deal, they exhumed a mass grave on the site which they said contained the bodies of 133 'auxiliaries,' women who worked until their deaths in the Magdalene Laundry of High Park, which closed in 1991.

There were ten of these laundries in Ireland. They are styled, by the nuns who ran them, as refuges for marginalised women where they endured, along with their keepers, an enclosed, monastic life of work and prayer. The women were described as 'penitents,' and the act of washing was seen as symbolic. The laundries were run as active concerns, washing dirty linen for hotels, hospitals and the army, and they undercut their rivals in the trade by the fact that their penitential workforce was not paid. So the laundries might also be styled as labour camps, or prison camps, where women were sent, without trial, for a crime that was hard to name. In 1958, 70 per cent of the women in the Magdalene Laundry in Galway were unmarried mothers. Asked how long they would be there, the mother superior answered: 'Some stay for life.'

To the apparent surprise of the Sisters of Our Lady of Charity of Refuge, 22 extra bodies were found in the opened grave at High Park. The nuns didn't appear to know the names of several of the women buried there, listing them by their religious names as Magdalene of St Cecilia or Magdalene of Lourdes, and more than one third of the 155 deaths had never been certified. It was clear the nuns were not used to dealing with outside authorities. Costs were high; they allegedly haggled with the undertaker to ask if he could get three bodies to a coffin. In the end, the remains were cremated, in contravention of Catholic custom, and everyone who heard the news then or read the reports knew, in the silence of their hearts, exactly what was going on, and what had been going on, and what all this meant.

It was another ten years before Mary Raftery wrote about the High Park exhumations. Raftery's documentaries, the three-part *States of Fear* (1999) and *Cardinal Secrets* (2002), provoked two commissions of inquiry, one into abuse in Irish institutions for children, which were usually run by the religious, and one into clerical abuse in the Dublin Archdiocese. These were published in 2009, as the *Ryan Report* and the *Murphy Report* respectively. Before her death in 2012 Raftery was hailed as the most influential broadcaster of her day, but she got what we used to call 'drag' from RTÉ television on these projects, especially States of Fear; the kind of delay, indifference and non-compliance that runs through an institution when someone seeks to disturb the status quo. Sheila Ahern, who worked with her as a lone researcher, remembers being told that the story was, in media terms, 'done already.' There was no budget, no resources, the whole thing was deemed, in audience terms, 'a turn-off' and Raftery was asked to 'lighten it up a bit.' Mostly patronising, this is an attitude that only turns aggressive at the last moment; it is particularly suited to dealing with women when they are troublesome, and Mary Raftery was very troublesome. Passionate for the victims of abuse, she had a bad attitude when it came to authority: non-compliant, endlessly tenacious and full of glee.

I don't think a man could have done what she did, but it would be wrong to cast Raftery as some kind of Antigone; all her concern was for the living. Her work was founded on the personal testimony of people who had been abused in institutions. She brought those voices into vision, and shaped an argument with and around them that was incontrovertible. For some reason they had been hard to hear: now you couldn't look away – their stories were unbearable and, for the country, deeply shaming. Bertie Ahern, the then Taoiseach, issued an apology before the third part of the series hit the air.

Raftery worked within the law, sharing the church's and the state's obsession with records, files, account books, ledgers, baptismal certificates, adoption papers, gravestones and mortal remains. She took an almost childlike pleasure in undoing the riddle of power. I knew her a little. She was good fun. One of our conversations was about the redress scheme established in 2002 as a result of her work, to compensate those who had suffered abuse in childcare institutions. This seemed to me like a good thing. But the money, Raftery said, was subject to a confidentiality clause and this recalled, for some victims, the secrecy imposed on them by their abusers, the small bribes they used: a bit of chocolate, a hug. 'You see?' she said. Back in the trap.

In the late 1980s I met a woman who had been committed to Saint Ita's, a mental institution near Dublin. The papers were signed by her mother and a priest. The priest had the power to sign a section order in those days – though a doctor might also have been involved. The priest was the woman's uncle, her mother's brother, and they were putting her away because she said that the priest had felt her up. This was a woman my own age, or younger. In St Ita's she was medicated for three months, and kept in for another three and then let go. The doctors, she said, knew there was nothing wrong with her. I remember laughing in horror at this story, and she laughed too: 'They have you every way.'

It is, of course, this woman's mother who is the most interesting person in this story; how she disbelieved her daughter and pushed her away. The graveyard at St Ita's is a walled plot that contains, by repute, five thousand bodies. There is only one personal headstone – raised by an inmate's uncle, on behalf of his grieving sister, in the early 1900s. The priest at Grangegorman, another huge asylum, got so lonely burying the abandoned mad that he requested company – just one other living person, to say the word 'Amen.' The dead, we feel, should be freed from their sorrows, from the projections of the living. The shame should die with them. They should be allowed back in.

*

'The boy is dead,' Tiresias says to Creon, 'stop killing him.' Instead, Creon kills Antigone. He kills his own future daughter-in-law, breaking his son's heart. Creon is concerned with anarchy ('obedience saves lives') and with keeping himself superior to womankind: '*never never never* let ourselves be bested by a woman.' He is also concerned with pollution. His son's nature has been 'polluted' by being subject to a woman. The pleasure of sex that women afford is 'an open wound in your house and your life.' Creon is speaking about all women here, but Antigone is a woman squared, being the product of an incestuous union between her father, Oedipus, and his mother, Jocasta. Their family, Ismene says, is 'doubled tripled degraded and dirty in every direction.' The line of kinship is hopelessly tangled, so when Ismene says, 'O sister don't cross this line,' she is speaking to someone in whom all boundaries are broken.

The line of Creon's edict is only one of the 'lines' in the play. There is the city wall, and there is also the horizon line, where Polynices' body lies on the unopening ground. Antigone is neither outside nor inside. She is 'a strange new kind of inbetween thing... not at home with the dead nor with the living.' As the play proceeds she moves deeper into the other world; 'my soul died long ago,' she says, 'so it might serve the dead.' This self-involvement makes her seem a bit adolescent in the face of Creon's unyielding, corporate fury – she is like a teenager 'doing' death – but this is not a rehearsal of adult autonomy. Antigone is buried alive by way of punishment for her crime. As she goes to her tomb – she calls it 'a bridal chamber' – she looks to her own incestuous contradictions, and goes to meet her people: father, mother and brother. According to the chorus, she is 'the only one of mortals to go down to Death alive.' The paradox of living death completes the incestuous paradox of her origins. It is like a bad joke. Antigone is a pun that was never funny. She never had anything to lose.

Creon, by contrast, is free of incestuous taint. 'A man who runs his household right/can run a government.' To be a man is to be a man. He will not get mixed up in her or by her. In order to stay whole and free he must assert his authority, he must kill Antigone. If he lets her get away with it then 'surely I am not a man here/*she* is the man.' He 'will be clean of this girl.' He will put some food in her burial chamber, 'just enough to avoid the pollution, a sort of/sacred technicality.' When his son kills himself, Creon bemoans his own folly and the god who was his undoing, but the sight of his wife's corpse makes him cry: 'O filth of death.' By trying to keep himself clean and separate – from the incestuous, from the female, from death itself – Creon has fallen into a different trap. 'If you find you're confusing evil with good/some god is heading you down the high road to ruin.' It is Tiresias, history's first transsexual, who puts him straight: 'for you've housed a living soul beneath the ground below/and held a dead man here/without his grave or rights.'

★

Sometimes, the things we have said all our lives look strange again, like the way the religious style themselves as family: Father this, Mother that, Brother, Sister.

It is hard to say if it is a question of aversion, of purity or of privacy, but the nuns' plot in High Park was as far as the land would allow from that of the auxiliaries. This is also true of Sunday's Well Magdalene Laundry in Cork: the nuns are in the north-east corner, in neat rows with a neat cross for each; the auxiliaries are in a mass grave, now vandalised, in an overgrown and inaccessible part of the complex. Ordinary Magdalenes were buried in the local public cemetery, though anxiety persists about the names on their headstones and the actual occupants of the graves. This anxiety was not alleviated by the most recent report, in a line of reports, by the Inter-Departmental Committee to establish the facts of State Involvement with the Magdalene Laundries (IDC), known as the *McAleese Report*.

Martin McAleese trained as a dentist and as an accountant and served the state well as the spouse of President Mary McAleese over 14 years, in which time he played an active role in the Northern Irish peace process. In his introduction McAleese says he wants to protect the privacy of the Magdalene workers, who have, for too long, suffered the stigma of being called 'fallen women.' They came to the homes through various routes: the courts, the industrial schools; by free will and at the behest of their families. He stresses that they were not prostitutes, as commonly thought, and hopes this label will not simply be replaced with the word 'criminal.' He does not discuss the anonymity of the nuns within the report, or their potential 'criminality': these are not at issue. The congregations have since refused either to apologise or to contribute to any redress scheme.

Published in 2013, the report is a strange document. The first mention that the women were not paid for their work comes in Chapter Fifteen, in a section about social insurance. There is another reference to their lack of wages in Chapter Nineteen. And that's it, really, on the slavery question. The report is a thousand pages long. And money is much discussed.

Accounts are provided, to show that the laundries operated on a 'break-even basis.' The documents were furnished by the congregations to their own accountants and were not subject to separate audit.

Some accounts are listed as missing, including that of Sunday's Well in Cork. During her time as an RTÉ researcher, Sheila Ahern came into possession of accounts for Sunday's Well dealing with the years 1957 to 1966. She photocopied them and posted the originals back to the nuns of the Good Shepherd; in March 1999 they wrote back, saying: 'The material you forwarded is a cash receipts record for the laundry... it bears no relationship whatsoever to profit.' Of course these accounts may subsequently have been lost, along with those that explained the absence of profit, so we cannot say that Martin McAleese was less than obsessive in his hunt for the truth. Still it's an odd – almost journalistic – thrill to look at documents on your own laptop that the public record says do not exist.

Broadly speaking, the report asks us to believe that women working an eight- or ten-hour day ('we never knew the time,' one of them says) six days a week, before falling asleep in unheated dormitories, could not earn enough to keep themselves fed. If the nuns were bad with money they were like no nuns I ever knew, but the issue of profitability is another distraction. The question is not one of business management, but of human rights. Why do we feel confused?

The advocacy group Justice for Magdalenes has challenged the IDC's findings about the number of women in the system and the average duration of stay. The report puts this at 3.22 years, with a median of 27.6 weeks, but this ignores women who went in before Independence in 1922, many of whom stayed for life. Claire McGettrick has checked electoral registers to find that 63.1 per cent of the adult women registered in the Donnybrook Magdalene Laundry in 1954–55 were still there nine years later. Local grave records show that over half the women at the institution between 1954 and 1964 were there until they died.

The Magdalene story, like the other stories here, is one of people maddened by information, misinformation, lies and ledgers, and there is much and persuasive talk of statistics. But it is the voices of the women that interest me. They spoke to McAleese in person. The report breaks down their testimony into different categories, moving from 'sexual abuse' through 'physical abuse' to 'lack of information and a real fear of remaining there until death.' Only one woman complains that she was not paid for her work. Perhaps the others did not feel entitled to pay, or entitled, indeed, to complain. Their idea of difficulty might be different from yours or mine. The report uses their voices in brief quotations to say that there was no sexual abuse, there was very little physical abuse (by which is meant beatings): there was ritual humiliation, long hours of thankless labour, bewilderment and fear.

But, you know, it wasn't as bad as you might think. Many, many times longer than any woman's testimony is the testimony offered by Dr Coughlan, who seemed to have a splendid time in the Galway Laundry: 'After I sat down at my desk [name] a jovial Resident would proudly arrive with a linen-covered tray laden with tea and buns.' The ladies wore colourful clothing, they brought him their small troubles, or bits of gossip – 'Do you like my hair, Doctor?' There was rarely anything wrong with them, medically: 'Overall, my experience with the Magdalene was a happy and gratifying one.' And as for death certs, he often had to tell people about death certs, we can assume he was worn out telling them. The women Dr Coughlan saw in 1984 were among the last Magdalenes. It is possible they were institutionalised, though he sees that damage as a kind of sweetness. It is possible – though it is really not possible – that it wasn't all that bad and, besides, it is fine now.

The fragmentation of the women's testimony – they are turned into a kind of chorus in the report – seems to show some unease. Justice for Magdalenes says that McAleese was at first reluctant to speak to the former inmates at all; they also say that 'survivors were not made aware their responses would be used to cast doubt over their abusive experiences.' Of course the report is not an oral history project, or even a history project, and it fulfilled its remit to prove there was significant state involvement in the laundries, but I felt I knew less after it than before. It is hard to describe how tiring it was to work through, chasing the sense that something is missing, that you are trapped within the paternalistic paradox: *I am in charge, therefore you are fine.*

So the Taoiseach said sorry, and there is now a redress scheme in place. The records, which McAleese said were so willingly opened to him by the congregations, have been anonymised and the originals returned.

Times were different, this is what the men in my life say: my husband, my brother, my father. Martin, my husband, says that for the Athenian audience Creon was the real hero of the piece; his was the hubris and his, the fall. Creon tries to control the natural order by his own will or ingenuity – a very Athenian impulse – and loses everything he loves. The death of his son, Haemon, is the real tragic event of the play, not the death of Antigone. At best, there are two parallel, dissonant tragedies here, two characters who cannot change their minds, with Antigone the unwitting agent and Creon the dupe of the gods. So it might even be time to feel sorry for the ageing Catholic congregations, who keep reaching for their PR companies and failing to understand. 'When the OH MY GOD – MASS GRAVE IN THE WEST OF IRELAND story broke in an English-owned newspaper (the

Mail) it surprised the hell out of everybody, not least the sisters of the Bons Secours,' wrote Terry Prone of the Communications Clinic, who went on to say that most of the nuns she represents are in their eighties now.

The Adoption Rights Alliance believes the state has a strategy of 'deny till they die': stalling until the nuns and the birth mothers are all dead. But though the children were sent away, they do keep coming back. In the *Examiner*, Conall Ó Fátharta keeps breaking a story about Bessborough, another Mother and Baby Home, also in Cork. A 2012 health service report is concerned that 'death records may have been falsified so children could be "brokered in clandestine adoption arrangements" at home and abroad.' Ó Fátharta says that according to figures given to the public health inspector, 102 babies died there in 1944, a death rate of 82 per cent. There are, however, only 76 deaths on the order's own register, and this pattern is repeated in the surrounding years. Where are the missing children? They may be alive and old, in America. If the problem in Bessborough and perhaps in Tuam, was one not of murder, neglect or the discarded dead, but one of baby trafficking, few people in Ireland would be surprised. One day we will all wake up and be shocked by it, but not yet. Meanwhile, the Sisters of the Sacred Hearts of Jesus and Mary may, in the interests of respectability, decline to open the records they hold on the deaths, births and adoptions of Irish citizens, except on their own terms.

In July 2015, the Adoption (Information and Tracing) Bill was discussed in cabinet. It would give as many as 50,000 adoptees the right to their birth certificate, if they promise not to contact their mothers directly. 'What we want,' says Susan Lohan of the Adoption Rights Alliance, is 'our file and nothing but the file.' In August, shortly before the reburial of Thomas Kent, John Buckley, the bishop of Cork and Ross, called for the exhumation of little Nellie Organ, from the graveyard of Sunday's Well in Cork. Nellie was a wonderfully pretty little girl who suffered a long illness and a terrible death – probably from tuberculosis – in the infirmary of the orphanage there. She was the darling of the nuns, and of all who came in contact with her. She died in 1908, at the age of four. On her last day, she received the host, and Irish schoolchildren were often told she died of happiness. Her story inspired Pope Pius X to lower the age of communion for children, from twelve to seven. The bishop calls her the unofficial saint of the city. She was buried in St Joseph's Cemetery but then exhumed and reburied within the convent grounds 'at the nuns' request,' Buckley said. At the time of the exhumation, a year after Nellie's death, her remains were found to be intact. She is currently buried in the locked nun's plot at Sunday's Well, her grave made distinctive, among the low plain crosses, by a large statue of the Infant of Prague. The Sunday's Well complex is now derelict. It is currently the property of Ulster Bank and the accountancy firm KPMG.

Three

The Lost Children of Tuam[1]

Dan Barry

Behold a child.

A slight girl all of six, she leaves the modest family farm, where the father minds the livestock and the mother keeps a painful secret, and walks out to the main road. Off she goes to primary school, off to the Sisters of Mercy.

Her auburn hair in ringlets, this child named Catherine is bound for Tuam, the ancient County Galway town whose name derives from a Latin term for 'burial mound.' It is the seat of a Roman Catholic archdiocese, a proud distinction announced by the sky-scraping cathedral that for generations has loomed over factory and field.

Two miles into this long-ago Irish morning, the young girl passes through a gantlet of grey formed by high walls along the Dublin Road that seem to thwart sunshine. To her right runs the Parkmore racecourse, where hard-earned shillings are won or lost by a nose. And to her left, the Mother and Baby Home, with glass shards embedded atop its stony enclosure.

Behind this forbidding divide, nuns keep watch over unmarried mothers and their children. Sinners and their illegitimate spawn, it is said. The fallen.

But young Catherine knows only that the children who live within seem to be a different species altogether: sallow, sickly – segregated. 'Home babies,' they're called.

The girl's long walk ends at the Mercy school, where tardiness might earn you a smarting whack on the hand. The children from the home are always late to school – by design, it seems, to keep them from mingling with 'legitimate' students. Their oversize hobnail boots beat a frantic rhythm as they hustle to their likely slap at the schoolhouse door.

A sensitive child, familiar with the sting of playground taunts, Catherine nevertheless decides to repeat a prank she saw a classmate pull on one of these children. She balls up an empty candy wrapper and presents it to a home baby as if it still contains a sweet, then watches as the little girl's anticipation melts to sad confusion.

Everyone laughs, nearly. This moment will stay with Catherine forever.

After classes end, the home babies hurry back down the Dublin Road in two straight lines, boots tap-tap-tapping, and disappear behind those Gothic walls. Sometimes the dark wooden front door is ajar, and on her way home Catherine thrills at the chance of a stolen peek.

Beyond those glass-fanged walls lay seven acres of Irish suffering. Buried here somewhere are famine victims who succumbed to starvation and fever a century earlier, when the home was a loathed workhouse for the homeless poor.

But they are not alone.

Deep in the distant future, Catherine will expose this property's appalling truths. She will prompt a national reckoning that will leave the people of Ireland asking themselves: Who were we? Who are we?

At the moment, though, she is only a child. She is walking home to a father tending to the cattle and a mother guarding a secret, away from the Irish town whose very name conjures the buried dead.

In Ireland, the departed stay present.

You might still come across old-timers who recall how families in rural stretches would clean the house and set out a drink on the first night of November – the eve of All Souls' Day – in the belief that the dead will return. How it was best to stay in the centre of the road when walking at night, so as not to disturb the spirits resting along the wayside.

Even today, the Irish say they do death well. Local radio newscasts routinely end with a recitation of death notices. In a country where the culture of Catholicism, if not its practice, still holds sway, this alerts the community to a familiar ritual: the wake at the home, the funeral Mass, the long gathering at the pub, the memorial Mass a month later and the anniversary Mass every year thereafter.

Wry acceptance of mortality lives in the country's songs, literature and wit. A standard joke is the Irish marriage proposal: 'Would you like to be buried with my people?' A standard song describes a thrown bottle splattering whiskey – from the Irish for 'water of life' – over a corpse. Thus the late Tim Finnegan is revived at his wake; see how he rises.

Respect for burial grounds runs deep, with crowds gathering in their local cemetery once a year to pray as a priest blesses the dead within. This reverence for the grave may derive from centuries of land dispossession, or passed-on memories of famine corpses in the fields and byways, or simply be linked to a basic desire expressed by the planting of a headstone:

To be remembered.

Some 60 years have passed since Catherine's primary school days. It is a gloomy June afternoon, and she is walking the grounds once hidden behind those shard-studded walls. As rain falls from the crow-flecked sky, she drapes her black jacket over her head, almost like a shawl.

Her name now is Catherine Corless, née Farrell. At 63, she is a grandmother with a smile not easily given, and any fealty to Catholicism long since lost.

True, she occasionally volunteers to paint the weathered statues outside the local country churches: the blue of the Blessed Virgin's eyes, the bronze in St Patrick's beard. But this is for the community, not the church. She finds deeper meaning in her garden, in the birds at the feeder outside her kitchen window, in the earth here at her feet.

Few photographs exist of the grim building that once loomed over this corner of Tuam (pronounced Chewm), perhaps because few desired the memory. In its place stand drab rows of subsidised housing and a modest playground. A silvery swing set, a yellow slide, a jungle gym.

One day, a few years back, Catherine began to inquire about the old home that had stoked her schoolgirl imagination. She set out on an amateur's historical quest, but whenever she focused on the children who lived there, so many questions arose about the children who died there – the ones who never made it to the classroom, or even past infancy.

What, then, of Patrick Derrane, who died at five months in 1925, and Mary Carty, at five months in 1960, and all those in between, children said to have been 'born on the other side of the blanket?' The Bridgets and Noras and Michaels and Johns, and so many Marys, so many Patricks, their surnames the common language of Ireland.

Would people pause at their graves? Would they be remembered?

In asking around, what Catherine heard was:

Ah, them poor children. Them poor children.

The more she dug, the more a distant time and place was revealed. Now, standing on the sodden grass, she can nearly see and hear all that was. The polished halls and bustling dormitories, the babies' nappies and nuns' habits, the shouts, the whimpers, the murmur of prayer.

The women and their newborns often arrived after the inquisitive streetlamps of Tuam had dimmed. They came from towns and crossroads with names like snatches of song. Portumna and Peterswell, Claremorris and Lettermore, Moylough and Loughrea.

And now they were here at the St Mary's Mother and Baby Home, a massive building the colour of storm clouds, a way station for 50 single mothers and 125 children born out of wedlock.

The building opened in 1846 as a workhouse, but almost immediately it began receiving victims of the Great Hunger, a famine so horrific that the moans of the dying, *The Tuam Herald* reported, were 'as familiar to our ears as the striking of the clock.' It later became a military barracks, serving the new Irish government formed after a treaty between Irish rebels and Great Britain in 1921. One spring morning during the civil war that followed, six prisoners – republicans who disagreed with concessions in the treaty – were marched into the yard and executed against the ashen wall.

The government repurposed the building to be among the institutions intended as ports of salvation where disgraced women might be redeemed. These state-financed homes were invariably managed by a Catholic order, in keeping with the hand-in-glove relationship between the dominant church and the fledgling state.

Given the misogyny, morality and economics that informed the public debate of the time – when a pregnancy out of wedlock could threaten a family's plans for land inheritance, and even confer dishonour upon a local pastor – imagine that naïve young woman from the country: impregnated by a man, sometimes a relative, who would assume little of the shame and none of the responsibility. She might flee to England, or pretend that the newborn was a married sister's – or be shipped to the dreaded Tuam home, run by a religious order with French roots called the Congregation of Sisters of Bon Secours.

Their motto: 'Good Help to Those in Need.'

You rose early and went down to the nursery with your infant. Mass at 8, then porridge and tea for breakfast. Breast feeding next, after which you rinsed your child's diapers before moving on to your daily drudgery. You might polish the dormitory floors with beeswax or clean bedsheets stained with urine.

'An awful lonely ould hole,' recalled Julia Carter Devaney.

Born in a workhouse and left in the care of the Bon Secours, Julia became an employee who lived in the home for almost 40 years. Although she died in 1985, her rare insight into this insulated world – one she described as 'unnatural' – lives on in taped interviews.

The gates remained unlocked to accommodate deliveries, but so powerful was the sense of cultural imprisonment that you dared not leave. Save for the chance gift of a cake from the bread man, you starved for love or consolation over the loss of your innocent courting days.

'Many a girl shed tears,' Julia said.

The Bon Secours sisters who watched your every move were doing the bidding of Irish society. They, too, existed in a repressive patriarchy with few options for women. They might have experienced a spiritual calling as a young girl, or simply desired not to be a farmer's wife, having seen overworked mothers forever pregnant, forever fretting. A vocation offered education, safety and status, all reflected in clean, freshly pressed habits.

And Julia remembered them all.

Mother Hortense had a big heart, yet was quick to punish; Mother Martha was more enlightened, but a thump from her could 'put you into the middle of next week.' This one hated the mere sight of children, while that one used kindness the way others used the rod. So it went.

The sisters frequently threatened banishment to the mental asylum in Ballinasloe, or to one of the Magdalen Laundries: institutions where women perceived to be susceptible or errant – including 'second offenders' who had become pregnant again – were often sent to work, and sometimes die, in guilt-ridden servitude.

You preferred instead to suffer at the Mother and Baby Home, bracing for that day when, after a year or so of penitent confinement, you were forced to leave – almost always without your child. Waiting for that moment of separation, Julia recalled, was 'like Our Lady waiting for the Crucifixion.'

Typical is the story of one unmarried woman who had been sent to the home from a remote Galway farm. Determined to remain close to her child, she took a job as a cleaner at a nearby hospital and, for several years, she appeared at the home's door on her day off every week to say the same thing:

That's my son you have in there. I want my son. I want to rear him.

No, would come the answer. And the door would close.

For the children left behind, there were swings and seesaws and donated Christmas gifts from town, but no grandparents and cousins coming around to coo. They lived amid the absence of affection and the ever-present threat of infectious disease.

'Like chickens in a coop,' Julia said.

Many survivors have only the sketchiest memories of those days, a haze of bed-wetting and rocking oneself to sleep. One man, now in his 70s, remembers being taken for a walk with other home babies, and the excitement of seeing themselves in the side-view mirrors of parked cars.

'We didn't even know it was a reflection of ourselves in the mirror,' he recalled. 'And we were laughing at ourselves. Laughing.'

Until they were adopted, sent to a training school or boarded out to a family, the older children walked to one of the two primary schools along the Dublin Road, some of them calling out 'daddy' and 'mammy' to strangers in the street. Shabby and betraying signs of neglect, they sat at the back of the classroom, apart.

'I never remember them really being taught,' Catherine said. 'They were just there.'

Teachers threatened to place rowdy students beside the home babies. Parents warned children that if they were bad they'd go right to 'the home.' And even though the babies were baptised as a matter of routine, there remained the hint of sulphur about them.

'They were the children of the Devil,' recalled Kevin O'Dwyer, 67, a retired principal who grew up just yards from the home. 'We learned this in school.'

Still, when a bully targeted a young Kevin during one recess, the child who came to his rescue was a home baby. You leave him alone, the older girl warned. *I see you doing that to him again, I'll get ya.*

The man has never forgotten his protector's name: Mary Curran.

One September day in 1961, a rare and ferocious hurricane howled across Ireland, downing power lines, destroying barley fields, battering cottages. As gales flicked away slates from the roof above, Julia helped lock the doors of the Mother and Baby Home for good. Its conditions were poor, some of its staff untrained, and County Galway officials decided not to proceed with a planned renovation.

Abandoned, the massive H-block building devolved into an echoing, eerie playscape, where games of hide-and-seek unfolded in dull halls once polished with beeswax. Even the old chapel became a place where children became the priests and confessors. 'Bless me, Father, for I have sinned. I shot Brother Whatever,' Kevin recalled. 'That kind of thing.'

The years passed. Galway County moved forward with plans to demolish the home and build subsidised housing. And the memories of hobnailed pitter-patter faded, replaced by the faint sounds of children outracing the home baby ghosts that inhabited the property at night.

Catherine still wonders what led her to the story of the Mother and Baby Home. Chance, perhaps, or distant memories of the little girl she once teased. Despite her bone-deep modesty, there are even times when she feels chosen.

She thinks back to her solitary childhood, her best friend a dog she called 'Puppy,' her time spent navigating the sadness that enveloped her mother. She admired the woman's deep empathy for others, but was puzzled by her refusal to say much about her own people back in County Armagh, a good 140 miles northeast of Tuam. Sure they're all dead and gone, is all she'd say, and God help you if you pried much further.

'A troubled soul,' her daughter said.

Catherine graduated from secondary school, left a Galway art college for fear of lacking the necessary talent, and found satisfaction as a receptionist. In 1978 she married Aidan Corless, a man as gregarious as she was shy, a fine singer, nimble on the accordion, comfortable on the community theatre stage.

Four children quickly followed. Before long, Catherine was minding the children of neighbours as well, immersing herself in the homework, play and exuberance of the young.

Her mother, Kathleen, died at 80 in 1992, leaving behind so much unsaid. Catherine eventually headed up to Armagh to examine public records that might explain why her mother had been so withholding, so unsettled.

As if part of some cosmic riddle, the answer was provided in the absence of one. On her mother's birth certificate, in the space reserved for the name of the father: nothing.

Her mother had been conceived out of wedlock.

Other tell-tale strands to the woman's early years came to be known: Fostered out, moving from family to family before finding work as a domestic. Then harbouring until death a secret she found shameful enough to keep from her husband.

'That she went through her life, that she didn't like telling us,' Catherine said. 'That she was ashamed to tell us....'

In this patch of pain and regret, a seed was planted.

The revelations about her mother fuelled in Catherine an interest in understanding the forces that shape who we are and how we behave. While attending a rigorous night course in local history, she learned an invaluable lesson:

'If you don't find something, you don't leave it. You ask why it's not there. You use "why" a lot.'

With the children grown, Catherine began contributing essays to the journal of the Old Tuam Society about local history, all the while grappling with debilitating headaches and anxiety attacks. The episodes might last for days, with the only relief at times coming from lying on the floor, still, away from light.

Burrowing deep into the past, though, provided welcome distraction, and at some point she chose to delve into the subject of the old Mother and Baby Home: its beginnings as a workhouse, its place in Tuam history, the usual. Nothing deep.

But there were almost no extant photographs of the home, and most of the locals were reluctant to talk. Every question Catherine raised led to another, the fullness of truth never quite within reach. Why, for example, did one corner of the property feature a well-manicured grotto centred around a statue of the Blessed Virgin?

Oh that, a few neighbours said. A while back an older couple created the peaceful space to mark where two local lads once found some bones in a concrete pit. Famine victims, maybe.

The story made no sense to Catherine. The famine dead weren't buried that way.

Who were these boys? What did they see?

Frannie Hopkins was about nine, Barry Sweeney, about seven. The two were at the fledgling stage of boyhood mischief as they monkeyed around some crab apple trees, all within view of the deserted home that figured in their fertile imagination.

Some evenings, Frannie's father would delay his pint at the Thatch Bar, at the top of the town, until he had watched his son race down the Athenry Road, dodging ghosts from the old home to his left and the cemetery to his right, all the way to the family's door. But on this autumn day in the early 1970s, the boys were daring in the daylight.

Jumping into some overgrowth at the property's southwest corner, they landed on a concrete slab that echoed in answer. Curious, they pushed aside the lid to reveal a shallow, tank-like space containing a gruesome jumble of skulls and bones.

Frannie nudge-bumped Barry, and the younger lad fell in. He started to cry, as any boy would, so Frannie pulled him out and then the two boys were running away, laughing in fun or out of fright. They told everyone they met, prompting Frannie's father to say he'd get a right kick in the arse if he went back to that spot.

County workers soon arrived to level that corner of the property. The police said they were only famine bones. A priest said a prayer. And that was that.

In adulthood Barry Sweeney would go to England to find work, and Frannie Hopkins would travel the world as an Irish soldier. Both would return to Tuam, where their shared story would come up now and then in the pub or on the street.

People would tell them they were either mistaken or lying. Barry would become upset that anyone would doubt a story that had so affected him, but Frannie would take pains to reassure him.

'Barry,' he would say. 'The truth will out.'

Now, 40 years later, here was Catherine Corless, amateur historian, trying to unearth that truth, applying what she had learned in her community centre research class: Use 'why' a lot.

When her headaches and panic attacks eased, she pored over old newspapers in a blur of microfilm. She spent hours studying historic maps in the special collections department of the library at the national university in Galway City. One day she copied a modern map of Tuam on tracing paper and placed it over a town map from 1890.

And there it was, in the cartographic details from another time: A tank for the home's old septic system sat precisely where the two boys had made their ghastly discovery. It was part of the Victorian-era system's warren of tunnels and chambers, all of which had been disconnected in the late 1930s.

Did this mean, then, that the two lads had stumbled upon the bones of home babies? Buried in an old sewage area?

'I couldn't understand it,' Catherine said. 'The horror of the idea.'

Acting on instinct, she purchased a random sample from the government of 200 death certificates for children who had died at the home. Then, sitting at the Tuam cemetery's edge in the van of its caretaker, she checked those death certificates against all the burials recorded by hand in two oversize books.

Only two children from the home had been buried in the town graveyard. Both were orphans, both 'legitimate.'

Neither the Bon Secours order nor the county council could explain the absence of burial records for home babies, although it was suggested that relatives had probably claimed the bodies to bury in their own family plots. Given the ostracising stigma attached at the time to illegitimacy, Catherine found this absurd.

In December 2012 Catherine's essay, titled 'The Home,' appeared in the historical journal of Tuam. After providing a general history of the facility, it laid out the results of her research, including the missing burial records and the disused septic tank where two boys had stumbled upon some bones.

'Is it possible that a large number of those little children were buried in that little plot at the rear of the former Home?' she wrote. 'And if so, why is it not acknowledged as a proper cemetery?'

She also shared her own memories, including that joke she and a classmate had played on two home babies long ago. 'I thought it funny at the time how those little girls hungrily grabbed the empty sweet papers, but the memory of it now haunts me,' she wrote.

Her daring essay implicitly raised a provocative question: Had Catholic nuns, working in service of the state, buried the bodies of hundreds of children in the septic system?

Catherine braced for condemnation from government and clergy – but none came. It was as if she had written nothing at all.

There was a time when Catherine wanted only to have a plaque erected in memory of these forgotten children. But now she felt that she owed them much more. 'No one cared,' she said. 'And that's my driving force all the time: No one cared.'

She kept digging, eventually paying for another spreadsheet that listed the names, ages and death dates of all the 'illegitimate' children who had died in the home during its 36-year existence.

The sobering final tally: 796.

Five-month-old Patrick Derrane was the first to die, from gastroenteritis. Weeks later, Mary Blake, less than four months old and anaemic since birth. A month after that, three-month-old Matthew Griffin, of meningitis. Then James Murray, fine one moment, dead the next. He was four weeks old.

In all, seven children died at the Mother and Baby Home in 1925, the year it opened. The holidays were especially tough, with 11-month-old Peter Lally dying of intestinal tuberculosis on Christmas Day, and one-year-old Julia Hynes dying the next day, St Stephen's Day, after a three-month bout of bronchitis.

Measles. Influenza. Gastroenteritis. Meningitis. Whooping cough. Tuberculosis. Severe undernourishment, also known as marasmus.

Nine home babies died in 1930. Eleven in 1931. Twenty-four in 1932. Thirty-two in 1933.

The Tuam home was not alone. Children born out of wedlock during this period were nearly four times more likely to die than 'legitimate' children, with those in institutions at particular risk. The reasons may be many – poor prenatal care, insufficient government funding, little or no training of staff – but this is certain: It was no secret.

In 1934, the Irish parliament was informed of the inordinate number of deaths among this group of children. 'One must come to the conclusion that they are not looked after with the same care and attention as that given to ordinary children,' a public health official said.

Thirty died in the Tuam home that year.

In 1938, it was 26. In 1940, 34. In 1944, 40.

In 1947, a government health inspector filed a report describing the conditions of infants in the nursery: 'a miserable emaciated child... delicate... occasional fits... emaciated and delicate... fragile abscess on hip... not thriving wizened limbs emaciated... pot-bellied emaciated... a very poor baby....'

That year, 52 died.

Catherine felt obligated to these children. Continuing to plumb the depths of the past, she eventually cross-checked her spreadsheet of 796 deceased home babies with the burial records of cemeteries throughout counties Galway and Mayo. Not one match.

'They're not in the main Tuam graveyard where they should have been put initially,' she remembers thinking. 'They're not in their mothers' hometown graveyards. Where are they?'

Catherine, of course, already knew.

Catherine lives simply, almost monastically. She favours practical clothing, usually black, and has never been one for a night at the pub. She doesn't drink alcohol or eat meat. Give her a bowl of muesli at the kitchen table and she'll be grand.

Those headaches and anxiety attacks, though, remain a part of her withdrawn life. Aidan, her husband, has become accustomed to attending wakes and weddings by himself. A few years ago, he booked a Mediterranean cruise for two; he travelled alone.

'A very quiet, introverted person, wrapped up in her own thoughts,' Aidan said of his wife. 'Suffering, if you like.'

But thoughts of the dead children of Tuam pushed Catherine beyond her fears. Believing that the body of even one 'legitimate' baby found in a septic tank would have prompted an outcry, she suspected that the silence met by her essay spoke to a reluctance to revisit the painful past – a past that had consumed her own mother.

Now she was angry.

Adding to her fury was the knowledge that when a Tuam hospital run by the Bon Secours closed in 2002, the religious order disinterred the bodies of a dozen nuns and reinterred them in consecrated ground outside the nearby pilgrimage town of Knock.

'I feel it at times: that those poor little souls were crying out for recognition, a recognition they never got in their little, short lives,' Catherine said. 'It was a wrong that just had to be righted some way.'

Seeing no other option, she contacted a reporter for *The Irish Mail on Sunday*, a national newspaper. Not long after, in the spring of 2014, a front-page story appeared about a certain seven acres in Tuam.

It became the talk of Ireland.

All who had been quiet before – the clerics, politicians and government officials – now conveyed shock and sadness, while the besieged Bon Secours sisters hired a public relations consultant whose email to a documentarian did little for the religious order's reputation:

'If you come here, you'll find no mass grave, no evidence that children were ever so buried and a local police force casting their eyes to heaven and saying "Yeah, a few bones were found – but this was an area where Famine victims were buried. So?"'

The news from Tuam had shocked many in the country, but the dismissive email reflected the lurking doubts about Catherine's work. She was, after all, only a housewife.

Mary Moriarty was getting her light-blond hair done at a salon in Tuam one day when the beauty-parlour chatter turned to this troublemaker Catherine Corless.

'The entire matter should be forgotten and put behind us,' someone said.

Mary, a grandmother well known in town for her advocacy work, would have none of it.

'Well,' she said. 'Every child is entitled to their name, and their mothers could be any one of us but for the grace of God.'

She left the salon, introduced herself by telephone to Catherine, and recounted a story that she rarely shared.

In 1975 Mary was a young married mother living in one of the new subsidised houses built on the old Mother and Baby Home property. One morning, close to Halloween, a neighbour told her that a boy was running about with a skull on a stick.

The boy, Martin, said he had found his prize in the overgrown muck, and there were loads more.

What the boy mistook for a plastic toy was actually the skull of a child, with a nearly complete set of teeth. 'That's not plastic, Martin,' Mary recalled saying. 'You have to put it back where you found it.'

Mary and a couple of neighbours followed the boy through the weeds and rubble, across the soft wet ground. Suddenly, the earth beneath her feet began to give, and down she fell into some cave or tunnel, with just enough light to illuminate the subterranean scene.

As far as she could see were little bundles stacked one on top of another, like packets in a grocery, each about the size of a large soda bottle and wrapped tight in greying cloth.

When her friends pulled her up, Mary's legs were scratched and her mind was on fire. What had she seen? That very morning, she reached out to a person in town who might know. Soon a stout older woman arrived on a bicycle, her faithful dogs trotting by her side.

Julia Carter Devaney, who used to work at the home.

'Ah, yeah, that's where the little babies is,' Mary recalled her saying as she came to a stop.

Julia bent down at the hole and peered in. Mary never forgot what the older woman said next: 'Many a little one I carried out in the night-time.'

Mary did not know what to make of this. Perhaps these were the bodies of stillborns – and therefore unbaptised. Stillborns. Yes, that's what they must be.

Eighteen months after falling into the hole, Mary gave birth to her son Kevin at a Tuam hospital run by the Bon Secours sisters. After breakfast, a nun presented her with her newborn, who was swathed like a little mummy. The young mother's mind instantly recalled those stacks of greying bundles, and straightaway she unwrapped her precious child.

Now, after listening to the woman's tale, Catherine asked whether Mary would be willing to tell her story on national radio.

Of course.

The veteran geophysicist guided her mower-like contraption over the thick grass, back and forth across a carefully measured grid. Equipped with ground-penetrating radar, the machine sent radio waves through the topsoil and down into the dark earth.

The curious machine was hunting for secrets concealed in the ground of the old Mother and Baby Home, all beneath the gaze of a statue of the Blessed Virgin.

This subterranean trawling was being conducted on an early autumn day in 2015 for the Commission of Investigation into Mother and Baby Homes, a panel created by an embarrassed government in response to Catherine's research. Its charge: to examine a once-accepted way of Irish life in all its social and historical complexity.

The commission's investigation into the homes – a network that by the late 1970s was falling into disuse – is focused on 18 institutions scattered across Ireland: in the capital city of Dublin, and in Counties Clare, Cork, Donegal, Galway, Kilkenny, Meath, Tipperary and Westmeath. The high infant mortality rate in some of these facilities was startling. In the Bessborough home in Cork, 478 children died from 1934 to 1953 – or about one death every two weeks.

The investigation's broad mandate also includes scrutiny of the network's links to the notorious Magdalene Laundries. The apparent coercion of unmarried mothers to surrender their children for adoption, often to Catholic Americans. The vaccine trials carried out on Mother-and-Baby-Home children for pharmaceutical companies. The use of home-baby remains for anatomical study at medical colleges.

It was all part of a church–state arrangement that, decades earlier, a long-time government health inspector named Alice Litster had repeatedly denounced, mostly to silence. This system marginalised defenceless Irish women, she asserted, and turned their unfortunate offspring into 'infant martyrs of convenience, respectability and fear.'

The Tuam case incited furious condemnation of a Catholic Church already weakened by a litany of sexual abuse scandals. Others countered that the sisters of Bon Secours had essentially been subcontractors of the Irish state.

But laying the blame entirely on the church or the state seemed too simple – perhaps even too convenient. After all, many of these abandoned children had fathers and grandparents and aunts and uncles.

The bitter truth was that the Mother and Baby Homes mirrored the Mother Ireland of the time.

As its investigation continued, the commission would occasionally provide cryptic updates of its work in Tuam. In September 2016, for example, it announced that forensic archaeologists would be digging trenches to resolve questions 'in relation to the interment of human remains.'

While she waited for the commission to complete its work, the woman responsible for this national self-examination, Catherine Corless, returned in a way to those days when her children and the children of neighbours packed the house. Only now the ones gathering about her were in their 60s and 70s, with hair of silver.

Home babies.

Often lost in the uproar over the many children who died at the Tuam home were the stories of those who had survived. And once Catherine's research became international news, they began calling and emailing her, seeing in this introverted woman their only hope of trying to find out who their mothers were, who their siblings were – who they were.

Catherine assumed the role of pro bono private detective, following paper trails that often led to some cemetery in England, where many unmarried mothers had gone to start anew. The children they were separated from, she said, needed to hear that their mother had 'fared all right.'

Before long, some of these survivors were gathering at the Corless house for a cup of tea and a chat. In their habits and manners of speech, they reminded Catherine of someone close to her who also had been born out of wedlock.

'They all have a kind of low self-esteem,' she said. 'They feel inadequate. They feel a bit inferior to other people. It mirrored, really, the way my mother was.'

During her research, Catherine had built a detailed, wood-and-clay model of the home, large enough to cover a dining-room table. It had helped her to visualise.

Now she and Aidan would occasionally remove the model from a high shelf in the barn out back so that survivors could do the same. They would touch the grey walls and peer into the small windows, as if to imagine themselves in the arms of their mothers.

P. J. Haverty, a retired mechanic, sat at the Corless kitchen table one day, sipping tea and eating a ham-and-butter sandwich. He was born in 1951, the son of a 27-year-old woman who had been left at the home by her father when she was eight months pregnant. Eileen was her name, and she seemed to vanish a year after giving birth.

The white-haired man remembers only a few snapshot moments of the home. Wetting the bed mattresses that would then be propped against the window to dry. Seeing himself for the first time in a car's side-view mirror.

Walking out the door with his new foster parents, the father choosing him because he looked sturdy for farm work, the mother because he had smiled at her.

P. J. was happy enough until his teens, when he was called a 'bastard,' and people avoided the pew he sat in, and girls at a dance tittered at the sight of him. 'If the parents found out,' he said, 'they'd tell them to keep away from that lad, you don't know where he came from.'

He considered drowning himself in the fast-moving river that coursed through his foster father's field. 'The things that I was called,' he said. 'I just thought everyone was against me.'

Thanks to a hint dropped here, a secret whispered there, P. J. managed in adulthood to locate his birth mother in South London. Plump and with greying hair, she reassured him that she hadn't abandoned him. After leaving the Tuam home, she had taken a cleaning job at a nearby hospital and, for more than five years, returned every week to demand that she be given back her child – only to be turned away at the door.

P. J.'s voice caught as he recalled what his mother, now dead, had said she told the nuns to no avail.

'That's my son you have in there. I want to rear him. I want to look after him.'

It was true.

In early March of this year, the Mother and Baby Homes Commission reported that 'significant quantities of human remains' had been discovered on the grounds of the Tuam home.

The ground-penetrating radar and delicate excavation had revealed what appeared to be a decommissioned septic tank. And in 17 of that septic system's 20 chambers, investigators found many human bones. A small sampling revealed that they were of children, ranging in age from 35 foetal weeks to three years, and all dating from the home's 36 years of operation.

Expressing shock, the commission vowed to continue its investigation into 'who was responsible for the disposal of human remains in this way.'

Once again, Ireland's past had returned to haunt it.

His voice trembling with passion, the prime minister, Enda Kenny, addressed the Irish legislature on what he called the 'chamber of horrors' discovered in Tuam. In the 'so-called good old days,' he said, Irish society 'did not just hide away the dead bodies of tiny human beings.'

'We dug deep and we dug deeper still,' he said. 'To bury our compassion, to bury our mercy, to bury our humanity itself.'

Though the prime minister said that 'no nuns broke into our homes to kidnap our children,' others directed their wrath at the Catholic Church and, of course, the Bon Secours order, whose only response so far has been to express its 'continued cooperation and support' for the commission's work.

The Corless household, meanwhile, became an international newsroom, with family members fielding the constant telephone calls and accommodating the television crews forever at the door. Catherine answered every question out of duty, not vanity. But when Ireland's most popular television program, *The Late Late Show*, invited her to appear as a guest, she balked.

There was her ever-present anxiety, which now limited her driving to little more than weekly five-mile runs to the SuperValu grocery in Tuam. More than that, she feared being accused of self-aggrandisement at the expense of dead children.

With her family all but demanding that she accept – *Imagine how many home-baby survivors, suffering in silence, might be reached* – Catherine reluctantly consented, but only if she would already be seated when the program returned from a commercial break. She did not want to be summoned from the curtain to unwanted applause.

Aidan drove her into Galway City to buy an outfit: black pants and a black top, of course, brightened slightly with a silver trim. Then up to Dublin.

'I was a mess,' Catherine recalled. 'But I said: "This is it. I have to do it."'

When she finished telling the story of the Tuam home on live television, the audience rose in what the host described as a very rare standing ovation. Catherine nodded, smiled slightly, tightly and exhaled. Watching on a monitor in an adjacent room, her husband fought back tears.

'I'm married to her for 40 years,' he said later, still astonished. 'And I don't know her at all.'

Photographs of grandchildren adorn the tan walls. A silver kettle rests on the stove. A laptop computer sits open on the counter, beside a window that looks out on a garden, a bird feeder and, beyond, an undulating field of grass.

This is the kitchen of Catherine Corless, and her office. She conducts her online research here, and keeps assorted documents on the kitchen table for easy retrieval when yet another call comes in. *Can you help me find my mother, my sister, my…* She never refuses.

The future of the Tuam grounds that her questioning disturbed has yet to be revealed. The government is grappling with many complexities, including the sad fact that the remains of infants and children, the Marys and Patricks, the Bridgets and Johns, are commingled.

One option is to leave everything as is. Another is to disinter the remains for possible identification and proper burial – although it is unclear whether

DNA evidence can be recovered from those who died so young, and so long ago.

Other issues also need resolution. Potential compensation for home-baby survivors; litigation against the Bon Secours sisters, who run a vast health-care network; the propriety of children playing above the bones of other children.

And there remains the maddening mystery of why a Catholic order of nuns would bury these children in such a manner. Was it to save a few pounds for the cost of each burial? Was it meant as a kind of catacombs, in echo of the order's French roots?

The baptism of these children entitled them under canon law to a funeral Mass and burial in consecrated ground. But perhaps the baptismal cleansing of their 'original sin' was not enough to also wipe away the shameful nature of their conception. Perhaps, having been born out of wedlock in an Ireland of another time, they simply did not matter.

Her auburn hair cut short, Catherine stands now at her computer, gazing through the window at the garden that blesses her with a sense of oneness with it all. Her begonias are blood-red bursts, her lobelias the bluest of blue, her mind forever returning to the past.

A candy wrapper. Empty.

She has searched school and government records many, many times. So far, though, she has been unable to find the name of one particular little girl from the Mother and Baby Home, her long-ago classmate.

'It would be nice to meet her,' Catherine says, leaving no doubt as to what she would say if given the chance.

Dan Barry reported from Tuam, Ireland. Kassie Bracken contributed reporting from Tuam, and Megan Specia from New York, edited for *The New York Times* by Christine Kay.

Among those providing guidance for this story were: Sarah-Anne Buckley, lecturer of history, National University of Ireland, Galway, and author of *The Cruelty Man: Child Welfare, the NSPCC and the State in Ireland, 1889–1956*; David Burke, editor of *The Tuam Herald*; Tony Claffey, historian; Stephen Dolan of the Irish Workhouse Centre; Lindsey Earner-Byrne, lecturer of history, University College Dublin, and author of *Mother and Child: Maternity and Child Welfare in Dublin, 1922–60*; the Rev. Msgr Thomas J. Green, professor of canon law, Catholic University; Kevin Higgins, solicitor; Liam Hogan, research librarian at the Limerick City Library; Yvonne McKenna, author of *Made Holy: Irish Women Religious at Home and Abroad*; Conall Ó Fátharta, reporter for *The Irish Examiner*; J. P. Rodgers, author of *For the Love of My Mother*; Paul Rouse, lecturer of history at University College Dublin; Salvador Ryan, professor of ecclesiastical history at Maynooth College and editor of *Death and the Irish: A Miscellany*; and James M. Smith, professor of English at Boston College and author of *Ireland's Magdalen Laundries and the Nation's Architecture of Containment*.

Other sources include: assorted government reports, historic and recent; *The Irish Examiner; The Irish Times; The Irish Independent; The Irish Mail on Sunday; The Connacht Tribune; The Tuam Herald;* RTÉ; IrishCentral. com; *Banished Babies: The Secret History of Ireland's Baby Export Business*, by Mike Milotte; and *Occasions of Sin: Sex and Society in Modern Ireland,* by Diarmaid Ferriter.

Four

Family Secrets[1]

Clair Wills

My baby's headstone stands taller than everyone else's. I mean this literally – it is a great, solid slab of Hornton stone that dwarfs the surrounding memorials in the graveyard in an almost embarrassing way, given his tiny dates: June 19th–20th, 1996. There is a practical reason for this mismatch. When my partner and I bought the plot, we learned that each eight-by-two-and-a-half-foot patch of earth could accommodate two and a half people. Better leave room to write in ourselves, we thought. Why waste the space? And I was rather comforted by the notion that I knew where I was headed in the end. But my partner and I are no longer together, and now when I think of the headstone I imagine my parents' names inscribed below my son's, and their bodies lowered into the plot alongside his small bones – although I do not tell them this.

The huge stone wasn't all about conserving resources, however. It was also a way of insisting on his little life. He died shortly after he was born in the small hours of the morning, in a hospital in the London borough of Hackney, after I haemorrhaged during labour. When the hospital chaplain came to see me later, I still had Thaddeus lying next to me in the bed, and I asked to have him baptised. Er, no, the chaplain explained, he couldn't do that, because he was already dead. He kept fiddling with the little metal paperclip he had used to attach some records to the inside cover of his black notebook. I was out of it on the morphine I had been given for the emergency Caesarean section, and I remember feeling not merely confused but astonished. He was so lately dead! Barely dead at all! Wasn't he still warm? Couldn't the chaplain do it anyway? The paperclip went up and down.

Later, the priest from my parish in Stoke Newington turned up and baptised away without any qualms. Or he blessed him, or something. It wasn't that I had faith; I just needed a ritual. After that I went into ritual overdrive. My partner and I drove out to graveyards all over London, surveying the desolate plots beneath overpasses and within hailing distance of the North Circular. And we arranged a big funeral mass, with all the works – the coffin on a little stand at the front of the church, cousins over from Ireland, readings, poems, hymns, flowers. All this for a baby who had lived for less than an hour. I look back and wonder why someone didn't take me aside, although I would have reacted as I reacted to the hospital chaplain, with uncomprehending blindness. The whole thing – the big Mass, the big stone, the big family event – it was madness, but it was also necessary.

The revelations in 2014 of the haphazard burial (would 'dumping' be a more accurate word?) of the bodies of nearly 800 babies and small children in the grounds of the Bon Secours Mother and Baby Home in Galway, where unwed mothers were sent to give birth between 1925 and 1961, were shocking for many reasons, but high up among them was that they offer incontrovertible, physical evidence that some lives mattered more than others in twentieth-century Ireland. Obviously that is not in itself a surprise, although Irish society is adept at pretending that it managed to escape the class system that apparently uniquely marred Britain. Its overlords were mostly foreign and Protestant, and were mostly got rid of; it escaped the Industrial Revolution (as though class only arrived with factories); its cities were small and in them community life was still possible; and anyway through much of the twentieth century no one (not even the well-off) had any money.

Weasel terms like 'status' have been used instead of 'class' to describe the rigid stratifications in rural, small-town and urban Ireland. But everybody knows there were the haves and the have-nots. Everyone knows that lots of the have-nots went to England, to become the underclass of the post-war industrial boom, to try to make good, or to have their babies in secret. For others there were the industrial schools, the county homes, the asylums, the laundries and the Mother and Baby Homes. Nearly everyone over the age of 40 knows of someone who was incarcerated in one of these institutions, if only for a time. Nowadays, blogs, advice columns and chat rooms online reveal thousands of people searching for information about their mothers, sisters, aunts and, weirdly, even about themselves.

There is an early painting by Giovanni Bellini that hangs in the Metropolitan Museum in New York. Madonna Adoring the Sleeping Child dates apparently from the 1460s, but has been overenthusiastically restored, so that there is something disturbing about the baby's china-like flesh, picked out in dark outlines, and something definitely off about his impossibly bent right arm. 'The sleeping child is a reminder of Christ's death and sacrifice,' says the catalogue note, and he certainly looks not too well. And then there is Bellini's Madonna Enthroned Adoring the Sleeping Child, in which Jesus's arm dangles in a positively dead-child manner. The dead weight of his arm mirrors almost exactly the dead weight of the crucified Jesus's arm in Michelangelo's Pietà at St Peter's. If he is alive, he is only a little bit alive.

One line on the parallel between the Madonna who breastfeeds her baby and the Madonna who weeps over her dead son is that her tears take the place of her milk, as Jesus's life comes full circle. This gap in time is short-circuited by the mother who gives birth to a child who dies. Her body bursts with milk and tears and blood. Her breasts harden with unwanted milk and her eyes seep. She puddles, like a stricken Witch of the West: 'I'm melting.' Her body cannot deny that the source of life is also the source of death. Baptisms – and even funerals, since funerals presume a life has been lived – are one way of repudiating this unwelcome knowledge.

My attempt to persuade myself, and those around me, that my own baby was barely dead at all extended beyond baptism. I wanted him beside me. I wanted to adore my sleeping child, and in fact if you cradle a small dead body close it does stay warm, or a little bit warm. But that brings its own problems. I kept Thaddeus next to me in the hospital bed until one of the midwives suggested she take him away and pop him in the fridge for a while. 'Don't worry, I'll bring him back.' Which she did, and over the next 24 hours or so he came and went, in his Moses basket. Once when she arrived to take him off for his chilling, I asked, What kind of fridge? I was imagining him in one of those crime-drama metal drawers. Um, she said, I think it's a Zanussi. It was one of the few really good laughs I got in those days – seeing him suddenly in with the milk and orange juice.

Later, at the funeral, my sons took over the task of keeping him alive. 'Why is it so big?' asked the three-year-old as, arms outstretched like a fisherman recalling his catch, he tried to measure the difference in size between the box in front of him and the tiny body he had seen. I must have given an inadequate answer – all I could see was how small the coffin was – because several months later he came to me in some distress to say that he was worried that Thaddeus would be getting too big for his coffin now. His older brother had a similar concern. They had each chosen a treasure to place in the coffin: a board-book version of The Very Hungry Caterpillar (I tried not to think about the worm holes) and a soft toy. Wouldn't he be getting very bored by now, with only those toys to play with?

A child who has never really been born cannot really die. It is immortality of a kind, but not the sort that anyone would hanker after – in a box, underground, just persisting, like Paddy Maguire in Patrick Kavanagh's poem 'The Great Hunger':

> *If he stretches out a hand – a wet clod,*
> *If he opens his nostrils – a dungy smell.*

It is a fiction, of course, to think of the dead who never made it fully into life as somehow less dead than the really dead. But it is a comforting fiction. The un-consecrated graveyards that dot the Irish countryside are home to unbaptised babies but also to criminals, suicides and the insane. In a secular age the natural burial that was forced on these outsiders brings them strangely closer to us – they fertilise the fields we farm and lie beneath the earth we tread. They are not set apart. It is, unfortunately, far harder to imagine the same of the 796 babies and small children who died at the Bon Secours Mother and Baby Home – aged between 35 weeks' gestation and three years old – or the nearly 500 who died at the Bessborough Mother and Baby Home in Cork City and for whom no official burial records can be found. Yet how comforting it would be to imagine that since the church and state institutions did not consider them persons – they were not worthy of proper burial – the rules of life and death do not apply. They did not survive, yet they have not gone away.

*

It was some time before Thaddeus's birth-and-death, back in the early 1990s, that I visited the Convent of Mercy in Clonakilty in order to try to find out more about my first cousin. I cannot remember when I first heard about the existence of this cousin, whom I had never met, and who had died more than ten years before I went searching for information. What I knew, or thought I knew, was that my mother's eldest brother, Jackie, had got a local girl pregnant in 1954. Jackie was then in his mid-thirties and living at home on the farm with his mother; most of the younger siblings were by this time working in Dublin or in London. My mother (nearly ten years Jackie's junior) was doing her nursing training at Whipps Cross, and she had to take several months out to go home and nurse her mother, who had reacted to news of the pregnancy with a sort of breakdown that everyone called a stroke.

My mother told me that during those months at home she talked to both Jackie and his lover, Lily, but they would not marry – and that this was in no small part because Lily was never going to be accepted by my grandmother. Lily was from a smaller, poorer farm, but my grandmother might have got over that. What she couldn't get over, apart presumably

50

from the fact that she regarded Lily as sexually wayward, was that she had 'a withered arm.' It was Social Darwinism that did for her. Lily went into a home to have her baby; Jackie went to work in England, and he never came home again. The farm he was to inherit was destined instead for the second son, Stephen, who came back from Dublin to take over running it.

I cannot remember exactly when I heard this story, but I believe it was 1989; I was in my mid-twenties and a graduate student. Nelson Mandela would soon be released from prison, the Berlin Wall had come down, and I had just given birth to my own baby. My boyfriend and I had agreed on friendly terms to go our separate ways. I would like to think I would have cared about Lily anyway, but I am sure that my shock had in part to do with the frightening difference in our situations. Although I vaguely understood that having a baby on my own was going to be hard (and it was), I never seriously doubted that I could manage it, alongside a future job, even future relationships, and possibly even future babies (and I could). I did not seriously doubt that I had a future. I felt outrage over my grandmother's behaviour. To destroy three lives (Lily's and the baby's, but also Jackie's) for the sake of some false – indeed wicked – ideals of morality, propriety and respectability, some bogus notion of genetic inheritance: I could not accept it. My mother's refusal to express the same sense of outrage puzzled and distressed me. Certainly she expressed sadness, but beyond that I could not penetrate. And to my shame, for a time I let the whole thing go.

It wasn't as though my grandmother hadn't been punished for her intransigence. She had kept the farm, but at what cost? She lost her eldest son; most of the others (two more brothers, two sisters) also lived in England, and came home rarely. How could the house and land possibly have been worth it?

Throughout the 1960s and 1970s we visited the farm where my grandmother continued to live with Stephen every summer, and sometimes at Christmas too. A slightly larger than average farmhouse stood (still stands – one of my cousins lives there now) on 33 acres of land, three acres of which is water: a lake, pretty from a distance, is just boggy land and tangles of reeds when you get close up. The 30-acre farm was meant to be the crucible of independent Ireland's rural economy, an area of land supposedly large enough for farmers to make an admittedly frugal but honest and mostly self-sufficient living. Whether that was ever possible is doubtful. In the 1940s my mother's brothers hired themselves out to dig ditches, lift potatoes and cut hedges in the summers, to make ends meet. Eventually either financial need or a rigid sexual morality, and probably both, was to send them away.

I remember our summers on the farm as idyllic, but they were so in part because the land was barely worked. It made no economic sense to invest in machinery; a visit to granny's was a visit to the nineteenth century. The fields were full of stones, thistles, dock and wild flowers. They were, of course, beautiful. My uncle Stephen borrowed machinery for larger tasks, but mostly he worked with a spade and a scythe. There was a donkey and cart for shifting stuff. He had no car. My grandmother looked after the sow – she seemed to be always making pigswill in the back kitchen. The hens wandered in and out of one of the barns, with its rotted doors and the broken roof slates opening up jagged shapes of sky.

I loved the inside of the house: the fireplace with its hook for the iron bastable, the settle with the horsehair stuffing coming out, the dresser and low benches painted that particular shade of brown, the blue-and-white-striped ware, the pile of copies of *Ireland's Own* to which I brought my puzzled, South London understanding, the daily baking of brown bread and sometimes sweet white bread with raisins, the enormous (horsehair-stuffed) mattresses on which we all (sisters and cousins) slept top-to-toe in rows, the cotton squares of curtains sewn onto plastic-covered wire. But the house was rotting like the barns. You could pass a broom handle through the wooden planks that formed both floor and ceiling. One of the three bedrooms was out of bounds, as you might fall through to the back kitchen below. And this beautiful but dying farm was apparently too good for Lily.

My uncle Stephen would sit at the long table and pour the tea from his cup into the saucer to cool it before drinking. In my memory I am always five or six and sitting on his knee. I had no interest then in where he was when he wasn't in the kitchen or out in the yard giving me a ride on the donkey. And there is so much about him that I do not know. The things that I do know are not enough. I know that he had rheumatic fever when he was a child – my mother recalls how they all had to tiptoe in whispers around the house for months as any sound or movement gave him pain – and that he was never physically strong; I know that he drank, though I don't recall him ever being drunk; I know that he socialised in the pub a few miles from the farm and I presume he used to walk there; I know (bizarrely) that he used to poach salmon by setting off small explosions in the river and waiting for the fish to float to the surface. I know for sure that he died when I was eleven, and when he was less than 50 years old. I can remember clearly my father taking the phone call from my mother, who had gone back home when Stephen was hospitalised with pneumonia. It was seven o'clock in the morning and we were supposed to be getting ready for school. The tears ran down my father's face.

All this I had stored up when I decided to find out more about Mary, my cousin, Lily's baby. 'I cannot remember when' is becoming a trope, but it is the case – I cannot remember when I learned that Lily had her baby in Bessborough Mother and Baby Home in Cork, and that later, when Mary was perhaps four years old, she moved to the Convent of Mercy in Clonakilty. I know now that four years was a very long time to stay in the home, and that the reason for it was Lily's arm. Mary was not adoption material. I cannot remember when I found out that Mary lived in the County Home until she was 16 – maybe longer – or that she went to England to train as a nurse, that she became pregnant by an Indian doctor, that she went to India to meet the family and was rejected by them, and that she killed herself in 1980. She is buried back in Ireland. I do remember the confusion and distress of trying to piece things together through conversations with my aunt, my mother, and my cousins, the guilt I felt about wanting to know more, the sense of a fog of information half-told and half-understood, the frustration of trying and failing to find her grave, and I remember going to the Convent of Mercy in the early 1990s.

I phoned first and spoke to a nun, explaining who I was and what I was looking for – information about my cousin. When had she entered the institution, how long had she stayed there, and was it possible to speak to anyone who had known her? She said she could show me the record of admittance. The old Convent is an imposing three-story nineteenth-century pile, built on a hill, on grounds set apart from the town. More than thirty windows look down on visitors entering the gates. I was terribly nervous as I drove up to the door. I had been at school in England. I didn't know nuns and convents, except by reputation, and that might have been part of the nervousness. But the larger cloud was that I was overstepping a boundary. I did not feel comfortable telling anyone what I was doing. What right had I? None of this belonged to me, though it touched me deeply. I was an outsider. I felt – and still feel – simultaneously attached to and ashamed of my desire to know.

The door was opened by a woman in her late sixties. She introduced herself to me as Sister Immaculata O'Regan. I began to explain again who I was but she put out a hand to stop me. 'I was at school with your mother,' she said. She saw the wild incomprehension track across my face. But she was indeed from the same townland, was brought up in a house a mile or so from my grandmother's farm, and was a few years ahead of my mother in school. It was perfect proof, if I could have understood it then, of the misguidedness of trying to distinguish the church from the local community when apportioning blame for the incarceration of children and young people in church-run institutions. When one in ten Irish children (the figure is from the mid-1960s) entered a religious life, either as priests, monks or nuns, what distinction could there be between the family and the church?

What I grasped at the time was that Sister Immaculata – a clear-eyed woman it was impossible not to warm to – was glad to help because she understood the sadness of the story, and my need to know. I wonder too now whether she also understood the condition of being an outsider. Like me she was both in on and excluded from the secrets of the family and the locale. As we leaned in together to the ledger where she pointed out the entry, we were complicit. I do not think I am making that up.

I don't doubt, however, that had I made the phone call to the convent a year or two later – after the beginning of the public outcry over the Magdalene Laundries and related institutions, where so-called 'fallen' women were confined, and forced to work without payment, for years and sometimes lifetimes – I would have been fobbed off. I would have been told that the records were lost, or that I needed permission from some institutional body or other to consult them. I would have been tied up in red tape, as the religious orders closed their doors to callers and instructed their solicitors. And as it was I got as much evidence as I could bear of the cruelty and lack of love in the system anyway. Sister Immaculata explained that she had not been in the convent when my cousin lived there, but there was an elderly retired nun, Sister Ciaran, who had known my cousin, and she was willing to talk to me. She gave me her phone number.

I knew I could not call from my aunt's house or any of my cousins' so I used our rudimentary mobile phone, though reception was terrible. I drove around looking for a signal, parked the car on a quiet street somewhere near Enniskeane, and called. Sister Ciaran was in her eighties and was now living in a retirement home. I imagined myself talking into a small, carpeted bed-sitting room, with an armchair, TV in the corner, crucifix on the wall. I began badly. A confused and possibly aggressive-sounding account of my desire to talk to someone who had known my cousin was met with a defensive counterblast. 'She was a moody girl, a moody girl,' she said.

In other circumstances I might have been able to interpret 'moody' as 'spirited,' and tell myself a story of resistance. But I knew, as Sister Ciaran knew, that Mary had later killed herself. 'Moody' opened up a world of misery on the part of my cousin and callous indifference on the part of her 'carers' that I had not properly prepared myself for. An already unsteady house of cards came cascading down. I sat back in the driver's seat of the Austin Metro, amid the muck and detritus of the kids (two of them by this time, different dads) – the discarded straws, empty crisp packets, baby wipes, torn colouring books, mashed wax crayons – and wept.

I should not have been so shocked. At the time I was editing an anthology of Irish women's writing, including contemporary journalism, autobiography and memoir. I was familiar with the campaigning articles by writers such as Mary Holland and Nell McCafferty on access to contraception, deserted wives, and the abortion referendum. I knew the stories of Joanne Hayes and Ann Lovett, young women who had tried to have their babies in secret. Both were scandals not so much of sex and reproduction as of the various official bodies (the church, the school, the police, and the judiciary) that let them and their babies down. Although the Ryan Commission report into sexual and physical abuse in industrial schools and reformatories would not be published until 2009, the silence about this systematic torture was beginning to break. There were stories in the papers and on the radio of the pervasive cruelty – rapes, beatings, broken bones – at Goldenbridge industrial school, at Artane, and at Letterfrack. As far back as 1970 the report of the Kennedy Committee into children living in residential homes had begun to uncover institutional cruelty and neglect.

For a long time I thought that my duty to my cousin and her mother was to uncover their story, to refuse to honour the association, once seemingly naturalised in Irish culture, between shame and secrecy. I made ineffectual stabs at getting to see various archives, with the aim of finding out 'what really happened.' But I am not so sure that I have the right to disturb the remains of Lily, Mary, Jackie and Stephen anymore. I am brought up short, first, by a sense of my own presumption. Although I would know more, by excavating dates and institutions, would I really know more of them? Moreover, it feels close to stealing. Lily and Mary belong to each other, and the people who knew them, but they belong to me, and to my sisters and cousins, only as lives lived in the dark.

All of the people involved in that mess in 1954, including my uncles, were condemned to live half-lives. While Jackie was consigned to labouring on building sites in England and an early death, Stephen was buried alive on the farm. And the half-lives lived by Lily and Mary are all too plain. Beyond the immediate family, however, this tragedy is interesting not for its particularity but for its typicality. Every family has a similar story, and sometimes they even come with happy endings. Tidying women away in Mother and Baby Homes or sending them to England, keeping children in county homes and industrial schools, was the norm. It was common from the mid-1960s to the mid-1990s for critics to comment on the peculiar docility of the Irish Catholic character – neither fired up by faith, nor particularly resistant either. The years when Mary lived at the Convent of Mercy were years in which religious observance in Ireland was at an all-time high for both men and women, measured by mass attendance and involvement in pilgrimages, devotions, and missions. The church provided far more than a religious home – it provided a social life and a community.

It is not what we know but how we know that matters. The difficulties I encountered in the 1990s in penetrating further into the half-understood story of my cousin and her parents were in part because of the secrecy that still surrounded them all those years later. But the secrecy was also a way of keeping them safe from the presumptions and condescensions of the next generation. Those of us, my sisters and cousins, born in the ten years after Lily gave birth in Bessborough Mother and Baby Home came of age as a generation as the inheritors of a history we half-knew, and the consequences of that half-knowledge were unpredictable. They include, surely, the fact that between us, in my family alone, we have had no less than five babies 'out of wedlock,' and we have tenaciously held on to all of them. As Patrick Kavanagh put it, we are all 'first cousins to the ghosts of the townland.'

FIVE

The Mother of Us All[1]

Emer O'Toole

On 31 January 1984, 15-year-old Ann Lovett left school to lie beneath a statue of the Virgin Mary in a grotto above her midlands town.

Is Mary your mother? My mother's Mary. Half my friends from home have a mother called Mary, and the rest have at least one Mary for a granny. Mary, the mother of us all.

Mary, my mother, was over six months pregnant when Ann Lovett pushed her baby out into winter. Mary was moulding me from the stuff of her flesh as Ann bled to ascension.

Ann would be in her early fifties now. Still young. Done with bleeding, maybe. Done with the years when her body could be wrest from her and declared a holy vessel. Out of danger. What would she be up to if her small town, her small nation, had not condemned her to die at the feet of an impossible ideal: virgin and mother; mother and virgin?

Would she be planning a week in the sun?

I wish Ann Lovett were fifty, a little overweight, one of those women with a 'fuck yis all' loyalty to smoking, out buying a swimsuit for Lanzarote.

I wish Mary had helped her.

The Mother of God was tired, maybe. The year 1983 had been a big one: she was invoked endlessly in the campaign to introduce a 'pro-life' amendment to the Irish Constitution;[2] she stood for hours on end as a symbol of the only appropriate reason for and response to a crisis pregnancy; statues of her were marched up and down in front of Ireland's family planning clinics in protest of the wanton distribution of lately legal (but only with a prescription) prophylactics. She'd had a lot on. Besides, she was gearing up for her 1985 moving statue tour, with plans to appear at over 30 locations around the country.[3]

If the statue at Granard refused to move that January day, the poet Paula Meehan makes her speak:

> ...and though she cried out to me in extremis
> I did not move,
> I didn't lift a finger to help her,
> I didn't intercede with heaven,
> nor whisper the charmed word in God's ear.[4]

Didn't. Not couldn't. Why?

My mother (Mary, you remember) worked as a nurse for the Galway Family Planning Clinic in 1984. She still tells funny stories of the Legion of Mary parading up and down outside the premises, holding a weighty effigy of the Virgin, chanting the rosary, keeping their beady eyes out for sinners to shame. Customers would nip in as the procession passed the doorway, and then wait for it to pass back again before running off in the opposite direction with their spermicidal spoils. Larks.

Eavan Boland says the voice of Meehan's Mary, 'turns the reader into a *we* – into an historical community, a receptive register for worn-out loyalties and disturbed religious feeling.'[5]

God. Who wants to be a receptive register for worn-out loyalties and disturbed religious feeling? No, *you're* a receptive register for worn-out loyalties and disturbed religious feeling, Mary.

The year 1984 gestated, and Mary stopped going to work because it was time to have me. On 14 April, at University College Hospital Galway, at 8.10 in the morning, I arrived. One week early. I continue to be a zealously punctual morning person. Mum says that a doctor took a picture of me as an example of a baby with perfect fat distribution. This characteristic, sadly, I failed to maintain.

On the same day, another baby was breaking the waters. A plastic bag washed up on the shore at Cahersiveen strand, Co. Kerry. In it, there was a newborn who had been stabbed 28 times.

One. Two. Three. Four. Five. Six. Seven. Eight. Nine. Ten. Eleven.

(This is upsetting to write. To *write* it is upsetting.)

Twelve. Thirteen. Fourteen. Fifteen. Sixteen. Seventeen. Eighteen. Nineteen. Twenty. Twenty-one. Twenty-two. Twenty-three. Twenty-four. Twenty-five. Twenty-six. Twenty-seven. Twenty-eight.

Sweet Holy Mother of Mercy.

It was known that a local woman, Joanne Hayes, had been pregnant. I am always fascinated by the 'it was known' in this story: how Hayes' pregnancy was seen and unseen; how no questions were asked until there was a corpse.

Hayes and her family were interrogated, and, by their accounts, intimidated until they confessed to the murder of the Cahersiveen baby, a murder that they did not commit. Afterwards, they produced another tiny body, Hayes' own child, buried in secret on the family farm. Hayes says her son died shortly after birth.

Hey, how many Irish Mammies does it take to change a lightbulb?

None.

Sure, I'll be fine here, on me own in the dark.

The Gardaí, not to be deprived of what Nell McCafferty designates 'a woman to blame,'[6] ludicrously accused Hayes of conceiving twins by two separate fathers, stabbing one and throwing it in the sea and burying the other.[7]

How many Irish Mammies?

April 1984: a cruel month. So soon after the Irish electorate wrapped the noose of the Eighth Amendment around the Republic's womb, bodies started to push up through the earth like shoots, refusing to stay quiet in *cillíní*,[8] refusing to be hidden within what James M. Smith calls Ireland's 'architecture of containment':[9] the Magdalene Laundries and Mother and Baby Homes designed to catch the ideological overspill of de Valera's dewy green dreams.

Margo Harkin's film *Hush-a-Bye Baby* (1990) is perhaps the most encompassing cultural text to address this moment in Irish history. In it, Derry teenager Goretti Friel hides a pregnancy against the backdrop of 1980s British army occupation, community devotion to both the blessed Virgin and Irish nationalism, enforced ignorance about reproduction and a performance of modern sexual liberation influenced by cultural imports from the USA.

Distressed and unable to confide in anyone, Goretti takes what is surely the most well-trodden journey in Irish cinema – she goes West. In the Donegal Gaeltacht she cries on a stony grey beach, trapped by her island, as a blue plastic bag reminiscent of Cahirsiveen washes against the shore. Or, baking bread in an idyllic cottage kitchen, she waits for the *Bean an Tí*[10] to leave before she tunes the radio to an English-language station and listens to two Dublin voices debating abortion and the death of Ann Lovett. When the *Bean an Tí* returns, Goretti adjusts the dial to listen to traditional music and the Irish language once more. From all directions, her history, her culture and her country close in on her. One of the few moments of respite comes when she and her friend Dinky stop at a grotto to the Virgin and pray. 'Lovely, isn't it,' says Goretti.

Indebted to international feminist avant-garde cinema, *Hush-a-Bye-Baby* gradually muddies the visual distinction between Goretti and the Virgin. Feverish dreams confuse her pregnant body with Marian statues, until on Christmas Day she goes into a nightmarish labour. Fidelma Farley astutely locates the film's contribution to Irish national discourse in its demonstration of 'an awareness of the pull and attraction of the fantasy maternal for women, at the same time as it deconstructs the myths that underpin that fantasy.'[11]

Mary, after all, is an unmarried teenage mother too. A small devotional figurine looks on as desperate Goretti tries to self-abort using castor oil, gin and a scalding bath. Could the Virgin be protecting her?

As tempting as the cool simplicity of a scathing atheism often feels to me, I understand what Farley calls the pull and attraction of the fantasy maternal. Embarrassing fact: I had a May altar in my room every year when I was little. This was encouraged by my Mum, who was perhaps trying to ensure that at least one Mary got the respect she deserved about the place. The altar was a cardboard box with a scarf over it, stage to a plastic virgin worshipped by wild flowers in jam jars. My friend from down the road still slags me about this, mercilessly.

It was nice to have a girl god, though.

No, *you're* a receptive register for worn-out loyalties and disturbed religious feeling.

I wonder if this pull and attraction might ripple with something deeper. Diana Taylor writes of the cult of the Virgin in Latin American. She cites the sixteenth-century Franciscan Friar, Bernardino de Satagün, whose letters gripe that the idolatrous natives are still performing their diabolical pilgrimages and sacrifices but under a Christian guise. The good friar complains of a hill where a temple to Tonantzin, mother of the Gods, once stood:

> and now that the Church of Our Lady of Guadalupe was built there, they also call it Tontanzin [...] and they come now to visit this Tontanzin from far off, as far off as before, which devotion is also suspicious because everywhere there are many churches of Our Lady and they do not go to them.[12]

But Our Lady of Guadalupe chose precisely this hill to appear to a Christian convert, Juan Diego, in 1531. This is the thing with Mary, she never seems to want to appear on the steps of St Peter's Basilica. She likes a heathen shrine, a West of Ireland village.

Taylor thinks about what it means when one deity is worshipped 'not only under the guise of another but at the same time as another – a form of multiplication and simultaneity rather than surrogation and absenting.'[13] She talks about how performances like those underpinning the cult of the Virgin of Guadalupe 'outlast the memory of their meanings.'[14] People end up repeating behaviours they have long since ceased to understand.

Indulge me, then, as I imagine that all this Irish devotion to a girl god is rooted far underground. With the Good People, the supernatural folk of the *Sí* maybe. With Brigid, daughter of the Dagda, who, even when Christianised, brewed beer and performed abortions.[15]

The Tuatha Dé Danann – Ireland's mythological indigenous tribe – were the people of Dana, a goddess who was mother of them all. Dana's daughters could kill just with their words.[16] They could shape shift,[17] prophesise[18] and curse the men who mistreated them in pregnancy down through the generations.[19] Sure, they could do all kinds of everything.

You can stop indulging me now if you like. I am probably just trying to spice up the conflicted conclusion of a childhood and adolescence in which every holiday, every milestone on the road to the age of reason, was drenched in priests and incense.

I remember picking road-side flowers with my Granny in Carraroe for the grotto tucked into the trees beside her cottage. With dozens of other grand-spawn for competition, having my witty, elegant Grandmother all to myself was a rare treat. When I was older she would tell me, 'if they'd had the pill in my day, there'd certainly be a few less O'Tooles.' She wasn't a Mary; she was an Ann. Nancy.

Nineteen-ninety-two brought the X case, in which a supreme court judge ruled that a pregnant and suicidal teenage rape victim had the right to an abortion. I was seven years old; Miss X was only seven years older. In the aftermath, the government put three referendums to the Irish people asking them, first, to remove the grounds of suicide for legal abortion; second, whether pregnant women and girls should have the right to travel for terminations; and third, whether they should have the right to access information about abortion. The electorate took a pro-choice stance on each of these issues. The government, however, did not legislate.

In 2002 the government tried once again to have the people remove suicidal intent as a potential ground for legal abortion. The people refused, by a hair's breadth this time. The government still did not legislate to allow for abortion.

In 2002 I was turning 18, but ineligible to vote in that referendum by one month. Probably a good thing. I had, after all, just spent most of my life being propagandised at Catholic school. I might even have voted to remove suicide as a ground for abortion in spite of my own pregnancy scare.

At 16 I started having terrible sex and, thus, paid a clandestine visit to a sympathetic doctor for the pill. I was told to wait until the first day of my period to start the prescription. But my period didn't come. I was so scared. For weeks, I ran to the toilets between classes to check for blood.

Buying a pregnancy test at the pharmacy in my village was inconceivable. I managed to get into Galway city alone and bought one in Boots on Shop Street. I'll never forget the look the woman behind the counter gave me.

The Legion of Mary might not have been out marching, but it was alive and well.

I took the test on a Sunday in a public bathroom after my dance class. I was so relieved it was negative that I didn't worry about the fact I'd become so thin that my periods had stopped.

'You don't look pregnant. Are you sure you don't have cancer or something,' says Goretti's best friend, Dinky.

'I wish to God I had cancer,' replies Goretti, not missing a beat.

A crisis pregnancy does not need to be worse than anorexia, worse than cancer.

In Áine Phillips' landmark performance art piece *Sex, Birth, and Death* (2003), she positions abortion as a point in a cycle of female sexuality, reproduction, nurturance and even pleasure. Milk pumps from her maternal teats (Fig. 1.). A traditional Irish fruitcake in the shape of a foetus lies in a kidney dish. Phillips chops it up and relishes a slice, offers some to her audience, invites us to chow down on a feminine ideal that tells us we shouldn't fuck or eat (Fig. 2).

[Figure 1. Sex, Birth, and Death. Image courtesy of Áine Phillips.]

[Figure 2. Sex, Birth, and Death. Image courtesy of Áine Phillips]

A crisis pregnancy should be as unterrible as possible.

But it was terrible for (are you ready for the oppression alphabet?): Miss X,[20] Miss C,[21] Miss D,[22] for A, B, and C[23], and for Ms Y (don't be fooled into thinking the progressive change of honorific represents a progressive change of anything else).[24] And for Amanda Mellet[25] and Siobhán Whelan.[26] And for the family of the brain-dead woman kept alive as a slowly decomposing cadaveric incubator for an unviable foetus.[27] And for the ten Irish female citizens who travelled every day to the UK.[28] And for all the girls and women who used abortion pills illegally and without medical support.

Crisis pregnancy was made as terrible as possible. Intentionally. Because women were supposed to suffer for their sexuality.

Mother and Baby Home survivor Ann O'Gorman tells of giving birth – terrified – at Bessborough. She was 17. The nun in attendance taunted her: 'You weren't roaring and shouting like that when you were having sex, were you?' Ann passed out from the pain of having the afterbirth roughly removed. When she awoke three days later, her daughter, Evelyn, was gone.[29]

The last of those hells might have shut in 1998, but, still, you couldn't have women getting off scot-free. So we were off to London for a fun weekend. We had a bit of a flu, actually, and we couldn't come in.

Even miscarriages had to be as terrible as possible. And at University College Hospital Galway, in October of 2012, Savita Halappanavar's was made the most terrible of all.[30]

> ...and though she cried out to me in extremis
> I did not move,
> I didn't lift a finger to help her,
> I didn't intercede with heaven,
> nor whisper the charmed word in God's ear.[31]

Didn't. Not couldn't. Why?

A mid-wife told Savita the truth – that she couldn't have an abortion to end her miscarriage because she was in a Catholic country. And, in the days that followed, the truth-teller was sent out into the wilderness bearing the sins of her people. Sure, everyone else was just repeating devotions they had long since ceased to understand.

Through his grief, Savita's husband Praveen said that maybe Savita was born to change Ireland's laws.

Her face appeared on gable walls. She looked down at us from lampposts. Shrines to her sprung up under bridges, in back alleys; her name was carved on bathroom doors and university desks and anywhere the wood was soft enough to bear it. Who could miss, in a Catholic country, that Savita had died for our sins?

What would she be up to, if she hadn't been condemned to die on the bed of an impenetrable precedent: virgin and mother; mother and virgin?

Would she be giving out to a toddler who has peed on the carpet and is trying to blame the cat, while a seven-year-old and a five-year-old scale the living room sofa?

I wish Savita was stuck in a 5.00 pm Galway bottleneck, late to get her kids from the childminder again, cursing the lady in the Green Mazda who's beatifically letting everyone out of the Merchant's Road car park. I wish she was looking forward to seeing three small faces with smiles just like hers – the kind of smiles that turn a rainy city into a festival of light; the kind of smiles that slit through apathy like a scalpel.

I wish I had never heard of her.

We lit candles and chanted her name. We sent up our sighs, mourning and weeping. Savita: our life, our sweetness and our hope. And her faithful started to testify to what they, too, had endured.

Comedian Tara Flynn sung her abortion story in a gentle, moving one-person show, *Not a Funny Word* (2017). It's a piece that, like Phillips' foetus cake, proclaims its right to be pleasurable. Flynn takes the stage and announces, 'Hello everyone, I'm Tara and I'm a filthy slut,' before launching herself into a number on Shame:

> Irish women are saints, if they're your mother
> Whores or virgins, one or the other
> Fáilte Fáilte Céad Míle Fáilte,
> 100,000 ways to fault you.[32]

Flynn brings us on the journey that so many Irish women have taken, overseas to an abortion clinic, then back to a country that considers them criminals. But she refuses to stay mired in what she designates 'the state of our shame,' and the piece ends with a silly, cathartic song on, well, riding. Flynn sings:

> Let's ride our way to freedom, it's a virtue not a vice
> Whips and chains might be a pain but if you like them do it twice
> Give them shocks in the confession box, give them more than swearing
> By the by, these hips don't lie, though they are not child-bearing
>
> Ride, for Ireland
> Take your turn on top
> Ride, for Ireland
> Don't ever stop
> Ride, for Ireland
> Might as well in this weather
> Ride for Ireland
> And maybe we will come together[33]

The day of the referendum to remove the Eighth Amendment from the Constitution, I walked down Shop Street and stopped to talk to campaigners on either side of the chasm. A young woman out for 'No' had an American accent. She explained that she was studying in Galway for the year, then shared her well-polished arguments with me. I thanked her, moved on. Three metres down the street, I swear upon my soul before you now that she manifested again from the crowd: an apparition.

Disbelieving, I looked back. Forward. Back. Forward. Back.

There were two of her. They were twins! Blessed American virgins.

I envied them their loyalties. Their undisturbed religious feeling. It was time to pray:

> Hail Mary, full of grace,
> Is the Lord with thee?
> No? He's out?
> Could I have a word?
> I'm not doubting the whole Gabriel story.
> As a feminist, I believe women

But, you and Joseph
You got down, right?
In fairness, that beard is hot.
To thee do we cry, poor banished Daughters of Eve.
We're sick of ferries and flights.
We don't want to be Ms Z.
Mary, oh most gracious mother of us all:
We know you're on our side.
Inter-fucking-cede, girl.

Now, the powers that be informed us we shouldn't celebrate the referendum result, but me and my mother Mary popped a bottle of prosecco all the same. Sure, who would begrudge us our pleasure?

In further contravention of our moral overlords, the night we won I went out dancing in the sweaty basement of The Black Gate Bar, where the DJ – my witty, elegant cousin – played only tunes by chicks.

She was there, the virgin, cavorting in her child's sky robes 'til dawn, with her homemade placard stashed in the corner. Rosaries. Ovaries. Loose. Incarnate. Of course, she was there.

On Christmas Day of 2018, the year we repealed the Eighth Amendment from the Irish Constitution, I peed on a stick in my partner's parents' bathroom and it was revealed that onto me a man and/or woman child would be born. And how much sweeter is a dream that's no one's nightmare.

After 35 years of the Eighth, after Ann, after Savita – the Virgin Mother is a mess, just like the rest of us. Our feeling for her might do most good when disturbed.

Of Meehan's poem, Boland writes, 'the voice of the virgin addresses a lost unity. But even in the moment of loss, what is shared is remembered. What is lost is recognised.'[34]

Unity is beautiful. It is. Then it comes to weigh heavy. The rupture is painful. Trust me, I know. But it's worth it.

So, Virgin, Mother (or whatever breed of a streeleen you might really be):

Just hear us. You can keep the pity.

IRISH STATE (IN)JUSTICE

State Responses to Historical Abuses in Ireland: 'Vulnerability' and the Denial of Rights[1]

Maeve O'Rourke

Introduction

This essay analyses the Irish state's treatment of victim-survivors of twentieth-century systematic institutional and gender-based abuses by reference to Martha Fineman's theory of vulnerability, including her warning of the dangers of a non-universalist approach. It argues that the Irish state has constructed victim-survivors as a 'vulnerable' group by denying them access to ordinary democratic accountability mechanisms and using this impunity to portray victim-survivors as requiring 'specialised' measures, which it then operates 'benevolently' without reference to human rights law. The essay argues that Fineman's work offers an unsettling lens through which to view reparation efforts for gross and systematic human rights violations, particularly involving systems of state care.

The defining feature of Martha Fineman's theory of vulnerability is her insistence that we are all equally vulnerable. According to Fineman, it is the universality of vulnerability – the inability of any person to escape their embodiment and embeddedness in society, and their consequent dependence – that is both the moral basis for the state's obligation to behave towards us in ways that enhance our resilience, and the touchstone for evaluating state action. Fineman resists absolutely the categorisation of individuals or groups as 'more vulnerable' or 'differently vulnerable' by comparison with others.[2] She identifies a 'vulnerability paradox': that is, the need to recognise and ensure equitable state responses to people's different positions (brought about by their inherent vulnerability and the extent to which they are denied or enabled to access the resources required for resilience), while at all times understanding vulnerability to be a universal human experience.[3]

Fineman's approach sets her apart from other scholars in the field. Catriona Mackenzie, Wendy Rogers and Susan Dodds note the alternative view among vulnerability theorists that distinguishing between sources and intensities of vulnerability is necessary in order to 'identify responsibilities owed to the "more than ordinarily vulnerable" and potential interventions to mitigate the effects of various forms of vulnerability.'[4] These authors highlight a prevalent concern that understanding the concept solely as an inherent experience may prevent identification of ways in which social arrangements cause and can ameliorate forms of powerlessness and dependency.[5] Mackenzie, Rogers and Dodds use the term 'situational vulnerability,' for example, to refer to powerlessness 'caused or exacerbated by the personal, social, political, economic or environmental situations of individuals or social groups.'[6] Fineman would describe these individuals and groups as 'differently positioned' while 'equally vulnerable.'[7]

When one considers Fineman's reasons for insisting on a universalist conception of vulnerability, the connections between her theory and the concept of human rights become clear. First, Fineman's key normative claim is that states are obliged to act in response to the fact that we all share a common, inherent, human condition.[8] She seeks to establish as the premise for state action every human being's equal moral entitlement to state intervention in ways that respond to their embodiment and social embeddedness. Second, Fineman posits that there is a (universal) conceptual core upon which an endlessly flexible and individually responsive state apparatus can be built,[9] and in defiance of which state action will lack legitimacy. Third, Fineman attends to the problem of discrimination. She contends that her theory of vulnerability challenges states' refusal to recognise their obligations towards people who do not occupy the position of the liberal stereotype. She also warns against conceiving of vulnerability as a group-based phenomenon because of the stigmatising impact of doing so.[10] Fineman is not alone in arguing that labelling certain people as uniquely vulnerable risks promoting measures that control, punish, and paternalise them on the basis that their needs for and entitlements to resources are understood not to derive from the same source or be of the same quality as the needs and entitlements of everybody else.[11]

Using the Irish state's treatment of victim-survivors of twentieth-century systematic institutional and gender-based abuses as a case study, this essay attempts to demonstrate how Fineman's theory can help to illuminate and explain human rights violations in contexts where the violations have been masked by the rhetoric of charity and benevolence on the state's part. Fineman pays intense attention to the underlying rationale for state action rather than the detail of its execution; as she explains, her approach is 'decidedly focused on exploring the nature of the *human* part, rather than the *rights* part, of the human rights trope.'[12] This emphasis is a powerful, unsettling lens through which to view patterns of state behaviour. It offers a thread by which the state's characterisation of certain people can be traced to the human impact of its treatment of them, and vice-versa.

The remainder of this essay discusses Ireland's responses over the past decade to the justice demands of victim-survivors[13] of Magdalene Laundries, Mother and Baby Homes and systematic forced family separation. Sections I and II describe the ongoing impunity for these so-called 'historical' abuses, evidenced by the Irish state's refusal to acknowledge responsibility for human rights violations and its foreclosing of the ordinary legal avenues of democratic state accountability to victims and survivors. Section III considers the state's rationale for its behaviour. Drawing on Fineman's theory of the dangers of a non-universalist conception of vulnerability, the essay argues that the Irish state can be seen to be using – and constructing – a notion of group-based 'vulnerability' to deny its human rights responsibilities. While refusing to acknowledge that it has caused victim-survivors' need to demand specialised measures of justice through public campaigning, the state portrays itself as responding benevolently to this 'hurt'[14] and 'vulnerable'[15] group. It has taken advantage of victim-survivors' lack of access to the ordinary democratic mechanisms of the courts, police investigations, inquests and archives to create mandates and procedures for these ad hoc mechanisms which do not meet human rights law requirements. Section III continues by describing how, as these mechanisms proceed without a human rights focus to their mandate or procedures, they reinforce the notion that the state is not responsible for human rights violations, allowing it to continue its pattern of impunity.

I. A State of Denial

To this day, the Irish state refuses to accept that it is responsible for constitutional or other human rights violations in Magdalene Laundries, despite the Taoiseach (Irish Prime Minister) issuing an official apology to survivors in 2013,[16] and the President of Ireland[17] and Minister for Justice[18] adding their own public apologies since. It is documented extensively[19] that Magdalene Laundries incarcerated, denigrated, and forced into unpaid labour – often for years, decades and whole lifetimes – well over 10,000 girls and women from the foundation of the Irish Free State in 1922 until the last institution's closure in 1996; that state agents placed over one quarter of those girls and women in the Catholic Church-run institutions; and that the state not only failed to regulate the institutions but actively supported them by contracting with the nuns for vast laundry services, ensuring under the Conditions of Employment Act 1936 that the nuns were not required to pay wages, and providing the assistance of An Garda Síochána (Irish police force) in returning escapees.

The government insists that there is 'no factual evidence to support allegations of systematic torture or ill treatment of a criminal nature in these institutions.'[20] It contends, further, that the available evidence does 'not support the allegations that women were systematically detained unlawfully in these institutions or kept for long periods against their will.'[21] A state report in 2015 to the United Nations (UN) Committee against Torture (CAT) asserted: 'No Government Department was involved in the running of a Magdalen Laundry. These were private institutions under the sole ownership and control of the religious congregations concerned and had no special statutory recognition or status.'[22] The Irish state's July 2020 Defence to Elizabeth Coppin's ongoing individual complaint to the CAT goes so far as to claim that her detention as a teenage girl in three Magdalene Laundries was not 'by reason of her gender' and therefore was not discriminatory.[23] For the past 11 years the government has repeatedly rejected recommendations from the Irish Human Rights and Equality Commission (IHREC)[24] and five UN human rights bodies[25] to establish an independent and thorough investigation into the allegations of widespread, grave and systematic human rights abuses in Magdalene Laundries.

Similarly, the Irish state refuses to accept that grave constitutional and human rights violations are disclosed or even indicated by the extensive publicly available evidence of systematic arbitrary detention of girls and women and neglect of their children in state-funded Mother and Baby Homes and County Homes,[26] and the widespread coerced or otherwise unlawful adoption of children born to unmarried mothers until the latter part of the twentieth century.[27] Numerous UN human rights bodies[28] have recommended an independent, thorough and effective investigation into all allegations of human rights violations in the family separation system that is estimated to have involved at least 182 agencies, individuals and institutions from independence onwards.[29] The government has declined to establish any independent investigation into historical adoption practices generally, within and from Ireland. State bodies continue to use the phrase 'incorrect registrations'[30] to describe the systematic illegal registration of 'adoptive' parents on a child's birth certificate, employed as a method of circumventing adoption laws and effecting de facto adoptions in the absence of legislation permitting domestic adoptions before 1953 and foreign adoptions generally.[31] Ó Fátharta has reported that staff in the national Child and Family Agency (Tusla) were instructed in 2017 not to refer to records of a 16-year-old mother being forced in 1974 to sign a false name on an adoption consent form as indicating an 'illegal adoption' because 'stuff is FOI'able... and it could be used against us if someone takes a case.'[32] The final report of the statutory Mother and Baby Homes Commission of Investigation (MBHCOI), published in January 2021, addressed the treatment of 56,000 mothers aged as young as 12 and an additional 57,000 children in 18 Mother and Baby Homes and County Homes between 1922 and 1998. Testimony provided by women to the MBHCOI described, among other abuses: detention without legal basis ('we were locked in and there was absolutely no way of getting out.'[33] ... 'I attempted to run away twice with two other girls, but they always found us and brought us back'[34]), forcible repatriation from England,[35] additional coercion to relinquish a child ('I told him I didn't want to sign but he just told me to shut up.'[36] ...'I was under continued pressure from the social worker to sign the adoption consent form')[37] and child stealing ('when my baby boy was six-seven weeks old, he was wrenched from my breast by one of the nuns whilst I was breastfeeding him and taken away for adoption').[38] Women reported denial of contact with relatives,[39] extreme neglect ('[my son was] in a closed off area called the dying room. I begged the nuns to take my son to a hospital, but they only did so after two weeks had passed. ...I do not even know whether he was buried in a coffin.'[40] ...'As the pain progressed, I was locked in what I can only describe as a cell. ...I was left there all night with no attention')[41] and subjection to forced unpaid labour ('[It was] heavy work scrubbing clothes and bedding on boards, washing and ironing all with our bare hands during a six-day week.'[42] ... 'We were made to work even if we were very ill, as I was. No excuses were ever accepted').[43] The survivor testimony and archival material which the MBHCOI summarised in its final report is further reflective and corroborative of the above excerpts.[44] Nonetheless the MBHCOI concluded that:

- 'There is no evidence that women were forced to enter mother and baby homes by the church or State authorities';[45]
- The girls and women in the institutions 'were not "incarcerated" in the strict meaning of the word but, in the earlier years at least, with some justification, they thought they were';[46]
- The girls and women 'were expected to work but this was generally work which they would have had to do if they were living at home';[47]
- There is 'very little evidence that children were forcibly taken from

their mothers... the mothers did not have much choice but that is not the same as "forced" adoption';[48]

- Regarding vaccine trials conducted by the Wellcome Foundation and Glaxo Laboratories between 1934 and 1973: 'It is clear that there was not compliance with the relevant regulatory and ethical standards of the time as consent was not obtained from either the mothers of the children or their guardians and the necessary licenses were not in place. There is no evidence of injury to the children involved as a result of the vaccines';[49] and

- In respect of the thousands of unknown graves of children who died: 'In cases where the mothers were in the homes when the child died, it is possible that they knew the burial arrangements or would have been told if they asked. It is arguable that no other family member is entitled to that information.'[50]

The MBHCOI's final report includes a chapter described as a 'compilation' of the testimony which 550 institutional survivors and adopted people gave to its 'Confidential Committee.'[51] Without identifying the extracts to which it refers, the chapter begins with the blanket accusatory statement that: 'The Commission has no doubt that the witnesses recounted their experiences as honestly as possible. However the Commission does have concerns about the contamination of some evidence. ...This contamination probably occurred because of meetings with other residents and inaccurate media coverage.'[52]

II. Exclusion from Democratic Accountability Mechanisms

Ireland's established mechanisms of democratic accountability and rule of law – its civil and criminal justice procedures, its coroners' inquest system and its information transparency mechanisms such as Freedom of Information, the National Archives and data protection laws – have been kept out of the reach of those affected by the above-mentioned, frequently termed 'historical,' abuses. Prompted by survivor- and adopted-person-led advocacy, the CAT has recommended that the Irish state ensure that civil actions 'can continue to be brought "in the interests of justice",' that the state 'promote greater access of victims and their representatives to relevant information concerning the Magdalene Laundries held in private and public archives,' and that 'information concerning abuses in [Mother and Baby Homes and related institutions] are made accessible to the public to the greatest extent possible.'[53] The CAT and other UN human rights treaty bodies have also repeatedly recommended the prosecution of perpetrators where appropriate and access to redress including as full rehabilitation as possible.[54]

An Garda Síochána has never announced that it is investigating the Magdalene Laundries nor asked for witnesses to come forward, notwithstanding the available evidence of systematic abuse and the fact that several survivors have made police complaints.[55] The government claims that '[i]t is open to anyone who believes a criminal act took place to make a criminal complaint and it will be investigated,'[56] while simultaneously asserting that all of the testimony and archival records available to it (which are mostly closed to survivors and the public) demonstrate the 'absence of any credible evidence of systematic torture or criminal abuse being committed in the Magdalene Laundries.'[57]

With the exception of one minor prosecution of a midwife in 1965 following which she continued to operate an adoption agency for over a decade, neither the adoption system nor the institutions that incarcerated unmarried mothers have been subject to criminal prosecution.[58] In recent years individuals have complained and various state bodies have delivered reports to the Gardaí regarding non-consensual vaccine trials in Mother and Baby Homes,[59] illegal adoptions,[60] the burial of thousands of babies' bodies, unmarked and unidentified, by nuns operating Mother and Baby Homes,[61] and the absence of death certificates for all children recorded by the nuns as dying in the institutions.[62] The Garda Commissioner announced in April 2021 that he does not plan to commence an investigation into the matters summarised in the 2,865-page MBHCOI's final report because the MBHCOI's anonymisation of its findings means that 'there is insufficient detail in the report to commence an investigation.'[63] The Garda Commissioner urged survivors of Mother and Baby Homes to come forward with their testimony while cautioning that 'there will be limitations as to the action we can take in some cases due to matters such as the loss of evidence over time or suspects and witnesses being deceased.'[64] He did not mention that his police force is statutorily barred from accessing the entire archive of records gathered by the MBHCOI, pursuant to the inquiry's underpinning legislation.[65] Meanwhile, in evidence to a parliamentary committee in early 2021, one survivor explained that when she approached the Gardaí regarding her missing brother who is recorded by the nuns as dying but regarding whom there is no death certificate or burial record, 'I was blocked and told by the Garda that it was dealing with the commission.'[66] Another survivor argued: 'more than 850 burials in Bessborough [Mother and Baby Home] are unaccounted for and we regard those babies as illegally missing. Accordingly, a full Garda investigation should be initiated, and it should include Garda access to the archives of the religious order and investigate all living personnel, no matter what age.'[67]

The civil courts are generally unavailable to survivors, and not only because of the secrecy of information (discussed further below). The Statute of Limitations presents an almost total bar to litigation of so-called 'historical' claims against either state or non-state actors.[68] There is no legislative provision for the exercise of judicial discretion to extend in the interests of justice the short limitation period for an action claiming personal injuries in tort, and the few existing exceptions to the limitation period are extremely narrow.[69] Strikingly, the publicly known nature of the Magdalene Laundries, Mother and Baby Homes and forced adoption abuses was recently found by the Irish High Court, Court of Appeal and Supreme Court to prevent the operation of the 'concealed fraud' exception to the ordinary limitation period for personal injury claims.[70]

The *O'Keeffe v. Ireland* case, concerning the state's failure to protect an eight-year-old child from sexual abuse at primary school in the 1970s, demonstrates the state's practice of pursuing litigants for its costs of defending even test human rights cases.[71] Although ultimately successful before the European Court of Human Rights in 2014, when Ms O'Keeffe lost her case at first instance the High Court awarded the state approximately €500,000 in legal costs, to be paid by the plaintiff.[72] Colin Smith and April Duff note that 'religious orders and State agencies are vigorous in seeking costs against litigants whose claims against them have failed… [and] victims of historic institutional abuse receiving legal advice will receive a stark warning from their lawyers that if their proceedings fail, they will face financial ruin.'[73] Further procedural obstacles to accessing the civil courts identified by Smith and Duff include: a narrow conception of vicarious liability in Irish tort law such that abuse in privately managed, state-funded social care services will not necessarily give rise to state responsibility; the difficulty of determining which defendant(s) to sue, particularly given that religious congregations in Ireland have no independent legal personality; the lack of class action legislation; and the inordinate delays that defendants can cause to the progress of proceedings due to the absence of modern judicial case management procedures in the Irish High Court.[74] In addition, in order to receive modest payments from an *ex gratia* 'restorative justice' administrative scheme established in 2013, Magdalene Laundry survivors were required by the government to waive all legal rights against the state regarding their abuse.[75]

The MBHCOI's final report indicates that no more than a handful of coroners' inquests have been held into deaths in Mother and Baby institutions,[76] despite the fact that 200 mothers and 9,000 (approximately 15 per cent) of children born in the institutions investigated by the MBHCOI died there[77] and no burial records have been produced for most.[78] Irish legislation throughout the twentieth century mandated an inquest where a death appeared unexplained or unnatural; current legislation additionally requires a coroner's inquest in every instance where a person has died while in state custody or detention[79] and permits the Attorney General to direct the holding of an inquest wherever it is deemed 'advisable.'[80] Several local coroners have been notified of the existence of mass unmarked graves at sites of former Mother and Baby institutions,[81] including in Tuam where 'significant quantities of human remains' were located in a disused sewage tank in 2017 and where they lie still, unidentified.[82]

Basic information, both about one's personal circumstances and about the systems within which individuals were abused, is withheld in numerous other ways. The National Archives Act 1986 does not designate health or social care agencies as sources of records that must be preserved and deposited for public access.[83] The list of state bodies to which the 1986 Act does apply is now 35 years out of date; it excludes the national Health Service Executive, for example, and the Child and Family Agency which holds approximately 70,000 adoption records deriving from its predecessors' activities and from now-defunct adoption agencies and Mother and Baby institutions.[84] Local authority records also fall outside the remit of the National Archives Act 1986,[85] as do the records of the Adoption Authority of Ireland (previously the Adoption Board).[86] Public access is constrained even to those state departmental records that should be available in the National Archives of Ireland (NAI) because government funding to the NAI is so low that its archivists are only capable of actively managing four government departments' records[87] and over one third of the NAI's limited holdings are not catalogued.[88]

The Freedom of Information Act 2014, meanwhile, creates a general right of access only to information held by public bodies that was created after 1998 (or 2008 for some public bodies) with narrow exceptions.[89] The 2014 Act specifically excludes from its remit adoption records held by the Adoption Authority of Ireland.[90] Decision-makers' discretion under the 2014 Act may be deployed to prevent access; Ó Fátharta, a journalist writing extensively on twentieth-century adoptions in and from Ireland, explains that the 2014 Act is becoming less useful to his research the more that the abuses in the adoption system are coming to public attention:

> Access to information is everything to a journalist. ... I would say in the last four or five years it has become far more stringent ...You don't get anything back on time, there's so many ways to drag it out. ... I've said this before: on all of the adoption stuff that I've done, I was accessing records to do with Mother and Baby Homes pretty easily through the HSE [Health Service Executive] and Tusla. I understand there are things you can't get. Then lo

and behold, since a lot of this stuff started to get more traction, I get nothing now.[91]

For many years, the government rejected survivors' and advocates' requests for legislation compelling the production of all historical 'care'-related records into a dedicated national archive. Ireland informed the CAT in 2018 that the nuns' records relating to Magdalene Laundries 'are in the ownership of the religious congregations and held in their private archives [and] the State does not have the authority to instruct them on their operation.'[92] This echoed a statement by the Minister for Justice in 2013 that:

> I have no control over records held by the religious congregations or other non-State bodies. ... It is not within my power to establish a facility that would allow the women who were admitted to the Magdalen Laundries and their families access to all genealogical and other records necessary to locate their families and reconstruct their family identities.[93]

In October 2020 the government finally announced that it will in the future create 'on a formal, national basis an archive of records related to institutional trauma during the 20th century.'[94] This announcement followed public pressure campaigns fought vigorously by survivor- and adopted-person-led groups in response to a government Bill in 2019 proposing to 'seal' for at least 75 years the archive of the largest statutory investigation to date on matters of historical church-related institutional child abuse,[95] and the government's announcement in September 2020 that it intended to 'seal' for 30 years the archive gathered by the MBHCOI.[96]

At present, the Department of the Taoiseach (Prime Minister) has custody of the entire archive of state administrative records concerning the Magdalene Laundries. These were gathered from numerous departments for the purpose of an Inter-Departmental Committee (IDC) examination between 2011 and 2013 of the state's historical interactions with the institutions.[97] For years the Taoiseach's Department insisted in response to Freedom of Information requests that: 'these records are stored in this Department for the purpose of safe keeping in a central location and are not held nor within the control of the Department for the purposes of the FOI Act. They cannot therefore be released by this Department.'[98] Following legal proceedings by one survivor, the Information Commissioner found this stance unlawful.[99] Nonetheless, the archive has not been deposited in the NAI nor made publicly available otherwise. The state argued as recently as July 2020 to the CAT that Elizabeth Coppin should try to piece together her own version of the Taoiseach's collected archive of Magdalene Laundry records by making individual requests to all of the original record holders using the Freedom of Information Act (which, as discussed above, does not apply generally to historical information).[100] The MBHCOI archive, which the Minister for Children announced his intention to 'seal' in September 2020, similarly rests in a government Department without any clear pathway to accessing it. Its contents are known to include financial, inspection, maternity, death and burial, adoption, statistical, research, baptism and other records of Mother and Baby institutions and related agencies, government departments, religious congregations, churches and dioceses, local authorities, foreign adoption societies, pharmaceutical companies, university anatomy departments, and cemeteries, for example.[101]

Finally, victims' and survivors' access to their personal data and to information about deceased or disappeared next of kin is stymied both by the absence of an explicit, detailed legislative scheme of personal access to historical care-related records and by the ad hoc, legally dubious decision-making of the wide range of state and non-state actors that hold relevant records and are subject to the European Union General Data Protection Regulation framework.[102] The CLANN Project has reported numerous incidences of mothers, adopted people and others affected by family separation being discouraged, delayed, demeaned and even lied to in their search for personal information in recent decades.[103] In 1997 the St Patrick's Guild adoption agency, which arranged more than 10,000 adoptions in Ireland during the twentieth century, acknowledged that it routinely gave false information to adopted people about their parents.[104] In summer 2019 a government-appointed Collaborative Forum of survivors of Mother and Baby Homes reported being informed by Tusla that when an adopted person requests their personal records, state social workers assess 'the likelihood of harm being caused to wider birth families by the release of personal information to an applicant.'[105] The Collaborative Forum noted that '[n]either the statutory basis for such a criterion, nor the nature of how harm is determined, was clear to forum members.'[106] Tusla has further stated as a blanket rule that when an adopted person seeks information it can only 'lawfully release information relating to other persons (e.g. birth parents) with their expressed consent,'[107] demonstrating that Tusla does not consider an adopted person's identity at birth or family circumstances to be their personal data.[108] The opaque and unpredictable manner in which the state manages the personal information of people subjected to unlawful family separation was further demonstrated in 2018 when the Department of Children publicly acknowledged (having been aware of many of these cases for several years)[109] that it knew of 126 people registered at birth by an adoption agency as the natural child of people who were not their natural parents.[110] Records of internal departmental discussions show the question being raised, 'whether the information will do more harm than good to those who have no indication of the problem to date,' and Tusla querying 'who to tell first – birth parents, adopted parents, subject of registration'; 'how much information are they entitled to'; 'if the subject matter is deceased, do we advise their children'; and 'how does the state manage litigation?'[111]

III. The Manipulation of 'Vulnerability' and Special Measures

The above section describes a labyrinth of obstacles barring victim-survivors from accessing what might be described as the 'ordinary' legal mechanisms of the democratic state. This is not a passive arrangement; rather the state has defended and strengthened it over the past decade in response to varied and persistent efforts by those affected to achieve justice, accountability and redress for their treatment. Fineman's theory – her strong resistance to the notion of group-based 'vulnerability' – urges an examination of the state's rationale for its behaviour, in order to understand more about why and how this state of impunity has persisted; what is required in order for the state to remedy its human rights violations; and whether an appreciation of the rationale can shed light on any further human rights violations.

It is contended here that state and public representatives have constructed victim-survivors of Magdalene Laundries, Mother and Baby institutions and the forced family separation system as a uniquely 'vulnerable' group and that, in the process, the state's human rights law obligations have been elided.

One method of this construction is explicit labelling. Government representatives have described Magdalene Laundry survivors as 'vulnerable' on numerous occasions.[112] In submissions to the UN Committee on the Elimination of Discrimination Against Women in 2017 the state described the purpose of the MBHCOI as follows: 'We established a statutory Commission of Investigation into Mother and Baby Homes in February 2015 to provide a full account of what happened to vulnerable women and children in these Homes during the period 1922 to 1998.'[113] Politicians reacted to the MBHCOI's final report in early 2021 as follows, for example:

- 'The commission's report is a reminder to us all of how vulnerable people are often removed from society.'[114]
- 'We commemorate the lives of soldiers who die for the nation and the State. Is it not fitting, then, that we should also commemorate the lives of the vulnerable who died and those who suffered because of the neglect of this nation and the State?'[115]
- 'We have to ensure that the survivors are heard. …We cannot

leave them again. They are so vulnerable and have gone through so much.'[116]

- 'The publication of this report is a first step on a very long road of national reflection, redress and reconciliation along with atonement for the wrongs and injustices committed against the most vulnerable and innocent in our society.'[117]
- 'As a practicing Catholic, I am deeply ashamed that such a system could exist, let alone be inflicted on the vulnerable in the name of mercy.'[118]
- 'There is a responsibility on all of us who have been affected by the publication of the report, and it is hard reading, to apply what we are feeling and what we have learned to help the many vulnerable people who are enduring shame and stigma as a result of personal issues in our society today. ... Such understanding and compassion were in short supply in the mother and baby homes.'[119]
- 'Following the publication of the report last week, the Government offered our apology and asked for forgiveness for the failings of the Irish State – failings that repeated over many decades and which had the most horrendous consequences for our most vulnerable citizens.'[120]

It is possible, I argue, to identify two further mainstays of the state's construction of these victim-survivors as an especially 'vulnerable' group, separate from other citizens who may suffer abuse (which category should, according to Fineman, be understood to be universal). The first is the practice of establishing ad hoc responses to their justice demands, such as a dedicated inquiry or administrative payments scheme, while at the same time dislocating them from Ireland's established democratic mechanisms of justice and accountability. This essay does not argue against the use of specialised investigation and reparation methods to address gross and systematic human rights abuses, per se. However, their deployment in a context where victim-survivors are being prevented from accessing the legal avenues that others in the state take for granted has the effect of portraying those for whom the specialised measures are designed as failing to meet the ordinary criteria for a remedy or response.

Civil servants have at times explicitly argued that 'historical' abuse victim-survivors' experiences do not meet the threshold for an ordinary legal response. A government report to the CAT in 2016 stated that while survivors had received an official apology and were entitled to *ex-gratia* financial payments, '[t]he majority of entrants into Magdalen Laundries were not "confined" there in any legal sense.'[121] The Department of Justice contended in correspondence to the Ombudsman that same year: 'There has been no court ruling that the State has any liability for women who entered such institutions, nor have we ever seen any legal advice or factual evidence that would give rise to the belief that the State has any legal liability.'[122]

The final report of the MBHCOI, by way of a further example, recommends that 'Adopted people should have a right to their birth certificates and associated birth information.'[123] It prefaces this recommendation, however, by asserting that adopted people have engaged in 'vitriolic criticism' of the state's decades-long practice of secrecy, and that their criticism is 'unfair and misplaced.'[124] The MBHCOI makes no reference to the existing laws of data protection in Ireland which grant a strong right of access to personal data held by state and non-state data controllers, including mixed personal data that relates to more than one person.[125] Nor does the MBHCOI acknowledge recent Irish constitutional law jurisprudence that identifies and protects the right to have one's identity correctly recognised by the state.[126] Recommending the creation of a bespoke scheme of access to adoption records, the MBHCOI asserts that adopted people currently 'do not have a right to access their original birth certificate nor do they have the right to access information on their families of origin';[127] and contends that '[d]iocesan records and the records of the religious orders involved in the institutions are the property of the holders and they have the right to determine who gets access.'[128]

The second supporting mainstay of the state's construction of these victim-survivors as uniquely 'vulnerable' is its characterisation of them as choosing not to pursue ordinary legal avenues. As noted above, the government repeatedly claims that police investigations would commence if any Magdalene Laundry survivor were to complain (ignoring that women have complained and that copious testimony of criminal abuse – including abuse perpetrated by Gardaí – is publicly available). Department of Justice officials considering in 2011 how to respond to the Irish Human Rights Commission's (IHRC) recommendation for a statutory inquiry into the Magdalene Laundries claimed: 'The IHRC conclusions ignore that the State already provides the mechanism of the courts where allegations of civil and criminal wrongs can be addressed [and] the groups/individuals concerned have apparently chosen not to make any complaints to the Garda or to pursue a civil action.'[129] Victim-survivors are described as though they are not willing to engage with the legal system in the way that others do, and therefore as people whose demands for remedies arise because they feel hurt, and not because the state and others have behaved towards them in an unlawful way.

Having othered victim-survivors in these ways, the state then portrays itself as benevolent – as generously choosing to respond because it is morally the right thing to do, rather than because human rights law requires the state to do so. In key public statements government representatives have substituted language of compassion for discussion of rights. One example is the former Minister for Children's deletion of references in a May 2019 Dáil debate motion to 'the ill-treatment of the mothers and babies in these homes' and 'the forced separation of single mothers and their babies from 1922 to 1998.'[130] The Minister replaced these words with the statement (among others) that Dáil Éireann 'acknowledges the lived experiences of Irish women and children who were in former mother and baby institutions in the last century and stands in solidarity with all former residents, and their loved ones.'[131] A more recent example is the current Minister's response to countless survivors' criticism of the MBHCOI's findings for ignoring their testimony of human rights violations.[132] The Minister characterised 'a legalistic approach' as antithetical to the needs of 'vulnerable' survivors:

> The Government published the commission's report a month ago. It was followed by an immediate State apology from An Taoiseach for the wrongs that we as a nation visited on our most vulnerable citizens and that was an acknowledgement of the fault on the part of the State and its failings regarding these vulnerable citizens. I know and understand that many survivors have been disappointed and angered by the report, finding its tone and language cold and overly legalistic. I recognise that some of the conclusions, which were grounded in a legalistic approach and analysis of 1.3 million pages of evidence, can feel removed from the grief, the breach of human rights and the trauma of the lived experience of many former residents.[133]

The following paragraphs illustrate that the mandates and procedures that the government has created for its ad hoc responses lack human rights as their focus or stated purpose. As the 'specialised' mechanisms undertake their work they reinforce the notion that the state is not responsible for human rights violations, allowing it to continue its pattern of impunity.

To begin with the most recent measure devised to respond to the deaths and unidentified burials in Mother and Baby Homes: although Ireland already has a coroners' system that makes provision for exhumation and identification, the government is currently progressing a Bill through the Oireachtas (parliament) that would create a dedicated agency to exhume and attempt to identify remains at institutional sites.[134] The Bill specifies that once such an agency is established, the existing legal powers and mandate of the coroners' system will be disapplied meaning that there will be no investigation into the circumstances of death (as many have argued, in contravention of the state's Article 2 ECHR obligations).[135]

The government's terms of reference for the MBHCOI made no mention of constitutional or human rights save for one clause mandating the MBHCOI to exercise discretion in relation to the scope and intensity of its investigation, having regard to, among other things, 'the need for the investigation to be prompt and thorough in accordance with the State's obligations under international human rights law.'[136] The MBHCOI was directed to examine 'the circumstances and arrangements for the entry of single women into these institutions and the exit pathways,' and 'mortality amongst mothers and children,' among other issues, without any link being made to the state's obligations to respect and protect rights in and arising from those contexts. That the MBHCOI's final report would avoid a constitutional and human rights law analysis was indicated by the fifth interim report, published in 2019. In the fifth interim report, the MBHCOI revealed that almost 1,000 bodies of deceased babies and children were distributed by Mother and Baby institutions to university medical schools for anatomical study up to the 1970s.[137] The MBHCOI noted that the legislative requirements concerning such donations frequently were not observed and stated that '[i]t is not known, but it seems unlikely, that the mothers concerned were made aware of the existence or requirements of the *Anatomy Act* at any stage during their stay in any of the institutions being investigated.'[138] The MBHCOI concluded simply: 'There can be little doubt that most people will find the arrangements made for anatomical studies prior to the 1970s distasteful at a minimum.'[139] It offered no analysis of the human rights implications of such practices.

The MBHCOI's final report noted simply that the government 'did not opt' to require it to analyse the evidence it received by reference to constitutional or human rights norms.[140] The MBHCOI made no reference to the existing requirement under the European Convention on Human Rights (ECHR) Act 2003[141] for statutory bodies to act compatibly with the state's obligations under the Convention.[142] Throughout its inquiry, the MBHCOI refused to allow affected individuals to see or comment on any of the evidence received; it even refused to grant access to one's own personal data or records concerning a disappeared family member.[143] It also refused all requests by victim-survivors for a public hearing despite having full statutory discretion to grant such requests.[144]

Regarding the Magdalene Laundries: the IDC examination between 2011 and 2013 was mandated 'to establish the facts of State interaction with the Magdalen Laundries' but not given the task of investigating questions of human rights abuse of the girls and women detained and working inside. Choosing nonetheless to include a chapter in its final report entitled 'Living and Working Conditions,' the IDC did not discuss in this chapter whether girls and women were arbitrarily deprived of their liberty in Magdalene Laundries or whether they were forced into unpaid labour[145] – two of the most prominent features of those institutions. The *IDC Report* contained no human rights-based analysis of the evidence revealed within it, although as is readily apparent and as the IHREC has concluded, 'the information published by the McAleese Inter-Departmental Committee established breaches of human rights.'[146] As explained above, the Irish state now relies on the *IDC Report* to claim that there is no 'credible evidence' of ill-treatment requiring the further investigation recommended by multiple human rights bodies.

Additionally, at a procedural level, the IDC breached the well-recognised right under ECHR Articles 2 and 3 to an effective investigation. The IDC was not independent, being composed of senior officials from six government departments involved with the Magdalene Laundries (although chaired independently). Furthermore, neither survivors nor the public have ever been allowed to scrutinise the archival or witness evidence gathered by it, given that it operated in private, returned all records it received from the nuns and created an archive of state papers that the government has censored.[147]

By way of a final example: in 2013 the government designated the Magdalene Laundries 'restorative justice' scheme (involving modest payments and limited healthcare) as an *ex-gratia* measure,[148] explicitly characterising it as a favour to survivors rather than an entitlement. In 2017 the Ombudsman issued a detailed report finding that the Department of Justice had 'maladministered' the *ex-gratia* payment scheme. Notably, the first sentence of the Ombudsman's report acknowledged human-rights abuses that the *IDC Report* and repeated state submissions to the UN never have: 'The incarceration of women in the Magdalen laundries and the forced labour to which they were subjected is one of the sorriest episodes in our history.'[149] Among the forms of malpractice criticised by the Ombudsman was the Department of Justice's method of assessing women's claimed duration of stay in a Magdalene Laundry. According to the Ombudsman's report: 'There was an over reliance on the records of the congregations and it is not apparent what weight if any was afforded to the testimony of the women and/or their relatives.'[150] The report continued: 'the Department advised applicants during the process that testimony would not be taken into account as consideration was purely "*records based*" ...This strict adherence to the records applied even in circumstances when the records turned out to be incomplete or incorrect.'[151]

Conclusion

In the case of Ireland's legacy of institutional and gender-related systematic abuses, the state's contemporary use of a group-based notion of 'vulnerability' to deny victim-survivors' human rights mirrors its behaviour during the twentieth century. Although space constraints precluded a detailed examination of the historical aspects of the abusive continuum, it should be noted that the brutalising and disenfranchising regimes of the Magdalene Laundries, Mother and Baby Homes and forced family separation system were frequently the state's response to situations in which women and children depended on it for care and resources following violence or community ostracisation. In other words, the state justified its abuse of women and children on the basis that they were in need.

In 2014 Sir Nigel Rodley used his concluding comments as Chairperson of the UN Human Rights Committee upon its examination of Ireland to criticise the complete absence of accountability for so-called historical abuse, despite years of purported responses by the state to the justice demands of victim-survivors.[152] Rodley identified a paradox worthy of sustained analysis: that there remains little to no 'accountability' for Ireland's gross and systematic institutional and gender-based abuses, notwithstanding that the Irish public has funded decades of inquiries and so-called 'restorative' measures, and government representatives have repeatedly proclaimed their desire, in the words of the Taoiseach to Mother and Baby Homes survivors in January 2021, 'to confront hard truths – and accept parts of our history which are deeply painful.'[153] Fineman's theory urges us to reflect carefully on the rationale for the Irish 'care' system's exploitation of so many women and children during the twentieth century, and to recognise the capacity of that rationale – if not vigorously identified, challenged and transformed – to reproduce further and compounding discrimination over time.

SEVEN

State Legal Responses to Historical Institutional Abuse: Shame, Sovereignty and Epistemic Injustice[1]

Máiréad Enright and Sinéad Ring

The history of the Irish state is littered with shamed bodies. For decades the state collaborated with religious orders in incarcerating children and single women, who were shamed by authorities for their poverty, race, disability or association with sexual transgression.[2] Practices such as head shaving, name changing, identifying children by number and flogging were used to punish and control.[3] Women and children in industrial or reformatory schools, psychiatric hospitals, county homes and Magdalene laundries were burdened with a stigmatised identity that meant total exclusion from society.[4] By beginning to speak publicly about their experiences, victim-survivors have forced the state and Irish society to acknowledge this history. Their testimony of neglect, beatings, forced labour, sexual assault and imprisonment is an indictment of the sovereign state's claim to protect its most vulnerable and to detect and punish crime within its territory. In response the state offers an architecture of apology, investigation, and redress. Scholars, however, have shown that this framework is built around patterns of violation of domestic and international norms.[5]

This essay contributes to the literature exploring transitional-justice processes by scrutinising the Irish state's responses to historical institutional abuse.[6] Scholars can analyse state actions through the lens of truth-telling, accountability, redress and reparations, and guarantees of nonrecurrence – the key objectives of transitional justice. But such processes are themselves contingent and potentially oppressive, especially where suppressed and marginalised knowledges are omitted or excluded in the name of transitional justice.[7] This essay develops a theory of state shame that describes and explains the harms experienced by victim-survivors of state institutions in their attempts to gain recognition and redress from the state. We present our argument in four parts. First, we distinguish between true shame as an ideal type on the one hand, and the Irish state's discourse of itself as shamed subject (state shame) on the other. We argue that true shame and state shame are very different modes of engagement with past wrongs. Whereas true shame involves a collapse of the sovereign self, state shame preserves the state from any loss of sovereignty. As we next show, a discourse of state shame has been employed to legitimate narrow legalist strategies such as limited inquiries, adversarial interrogation, adherence to fixed evidentiary standards and a focus on monetary redress to the exclusion of other aspects of reparation. Examining the state's use of law and legalism to respond to the claims of victim-survivors of institutional child abuse and of the Magdalene laundries, we show how the state produces unitary official histories, monetises and commodifies harms raised in personal testimony, and preserves old hierarchies of power between state, religious orders and victim-survivors. In the third section we argue that in their encounters with these legal measures victim-survivors experience epistemic injustice. This term refers to forms of unfair treatment relating to issues of knowledge, understanding and participation in communicative practices.[8] Miranda Fricker identifies two forms of epistemic injustice, testimonial and hermeneutical. Both involve wronging someone in their capacity as a knower.[9] We suggest that the legal responses to victim-survivors enact a refusal to listen (testimonial injustice) or to alter the conditions under which victim-survivors can be heard (hermeneutical injustice). Finally, we show that state professions of shame and state responses to institutional abuse are linked by an investment in sovereignty. In this economy of shame, testimonial injustice is the cost of ensuring that the sovereign state narrative, not victim-survivor testimony, dominates public responses to historical abuse. Hermeneutical injustice is the cost of exalting the state's sovereign ways of framing and knowing historical injustice. State shame therefore maintains state sovereignty through unaltered legal technique. We conclude by exploring what engagement with the radical potential of shame might mean for imagining new state and community responses that attempt to do epistemic justice to victim-survivors.

Theorising State Shame

We use true shame as a heuristic to convey an ideal type that we can productively compare with the Irish state's discourse of itself as a shamed subject. Borrowing from the work of Giorgio Agamben, we understand true shame as an experience of the collapse of the sovereign self.[10] For Agamben shame is more than 'a feeling that man has.' Rather, it is part of the 'hidden structure of all subjectivity and consciousness.'[11] Shame comes from our fundamental inability to separate ourselves from how others see us. There is no escape from who we are to others; this intense relationality is what makes shame so devastating.[12] We want to flee from our visibility to others but know that we cannot. Agamben describes shaming in vivid terms: 'In shame the subject... has no other content than its own desubjectification; it becomes witness to its own disorder, its own oblivion as a subject.'[13] True shame is thus 'a kind of existential nakedness' inseparable from a devastating loss of sovereignty, subjectivity and speech.[14] In shame we witness our own ruin.[15] We do not wish to be definitive or proscriptive, and we recognise the diversity of responses to abuse. However, we suggest that it is possible to understand these accounts of shame as loss of sovereignty, as resonating with testimony of victim-survivors to the experience of historical institutional abuse in Ireland.

When speaking about historical institutional abuse, state actors have positioned the Irish state as ashamed of its past. Former Taoiseach Brian Cowen has stated:

> The Ryan commission report has shone a powerful light into probably the darkest corner of the history of the state. *What it has revealed must be a source of the deepest shame to all of us*....Everyone, including the general public, must reflect on what the report has stated about how vulnerable children were treated in Ireland in the past and resolve that from *this shame and evil* we will make Ireland a model of how to treat children.[16] [emphasis supplied]

Ruairí Quinn, former Minister for Education, asserted that 'we cannot, nor will we try to, rewrite history; the conclusions and records of the courts must stand for future generations to see what shame we brought upon ourselves.' And Taoiseach Leo Varadkar stated that 'as a society we inherit a deep shame for what was done back then, and we must now endeavour to learn, to atone, and to put things right.'[17] But state shame as performed in statements of this kind entails no loss of sovereignty. Rather, the post-authoritarian Irish state's identification with shame has run alongside new, intensely productive politics of nation-building, reinforcing state sovereignty and inaugurating new techniques of government.[18]

This observation is not unique to Ireland. Writing about Australia, for example, Povinelli shows that shame is used to preserve the 'good intentions' of a society as it reconfigures its self-understanding in the encounter with its own history.[19] By confessing to being 'ashamed' of the past, the state establishes a temporal logic of exceptionalism rooted in a sense of national change and overcoming.[20] Instead of experiencing a collapse of its sovereignty, the state claims ownership of the injustice that must now be overcome. As Sara Ahmed writes of Australia, such performances of state redemption detach shame from victim-survivors' experiences, transforming it from a deeply personal injury to a matter of national authority and identity, which the sovereign state is uniquely competent to understand and address.[21] For instance, in apologising to survivors of the Magdalene laundries in 2013, former Taoiseach Enda Kenny acknowledged their suffering as a 'national shame' and announced that the country would 'take [their hurt] back.'[22] Accordingly, the state seeks to dictate the terms on which the shame of the past is cleansed. It vests itself with the power to revisit others' shaming, to appropriate their experience, and to act to end certain injuries. It owns both the injury and the remedy, and it can control and contain how both are understood.

The legal responses to abuse in industrial and reformatory schools and Magdalene laundries provide two case studies for developing the theory of state shame in Ireland. Such schools and laundries were part of a wider network of institutions, which also included psychiatric hospitals, county homes and Mother and Baby Homes, designed to contain marginalised and stigmatised people. During the middle of the twentieth century over one percent of the country's population was involuntarily detained in one of these punitive institutions.[23]

Case Study 1: Institutional Child Abuse

Industrial schools were designed to contain children who were powerful reminders of the shame of poverty and unmarried motherhood, and in some cases the shame of having been abused or neglected at home.[24] Reformatory schools were created to discipline deviant and criminalised boys and girls. Shame was a governance technique in these institutions. In St Joseph's Industrial School, Artane, Dublin, boys were known by numbers rather than their names and were subjected to public inspections of underwear.[25] Children who had wet their beds were humiliated and forced to parade their wet sheets in front of the other children in St Vincent's Industrial School, Goldenbridge, Dublin.[26] In St Conleth's Reformatory School, Daingean, Offaly, boys were subjected to arbitrary torture in front of their peers.[27] Sexual violence in these institutions thrived, bolstered by the victims' feelings of shame and self-blame.[28] And when they attempted to report sexual abuse, children were ignored or even blamed by institutional actors and punished severely.[29]

Institutional abuse of children entered public discourse in earnest in the 1990s when people began speaking out about their experiences. Public concern about child sexual abuse was heightened by the Fr Brendan Smyth scandal.[30] The state was finally forced to respond following the outcry provoked by the television documentary series produced by Mary Raftery, *States of Fear* (1999), which exposed systematic abuse of children in the former industrial-and reformatory-school system. On 11 May, prior to the airing of the third episode highlighting years of inaction and the previous government's suppression of details of an official report into child abuse in the Madonna House residential home in the 1990s, former Taoiseach Bertie Ahern apologised for the state and its citizens' 'collective failure to intervene, to detect their pain, and to come to their rescue,' and promised to learn the lessons of the past.[31] These promises took legal form with the creation of a statutory Commission to Inquire into Child Abuse (CICA) in 2000, a statutory Residential Institutions Redress Board in 2002, and in 2013 an agency to support victim-survivors with their ongoing health, education, and housing requirements.[32] Examination of the operation of each body reveals not a truly shamed state but one primarily concerned with the management and containment of victim-survivors' justice claims.

The CICA was comprised of two committees: the Confidential Committee and the Investigation Committee. The Confidential Committee provided a forum where victim-survivors could report their experiences in a confidential setting. The Investigation Committee was tasked with investigating the abuse of children in institutions, including, among other things, the extent to which institutions contributed to the occurrence of abuse.[33] After the Investigation Committee's public and private hearings, the commission's final report (known as the *Ryan Report*, after chairperson Justice Seán Ryan) found that sexual abuse was 'endemic' in boys' schools, and that there was pervasive neglect and physical and emotional abuse against boys and girls throughout the institutions examined.[34] It also found that the state failed to protect children in industrial and reformatory schools. However, despite its immensely significant findings, its work was far from satisfactory in terms of achieving truth recovery or accountability.[35] The commission prioritised religious orders' respectability over accountability to victim-survivors and the public. Pseudonyms were granted to everyone accused of abuse, regardless of whether they had been convicted or not.[36] The evidence gathered during the process was not permitted to be used in criminal prosecutions. This cloak of anonymity and effective immunity created a partial history and left many victim-survivors feeling exposed and ignored by the state. As victim-survivor 'Alex' remarked, 'For me, not naming the abusers shows that nothing has changed; the attitude from the state towards us hasn't changed. That apology really meant nothing. As long as they (the religious orders) have money and powerful people behind them, they'll get away with it.'[37]

Efforts to provide redress, moreover, have focused on limiting the exposure of the state and the religious orders to compensation claims. Under the indemnity agreement reached on 5 June 2002 between the state and the organisation representing the relevant eighteen religious orders, the Conference of Religious in Ireland, the orders promised to contribute €128 million to the costs of redress.[38] This promise, which has not been honoured in full, was given in return for an indemnity against all future legal actions taken by those who as children had been in institutions run by these orders.[39] However, the indemnity was not based on any apportionment of responsibility for abuse and has not in fact been invoked in many cases because the state established a redress scheme in December 2002.[40] Under this system payments were made following a paper application or a hearing. Provision of financial redress was on an ex-gratia basis without admission of liability by the religious order or the state. No blame was assigned or accepted. In accordance with normal legal practice, the scheme required awardees to agree that they would sue neither the state nor the religious order. When details of the scheme were originally announced, it was declared that compensation payments would be broadly equivalent to those awarded in the courts for similar cases. However, the average award was €62,250, roughly half that made in successful civil cases against religious orders (and in which, under the indemnity agreement, the state was liable).[41]

Operational for only three years, the scheme proved harrowing for many victim-survivors.[42] Participants have described the board as retraumatising and as discouraging future help-seeking.[43] Some felt so strongly about their treatment that they never spent their awards.[44] The hostile environment of the panel hearings distressed many survivors who appeared before them.[45] Partners or friends of victim-survivors were not allowed to be present when they gave their evidence. In contravention of the ordinary principles of legal procedure, victim-survivors taking part in panel hearings were subjected to cross-examination by legal advisors to the board on the information provided by the religious orders, but without any oral evidence having been given by the orders.[46] Despite the no-fault basis of the scheme, the Christian Brothers were permitted to issue repeated letters denying that any abuse took place in their institutions, thereby adding to victim-survivors' distress.[47] One consultant psychiatrist who gave evidence to the board on behalf of three patients described the experience as 'contraven[ing] the most basic of human and civil rights.'[48]

The overall impression of the legal framework for redress is of secrecy and control. Information provided by the religious orders in response to applications cannot be made public.[49] Awardees were required to sign a confidentiality agreement promising not to talk about their experience of the scheme or divulge how much compensation they received. They were also sent a letter quoting legislation criminalising the publication of information relating to a redress application or award that could lead to identification of a person or institution.[50] The maximum punishment is a fine of €25,000 and two years' imprisonment.[51] This theme of censorship is continued in current draft legislation that would seal the archives of the Commission to Inquire into Child Abuse and those of the Redress Board and the Review Committee for seventy-five years. Under the Retention of Records Bill (2019) currently under review, no one would be allowed access to these bodies' records, including people who gave evidence, their family members or researchers. Thus the state continues to control victim-survivors' access to their own testimony and is preventing academic and community exploration of these histories, information that could usefully inform child-care policy and practice in the present.[52]

The statutory agency created to support victim-survivors' health, housing and educational needs, Caranua, was characterised by its administrative ethos.[53] Engagement with clients was primarily through a website, which created particular challenges for people who cannot read or who do not have access to a computer. Victim-survivors reported inordinate delays in processing applications and inaction even following successful appeals. The agency imposed an upper limit of €15,000 on each claim, despite clear evidence that some victim-survivors have ongoing medical and related housing needs that will inevitably exceed that amount.[54] Victim-survivors have described Caranua as abusive and disempowering.[55] And yet the government has refused requests to carry out a full review of the operation of the scheme and claimed (incorrectly) that Caranua was independent of the state.[56] Caranua closed on 23 March 2021 but the state has yet to explain how it will fulfil its continuing obligations to victim-survivors in the future.

Finally, despite Ahern's promise in 1999 to learn the lessons of the past, the state continues to extend extraordinary deferential treatment to the religious orders. In the years since the indemnity agreement the costs relating to historical institutional child abuse have risen far beyond anything imagined in 2002. Following the publication of the *Ryan Report* in 2009 the state asked the religious orders to increase their contributions. They offered a further €352 million in cash, property, and other resources, a sum that was later revised downwards to €226 million. As of 2021, approximately €116.24 million of this amount had been paid.[57] The total costs of the commission, redress, and survivor supports are approximately €1.5 billion.[58] In short, the state continues to indemnify the religious orders from legal liability, while the orders' contributions (under 2002 and the 2009 agreements) come to approximately 16 per cent of the total cost. This is far short of the fifty-fifty split originally envisaged by the Department of Finance during the indemnity-agreement negotiations.[59] Nevertheless, deference to the property rights of the religious orders seems to have stymied any suggestion of compulsory acquisition of the orders' assets. Instead there have only been appeals to the orders' 'moral responsibility.'[60]

Case Study 2: The Magdalene Laundries

The Magdalene laundries were commercial laundries and places of detention run by religious orders with the cooperation of the state. It is believed that from 1922 to 1996 at least 10,000 women who had transgressed prevailing Catholic gender norms were incarcerated in such institutions.[61] These institutions operated in plain sight as a normalised part of Ireland's social and economic landscape.[62] However, laundries were also places of shame and seclusion where women were segregated from wider society so that their impurity would not taint others.[63] In the laundries they were punished as 'penitents' who should work for their redemption.[64] Shame defined Magdalene women as a distinct legal category.[65] Although the courts sometimes substituted detention in a laundry for imprisonment, women were incarcerated without any statutory basis and without being given reasons for their detention, information as to how long they would be held, or opportunities to secure their release.[66] They were deprived of their names, forbidden to speak, systematically assaulted and neglected with impunity.[67] They worked long days unpaid, often for years.[68] Women pregnant on entry into a laundry (or who became pregnant during their incarceration) were transferred to a Mother and Baby Home where they invariably lost their children to a wider system of coerced adoption.[69] Most women were released after two to three years, but others remained in the laundries until death. Such deaths in the system were not always recorded, as the deceased were often buried in unmarked graves.[70] Although the law did not explicitly prescribe the shaming practices endured by these women, the state enforced them through the efforts of the police, who returned women to the institutions from which they had attempted to escape.[71] For many victim-survivors of these institutions the destabilising effects of the laundries' shaming practices have endured.[72] As one woman attending the Dublin Honours Magdalenes gathering in June 2018 explained, 'I'd still feel a shame and that I'm not the same as other people.'[73] Shame has inhibited women's ability to speak about their experiences. Another survivor affirmed this reality: 'We don't tell everybody that we've been in the laundries. We're ashamed of it, we're embarrassed by it.'[74]

Initially, the state denied all responsibility for the laundries. A formal institutional response to survivors began in 2013 following a long advocacy campaign by the Justice for Magdalenes group and others.[75] The *McAleese Report*, published in February 2013, found that state agents placed women in the laundries and returned them if they escaped, subsidised the laundries' activities with state contracts and grants, and sanctioned non-payment of wages.[76] Two weeks later, Enda Kenny offered a state apology to the women that was initially well received by survivors.[77] In May 2013 Justice John Quirke published the terms of the Magdalene Restorative Justice Ex-Gratia Scheme, which offered ex-gratia payments to survivors in an attempt 'to reflect the shame of the nation.'[78] Payments were not individualised and do not compensate for lost wages or suffering; a pre-set tariff was applied based only on each woman's duration of stay as verified, in large part, by the religious orders' records. The average payment was €37,386. Although Quirke recommended that women should receive access to enhanced health services for life, this redress has not yet been secured.

Three features of the state response are key. First, as with the *Ryan Report*, the *McAleese Report* produced a supposedly authoritative 'official history' of the laundries that minimised state liability. The McAleese inquiry was offered as an alternative to the 'prompt, independent and thorough' investigation twice requested by the UN Committee Against Torture.[79] This inquiry was not independent of the government, had no statutory powers to compel evidence, and it commissioned no public testimony. Despite Justice for Magdalenes' efforts, victim-survivors' voices were marginalised within the report. For example, an archive that they had created to inform the process was ignored.[80] The report included women's testimony only as scant, disjointed quotations. As Gallen and Gleeson note, McAleese presented women's accounts of the Magdalene laundries as mere 'stories.'[81] These stories were the fragmented remnants of an unsettling and demeaning process in which women's credibility was not taken for granted. Claire McGettrick recalls:

> Initially, the committee didn't even want to speak to women in person, but we fought for that. The women gave their testimony verbally and then we were given very little notice of a second meeting where we were to look at the format of the initial testimony. Instead, the women were brought in one by one for a meeting with the commission where they asked repeated questions. Their overall impression was that they were being checked to ensure that their memories were correct. The women came out of those meetings very quiet and subdued. None of them, none of us, had been expecting for them to be questioned like that.[82]

Secondly, survivors had little opportunity publicly to contest the McAleese account once it was published. The state discouraged victim-survivors from bringing claims to the courts by contractually requiring them to waive their right of action against the state or state agencies as a condition of participation in the redress scheme. Women were required to accept this decision before the state had provided any guarantees on welfare or health provision, and the denial of access to the courts was framed as an act of care. For example, the Quirke scheme promised to avoid 'mutually antagonistic roles and positions and… invasive and painful inquiry and interrogation.' While it spoke of collaborating with women and giving effect to their voices, in practice the operation of the waiver meant that even those few cases that were not already stymied by the statute of limitations could not be brought to court.[83] Women's total containment within the redress scheme also has had the effect of denying access to a state forum in which alternative accounts of women's experiences might be shared in public and reframed as legally cognisable wrongs.[84] O'Rourke notes that in seeking to deny further liability, the state has repeatedly pointed to the absence of successful litigation by Magdalene women for the harms that they suffered.[85] The state has done little to assist women in disseminating their own histories in other forums or in making sense of their own personal stories. Records of women's time in the laundries remain in the possession of religious orders, and the state will not make its own related administrative records available for examination by victim-survivors.

As in the case of institutional child abuse, the state's response to laundry survivors has done little to unsettle perpetrators' privileged social position. McAleese made no recommendations about prosecution or accountability. The waiver, a condition of participation in the redress scheme, also immunised the state from further litigation. Moreover, because the report made no findings as to ill-treatment of women in the laundries (holding that this was 'outside its remit'), the state is able to maintain that there is no 'credible evidence' that women were detained for long periods, tortured or subjected to criminal abuse.[86] The state has also protected religious orders. After the *McAleese Report* some religious sisters could defend their role in the laundries as providing social service.[87] A similar defence of the religious orders appears in the *McAleese Report*, which downplays the suggestion that the orders profited from women's forced labour.[88] The four orders that ran Magdalene laundries were not compelled to contribute to the redress scheme, despite receiving four separate invitations to do so. They have ongoing economic relationships with the state, particularly in healthcare and the provision of services for sex workers.

Finally, the state has limited its duties of reparation to financial redress, privileging limited monetary restitution over responding to demands to facilitate survivors in memorialising the dead or in preserving institutional buildings as museums.[89] Translating the demand for reparation into a demand for money had two effects. First, it constructed victim-survivors as a drain on the state's finances. Indeed, Quirke emphasised concern for the then-recent economic recession as a check on the scheme.[90] Relatedly, it subjected individual victim-survivors to state scrutiny and control. Survivors remain, in a sense, objects to be administered. A 2017 Ombudsman's report examining the scheme found that eligibility criteria were narrowly interpreted, and the scheme's administrators preferred to rely on (often incomplete) records held by religious congregations rather than on survivors' affidavits. These practices work against women's ability to prove length of stay in a laundry, which meant that they received reduced compensation payments.[91] In addition, women who should have benefited from the scheme were initially excluded; for example, some women who worked in laundries as children registered in an adjoining institution were refused access to the redress scheme because they had not been laundry inmates. Although the High Court found that this exclusion was in violation of their rights to natural justice and fair procedures, these women did not receive redress payments until after the publication of the Ombudsman's report in April 2019.[92] A subsequent process found that 214 applications to the redress scheme required review.[93] Women found the assessment process distressing. Mary Cavner recently spoke about her experience: 'It took all of my courage to admit what I had been through and then they called me a liar... I have had really low points as they have made me live this again, and to be accused of not telling the truth made me feel rejected.'[94] Another woman explained the health consequences of engaging with the state redress scheme: 'Of all the things I've been through in my life, I've never been through anything as stressful as this.'[95]

In an ex-gratia scheme redress is always constructed as a gift of the state rather than an entitlement of victim-survivors. Elizabeth Coppin speaks of her experience of the Magdalene redress scheme in terms of reinforcement of hierarchies of entitlement: 'For me, they're saying again that I don't matter. Again they're ignoring my basic human rights... I bet you all those people in government are getting their full pension and expenses, yet the Irish women are still being deprived of their entitlements.'[96]

The state expressions of shame following survivor campaigning around institutional child abuse and the harms of the Magdalene laundries were notionally transformative moments. However, as the above examples illustrate, the state refused in these efforts to engage with the full implications of survivors' testimony: its capacity to judge and remedy past injuries of neglect, physical and sexual abuse, and forced labour. In the state's legal responses we can observe a common pattern. First, the state claims shame at its past (in)action(s). Secondly, it produces a narrow 'official history' immunised from victim-survivors' alternative narratives. Rather than seeking to construct a shared memory of past harm, this 'official' narrative becomes the evidentiary basis for restricting or denying reparations. Thirdly, it preserves the status of both state and nonstate perpetrators of abuse, limiting their exposure to liability and preserving their reputations. Finally, it reduces reparation to limited monetary redress, delivered via exclusionary schemes that construct victim-survivors primarily as financially interested claimants. We argue that this engagement works an epistemic injustice against victim-survivors.

Legal Responses and Epistemic Injustice

In the 'shamed' state's legal responses to victim-survivors' testimony we can observe epistemic injustices that compound their injuries.[97] Literature on the 'impossibility of bearing witness' doubts whether survivors can ever perfectly recount a traumatic event in terms that represent the atrocity they have experienced.[98] Questions of justice thus arise around how the law treats those who offer such testimony. In this section we draw on Fricker's two varieties of epistemic injustice. The first, testimonial injustice, occurs when prejudice causes a hearer to give a deflated level of credibility to a speaker's word.[99] Testimonial injustice is a transactional or inter-personal form of direct discrimination against the speaker.

State actors tasked with assessing redress failed to take victim-survivors seriously or to deem their accounts credible and worthy of belief. This denial of credibility is rooted in a prejudiced perception of the individual victim-survivor's social status as a former resident of an industrial school or an inmate of a Magdalene laundry. Such unjustified assignment of a credibility deficit to the speaker is an epistemic harm, as evidenced by a man who engaged with the Residential Institutions Redress Board:

> [The board] made me feel like I had done something wrong, the way I was on trial in front of a judge, and when she questioned my statement by saying that I would have to be believed because the bastard that abused me was not there to defend himself, I wanted out of there as quick as I could. That was my experience of redress; all it done for me was made me bitter and angry; I was sorry I did not go to court and expose everything that went on in Letterfrack.[100]

Diane Croghan recalls a similar sense of exclusion and misrecognition when engaging with the Magdalene scheme: 'I felt like I was a liar; that I was trying to claim for years I wasn't [in a Magdalene laundry], and that's not true. I accepted what they said because I took a stroke and I said no money would repay my good health. I felt I was being punished. I was bullied into accepting it, so I accepted it.'[101] We understand these experiences as resonating with Fricker's conception of testimonial injustice, where victim-survivors are prevented from acknowledgement as a giver of knowledge and as an informant.[102] What is perhaps particularly unjust here is that the knowledge concerns one's own childhood.

The construction of redress within state schemes can also work a testimonial injustice. Redress schemes have financialised the wrongs done to victim-survivors and eclipsed other dimensions of their claims. Victim-survivors feel that the injuries they suffered are not heard and recognised as wrongs[103]: 'I was so disgusted when I received the cheque from the redress board. They did not say they were sorry; they denied they were responsible, and I had to accept the money on that basis. I wanted to rip the cheque in half. I never spent a penny of the money; I gave it to my children. It was never about the money.'[104] This financialisation of harm suffered is even more objectionable because the state has yet to act on the first recommendation of the Commission to Inquire into Child Abuse, that a memorial to survivors of institutional abuse be created.[105]

Fricker's second form of epistemic injustice, hermeneutical injustice, occurs when a gap in collective resources puts someone at an unfair disadvantage when it comes to making sense of their social experiences and/or getting others to comprehend an experience of that kind.[106] Scholars do not fully agree on the completeness of the barriers facing marginalised people. Kristie Dotson, for instance, criticises Fricker's account of hermeneutical injustice as failing to account for a marginalised community's capacity to develop hermeneutical resources that help members to explain their experience to themselves and one another – even if these resources are not widely accepted by dominantly situated knowers.[107] Certainly, there are many examples of victim-survivors of institutional abuse developing their own frameworks for understanding and expressing their experiences by establishing support groups and engaging in forms of artistic expression.[108] Such communities even develop parallel methods for recording their engagements with legal institutions.[109] The state's power and ignorance has not prevented victim-survivors from understanding their own oppression and marginalisation or from engaging in consciousness-raising.

However, if we understand hermeneutical injustice as the structural gap in conceptual resources with which to articulate experience to the state, it is clear that the Irish state has allowed this shortcoming to persist and even widen. As we have shown, the state has refused to engage fully with victim-survivors' ways of knowing about the nation's dark past. It has failed to reimagine or supplement frameworks of civil and criminal liability, leaving victim-survivors without adequate conceptual means to give public legal expression to their experiences or to establish new legal discourses of unashamed authority and credibility that might enable them to speak to the state without fear of sanction.[110] For example, by insulating itself (and religious orders) from meaningful accountability, the state has deprived victim-survivors of opportunities to use legal means to contest the partial accounts of responsibility dispersed through official histories. By limiting access to archives, the state has denied them the evidence with which to contest the state's version of events. By subjecting them to ongoing discipline in the determination of their personal histories and in the administration of their affairs, it has blocked opportunities to build relationships with the state that escape older abusive dynamics of power and control – and that might allow for full public articulation of the wrongs done. In each of these practices the supposedly ashamed state is benefitting from and continuing the prejudicial exclusion of victim-survivors from participation in the spread of knowledge about Ireland's history of abuse of marginalised women and children.[111]

State Shame, Sovereignty, and Epistemic Injustice

True shame is an extraordinary and devastating ethical situation in which we are inescapably exposed to another's judgment. Shame cannot be controlled or assimilated to the self.[112] As we have sought to demonstrate, the Irish state's response to institutional child abuse and the Magdalene laundries does not resemble anything approaching this disorder. By subjecting victim-survivors to damaging processes, by substituting partial official histories for their testimony and by censoring access to the archives of the bodies created to learn from the past, the state has co-opted victim-survivors' primary source of power: their unique knowledge of Ireland's recent history of institutional abuse of children and women. Redress schemes have commodified and financialised the wrongs done to survivors, eclipsing other dimensions of their testimony, such as the need for an apology from representatives of the abuser's community.

This use of law makes sense given that what is at stake is the right to govern. Victim-survivors' testimony reveals the history of the state as a story of subordination to religious power, which rendered the Irish government unable and unwilling to protect its most vulnerable citizens.[113] Victim-survivors' testimony (if it were taken seriously as a source of knowledge about the nation's history) could fully expose the state's complicity in its past failure to protect women and children and its present inability effectively to judge, determine, and redress that failure. Articulated within the politics of representative groups and offered in multiple forms, such testimony could engender true shame: a revelation of inescapable truth that acts as an existential threat to sovereignty. But what appears to be a response to victim-survivor testimony is actually an avoidance of such a threat. The state has multiple means of controlling and containing such testimony. Its use of law, moreover, is especially pernicious because it attempts to end contestation surrounding past wrongs by bringing about 'closure.'[114] It responds to the uncertainty produced by victim-survivor testimony so as to render the state's liability 'finite and calculable.'[115] It offers recognition to victim-survivors, but only of a kind that subordinates their testimony to the state's preferred frameworks for knowing about institutional abuse of women and children. Testimonial injustice is thus the cost of ensuring that responses to historical abuse protect the state, and hermeneutical injustice is the cost of privileging the state's sovereign ways of knowing and determining historical injustice. Epistemic injustice becomes a symptom of the state's prioritisation of the status quo of sovereignty in moments of supposed transition and change.

Conclusion

This article explores the implication of shame in the Irish state's response to the public revelations of institutional abuse of children and women. It has shown that the state has professed to be ashamed of its past but has responded through law in ways that are antithetical to true shame. Exploring two case studies – institutional child abuse and abuse of women and girls in Magdalene laundries – we demonstrate that the state's responses have centred on an investment in sovereignty and a juridical sense of responsibility for victim-survivors that is readily exhausted by legalist conceptions of fault, certainty and compensation.

When this paper was first written, the final report of the Mother and Baby Homes Commission of Investigation (MBHCOI) had not yet been published. On the day after it was made public, the Taoiseach Micheál Martin apologised on behalf of the state to 'Irish mothers and their children who ended up in a Mother and Baby Home or a county home.'[116] He apologised for the state's past failures to control the institutions, and to protect its citizens. He apologised in particular for the 'shame and stigma' to which they were subjected and professed the state's own shame at their treatment:

> The shame was not theirs – it was ours. It was our shame that we did not show them the respect and compassion which we as a country owed them. It remains our shame.[117]

In his apology, the Taoiseach calls the MBHCOI's final report 'the definitive account' of how the country responded to unmarried women and their children. We can already say with some confidence that this 'definitive' history is deeply marked by epistemic injustice and that this injustice is tightly bound to legalism.

During spring 2021 several witnesses, including Mary Harney and Philomena Lee, commenced High Court actions challenging elements of the report's findings[118] and the Commission's procedures.[119] Numerous witnesses who are identifiable, despite anonymisation, from the fragments of their testimony reproduced in the final report argued that they should have been given the opportunity to review and make submissions on the report in draft.[120] In December 2021, the state settled Harney and Lee's cases. It consented to a declaration that it had failed in its statutory duty to provide drafts of the relevant sections of the report to each woman before the report was finalised. An acknowledgment that each woman takes issue with parts of the report will be published alongside the report in the Oireachtas library and online. However, the report has not been withdrawn. The Minister for Children offered a vague defence of the report suggesting that while some survivors did not accept its findings, others did.[121] The question of whether Confidential Committee testimony influenced the report's findings emerged almost immediately. By far the majority of people with lived experience of the 'homes' who engaged with the Commission spoke to the Confidential Committee.[122] In June 2021 Professor Mary Daly, who had served as one of the three Commissioners, spoke at an online seminar hosted by Oxford University. She explained that, as far as she understood, the law demanded that testimony given to the Confidential Committee could not be used in the main body of the report.[123] In her view Confidential Committee evidence could not be used because it was not given 'under oath,' and because incorporating it in ways that would satisfy the applicable legal standards would require hours of additional work. In a subsequent letter to the Oireachtas, former Commissioner Yvonne Murphy insisted that Confidential Committee evidence had influenced the report's findings but did not explain how.[124] The Commissioners twice refused to appear in person before the Oireachtas to answer these claims and have said that they stand over the report in its entirety.[125]

In this episode as in others victim-survivors suffer epistemic harms when the supposedly shamed state reaches for law. They suffer testimonial injustice because their testimony is framed as risky and untrustworthy in ways that directly undermine their credibility. They also suffer hermeneutical injustice because they are repeatedly denied opportunities to contribute directly to the shared knowledge produced by the Commission. We have argued that a truly ashamed state, committed to dwelling in and learning from histories of abuse, would uncouple its official histories from legal process. Nothing of that kind has happened so far in the state's response to the mother and baby homes and county homes. On the contrary, it is clear that legalism actively shaped the production of official history through careful management of the risks associated with victim-survivor testimony. Despite these legal efforts to impose closure on the state's engagement with its past, the 'official history' remains open to public challenge and displacement by other bodies of testimony produced in solidarity with and on behalf of victim-survivors.[126]

Epistemic justice would require the ashamed state to engage in a risky exposure to victim-survivors' testimony and to the possibility that doing so may transform the state and its law.[127] Such exposure would require a different understanding of state shame than the one used in the past. Despite its misappropriation by the Irish state, shame has radical potential; its 'ambivalence bears the possibility of *both* abjection and solidarity.'[128] Precisely because it is destabilising, shame can be transformative. It can awaken a community to new knowledge of its own actions of which it formerly professed ignorance.[129] Often, this radical potential is not grasped because shame brings with it the radical risk of desubjectification – of utter loss of control. Accessing the transformative potential of shame, Bersani and Phillips explain, requires a willingness to dwell with it: 'The most difficult thing about shame is to go through with it. This might require an ascetic self-discipline.'[130] The ashamed state is useful to victim-survivors only if shame imposes an ethical duty on the state to 'go through with it': to bear the risks of engagement with victim-survivor testimony. For Agamben, the fundamental structure of shame generates such a duty. It is, strikingly, a *limitless* duty to bear witness to the wrongs done to others and to make space for testimony – a duty obviously incompatible with the urge to subject that testimony to the controlling forces of legal judgment.[131] From this perspective the relationship between state shame and epistemic injustice shifts. Epistemic justice can no longer be the casualty of the state's failure to engage with its shame. Epistemic justice is incompatible with mere professions of shame unaccompanied by any radical change in the state's normal legal practices.

That realisation, however, generates a problem: What sort of radical change is required? It may be that a law-making state can never go through desubjectifying and devastating shame of the kind that Agamben describes. It may be that we would not wish it to do so, if that kind of state shame implies a radical passivity that paralyses the state and renders it incapable of acting on victim-survivors' demands for justice – incapable of anything but permanent withdrawal, 'speechless and inert.'[132] At the same time the state must find a way to negotiate shame's demands while resisting the urge to repair its unsettling effects. Addressing this problem, Gillian Rose wrote about a 'broken middle,' about an approach to social and political relations recognising that social ruptures cannot be repaired or overcome. We can only negotiate and attempt to comprehend them. The 'broken middle' may lie between a paralysing limitless exposure to testimony of past wrongs and the insistence that rational formal legal process overcome those wrongs. Following Rose, we would argue that the state cannot choose, ethically, between shame-induced paralysis and a perfect legalism that will dissolve the challenges of history. In particular, an ashamed state would understand that it could no longer indulge in unaltered legalism in its engagement with victim-survivors' testimony. Instead, we must negotiate open and responsive paths between limited law and endless shame. Embracing shame as a mode of doing justice to the past in Ireland must mean decentring and reconfiguring established state attitudes to law, allowing new epistemic frames for the voicing and witnessing of traumatic experiences of historical institutional abuse to emerge. This is a process of anxious struggle, far removed from the comforts of the old sovereignty; the state must risk established practice and 'act, *without guarantees*, for the good of all.'[133]

EIGHT

Access to Justice for Victims of Historic Institutional Abuse[1]

Colin Smith and April Duff

This article focuses on the procedural obstacles to gaining redress for physical and sexual abuse, neglect, and other serious human rights violations perpetrated against children and adults in Irish institutions throughout much of the twentieth century. These institutions were owned and operated by various religious organisations, most of them affiliated with the Catholic church.[2] Although they were integrated into the state's system of criminal justice, social welfare and child protection (such as it was), the state failed to exercise meaningful supervision or control of conditions over them.[3] Residents therefore had no effective state protection against mistreatment or neglect. Children could be subjected to sexual and physical abuse in industrial schools, women to detention and forced labour in Magdalene laundries, and mothers and their babies could be forcibly and permanently separated in Mother and Baby Homes.

In addition to being subject to criminal prohibition and sanction when they occurred, these human rights violations gave rise to civil liability as violations of the personal rights protected by Article 40.3 of the Constitution. By the 1960s and 1970s such basic guarantees included the right to bodily integrity; to be reared with due regard to one's religious, moral, intellectual, physical and social welfare; and to be safeguarded from inhuman or degrading treatment.[4] These rights were protected by the law of tort through causes of action for trespass to the person such as assault, battery, false imprisonment and infliction of emotional suffering.[5] Where no adequate remedy was available in tort law, these rights were protected by the ability to bring a claim for breach of constitutional rights.[6]

The first such civil actions for damages appear to have been related to sexual abuse in Madonna House, a state-licensed residential home for children run by the Sisters of Charity in Stillorgan.[7] The official report on Madonna House in 1996 was never published in full,[8] but revelations about horrific abuse of children by staff were incorporated into Mary Raftery's *States of Fear* documentary series for RTÉ in 1999. A number of civil actions were issued against the sisters and the Eastern Health Board in the early 1990s, yet although in 1999 one High Court case ran for 22 days, these cases appear to have been settled; therefore no guiding precedent has been established.[9]

For the state and the religious orders involved in administrating such institutions, the cost of resisting or settling such proceedings motivated the establishment of nonjudicial victim-redress schemes, the first created by the Residential Institutions Redress Act (2002). Such awards by the Residential Institutions Redress Board (RIRB) were conditional on the victim signing the following waiver:

> I, [name], hereby accept the award of the Board in the sum of [amount of award] communicated to me by notice dated [date] and in accordance with section 13(6) of the Residential Institutions Redress Act 2002, I hereby waive any right of action which I might otherwise have had against any public body within the meaning of section 1(1) of the Act or against any person who has made a contribution under section 23(5) of the Act, and I further agree to discontinue any other proceedings instituted by me against any such public body or person arising out of the circumstances of my application to the Board.[10]

Subsequently, an administrative scheme based on the RIRB model was established to address further potential liability in regard to claims by women and girls detained and compelled to perform forced labour in the Magdalene laundries. In the wake of the *McAleese Report*, awards of redress offered under the so-called Restorative Justice Scheme were conditional on the signing of a waiver.[11] Although the waivers obtained from victims under these schemes protected the state and the religious congregations against many civil actions, these institutions could still be exposed by victims who were unwilling to waive their rights – or by those ineligible for redress. But many other barriers stand in the way of victims of institutional abuse who wish to obtain justice in Irish courts.

Obstacles to the Commencement of Proceedings

I. Statute of Limitations

The Statute of Limitations (1957) remains a significant barrier to litigation by victims of institutional abuse.[12] It generally requires victims to bring cases within a period of six years from the abuse occurring.[13] Various exceptions have been carved out of this rule over the years. The limitation period for personal-injury actions arising out of negligence, nuisance or breach of duty was reduced to three years in 1991, then to two years in 2004, the period to run from the injured party's date of knowledge of the injury rather than the date of injury itself.[14] A further adjustment was made in 2000 to lift the statute bar for victims able to show that they were suffering from a significant 'psychological injury' as a result of being sexually abused during childhood – such that their will or ability to make a reasoned decision to institute civil proceedings in respect of such abuse was substantially impaired.[15] But as James Gallen has observed, these rigid limitations still raise formidable difficulties in accessing legal remedies for such abuse:

> The Irish limitation regime is highly inflexible when compared with other common-law jurisdictions in failing to provide sufficient judicial discretion to enable consideration of whether, despite the time limits for civil action otherwise elapsing, a fair trial should be allowed to proceed in the interests of justice. The approach in Ireland has privileged the experience of victims of child sexual abuse to date, due to recognised psychiatric illnesses and injuries that victims of such abuse can experience. Recent expert evidence suggests, however, that this approach should justifiably be extended to victims of other forms of historical abuse, who also suffer from post-traumatic stress disorder and related injuries.[16]

As referred to in repeated Irish state apologies, the limitation regime established in Ireland ignores how such abusive treatment was officially and socially approved at the time it occurred.[17] That the law holds against victims the fact that they did not then take on the allied might of the church and state appears fundamentally unjust now that society's views have changed. Furthermore, although delay in instituting proceedings can prejudice an individual defendant's right to a fair trial, this logic does not necessarily apply with equal force to institutional and state defendants, whose liability may depend less on human memory than on their own records. Nevertheless, a *prima facie* defence based on the statute of limitations will arise in almost all historic institutional-abuse cases. Even where such a defence does not arise, there is a risk that the court's jurisdiction to dismiss proceedings for 'inordinate and inexcusable' delay[18] will be successfully invoked by the defendants. For example, in *McNamee v. Boyce* (2016), the Court of Appeal overturned the award of nearly €500,000 to a victim of sexual abuse against her abuser on the grounds of inordinate and inexcusable delay – although he had been convicted of the abuse in 1999.[19]

II. Vicarious Liability

Apart from rules of limitation, the judgment of the European Court of Human Rights in *O'Keeffe v. Ireland* (2014) illustrates that Irish law on vicarious liability is too narrow to provide an effective remedy against historic institutional abuse.[20] Ms O'Keeffe had suffered sexual abuse at the hands of her school principal, who was employed by a school operated under the patronage of the local Catholic bishop. She was not eligible for the RIRB scheme because her abuse took place at school rather than in a residential institution. Her abuser did not defend the civil case against him, but her case against the Minister for Education for failure to protect her was unsuccessful before the domestic courts because, as the Minister did not control the school or hire the principal, he could not be held vicariously liable for the abuse.[21] But the Strasbourg Court held that the state had failed to fulfil its positive obligations under Article 3 of the Convention to establish a mechanism of effective state control against the risks of child abuse in schools, a risk that was known even in the 1970s.[22] Whether this judgment will lead to any meaningful alteration in the approach of the courts to vicarious liability for human rights violations remains to be seen. But the Department of Education has interpreted the judgment as applying only where the victim made a prior complaint of abuse, and where the state had failed to act in response to that complaint. Such an interpretation means that victims in other cases are faced with threats to pursue them for very substantial costs if they do not abandon their proceedings.[23]

The example of *O'Keeffe v. Ireland* demonstrates that the rules on limitation and vicarious liability are not absolute barriers to justice, and that a civil action for damages arising out of historic institutional abuse can succeed – even if that means taking the case to the European Court of Human Rights. The exceptionality of that case has to be recognised, however, as does the fact that there are other less obvious barriers to litigation by victims of historical institutional abuse that they must navigate.

III. No Class Action

For any victim of injustice, deciding to go to law is daunting. That the injustice occurred in the past makes the decision even more painful since it involves confronting long-suppressed memories. This choice would be less difficult if the law provided some mechanism of collective redress whereby a victim could pursue a case with others in similar situations. Unfortunately, Irish procedural rules generally mandate that victim-plaintiffs act alone in taking on their abuser and in finally confronting the state that failed to protect them.

Significantly, Ireland has no mechanism comparable to class-action suits as they exist in the United States. Such actions, provided for in U.S. rules of procedure in the various states and in Title IV, Rule 23 of the Federal Rules of Civil Procedure, allow an individual or group to bring proceedings on behalf of a larger group – the class – that has suffered a similar kind of harm. This procedure requires identification of the class's existence, but not of every individual member within it. A principal benefit of class-action suits is that they provide a measure of solidarity for victims of harm by large or powerful entities; additionally, they permit victims to pool their resources and allow them to exert more pressure on defendants than a single plaintiff suing alone. In Ireland the only comparable mechanism available to plaintiffs is representative action. RSC Order 15, Rule 9, makes provision for such proceedings in the following terms:

> Where there are numerous persons having the same interest in one cause or matter, one or more of such persons may sue or be sued, or may be authorised by the court to defend, in such cause or matter, on behalf, or for the benefit, of all persons so interested.

But even if this mechanism may be employed by plaintiffs who have similar rather than the same interests in a particular matter, the problem with Order 15, Rule 9 – and the main distinction between Irish representative action and American class action – is that Irish representative actions require that all of the individual claimants be identified and give consent to have their interest represented by the plaintiff before the court will authorise the representative action.[24] Gerry Whyte observes that recourses to this mechanism are few; he notes that the onerous requirement to shepherd those seeking representation gave rise to grave administrative difficulties in the only large representative Irish action ever attempted. That action on behalf of 1,800 women, organised through the Free Legal Advice Centres (FLAC) to recover social-welfare arrears caused by discrimination on the grounds of sex was ultimately settled. But it occupied FLAC's resources for many years, and the settlement applied only to the women who had participated, not to the many thousands more who had also been affected by the discrimination.[25] The case suggests why Ireland's provision for representative action is so seldom invoked.

IV. Limitations on Litigation by Representative Organisations

As well as excluding the possibility of collective action by victims of historic institutional abuse, the Irish rules relating to standing also prevent representative organisations taking actions on their behalf. In *Cahill v.*

Sutton (1980) the Supreme Court ruled that a proceeding should only be brought by parties with sufficient interest in the outcome.[26] In the subsequent cases of *Construction Industry Federation v. Dublin City Council* (2005) and *Garda Representative Association v. Minister for Public Expenditure and Reform* (2014), the representative organisations were found not to have standing to litigate on their members' behalf because the members could have been plaintiffs in their own right and were better situated to bring the actions in question.[27] In *National Maternity Hospital v. Information Commissioner* (2007), the High Court found that a company formed by parents of deceased children whose organs were retained after post-mortem procedures did not have standing to participate in proceedings because it had not provided evidence that its members were incapable of financing the appeal themselves.[28] Existing mechanisms for collective action are therefore of little practical use in aiding victims of past institutional abuse who seek judgments against abusers or the state.

V. The Costs of Litigation

The financial burden of litigation raises further issues of access to justice. Although legal aid may be available to victims of past abuse under the Civil Legal Aid Act (1995), the grant of a legal-aid certificate is generally subject to a merits test.[29] But given the issues of limitation and the law of vicarious liability discussed above, the prospect of success in such litigation is small since the Legal Aid Board's merits test is difficult to pass. As a source of financial support, private third-party litigation funding – known in Irish law as 'maintenance' – can essentially be excluded. In *Persona Digital Telephony v. Minister for Public Enterprise and Others* (2017), the Supreme Court confirmed that the prohibition on maintenance in section 3 of the Maintenance and Embracery Act (1634) remains in force. Additionally, the court ruled against the legality of parties without interest or legally recognised motive in an action to give plaintiffs assistance or encouragement.[30] The remaining options for victims are *pro bono* legal representation and representation by lawyers acting through contingency arrangements in which they will be paid only if the action is successful. Unfortunately, historic institutional abuse cases are problematic even for lawyers willing to work under such arrangements; these cases are invariably long, complex and onerous. Even lawyers accustomed to working on contingency are unlikely to be enticed, given how difficult they are to win.

Victims considering litigation related to institutional abuse must consider not only their own costs but also those of the defendants, for which the plaintiff will in principle be held liable if the action is unsuccessful.[31] The risk of an adverse-costs order cannot even be allayed by obtaining a protective-costs order – that is, an order insulating those taking proceedings against having to pay their opponent's costs if the litigation is not successful. The test set down for the making of such orders includes a requirement that the plaintiff have no personal financial interest in the outcome of the case – a requirement that no victim of institutional abuse will ever be in a position to fulfil.[32]

The courts retain some discretion to depart from the general rule that 'costs follow the event,' that is, that a successful party to litigation is entitled to recover legal costs against the unsuccessful party.[33] One might expect that church and state defendants would be slow to pursue alleged victims, and that courts might exercise their discretion generously so as to excuse victims of abuse of having to discharge costs orders if their proceedings ultimately fail. Far from turning the other cheek, however, religious orders and state agencies are vigorous in seeking costs against litigants whose claims against them have failed; thus the threat of adverse-costs is a standard weapon deployed by defendants to intimidate plaintiffs.[34] Furthermore, discretion on the part of the courts to depart from the general rule on costs is exercised sparingly and only in accordance with established principles. Although unsuccessful plaintiffs in test cases (cases designed to set a precedent for further cases) and public-interest cases may escape costs orders against them, most historic institutional abuse cases will not be test cases and, similarly, few will have any general public-interest objective. In these circumstances victims of historic institutional abuse will receive a stark warning from their lawyers that if their proceedings fail, they will face financial ruin. Given their prior experience of abuse, it is hardly surprising that so few elect to commence legal proceedings in the first place.

VI. Whom to Sue

Yet another obstacle for victims lies in deciding whom they should sue. This step is fraught for plaintiffs and their lawyers. If a defendant who should have been sued is omitted, the plaintiff will have to bear that defendant's liability.[35] The problem cannot simply be solved by erring on the side of caution and including all defendants who might possibly be liable, however remotely; if a claim against any defendant does not succeed, the plaintiff will be liable for that defendant's costs. Furthermore, multiple defendants mean multiple legal teams – usually very well-funded ones. Such developments add to the complexity of the proceedings and open up further fronts across which the legal team's scarce resources of money, time, and energy must be stretched.

In *Hickey v. McGowan* (2017) the Supreme Court expressly recognised that there are risks for plaintiffs in deciding whom to sue. In that case damages awarded to the plaintiff for abuse by his former schoolteacher were reduced by 50 per cent by the Supreme Court on the basis that the school manager, who had not been joined, was vicariously liable for the abuse of the plaintiff and not just the provincial of the abuser's religious order who had been sued. Mr Justice O'Donnell noted in his judgment that 'questions as to whether the correct defendant has been sued are major traps for plaintiffs and their advisors.'[36] His use of the word 'traps' is particularly apposite, suggesting that for the victim of institutional abuse such rules can appear as devices designed by a hostile system to confound and defeat them.

Religious congregations against whom a victim may seek to commence proceedings – on the basis that the congregation is vicariously liable for the acts of its members – have no independent legal personality.[37] In other words, a plaintiff abused by a Christian Brother in an industrial school or forced to work without pay by a Sister of Mercy in a Magdalen laundry cannot simply sue 'the Christian Brothers' or 'the Sisters of Mercy' because in law these entities do not exist. The extraordinary procedure such a plaintiff is required to adopt was set out in *Hickey v. McGowan*:

> The appropriate course in such a case is to write to the order or provincial threatening to sue all individual members of the order unless a defendant is nominated. If that course is not taken, then all members who can be identified can be joined as defendants.[38]

Unsurprisingly, members of religious congregations do not readily cooperate with those threatening to sue them; an order can simply refuse to nominate a representative or even to respond to the plaintiff's request to do so. The facts in *Hickey v. McGowan* illustrate the problem. The plaintiff's solicitors sought agreement from the provincial of the abuser's order that he could be sued as its representative, and the provincial, as he was entitled to do, refused the request.[39]

Obvious practical difficulties exist for a plaintiff who must resort to suing all members of a particular religious congregation. Data protection rules mean that lists of a congregation's past and present members are likely to be closely guarded. Additionally, the members at the time that the harm complained of was committed would be liable, not the members when the proceedings are commenced.[40] The judgment in *Hickey v. McGowan* shows that the courts will permit defendants to be evasive in seeking to frustrate the plaintiff's claim. Reflecting on the efforts made by the victim of abuse to identify an appropriate defendant, Mr Justice O'Donnell remarked:

> This pattern of sporadic and somewhat ineffectual efforts on behalf of the plaintiff which were met with a barrage of technical complications raised by

the first named defendant characterised the progress of this case. However, a defendant is entitled to be punctilious, technical, and difficult, though such a course is not without risk. There is no such excuse for ineffective efforts on behalf of a plaintiff.[41]

Thus, even the simple rules of pleading assist institutional defendants in frustrating access to justice by plaintiffs.

Attrition in Proceedings

Even when victims of institutional abuse successfully navigate the many obstacles to commencement of proceedings, they face further hurdles in prosecuting a case to the point of its hearing and judgment. Indeed, the procedures laid down by the rules of the superior courts might be said to permit a form of harassment of plaintiffs by defendants. Since their cases are legally and factually complex, and their lawyers are unlikely to be well-resourced, plaintiffs in historic institutional abuse cases – especially if elderly – are particularly vulnerable to such tactics. Aside from the chance that delay may resolve a defendant's problem by simple attrition, procedural chicanery – even if not ultimately successful – can wear down a plaintiff's stamina and diminish the resolve of even the most committed legal team. Thus procedural delay in historic institutional abuse cases operates in favour of the defendants.

Tracing the 'life cycle' of an Irish civil action in the High Court reveals how procedures that may appear neutral operate to the advantage of well-funded institutional defendants. An action in the High Court claiming damages for historic institutional abuse will commence – depending on the type of claim being brought – by way of plenary summons or personal-injuries summons.[42] A personal injuries summons sets out the facts of the case being pleaded, the basis for the claim that the defendant is liable, and the nature of the harm suffered.[43] If the proceedings are commenced by plenary summons, these details are contained in a separate document called a statement of claim, which follows the plenary summons.[44]

Before the defendant enters any substantive defence to the claim, they can raise a notice for particulars: a list of questions asking for more details in regard to the claim being made by the plaintiff.[45] Although its purpose is merely to define the issues between the parties and not to set out the evidence supporting the parties' cases, in practice defendants routinely raise notices for particulars seeking extremely detailed accounts of the plaintiff's claim and evidence. Multiple defendants mean multiple notices for particulars, causing the plaintiff to expend yet more resources and to lose more time. If the defendant is not satisfied with the plaintiff's replies to particulars, the rules permit a notice for further and better particulars to be raised, occasioning yet more delay and more expense. Where, as is often the case, the defendants seek to interrogate the plaintiff's claim further, they can issue a notice of motion to bring the question before a judge, who may then direct that the plaintiff furnish the particulars sought.

If a defendant wishes to contest the case, the rules of the superior courts require the delivery of a 'defence.'[46] Time limits for defences vary depending on the type of action, but in practice these limits are rarely adhered to or enforced.[47] For defendants, foot-dragging in delivery of a defence can be an effective delaying tactic since the case cannot progress without one. The plaintiff has then to bring a motion seeking judgment in default of defence.[48] Before such a motion can issue, a 21-day warning letter must be sent, giving the defendant yet another opportunity to deliver a defence.[49] After a further opportunity for the defendant to do so, the motion can be heard.[50] In reality there is almost no prospect of a court actually granting judgment in default of defence. The usual pattern is that the defendant undertakes to file a defence within a particular period, now with the backing of a court order. The absence of meaningful enforcement of the time limits provided for in the rules is a pervasive feature of Irish civil procedure. This failure of enforcement allows defendants to waste a plaintiff's time with impunity, making it difficult and costly for plaintiffs to manage proceedings to a conclusion.

Still other tactics operate to favour defendants. The rules of the superior courts include a mechanism whereby defendants can turn the tables on the plaintiff even before a defence is filed by bringing a motion to dismiss the plaintiff's proceedings on the basis of delay. This tactic is employed to great effect by religious congregations in defending historic institutional abuse cases.[51] It typically involves asking the court to strike out the plaintiff's proceedings because of inordinate and inexcusable delay in their commencement, such that the defendant's right to a fair trial has been prejudiced. Any case of historic institutional abuse stretching into the 1990s or earlier, however, will involve delay that the courts will consider inordinate.[52] In theory the onus of proof in an application to dismiss is on the defendant; yet Irish case law suggests that in practice the defendant may meet this threshold by arguing that no credible explanation has been offered for the delay.[53] Because no evidence has been exchanged, this is a straightforward matter – shifting the onus to the plaintiffs to justify their delay in commencing proceedings. For victims of historic institutional abuse the effect of having their ordeals critiqued by parties allegedly implicated in the abuse is obvious. Dismissal on the basis of delay is the ultimate fate of many historic institutional abuse cases. For a plaintiff whose search for justice ends in dismissal, the experience compounds the pain of the original abuse.

For the fortunate plaintiff who navigates these obstacles, further difficulties lie ahead. When a defence has been delivered – and, if necessary, the plaintiff has replied – the case moves to the discovery phase. At this point either side may seek discovery of documents held by or available to the other side that are relevant to the case and necessary for its fair determination.[54] Again there are ample opportunities for the defendant to delay and harass the plaintiff. For example, the defendant can exploit the rules to obstruct the plaintiff's access to documents within her/his possession by ignoring letters seeking voluntary discovery and by forcing the plaintiff to bring the matter before a judge. Even the discovery hearing can be delayed by repeated adjournment applications; when it eventually comes on for hearing, it can be vigorously opposed by the defendant's counsel. If the defendant is then ordered by the court to make discovery, a lackadaisical approach can be adopted toward compliance in the certain knowledge that the sanction for failure to make discovery on the part of a defendant – the striking out of the defence – is applied in only the most exceptional cases.[55]

In addition, the defendant can seek discovery against the plaintiff. Frequently, the defendant will seek categories of documents so expansive that the plaintiff will have no choice but to object. The necessity for the issue to go before a judge adds to the length and cost of the proceedings. If the application is successful, the plaintiff will be required to go through the costly and time-consuming process of listing, compiling, and handing over the documents.

The courts are aware that procedural devices such as notices for particulars and requests for discovery may be used for purposes other than those for which they were designed. In *Armstrong v. Moffatt* (2013) the High Court criticised an excessive and extremely lengthy request for particulars, tellingly observing that the tactic was 'representative of current practice.'[56] The court noted that in personal injuries proceedings, section 10 of the Civil Liability and Courts Act (2004) now sets out the information that must be contained in a personal injuries summons. Mr Justice Hogan said that where a personal injuries case is properly pleaded in the manner required by section 10, the necessity for further extensive particulars 'should be very much the exception, not the rule.'[57] Yet the oppressive practices criticised in that case continue. Furthermore, in *Irish Nationwide Building Society v. Charlton* (1997), the Supreme Court recognised that in the context of discovery 'there is a danger that this valuable legal procedure may be invoked unnecessarily or applied oppressively.'[58]

Concerns about delays caused by unnecessary procedural wrangles, coupled with a general increase in the volume of litigation, led the judiciary to adopt a new, more interventionist approach to case management.[59] The judgment of the European Court of Human Rights (ECHR) in *McFarlane v. Ireland* (2010) gave particular impetus to this project, for the Strasbourg Court held that delays in the Irish legal system were so severe as to violate the right to due process guaranteed in Article 6 of the ECHR.[60] Although introduction of case management had already been recommended by the Law Reform Commission in 2010, only in 2016 were the rules of the superior courts amended to provide a framework within which case management could actually be carried out. It was anticipated that the adoption of the rules of the superior courts would streamline civil procedure and prevent delay.[61] Regrettably, personal injuries were excluded from this new mechanism – and a shortage of judges meant that the system was never actually put into operation.[62]

What Is to Be Done?

Although this article identifies some of the principal procedural impediments to justice for victims of historical abuse in Ireland, such obstacles are not beyond solution. The Statute of Limitations (1957) could be amended to provide for judicial discretion to lift the statute bar in the interests of justice. Under the European Convention on Human Rights Act (2003), a mechanism for claims arising after 2003 had already been made possible in Ireland – and has existed in England and Wales since 1980 without their legal systems collapsing under the weight of stale claims.[63] For further limitation reform, the test for inordinate and inexcusable delay could be adjusted by statute to take account of what was reasonable given social reality in Ireland before the liberalisation of the 1990s.

A mechanism for class actions will also improve access to justice. In 2005 the Law Reform Commission recommended the introduction of a system for multiparty litigation; yet the Multi-Party Actions Bill (2017), introduced by Sinn Féin on 9 November 2017, remains at committee stage. In a submission to the Review Group of the Administration of Civil Justice, the Bar Council of Ireland recently recommended that American-style class actions be introduced in Ireland; the council also noted some of the obstacles to justice posed by the current system as justifications for reform:

> A strong public policy argument favouring the establishment of class-action litigation is that such cases assist in ensuring that large corporate entities are held accountable for their behaviour in relation to groups such as consumers which on an individual basis may not have cost a significant amount, but

when repeated across the class of individuals concerned, has enabled the defendant to realise very significant gains from its wrongful behaviour.

The opposition to such an approach has traditionally come from those that might be seen as possible defendants (large institutions, finance houses, the state, etc.). These parties have used the fact that class action suits are not permitted to wear down individual claimants by making them pursue lengthy and cost-prohibitive claims through the courts. The current system effectively encourages this, with the effect that more court time is taken up with these cases.[64]

As a measure to facilitate access to justice, introduction of class actions could be supplemented by a relaxation of the rules of standing to allow representative organisations to litigate on behalf of their members without the need to demonstrate that there is no individual plaintiff willing and able to take the case – and additionally by reform of the rules on third-party funding of litigation. Such reforms would be in line with developments at the level of the European Union. The European Commission recommendation of 11 June 2013 concerned common principles for injunctive and compensatory collective-redress mechanisms in the member states in regard to violations of rights granted under EU law.[65] This nonbinding recommendation recognises that 'the possibility of joining claims and pursuing them collectively may constitute a better means of access to justice, in particular when the cost of individual actions would deter the harmed individuals from going to court.'[66] It suggests that member states introduce mechanisms for collective redress for violations of EU law into their domestic legal systems.[67] The commission also recommends that third-party funding of litigation be permitted as long as it does not create an incentive for abusive litigation or conflicts of interest.[68] Whereas most historic institutional abuse cases do not involve the implementation of EU law, aspects of complaints may raise issues – data protection, for instance – that do fall within the European Union's scope. Because it would be impractical to provide for collective-redress actions in cases covered by EU law while not in others, the recommendation provides further justification for urgent and overdue review of the rules around standing and funding.

In regard to historic abuse actions posed by the standing of institutional defendants, in 2005 the Law Reform Commission recommended introducing a new legal form for the structures of charities: the Charitable Incorporated Organisation (CIO). The commission's report suggested a process of gradual replacement of charitable trusts and unincorporated associations with charitable purposes by CIOs.[69] Unfortunately, even this moderate reform failed to appear in the Charities Act (2009). Because the position of religious congregations continues to be problematic, the introduction of legislation to regularise their legal status should be considered again.

Finally, a formal system of judicial case-management applicable to all High Court cases – including claims for personal injuries – is essential to address the current structural problems that can be exploited by defendants in historic institutional abuse claims. The stalling of the 2016 case-management initiative needs to be addressed, and the work of the Review Group of the Administration of Civil Justice will, one hopes, lead to radical reform. The application of imagination and resources to the problem of case management will unquestionably result in efficiencies elsewhere in the system; more importantly, it will mean that cases can proceed to the point of settlement or trial more rapidly. This would be an important improvement for all users of the judicial system, but for victims of historic institutional abuse, it would permit a radical rebalancing of their relationship with those whom they believe responsible for their suffering.

Conclusion

Those familiar with the accounts of individuals abused in industrial schools, incarcerated and exploited in Magdalene laundries, or separated from their mother or their child in a Mother and Baby Home cannot say that justice has yet been done to either victims or perpetrators. This article argues that significant responsibility lies with the judicial system and with the rules governing its operation. If the Irish legal system is to reflect more than a national talent for hypocrisy, a broad reform of the system of civil procedure is in order. The obstacles to litigation by victims of historical abuse here identified should be removed, and a balance must be struck between the right of victims to an effective remedy and the due-process rights of those they accuse. Ireland is fortunate in that history has granted a last opportunity to afford some measure of justice to surviving victims of historic institutional abuse. But time passes, and their numbers become fewer. If change is to have meaning, it must happen soon.

NINE

State's Reaction is to Deny, Delay and to Buy Silence[1]

Conall Ó Fátharta

Magdalene laundries, Mother and Baby Homes, industrial schools, illegal adoptions – Taoiseach Leo Varadkar listed them all out to the Pope in Dublin Castle this summer [2018]. He told the Pontiff that the sorry litany of scandals 'are stains on our State, our society and also the Catholic Church.'[2]

In doing so Varadkar trod a well-worn path of previous governments, treating all these issues as if they are distinct and separate scandals, instead of part of the same story.

Instead of examining and investigating the bigger picture of how unmarried and vulnerable women and children were treated in a sprawling network of interlinking institutions, private agencies and state authorities, the state breaks it down into separate scandals. 'Focus on the narrow and obscure the broader picture.'

Identifying all of these issues as individual scandals deflects from what they are really about – namely the collusion of Church and State in the construction of a system of confinement of single women and the removal of their children.

What flows from that system are the related practices which have shocked the world – like the infant remains interred in a disused septic tank at Tuam, but also the spectre of forced and illegal adoptions, infant trafficking, alteration of identities and records, medical and vaccine trials, infant mortality and the use of infant remains for anatomical research.

Mother and Baby Homes, Magdalene laundries, industrials schools – these not are not individual aberrations. They are one story; one scandal which, when seen in its totality, tell us about the fundamental character of the Irish State – right from its very foundation.

Controlling the narrative has always been an important method by which the government limits the impact of this story.

'Scandal' has been the word used in relation to the treatment of women and children in Ireland for decades. And, the reaction to scandal hasn't changed much down the generations.

Catherine Corless' research and the shocking revelations at Tuam were the match that lit the touch paper in 2014. In its wake, we witnessed the usual procession of TDs and ministers expressing shock and outrage about this latest scandal.

Seventy years earlier, in 1945, the same word was used by parliamentary secretary to the then Minister for Local Government and Public Health, Dr Con Ward, in relation to an 82 per cent infant mortality rate at the Bessborough Mother and Baby Home in Cork. That rate had been reported to state inspectors.

The government of the day took notice, intervening to ban pregnant women being sent to the home and Dr Ward wrote to then Bishop of Cork, Daniel Cohalan, to express fears about a 'public scandal' over the deaths.

The key word here is 'public.' A scandal is one thing to an Irish government; a public scandal is a very different animal.

Children's Minister Katherine Zappone's recent letter to Pope Francis also stressed that the issue of Mother and Baby Homes only came to 'public attention' in Ireland during the summer of 2014.[3]

In short, as far as the Government's narrative is concerned, the start date for dealing with the 'Mother and Baby Homes scandal' was 2014. From that perspective, it looks like the state reacted swiftly to revelations at Tuam.

Of course, there is a different narrative, one which focuses on institutional rather than public knowledge. This narrative reveals that regardless of whether it's Magdalene Laundries, Mother and Baby Homes or illegal adoptions, the state reaction is to deny, to delay and, when an issue becomes 'public' in a manner that can no longer be controlled, to launch an inquiry – but a limited one. A redress scheme which buys silence with compensation usually follows.

Mother and Baby Homes

Three years before Catherine Corless' revelations about a mass grave in Tuam sent shockwaves around the globe, the Cabinet was grappling with how to deal with another part of this story – the Magdalene Laundries.

Even in 2011, the issue of Mother and Baby Homes – and how to limit calls for inquiries into such institutions – was on the Cabinet's agenda.

In a memorandum for Government seeking permission to establish what would become the McAleese Committee, concerns were expressed that if there was an inquiry into Magdalene laundries, it could lead to calls for inquiries into abuses in mother and baby homes, psychiatric institutions and foster care settings.[4]

Controlling the narrative and limiting the scope of the Magdalene inquiry was the order of the day. Some seven years later, the Mother and Baby Home system and the treatment of more than 40 vulnerable adults in a foster care setting are now the subject of state inquiries.[5]

By 2012 the Health Service Executive (HSE) was expressing stark concerns about records it had uncovered related to Mother and Baby Homes.

The McAleese Committee had requested that the HSE examine records relating to the 10 Magdalene laundries under investigation.

Ultimately, permission was granted to include two mother and baby homes in this trawl – Bessborough in Cork and Tuam in Galway. This decision was 'based on potential pathways references by the advocacy group Justice For Magdalenes (JFM).'[6]

Prof. Jim Smith of Boston College and the JFM group had written to the chairperson of the Committee, then-senator Martin McAleese, on 21 February 2012 outlining a circular he had discovered relating to a 1948 Government survey which revealed 'disturbing' infant mortality rates in excess of 50 per cent at the Tuam Mother and Baby Home.

Within eight months, HSE staff in Cork and Galway had turned up enough shocking material that concerns were being expressed about whether or not these issues warranted a state inquiry in and of themselves.

By October 2012 such was the level of consternation caused by the material that Dr Declan McKeown – consultant public health physician and medical epidemiologist of the medical intelligence unit in the HSE – prepared an internal memorandum and in which he relayed the details of a teleconference with then assistant director of children and family services Phil Garland, who was co-ordinating the HSE project for the McAleese Committee, and then head of the medical intelligence unit Davida De La Harpe.

The memo outlines concerns raised by the principal social worker for adoption in HSE West who had found 'a large archive of photographs, documentation and correspondence relating to children sent for adoption to the USA' and 'documentation in relation to discharges and admissions to psychiatric institutions in the Western area.'[7]

It notes that there were letters from the Tuam Mother and Baby Home addressed to parents requesting money for the upkeep of their children and suggests that the duration of stay for children may have been prolonged by the Order for financial reasons.

It also refers to letters asking parents for money for the upkeep of some children that had already been discharged or had died.

The social worker, 'working in her own time and on her own dollar,' had compiled a list of 'up to 1,000 names,' but said it was 'not clear yet whether all of these relate to the ongoing examination of the Magdalene system, or whether they relate to the adoption of children by parents, possibly in the USA.'

At that point, the social worker was assembling a filing system 'to enable her to link names to letters and to payments.' Ultimately, the memo contends that:

> This may prove to be a scandal that dwarfs other, more recent issues with the Church and State, because of the very emotive sensitivities around adoption of babies, with or without the will of the mother.

A concern is that, if there is evidence of trafficking babies, that it must have been facilitated by doctors, social workers etc. and a number of these health professionals may still be working in the system.

The memo ends with a recommendation that an 'early warning' letter be written for the attention of the national director of the HSE's quality and patient safety division, Philip Crowley, suggesting 'that this goes all the way up to the minister.'

'It is more important to send this up to the minister as soon as possible: with a view to an inter-departmental committee and a fully-fledged, fully resourced forensic investigation and State inquiry,' concludes the memo.[8]

The Department of Children and Youth Affairs has said the minister was never made aware of the issues surrounding Tuam in 2012.[9]

In September 2012 a 20-page report had been prepared on the Bessborough home in tandem with the internal memorandum.[10] It revealed that the HSE was in possession of a death register from 1934 to 1953 maintained by the Order that ran the institution.

The report outlined that the almost 500 deaths recorded in this period were 'shocking' and 'a cause for serious consternation.'

It also expressed concern that death certificates may have been falsified so children could be 'brokered into clandestine adoption arrangements, both foreign and domestic' – a possibility the HSE report said had 'dire implications for the Church and State.'

The report notes that the records reveal a culture 'where women and babies were considered little more than a commodity for trade amongst religious orders' and that they were 'provided with little more than the basic care and provision afforded to that of any individual convicted of crimes against the State.'

It also highlights the 'intricacies of Bessboro[ugh]'s accounting practices,' and that 'detailed financial records and accounts were not handed over to the HSE by the Sacred Heart Order.'[11]

This report was seen by both the Department of Health and the Department of Children and Youth Affairs.

Given the level of concern surrounding what was uncovered in relation to both institutions, Dr McKeown began work on a briefing paper summarising the situation for Mr Crowley. This brief was also forwarded to the then national director of children and family services at the HSE, Gordon Jeyes on 19 October 2012.[12]

In one of the drafts of this brief, marked 'strictly confidential,' Dr McKeown states that the records show that one child was sent to a US couple in 1957 in return for a cash payment.[13]

Dr McKeown added that adoption records contained in the archive showed clear examples of multiple illegal adoptions that were not processed by the Adoption Board – the regulatory body for adoption at the time.

Dr McKeown's brief also revealed letters from 'senior Church figures requesting the nuns to identify babies for adoption to the USA' – indicating that the Catholic Church hierarchy was also directing this practice.

'The archives need to be examined for clinical, accounting and ethical irregularities, of which there are numerous clues in the material already uncovered.'

'Additionally, there may be legal or criminal issues underlying the documentation, and it is critical that these potentials are outruled as soon as possible, given the increased public interest in the issue of adoption practice in Ireland, particularly in the 1950s,' he wrote.[14]

None of these concerns appear in the final HSE submission to the McAleese Committee which only addressed concern with Mother and Baby Homes in so far as referrals took place with Magdalene laundries.

In a cover letter attached to a draft of the HSE report sent to the principal officer at the Department of Children and Youth Affairs (DCYA) and member of the McAleese Committee, Denis O'Sullivan, on 1 November 2012, Dr McKeown states that:

> Evidence in the form of higher than expected Infant Mortality Rates in Bessboro Mother and Baby Home has led the team to refer the issue of the Mother and Baby Homes directly to the National Director of Quality and Patient Safety within the HSE. Adoption, birth and registration and the recording of Infant Mortality are issues that may require a deeper

investigation, therefore Bessboro and Tuam Mother and Baby Homes no longer form part of the core investigation into the Magdalene system.[15]

Six days later, Mr O'Sullivan emailed Gordon Jeyes on 7 November 2012, to advise that any issues related to Mother and Baby Homes were outside the remit of the McAleese Committee.

'Material included beyond that is beyond the scope of our work – e.g. the scope does not extend to an examination of other places of refuge, e.g. mother and baby homes, other than in the context of referrals from Magdalene laundries. If there are separate and validated findings of concern emerging from such additional research, obviously they should be communicated by HSE and through a separate process.'[16]

It remains unclear where the HSE investigation went from here, if anywhere. No investigation was launched. Nothing happened.

The *McAleese Report* was published in February 2013. It addressed none of the concerns around mother and baby homes as they were deemed outside its remit.

But, within two years, Tuam was making headlines around the world. The Government launched another inquiry into the treatment of women and children – this time it was to be called the Commission of Investigation into Mother and Baby Homes.

From the outset, this Commission was criticised for being too narrow in scope and limited only to institutions labelled Mother and Baby Homes. Adoption would be addressed in so far as it related to the 14 named Mother and Baby Homes and four sample county homes under investigation. Calls for the probe to be widened to include adoption agencies and other institutions once again went unheeded. Calls for the inquiry to focus on the scale of forced and illegal adoptions across the institutional system fell on deaf ears.

Three years later, in May 2018, illegal adoption was to become the newest 'public scandal.' Once again, a piece of the same story was viewed in isolation.

Illegal Adoptions

The announcement came at a press conference with Children's Minister Katherine Zappone in May 2018 – Tusla (Ireland's Child and Family Agency) had discovered 126 cases where births were illegally registered between 1946 and 1969 in the records of former state-licensed, religious-run adoption agency, St Patrick's Guild.[17] A blaze of publicity ensued.[18]

The media declared the discovery 'Ireland's adoption scandal,' as if this news had come like a bolt out of the blue.

Of course, the issue of illegal birth registrations and other forms of illegal adoptions has been circulating in adoption-advocacy circles for years. That these practices occurred at St Patrick's Guild was already well known.

You can go back more than 20 years and find references to St Patrick's Guild in the news for all the wrong reasons.[19]

Of course, Minister Zappone rightly acknowledged that the problem of illegal birth registrations had been known before the Tusla discovery. However, the Minister quickly provided us with the state's new narrative: this time was different, whereas previously there were suspicions, now there was established fact.

'While there have been suspicions about the practice of incorrect registrations for many years, it has been extremely difficult to uncover clear evidence of the practice because of the deliberate failure by those involved to keep records. The 126 cases announced by the minister on 29th May represent the first time this threshold of a high level of certainty has been reached,' the DCYA told this newspaper in June.[20]

The DCYA went even further and said that where such evidence is found, the state's responsibility, 'is to inform the individuals concerned.' DCYA's statement is unique; it is both untrue and a significant U-turn all in one.

Firstly, the 126 cases are not the first evidence of illegal registrations. The DCYA and multiple government ministers have been aware of this issue for years. They chose to do nothing.

Take the case of Tressa Reeves – who recently settled a case against St Patrick's Guild and the state on this very issue.[21]

Tressa's son, was the victim of an illegal registration facilitated by St Patrick's Guild. Her story first appeared in *The Irish Examiner* in 2010.[22] Tressa had evidence to support her claim since 1997. The former Adoption Board, now the Adoption Authority of Ireland (AAI), knew about her case since 2001. In the years that followed, three former children's ministers were informed of Tressa Reeves' case.[23]

If, as the DCYA claims, the state has a responsibility to tell victims of illegal registrations the truth about their identity, why didn't it see fit to do this for Tressa's son?

For more than a decade, all Tressa asked for was that the state tell her son the truth. It took until 2012 – and the threat of a public scandal – for that to happen.

Remarkably, despite full knowledge of St Patrick's Guild's involvement in such practices, it was the very first adoption agency accredited under the Adoption Act 2010.

And, if Tressa's case wasn't enough evidence for the DCYA, the department's own regulatory body, the AAI, had been communicating its concerns for years.

Following *The Irish Examiner*'s story on Tressa Reeves, the AAI committed to an audit of its records.[24] It found approximately 45 cases which 'definitely related to illegal birth registrations' post the introduction of legal adoption in 1953 along with a further 50 cases pre-1953. A further twenty illegal birth registration cases were identified in the following years. This has subsequently risen to 131. Not all of these cases refer to St Patrick's Guild.

In a report prepared for the DCYA in June 2011, the AAI said it considered carrying out a more comprehensive audit of the cases it uncovered, but because of the transfer of senior personnel and the 'pressure on resources of the imminent establishment of the Adoption Authority no further action was taken.'[25]

In June 2013, an AAI delegation told the DCYA again of there being 'at least 120 [confirmed] cases' of illegal registrations found as the result of the 2010 audit.[26]

The AAI name-checked St Patrick's Guild for the department, stating that the agency was 'aware of several hundred illegal registrations,' and that it was 'not seeking the people involved' but were, rather, 'waiting for people to contact them.' The AAI went further, stating its belief that this could well be the tip of the iceberg and that there 'may be thousands' more.[27]

In 2015, the DCYA was again notified by its regulatory body about illegal registrations. This time the AAI sent three reports – including a spreadsheet of ninety specific cases it believed were likely illegal registrations.

Clearly, the department has been put on notice about this issue for years, had been informed of specific cases even, and has chosen to do nothing.

DCYA has defended its lack of action on the 90 cases it was notified about in 2015. It claimed these were cases 'where the appearance of irregular activity suggested the possibility of an incorrect registration having occurred,' before pointing out that the 126 cases found by Tusla in 2018 were confirmed cases of illegal birth registration.[28]

'The 126 cases currently being dealt with by Tusla were confirmed, once a rigorous process was completed to ensure that the state could be as sure as possible that these individuals' births were, in fact, illegally registered,' said the department.[29]

Why were the three AAI reports – including the spreadsheet with evidence related to ninety specific cases – not subjected to the same 'rigorous process' that Tusla's cases were? Do the concerns of the AAI, the regulatory body for adoption, count for nothing?

Just five months after the June 2013 meeting, then children's minister

Frances Fitzgerald told the Dáil she 'had no plans to initiate an audit of all [adoption] files.'[30]

She also claimed that all adoptions 'which the Irish State has been involved in since 1952 have been in line with this [Adoption Act 1952] and subsequent adoption legislation.'[31]

This claim was repeated on two separate occasions by her successor, Charlie Flanagan. Both made the claim despite the fact that no state agency had ever examined all the records.

The ministers' claim is also supported by the AAI, which said that to 'its knowledge,' all adoptions carried out by the regulatory body 'have been conducted in accordance with the relevant legislative framework for adoption.'

'Certain illegal birth registrations have been found to have occurred but these were conducted outside the legislative framework for adoption and can therefore not be classified as adoptions,' said the AAI in a statement.[32]

However, as *The Irish Examiner* revealed last week, we now know that some illegal registrations also resulted in adoption orders.[33]

Jackie Foley (named changed to protect identity) was instructed as a 16-year-old in Bessborough to sign a false name on an adoption consent form. All of the paperwork that followed – including her son's birth certificate and the adoption order – are made out in false names.

St Patrick's Guild could have been included in the Mother and Baby Homes inquiry in 2015 on foot of the AAI's notifications to the DCYA but it was not. By contrast, the cases found by Tusla were reported to the Commission this year. Once again, the inevitable was delayed.

When *The Irish Examiner* published details of the 2013 meeting in 2015,[34] it asked the DCYA did it not think that the AAI's belief that thousands of people in the country had their identities falsely registered – a criminal offence – warranted investigation?

The department declined to respond to the specific questions asked, but said a full audit of adoption records would be 'of very limited benefit.' Said a statement:

> It is important to note that the only way information generally becomes available is when someone with knowledge about the event comes forward… There is little, if any, supporting information in relation to these arrangements… Accordingly, an audit of all adoption records would be of very limited benefit in establishing the number of illegal registrations that took place.[35]

Recently, Minister Zappone has acknowledged the cases found by the AAI and says 'a validation exercise is underway' in relation to them.[36] However, she did not acknowledge that these cases had been found as far back as 2010. This action could and should have been taken years ago.

The DCYA's earlier view that an audit of the records would be of little use has also been exposed as flawed. Indeed, the 126 cases Tusla uncovered were specifically marked 'adopted from birth.' No detective work was required.

The DCYA has now committed to 'a scoping exercise' led by independent reviewer Marion Reynolds and involving the AAI and Tusla.[37] This exercise will clarify whether or not a full audit – which up to now was deemed a waste of time – is in fact necessary.

The DCYA has now declined to reveal how this scoping exercise will work. It won't say what sample of records will be examined or what methodology will be followed.

Of course, the real point of the scoping exercise is to delay and buy time. Like the decision at Tuam, we all know there is only one decision to be made. These matters require a full and thorough investigation.

The report of the scoping exercise originally due at the end of October 2018, won't be with us now until mid-December.[38] Word is the December deadline won't be met either.[39]

Everyone knew that the right call was for the fullest possible exhumation at Tuam and other sites like it. Similarly with illegal adoptions, everyone knows that the fullest audit of adoption records is also the right decision.

Even the DCYA knows this. A note from a meeting between department representatives and the AAI, and prepared by the department's adoption policy unit, contains an acknowledgment that evidence of illegal registrations was not confined to St Patrick's Guild.

The note stressed that a full investigation of these issues would be 'onerous, requiring massive resources.'[40]

Indeed, Tusla itself has raised concerns about a further 748 cases from St Patrick's Guild. These cases contain evidence of names being changed, payments being made to the agency, placements of children with no corresponding adoption order and other 'irregularities.'

So everyone knows – the DCYA, Tusla and the AAI – that this is an issue that requires a full investigation of all adoption records held by the state. Yet it persists with a scoping exercise that the public has been given no information about and which will satisfy no one.

Magdalene Laundries

The Magdalene laundries, yet another tale of denial and delay, represent a different chapter of the same story. It is now taken as fact that the state was directly involved in referring large numbers of women to the Magdalene laundries and indeed paying the religious orders for the privilege of providing for their 'care.'

State involvement, finally acknowledged in the 2013 *McAleese Report*, was long taken as accepted fact by a number of groups and survivors who spent decades campaigning on the issue. As with much of this story, their voices went unheard.

In the early 2000s, the then-government refused to include the Magdalene laundries in the Commission to Inquire into Child Abuse and the related Residential Institutions Redress Board scheme.

This stance was defended by then education minister Michael Woods in 2002 on the grounds that the laundries were 'entirely private institutions, in respect of which public bodies had no function.'[41]

This was the Government's line and it was stuck to rigidly.

By 2009 the country was reeling from the revelations of the *Ryan Report* and the Government was again facing down calls to examine the Magdalene laundries. The official policy remained the same.

In 2009 then education minister Batt O'Keeffe said categorically that the 'State did not refer individuals to Magdalen laundries nor was it complicit in referring individuals to them.'

He also said that they 'were not subject to State regulation or supervision.'[42]

Of course, survivors and campaigners knew this was categorically untrue. In 2010 Justice For Magdalenes (JFM) made an application to the Irish Human Rights Commission (IHRC) seeking an inquiry into the state's failure to protect the human rights of girls and women detained in the Magdalene laundry system.

Later that year, the IHRC issued a recommendation to government to immediately launch a statutory inquiry into abuse in the laundries.

With the Government failing to respond, JFM went to the United Nations Committee Against Torture (UNCAT), which in June 2011 recommended the same course of action to the Government as the IHRC.

The Government finally relented and launched an Inter-Departmental Committee to investigate the issue – the McAleese Committee.

The *McAleese Report* was published in February 2013 and confirmed what everyone knew. Indeed, the report confirmed that at minimum one-quarter of all referrals to Magdalene laundries were made or facilitated by the state.

Despite this confirmation, an official apology took two weeks to come.

The *McAleese Report* and the ensuing *ex-gratia* restorative justice scheme have been subjected to persistent scrutiny and criticism in the five years thereafter.

The Department of Justice finally allowed a small cohort of women access to the scheme in 2018. They had been wrongfully excluded. Some had gone to the High Court to fight their case. Revelations by this newspaper and a scathing report by the Ombudsman following a year-long investigation eventually led the Department of Justice to grant them access.[43]

However, campaigners say women are still not getting the full range of healthcare provisions promised to them.[44]

When Taoiseach Leo Varadkar addressed the Pope and asked him to use his 'office and influence' to ensure that 'justice and truth and healing' is granted to survivors of institutional and clerical abuse, he specifically name-checked the Magdalene laundries.

However, at the same time his Government recently told the United Nations Committee Against Torture (UNCAT) that there is 'no credible evidence of systematic torture or criminal abuse being committed in the Magdalene laundries' and that it has no intention of setting up a formal state inquiry into the matter.

Indeed, the Government has been accused of 'walking back' the state apology offered by then Taoiseach Enda Kenny in 2013, now claiming, repeatedly, that the report made 'no finding' in relation to state liability with regard to Magdalene laundries.[45]

It continues to cite the *McAleese Report* as the de-facto narrative of how the Magdalene laundry system operated in Ireland.

That would be fine if researchers could access any of the material in order to challenge the findings of the *McAleese Report*. However, they can't.

The archive has been held in the Taoiseach's own department for 'safekeeping' since 2013. It is exempt from Freedom of Information and the department told *The Irish Examiner* it has 'no plans' to open it up to public inspection.[46] We must simply accept that the *McAleese Report* as we find it.

So, while Mr Varadkar is quick to call on the Pope to use his 'office and influence' to offer 'justice and truth and healing,' he declines to use his own office to open the archive so people can challenge or confirm the findings of an investigation into the Magdalene laundry system.

TRANSITIONAL JUSTICE: OPPORTUNITIES, LIMITS

Reparations for Historic Institutional Gender Violence in Ireland: Learning from Transitional Justice

Ruth Rubio Marín

Keynote address at the international conference: Towards Transitional Justice? Recognition, Truth-Telling and Institutional Abuse in Ireland[1]

The forms of historic injustice that states have orchestrated or facilitated are many. Indeed, as Dinah Shelton rightly observes, 'to a large extent the existence and boundaries of modern states are the result of past acts and omissions that would be unlawful today according to international law, and most national constitutions and laws.'[2] Yet it is a very specific chapter of historic state-related abuse that brings us here today, this lecture being part of a two-day conference at Boston College devoted to discussing truth-telling and institutional abuse in Ireland.

This lecture is consecrated to the thousands of victims and survivors affected by a policy that sought to encourage prolific Catholic marriages as much as to prevent or to hide unmarried motherhood: a joint venture between the Catholic Church and the Irish Republic since its very inception and lasting to some extent until the 1990s.[3]

The lecture is also consecrated to the 1,500 Irish women and girls subjected to symphysiotomy, a childbirth operation that severed the symphysis pubis (the joint that binds the two sides of the pelvis) without free and informed consent from the 1940s to the 1980s.[4] The so-called 'rule of three' limited the number of caesarean sections that could safely be performed on the same woman, hence such operations were seen as leading to the use of contraception, sterilisation and abortion, all practices prohibited by Roman Catholic doctrine. A symphysiotomy, by contrast, would enable subsequent children to be delivered vaginally.[5] As the 'Survivors of Symphysiotomy' group has informed the United Nations, survivors recall being physically restrained as they screamed and struggled against the surgery, fully conscious in the heat of labour, often in front of large groups of generally male medical students.[6] Symphysiotomy inflicted serious bodily injury, depriving many women of their ability to walk. Some have experienced continuing pelvic instability, urinary incontinence, chronic urinary tract infections and chronic pain, besides huge trauma.[7]

In addition, this lecture also consecrated to mothers who were ill-treated in Ireland's Mother and Baby Homes, and in County Homes, for much of the twentieth century. The Mother and Baby institutions were funded, regulated and inspected by the State between the 1920s and 1990s and run by various religious orders solely for the purpose of housing children born outside of marriage prior to their enforced adoption and the mothers while pregnant and after giving birth: an estimated population of at least 56,000 girls and women and their 57,000 infants.[8] Many of the illegally adopted persons – a practice facilitated by the state including through the falsification of birth certificates and the issuance of passports to transnational adoptees – still anguish at the impossibility of accessing information about their natural families and some suffer the lingering traumas from when they were given to abusive adoptive families, some in the U.S., many such families chosen without proper scrutiny.[9]

Lingering trauma also haunts the survivors of State-funded, Church-run Reformatory and Industrial residential schools for children, which operated between the 1920s and 1990s, affecting at least 42,000 children who were systematically subjected to physical, sexual and emotional abuse and neglect in the midst of a conspiracy of silence, fear and coercion.[10] As documented in the Report of the Commission to Inquire into Child Abuse, complaints were ignored, witnesses were punished, and pressure was brought to bear on the child and family to deny the complaint and/or remain silent.[11]

A similar conspiracy of silence surrounded the more than 10,000 women and girls, some as young as nine, who were incarcerated between 1922 and 1996 in Ireland's Magdalene laundries. Here, they were involuntarily detained behind locked doors and high walls with no information as to whether or when they would be released. They were stripped of their identity, including through imposition of house names and/or numbers, uniforms, haircuts and the prohibition of speaking. They were banned from communicating with the outside world except under strict surveillance, verbally denigrated and humiliated, kept in cold conditions with minimal nourishment and hygiene facilities, denied any education and forced to work constantly and unpaid at laundry, needlework and general chores.[12]

We have learned from the Minister for Children, Dr Katherine Zappone, in her remarks to this conference, that the government's decision regarding the unmarked burial site at the Tuam institution is to conduct a full exhumation and forensic DNA analysis, in order to support individualisation and identification and dignified reburial.[13] This is to be celebrated while of course we have to remember that there are similar end-of-life concerns and unmarked burial sites at many of the other Mother and Baby Homes and at the Magdalene laundries.

This lecture, then, is a tribute to victims, many of whom unfortunately as we have heard still lie in unmarked graves, and to survivors, many of whom finally freed from societal shaming and blaming continue restless in their unstoppable battle for justice. It is also a tribute to the people and organisations who tirelessly seek redress for the injustice of these past forms of institutional violence and for the present-day injustice of lack of redress, truth and recognition by the responsible authorities. It is from those personally affected that I have learned much of what I will now go on to discuss.

Structural Gender Violence

One of the first things to notice is that the institution-centred – and even activist dynamic – approach to these events has evolved in such a way that one could easily be tempted to see them as separate and distinct thus losing sight of the larger picture of what, when put together, they collectively represent. And what they collectively represent is a repressive disciplinary regime that sustained a State-/Church-imposed social and moral gender order which saw women's citizenship as confined to the private sphere; married women's bodies viewed primarily as reproductive vessels to breed Catholic offspring, and women's souls as repositories of an Irish national Catholic identity which was, aspirationally at least, to define itself in contraposition to that of its Protestant neighbour.

After all, the great physical and psychological harm, the exploitation, and the severe deprivation of liberty and autonomy – both physical and reproductive – that victims endured, resulted from the need to punish (justified in redeeming terms) those women who deviated from the normative motherhood script or were seen as being in danger of doing so. These abuses resulted from the need to hide from public sight the traces of the failure of a system which confined sexual relations to marriage (for many of the institutionalised were not 'fallen women,' but rather victims of sexual abuse), as well as from the need to ensure, no matter how high the price to be paid in human suffering, the possibility that married women would be able to receive as many offspring as God's will dictated. This deeply gendered project relied on what author James M. Smith has called an 'architecture of containment,' resting on an array of interdependent institutions acting as its repressive apparatus which allowed the historically powerful Catholic Church and the fledgling Irish Free State to cooperate as self-appointed guardians of the nation's moral climate.[14] Together they placed emphasis on the virtues of chastity, virginity, modesty, piety: virtues primarily directed towards women and children, denying any male moral responsibility for either the sexual practices leading to illegitimacy or the violence of sexual abuse.[15] In this climate, as Anne-Marie McAlinden has written, 'sex and sexuality became associated with the precarious undertones of silence, denial and secrecy,' which, ironically, 'set the stage for the abuse of children and its subsequent cover-up.'[16]

Simply put then, we are talking about institutional and structural gender violence justified in the name of Catholic morality turned into State ideology, and about it supporting a repressive moral architecture, which failed until well into the 1990s to live up to basic liberal democratic standards promising women full and equal citizenship.

Gendered Human Rights Violations and a Survivors' Centred Approach to the Statute of Limitations

With this in mind, let me turn to discuss survivors' right to reparation under current human rights law standards. Doing so also allows me to raise the specific question of whether a transitional justice framework can be useful to address these episodes of historic injustice and, if so, what we can learn about transitional justice that would inform the way Ireland and countries with a similar past of structural gender violence should act when confronting claims that are starting to appear now and are not likely to be contained once the silence has been broken.

Let us delve for a moment into the technicalities of the law. In translating the harms endured by victims, several key human rights provisions come to mind, including those that appear in the main and initial international and regional human rights treaties adopted as part of the post-war human rights revolution and that, therefore, were binding at much of the time when these abusive practices were taking place. Think of the European Convention of Human Rights, binding on Ireland since 1953, and of the International Covenant on Civil and Political Rights, adopted in 1966 and which Ireland ratified in 1989 – but think also of the Irish Constitution, which dates from 1937. So think of the right to life, the prohibition of slavery and forced labour, the prohibition of torture or inhuman or degrading treatment, the right to liberty, the prohibition of forced detention, not to mention other rights that are also included in early human rights treaties and were severely violated by these practices such as freedom of expression, the right to private and family life, freedom of conscience, and certainly the right not be discriminated against on the grounds of sex and birth.

Thus, it does not seem plausible to argue that the practices did not contravene human rights standards that were valid at the time. What seems to have changed or is changing is not so much the affirmation of certain moral standards as embodied under these constitutional and human rights norms, but rather two other things. First and most importantly, we see the de-legitimatisation of states' delegation of their jurisdiction in favour of the Church and its institutions; human rights norms are increasingly understood to bind across the board and limit power in every site of power. Secondly and relatedly, there is the increasing affirmation that women's rights are human rights and that the public/private divide cannot serve as an ideological construct to abandon women and children into spaces constructed as 'private' where they can be abused with impunity. These two things are changing.

That the abuses I describe contravened human rights provisions has now been denounced by many human rights bodies, which have called on the provisions I mention as well as others. I am referring here to the Human Rights Committee,[17] but also the Committee on Economic, Social and Cultural Rights,[18] the Committee on the Elimination of Discrimination Against Women,[19] the Committee Against Torture;[20] this is a position shared also by the Irish Human Rights and Equality Commission.[21]

In spite of this condemnation by the treaty bodies, it is worth noticing that these human rights instruments are insufficient in terms of an adequate and explicit portrayal of the different forms of reproductive violence. Reproductive violence broadly understood encompasses severe interference with reproductive free will or autonomy, the impairment of reproductive bodily functions or forms of motherhood and fatherhood deprivation (such as the removal through force or illegal adoption or otherwise of offspring), or the removal of the capacity to raise or otherwise care for one's children. Now think of what illegal detention in prison-like conditions meant for women who lost the possibility to mother; or think, for instance, of the loss of parental skills because of the neglect that institutionalised children were subjected to, a loss that survivors attending this conference addressed earlier.

In other words, still to this day and in spite of the fact that the human rights corpus has gradually become more gendered, there is insufficient spelling out of the different modalities of reproductive violence that women are subject to – maybe with the exception of forced abortions and sterilisations which have been recognised as international crimes. Now, true, one can always take some forms of violence as expressions or modalities of other forms of more broadly or generically defined violence, but one does wonder about the consequences of making women's experience of violence always fit into categories that have first been inhabited by other forms whose primary victims were often thought of as male. So, when the Irish government argues that the findings of a governmental enquiry into state involvement in the Magdalene laundries, which confirms the practices I described, demonstrates that there is 'no factual evidence to support allegations of systematic torture or ill-treatment,' one has to wonder what constitutes the Irish government's default understanding of torture or ill-treatment.[22]

Also, while gender violence has come to the fore in the human rights world in recent times (think, for instance, of the adoption and entering into force of the Istanbul Convention[23] in the framework of the Council of Europe, or ongoing conversations about the possibility to adopt a general UN level Convention Against Violence Against Women), we often find that gender violence is too narrowly conceived as sexual violence or intimate partner violence, leaving out expressions of coercive imposition of gender roles that would allow us to see the compound effect of multiple forms of structural discrimination on women's lives. And in this sense, it is interesting to notice that the Irish government when assessing the gravity of the Magdalene laundries chose particularly to focus on the lack of evidence of sexual violence in the laundries.[24]

Now, when discussions about human rights appear there is of course the question of the relevance of the passage of time, and the statute of limitations. Are these historic violations which can no longer trigger remedial response? There is an evolution in human rights law and doctrine about what needs to be done around this question and, although it is not possible to go into detail, I would say that this doctrinal evolution rests on two premises: first, that rights must be effectively enjoyed and, second, that when it comes to statutes of limitations, we have to prioritise the harm that is done to victims and the way it operates and has ongoing effects on victims, rather than the vision of a ticking clock that starts at the moment of the action of the perpetrator and essentially seeks to protect legal certainty for the perpetrator.

In general, I would say when it comes to the doctrine of statutes of limitations, one must also consider the hierarchy of norms. We cannot simply take existing statutory limitations and automatically apply them to human rights violations contained in norms that must prevail and have their own internal logic. Legal certainty is certainly a central value in rule of law, but the time to react against human rights violations of such gravity can only count from the moment in time in which the conditions exist for victims to be reasonably able to claim justice. I would say that for victims who endured severe forms of disciplinary repression around a normalised coercive gender order, only the sufficient demise of that gender order – a task that is low in its progression and in fact is a work in progress – can create an environment that reasonably allows claims of justice to come to the surface. So, whether it be because of procedural obstacles, or because of what we can reasonably assume to be personal conditions (in terms of trauma effects) or societal conditions (in terms of lingering shame or stigma), those barriers need to be taken into account as possibly impeding survivors from coming to the fore to claim justice. As a rule of thumb, I would say that systemic forms of gross violations of human rights should not be treated as 'historic' injustice for as long as survivors and their immediate relatives are alive, enabling conditions for justice have not been generally given and redress has not been granted.[25]

The Right to Reparations and Forms of Reparation

Now, what about reparations under human rights law? What is the relevant legal framework? Although a coherent theory and practice for remedies for victims of human rights violations does not yet exist under international law, the right of individuals to reparations for the violation of their human rights has been increasingly recognised. The principle of reparations was initially affirmed as a principle of interstate responsibility, but it is true that since World War II a shift of focus can be observed to national arenas and away from international disputes. The legal basis for a right to a remedy and, linked to it, a right to reparations has since then become firmly enshrined in the corpus of international human rights and humanitarian instruments. This includes human rights treaties that focus specifically on violence against women, like the Inter-American Convention on the Prevention, Punishment and Eradication of Violence against Women, which espouses that states must undertake to establish the necessary legal and administrative mechanisms to ensure that women subjected to violence have effective access to restitution, reparations and other just and effective remedies.[26] Similar provisions can be found in the Protocol to the African Charter of Human and People's Rights and the Rights of Women in Africa,[27] and in the aforementioned Istanbul Convention.[28]

But what does the obligation to provide reparations encompass under human rights law? A basic guide to the substance is the UN General Assembly's *Basic Principles and Guidelines on the Right to a Remedy and Reparation for Victims of Gross Violations of International Human Rights Law and Serious Violations of International Humanitarian Law*, adopted in 2005.[29] *Basic Principles* tellingly defines the contours of state responsibility for providing reparation to victims not just for acts but also for omissions that can be attributed to the state. This is because states are responsible for the failures to meet their international obligations even when substantive breaches originate in the conduct of private persons. *Basic Principles* lists what can be considered different reparations modalities; it describes what, in a perfect world if these breaches of human rights occur, are the kinds of modalities and measures that should be provided in terms of redress.[30]

It is useful to dwell momentarily on the technicalities which might be relevant for our understanding of what might be required to satisfy survivors' needs. The first modality referred to in *Basic Principles* is restitution. In theory it means restoring the victim to the original situation before the gross violation – which, as we know, taking into account the kinds of violations we are talking about, would not be possible in reality. Restitution includes restoration of liberty and enjoyment of human rights, identity, family life and citizenship. So, recovering one's identity is a matter of restitution.

Compensation is the second modality and should be provided for any economically assessable damage as appropriate and in proportion to the gravity of the violation; it should include damages linked to physical or mental harm but also lost opportunities (such as employment and education) and material and moral damages. The third modality is rehabilitation, and this should include medical and psychological care as well as social services.

There is a fourth very interesting modality that is broadly identified as 'satisfaction' measures. It combines measures that are related to truth-telling such as verification of the facts, full and public disclosure of the truth and the search for the whereabouts of the disappeared – for the identities of the children abducted and for the bodies of those who died – and assistance in the recovery, identification and reburial of the bodies. Satisfaction measures are also inclusive of symbolic redress measures such as public apologies or commemorations and tributes to victims. Satisfaction measures also include accountability measures such as judicial and administrative sanctions against persons liable for the violations. So, reparations are not either/or, but calls for some measure of all of the above.

And finally, there is a modality of reparation that is forward looking and has the greatest transformative potential, that of 'guarantees of non-repetition.' These of course look at the individual victim and survivor, trying to ensure that the violations will not recur, but in most cases the only way of ensuring that is by tackling the structural and systemic problems that have led to the massive and systemic violations, hence the transformative potential. *Basic Principles* lists many measures that may provide such guarantees, such as strengthening the independence of the judiciary or providing human rights and international humanitarian law education to all sectors of society.

Transitional Justice and Reparations in Unfinished Democracies

Let me turn now to consider the transitional-justice framework and ask: is it helpful? And, if so, how?

As many of you know, transitional justice emerged in the late 1980s and early 1990s, mainly in response to political changes and demands for justice in Latin America and Eastern Europe.[31] These political and legal responses sought to address the systematic abuses of previous regimes, without jeopardising the ongoing political transformations, acknowledging and understanding that the numerous problems that arise from massive and/or systematic violations of human rights of the past are often too complex to be solved with a single action or by seeking perfect justice. Because of this, the term 'transitional justice' came to imply the plurality of complementary approaches that might be required to properly confront the legacy of mass human rights violations in a comprehensive and holistic manner. These complementary approaches would include truth, justice, reparation and guarantees of non-repetition and ideally be also supplemented with other parallel interventions such as development, humanitarian assistance and peace building measures.[32] The strength of the transitional justice framework relies, among other things, in bringing victims to the fore and in endorsing a holistic approach. The idea is that, even under conditions of imperfect justice (given the number or the gravity of the violations), some measure of justice still needs to be provided. A page cannot simply be turned. Truth, accountability, reparations and structural reforms are called for.[33] Among these elements, truth recovery in particular has emerged as a vital element in dealing with legacies of the past. Fundamentally, truth recovery – often via the conduit of truth commissions – entails investigating patterns of abuse or crimes of a past regime, usually uncovering information previously concealed by the authorities, in order to make the transition from one order to another.

Typically, transitional justice approaches have succeeded in societies that have self-reflectively identified as undergoing what in Bruce Ackerman's terms we could call a 'constitutional moment,'[34] such as those that appear in the wake of an authoritarian regime, a dictatorship or a civil conflict, all of them situations traditionally identified as instances of 'political violence.' However, I would argue that in general – but especially when we make the state responsible not only for inflicting harm but also for failing to protect its citizenry – the naming of certain forms of widespread violence as 'political violence' is itself a political act.

Let us consider an additional question: which are the violations under authoritarian regimes that have deserved the attention of transitional justice mechanisms so far? If we consider the Latin American dictatorships, which provided many of the examples around which the transitional-justice field was defined, the set of violations which became the object of analysis by truth commissions and reparation schemes include illegal detention, enforced disappearance, severe ill-treatment and, more recently, and as a result of women's struggle, sexual and reproductive violence. Well, are these not precisely the types of violations that Ireland's victims of institutional abuse suffered because they were dissidents in the State-Church imposed 'gender order' or, at least, collateral victims thereof?

So maybe we should broaden our imagination when we define the typologies of what we call 'political violence.' Professor Fionnuala Ní Aoláin, a fellow contributor to this volume, uses the term of 'conflicted societies' to expand the reach of transitional justice paradigms to situations that do not strictly refer to authoritarian regimes or armed conflict and yet still offer patterns of systemic violence.[35] Maybe we could add to it the term of 'unfinished democracies.' If we do, I would argue that a state/church/patriarchal regime that treats women as second-class citizens, imposing on them a gendered moral order, including through violent methods, cannot be but an unfinished democracy so that the self-reflective effort to overcome it can indeed be identified as a constitutional moment for the country.

How then does our understanding of reparations change when we think of reparations in a transitional justice framework? What does the transitional-justice framework add? In essence, there seems to be something problematic about endorsing a notion of reparations that focuses on (mostly) individual types of remedy aimed at full restitution or compensation of the harmed person to cope with a legacy of systemic and gross violations of human rights. The main reason for this inadequacy is that in those scenarios the basic presumption on which the notion of reparation for the violation of a right rests – namely, an overall well-functioning system based on the rule of law and commitment to a human rights ethos where violations are the exception rather than the norm – does not apply. The very fact that the violations took place on such massive scale is precisely the result of the state's fundamental lack of commitment to a certain rights order or, at best, its fundamental failure in ensuring the respect for such an order by others.

This is why I think Pablo de Greiff is right in arguing that when confronted with a legacy of widespread and systemic violations, governments do best conceptualising reparations as political projects.[36] Yes, legally grounded and rights-based, but political projects aimed at the reconstitution of a new political community through the promotion of a minimal degree of both interpersonal trust and trust in the institutions of the state. In this light, reparations then become modest acts of (re-)creation of the 'new' democratic state representing a commitment to overcome the underlying structural flaws and to confirm the new basis of legitimacy in a given political order that claims to be grounded on the idea of equal citizenship.

Now, if this is the case – if reparation is not seen as attempting in a futile way to provide each individual victim with full restitution and compensation for the harm endured but is rather seen as part of a societal endeavour to overcome severe structural flaws in 'unfinished democracies' – then the key element in reparation is that of victims' recognition. Recognition of the wrongdoing, the ensuing harm, the responsibility of all the institutions and parties involved, and the resulting reparative needs becomes a centrepiece of reparations when reparations are to help survivors reclaim their equal citizenship status in a more perfect democracy whose institutions can be trusted.

Recognition-Centred Reparations

If we find the idea of recognition-centred reparations compelling, what follows? I think that the main consequence that follows from recognition-centred reparations is that truth is an absolutely indispensable precondition. By truth I mean full disclosure and information to survivors – individual truth, if you will – but also public acknowledgement of facts: call it collective truth, concerning rights violations. This requires serious, comprehensive and independent investigations. It requires access to archives, the gathering and preservation of survivors' testimonies, and the holding of public hearings that can reach the wider citizenry.

Why are these elements of private and public truth so important? Mainly for three reasons. First, compensation efforts without individual truth are not bound to have any reparative effect. Rather, they tend to be seen as efforts of buying victims' silence – especially if payments come, as they have done so far in Ireland, with legal waivers as a condition. They can also be interpreted by family members as selling out on their beloved ones, with the most in need not being able to afford what we could call dignity-based conscientious objection to the payments. Let me explain. One of the problematic issues about the process followed by the Moroccan Equity and Truth Commission, as became clear to me in my fieldwork in the country, was that compensation payments were being provided to the wives of many of the disappeared before they had information about the whereabouts of their husband – so, many of them refused to take the money. But what I noticed in Morocco was that in reality there were two groups of survivors.

Whereas some of them could afford to say no, others simply could not because they were in dire need. I felt this was a serious injustice.

Second, without collective truth and acceptance of responsibility, stigma will not go away; this prevents more survivors from stepping to the fore and impedes their psycho-social rehabilitation. Survivors need to know why. They need to know why this happened to *them*. And they need the wider community to know as well. They cannot be expected to be the ones who individually expose themselves to facilitate the transformation of the interpretive lenses through which society judges what was done to them. If they freely decide to do so, we must all be thankful. But survivors should not be bearing that weight.

And third, only truth telling signals the collective act of self-reflection and invites a future-looking debate that allows society to identify historical continuities and to plan for needed ruptures. Guarantees of non-repetition offer precisely this way forward, but they cannot be adequately discussed without the prior exercise of collective truth disclosure. In fact, what one sees in many transitional processes is that the discussions of certain forms of historic violence – for instance, conflict-related sexual violence – is what allows to break the taboo and facilitate conversations about ongoing, present, 'ordinary' forms of sexual violence. Moreover, it is important to recall that guarantees of non-repetition not only offer the greatest potential for transformation of pre-existing gender relations, but they can also help survivors feel their contribution as actors of change, something which especially those who have turned their experience of victimisation into a struggle for justice (something which many survivors certainly do even if not a single one has a moral duty to).

Now, in view of this, we can ask ourselves about the soundness of the Irish process so far, in that numerous ongoing and past investigations into these historical abuses have been said to suffer from serious flaws such as limited reach, lack of transparency, withholding of evidence, failure in collecting and putting together and ensuring access to archival evidence, or failure to offer public hearings.

The second lesson that I think emerges from making recognition the cornerstone of reparations, and reparations a part of a political project of recovering citizens' horizontal and vertical trust, is that the symbolic dimension of redress is as important as the material dimension. And this is because the symbolic dimension of redress is what shapes the meaning of whatever material measure accompanies it. I would add that the symbolic dimension of reparation hinges not just on the specific acts of symbolic redress that are undertaken (such as, for instance, a public apology or a commemoration event), but also on the rest of the features of the

143

reparations and transitional justice process altogether. Let me say a few words about this.

Acts of public apology are key to societal recognition, psycho-social rehabilitation, the overcoming of stigma and the expression of future commitments. Much can be learned from experiences in other parts of the world. Maybe the single most organised and well-documented historical movement for reparations for women is that of the so-called 'comfort women' (women who were forced into sexual slavery during World War II by the Japanese army). Since the late 1980s, survivors have come forward to bear witness and mobilise international public opinion asking for an official apology and reparations. Survivors have rejected financial aid gestures as inadequate and reiterated their desire for a formal apology and individual compensation through public funds rather than a welfare or benevolence type of assistance based on socioeconomic needs. As victims of sexual crimes, they do not want to receive economic compensation without an official apology and official recognition of state responsibility.

But apologies have to be delivered in a way that they acknowledge not only the harm done but also the rights violations – that is, the wrongdoing – and express not only regret or sorrow but the responsibility of all responsible parties. Moreover, the recognition dimension of apologies must in turn be reflected in other features of a redress scheme and broader transitional-justice process. Calling a redress scheme *'ex gratia'* suggests that solidarity, when not pure mercy, instead of responsibility is the underlying rationale. Failing to name or undertake any legal action against perpetrators (who are instead offered cover-ups and indemnity deals) is also a poor way of acknowledging direct and due diligence-based responsibility.

Finally, form and process in the delivery of redress measures matter as much as substance to convey proper symbolic meaning. Forms of denigration in the act of compensating or procedural secondary victimisation can kill whatever reparative dimension a redress scheme might have had, precisely because they defeat the goal of recognition. Unfortunately, many of those ill-treated in Industrial and Reformatory Schools, Magdalene laundries and Mother and Baby Homes in Ireland have experienced the procedures of various state bodies responsible for providing assistance and shedding light on historical injustice as seriously re-victimising and continue to do so to this very day.[37]

Conclusion

To conclude, debates about reparations in consolidated democracies provide a forum to discuss whether the liberal democratic aspirations nominally embraced have in fact delivered the promise of equal citizenship. In particular, reparations discussions offer the possibility to address historical injustices against groups that have not been adequately recognised so far and to draw lessons about the measures needed to overcome violence, prevent discrimination and ensure intergroup equality. The conclusions and deficits identified in each national conversation stirred up by reparations claims will vary, in part because there are competing and changing conceptions of what equal citizenship means. These variations show how, although inspired by a universalist ethos, democracy remains a historically grounded and shaped venture, always open for revisitation with an eye both to the past and to the future.

This becomes even more obvious when we underscore, as I think we must, the fluid boundaries between the 'ordinary' and the 'extraordinary' forms of violence, marginalisation and exclusion signalling the 'before' and the 'after' of a certain historical period which at some point in a country's history comes to be collectively understood as a period of 'the dark ages.' Rather than taking place at a single point in time with final closure as a necessary end station, the struggle for reparations can recur whenever sufficient progress in either democratic conviction or practice has been made to 'signal' the need for a foundational break with the past. This foundational break centrally requires the disclosure of truth and acceptance of responsibility in front of the larger community, precisely to enable a collective reinterpretation of the meaning and the relevance of both past and present forms of exclusion. For women, who have thus far rarely been the protagonists of discussions about historical injustices and reparations, this opens up the possibility that, in time, all of the gender-based forms of systemic discrimination, violence and subordination will come to be judged as 'extraordinary' and, hence, as essentially antithetical to the democratic promise, triggering, among other things, a call for reparations.

ELEVEN

The Inner and Outer Limits of Gendered Transitional Justice[1]

Fionnuala Ní Aoláin

There is a door that you have closed for good
A mirror that waits in vain to hold your face;
A four-faced Janus guards your next crossroad,
Though it seems you might go any of its ways.[2]

For decades gender-justice advocates have placed much hope in transitional justice as a vehicle to address the sustained, systematic and deeply wounding human-rights and humanitarian-law violations experienced by women. Transitional justice itself is a vehicle of new aspirations and bespoke mechanisms that holds significant promise to close impunity gaps, focuses on the needs and demands of victim-survivors and offers the hope of accountability, reparations and guarantees of nonrepetition.[3] Since transitional justice has consolidated as a field, outgrowing its early beginnings as a tool primarily for use in post-authoritarian and post-conflict societies, its pull toward other sites of grievance and need has gathered pace.[4] Despite marked success – for example, in producing a vocabulary to name certain harms, new institutions such as truth commissions that have demonstrated the specificity of harms in particular sites, institutional reforms that can be measured by lustration accomplishments, and a global institution of international criminal justice created by treaty – the field and practice of transitional justice continue to experience challenges. These include the tensions of rapid growth in application to new arenas balanced against the need to consolidate success in core areas, the highly sophisticated resistance strategies that have emerged to confront institutional gains, the rewriting of histories of harm by populist and nationalist successor regimes and, most of all, the lack of specific remedies and reparations to individuals despite the lofty articulations of transitional justice at a metapolitical level.

This article addresses the contemporary boundaries of the transitional-justice field with a particular focus on the limits of gender justice. These limits are important to confront squarely as Ireland considers the adoption of transitional-justice mechanisms to face its painful past of systematic institutional abuse. I address the issues in transitional justice outlined above as they impinge on the experiences of gender harm.[5] The starting premise offered below holds that despite scholarly, policy and political attention, gender justice has been given only limited attention in what might be regarded as traditional transitional-justice contexts, with little consistency in application or outcomes. This makes the extended application of transitional-justice theory and practice beyond its core domain a haphazard enterprise – one that lacks solid and sustained jurisprudence, normative content and precedent to guide it. In this context advocating for a transitional-justice mechanism to address historic institutional abuse in Ireland demands attention to the foundations and scaffolding of transitional justice, and wariness of overconfidence regarding what justice can actually be achieved in practice.

The article is structured in three parts. First, I offer a short institutional history of transitional justice. I pay attention to the ways in which gender justice has been subverted in institutional contexts with a highly selective approach to what gender justice means in implementation. I illustrate how the field of transitional justice continues to exclude gender justice and the challenges faced in the meaningful integration of gendered concerns in practice. Part two examines the external challenges to transitional justice and how they affect the goal of gender-transformative justice. I concentrate on the amplified focus on sexual violence in national and global debates that has failed to bring with it sufficient attention to the socioeconomic and cultural conditions that produce violence and inequality in the first place.[6] I examine how global revisionism of the experience and scope of historical harms has placed significant strains on maintaining narrative truths and sought to undo parallel accountability work arduously carried out over decades.[7] In these contexts, gender ideologies have been deeply interwoven into national revisionism as the ideology of the patriarchal, heterosexual family based in marriage triumphs. The denial of the word 'gender' itself manifests in national and international law, and restrictions on reproductive rights (one of the few remedies available to women in conflict and post-authoritarian regimes) re-emerge and consolidate.[8] These narrative strains have national resonance and have weakened the overall impact of transitional justice globally, with consequent effects for adoption at the local level. Finally, with a specific eye to the Irish context, I argue that despite the rhetoric of victim-centred justice, transitional justice has always struggled to deliver on the ground for victims. Some of that struggle is not unexpected. The scale and scope of violations, the distance from the primary harm, and the vicissitudes of memory mean that while the lofty goal of achieving justice is well-intentioned, in practice it may be impossible to deliver at the granular individual level. This gap between promise and delivery haunts all transitional-justice processes and should be keenly felt in any national endeavour, including in Ireland.

Internal Limits: A Short Gender Genealogy in Transitional Justice

With some notable exceptions in its creation and early framing, transitional justice was a predominantly masculine field.[9] In the authoritarian transitions that dominated the early construction of the transitional-justice domain, a feminist discourse was largely absent. Or more precisely, it was absent in the globalised settings and spaces that facilitated comparative exchange about how successor regimes would 'reckon with the past.'[10] An engaged history of feminist activism, combined with a substantial scholarly agenda on the issues of war and peace as they affected women, influenced the emergence of feminising transition as applied to conflict.[11] This backdrop profoundly reshaped conceptual framing of the transitional-justice arena and prompted an array of scholarly insights, sharpening and expanding the extent to which the concept of transitional justice was seen to engage issues involving women. Once activated, feminist interventions aimed at shaping the field and scope of transitional justice concentrated in particular on widening the range of harms visible in the process of societal transformation.[12] To this end, activating international accountability and deepening domestic criminalisation of sexual violence in times of conflict and societal repression was an early priority. Connectedly, exploring the relationship between truth-telling and gender, amnesty and gender, as well as the relationship between gender and peace-making, were also high on the feminist agenda.[13] Thereafter, engendering the conception and practice of reparations and institutional reform advanced as important aspects of a gender-conscious transformative justice.[14] Feminist scholars also challenged the presumed advantages of key transitional-justice mechanisms, particularly those engaging restorative-justice practices that have been offered as meaningful alternatives to formal justice systems in post-conflict and post-repressive settings.[15]

Thoughtful feminist critiques of transitional justice as a practice give deep insight into why the study of gender struggles for space in transitional-justice arenas. The evolution of transitional justice as a discourse based in the legal framework of international human-rights law has been criticised for an overly narrow, legalistic focus that elevates certain civil and political rights and fails to encompass other pervasive social and economic realities.[16] Systemic structural inequalities that may have precipitated civil protest and fuelled violent conflict in the first place are often deprioritised and treated as policy matters to be dealt with 'down the road.' Economic and social-justice conversations have been stymied as a result of being deemed insufficiently urgent or relevant to bring into the fulcrum of transitional-justice bargaining. Acknowledgment of the locations of capacity, insight, knowledge and strategy goes hand in hand with the ongoing realities of power and exclusion. Despite gains for marginalised groups, including indigenous, youth, women, minorities, LGBTQIA+ and economic and socially marginalised persons, there are insidious gaps in what we know of the experience of certain others, how they are heard and the patterns of knowledge production and sharing that exclude them. Moreover, transitional-justice settlements benefit some more than others, and there are distinct patterns as to who is privileged and who is left out. Marginality, however constructed, is often not compressed into a single category (e.g. women), but rather consistently intersects with other socially excluded experiences (social and economic disadvantage, religious status, race, ethnicity, and sexual orientation).

One of the comparative insights that we have gleaned is that at best the narrow gender lens of transitional justice has fixated on women's individualised gender-based experience of sexual violation at the cost of ignoring other power and identity dynamics that underpin/mandate/authorise violations in the first place. In a forthright appraisal Canadian scholar Sherene Razack characterises transitional-justice discourse as a form of 'stealing the pain of others.'[17] This focus on individualised violent incidents can be a form of othering that decontextualises social oppression, renders institutional racism invisible and fosters a wilful lack of awareness of racist and sexist discourse within transitional justice. At the forefront of hard conversations about transitional justice, many of us are painfully aware of the commodification of victims, their stories, pain and misfortune, and the fundamental contradiction in the reality that the field of transitional justice needs victims sometimes more than victims need transitional justice. Victims are increasingly aware of this positionality, struggle to make sense of it, and are sometimes able to reposition their own strengths in light of it.[18]

External Limits: The Contemporary Strains on Transitional Justice

The external constraints and impositions on transitional justice also pose considerable contemporary challenges relevant to the application of transitional justice to non-conflict and nonauthoritarian sites. First and foremost, there has been the co-option and narrowing of gender-focused transitional justice to concentrate primarily on one set of specific harms experienced by women, specifically penetrative sexual violence and sexually specific sex-based harm in repressive or violent-conflict settings.[19] This includes multiple manifestations of violence that may reach both the 'tactic of war' threshold as well as the wider sexual violence against civilians that takes place in the context of the conflict/repression. In conflicts that do not demonstrate this kind of pervasive sexual violence, it is frequently presumed that gender-based harms are not a relevant category of analysis or accountability. A substantial case in point is the struggle for recognition in Northern Ireland of the gender- and sex-based dimensions of the conflict.[20]

Sexual violence as experienced in situations of conflict can be individual and collective, and the harms that ensue can be physical and moral, emotional and social, immediate and intergenerational. Acts falling within the definition of conflict-related sexual violence or repression include rape, forced pregnancy, forced sterilisation, forced abortion, forced prostitution, trafficking, sexual enslavement and forced nudity.[21] The attention to sexual violence in war is long overdue, and it addresses historical and legal lacunae in accountability. Scholarly and policy attention has demonstrated that sexual violence in war and repressive contexts has highly complex characteristics manifested in a variety of compelled social practices forced by the combatants on the female subject.[22] However, it is also true that attention to sexual violence in conflict has failed to fully grasp the relationship between the functionality of sexual violence in armed conflict and its linkages to the ordinary, regularised and socially embedded violence that women experience across multiple jurisdictions every day.

Several points merit emphasis as I underscore the pervasiveness of attention to penetrative sexual harms over all other gender-based violence and exclusions. Despite the fact that much of the policy literature has recognised a broad variety of sex-based harms, in practice rape remains *primus inter pares* among conflict/repression identified female harms.[23] Sex-based harms is used here as conceptual tool to go beyond the narrow category of sexual violence often used in international legal discourse concerning sexual harms. Collapsing the totality of sexual harm to rape entirely evacuates the broader experiences of sexual violence and assumes that such aggression as forced abortion, forced sterilisation, forced nudity, and other serious physical intrusions are demonstrably of lesser importance than penetrative and non-consensual sexual intercourse.[24] It further assumes that even in the context of sexual harm the act of rape itself is worse than any other harm, including death.[25] Evidence would suggest that even as we acknowledge the gravity of rape, the assumption of its evil above all others is at least open to discussion when contextualised within the totality of harms experienced by women. Such positioning may have substantial unintended consequences for conversations on female equality, agency and status.[26] One troubling unintended consequence of the attention taken by the analysis and visibility of rape in war is that it has de facto operated to frame any subsequent conversation about sexual agency and autonomy in situations of exigency.

The related consequences of singular focus on penetrative sexual violence is the failure to address intersecting institutional violence, including the contribution of institutions, legal norms and political culture, to enabling, supporting and facilitating violence. The evacuation of social and economic harms from the fulcrum of recognition of sex-based harms for women and men is deeply troubling in societies where it is precisely the matrix of economic vulnerability and social exclusion that is the enabler of multiple forms of violence. Moreover, while this author profoundly acknowledges the need for criminal accountability in the context of sexual violence, there are two prescient dangers that follow from the emphasis on individual harms in a criminal-justice context. First is the proven inability of transitional-justice mechanisms, for explicable reasons of capacity, to process the totality of criminal accountability in the context of mass and systemic violence, including mass sexual violence. Second, the logic of criminal prosecutions, which requires proof of both *actus reus* and *mens rea* for each individual being prosecuted,[27] functions to erase the broader systemic causes and prompts for sex-based harm and limits our overall understanding of the logic, structure and pathways of sex-based harm in transitioning societies.

Another fundamental external challenge is the lack of success and the lacklustre pursuit of gender justice even within those transitional-justice frameworks and institutions where it has been formally embraced. The point I emphasise here is that what might be regarded as success stories for gender justice in transitional justice are limited. Thus transposition to new national settings, including gender-justice goals for institutional abuse in Ireland, must be realistic about what has been achieved to date and what may be possible in accountability terms. In terms of criminal-justice success, Louise Chappell's ground-breaking work on gender justice at the International Criminal Court confirms the patchy advancement of criminal justice accountability for serious crimes under international law.[28] Despite early jurisprudential success in a small number of sexual-violence cases, there has been no fundamental transformation in the landscape of accountability for sexual harms in conflict. The reasons for the failure to fully and adequately prosecute sexual crimes on an international scale align with the reasons commonly identified for the miserable rate of success in state-level prosecutions of gendered violence.[29] Despite advances, impunity for sexual violence and rape continues, as evidenced by low victim-reporting, a significant decline in pursuit of proceedings by police (from reporting to investigation), low conviction rates and desultory sentencing practices.[30] After decades of domestic lobbying in many highly sophisticated legal systems, efforts to address violence against women through statutory regulation and modification has yielded, relatively speaking, modest results. The range of offenses against women as articulated by domestic criminal-law statutes remains rather static,[31] and undergirding doctrines and myths (fresh complaint, mistake of fact, passivity/fighting) exercise ongoing effects on the likely outcomes of any criminal proceeding.[32] Thus knowledge-share from domestic legal systems concerning the challenges of adequately prosecuting crimes of sexual violence is highly relevant to the potential for indictment, prosecution and conviction at the international level. This point is no less relevant when dealing with historic and long-standing harms in which the legal impediments in formal legal systems have unexpected but real crossover to transitional-justice mechanisms.

Truth commissions may have fared somewhat better in terms of the scope and scale of harms addressed, but despite some high-profile exceptions emerging from truth processes globally, overall the wins for bringing attention to gender have been few. Even in the most lauded of truth processes, the South African Truth and Reconciliation Commission, women's voices and women's experiences of the apartheid era were largely marginalised. It was only as a result of sustained work by key feminist scholars and activists in South Africa that attention was brought to the lack of a coherent gender strategy at the Truth and Reconciliation Commission – ultimately forcing one set of hearings on the experiences of women *qua* women through the apartheid period.[33] While welcome, these hearings did not reframe the focus of the commission or even come close to mainstreaming women's voices in its final report.[34] In more recently established truth processes women are still brought belatedly to the conversation, and then struggle to insert voice and experience into truth recovery when the terms of reference and worldview are already largely negotiated through male-dominated security arrangements and political settlement.[35] Again, Northern Ireland's fractured engagement with truth recovery illustrates this absence of a gender reckoning and the efforts that women's rights organisations have made to steer a conversation about gendered truth into the mainstream discussions.[36] This fragmented history of women's place in the practice of transitional justice affirms that transition remains a place of struggle for voice and agency by women in particular and for gendered narratives more broadly. In short, gendered absences underscore the significant precedential limits of what is recognised as good practice in this regulatory space, and the sizeable gap between aspirational rhetoric and actual reality.

Transitional justice, like other rule-of-law-based movements, is facing considerable contemporary backlash from nationalist and populist discourses. While these movements have unique national identities and specific prompts, they share apathy and hostility toward efforts to deliver past-focused accountability for repressive regimes and wartime misconduct, concurrent with nostalgic recalls of militaristic, authoritarian and rights-purging pasts. Their imprints are realised on newly found enthusiasm for military amnesties from Northern Ireland to Washington.[37] Efforts to undermine the work of the International Criminal Court have emboldened the new populists[38] and dented global confidence in the capacity of these post-Cold War institutions to thrive. These new movements are also driving global retrenchment on gender advances in international law, including but not limited to the use of the term gender itself in international legal discourse.[39]

The language retrenchment is seen in recent UN Security Council Resolutions addressing sexual violence against women in conflict settings known as the Women, Peace and Security Agenda.[40] Until now the United Nations had established a long and fairly distinguished history of addressing the harms caused by sexual violence in war, advancing legal prohibitions and seeking to provide redress for survivors. Central to the political work captured by this agenda was the commitment of numerous states, including the United States, to highlighting the harm of sexual violence in war, the needs of survivors, and the validity of accountability for such harm. In Security Council Resolution 2467, passed in April 2019, pressed by the United States and supported by Russia and China, the resolution generated massive controversy concerning its use of the word 'gender.' The resolution also explicitly avoided direct references to the rights of victims to reproductive health. Given the centrality of reproductive rights to redeem and repair the rights of women harmed by sexual and other violence,[41] Resolution 2467 signals the emerging boundaries of women's right to remedy in the current global political climate. This is but one example of linguistic (and therefore policy) rollback that signals a deeper retrenchment of women's rights while also expressly excluding the rights and identities of sexual minorities from the ambit of accountability, repair and concern. In parallel the rise of traditional and conservative ideologies, coalescing around claims that 'gender ideology' is a product of western elites seeking to destabilise the traditional family and the natural order of society, is placing the broader claims of women's rights, including the rights of the most vulnerable women, in legal and political jeopardy.[42] These cross-cutting movements place sustained stress on the nascent efforts to engage and mainstream gender harms and gendered practices in transitional justice. They have broadly made the capacity to engage transitional justice more challenging in multiple conflict, post-conflict and accountability-deficient regimes, not least because mobilising the necessary international support for such efforts has been virtually impossible; the case most relevant here is that of Syria. We have yet to fully map the trickle-down effects of resistance to transitional justice generally, and gendered transitional justice in particular, from these multiple and intersectional global trends.

Limits and Possibilities: Transitional Justice in Ireland

My conclusion addresses the implications of these multiple and layered limitations and challenges in the Irish context. Various contributions to this volume reflect positively on transitional justice and embrace the evocativeness of its philosophical underpinnings, its institutional capacity and its normative content to bridge an acknowledgment, accountability, and remedy gap for decades of institutional abuse in the Irish republic. While not closing off the capacity to deploy transitional justice to the Irish legacy of silence, harms and the gaping holes of collective and individual narrative, this conclusion explores the limits of the transitional-justice oeuvre in Ireland.

I start by noting that the development of transitional justice was required by the complete absence of law, legal systems and legal capacity in authoritarian and conflicted sites. It was the gaps in legal capacity and/ or willingness to invoke the formal capacities of the law that gave rise to transitional justice – a justice in part always lesser than the full quota of justice, premised on a set of compromises about law, not available in the absence of fully functional legal systems and the rule of law. Transitional justice exists in spaces where law in practice is rendered inoperable for a variety of reasons. Hence, as my colleague Colm Campbell and I have pointed out, there is an inherent paradox in invoking transitional justice in democratic states where the rule of law is fully operative and largely functional.[43] Given the obvious limits of even what might be regarded as best-case transitional justice, the paradox of resorting to transitional justice to gap-fill for accountability and remedy underscores a further paradox when states utilise transitional-justice measures to avoid the full engagement of their criminal, civil, and administrative-justice systems. The responsibility of the Irish legal system to transpose its obligations under law to remedy the gaping legal issues (access to documents including prior testimony, the right to one's own identity, the barriers to effective individual remedy) are not displaced by any transitional-justice mechanism. There is a grave danger that the state may view its remedial work as done by enabling a truth-recovery process and not address the legal lacunae exposed by decades of largely unrewarded legal challenges in the Irish courts by individual victims.[44] Concerning institutional abuse in Ireland, the abject failure of those multiple (and broadly functional and capable) legal capacities of the state has been well documented.[45] But it should be restated that the legal responsibilities of those institutions and legal processes are not displaced by invoking transitional justice, even if transitional justice tends to occlude those obligations in the short term.

Paradoxically, while transitional justice may operate in democratic settings to displace temporarily the role of the criminal-, civil- and administrative-law systems, after the outcomes of particular mechanisms (truth commissions in particular) have been delivered, the pushback to produce concrete versions of those same legal outcomes may intensify rather than abate.[46] This demand will arise in a highly constrained legal environment in Ireland, where the right to ordinary legal remedy for women and children has already been severely compromised, likely in breach of Ireland's international human-rights treaty obligations. First, under the legislation establishing the recently concluded Commission of Investigation into Mother and Baby Homes, all evidence will be unusable in civil or criminal proceedings and seems likely to be sealed from public view upon the conclusion of the investigation for at least twenty years.[47] Second, the archive of the Ryan commission was not made available to An Garda Síochána and under current regulatory provisions appears to be fully sealed for at least 75 years. This provision may also impinge on Ireland's human-rights treaty obligations, specifically the right to a remedy under international law and the right to equality of arms for victims.[48] Finally, the archive created by the McAleese process, which contains all state records concerning the Magdalen laundries and is held by the Department of An Taoiseach, is being withheld from public view by that office, which states that it possesses the archive for the purpose of 'safe keeping' and 'not... for the purposes of the FOI Act.'[49]

On the positive side a truth-recovery process may provide the evidence, political will and public enthusiasm to engage multidimensional legal accountability. A truth-recovery process may create the political and legal momentum to address the documentary lacunae in Ireland, an objective that may also be achieved by bringing strategic litigation at the European Court of Human Rights, seeking investigation by the Convention on the Elimination of All Forms of Discrimination Against Women, or submitting individual complaints to the United Nations Human Rights Committee. Such truth recovery may be a necessary precursor to give expression to legal capacity and expose culpability sufficient to trigger and sustain parallel legal processes. But it is important to underscore that for long-standing grievance and historic harms, despite the power of individual testimony, the evidential basis may not be sufficiently dense to advance formal legal proceedings for accountability and liability. It is obvious but important to state that the disappointment and further injury sustained by victims from the inability to pursue expected redress through ordinary legal process may be substantial when expectations have been raised by the truth-recovery process itself.

The limits of transitional-justice mechanisms are often overlooked in the enthusiasm to deploy open-ended processes to address the compelling and immediate needs of victim-survivor communities, many of whom are aging and in poor health, thus compounding the sense of urgency to acknowledge, put formalities in place, and engage grievances. But commentators have consistently demonstrated that no matter how friendly to victim-survivors transitional-justice processes may be (and not all have been particularly cognisant of gendered needs and sensitivities), they have their own formalities, necessary rules and structures that are often extremely difficult for vulnerable and harmed persons to navigate. Law is a power-based structure, and even those legal institutions that are relatively malleable and open-ended still function to transmit and manage the power of the state vis-à-vis the subject individual. Transitional-justice mechanisms use their power to shape narratives and subjectivities, and no observer expects such processes to be value-free or neutral. Although human-rights frameworks are intrinsic to transitional-justice institutions – including truth processes – other legal frames play a role, including the legal culture and context of the country engaged in truth recovery. That the legal culture and political context has both positive and negative dimensions underscore the complex interplay of legal rules and institutional constraints in the transitional-justice arena. To date, a human-rights-based approach has not played any meaningful role in the legal processes investigating industrial and reformatory schools, Magdalene laundries, or Mother and Baby Homes. Transitional justice has the capacity to inject a rights-based dimension into a much-needed accountability vacuum, notwithstanding the caveat articulated here that transitional justice is not per se a human-rights frame only.

It remains true that in the complex Irish histories of historical institutional abuse, there is little neutrality, and the costs are substantial to opening up the narrative, particularly where evidence of collusion between state and private actors in the perpetuation of sustained human-rights violations is substantial. The point here is that no matter how well-disposed the state may be to the creation and validation of particular harms, the exposure creates risks and challenges for state institutions and actors. The risks include the substantial costs of fully human-rights-compliant legal proceedings, legal liability, political embarrassment and the flux that inevitably follows from exposing massive human-rights abuses that are rarely if ever fully resolved as a legal matter. Truth recovery also clearly exposes potential liability (if only reputational and symbolic) for private religious actors. This is evidently true in the context of institutional abuse in Ireland, where the state was implicitly and explicitly responsible for harms and complicit in the unwillingness to redress them in a transparent and human-rights-compliant manner. What we have learnt from comparative truth-recovery processes is that few if any processes can reveal the systematic and total nature of the harms, the absolute allocation of responsibilities and the totality of violation patterns.[50] Even as transitional justice may be the only tool available to reveal certain types of systemic harms, it is also a limited and constrained tool.

In sum, the structural limits of transitional justice should not be underestimated in the Irish context, and there are few roadmaps to address the deficits exposed in other truth-and-reconciliation processes.[51] Moreover, the capacity of the state and private actors to resist the concrete consequences of liability, exposure, and reparations has been well demonstrated in other national contexts.[52] We should assume that the same patterns of institutional resistance will be manifested in an Irish truth-recovery context. There is of course opportunity to create a bespoke Irish transitional-justice process. Even as this article has charted the global pressures being faced by the field and institutions of transitional justice, there remains a glimmer of optimism that an Irish commitment to addressing the deeply gendered experience of institutional abuse might not only provide historical and individual reckoning but would offer a revitalised approach to gendering transitional justice to a global audience. This is in part premised on the recently evidenced national capacity to address thorny and difficult pasts, including the provision of full reproductive rights, marriage equality, the decriminalisation of sodomy and the constitutional abandonment of blasphemy. Truth recovery is not an insignificant endeavour, and it would not be easy to deliver. It would require both a commitment to the highest standards of gender justice in theory and practice and a clear-eyed capacity to withstand the multiple external and internal fault lines of transitional-justice limitations. This is the prescient challenge for transitional justice in Ireland as it faces the grim history of institutional abuse.

Twelve

Transitional Justice and Ireland's Legacy of Historical Abuse[1]

James Gallen

This essay evaluates the application of transitional justice to the context of historical abuse in peaceful, consolidated democracies, in particular the Republic of Ireland.[2] Examining Ireland's efforts at repairing its past from such a perspective reveals an unwillingness by state authorities and Christian churches and religious orders to embrace the necessity of fundamental social, legal and political transformation when addressing widespread and systemic historical abuse.[3] In Irish efforts to address historical abuse across a range of contexts, power remains out of the hands of victim-survivors and of those traditionally marginalised in society. Instead, in agreement with Georges Balandier, I argue that 'the supreme ruse of power is to allow itself to be contested ritually in order to consolidate itself more effectively.'[4] Recent state responses to historical abuse contribute to such a consolidation of power. Although public inquiries, legal accountability and redress schemes claim to serve the interests of victim-survivors of historical abuse, these mechanisms fail meaningfully to empower or support their voices, participation and ownership in shaping how Ireland addresses its historical abuses. The Irish state designs mechanisms and engages in practices that marginalise victim-survivors in the present and thereby risk creating new forms of harm and distress. As a result, Irish 'transitional justice' risks claiming the legitimacy of serving survivors' needs without any meaningful transition in how they are treated by the state, churches or society.

Section one of this article introduces the framework of transitional justice and considers its application to the Irish republic. Section two assesses the Irish experience of investigating and truth-seeking regarding historical abuses and draws comparisons with the 'truth commission' model in transitional justice. Section three evaluates the Irish approach to accountability for historical abuses and demonstrates its limitations despite the different expectations for accountability for historical criminal and civil offenses. Finally, section four assesses Ireland's redress schemes for victim-survivors of historical abuse, drawing on approaches to reparations in transitional justice, and briefly examines Ireland's apologies regarding historical abuse and their potential impact on reform and reconciliation.

Transitional Justice and Consolidated Democracies

Ireland is not unique in dealing with a national legacy of past systemic violence. Although it has deployed several mechanisms since the early 2000s to address historical abuses, it has typically not employed the language or framework of transitional justice. It was only in March 2017 that TD Katherine Zappone, the Minister for Children and Youth Affairs, announced that she would initiate a transitional-justice approach to meet the needs of survivors of Mother and Baby Homes (maternity homes).[5] As a result, transitional justice forms only a small part of the explicit approach used by the Irish state to address its past. But transitional justice – as a body of scholarship and comparative international best practice – can also be employed as a conceptual and legal tool to evaluate the entirety of how countries such as Ireland have addressed their legacy of past violence.

Transitional justice typically addresses how societies reckon with a legacy of gross violations of human rights in the specific contexts of a transition from armed conflict or authoritarian rule to stable, peaceful liberal democracy.[6] It includes several discrete but linked 'pillars': investigation and truth-seeking (typically through truth and reconciliation commissions), accountability, reparation, guarantees of nonrecurrence and reconciliation.[7] Though a field dominated by law and lawyers, transitional-justice discourse claims to institute an interdisciplinary practice, with several ethical commitments to how justice is to be achieved; the process matters as much as the outcome.[8] To this end a number of key tenets have informed scholarship and practice in this area that must be highlighted in any application of transitional justice to Ireland. First, an approach recognising victim-survivors as legal subjects, bearers of human rights and key participants in any decision affecting transitional justice is central to international transitional-justice policy.[9] Second, each transitional-justice mechanism is designed to complement rather than compete with the others and is designed to form part of a single holistic process.[10] Transitional justice is not comprised of elements of 'either/or' but of 'both/and.'

Third, the process of transitional justice should not be seen as optional or discretionary, but as reflecting and embodying a state's legal commitments to its citizens in national and international human-rights law.[11]

This commitment to legal rights and obligations counteracts the risk that governments frame the addressing of historical abuses as a matter merely of charity or political benevolence. A focus on law, however, may also risk slipping into a legalistic and lawyer-led approach that provides only a perfunctory nod toward a victim-survivor-led process. It remains essential to assess whether legal rights, materials and resources empower and support the interests and preferences of victim-survivors and advocates, or are instead used as institutional means to silence and further marginalise them.

The effectiveness of transitional justice is often challenged despite its rapid growth as a field of inquiry. Some critics suggest that it remains 'faith based rather than fact based' as a result of limited empirical measurement of success in achieving its stated goals.[12] Others have highlighted its lack of emphasis on addressing violations of socioeconomic rights such as the right to health or right to an adequate standard of living, a reflection of a similar shortcoming in mainstream human-rights discourse.[13] Further criticism has suggested that transitional-justice practice retains a significantly gender-blind approach, with the result that women are typically disadvantaged and deprioritised in the provision of testimony, accountability, prosecution strategies and access to effective remedies and redress.[14] Nonetheless, transitional-justice scholarship remains a highly self-reflective and self-critical area that seeks to reimagine and reinvigorate its own practice.[15] Simon Robins and Paul Gready prefer the concept of transformative justice, 'defined as transformative change that emphasises local agency and resources, the prioritisation of process rather than preconceived outcomes, and the challenging of unequal and intersecting power relationships and structures of exclusion at both the local and the global level.'[16] Dáire McGill positions transformative justice 'at the radical end of a transitional-justice continuum' and concludes that it has thus far worked to diagnose its problems, among them the need for a constructive or practical dimension.[17] A transformative-justice approach thus has the potential to align strongly with the principle expressed by many survivors and activists: 'nothing about us without us.' However, transformative justice remains in need of explicit alternative practices and examples of its use as a concrete alternative to existing transitional-justice institutions and practices.

In recent years transitional-justice scholarship and practice has extended beyond its paradigmatic context of post-conflict or post-authoritarian societies to consider other large-scale or systematic human-rights abuses in peaceful consolidated democracies. Examples include Canada's investigation of the abuse of indigenous children in residential schools through the Truth and Reconciliation Commission, Australia's commissions of investigation addressing the forced child-removal from indigenous populations (known as 'The Stolen Generation'), and Australia's recent Royal Commission into Institutional Responses to Child Sexual Abuse.[18] This expansion demonstrates the shared logic of requiring more than the ordinary criminal law to redress large-scale human-rights abuses regardless of context. Stephen Winter argues that redress activity undertaken in established democratic states can be seen as a form of transitional justice because public inquiries, official apologies, and survivor compensation schemes aim to respond to the delegitimation of the state as a result of past state violence.[19] Nicola Henry has argued that transitional justice may serve to provide a distinctive cohering or unifying function by bringing together discourses, academic disciplines and fields of practice that seek to address large-scale human-rights abuse across different jurisdictions.[20] I have previously argued that transitional justice should operate as an evaluative and analytical framework for responding to a legacy of historical abuse across several peaceful consolidated democracies and in the context of historical abuses committed by institutional Christianity, especially the Roman Catholic church.[21]

Transitional justice in Ireland has typically addressed the Troubles on the island of Ireland.[22] It is a legitimate question to consider why transitional justice should extend in Ireland to the context of historical abuse by church and state actors. As noted above, it was only in 2017 that Minister Zappone introduced the concept to Irish political discourse, prompted by scientific evidence confirming the presence of significant amounts of human infant remains on the site of the former mother and baby home in Tuam, Co. Galway.[23] Anne-Marie McAlinden suggests that the regime change resulting from Irish inquiries into institutional abuse of children represents a 'defining moment in Irish political and legal history' because it 'offers a unique opportunity to make a permanent break with the past' and to transition from an 'amorphous or undefined' relationship to one of greater state control of church authority.[24] Balint, Evans and McMillan conceive of transitional justice as a harm-centric 'justice model,' a contrast with a more traditional model that would exclusively address post-armed conflict and post-authoritarian states.[25] In particular, the model of Balint et al. contemplates the possibility of transitional justice responding to 'structural harms,' understood by Ratna Kapur as 'the institutional arrangements and structures [that] may be deeply implicated in the production of the violation or the harm in the first place.'[26] Such an approach could be extended to contexts such as Ireland, Canada or Australia, where significant structural violence emerged outside of the context of armed conflict or authoritarian rule. Paul Gready in turn proposes that structural violence can be conceptually divided into three major pillars: social marginalisation, political exclusion and economic exploitation.[27]

The harms in the context of Irish historical abuses have been found to be widespread, endemic and profound, reflecting each of Gready's categories of structural violence. Over sixteen thousand people received compensation from the Residential Institutions Redress Board scheme, which sought to compensate persons who were abused as children while resident in industrial schools, reformatory schools and other residential institutions subject to state regulation or inspection.[28] More than 1,000 former pupils testified before the Commission to Inquire into Child Abuse (CICA), also referred to as the Ryan commission, alleging physical and sexual abuse in these institutions.[29] Three state inquiries into allegations of child sexual abuse against priests in Irish dioceses – Ferns, Dublin and Cloyne – found significant numbers of allegations of sexual abuse in non-residential settings.[30] The full extent of clerical sexual abuse in Ireland remains unknown. The National Board for Safeguarding Children in the Catholic Church in Ireland (NBSCCCI), established by the Catholic church, has issued reports across all dioceses and religious orders in Ireland. According to NBSCCCI figures, between 1975 and 2014 there were 4,406 allegations of child sexual abuse by priests reported to church authorities and gardaí.[31] The overall figure of complaints is likely greater, as not all complainants would have engaged with either the church authorities or the police.

Widespread systemic and profound historical abuses in Ireland have extended beyond child sexual abuse. At an absolute minimum,10,012 women and young girls are known to have been detained in a Magdalen laundry between the foundation of the Irish state in 1922 and the closure of the last laundry in 1996. Victim-survivor and advocacy groups suggest that these figures are underestimated.[32] Women detained in Magdalene laundries were arbitrarily detained, denied their given identities and obliged to engage in compulsory labour. Unmarried mothers, resident in Mother and Baby Homes, were also obliged to pay through uncompensated manual labour for maintenance during their stay and that of their baby after birth.[33] According to the Commission of Investigation into Mother and Baby Homes, there were about 56,000 unmarried mothers and about 57,000 children in the 14 Mother and Baby Homes and four county homes investigated by the Commission.[34] In 1966 there were 47 county homes across the Republic of Ireland; approximately 300 private maternity homes were registered under the Registration of Maternity Homes Act (1934).[35] The full extent of illegal adoption in Ireland remains unknown.

Mike Milotte, for example, presents data sourced from the Department of Foreign Affairs and Trade archives identifying at least 2,100 children sent for adoption to America between 1949 and 1973 in the absence of laws regulating domestic adoption until 1952.[36] In addition, symphysiotomies – a surgical procedure designed to enlarge a woman's pelvis during childbirth by partially cutting the fibres that join the pubic bones at the front of the pelvis – were carried out on an estimated 1,500 women during childbirth between 1944 and 1984, with significant numbers contesting that they ever effectively consented to or were informed of the procedure.[37]

It is in this context of significant numbers and forms of harms that transitional-justice concepts can operate as a useful tool to evaluate the existing Irish practice that addresses historical abuse. Prompted by the submissions of voluntary advocacy groups, several United Nations bodies have criticised Ireland's record in addressing historical abuse, including one incident as recently as March 2017.[38] For instance, in response to advocacy, the Committee on the Elimination of Discrimination against Women (CEDAW) noted that despite an interdepartmental committee to establish the facts of state involvement in Magdalene laundries (also known as the McAleese committee), Ireland had 'failed to establish an independent, thorough and effective investigation in line with international standards into all allegations of abuse, ill-treatment or neglect of women and children in the Magdalen laundries in order to establish the role of the state and the church in the perpetration of the alleged violations.' The committee went on to note that no effort has been made to establish an independent investigation to 'identify, prosecute and punish the perpetrators who performed the medical procedure of symphysiotomy without the consent of women,' and that 'the scope of the terms of reference for the Commission of Investigation into Mother and Baby Homes and Certain Related Matters is too narrow to cover all homes and analogous institutions and therefore may not address the whole spectrum of abuses perpetrated against women and girls.'[39]

Ireland has expended considerable time, energy and resources in addressing its legacy of historical abuses arising in state and church institutions. In responding to these harms, a range of entities, including national legislatures, criminal- and civil-justice systems, mental-health and social-welfare agencies and victim-survivor interest and advocacy groups, have all contributed to date. However, no overarching framework has been employed to address the range of moral, legal, spiritual, policy and psychological issues relevant to historical abuse.[40] At its best, a transitional-justice approach can offer the tools for a comprehensive and coherent evaluation of a victim-and survivor-centred response to legacies of historical abuse. Such an approach can draw not only on academic theory and international policy but also on the comparative practices of other jurisdictions addressing gross violations of human rights. A transitional-justice methodology also provides guidance toward legal and policy alternatives to the existing Irish practice across the areas of investigation through public inquiries, legal accountability, redress and compensation, and guarantees of non-repetition through state apologies and reconciliation. By evaluating Ireland's approach through the lens of transitional justice and across its four 'pillars,' lessons can be learned for present and future attempts to address the abusive elements of our past.

Investigation and Truth Seeking

To address a violent past meaningfully – to know what happened, who was responsible and what should be done – the truth about past wrongdoing must be established. Several states, including Ireland, have chosen public inquiries as the mechanism to verify historical abuses.[41] McAlinden and Naylor note that public inquiries are typically chosen 'to address a range of state – or state-supported – harms chiefly because of their organisational and "curative properties" as a form of scandal management.'[42] Ireland's initial examination of its past focused on abuse in industrial and reformatory schools under the Ryan commission, which was established in 2000 and reported in 2009. A series of investigations into child sexual abuse in non-residential clerical settings followed across the dioceses of Ferns, Dublin and Cloyne, with reports presented in 2005, 2009 and 2010, respectively. Investigations have expanded to include inquiries into nonsexual forms of historical abuse, particularly those involving institutionalisation in Magdalene laundries – reviewed in the 2013 *McAleese Report*[43] – and in Mother and Baby Homes – with a report made public in 2021.[44] A range of human-rights abuses allegedly occurred across these institutions, including rape, sexual violence, physical violence, illegal adoptions, forced labour and arbitrary detention.[45] As discussed further below, neither the *McAleese Report* nor the Mother and Baby Homes report engaged meaningfully with allegations of human-rights abuses. In the context of the Commission of Investigation into Mother and Baby Homes, this lack of human rights focus led 25 academics to produce an alternative executive summary of the Commission report.[46]

Ireland has employed a tribunal-of-inquiry model (the Commission to Inquire into Child Abuse), related commissions of inquiry (Murphy, Cloyne, Ferns, Mother and Baby Homes), and non-statutory investigations established by church and state (the McAleese inquiry into Magdalen laundries, the Harding Clark investigation into the symphysiotomy ex-gratia-payment scheme, and Catholic church child-protection audits). No inquiry to date has examined the relationship between different forms of coercive institutional confinement, such as pathways between an industrial school, Magdalene laundry and Mother and Baby Home. Nor has there been adequate examination of the shared social and structural conditions accounting for the extent of Irish historical abuses – or the conditions by which such abuses were ignored and/or went unaddressed politically and socially for decades.[47] The most recent inquiries into Magdalene laundries, symphysiotomies and Mother and Baby Homes – all primarily affecting women and girls – failed to address the nature and persistence of patriarchal social norms that influenced the establishment and operation of these institutions and practices.

Truth-and-reconciliation commissions have formed a key part of transitional-justice practice since the 1980s.[48] But Irish approaches to these commissions contrast significantly with international best practice as part of a broader program of transitional justice. The United Nations, for instance, defines truth commissions as 'official, temporary nonjudicial fact-finding bodies that investigate a pattern of abuses of human rights or humanitarian law committed over a number of years.'[49] Though truth commissions offer a more comprehensive model of investigation, both commissions of inquiry and truth commissions present risks to victim-survivors. And as Adam Ashforth has warned, commissions of inquiry risk becoming 'theatre in which a central received "truth" of modern state power is ritually played out before a public audience.'[50] I believe that this ritual contestation of power is played out in Irish public inquiries into historical abuse. To illustrate this point, this essay examines the practices of Irish inquiries across several criteria. I review the inputs to commissions (victim-survivor consultation, mandates, commissioners, resources), the processes (statement-taking and public hearings), and the outputs (reports and impact), to compare Irish inquiries with the practices of truth-seeking commissions in transitional justice. These criteria reflect an increasing convergence of best practices and soft-law norms regarding investigation into gross violations of human rights, and they can be applied in evaluating Irish practice through a transitional-justice lens.

I. Inputs

A. Victim-Survivor Consultation

Best practice seeks to guarantee that the design, proces and outcome of transitional-justice mechanisms involve consistent consultation and collaboration with victim-survivors and their families. As Robins suggests, 'an awareness of the centrality of victims/survivors and their needs to the whole process drives it.'[51] Victim-survivor engagement is thus essential to the legitimacy and effectiveness of the enterprise.[52] The Irish experience of such engagement is limited and inconsistent at best. Although emergent victim-advocacy groups were involved in the establishment of the Commission to Inquire into Child Abuse and consulted throughout the Ferns inquiry,[53] limited evidence of consultation appears in the reports of the Murphy, Cloyne and McAleese investigations. Meanwhile, the Harding Clark report on symphysiotomy was critical of 'intense' publicity and activism leading to the establishment of the scheme.[54] By contrast, the adoption by the Department of Children and Youth Affairs of an explicitly transitional-justice approach to addressing the needs of Mother-and-Baby-Home survivors prompted subsequent consultations and the establishment of a collaborative forum with victim-survivors.[55] But such collaboration did not lead to any public, substantive changes in the practices of the Commission of Investigation and was undermined by the department's failure to publish the collaborative forum's first report.[56] Ireland's approach to victim-survivor engagement has missed the opportunity to frame its response to historical abuses as a pivotal, comprehensive governmental moment – one in which the state reimagines how it engages citizens by demonstrating that the purpose of addressing historical abuses includes the empowerment and recognition of victim-survivors' needs.

B. Commissioners

Public inquiries are typically led by individuals appointed to the role of commissioner of the inquiry, who are often judges or experts in a topic relevant to the commission's mandate. These commissioners represent the public and symbolic face of such inquiries. Accordingly, the majority of appointments to historical-abuse inquiries in Ireland involved legal professionals chosen to lead the process. Transitional-justice practice, however, attempts to include victim-survivors and representatives of civil society as commissioners rather than relying exclusively on so-called 'expert' commissioners.[57] Furthermore, none of Ireland's recent inquiries involved consultation with victim-survivors on the suitability of appointments, the potential to include international expertise or victim-survivor representation. The Irish inquiries thus failed to collaborate meaningfully with victim-survivor communities and civil society; they also failed to establish a perception of publicity, transparency and fairness expected in public investigations.

C. Mandate

Ireland's approach to the mandates of commissions fails to capture the full range and depth of historical abuses or their causes and contexts. The Ryan commission has been criticised for its failure to emphasise the nature and extent of state involvement in abuse.[58] Several commissions (Mother and Baby Homes, Murphy, Ferns, and Cloyne) have adopted the sampling of potential institutions or complaints rather than engaging in a comprehensive account. The Murphy and Cloyne inquiries concerned themselves only with investigating the handling of allegations rather than evaluating the truth of those allegations.[59] The terms of reference of the non-statutory Ferns inquiry limited its mandate to identifying complaints made to the diocese and to reporting on 'the nature of the response to the identified complaints or allegations on the part of the church authorities and any public authorities to which complaints or allegations were reported.'[60] As a result, the Ferns report was unable to assess the truth of any allegations regarding sexual abuse or to verify whether sexual abuse took place. The mandate of the McAleese inquiry was limited to the examination of state involvement in the operation of the laundries, excluding an assessment of individual allegations of abuse or the legal responsibility of religious orders operating these commercial, for-profit concerns. The terms of reference for the inter-departmental committee, specifying its mandate, powers and ability to make factual determinations or recommendations, were never made public.

The Mother and Baby Homes Commission's mandate expressly excluded accounts of cases related to individuals seeking their birth identities or relatives. To achieve a cost-effective and efficient investigation, the commission had discretion 'to use such sampling techniques or selection of samples as it may determine.'[61] The design of this mandate privileged a 'literature based academic social history module to establish an objective and comprehensive historical analysis of significant matters.'[62] This choice proved significant in shaping the Commission's final report and findings and minimising consideration of the State's legal and human-rights obligations and responsibility. As a result, in its final report the Commission did not address, as human-rights violations, those violations raised in the civil-society *CLANN Report*, such as 'gender and socioeconomic discrimination, stigma, racism, forced adoption, illegal adoptions, arbitrary detention, forced labour, physical and psychological abuse, punishments, neglect (including medical neglect), and the deaths of infants in Mother and Baby Homes and related institutions.'[63] Instead, for instance, the Commission concluded that it 'found very little evidence that children were forcibly taken from their mothers; it accepts that the mothers did not have much choice but that is not the same as "forced" adoption.'[64]

These limitations to individual mandates aside, several issues relevant to historical abuse also remain unexamined through official inquiry. The state has yet to address Ireland's network of psychiatric hospitals and the entire system of forced adoption, illegal registrations of adoptions and alleged trafficking of children for adoption outside the national jurisdiction. Mandate limitations are familiar in transitional justice, but for reasons that do not apply to Ireland. Early truth-and-reconciliation commissions (TRCs) operated in the context of ongoing political repression and violence, rendering a comprehensive public commission unviable. These concerns do not exist in Ireland, where the mandate limitations can best be explained by a limited political will to examine the past.

D. Resources

Uneven expenditure characterises the resourcing of public inquiries in Ireland. The cost of the Ryan commission and concurrent tribunals of inquiry unrelated to historical abuse resulted in a desire among government officials for a more cost-efficient approach, especially after the global financial crisis in 2008. For example, in 2011 the Committee of Public Accounts reviewed the experience of tribunals of inquiry and endorsed a recommendation that the terms of reference of inquiries be tightly drawn and that new lines of inquiry be limited.[65] The administrative costs of operating public inquiries have typically shrunk over time, although the ongoing Mother and Baby Home investigations are likely to change that trend. The Ryan commission cost approximately €86 million.[66] The Murphy inquiry estimated a cost of €3.6 million, with €1.9 million for Cloyne and €1.9 million for Ferns. The McAleese inquiry cost a mere €11,000.[67] The Commission of Investigation into Mother and Baby Homes was estimated to cost at least €21.5 million, but expenditure totalled only €11.5 million.[68] Cost minimisation features explicitly as a motivating factor in government reports on inquiry design for both symphysiotomy and Mother and Baby Homes.[69]

II. Processes

A. Statement Taking

Victim-survivors' testimony is the defining feature of institutional-abuse inquiries in the current era.[70] Although this process may be cathartic for some, for others it can be distressing or retraumatising.[71] In the Ryan commission inquiries, victims had to decide whether to approach either the Investigation Committee or the Confidential Committee.[72] The Investigation Committee was tasked to 'receive evidence under oath and to make findings of fact upon the civil burden of proof.'[73] The Confidential Committee served a private therapeutic function whereby victim-survivors were aided by witness-support officers. Whether this proved therapeutic remains largely unassessed.[74] Carol Brennan concludes that 'the failures of the Irish state in its duty of care for children may have unwittingly or carelessly been replicated in its attempts to acknowledge and remedy the situation,'[75] specifically by disabling victim-survivor ownership of the process, by disavowing their needs for redress, and by compelling them to engage with a purported therapeutic model.[76] Also remaining unclear is how the Murphy, Cloyne and Ferns commissions affected victim-survivors who provided testimony or otherwise engaged with their processes. The McAleese committee exacerbated the discriminatory and gendered forms of harm experienced by victim-survivors of the laundries, describing their testimony as 'stories' and that of religious orders as evidence.[77] Claire McGettrick, cofounder of Justice for Magdalenes Research (JFMR), describes how the committee interviewed survivors:

Initially, the committee didn't even want to speak to women in person, but we fought for that. The women gave their testimony verbally, and then we were given very little notice of a second meeting where we were to look at the format of the initial testimony. Instead, the women were brought in one by one for a meeting with the commission, where they asked repeated questions. Their overall impression was that they were being checked to ensure that their memories were correct. The women came out of those meetings very quiet and subdued. None of them, none of us, had been expecting for them to be questioned like that.[78]

The Mother and Baby Homes Commission replicated the dual structure of the Ryan commission, with investigative and confidential committees. It appears that the Commission did not adequately advertise the alternative of appearing before the Investigative Committee or sending a sworn written statement.[79] A presentation by Commissioner Mary Daly to an Oxford University seminar in 2021 indicated that the statements of survivors given to the Confidential Committee were not integrated into the main text of the commission's report, owing to claimed legal concerns regarding the lack of cross-examination of this evidence and the 'hundreds of hours of cross checking' that might have been involved.[80] Such a disclosure reveals a fundamental lack of concern with centring the lived experience of victim-survivors in the Commission's approach.

Other practices by the Mother and Baby Homes Commission suggest a similar lack of concern for victim-survivors. The commission refused to give survivors or family members of the deceased a copy of the transcript of their own testimony to the commission or copies of personal records that the commission held relating to them or their family members, even if deceased. It also refused survivors any access to other evidence that it was considering.[81] The statement-taking process was a primary way in which victim-survivors experienced the state's investigation. A lack of care as to how victim-survivors experience providing testimony risks the perception that statement-taking serves only to legitimate the inquiry process, without empowering or promoting the voices of those who suffered historical abuses. This approach then threatens to create a new form of harm, especially if it results in re-traumatisation. The commission's methods contrast significantly with those of the advocacy CLANN project, which facilitated survivor statement-taking in an informed, ethical and effective manner.[82] The CLANN report is dismissed curtly in the commission report, where the commission states, without engaging with the substance of the CLANN submission: 'While the Commission wishes to record its appreciation of these contributions it was disappointed that no attempt was made to quantify the costs involved.'[83]

B. Public Hearings

The Ryan commission remains unique in the Irish context as being the only inquiry to hold public hearings. The Commissions of Investigation Act (2004), which governed the Murphy and Cloyne inquiries and the Mother and Baby Homes inquiry, gave the power to hold public hearings, but each of these commissions declined to exercise that power. Comparatively, the failure to hold public inquiries is often framed in terms of confidentiality and/or privacy, concern for vulnerable persons, and the potentially defamatory nature of charges made against alleged perpetrators and institutions.[84] None of these concerns are unique to historical-abuse inquiries or to Ireland; Canada, Australia and the United Kingdom have all managed public hearings into historical abuse. The failure to hold such hearings in Ireland represents another missed opportunity for the public scrutiny of those responsible for abusive institutions, as well as for the public affirmation and acknowledgment of the rights and suffering of victim-survivors.

III. Outputs

In transitional justice a truth commission's final report will serve as its most enduring legacy.[85] Although Irish reports have detailed significant harm in institutions, the drafting of Irish reports has inhibited the potential impact of such a legacy. Regarding the Ryan commission, Sköld notes that the sections on each institution are structured around the alleged abuse and the alleged perpetrators, dealt with case-by-case in a more or less judicial manner.[86] But the report failed to name alleged perpetrators after a legal challenge by a religious order.[87] McAlinden and Naylor note that this approach was problematic:

> A narrow legal construction of victimhood and focus on selected testimonies also tend to create "hierarchies of pain" by excluding particular accounts of victimhood and subordinating the experiences of some victims. Moreover, the singular focus on the direct victims of institutional abuse also fails to acknowledge secondary and tertiary victims, including the families of victims, as well as the wider faith community.[88]

Similarly, the Harding Clark report into symphysiotomy failed to document the testimony of women subjected to the procedure. The *McAleese Report*, claiming limitations arising from its mandate, did not issue recommendations regarding accountability, responsibility, or criminality.[89] It emphasised that harm experienced in the laundries compared favourably to harm experienced in industrial schools and in diocesan settings.[90] Two oral-history projects, however, counter the minimisation of harm in the lived experience of survivors as presented in the *McAleese Report*.[91] In addition, reports of public inquiries have typically failed to use the language and framework of human rights. Maeve O'Rourke, James M. Smith and Claire McGettrick have consistently argued that the state's failure to prevent the arbitrary detention, slavery, servitude and forced labour experienced by women detained in the Magdalen laundries should be understood as human-rights violations.[92] In their submission to the UN Committee Against Torture in 2011, Justice for Magdalenes argued that the continuing effects of the Magdalene laundries on survivors 'amount to degrading treatment under Article 16 CAT, which the state has a duty to prevent under Article 16 and to investigate and redress under Articles 12, 13 and 14.'[93] This argument led the Committee Against Torture to express 'grave concern at the failure by the state party to institute prompt, independent and thorough investigations into the allegations of ill-treatment perpetrated on girls and women in the Magdalen laundries.'[94] In 2017, in light of the limitations of the *McAleese Report*, the Committee Against Torture concluded that 'its recommendations to investigate allegations of ill-treatment of women at the Magdalen laundries operated by religious orders of the Catholic church, prosecute perpetrators, and ensure that victims obtain redress and have an enforceable right to compensation have not been implemented.'[95] The *Mother and Baby Homes Commission Report* does not adopt a human rights centred approach, either. Chapter 36 of the Report does address

Ireland's human rights obligations but in a dismissive fashion that does not engage the question of continuing human rights violations.[96] In particular, where human rights abuses are identified, the report does not analyse them as such. The lack of human rights focus led 25 academics to produce an alternative executive summary of the Commission report, which analysed the evidence contained in the Report using the constitutional and human rights law in force during the period under examination.[97] While the Commission concluded that families, especially fathers, were primarily responsible for the treatment of unmarried women and girls and their children,[98] the alternative executive summary reasserted the primacy, in law, of state responsibility for addressing human rights abuses.

In the context of these inquiries and their processes, I suggest that there are significant gaps in the investigations into historical abuse in Ireland to date; a fully mandated inquiry into Magdalen laundries, illegal adoptions and psychiatric hospitals (to name but a few areas for further investigation) remains outstanding. A process that involves public hearings that address themes such as gender, class and race would constitute a significant shift from the processes adopted under the Commissions of Investigation Act or state-led internal processes. The facilitation of a restorative-justice mechanism based on comparative practices of international truth-and-reconciliation commissions, with the ability of victim-survivors to meet state and religious representatives responsible for their alleged harm or institutionalisation, would offer a significant change in practice that may better meet the needs of those most directly impacted.[99] Any such mechanism should be driven by the preferences of victim-survivors and their representatives.

Critically, given the considerable data and information gathered by existing inquiries, the archives of relevant religious orders, state records and the archives of existing inquiries all remain closed to victim-survivors, family members, academics, and members of the public.[100] The state's attitude toward victim-survivors accessing information related to historical-abuse inquiries affirms the nature of the inquiries as a ritual contestation of power rather than as meaningful empowerment or support for survivors. The Retention of Records Bill (2019) sought to seal and withhold entirely from public inspection for no less than 75 years all records of the Commission to Inquire into Child Abuse, the Residential Institutions Redress Board and the Residential Institutions Review Committee.[101] A majority of survivors surveyed have objected to this approach; it was 'seen by some as a violation of their rights to their own stories, by others as excessive, while a smaller number who spoke about it expressed relief.'[102] The bill was also opposed by Catriona Crowe, former head of special projects at the National Archives of Ireland, who argues that 'there is no reasonable argument for setting them aside in the case of these particular records, which will be extraordinary sources for scholars in the years ahead. The department's action opens the gate for future restricted access to any records the state may not wish citizens to see.'[103] On foot of extensive campaigning from survivors and advocates, the Irish government agreed to 'delay and re-examine' the bill.[104]

In addition, the Department of the Taoiseach has for years insisted that it is holding the archive of the McAleese committee 'for safe keeping' and 'not... for the purposes of the FOI [Freedom of Information] Act.'[105] The state's strategy of constraining access to information related to potential historical abuses also extends to its proposals regarding reform of access to adoption information. In May 2021 the Minister for Children, Equality, Disability, Integration and Youth, Roderic O'Gorman, TD, published the General Scheme of the Birth Information and Tracing Bill 2021. Although Minister O'Gorman stated the intention of the bill was to provide 'full and clear right of access... to birth certificates, birth and early life information,'[106] as currently drafted the bill would exclude large categories of personal data from what is made available to adopted people. The Scheme of the Bill ignores the rights of natural mothers to their personal information and provides no mechanism for adopted people and natural mothers to access the administrative files of institutions, agencies and individuals involved in forced family separation, and adopts a narrow definition of personal information.[107]

Establishing an Irish truth-and-reconciliation commission would have the potential to offer significant added value, particularly if it is designed to complement existing inquiries across all institutional forms of abuse, clerical sexual abuse, and illegal adoptions – and especially if it facilitated the centralisation, digitisation and analysis of all related administrative and personal records. Such a design would overcome the tendency toward a representative-sample approach that we have seen in several commissions to date (Murphy, Cloyne, and Mother and Baby Homes). However, state practices in addressing historic abuse seem intent on managing scandal, reducing cost and avoiding recognition of state liability wherever possible, especially through retaining control of official narratives about the past and controlling access to personal information related to abusive contexts.

Accountability

Accountability is a central organising principle of international human-rights law, international criminal law and transitional justice; it is principally understood to entail investigation, prosecution and conviction of perpetrators of gross violations of human rights, particularly genocide, war crimes and crimes against humanity.[108] Successfully prosecuting historical-abuse offenses, especially sexual offenses, remains deeply challenging despite a raft of legislation that has changed procedures across jurisdictions globally.[109] Some transitional-justice scholars maintain that as a result of the overwhelming scale and complexity of mass atrocity and the number of potential defendants, the purpose of such prosecutions cannot support the traditional goals of criminal law associated with isolated cases of harm.[110] The vast majority of perpetrators of widespread or systemic crime typically go without prosecution or conviction.[111] Instead, accountability must privilege the symbolic and communicative power of holding perpetrators responsible and of framing moral wrongdoing as crimes, as legal harms, and as violations of rights. Shuman and McCall Smith suggest that a failure to punish a historic crime sends a message that this wrong is one about which society is indifferent.[112] However, if the state only prosecutes selectively, it cultivates silence regarding accountability for other historical wrongdoings. This seeming failure of accountability can distress victim-survivors and create the image for wider society that such offenses are acceptable – or do not warrant prosecution because they occurred in the past. In recognition of the challenging nature of criminal justice, recent transitional-justice practice and literature seeks to incorporate victim-survivor ownership of and participation in accountability mechanisms.[113] Ireland has procured only limited criminal accountability for historical abuse despite claims in the *Murphy Report* into clerical sexual abuse in the Dublin archdiocese that the police investigation was 'an effective, coordinated and comprehensive inquiry.'[114] Between 1975 and 2014 there were 4,406 allegations of child sexual abuse by priests reported to church authorities and gardaí from across Ireland. These allegations related to abuse in non-residential settings and were subject to state investigation in only a subset of dioceses nationally – Ferns, Cloyne and Dublin. Based on the *Ryan Report* regarding abuse in child residential institutions, only 11 criminal cases were forwarded to the director of public prosecutions.[115] There have been no recent criminal prosecutions related to Magdalen laundries, Mother and Baby Homes , illegal adoptions or symphysiotomy.[116] The Irish criminal-law experience frames responsibility for historical abuse in only a partial and fragmentary way that fails to reflect the systemic nature of abuse in institutional settings, including the cover-up of abuse or the overall responsibility of state and church institutions. Although the challenges in successfully prosecuting historical cases are considerable, other jurisdictions seem to have significantly greater success in pursuing accountability as a result of inquiries into historical abuse. The Australian Royal Commission into Institutional Responses to Child Sexual Abuse, for example, referred over two thousand matters to the authorities, including the police.[117]

In other instances the Irish state has sought to limit the impact of accountability mechanisms. In *O'Keeffe v. Ireland* the European Court of Human Rights asserted that Ireland should have been aware of the risk of child sexual abuse in schools owned and managed by the Catholic church. Given the state's role of fully funding these schools, there was ineffective legislative and policy protection for children against the risk of physical and sexual abuse.[118] Although Louise O'Keeffe successfully sued in Strasbourg, the state structured its response to the judgment to prevent other survivors from obtaining compensation. It established an ex-gratia compensation scheme, but applicants could qualify only if they could prove that their abuse occurred in the aftermath of a prior complaint made against their abuser. As Conor O'Mahony notes, 'this condition was effectively impossible to prove; and moreover, it was incompatible with the judgment in Ms O'Keeffe's case. Every single application to the scheme was rejected for failure to prove prior complaint.'[119] An independent assessor appointed to review applications to the scheme, retired High Court judge Iarfhlaith O'Neill, ruled in June 2019 that the condition was 'an inherent inversion of logic and a fundamental unfairness to applicants' and was 'inconsistent with the core reasoning of the judgment of the ECtHR in the Louise O'Keeffe case.'[120] Such an approach from the Irish state reveals a fundamental unwillingness to cede to others, including the European Court, any say in how it addresses historical abuses.[121]

Redress and Reconciliation

'Reparation' has been recognised as an umbrella term for different forms of redress, embracing related conceptions of restitution, rehabilitation, compensation and symbolic measures such as apologies or memorials.[122] Whereas trials are a struggle against perpetrators and inquiries seek to benefit victim-survivors and society as a whole, reparations are the only measure designed to explicitly and primarily benefit victim-survivors.[123] Reparations represent an opportunity for those responsible for harm in the contexts of state and church to acknowledge and accept responsibility for wrongdoing and to engage directly in a process with victim-survivors that acknowledges their fundamental human dignity. The granting of reparations as redress seeks through its operations to rebuild trust and commitment to the rule of law. Unfortunately, the Irish approach to redress has been largely adversarial and risks retraumatising victim-survivors.

The first and most significant redress scheme in Ireland was the Residential Institutions Redress Board (RIRB).[124] In introducing the legislation in November 2001, following a proposal to include foster homes, orthopaedic hospitals and Magdalene laundries within its terms, then

Minister for Education Michael Woods TD urged against that initiative, referring to the draft legislation as 'a proposal addressed to a particular set of circumstances, not as a vehicle for dealing with every injustice and abuse committed on children and young people in the past.'[125] Two primary motivations can be identified in establishing the redress scheme. First, government statements indicate a perceived urgency in responding to the needs of victim-survivors of historical abuse given the delay in social and political acceptance of serious injustice. Second, the scheme was established in a context in which, 'without a commitment by government to establish such a scheme, solicitors for persons who had applied to the commission were adamant that their clients would not cooperate with the commission until the matter had been decided upon.'[126] Gag orders on applicants discussing engagement with the RIRB have made assessment of its work highly challenging.[127] Under section 28(6) of the Residential Institutions Redress Act (2002), a person shall not publish any information concerning an application or an award that refers to any other person or institution by name or which could reasonably lead to the identification of any other person or institution. The government agreed to an indemnity with eighteen Catholic congregations in exchange for a contribution of €128 million. As of 2017 the total cost of the RIRB exceeds €1.4 billion.[128] In 2017 the religious congregations challenged calls for their further contribution to the state's scheme: 'The bill incurred by the government for the redress fund is not a benchmark of the responsibility of any of the others who were involved, including the religious. It was a bill incurred by a government and Dáil on their own legal and moral responsibility.'[129] The operation of the Residential Institutions Statutory Fund Act (2012), popularly known as Caranua, has proved dysfunctional and unsatisfactory to many victim-survivors. It received as many as 5,637 applications, but applicants, most of whom are elderly, complained about the long delays in the decision-making process and about being treated with disrespect.[130]

Since the 1990s payment of compensation to victims of clerical child sexual abuse in non-residential settings has also become a significant practice in Ireland.[131] The latest figures indicate that the Dublin archdiocese spent €12.3 million in 2017 and €14.1 million in 2016;[132] however, it is hard to gather systemic data across the range of dioceses and religious congregations that settle cases. The lack of transparency in church settlement of clerical sexual-abuse cases makes it difficult for survivors to compare settlements, share experiences of engaging with church authorities and lawyers, and gather a systematic picture of what abuse has been addressed and compensated.

In addition, following the McAleese inquiry into Magdalene laundries, Mr Justice Quirke, a High Court judge, was asked to provide a report on the establishment and potential contents of an ex-gratia scheme and related matters for the benefit of those women who were admitted to and worked in the laundries.[133] In June 2013 the Irish government accepted Judge Quirke's recommendation for an ex-gratia lump-sum-payment scheme for the women affected. The report concluded that the Magdalene women should be paid a minimum sum of €10,000 and up to a maximum of €100,000 to reflect 'work undertaken.' Further recommendations included a memorial, payment equivalent to the state pension, and assistance and other supports to Magdalene survivors. Quirke recommended that under the scheme, survivors should be 'put... in the position that they would have occupied had they acquired sufficient stamps to qualify for the State Contributory Pension.'[134] However, the Department of Justice and Equality, which managed the scheme on behalf of the state, interpreted the start date for payments narrowly as the beginning of the scheme's operation rather than back-dating to the women's pensionable age.[135] The Redress for Women Resident in Certain Institutions Act (2015) also provided that the state make available health services to participants in the scheme without charge, including general medical practitioners, counselling services and physiotherapy. However, this law did not provide for more extensive healthcare as recommended by Justice Quirke. Instead, the services offered were 'almost identical to an ordinary medical card – which the majority of the women resident in Ireland already hold.'[136] And in contrast to the Industrial and Reformatory Schools redress scheme, the relevant religious congregations have refused to contribute to the compensation fund for Magdalen victim-survivors.

The scheme also initially failed to include all relevant institutions associated with Magdalen laundries, in particular An Grianán Training Centre, which formed part of St Mary's Refuge in High Park, Drumcondra, Dublin.[137] In *MKL v. Minister for Justice and Equality* (2017) two applicants sought and were granted judicial review of the decision to exclude their entry into the ex-gratia scheme.[138] In the High Court, Judge White concluded that the Department of Justice and Equality did not apply fair procedures owing to its failure to exchange any documentation that it was considering in dealing with the eligibility of the applicants for their consideration and comment.[139] The operation of this scheme demonstrates the pursuit by the state of the most narrow interpretation of eligibility and of the content of redress, even where such interpretation results in subsequent expense in fighting legal challenges.

In addition, 27 complaints regarding the administration of the Quirke scheme were brought to the Office of the Ombudsman, relating primarily to admission to the scheme and the assessment of the duration of stay by the Department of Justice and Equality, the entity charged with administering the program. These complaints led to an investigation by the Ombudsman into the operation of the scheme by the Department of Justice and Equality. Regarding the administration of the scheme and the exclusion of women detained in An Grianán Training Centre, the investigation concluded that 'the actions of the department in this regard constitute maladministration, being actions based on erroneous or incomplete information and an undesirable administrative practice.'[140] The finding of 'maladministration' resulted from the Ombudsman's view (among other issues) that the department had adopted an unreasonably narrow interpretation of the admission criteria for the scheme – crucially, not that the department should have added further institutions to the scheme. The Ombudsman found that the women who were on the rolls of these additional institutions should simply have been admitted to the scheme, as it was known that they had been present and working in one of the Magdalene laundries originally included in the process of redress.[141]

Although Ireland has provided redress to victim-survivors of other forms of abuse, this response was framed as ex gratia without admission of responsibility; such compensation can be seen as 'hush money' or 'blood money' by victim-survivors.[142] International human-rights bodies and national civil-society organisations have criticised such Irish redress schemes.[143] As AnneMarie Crean and Fionna Fox write, 'Within the remit of institutional child abuse there is a continual imbalance of power dynamics between victims and state, particularly visible through the state's continued dismissal of victims' concerns.'[144] Revisiting the 2002 indemnity deal that the state granted to religious orders for child sexual abuse seems more and more appropriate as further forms of abuse become publicly acknowledged. The inadequacy of money as a form of reparation in transitional justice is well recognised,[145] but the lack of willingness to empower and support victim-survivors as they seek to access redress critically undermines whatever potential value such schemes may have. Given these limitations of investigation, accountability and redress, it remains premature to discuss reform of Irish institutions or social and individual reconciliation. Although there have been three state apologies and apologies from several religious congregations related to industrial schools and recently Mother and Baby Homes,[146] the leadership of the Catholic church remains unwilling to apologise for covering up abuse or to concede any responsibility for wrongdoing in Magdalene laundries. Almost every opportunity to transform the relationship between victim-survivor and state and church institutions has been missed.

Conclusion

Examining Ireland's attempts to address historical abuse from a transitional-justice perspective reveals a consistent bureaucratic approach designed to retain state control of information, resources, and reputation across the areas of investigation, accountability and redress. The Irish approach to each of these processes differs significantly from international best practice and from actions undertaken in comparable jurisdictions. Ireland's historical abuses were profound, widespread, and systemic. They warrant an equally profound, widespread and systemic reform of how the state engages with victim-survivors, a reform embracing the challenge of transitioning from a society that marginalised those deemed 'other' to one that meaningfully recognises, protects and promotes the dignity and value of all.

MOTHERHOOD AND ADOPTION

THIRTEEN

Creating 'Common Sense' Responses to the 'Unmarried Mother' in the Irish Free State[1]

Paul Michael Garrett

To better understand the treatment of the 'unmarried mother' in twentieth-century Ireland, it is important to have regard to the encompassing institutional order that evolved after the Free State attained a limited measure of independence in 1922.[2] This economic, societal and cultural order furnishes the context for the construction of the unmarried mother as a 'social problem' demanding a solution. In this essay Antonio Gramsci's theorisation of hegemony offer conceptual tools to comprehend how such a climate of opinion was created and nurtured in Free State Ireland. I will argue, moreover, that Father Richard Stanislaus Devane, S.J. (1876–1951), as well as other Catholic intellectuals in the period, operated as 'primary definers' of the unmarried mother.[3] Particularly significant for the essay's argument is the rarely examined testimony heard by the Commission on the Relief of the Sick and Destitute Poor, Including the Insane Poor (1927), which listened to evidence from 180 witnesses during 32 public sittings between May 1925 and December 1926.[4] Evidence provided by witnesses and members of this commission further conveys how the unmarried mother in Ireland became a criminalised figure.

A somewhat neglected presence in Irish historiography, Devane was a public intellectual whom Aidan Beatty describes as one of the 'most important figures in the legislative history of the Irish Free State, with a strong influence on the soft authoritarian world of post-1922 social reform and social control.'[5] Devane gave evidence to the 1927 commission and later to the Committee on the Criminal Law Amendment Acts, 1880–85, and Juvenile Prostitution (1931), which produced the Carrigan Report (1931).[6] A prominent Jesuit, he wrote a number of articles for the *Irish Ecclesiastical Record* on a range of interrelated topics such as jazz, the 'dance menace,'[7] and the 'indecent' literature found in the 'reptile press' – especially the 'English Sunday and other weekly gutter journals.'[8] He was committed to safeguarding a particular form of Catholic Irishness that he viewed as threatened by young people's capacity to expand – through, for example, the growing popularity of the motor car – the 'circle of their enjoyments.'[9] Such fears applied particularly to 'girls' and young women who appeared increasingly able to slip through the nets of community surveillance.

Hegemony and the Emergence of the 'Social Problem' of the 'Unmarried Mother'

Gramsci's theorising of hegemony focuses on how a dominant class organises, persuades and maintains the consent of the subjugated by ensuring that its own ideas constitute embedded 'mental conceptions'[10] and 'common sense' within a particular social formation.[11] Hegemonic power does not 'flow automatically from the economic position of the dominant group,' but has to be 'constructed and negotiated.'[12] This imperative becomes key at specific historical conjunctures at which 'levels of society, the economy, politics, ideology, common sense... come together or "fuse".'[13] During such a period a constellation of seemingly unrelated circumstances cluster, particular thematic concerns and preoccupations appear to accumulate or condense to highlight broader questions within an emerging hegemonic apparatus. This essay contends that the figure of the unmarried mother functioned as such a nodal point during the early years of the post–Civil War Irish Free State. In the mid-1920s the Free State could best be perceived as transitional – that is, it was in the process of developing what Michel Foucault would view as specific ideologies concerning the 'just' treatment of 'deviant' and 'shameless classes.'[14] Located at a conjuncture marked by an evolving postcolonial hegemony, the new polity slowly achieved both conservative stability and a modernisation of the state's social apparatus.[15] Breathnach and O'Halpin suggest that the first decade of Irish independence was characterised by 'unprecedented centralisation in public administration, a process marked by an almost puritanical zeal for efficiency, modernity and probity.'[16]

An institutional social order was being crafted to serve the material interests of a new national ruling class. In 1914 James Connolly had accurately predicted that the partition of Ireland was likely to result in a 'carnival of reaction' in both the north and south.[17] Despite operating under different dominant religious traditions, each of the separate jurisdictions did indeed become culturally repressive. Thus the social order established in the Free State, suggests Beatty, was not 'drastically altered' in that 'agrarian and labour agitation were undercut and ultimately suppressed, and the country's status in the world-economy remained largely the same.'[18] Prior to 1922, according to Karl Marx, Ireland had largely functioned as an 'agricultural district of England' that furnished 'corn, wool, cattle, and industrial and military recruits.'[19] This subservient economic role remained fundamentally unchanged, with most Irish exports still being transported across the Irish Sea. More fundamentally, a state constructed by economic and political elites largely conformed, in the words of David Lloyd, to their 'interests and ideology: conservative, principally agricultural, and dominated by the most conservative type of Catholicism imaginable.'[20]

The conservatism of the Free State was additionally founded on an institutionalised gendered order. Irish women had been active both politically and militarily during the Easter Rising, the War of Independence, and the Civil War.[21] In 1922 women over the age of 21 were enfranchised by the Free State – in contrast to their situation in the six counties of Northern Ireland and in Britain, where women between the ages of 21 and 29 were denied the vote until 1929. Nevertheless, in the Free State the period between the signing of the Treaty and the 1937 approval of the new constitution witnessed, in Liam O'Dowd's words, a 'contraction of women's public and political role.'[22] Before independence their roles in civil society were limited, but further measures were introduced to ease women out of the public sphere after 1922. In short, the ruling administration began to more emphatically delineate biological reproduction from economic production.[23] Women, therefore, found themselves increasingly excluded from sectors of employment: in 1925 the Civil Service (Amendment) Act limited the opportunities to enter the civil service and two years later the Juries Act eroded women's right as citizens to jury service. Although the Irish government was far from unique in its approach, the Conditions of Employment Act 1936 further curtailed women's employment options. While, in theory, divorce had formerly been available, in practice only the wealthy could afford its exorbitant cost. In 1925, however, a ban on divorce came into effect, which persisted for 70 years.[24] Women's reproductive rights and sexual morality also featured as controversial issues throughout the Irish Free State period. Policy regulating birth control derived from the Censorship of Publications Act (1929) and the Criminal Law (Amendment) Act (1935), measures that banned birth-control literature and the sale and importation of contraceptives. As Mary Clancy avows, underlying the entire censorship debate was a 'desire to extend control over aspects of women's lives in general.'[25] Her assessment draws our attention to the structural factors shaping women's notion of their place in the world and their sense of 'habitus.'[26] Harsh measures were meted out to women whose disposition and conduct opposed the corrosively conservative hegemonic order. Such sanctions for sexual transgression against the social order reveal how the new state perceived and punished unmarried mothers.[27]

Reflecting Gramsci's alertness to the role of coercion in hegemonic projects predicated on consent, a newly institutionalised authoritarian Irish society resorted to a panoply of confinement strategies.[28] For example, the Ryan Report (2009) remarks on 'the culture of obeying orders without question' within abusive industrial schools; according to James M. Smith, a similar reliance on obedience and social conformity arose in other spheres of life within the Republic.[29] Indeed, a grid of interlocking incarcerating institutions were established to contain what Bauman critically labels 'social waste,' those perceived as 'out of place,' 'deviant' or ambiguously 'troublesome.'[30] Children of unmarried mothers could easily find themselves in industrial schools or boarded out either at home or abroad.[31] By the middle of the twentieth century a high proportion of Ireland's population was dispatched to various locations of coercive confinement.[32]

Intellectuals, 'Common Sense,' and the 'Unmarried Mother'

Warranting further analysis, however, is how 'common sense' responses to the unmarried mother were assembled by Irish intellectuals in the 1920s. Unlike the English use of the term, notes Peter Ives, the 'Italian notion of common sense (*senso comune*)' conveys not 'sound, practical sense,' but an 'average understanding' of the social world.[33] Generally averse to novelty and change, Gramsci views common sense as 'crudely neophobe and conservative.'[34] Here intellectuals play a vital role, for he redefines the 'intellectual' as 'anyone whose function in society is primarily that of organising, administering, directing, educating, or leading others.'[35] Furthermore, the 'mode of being a new intellectual can no longer consist in eloquence, …but in active participation in practical life as a constructor, organiser, "permanent persuader".'[36] Within this Gramscian framework, therefore, intellectuals can be perceived as helping either to consolidate or to undermine the exercise of hegemonic power.

Although never an omnipotent presence within the Free State, the Roman Catholic church undoubtedly remained a key component within the governing hegemonic apparatus. Joe Lee, however, views the church as having by the mid-1930s established itself as 'virtually a state within a state,'[37] with male clerics asserting themselves as the 'primary definers,' enunciators and articulators of social policy.[38] Subsequently, the symbolic and material power wielded by John Charles McQuaid, the Catholic primate of Ireland and archbishop of Dublin between December 1940 and January 1972, reflected such growing clerical dominance. Catholic intellectuals now saw their role, in Gramsci's terms again, as constructors, organisers and permanent persuaders – as aspiring to influence state policy and to manufacture 'common sense' among the wider public.

Occasionally, the church's growing role would be fulfilled at the behest of the state. For example, Devane's interventions against 'indecent literature' in the 1920s appear to have been 'suggested' to him by the minister for justice, Kevin O'Higgins, who according to Jesuit archives was 'conscious' of the need to 'excite an atmosphere in advance so as to facilitate legislation' on the matter.[39] Beatty remarks on an:

> important dynamic on display here; the 'state,' represented by the minister of justice, requested that 'the church,' personified by Devane, write an article that will publicly tell 'the state' what to do. The circularity of all this reveals a conceptual problem in Irish historiography; it is rarely clear where the church ends and the state begins in modern Ireland.

Beatty's analysis rebuts crude portrayals of an omnipresent church covertly levering a compliant state to act in line with clerical precepts and Catholic social teaching.[40] More fundamentally, the state and the church might be better perceived as an integrated totality, albeit one imbued with tension and instability; both were part of the ruling bloc endeavouring to provide, as Gramsci would have it, 'ethical' leadership within the newly created state.

Those now regarded as 'experts' played a key role in formulating policy about how to intervene in the lives of supposedly 'deviant' women in Ireland.[41] Concerns about such women, of course, preceded revolutionary change, for prior to the July 1921 truce in the War of Independence, solutions to the 'problem' of the unmarried mother had already been discussed. Maria Luddy reports that at least 23 nineteenth-century asylums or refuges had been established to 'rescue and reclaim' women who had 'fallen.'[42] Although such institutions were not exclusively concerned with unmarried mothers, their ethos and modalities of operation were to influence the character of institutional provision for this group of women for over 200 years.[43] Nevertheless, it is significant that in 1922, the initial year of the Free State, the first Mother and Baby Home – an institution aimed at reforming 'first time' unmarried mothers – was founded by the Sisters of the Sacred Hearts of Jesus and Mary at Bessborough in County Cork. This home provided a prototype for other envisaged services, with the proliferation of such establishments advocated by a range of organisations and individuals – among them Devane in his role as one of a number of constructors, organisers and permanent persuaders.

Devane's Organising of Public Opinion

Close to the government and something of a 'consultant-at-large' in the 1920s and 1930s,[44] Devane aspired not only to shape the state's agenda but also to craft 'common sense' during this era. Public opinion, he observed, 'becomes vocal only by its being systematically organised.'[45] Seemingly marginalised by Fianna Fáil, which had come to power in 1932, Devane drifted into the orbit of European fascism and in the 1930s expressed support for Salazar in Portugal and Mussolini in Italy.[46] In the Irish context he represents a complex champion of what Smith dubs the 'architecture of containment' central to the construction of the institutional social order in the Free State.[47] According to Pierre Bourdieu, within any social formation, the state and 'primary definers' strategically positioned within civil society are crucial to the 'labour of categorisation' and the delineation of 'social problems'[48] – and Devane was wholly committed to honing techniques of tabulation and classification.[49] Responding to previous articles by clerical figures M. H. MacInerny, Joseph Glynn, and 'Sagart' on the theme of the unmarried mother, he focused on the issue of the age of consent in the new state.[50] The 'woman, and the girl especially,' must, he argued, get the protection that was 'their due from a chivalrous and Catholic nation.'[51] One problem for him was the vulnerability of girls appearing to have reached the age of 16, the legal age of consent to sexual intercourse. Pressing for legislation to increase that age, Devane maintained that if a 'girl be prematurely developed and... appear to be sixteen when in reality she is but fourteen, there is no action in law against the man who ruins such a child in southern Ireland.' Although this issue had been dealt with in England, he argued that the Free State had failed to provide 'adequate protection to the growing girl against her own simplicity as well as against the seduction of the designing blackguard.' Expressing anxieties about the encroachment of capitalist modernity and its new patterning of mobility and freedom, the Jesuit priest asserted that 'raising of the age of consent' was clearly a matter of 'very grave importance, especially if one considers the independent and free and easy airs of the growing girl of today, and the greater need for protection accordingly, not only against others, but against her own silliness and stupidity – and perhaps even against the too-frequent negligence of unnatural parents.'[52] Alert to the unfairness of gendered double standards, Devane also raised the issue of the man's responsibility when an 'illegitimate' child was born: 'The father? The law in Ireland practically absolves him of all responsibility.'[53] In comparison, the mother becomes a 'poor creature' left to 'bear the disgrace and all the expenses incidental to the pre-birth inability to work, to the birth of the child, and to its maintenance through life'; this state of affairs, he maintained, amounted to an 'unchristian dual standard.' Devane's articulation of the mother's predicament reveals that financial compensation was available only to third parties who were able to prove a loss of labour power resulting from the mother's untimely absence. That is to say, action could be taken only with 'regard to 'loss of service' owing to the enforced idleness consequent on child-bearing and child-birth, and only by the employer or the father of the 'girl.'[54] But central to Devane's strategy too was the importance of impressing upon the unmarried mother the 'guilt of her sin' in order to 'leave her with an abiding memory and sorrow.'[55] Conflating the issue of unmarried mothers with prostitution, he speculated that some 'girls,' feeling abandoned and penniless, might 'fling shame to the winds and take up sin as a profession.' Required for Devane in such cases was an effective taxonomy, and he identified three distinct categories of fallen women: those under 21, the 'semi-imbecile and the mentally deficient,' and the 'perverse, who lead such a life by preference.' More robust classification, he maintained, should result in different forms of treatment, with the first (youthful) group housed in a female Borstal institute. (All that was needed was the 'transformation of some derelict government building' and its use as a training place for the 'wild girls' situated in that first category.) The second class of 'poor, irresponsible creatures' ought to be committed to a Good Shepherd Home.[56] The third category of unmarried mothers, those choosing to be prostitutes, should face differing degrees of incarceration and hard labour.

The 1927 Commission: On 'Unmarried Mothers'

Appointed on 19 March 1925, the ten-member Commission on the Relief of the Sick and Destitute Poor included supporters of Cosgrave's Cumann na nGaedheal government and representatives from wider civil society. Its membership reflects a coalition of interests forming the scaffolding for the emergent – largely male – hegemonic apparatus in the Free State: the ruling administration, the church, local government officials, the legal and medical profession and reformist elements in the labour movement.[57] With a wide remit the commission heard evidence on an expansive range of topics. However, a number of 'expert' witnesses also offered significant testimony relating to the unmarried mother.[58] They included Devane and Anneenee Fitzgerald-Kenney, inspector of the Department of Local Government and Public Health.[59] Others providing relevant information on the subject included Mary Josephine Cruice, secretary of the St Patrick's Guild; Lucy Desmond of the Catholic Aid Society in Liverpool; and two commissioners from the Dublin Union, Seamus MacLysaght and Jane Power. Their contributions can be summarised under three interrelated headings: the classification of the unmarried mothers, the role of state intervention in the 'social' domain, and observations about the industrial schools to which the children of many unmarried mothers were sent.

Evoking and Classifying the Unmarried Mother

Witnesses were keen to evoke images of the unmarried mother. From the St Patrick's Guild, Mary Cruice believed that the 'illegitimate' child branded the unmarried mother and – somewhat elliptically – that 'they go down.' When the commission wondered if the child might act as a 'magnet' tending to 'draw the mother from her evil ways,' Cruice remained unconvinced. Indeed, she claimed that many unmarried mothers dropped their 'children just like an old garment. They never want to see them again.'[60] This account was entirely at variance with the testimony of a commissioner from the Dublin Union, Seamus MacLysaght, who told the commission that the union had introduced a 'system of boarding out' – or fostering – for children left behind in the county homes by unmarried mothers. But as soon as the mothers learned of any plans to board out, they returned to reclaim their children.[61] Cruice's perspective, however, converged with the practice of St Patrick's Guild: ensuring that 'illegitimate' children were removed from their mothers at birth. The babies were sent to St Patrick's Infant Hospital in Temple Hill before being informally adopted.

The evidence presented to the commission often revealed a consistent distrust and disapproval of the unmarried mother's capacity to rear a child or to become usefully employed. Lucy Desmond, of Liverpool's Catholic Aid Society, informed the commission of her organisation's procedures: Cruice 'takes the baby, and… I write round and see if there is any possibility of getting her [the unmarried mother] into service. Sometimes I lose the girl and she goes into a common lodging house in Liverpool and takes her baby, which is really a terrible thing.' Desmond also expounded on unmarried mothers who found their way to Liverpool. They were, she bemoaned, mostly 'domestics, or not even domestics. They come even from their homes on small farms where they have been living. [T]hey are not fit for service.'[62] Cruice added that the 'girls' tended to be 'typists, post office assistants, nurses, and farmers' daughters.' There were 'quite a large number of girls over thirty years of age,' and the 'old fools' appeared to be the 'worst of all.' The 'most difficult person to deal with,' avowed Cruice, was the 'illegitimate child of the illegitimate mother.'[63] Devane further claimed that this sort of figure was in 'many cases the prolific mother of degenerates; imbecility, insanity, venereal disease, blindness.' In other words, 'physical and moral degeneracy can to a considerable extent be referred back to her as source.'[64] As the casual use of the term 'offenders,' by both commissioners and witnesses suggests, the female subject of their discourse was becoming criminalised. Witnesses like Devane stressed the importance of systematically classifying unmarried mothers. Anxious about all 'grades' being 'herded together,' the commission raised this issue with Dublin Union's Jane Power, who favoured special provision for 'first offenders.'[65] Always visible in the commission's testimony is the pervasive need to differentiate, rank and arrange the unmarried mothers into particular categories from which flowed specific types of intervention and treatment. Although the Pelletstown institution in Dublin recognised no distinction between 'first and second offenders,' MacLysaght, also of the Dublin Union, surmised that two-thirds of offenders belonged in the former category and proposed that the two groups of women be maintained in different houses and 'in a different atmosphere if at all possible.'[66] For Power, a problem was that the unmarried mother waiting to give birth in the Dublin Union prior to transfer to Pelletstown risked associating with 'ex-prostitutes.'[67] MacLysaght confided that it was better to get 'rid of the very 'wicket' [*sic*] women,' even if this might risk 'contaminating the outside world?'[68] Commission member Joseph Glynn, believing that 'every woman should be able to use a needle,' voiced a more mundane concern: unmarried mothers often left the union 'untrained.'[69]

The testimony revealed some differences in attitudes toward the unmarried mothers. Power, for example, raised the possibility of introducing a more honed and refined classification system, because 'you will get some very good mothers in the second offenders.' Aligning herself with MacLysaght, she supported the 'boarding out' of the children of unmarried mothers, but felt that institutional provision was important for a 'residue' comprised of 'delicate children, ...the sub-normals and the cripples.'[70] Devane opined that 'first fall cases should get every help to reform and even some second falls – after that some more drastic measures should be taken.' The 'normal steady-girl should be left twelve months with the child, and [the] giddy or unstable girl should be locked up for two years, otherwise they would come to grief in all probability again.' In relating his own experience providing a religious retreat for fifty-six unmarried mothers at an undisclosed location, Devane casually alluded to the punishing outcomes for some women of such classification: 'These girls went through the spiritual exercises – I gave them four instructions a day. I concentrated and "strummed" on one string – put before them their fall and their future. The consequence was that two of those girls would not return to the world.'[71]

Fitzgerald-Kenney, one of the commission's most assertive and outspoken witnesses, was a champion of the 'strictest classification.' She did not believe first offenders ought to 'come into touch with' those who had fallen more than once. Those she disparagingly termed 'old offenders' should 'enter a state penitentiary,' since in this category they were 'always a charge on the rates'; they needed to be 'sent there for a sufficiently long period to enable you to do something with them.' Revealing the harsh class-based perceptions at play in her discourse, Fitzgerald-Kenney confided that 'first offenders' required an entirely different approach. Many of these young women were the products of 'comfortable and clean homes, and just at this period when they want care and kindness they have to live under conditions of the greatest discomfort and privation.'[72]

Delineating the Role of the New State

The number of so-called 'maternity homes' that appeared to be proliferating in Dublin generated significant discussion among commission members. Despite advertising themselves as specialist providers, these lodging houses were rarely subject to regulations and new births remained unregistered. On occasions, asserted Power, they would send the child of a resident unmarried mother to England, yet the parent would not be informed.[73] Fitzgerald-Kenney likewise expressed concern that these 'maternity homes' were 'not licensed.'[74]

Fitzgerald-Kenney's comment might imply the need for the state to assume a more interventionist role in regulating and curtailing the imperatives of the market. However, such concern did not translate into the commission and its witnesses asserting a need for more public spending. In fact, responding to prompts from Sir John Keane, a supporter of the government's welfare-retrenchment policies, Fitzgerald-Kenney complained that there was already a 'tendency' to 'tax people out of existence'; she preferred in fact the 'American system of budgeting for the charities.'[75] This opinion may have been connected to the Charity Organisation Society (COS) that in both the United States and the United Kingdom had striven to restructure interventions in order to moralise about the feckless poor.[76] Such projects reframed debates on poverty by shifting attention from structurally generated social suffering to the deficient morality, behaviour and disposition of the indigent. In discussing the need for a home for 'destitute girls,' Fitzgerald-Kenney asserted that she was not in 'favor of state hostels at all.' Fundamentally, she opposed the 'state doing too much,' arguing that 'a state-aided business turns out to be nobody's business.'[77] A number of witnesses were still keen to establish more holistic and strategic approaches to children's services. Fitzgerald-Kenney herself called for what in contemporary parlance is referred to as 'aftercare,' a belief that children at age fifteen were 'too young to be at large in the world.' She did not 'approve of the withdrawal of supervision.

I should like to keep them under supervision up to eighteen, with further power to vest in ourselves authority to deal with them up to twenty-one.'[78] Some testimony revealed uneasiness or unnerving responses to Ireland's high rate of child mortality in institutional care. Along with Devane, Fitzgerald-Kenney championed a 'state children's department to deal with all children,' asserting that there was 'no other country in Europe where children are so badly looked after.'[79] And indeed mortality rates for 'illegitimate' children support her perspective. Observing that 53 children had died in the care of St Patrick's Guild in 1924, Glynn remarked that Irish children appeared to be 'dying like flies.' But Mary Cruice responded chillingly, 'it is a pity very often for the poor children themselves that they live at all.'[80]

The Critique of Industrial Schools

Along with the issue of unmarried mothers, the industrial schools that so many of their children were destined to enter featured prominently as a topic in witness testimony. Glynn declared, 'I want to kill the industrial schools.'[81] Cruice, less emphatically, argued that the 'training' provided in industrial schools was too routinised, 'too automatic.' If industrial schools had a role to play, particularly in relation to 'wild boys,' she added that in 'young children the heart is not cultivated at all. I am against these schools until the children come to nine or ten years of age.'[82] Fitzgerald-Kenney also declared herself 'opposed altogether to institutions' where 'life for a child is wicked.' She declared herself a vociferous opponent of industrial schools, where children functioned as 'mere machines,' without 'domestic ties' and uninfluenced by 'affection for anybody.' Institutionalisation was not to the 'advantage of the child or the population' and should be discouraged. But in contrast to the dominant opinion, she argued that institutions were 'bad' even for children with 'criminal tendencies.'[83]

In her evidence Fitzgerald-Kenney starkly denounced the canvassing taking place to ensure regular supplies of children to industrial schools in order to boost the payable capitation fees: a 'tremendous effort' was being made to place children in industrial schools and 'pressure was put on the boards of health.' She also claimed that at present the 'idea' seemed to be to 'institutionalise children much more than it was formerly.' But although such a charge seemingly alluded to the growing power of the church and of particular religious orders, Fitzgerald-Kenney did not identify those who were responsible for such pressure or may have interfered in the 'peculiar circumstances' of industrial schools. Instead, she redirected the commission to alternatives such as the significantly less expensive practice of boarding out children. Although a foster home should, of course, be a 'moral home,' she maintained that there was no difficulty in locating suitable foster caretakers if the payments were adequate. If, argued Fitzgerald-Kenney, 'you want to screw people down and not pay them enough, you will not get homes.'[84]

Yet another theme in the commission's discourse focused on the location of care. Jane Power preferred country rather than town or city placements for children.[85] Fitzgerald-Kenney added that if children 'go to the country, they can become farm labourers and can work' rather than becoming engaged in the light and 'blind alley' employment of urban life (such as serving as message boys).[86] Some exchanges, however, touched on the exploitation of boarded-out children as cheap farm labour, as with Myles's disapproving question to Fitzgerald-Kenney: 'You want to bring up all these children as agricultural labourers?' To which she responded, 'I do.' Reinforcing Myles's concerns, Fitzgerald-Kenney added that boarded-out children were 'very useful in the house, and it is helpful to have a child to drive in the cattle and to bring the water and to get the turf, and it is very useful for the child to be trained to do these *little things*' [emphasis supplied].[87] Her casual remark fails to register that farmers were not only receiving state allowances to accommodate children but also acquiring freely exploitable labour power. In short, the lifetime of the boarded-out child was being transformed into mere labour-time.[88] One commission member was prompted to remark that he had the impression that the children 'all drift into the lower form of agricultural labourer,' becoming the 'hewers of wood and drawers of water.'[89] Indeed, these young workers appear to have constituted part of what Marx refers to as the 'relative surplus population' of exploitable and precarious agricultural labour.[90]

This article has argued that the Gramscian concepts of hegemony and 'common sense' may illuminate how and why the figure of the unmarried mother became constructed as such a pernicious 'social problem' at a particular conjuncture in Irish history. Every hegemonic apparatus appears to require its outcasts, figures of opprobrium who must be identified and managed with a mixture of coercion and, when deemed suitable, patronising kindness. In post-independence Ireland public intellectuals and commentators such as Devane were primary definers and organisers of 'common sense.'

Foucault maintains that the 'first of the great operations of discipline' is the 'constitution of *tableaux vivant* which transform the confused, useless, or dangerous multitudes into ordered multiplicities.'[91] Indeed, the women discussed by Devane and other witnesses before the 1927 commission were configured into two classes of unmarried mothers: those 'who may be amenable to reform' and the 'less hopeful cases.' As already noted in relation to the witness testimony, the commission's tone toward these women signalled a shift in favour of criminalising them. In county homes and Dublin workhouses some unmarried mothers would be classified as 'first *offenders*,' whereas those who had 'fallen more than once' were 'hopeless cases' [emphasis supplied]. This crucial distinction led to their being assigned to specific types of institutions. The treatment of the first-time offender necessitated 'moral upbuilding, ...firmness, and discipline... blended with a certain amount of individual charity and sympathy.'[92] Correction for these women occurred in special establishments, for example in the home founded by the Sisters of the Sacred Hearts of Jesus and Mary at Bessborough. For the 'less hopeful' cases – the disreputable residue viewed as impervious to good influences – the commission envisaged periods of lengthy detention. The impulse to sift and sort unmarried mothers, moreover, was characterised by a powerful class-based rationality. The middle-class 'girls,' whose parents were more likely to be able to pay the fees, tended to be accommodated in Mother and Baby Homes, whereas working-class women were, in the words of one historian, 'by default thrown upon the county home system.'[93] Those women refusing to be coerced and corralled into any form of institutional provision embarked on strategies of resistance and fled the country to give birth across the Irish Sea.[94] Despite their animosity toward the 'less hopeful' women, the testimony of some witnesses hinted at 'emergent' and somewhat more progressive policy departures in respect to, for example, integrated children's services and better aftercare for those boarded out.[95] Nevertheless, such ideological possibilities were largely conditioned by the myopic 'common sense' of those Fitzgerald-Kenney termed the 'leisured people,' the power elite within Irish society. The restricted gendered order that such an elite crafted in the early years of the Free State began to unravel only in the 1970s; the 1973 Social Welfare Act introduced the Unmarried Mothers' Allowance and the Unfair Dismissals Act of 1977 ensured that women would not lose their jobs as a result of pregnancy. Following an embryonic women's movement in the late 1960s, these measures afforded some degree of protection and freedom in regard to reproductive choices.

In the final quarter of the twentieth century, however, Irish society was approaching yet a new conjuncture as it increasingly perceived restrictively gendered norms and practices as anachronistic – as likely to curtail more 'flexible' patterns of capital accumulation. Although a fuller exploration of this question lies beyond the scope of this article, within this emergent hegemonic order, arguably, the issue of 'unmarried motherhood' was becoming irrelevant.[96] Although still discriminatory to the interests of women, society became constituted, differentiated and hierarchised in an alternative way. Driven by a different set of imperatives and remade forms of 'common sense,' the omnipresent demand placed on women (and men) would be that they fit seamlessly into their allotted spaces as compliant workers and docile consumers.[97]

FOURTEEN

'Disremembrance':
Joyce and Irish Protestant Institutions[1]

Mary Burke

The dominance of Catholicism following independence in Ireland has led to the assumption that all institutions for the vulnerable were run by clergy of that denomination, though numerous Protestant asylums for women and children operated from the colonial era. Indeed, Smyly, a trust with roots in the Famine period, still operates today. Recent accounts of historical mistreatment within Catholic establishments create the misleading impression of an intrinsic connection between Irish Catholicism and child abuse, with little consideration of what may have occurred in otherwise affiliated institutions. Beginning with the nineteenth century, this essay queries conditions in certain Protestant-run establishments and explores the underexamined role played by the post-World War II Protestant-managed adoption system within the unregulated and illegal trade in Irish adoptees. In considering assumptions that allowed non-Catholic institutional abuse of women and children to escape scrutiny and to remain absent from current redress schemes, this essay turns to an array of sources: investigative journalism, memoir, historical scholarship and James Joyce's encyclopaedic fictional evocations of Dublin.

Antagonistic Protestant–Catholic relations in colonial nineteenth-century Ireland siloed the inner workings of what were considered 'rival' institutions, undoubtedly to the detriment of vulnerable internees of charitable establishments of both denominations. The sectarian tensions that culminated in the 1921 partition of Ireland shaped a charitable scene that 'divvied up' vulnerable citizens according to religion, with sectarianism surviving south of the border under a guise of Protestant 'difference' that helped to maintain the invisibility of abuses within Protestant institutions. The perception of Irish Protestants as colonial holdovers who were less than full citizens of a de facto 'Catholic republic' further facilitated the overlooking of that denomination's participation in institutional abuse. This essay argues that mistreatment in Protestant institutions for women and children has been ignored rather than hidden, and further suggests that Ireland has been told over and over about such abuses, but seems surprised at each reminder. I have searched for a term to encompass the paradox that Ireland has repeatedly forgotten revelations regarding abuses in Protestant institutions. The word that occurs is 'disremember,' a dialect term meaning 'to forget,' but that I use here to refer to a continual failure to recall something of which one has been repeatedly reminded.

Joyce and Dublin's 'Disremembrance'

In James Joyce's complex and interconnected oeuvre bookending this essay, the memory of abuses in Protestant-run institutions arguably operates at multiple registers that recognise the working of disremembrance at a societal and even personal level. Moreover, as evidenced by the contemporary state's disregard for survivors of abuse at Dublin's Bethany Child and Mother Home (1921–72) and other non-Catholic institutional settings, this disremembrance continues in Ireland. Joyce's *Dubliners* (1914) audits the varieties of degradation to which women and children are subjected and for which no common vocabulary existed in Edwardian Ireland: clerical abuse in 'The Sisters,' child sexual endangerment in 'An Encounter,' a father's beating of a child in 'Counterparts,' and conditions in the Protestant, lay-managed Dublin by Lamplight Laundry for 'penitent females' that employs Maria in 'Clay.'

In a 1906 letter Joyce assesses the hypocrisy of such institutions when he acknowledges his own disremembrance in making use of the cheap service that the real laundry of that name offered Dublin's male citizens – the very cohort whose exploitation of prostitutes led to female incarceration and the unpaid labour that residents of Magdalen homes provided:

> The meaning of Dublin by Lamplight Laundry? That is the name of the laundry at Ballsbridge, of which the story treats. It is run by a society of Protestant spinsters, widows, and childless women – I expect – as a Magdalen's home. The phrase Dublin by Lamplight means that Dublin by lamplight is a wicked place full of wicked and lost women whom a kindly committee gather together for the good work of washing my dirty shirts. I like the phrase because it is a gentle way of putting it.[2]

Joyce's descriptions of the internees and their workplace as 'wicked' and of the committee as 'kindly' and 'good' drip with irony; 'a gentle way of putting it' suggests a barely controlled narrative anger directed toward the hypocrisy of the laundry's lay Protestant committee and all those who publicly condemn prostitution. Such shaming rhetoric does not name the women's male clients that Joyce's phrase about the washing of his dirty linen so evocatively implies.

Maria's unquestioning belief in the moral superiority of those in charge, and in particular her complicit reticence regarding Dublin by Lamplight's inmates, have received critical attention,[3] but the culminating story of *Dubliners*, 'The Dead,' is haunted by the more thoroughly effaced inmates of another such Protestant institution for 'penitent' women, the Bethesda Asylum (founded 1794). My own exploration of Bethesda arose from specific details I had included in the footnotes of an article about the lost histories of women and the poor in 'The Dead'; this origin in the textual margins is telling, implicating me in the forgetting that I will audit.[4] My interest in this essay is the forgotten inmates of Irish Protestant institutions for women and children – victims who also haunt the edges of contemporary reports pertaining to Catholic establishments. Just as a séance must suffice when the dead victim alone can testify to a crime, I challenge 'disremembering' with necessarily speculative investigation in order to provide a voice for mute ghosts.

In his travelogue-cum-directory *The New Picture of Dublin: Or, Stranger's Guide through the Irish Metropolis* (1831), Philip Hardy describes Bethesda as 'an asylum for female orphans… and a penitentiary for the reception and employment of such women dismissed from the Lock [venereal diseases] hospital, as wished to return again to the paths of industry and virtue. About 50 [adult women] are generally in the asylum, where they are employed in washing, mangling, and plain work.'[5] The asylum had been built in 1794 as an annex to a chapel and orphanage for girls of the same name at Granby Row and Dorset Street. Although its ethos was evangelical, Bethesda Chapel and its orphanage were endowed in 1786 by a nephew of Arthur Smyth, the Anglican archbishop of Dublin.[6] In contrast to the stigmatised women housed in Bethesda Asylum, the house of worship that funded the attached charitable institutions for females boasted 'one of the largest and most elite congregations in Dublin'; the wider social circle from which congregants were drawn included, for example, members of the prominent Guinness and Maturin families, while guest preachers of the calibre of John Wesley visited the chapel.[7] Perhaps because of this link to the city's establishment, Bethesda's fate on the eve of the Great Famine during the most destructive storm in Irish recorded history received a degree of attention in Dublin's newspapers.

Joyce sets 'The Dead' on 6–7 January 1904, the anniversary of the 1839

'Night of the Big Wind,' a storm that, like all such natural catastrophes, disproportionately affected Dublin's poor and socially marginalised. The *Dublin Evening Mail* described the capital in the storm's aftermath as a 'sacked city,' with 'houses burning' and thousands more unroofed.[8] In a report dated 7 January 1839 the London *Times* correspondent concentrated on an immense conflagration that lit up Dublin's night sky:

> In the very height of the tempest the north side of the city was thrown into consternation by the bursting out of a fire at the Bethesda, a large Protestant church and asylum for females; I never witnessed a more awful scene. The extensive building was soon a huge volume of flames, and the streets surrounding were rendered impassable by the drifting fire. The Bethesda and the buildings adjacent are complete wrecks.[9]

Decades later, a witness recalled that 'the lurid glare of flames from the Bethesda made still more striking the pall of gloom which overhung the city' during the storm, echoing immediate accounts of the 'vivid blaze of light' produced by the 'awful burning' in the sky above the chapel complex.[10]

In the early hours of 7 January in Joyce's 'The Dead' the strained Conroys – he by growing desire and she by having heard a song evoking her past – travel northward to the Gresham Hotel, the direction in which the sky would have been lit up by the Bethesda fire on that date that occurred a ten-minute walk to the immediate northwest of the hotel: the blaze 'commenced soon after midnight on Sunday [6 January] and has not ceased at half-past 4 on Monday afternoon [7 January].'[11] On the Night of the Big Wind the meteorologically rare event of snow falling all over Ireland – an occurrence that closes 'The Dead' – was just the beginning of the horrific weather. Anomalous weather is a form of shared public trauma that often evokes the memory of previous storms and their consequences. Thus the troubled sky that greets the emotionally overwrought Gabriel and Gretta as they depart Usher's Island south of the River Liffey and look northeast ('A dull yellow light brooded over the houses and the river; and the sky seemed to be descending. [...] The lamps were still burning redly in the murky air and, across the river, the palace of the Four Courts stood out menacingly against the heavy sky') augurs the traumatic return of one of the most discussed consequences of the 1839 storm in its immediate aftermath, the Bethesda conflagration.[12]

Newspaper accounts noted without comment that a fire had been put out in Bethesda on the morning of the day of the storm. However, the London *Times* report baldly states that the 'most melancholy feature in the case is that this dreadful fire is supposed to have been the work of an incendiary [arsonist].'[13] This single journalistic claim of arson by seditious inmates in the case of either or both fires at Bethesda is provocative; it fails to reappear in other immediate coverage and remains unrecorded in subsequent histories. However, and in recognition of the necessity of speculation in challenging disremembrance, I conjecture that the ghostly trace of a possible deliberate burning of Bethesda by inmates emerges in *Dubliners*, given the collection's emphasis on the unnameable histories of vulnerable women and children. Although the *Dublin Evening Mail* called the storm 'the vengeance of Providence' visited upon 'peer and peasant' alike, newspapers from the principal towns concentrated on the losses of named landowners and substantial urban proprietors of the sort that made up the Bethesda Chapel congregation.[14] By contrast those that the *Times* called the '23 orphan girls' and '40 female penitents' of Bethesda who fled the conflagration are anonymous and unindividuated in press accounts.

In depicting a traumatic past that refuses to remain dormant, Joyce contests the periodisation of official history: the weather of 6–7 January 1904 in 'The Dead' uncannily echoes the storm of 1839 on the same date in January, just as Maria's equivocation in 'Clay' revives Bethesda's voiceless inmates on the anniversary of their possible mutiny. Joyce's 1906 letter regarding the real Dublin by Lamplight draws attention to Maria's pregnant silence regarding the true nature of the fictional workplace of that name in 'Clay.' Thus Bethesda's haunting of 'The Dead' suggests how traces of possible abuses in Protestant asylums may be glimpsed between the lines of *Dubliners*. Moreover, this effaced history of poor and marginalised women also leaves traces in the juxtaposition of two entries in Hardy's directory. The latter's laudatory item on Bethesda comes one page after the equally admiring entry on the Protestant-run Magdalen asylum on Leeson Street (founded 1766), the first of many such in Ireland. In the wake of efforts by contemporary survivors' advocacy organisation Justice for Magdalenes (founded 2003) and twenty-first-century scholarship targeting institutional abuse in Catholic-run 'homes' and laundries for female 'sinners,' Hardy's entries strongly suggest obfuscations regarding far less investigated Protestant-run institutions such as Bethesda and its ilk.[15]

Wages of Sectarianism: Children as Commodities for Export

Dubliners was published just seven years before independence, but the legacy of nineteenth-century Ireland's toxic Protestant–Catholic sectarianism shaped the experiences of institutionalised children into the middle of its century of publication and structured a subsequent criminal Irish adoption policy and practice. In noting that Catholic Maria's one concern about her Protestant employers was the 'tracts on the walls,' Joyce's 'Clay' reflects an ongoing fear of proselytism within Edwardian Dublin's charitable institutions.[16] Anxieties regarding the 'loss' of children of one faith to that of the other manifested themselves far earlier, however, as fears of a growing Catholic ascendancy following emancipation in 1829 arguably shaped charitable responses to Ireland's many needy children.[17] Indeed, most early nineteenth-century Protestant orphan societies – generally Anglican or Presbyterian in ethos – were founded in direct response to this ending of strictures against Catholicism, which Joseph Robins argues heightened the Protestant community's anxiety about their own orphans falling into the hands of Catholic charities (and vice versa).[18] An instance of the horror of 'mixed' (Catholic–Protestant) union occurred in 1830, the year after emancipation, when the Orphan Refuge for the Education and Support of the Destitute Orphans of Mixed Marriages declared that its remit was 'to care for Protestant orphans whose additional misfortune, superadded to orphanage, is to have one parent a Roman Catholic.'[19]

Echoes of anxiety about one denomination snatching or converting the other's orphans survived, most notably in the case of the Smyly homes and subsequent Smyly Trust, named after wealthy Protestant activist Ellen Smyly. After founding several schools for poor children in Dublin, she opened the Bird's Nest in Kingstown in 1859, an institution notorious among Irish Catholics – and even among other Protestant charities – as a 'self-confessed proselytising agency.'[20] Such religious divisiveness became a factor facilitating abuse in institutions serving the vulnerable: the author of an 1884 guide to Dublin charities complained of the lack of cooperation between charities of differing denominations but similar remits, which led to an absence of agreement regarding oversight.[21]

Not only sectarianism but racism and a view of illegitimacy as conferring chattel status on nonmarital or 'mixed' births structured the experience of institutionalised children. Australia's recent recognition of 'orphanage trafficking' as a form of modern-day slavery organised for economic gain illuminates the profit motive of mid-twentieth-century Irish institutions that passed off 'illegitimate' children as orphans for export to a lucrative American adoption marketplace.[22] Elizabeth Raleigh's work on contemporary transracial adoption pointedly deploys the language of consumerism, transaction and the marketplace to describe the process whereby certain adoptees 'embody a greater market value than others.'[23] In the post–World War II Irish case the most 'valuable' children for the American adoption market-place were fair-haired, blue-eyed, and Catholic – the combined result of the racism of the target market (the United States) and the ongoing sectarianism of the country of production (Ireland).[24]

The infrastructural development that aided mid-century Irish exports and tourism likewise facilitated this traffic and helped to commodify institutionalised Irish children. State agencies and various manufacturing industries cooperated in creating an international image of Ireland centred on the making, selling, exporting and marketing of heritage and designer clothing and other luxuries requiring traditional materials or skills. This was aided by the evolution of Ireland's air-transportation industry: the Irish American tourist ritual of shopping for quality 'native' products emerged at Shannon Airport in 1947 in the form of the world's first duty-free shop; Aer Lingus cosponsored Irish crystal and woollen and linen fashion promotions in America; and a de facto Irish fashion season became an international-trade pit stop owing to improved Aer Lingus flight times into Dublin as of 1954. As a result of such developments, the terms 'quality,' 'authentic' and 'Irish' converged in the mid-century American marketplace.[25]

One might envisage the first leg of the Ireland-United States flight in those heady days. Seated near an Irish designer on a state-subsidised promotional trip might be a well-to-do American couple bearing the era's ultimate trophy of pure Irish provenance: a newly acquired Irish baby. This child's passage would have been surreptitiously smoothed by Ireland's Department of External Affairs, although the market was otherwise barely regulated. In a development that would have pleased the speaker of Jonathan Swift's 'A Modest Proposal' (1729), the mid-century reach of transportation and of the high-end Irish export trade also facilitated a process whereby Irish babies became exportable commodities.[26] An Aer Lingus employee of the 1950s has recalled seeing a nervous American male passenger with a child on his knee who 'had bought the baby from an orphanage.'[27] That Shannon's duty-free shop was created in the very year in which the first Irish adoptee was sent to America from that airport suggests how transatlantic adoption and air transportation developed in tandem.[28] (However, the profitable eighteenth-century trafficking of kidnapped Irish children by ship was a precedent.)[29] A single page of the 18 March 1950 *New York Times* revealingly juxtaposes the two lucrative transatlantic Irish trades: the article 'Irish Orphans Fly in [to] Meet New Parents' appears next to an advertisement for a 'Yankee Donegal' overcoat – evidence of the emerging cachet of garments with Irish associations.[30] As suggested by *Life* magazine's 1953 promotion of a 'relatively low' priced $400 Irish couture ball gown 'embroidered by Donegal cottagers' earning $25 per week, the poverty and powerlessness of marginalised producers of both Irish designer-wear and 'exportable' Irish babies made the commodities concerned a relative bargain for wealthy Americans.[31]

Irish babies were also desirable acquisitions because of the initial lack – or enforcement – of regulation. Mike Milotte's *Banished Babies* (1997), a study of Irish children exported for adoption to the United States, records that the market kicked off in July 1949 when the wealthy American businessman Rollie William McDowell removed four-year-old Michael

James and four-month-old Patricia Frances from Cork's Braemar Rescue Home.[32] The ensuing U.S. coverage of the ease and pace with which McDowell had acquired the children without his wife's knowledge led to a huge demand for Irish adoptees in America. *The New York Times* account of McDowell's escapade jocularly describes the children as a 'surprise' gift for the wife, akin to flowers or candy.[33] Similarly, a 1950s *Chicago Tribune* story about the arrival of an Irish 'orphan' on U.S. soil describes the child as a 'fifth wedding anniversary' gift to which the adoptive parents had treated themselves.[34] These 'illegitimate' babies were generally – and inaccurately – described as 'orphans' in breezy U.S. press accounts of their arrival by air, often accompanied by endearing photographs and telling details that should have prompted more probing coverage of the conditions from which these children had come and to which they were destined.[35]

Milotte stresses the lack of records of children adopted from Ireland before 1949, but some few thousand removals are recorded in the two following decades, with traffic peaking in the 1950s and becoming a trickle after the early 1960s.[36] As the market developed, he reports, babies were generally taken from women interned in institutions for unmarried mothers (popularly known as Mother and Baby Homes and County Homes), by Catholic intermediaries, or effectively purchased from the nuns in charge. Although Milotte suggests that it was generally the brokering nuns who profited, Reuters reported that Donogh O'Malley charged in the Dáil in 1956 that 'money was being given to poor women in Ireland to facilitate the adoptions.'[37] At any rate, when this trade took off in the wake of the McDowell case, Ireland did not have laws prohibiting the removal of such children, restrictions on their entry to America, nor initially, criteria for establishing the suitability of the would-be parents.[38]

Milotte presents the export of 'illegitimate' children as regulated by the de facto 'Catholic republic,' with official sanction by the Catholic archbishop of Dublin, John McQuaid: 'Facilitated by the state, with the Department of External Affairs issuing passports,... the whole business was conducted in conditions of secrecy ... [and]... the matter was only discussed once – and briefly – by the full [government] cabinet. It was rarely mentioned in the Irish press [at McQuaid's request].'[39] Protestantism, however, is a shadowy presence in this arena too, since a sectarian response to the McDowell case helped to shape the subsequent evolution of adoption legislation in Ireland. McDowell's Scottish surname, his Irish Methodist heritage,[40] his choice of the 'pan-protestant' Braemar 'orphanage,'[41] and his arrival in Ireland on 12 July, a date associated with triumphalist Orange parades, would have, in combination, prodded a reading of him as 'Scots-Irish' or 'Ulster Protestant' in 1940s Ireland.

Unsurprisingly, then, the publicity generated by the McDowell case caused consternation in the upper echelons of the Dublin Catholic archdiocese, ruled as a fiefdom by McQuaid. A reluctant concession emerged in the archbishop's inner circle: that adoption had to be legalised in order to prevent the possibility of Catholic children being placed with Protestants or of Catholic inmates of Protestant institutions being sent abroad for adoption. At McQuaid's episcopal seat in Dublin Fr Cecil Barrett voiced concern that Irish Catholic children adopted by Americans were in danger of having their Catholic education 'neglect[ed].'[42] In a 1951 letter Barrett worried that 'non-Catholic agencies have been sending children abroad'; he singled out Irish Church Missions (a Protestant proselytising organisation founded in 1849 that had aided Smyly) as having sent a Catholic child 'out of the jurisdiction,' almost certainly a reference to Northern Ireland.[43] Moreover, Barrett headed the Catholic Protection and Rescue Society of Ireland (CPRSI), which repatriated unmarried Irish mothers so as to prevent Irish babies born in England from being adopted by Protestant families.[44]

The initial regulation of the American adoption trade speaks to sectarianism rather than to child-welfare concerns; under pressure from McQuaid and with the aid of American Catholic organisations, Irish authorities decided in 1951 that only Catholic U.S. parents might obtain Irish babies, although children whose American adoptive parents were unvetted continued to be issued passports to leave Ireland even after this date.[45] An unattributed quotation from an Irish source in the *Chicago Sunday Tribune*'s coverage of the change, which candidly discussed the 'illegitimacy' of such adoptees, suggested that it was preferable to have such children boarded out with Irish foster parents rather than have them adopted by 'wealthy Americans [because] "at least [Irish foster parents] are good Christians",'[46] a coded insult with regard to the presumed Protestantism of many wealthy Americans.

Sectarian sentiments also informed McQuaid's long-standing opposition to legal adoption within Ireland,[47] for he feared that the state administration could not guarantee that adoptive couples were Catholics. When the Adoption Act came into force on 1 January 1953, at the express direction of McQuaid it prohibited interdenominational adoption and outlawed the export of legitimate children.[48] These measures reflected a goal of preventing adoption of Catholic Irish children by Northern Irish Protestants rather than concern for the welfare of adoptees, in this case that of children sent to American Catholics. Such a Catholic agenda had been ensured by successful manoeuvres to remove 'those with T[rinity] C[ollege] D[ublin] and other non-Catholic qualifications' from the advisory board on adoption.[49] Moreover, once the legislation was in place, as Milotte tellingly reports, 'it remained perfectly legal to dispatch 'illegitimate' children overseas for adoption.'[50]

Restrictions meant to control the denomination and/or Irish regional origin of adopting parents as well as the secrecy of the child-export scene led to the very 'danger' to Catholic children's heritage that the highly sectarian McQuaid had sought to control, as seen in the following criminal case. Light-hearted accounts celebrating the arrival of Irish 'orphans' on American soil continued in U.S. media into 1955, the year of an Irish police report alleging that as a result of demand and to avoid oversight, Irish babies were being kidnapped to order for the lucrative American adoption market. The surmise originated in a spate of successful or attempted kidnappings in inner-city Dublin during the mid-1950s. The ensuing massive police manhunt inadvertently uncovered an '"illegitimate"-baby-for-sale' ring organised by an illegal international adoption agency suspected of smuggling children into Belfast en route to the United States.[51] Availed of by United Kingdom- or Germany-based American military families, the scheme involved falsified birth records that effaced the child's biological Irish mother and named the American couple as parents – thereby bypassing any need for formal adoption.[52] The trade appears to have been an open secret on both sides of the Atlantic in that decade: In American author Eudora Welty's 'The Bride of the Innisfallen' (1955), set aboard a London train, Irish passengers whisper that an English nurse carrying a red-haired and beautifully dressed baby presumed to be Irish 'must have kidnaped the lad.'[53] The kidnappings that had accidentally uncovered the 'baby-for-sale' ring eventually led to the discovery of two of the children on Belfast's mixed-religion White City housing estate, where a woman was passing them off as her own.[54] Here was McQuaid's worst nightmare, as Mary Morrissy's fictionalisation of the incident intimates in her novel *Mother of Pearl* (1995).

Nevertheless, this trade was perceived to be – even in the wake of Milotte's exposé – Catholic Ireland's scandal alone; any specific background about the two children taken from Braemer House whose bewildered faces look out from the photo accompanying the jovial 1949 article on McDowell's acquisitions remain effaced.[55] The willingness to ignore these adoptees' origins suggests the relative invisibility of Protestant institutions and their inmates in discussions of mid-century Ireland's vulnerable children. Moreover, an official silence *still* surrounds cases of children in such institutions in the period, as in that of Derek Leinster, whose story began in the decade when transatlantic trafficking took off.

'Disremembered': Institutionalised Irish Protestant children

The fear of 'miscegenation' through Protestant–Catholic union that influenced the lives of nineteenth-century Dublin's institutionalised children would shape later attitudes toward 'mixed' parentage as well as McQuaid's adoption policy in the 1950s. In 1941, the year of Joyce's death, Derek Leinster was born to a Protestant teenage mother. At four months of age he was placed in the Bethany Home, a Protestant evangelical-run Dublin institution that housed unmarried pregnant women and their children. Derek was eight years old when McDowell obtained his two Braemar charges in 1949 and remains, more than 70 years after that pivotal event, the most vocal spokesperson for Protestant survivors of institutional abuse. In his memoir *Hannah's Shame* (self-published in 2005), Leinster relates how, being the result of what post-independence Irish society would pejoratively term a 'mixed' relationship, he was removed from the care of his Catholic father. His Protestant maternal family's unwillingness to countenance the child being raised Catholic led to the four-month-old baby's commitment to Bethany Home. Fostered out with poor rural Protestant families unable to afford even minimal care for him, Leinster was subjected to physical neglect and missed schooling. He left formal education early, unable to read or write, and drifted into casual farm labouring. In an echo of mid-century Ireland's rigorous screening of potential American adoptive parents for Catholicity alone, he claims that the Church of Ireland's only concern was that his foster family was Protestant, 'not whether I was being looked after properly.'[56]

In 2010 journalism and media scholar Niall Meehan discovered that more than 220 children had died at the Bethany Home between 1922 and 1949, many seemingly as a result of serious neglect; 219 were buried in unmarked graves in Mount Jerome Cemetery.[57] (With the benefit of hindsight, *Ulysses* – Joyce's encyclopaedic fictional account of Dublin's past, present, and future – seemingly evokes this hidden history: 'Then Mount Jerome for the protestants… Shovelling them under by the cartload doublequick. Thousands every hour.'[58] Having traced and confirmed Bethany's Church of Ireland affiliation, Meehan concludes that 'if the Irish government disclaims responsibility for what happened in Bethany Home, so too does the Church of Ireland.'[59]

Meehan and Leinster, as well as journalists Victoria White and Carol Coulter, have repeatedly drawn attention to the issue of abuse in Protestant institutions. Nevertheless such historical experience remains absent from general public discourse and from the state's political response to Ireland's carceral regime. The silence that Joyce alludes to with regard to the Dublin of 1839 in 'The Dead' and the contemporaneous Dublin of 'Clay' persists. In

The Irish Times Coulter reported a 2001 investigation into alleged historical abuse at a Smyly Trust institution.[60] Her subsequent 2003 article noted the lack of response to such reports owing to the persistent narrative that child abuse was limited to Catholic institutions. Referring in the later article to Mary Raftery's *States of Fear* – an RTÉ documentary about decades of abuse in Catholic reformatory and industrial schools and the public inquiry in its wake – Coulter targeted an absence: 'no one thought to inquire about the children in Protestant orphanages' because vulnerable Protestants 'fell outside the known boundaries of public discourse about Catholic and non-Catholic, rich and poor, privileged and marginalised.' Ireland's 'longest-standing minority... has been presented as a homogenous group whose minority status somehow puts it beyond any criticism.' Coulter, from a farming west of Ireland Protestant background, found the 'vastly different' Protestant south Dublin of the 1960s to be 'an intimate, smug, and complacent world,'[61] with certain allegedly abusive Protestant institutions seemingly nestled in such affluent Church of Ireland enclaves: evangelical British former nurse Adeline Mathers ran the Westbank Orphanage in Greystones for decades from the 1940s, presiding over a regime whereby the mostly Protestant Irish children, many former Bethany residents, are alleged to have been forced to carry out manual labour, deprived of food and beaten. Mathers exploited the period's marked sectarian divide by parading the Westbank residents as 'poor Protestant orphans from the South' at Orange Halls in Northern Ireland in order to raise funds.[62] In the 1980s a teacher alerted authorities on finding evidence of severe physical abuse of a Westbank child, but no investigation ensued.[63]

Leinster notes that 'the poverty-stricken conditions I was raised in and the pain and suffering I endured were not usually considered to apply to Protestant children like me.'[64] Similarly, Coulter recalls her irritation with the 'extraordinarily benign view' that Catholic friends had of her Protestant community as 'economically comfortable, diligent, hard-working, tolerant, ...a view [that] does not accommodate differences in historical origin, geography, or class.'[65] In light of such positive stereotypes, abuse in Protestant homes becomes, in Meehan's words, 'an unclassifiable curiosity,'[66] unassimilable into the standard view of the intrinsic connection between Irish Catholicism and child abuse. However, as Leinster notes of victims of historical institutional abuse of all stripes, 'just being Irish was reason enough. That and being poor.'[67]

Arguably, one root of Ireland's disremembrance of abuse in Protestant homes is the loose use of the word 'Protestant,' often mistakenly turned to as an equivalent of the class denomination 'Anglo-Irish' – especially in literary studies. To be Anglo-Irish, as the positive stereotype of that label goes, is to belong to the landed or professional classes and to be educated, sophisticated and liberal. Writing in 2012 with considerable irony in an article touching on the Westbank Orphanage, journalist Victoria White implicates what we might label the Irish myth of the 'honourable Protestant': 'We're the Prods, you see. We don't abuse children....'[68] Such positive generalising effaces the ethnic, class, and religious denominational differences that are crucial to understanding why abuse in Protestant institutions remains ignored.

Maria in Joyce's 'Clay' thought that Protestants 'were very nice people,'[69] though recent research on positive stereotypes suggests that favourable beliefs about Protestants in late twentieth-century Ireland were merely a watered-down version of the overt sectarianism of an earlier period.[70] Breda O'Brien similarly argues that Bethany was left to its own devices because of a tacit agreement in post-independence Ireland that Protestants should look after their own.[71] Thus silence at the state level is a legacy of colonialism. The post-partition assumption that Protestants were a vestigial fifth column that really belonged with the former colonial master aligns with the reality that children from Protestant institutions were repeatedly trafficked to Britain and to Protestant families located north of the border or in nine-county Ulster.[72] The old nationalist suspicion that Protestants cannot fully be Irish citizens feeds the state's apparent contemporary stance that they cannot be fully recognised as victims of institutions that were ultimately the state's responsibility. The 2009 Commission to Inquire into Child Abuse in Residential Institutions (and its subsequent Ryan report) included no Protestant homes, and Bethany was excluded from the McAleese inquiry into the Magdalene laundries despite the support of Justice for Magdalenes.[73]

This essay eschews calling for a revisionist shift of blame from the Catholic to the Protestant churches. Rather, it argues that the Irish state – instead of any one denomination – should be consistently framed as bearing responsibility for what occurred to some of its most vulnerable Protestant as well as Catholic citizens.[74] Since a disordered eighteenth-century colonial Ireland failed to provide a legislative infrastructure to deal adequately with the organised kidnapping of children, citizens took it upon themselves to punish the kidnappers.[75] By contrast the politically independent contemporary Irish state, with resources to confront and deal with historic abuse in Protestant institutions, *chooses* not to do so.

I suggested earlier that Joyce implies abuse in Protestant institutions through meaningful silences and oblique references well before knowledge of such occurrences emerged into public consciousness. However, an extraordinary legal case, well publicised on both sides of the Atlantic when Joyce was young, suggests that such unsavoury facts had emerged even in his lifetime, and that his generation too disremembered. Reverend

Samuel Cotton, perpetual curate of Caragh (or Carogh), Co. Kildare, author, and founder with his wife of the private-subscription-funded Caragh Orphanage for Protestant children, was charged in 1892 with the ill-treatment of five 'shockingly neglected' and 'inadequate[ly] nourishe[d]' children found in an emaciated and diseased condition at the institution. Although in court Cotton claimed that he was too busy fundraising to be aware of the orphanage's conditions, witnesses spoke of a building in a 'filthy condition, while the children were ill-clad, dirty, starved, and covered with vermin.'[76] Such facts make Cotton's short story 'The Foundling' (1870) – which concerns the tender care given to an illegitimate Catholic foundling (and willing Protestant convert) by a kindly Anglican minister – a grimly amusing read.[77] In July 1892, and despite having been eloquently defended by Edward Carson, the man whom *The New York Times* labelled a 'Reverend Brute' was given six months in jail and fined £400 for cruelty toward children.[78]

Other than a brief discussion in Joseph Robins's *The Lost Children: A Study of Charity Children in Ireland, 1700–1900* (1980), the Caragh scandal is almost forgotten today. Robins interprets the case as a terminal revelation of horrors understood to be long past: 'In the long and sad history of the Irish pauper child it was the last incident involving cruelty on a significant scale to children supported by a charitable institution.'[79] The horrors were not past, however, and other cases of abuse in Protestant institutions for children occurred and were discovered over and over again in the years following Cotton's conviction. Joyce's *Finnegans Wake* (1939) is written in a style that generates near-endless meaning, and I speculate that it includes an embedded record of the Caragh case as well as a prediction of its disremembrance. A self-referential passage on the continuous return required of both reader and writer of the *Wake* appears to include a reference to cruelty at Reverend Cotton's Caragh home for orphans ('the barbar of the Carrageehouse') and, five lines later, to the inevitability of its disremembrance and repetition: 'to this [...] cotton [...] we must ceaselessly return.'[80]

Robins's subtitle (*A Study of Charity Children in Ireland, 1700–1900*) further suggests that the dawn of the twentieth century witnessed the end of the abuse of vulnerable children. However, Joyce's *Dubliners*, set in that very period, refutes this narrative of linear progress and depicts an unquiet past by moving from the scattered individual traumas of the earlier stories to the closing panorama on vast suffering unbound by the constraints of chronological time or individual consciousness of 'The Dead.' The closing story posits an unprocessed traumatic past that repeats itself, for repressed trauma is not locatable in the original event, and so returns belatedly. Its unassimilated nature, as Cathy Caruth notes, 'the way that it is precisely *not known* in the first instance – returns to haunt the survivor later on.'[81] In this reading the meaning of the Bethesda conflagration was illegible at the time of its occurrence for the most part. Joyce's oblique inclusion of it as a possibly seditious act by nameless women or girls that haunts Edwardian Dublin suggests that even in its brief reappearance in the twentieth century, it remained only semi-legible. The suffering of the child and women inmates of Bethesda and other Protestant institutions remains in the liminal realms of subtle allusion, self-published memoir, textual margins and addenda; they have yet to enter fully into an official history of institutional abuse in Ireland that would stretch from Joyce's century of birth into our own.

Postscript

In June 2019, after completing a late draft of this essay, I went in search of the former Bethesda site at the corner of Granby Row and Dorset Street in Dublin's north inner city. I queried staff at the desk of the Maldron Hotel – built at the same location in 2006–7 – about any trace of the site's use in the mid-nineteenth century. Although I refrained from asking any leading question or mentioning the nature of Bethesda, a manager answered, 'Oh, you mean the jail?' She revealed that at the time of the 2006–7 renovation a tiny portion of 'the jail's original wall' to which some kind of plaque may have been attached had been removed, but to where she did not know.[82] Once more, the lost history of the women and girls of Bethesda had emerged as briefly and incoherently as it does in the ghost conflagration that Joyce records in the glowing sky of 'The Dead.' Nevertheless, this residual memory of Bethesda as a jail may be a more truthful representation of the conditions under which inmates possibly driven to mutiny existed than the cheery picture that Hardy painted in his Dublin directory eight years before the 1839 fire.

FIFTEEN

'Illegitimate' Knowledge: Transitional Justice and Adopted People[1]

Claire McGettrick

Over the past two decades the Irish state has vigorously pursued a genealogical tourism strategy that encourages citizens at home and abroad to research their family histories.[2] Incentives include the provision of free online access to the 1901 and 1911 censuses, thousands of parish records, and historic birth, death and marriage records. Concurrently, however, through a series of legislative and other obstacles the state impedes attempts by adopted people to access their personal data. Why are non-adopted people actively supported in the quest for family and personal information even as such searches are considered illegitimate for adopted people? This chapter explores Ireland's closed, secret adoption system, including various state proposals to legislate on information rights. It also considers the many obstacles that deter adopted people from constructing their own identity narratives and exposes the challenges they face in the campaign for adoption rights. I argue, moreover, that a sociological research paradigm offers a possible alternative to the emphasis on emotional damage evident in some fields of adoption research – and also suggest that transitional-justice principles might help the Irish nation to address this troubled legacy.

Closed, Secret Adoption in Ireland

The history of adoption in Ireland is fraught with decades of state-initiated barriers preventing adopted people from accessing their personal data.[3] Legal adoption was first introduced on 1 January 1953 when the Adoption Act (1952) came into force.[4] That legislation facilitated a legal and genealogical fiction that the adopted person had been born to her/his adoptive parents and provided for the transfer of parental responsibility of children born outside of marriage to eligible applicants. To ensure that the adopted child passed as the natural offspring of the adopting parents and to facilitate a 'clean slate' with no interference from natural mothers, section 24(a) of the act states that after an adoption order is made, the child is considered to have been born to the adopting parents.

Section 22(5), moreover, prohibits public viewing of the index making traceable the link between the register of adoptions and the corresponding entries in the register of births.[5] Under the Irish civil-registration system birth certificates have been public records since 1864, and members of the public can visit the General Register Office (GRO) research facility and view the registers of births, deaths and marriages.[6] The index to the adopted children's register is also a public record available for inspection.[7] In practice, however, adopted people have no automatic right to their birth certificates and adoption files, and the absence of explicit statutory rights has resulted in ad-hoc policies and practices, often unprofessional and discriminatory. Witness testimony provided to the CLANN project depicts an obstructive system suspicious of adopted people making requests for information:

> The... social worker... seemed more interested in finding out about my state of mind than in giving me information about my identity.

> I can honestly say that [the religious sister] made me feel like a criminal, someone unworthy of her time and attention.

> I felt like I was treated as a threat to my mother, and that the social worker tried to keep us apart for as long as possible.

> It has been the most daunting, depressing, miserable, and lonely search. I have faced umpteen brick walls, and I don't know how to express it. All I know is that it has worn me out.[8]

Although the first people adopted under the 1952 legislation came of age in 1970, the state failed to offer concrete proposals on information access until 2001, when the Department of Health and Children published a 'draft scheme of a bill on adoption information and post-adoption contact.'[9] Had it been enacted, the legislation would have facilitated access to birth certificates for adopted people. However, the bill also provided for a 'contact veto' mechanism whereby natural mothers who did not want contact from their adult children could register a veto to this effect. Most significantly, adopted people acting in breach of the veto would be fined or imprisoned.[10] Mary Hanafin, then Minister for Children, declared that she hoped the proposed contact veto would provide reassurance that the legislation granting information rights would 'not constitute a threat.'[11] In 2003 that draft scheme was published as part of an adoption-legislation consultation established to facilitate discussions on adoption reform.[12] After proposals to imprison adopted people who disregarded a contact veto were severely criticised, at the consultation's oral stage the new minister announced removal of this threat of criminalisation.[13] The 2001 information bill progressed no further, and in the years that followed, access to birth certificates for adopted people was repeatedly stalemated. The only concrete outcome of the consultation was the establishment in 2005 of the National Adoption Contact Preference Register (NACPR) – though it has never been placed on a statutory footing.[14] The consultation had been designed to discuss the modernisation of 'all aspects of adoption legislation,' yet information rights remained unachieved.[15] In 2010 Ireland ratified the Hague Convention on Protection of Children and Cooperation in Respect of Intercountry Adoption, but the minister of the day refused to legislate for information rights in the Adoption Act (2010).[16] He claimed that 'an effective administration system' (i.e. the NACPR) was already in place for the provision of information and tracing services, although testimony provided to the CLANN project disputes this assertion.[17]

In the wake of revelations about the deaths of children at the Tuam Mother and Baby Home, the state once again turned its attention to adoption-information legislation.[18] In July 2015 the Department of Children and Youth Affairs published the General Scheme and Heads of the Adoption (Information and Tracing) Bill.[19] It included a requirement for adopted people to sign a statutory declaration that they would not attempt to contact their natural parent(s) directly as a condition of obtaining their birth certificate.[20] This proposed scheme also envisaged that there might be 'a compelling reason, such as may endanger the life of a person, for not disclosing... information' to an adopted person [emphasis supplied].[21] Although the scheme was widely criticised, nonetheless the new Minister for Children brought forward virtually identical proposals under the Adoption (Information and Tracing) Bill (2016).[22] This bill was also rejected by advocacy groups.[23]

The 2016 bill lay dormant until mid-2018, when adoption came under the spotlight once more as Tusla (Ireland's child and family agency) announced it had identified 126 illegal adoptions in records that were transferred to it by a former adoption society.[24] Advocacy groups continued to object to the bill, and in February 2019 the minister obtained cabinet approval to amend the legislation.[25] In June 2019 the minister signalled her intent to legislate for a new administrative system whereby Tusla would attempt to contact both natural parents when an adopted person requests access to their birth certificate and other personal data.[26] Under the new proposals natural parents who opposed the release of information had a right to a hearing before the Adoption Authority of Ireland (AAI), which would then make a decision balancing the rights of everyone concerned.[27] Activist groups, including the Adoption Rights Alliance (ARA), raised concerns about the AAI hearings and characterised the proposals as 'a grave interference with the privacy of both natural parents and adopted people.'[28] The ARA engaged in an intensive two-week consultation process with the minister and other members of parliament.[29] Additionally, ARA launched an email campaign calling on adopted people, natural family members and the general public to contact members of parliament about the bill.[30] The Irish Examiner reported that over 650 emails were received by the office of the minister for children, and on 19 June 2019 the minister announced that committee stage of the bill would be deferred pending a consultation process.[31]

The 2016 bill would eventually lapse with the dissolution of the last government. The current minister introduced the new Birth (Information and Tracing) Bill 2022, which is currently making its way through the Oireachtas. The Joint Committee on Children, Disability, Equality, Integration and Youth carried out pre-legislative scrutiny on the General Scheme of the bill and ultimately published 83 recommendations in December 2021.[32] The recommendations sought to address key areas of concern; for example, the removal of a mandatory Information Session for certain adopted people, and several proposals to strengthen the right to information and records for adopted people, mothers and relatives, which were in jeopardy under the General Scheme. When published on 12 January 2022, the draft bill ignored many of the committee's principal recommendations. If enacted as written, an adopted person who applies for their birth certificate but whose parent has registered a 'no contact' preference on the new Contact Preference Register must attend a mandatory Information Session, one of the express purposes of which is to inform the adopted person of the importance of respecting the privacy rights of their parent. Myriad other concerns include unlawful restrictions on the right to access personal data and the absence of information rights for most mothers and relatives. The bill has been widely criticised, including by the chair of the Children's Committee who said: 'The extensive work undertaken by the committee, the hours and hours of testimony from adoptees, mothers, survivors and their advocates; the significant and all-encompassing report and comprehensive consultation all appears to have been in vain. This makes a mockery of the committee and its work.'[33] At the time of writing, the bill is awaiting committee stage in the Dáil, and opposition members of the Children's Committee have pledged to try to implement amendments reflecting their 83 recommendations.[34]

Information Rights or a Protective Service?

As evidenced above, the Irish state has consistently taken a punitive and restrictive approach to providing adopted people with their personal data. Rather than advocating reparation for a closed and secret adoption system, government proposals have framed adopted people as untrustworthy individuals from whom their mothers need to be protected. Examining the enactment and implementation of Section 26 of the UK Children Act (1975), which gave English and Welsh adopted people the right to access their birth certificates, provides useful context for Irish policy. If, on one hand, the 1975 act was 'a law for the provision of information,' Erica Haimes and Noel Timms argue that it was also conceived of as legislation protecting natural parents.[35] Haimes (a sociologist) and Timms (a social-work professor) conducted a three-year study on the compulsory-counselling requirement under the legislation. This often-overlooked study is a hidden gem in adoption research; indeed, I argue that Haimes and Timms's approach remains largely unmatched in the field, and throughout this essay I highlight pertinent elements of their findings.

Adopted people are managed as a distinct social group in policy and practice. Haimes and Timms argue that in the UK context they are 'made marginal by a set of social processes embodied in the structural arrangements for adoption,' and similar treatment occurs in Ireland.[36] They maintain that:

> adoption... presents problems for practitioners and for society as a whole. Consequently, adoptees also present a problem: we cannot place it or them easily. The uneasiness that is felt about the process is attributed to the individuals and extends to questioning their stability. In viewing adoptees potentially at least as damaged and in need of help, the psycho-pathological model attributes the uncertainty about adoption to the adopted people themselves.[37]

According to John Triseliotis, in the months prior to the enactment of the Children Act strong opposition developed to birth-certificate access, with some members of parliament portraying adopted people as potential 'blackmailers.'[38] Supporters of this position argued that Section 26 raised the likelihood of adopted people destroying the lives of others, and maintained that requiring compulsory counselling prior to the release of birth certificates would provide 'a check or restraint against possible hasty actions by adoptees.'[39] Indeed, as Triseliotis notes, when the law came into force, some elements of the media represented adopted people as 'potentially vindictive "second class" citizens' and anticipated harassment of natural mothers.[40] However, in his analysis of the research carried out on the impact of the act, he reports that 'the calamities anticipated by sections of the media, politicians, and some organisations have not materialised.'[41] This divergent treatment of adopted people extends to Ireland. Irish adopted people must use an extract from the Adopted Children's Register in lieu of a birth certificate. They are registered twice in the civil-registration system,[42] once under their original identity in the register of births, and again in the index to the Adopted Children's Register under their adoptive identity, but they are denied access to the index linking the two registers. Adopted people are perpetually classified as children in the index to the Adopted Children's Register and are further infantilised by being placed under the remit of the Department of Children and Youth Affairs despite reaching the age of majority.[43] And when they make subject-access requests under the General Data Protection Regulation (GDPR),[44] a significant effort is invested in redacting their files prior to release.

Fears associated with providing information rights to adopted people in Ireland today, as in the United Kingdom prior to 1975, rest on the mistaken belief that a release of records leads inevitably to an adopted person's decision to trace and contact natural family members and demand the right to a relationship.[45] In reality, however, information and actual contact remain separate issues; many choose to wait after obtaining their information before considering tracing their natural mothers.[46] Indeed, some adopted people who have obtained information about themselves and their natural family choose not to make contact at all – and if they reach out, asserts Triseliotis, the vast majority of them act thoughtfully and discreetly.[47]

In their research on the counselling requirement under the Children Act, Haimes and Timms argue that focusing on adoption tracing can emphasise a 'psychopathological image,' 'instead of a picture of adoptees as "psychological vagrants" rushing around looking for a new set of family relationships, a more rational picture is available: that is, of adoptees seeking to place themselves socially.'[48] These researchers maintain that adopted people are 'seeking to place themselves in a narrative... in order to correct that part of their lives which gives them a marginal identity, that is, their ignorance about certain key people and events in their lives.' Haimes and Timms also contend that the so-called search for identity can best be understood as 'a desire for the *ability* to ask, without censure, about one's story and to ask others about their part in one's story' [emphasis supplied].[49] They further observe that adoption inquiries made by participants in their study prior to the 1975 act were 'secretive, individual, and fragmentary,' whereas afterward such inquiry was a legal and thus 'socially sanctioned' procedure – helping to alleviate the shame they felt about being adopted.[50]

Adoption Narratives

With some notable exceptions cultural representations of adoption too often reflect extremes having little basis in reality.[51] But adopted persons who come of age under a closed and secret system lack the necessary facts about their personal stories and must depend on available versions of their experience. However, as Jo Woodiwiss warns, contemporary story-telling practices are dominated by a single narrative shaped by 'therapeutic culture, pop-psychology, and self-help literature.'[52] In the absence of alternatives adopted people rely on popular adoption literature by authors such as Betty Jean Lifton and Nancy Newton Verrier not only to learn about the emotional aspect of adoption but also as a tool in constructing their own stories.[53] Such strategies are inherently problematic since in Lifton and Verrier's popular paradigm adopted people are susceptible to mental illness, drug abuse, crime, promiscuity and a host of other manifestations of the 'primal wound' or 'cumulative adoption trauma.'[54] For Woodiwiss, then, popular self-help literature confronts readers 'with a narrative framework... [that] makes it difficult to construct biographies that are not centred on damage.'[55]

Heidi Marie Rimke, moreover, contends that such literature 'exalts the individual over the social' and 'ensures that norms of obligation, accountability, and responsibility continually turn the subject back on itself.'[56] Her argument resonates with the Irish case; for example, on one hand the government has yet to publish the report of an examination of illegal adoptions, but on the other, the public has been assured that the people who are affected have been offered counselling.[57] Moreover, in April 2019 the Department of Children and Youth Affairs refused to publish the full report of the Collaborative Forum on Mother and Baby Homes, instead announcing a suite of 'well-being supports' for people who were in these institutions.[58] Whereas counselling and services are to be welcomed, such supportive measures are provided in the absence of transparency and accountability (including access to state reports as well as personal and administrative records for adopted people and natural family members). This lack of access renders invisible and impenetrable the very system that is under investigation in the first place.

Adopted people living under such closed, secret systems are further disadvantaged in constructing their own life narratives because they are prevented from accessing their birth certificates and their personal adoption records. Moreover, because they were infants or very young children when adopted, they cannot rely on their own memories to reconstruct their individual life stories. They are denied access to the administrative records of the agencies and individuals involved in their placement and are thus impeded from understanding how those narratives fit into the wider historical picture. Haimes and Timms report that participants in their study considered 'their name, more than any other piece of information,' as associated with 'the essence of their identity.'[59] And Anselm Strauss argues that a name 'is a container; poured into it are the conscious or unwitting evaluations of the namer.'[60] But most adopted people in Ireland grew up without any knowledge of their original names – or indeed their natural parents' names. And without access to their adoption files or contact with their natural families, they are unable to inquire about the reflections informing the choice of their own names.

Equally lacking for the adopted is information explaining why and how they were placed with particular families. In most cases names were given by the adopting parents, yet the decision-making process about placing children lay with the adoption agency and the Adoption Board.[61] Subjective evaluations on the part of social workers thus determined the family that adopted a daughter or son. But here too Irish adopted people lack access to their personal files, the administrative records of the relevant adoption agency, and the records of the institutions in which they may have been born. Those who have managed to obtain personal data through subject-access requests under the GDPR report that these materials are heavily redacted, with the names of third parties, including social workers, effaced.[62] It is currently impossible, therefore, for an Irish adopted person to make 'a request for an account' of how they came to have their adoptive identity because they do not know the names of those individuals holding the answers.[63]

Adoption Activism: Civil Rights or Psychological Needs?

Since adopted people remain disadvantaged in compiling their own life histories, popular-psychology texts often fill the resulting lacuna. But adopted people experience what Miranda Fricker terms 'hermeneutical injustice,' occurring when there is a gap in the shared tools of interpretation available to marginalised individuals and groups in articulating their experience.[64] For adopted people this means that it can be difficult to put into words what it means to be adopted. And in the absence of alternative understandings, the alleged psycho-pathology of adoption has become the dominant narrative propelling information-rights campaigns. Much psychological and self-help literature suggests that the wish to trace one's origins stems from a deep psychological need – as a 'self-therapy, correcting a psychopathological condition.'[65] But Haimes and Timms argue the contrary: participants in their study were 'normal, well-adjusted adults' who did not conform to such assumptions.[66] Indeed, despite the failure of empirical evidence to support claims that adopted people suffer from a pathological condition, psychological research and psycho-pathological theories have played a prominent role in campaigns for adoption-information rights since the 1980s and 1990s, particularly in the United States.[67]

Ireland's adoption-information rights movement emerged against an international backdrop focusing on the psychological damage of adoption and the need for healing and support. In 1990 Eileen Ryan and Patricia Murray founded the Adult Adoptees Association (AAA) as a support group holding monthly meetings.[68] To protect this foundational ethos of support, the organisation's leaders dissuaded the group from engaging in political activism.[69] Two years later, Adoption Action was founded, initially as the 'information and action committee' of the AAA, and later as an activist organisation in its own right.[70] Although the history of the Irish adoption-rights movement has yet to be written, available evidence indicates that in these early years campaigners followed the lead of their American counterparts in basing their appeals on psychological need. In a 1992 letter to the Irish Press, Ryan makes her case clear:

> Telling a child that he is adopted but that he has no right to his original records and birth history is not acceptable... Growth into whole adulthood, with a secure sense of identity and capacity to achieve full potential, is seriously hindered by lack of birth information and cutting off from one's mother... Dr. Betty-Jean Lifton, herself an adoptee, speaking on the psychopathology of adoption in Dublin recently, urged psychiatrists, therapists, and counsellors to tune into the 'forbidden self' when treating adoptees and birth mothers who present with depression, eating disorders, adolescent acting-out, asthma, and many other psychological problems in numbers which exceed their proportion of the population.[71]

In the same letter Ryan stresses that 'the 'need to know' is not motivated by dissatisfaction with the adoptive parents.'[72] But Haimes and Timms's reflections on their research participants' use of language offers a critical perspective in understanding the motivation to justify the 'need to know.' They observed in their participants an attribute they labelled 'just-talk,' in which adopted people used the word 'just' in order to 'normalise their request [for information], thus minimising its dramatic and therefore potentially threatening nature.'They argue that 'something so self-evidently reasonable as... wanting to know who your parents are becomes immediately complex when needing explanation.'[73] Ireland was in the early stages of confronting its history of injustice against women and children in the early 1990s when

Ryan and others began to speak out against a system that prevents adopted people from accessing their records. The only available script at the time – underscored by Lifton's lecture in Dublin – was a model emphasising the psychopathology of adoption. Hardly surprisingly, then, that these early adoption advocates in Ireland campaigned on the basis of psychological need. However, strategies that pathologise adopted people run the risk of backfiring on the open-records movement by misrepresenting adopted people as potentially dangerous.

From Psychopathology to Sociology

How can the injustice of sealed records be acknowledged without simultaneously pathologising adopted people? I argue that a sociological rather than a psychological lens offers one way forward. From the psychopathological perspective adopted people seeking information rights are considered, in Haimes and Timms's memorable phrase, as 'psychological vagrants' looking for new relationships with family members.[74] This perspective rests on two assumptions: that accessing information automatically means contact with one's natural family, and that reunion with that family represents a needed form of therapy. But, as already pointed out, such assumptions do not rest on empirical evidence, even if informed by adoption-psychology literature, both academic and popular.[75]

Many fields of psychology focus on traits of the individual rather than on the social structures that shape individual lives. But if the expert gaze in adoption research is steadfastly focused on the personal, findings will tend to emphasise the individual's triumphs or failings (for example in adoption-outcome studies); such findings can sometimes be used to draw dubious and unverified assumptions.[76] Psychologist Myrna L. Friedlander's pronouncement that 'adoption works' stands out as one example, for she arrives at that assertion after reading literature reviews on the high levels of resilience among adopted children.[77] Such logic promotes adoption as a viable institution because adopted children are resilient; its conclusion is not only empirically dubious but also elides the power relations, inequalities and other factors that can make children 'adoptable' in the first place.[78]

Although I do not suggest that all psychologists arrive at false assumptions or view adopted people as unstable, I would nevertheless argue for significant rethinking among the disciplines traditionally associated with adoption research: psychology, medicine and social work. I further suggest that the discipline of sociology, which has long neglected adoption studies, expand its boundaries of research.[79]

From a sociological perspective adopted people seeking information are far from psychologically impaired; they are attempting to place themselves within a system that has marginalised them. Haimes and Timms's research focused on the compulsory counselling requirement of the Children Act. In order to examine the relationship between 'social identity and certain aspects of social policy,' they studied the various social actors involved in this process, including parliamentarians, experts, local administrators, practitioners, and adopted people themselves.[80] They examined the impact of secrecy on an adopted person's social rather than ego identity, viewing the latter as insufficient to explain the phenomenon of adopted people making information requests. Haimes and Timms advocate shifting the focus to the social organisation of adoption. This framework enables us to see that adopted people are at a disadvantage because they are unable to narrate their life histories – as when asked to provide basic information such as medical history, family background or simply their name at birth. Haimes and Timms argue that a person's social identity 'is precisely that which opens them to question, suspicion, friendliness, rejection, special-ness on the grounds of that which distinguishes them socially.' For adopted people, 'what distinguishes them from others is their adoptive status.'[81] The inequity of closed adoption records is central to this paradigm, but – and this is pivotal – there is no inference of associated psychological damage. Again in the words of Haimes and Timms, a 'social identity open to questioning does not imply, as a damaged ego might, a degree of psychological disturbance, but rather that extra care is needed to ensure the individual is taken as a serious, competent but non-threatening member of society.'[82]

Transitional Justice and Adopted People

Although the Irish state has begun to redress the nation's treatment of women and children,[83] current discourses around such human-rights violations generally characterise historical abuse as entirely institutional rather than systematic, widespread and dependent on social classifications. Those discourses, moreover, have too often ignored closed and secret adoption as a form of injustice. Because all parties were expected to get on with their lives after the signing of an adoption order, silence and secrecy were inculcated within the adoptive family. Consequently, adoption was rarely discussed beyond being a given fact, and in some instances adoptive parents hid the fact that their daughter or son was adopted. Fearful of appearing disloyal, many adopted people have waited until their adoptive parents have died before seeking information.[84] For adopted people, conforming to expected norms – for example, dutifully reporting a happy adoption experience – has been seen as 'success,' whereas deviance from such norms – as in protesting against the closed system – has implied 'failure.'[85] These factors exacerbate the difficulties faced by Irish adopted people, explaining why so few recognise that they are affected by historic injustice. Consequently, adoption-rights campaigners confront challenges in their efforts to achieve recognition of adoption as a key element underpinning the Irish state's systemic human-rights violations against women and children.

Transitional justice includes four core principles: the right to know the truth about historic abuses and the fate of the disappeared, the state's obligation to investigate and prosecute human-rights abuses, the right to reparations and, finally, the state's obligation to prevent the recurrence of human rights abuses in the future.[86] For adopted people reparation and the right to know the truth are inextricably linked. In essence 'redress' means equal access to personal data, for without these records no form of reparation is either possible or meaningful.[87] In 2015 the Irish government established a Commission of Investigation to examine abuse in Mother and Baby Homes; however, its focus is almost entirely on institutional abuse – thus excluding the adoption system and adopted people as a core component of its investigative process, even though many adopted people were born and adopted from these very institutions.[88] In the CLANN Project Report, Adoption Rights Alliance and JFMR called on the Irish state to move from a fragmented, compartmentalised approach in investigating historical abuse, advocating instead a comprehensive transitional-justice process, including a capstone investigation.[89] This call has fallen on deaf ears.

Reform and a guarantee of nonrecurrence are vital components of the transitional-justice process, but Ireland's adoption history throws these components into sharp relief: the oppressive policies imposed on adopted people still today assure that past injustices continue.[90] More positively, significant progress has been made in reforming intercountry adoption in Ireland, both at policy and practice level.[91] Stricter regulations have ensured more child-centred policies; however, a culture of entitlement persists, with some accusing the state of ruining their chances to parent children.[92] A comprehensive and independent investigation of the twentieth-century adoption system in Ireland would expose the underlying processes and power structures of the past.

Closed, secret adoption represents one of the last bastions of Ireland's twentieth-century system of oppression against women and children. Despite significant social change in recent years, as well as a new culture of embracing family genealogies and histories, much of the 'old Ireland' survives for adopted people. The psychopathological research paradigms and literature associated with adoption further compound this situation.

As I argue, however, embracing transitional-justice principles and shifting to sociological rather than psychopathological research frameworks will illuminate these injustices. Acting on such principles will mark the beginning of an effective response to historical abuse in Ireland, but only if access to information is prioritised as a fundamental right and a cornerstone of the reparations process.

Sixteen

'It Steadies Me to Tell These Things': Memoir and the Redemptive Power of Truth-Telling[1]

Caitríona Palmer

In March 2016 I published a memoir, *An Affair with My Mother*.[2] It told the story of my life and that of my birth mother Sarah – not her real name – who gave birth to me outside of marriage in Ireland in 1972 and, with no other choice, handed me over to a Catholic agency for adoption. In 1999, when I was 27 years old, Sarah and I reunited. An affair is a provocative word to describe a relationship between a parent and child, but it was the only way I knew how to portray the subsequent 15 years that I spent getting to know Sarah on condition of the strictest secrecy. Our relationship – hidden from her husband, children and friends – was conducted entirely undercover. Bound by conditions set by Sarah, we emailed, texted and met at locations far outside the perimeter of her social circle. Not once did I knock on her door or call her cell phone outside the appointed time. Desperate to keep her in my life, I obeyed the rules. 'Take your time,' I repeatedly told Sarah, 'I can wait.' What I did not understand in those early days of our relationship was that Sarah would need a lifetime.

In truth I wrote *An Affair with My Mother* with just one reader in mind: Sarah. As a journalist and daughter, I wanted to understand the competing forces that kept Sarah and me at arm's length: her desire to preserve a life carefully constructed in the wake of my loss and my desire to be fully acknowledged as the child she once gave away. I saw the book as a love letter to her: an attempt to explain to Sarah the powers that had conspired to destroy her life back when she was 22 years old and in love. I wanted to publicly exonerate a woman who still believes – to this day – that she alone is to blame for falling pregnant outside of marriage in Ireland in 1972. Blinded by her shame, she does not consider the responsibility of the man who impregnated her and walked away, nor the culpability of the Catholic church, with its culture of institutional dishonesty and shame, and the Irish state, which allowed the church to dictate the terms on which unmarried mothers and their children were treated.

It seems strange to admit this now, but in the process of writing the memoir I never thought of other readers. I imagined Sarah reading the book, and my parents Liam and Mary, and I agonised over what they might think. But I found it hard to visualise how the words I was writing might travel beyond my laptop and into the lives of others. Imagine my astonishment in the anxiety-filled days following publication when dozens of emails and social-media messages began to pour in. They came mostly from Ireland but also from around the globe: the United Kingdom, the United States, Canada, Spain, France, Malta, Australia, New Zealand, Tunisia, South Africa and Zimbabwe. Most were from secret adoptees like me, insisting that the story I had written belonged to them. Many more were from birth mothers, anxious to explain why Sarah felt the need to keep me hidden. I heard from adoptive parents and from people who had discovered late into adulthood an older sibling given away. I heard from adults who had grown up without a parent and others raised in a home weighed down by a family secret. I heard from a woman who had undergone an abortion, and another who wished she had never been born. An email from a woman in Boston was typical of the messages that arrived in the immediate days following publication: 'My Irish mother also has kept me a secret for almost fifty years. She has also completely rejected me. The pain is too much to bear without a feeling of connection with other adoptees who can understand and relate.' As was this communication from an Irish woman living in London: 'Since I met my birth mother almost a year ago, I have been saying these exact words – "It feels like we're having an affair." How strange but comforting to then see the title of your book.'

For more than three years, long after the memoir had faded from public view, the emails and messages continued to pour in: a constellation of confessions, of revelations, of sorrow and loss. Each one took my breath away. To be summoned into the lives of strangers, to be invited into such intimacy, felt like a gift. I responded to every email even when my heart was not up to it, or when I did not know what to say. These innermost outpourings, and the expectations directed toward me, were one and the same. In the absence of an approach to deal with the toxic legacy of adoption in Ireland, I had become the unwitting inheritor of other people's secrets. I was a sounding board, a conduit to validation and a way for others to unburden themselves of their pain. The responsibility felt like both an honour and a terrible burden.

Before writing my memoir, I mostly shied away from other adoptees. I was cloistered in what the adoption community refers to as 'the fog': the belief that losing one's biological family at birth is inconsequential. I saw my adoption as a quirky footnote in an otherwise unremarkable biography, and I struggled to connect with other adoptees who so clearly showed their pain. But in November 2004, face-to-face with my newborn son, the first biological relative I had ever seen, I understood – with horrifying clarity – what I had lost. A year later, I joined an adoption support group. Still, even then, the pain of those in the room overwhelmed me and after two or three sessions I quit. But now, over a decade later, in the weeks and months following publication, adoptees from around the world were seeking me out. Some, like this woman from the United States, wrote to express thanks 'for the hard and sometimes agonising work of writing' my book:

> I underlined just about every time you wrote about your emotions and effects adoption had on you, for your words cracked open my closed-off emotions for most of my life. It was like a free counseling session. I too fractured when I was told I was adopted at age eight. I was afraid if I began to cry that I would hurt my parents and also go crazy. I... finally located my mother this summer, who is still alive and doing well at eighty-seven. Even though I sent her a most lovely letter with pictures, I never heard from her. I finally... received a one-page terse response saying to leave her alone, and that I was never really her child. All I wanted was ancestry and medical info.

Another young Irish woman, in the first flush of a secret relationship with her birth mother, wrote to say that my book had provided an unwitting roadmap to help navigate around her mother's appeal for secrecy: 'Even though it's only been a few months, I have been struggling daily with the burden of her request, and so many of my thoughts, feelings, and insecurities match those expressed by you in your book. It is great to know – even remotely – that someone else "gets it", meaning what it's like to walk in these "secret" shoes.' Another writes to tell me that, just like Sarah, her birth mother is 'living in fear and anxiety' in Ireland. 'I've struggled with my reunion and rejection since 2007,' she admits, 'and I open up to my parents with a drink every now and then.' An adopted woman in her seventies writes to me from Northern Ireland. 'My story is still unfolding after nearly forty years,' she writes. 'Becoming a mother, and now a grandmother, is an incredibly healing experience. Yet there's a fragility and separateness which has never left me. It just has to be held tenderly.'

Several years earlier, I had read a memoir by the American novelist A. M. Homes about her own adoption experience and traumatic reunion with her birth mother Ellen. Homes wrote about how she grew up 'furious' and 'perpetually in mourning,' grieving for a life – and a phantom mother – that felt far out of reach. Her writing seethed with anger.[3] Her willingness to call out the ugly side of adoption – the grief, the loneliness, the emotional whiplash of never truly knowing who you are – hit me with lightening force. I underlined passages on practically every page. I found Homes's email address and sent her a note gushing about how her memoir had allowed me to access a fresh awareness of my own relationship to adoption. I never received a reply, but I did not care. Homes's writing had already validated my own experience and made me feel less alone. Now in turn others were writing to say that my own narrative resonated with them.

In the process of writing my memoir, I stumbled across multiple stories of adoption reunions gone wrong. But one that stood out involved an Irish woman whose birth parents had gone on to have three more children following her adoption. This couple, who had married, refused to enter a relationship when contacted by their long-lost child, telling her that the shame of her existence – three decades later in a post-Celtic Tiger Ireland – was still too toxic to bring to light. The cruelty in that story astonished me, and I assumed that it was a once-off. But later, with my memoir making the rounds on radio and television talk shows, other adoptees with similar stories began to contact me. A woman from the west of Ireland, once a resident of the same Dublin baby home where I spent the first six weeks of my life, wrote to say that her birth parents had married shortly after her birth and subsequently had five additional children. Now reunited, this woman's birth parents had introduced her to her siblings but kept her a secret from their extended family – aunts, uncles and grandparents – and wider social circle. 'Seven years later, no one knows of my existence,' she wrote. 'I attended a [family event] in May and was introduced to my cousin by my birth mother as a really good friend of my sisters. This broke my heart, and I felt as if I had been kicked in the stomach.' Diminished, this woman confronted her birth mother. 'I told her I find this upsetting, but there was no huge acknowledgment of her feelings or mine,' she wrote. 'I am going to leave it there because I am not as brave as you, and despite it all, I crave whatever she can give me.'

I did not consider myself brave, and I was intimately familiar with this craving. For years I had tiptoed around Sarah, fearful that my quest to uncover my identity might scare her away. It was five years into our relationship before I could press for more details about my birth father, a subject that Sarah – gentle in nature – kept forcefully off limits. Even then my hesitant prodding about this man seemed impertinent, and I worried that I would chase Sarah away. But I was not alone in navigating this emotional tightrope. 'It's like you are standing outside a window of a house and you can see all that is going on inside, but the people inside don't even know you are there and you're not allowed to go in.' This from another Irish woman who wrote about the pain of being kept at arm's length from birth parents who had also married following her adoption. 'I'm still a secret after all these years to the rest of their family, including my birth siblings, which I find very difficult, but they cannot bring themselves to tell them,' she wrote. 'The first few years of reunion it didn't bother me as I got to know them…, but for the last few years it's really difficult.' Held hostage to their shame, this woman continues to meet her parents occasionally, mostly in an Irish hotel far beyond the borders of their social life. In between rendezvous she sends pained letters confessing to the difficulty of being kept in the dark. But her birth mother and father have never acknowledged the letters. 'Some people say I should give them an ultimatum, threaten to contact my siblings,' she explains, 'but I could never do that, as much as it pains me. I don't want to damage our relationship.' I want to write to this woman and urge her to walk away, but it is not my place. I am projecting my own feelings, wishing that I could have had the courage in those early days to take Sarah's delicate hands in mine, to look her in the eyes and say gently, convincingly, with as much love as I could muster, 'This isn't working, Sarah. I can't do this anymore.' I reasoned that it was I who had initiated the relationship, I who had intruded into Sarah's life, not the other way around. It wasn't for me to issue an ultimatum.

On the dedication page for *An Affair with My Mother* I expressed my desire that 'love and compassion' would set Sarah – and every birth mother burdened by secrecy – free. Despite writing the book for Sarah, I hoped that other birth mothers struggling to reveal their secret children might find a connection in her story. From Canada a 70-year-old woman wrote to tell me about living with a 'grief unspoken to a soul for fifty years' and the 'madness of the confiscation of her own baby under the guise of "the right thing to do".' Self-loathing had governed this woman's life since losing her son to adoption, she confessed, as was the strange experience of becoming a 'facsimile' of the person she was once before:

> Your words have pierced my heart. For me, as a seventy-year-old birth mother, recently found by my son, I can say that you have unveiled my secret life completely, … always trying to make up for the unthinkable price I had to pay for innocent love, …camouflaging my shame with my best efforts to be acceptable.

There is just no way to forgive oneself, this woman writes, for the crime – however forced – of giving a child away. Nor is it easy to forgive those who took that child, excising her from the cycle of nature by 'experiencing the miracle of life and enabling a child to live, but then being eviscerated of all traces of motherhood.' Her email ended with this declaration: 'I believe that Sarah is not hiding YOU but hiding the "horrible" person who gave you away. I am so glad you are on this earth writing so carefully about your experience.'

Many emails are from birth mothers like Sarah who insist on keeping their newly found children hidden. They offer love and reassurance. 'In the first instance,' one email began, 'I would love to hug you.' Often tentative, many attempt to explain Sarah's behaviour. 'I am a natural mother who has connected with my son in the past four years,' reads a Facebook message from Ireland. 'I haven't told anyone of his existence, which I can't explain why. The shame is still instilled in us, and it's extremely difficult to confide in others, even our closest friends.' An Irish woman writes to say how she gave birth at 18 years old but was forbidden from holding or even looking at her child. Delivery-room nurses immediately spirited the baby away. For 45 years she had no idea whether she had given birth to a girl or a boy, and her own mother, despite this woman's pleas, refused to tell her. 'I carried the sound of my babe's first cry in my heart all those years,' she wrote. 'I know of the shame, the secrets, which are truly soul destroying.' Another woman emails to ask if we can speak by phone. When I call, the woman sounds panicked. She asks that I wait. I hear the tip tap of shoes on a wooden floor, the crunch of gravel underfoot, and then the soft closing of a car door. Only when seated in her driveway, far from earshot of her family, does she begin to tell me about her secret child. 'Nobody else knows anything about her,' this woman tells me. 'You are the first to know.'

The birth mothers who write to me are mostly Sarah's age and older. But one day an email arrives out of the blue:

> Dear Caitríona,
> I am around the same age as you, but I am a birth mother. My Irish parents were horrified at my teenage pregnancy. I was told without question that I would not be allowed to keep my baby. I was mortified at having caused them such shame and horror. I felt I had to do the thing that everyone told me was 'for the best.' I can relate to so much in your story, and the sadness that 'Sarah' experiences. Although I have many blessings in my life, I too feel that death will be a release from all the pain and guilt. People forget that this situation continued well into the 1980s. Thank you for sharing your story.

I read and reread the email. I am transported back to an autumnal afternoon, nearly a decade before, when Sarah and I met for lunch at the Marine Hotel in Sutton, Sarah's preferred location for our secret meetings. That day, at a window table overlooking Dublin Bay, Sarah was unusually candid about her feelings. She spoke about the bifurcated life she had lived since I was born, internalising the shame that began the moment she discovered she was pregnant, limping through life believing that she was undeserving of happiness, trapped inside a secret. 'I'll be sixty-five soon,' Sarah told me that afternoon. 'And then I'll be seventy, then seventy-five, then eighty. It's a case of wishing my life away.' The thought of Sarah trying to rush through her life, to outrun the secret, filled me with an unbearable sadness. I wondered in that moment how many other women like her, secret birth mothers, carried the same burden? 'I'm just delighted that I am the age I am,' Sarah continued. 'That I'm older now. I say, "Another five years, and then another, and then another, and that will bring me up to eighty." And hopefully it won't be long after that. And that's fine.'

This is the scene that plays out in my mind as I compose a reply to this woman, even though I am at a loss for words. She and Sarah are living a life sentence without parole, I write, unwitting victims of a country – and an entire society – that allowed such cruelty to happen.

A few weeks later there is a reply:

> I just wanted to update you on my situation, as I feel that your book has influenced my decision to speak to a therapist about all that has happened to me. A few weeks ago my son said that he would like to meet me! How wonderful this was to hear, and I readily agreed, and we hope to meet in the next couple of weeks. Emotionally, however, I completely lost it. I think I cried solidly for a week (when the children were not around) and it felt like all the torment, grief, regret, and loss that I had become so good at hiding had decided to emerge. I knew I could not carry on like this, but I did not know where to turn. …An internet search led me to a therapist who stated she had experience of adoption issues. Being made to give away my baby turned me into a quiet, private person. I instinctively turn any questions away from me, but for the first time I have opened up and told my story to someone other than my husband. I have cried a lot. …The grief of 'what might have been' will never go away … I want to live and be happy, not to be so low at times that death seems preferable. … It's not that you want to die, as death is scary. It's more like not wanting to be alive, to escape the pain. I recognize now that I have had periods of depression because of losing my child and being prevented from mourning the loss.

I print out this email and place it in my wallet. It becomes my talisman. In the moments when the weight of the memoir becomes too crippling – when I am excoriated in the online-comments section of an article or review, or taken to task for a perceived greediness in searching out my past – I take it out and reread it. We are strangers, this woman and I, and yet we have found resonance in the other, united in a loss caused by forces beyond our control. Her words and courage ignite in me something that feels a lot like love.

The emails and messages that arrive are mostly from women, but every now and then a male reader writes. One man, an adoptee from Dublin, writes to tell me of the happiness he shares with a wife of over two decades and two daughters. 'But there is always that missing piece of the jigsaw that nonadopted people just don't understand. They say, "Sure, you have a great family, shouldn't that be enough?" and it is, but there is always that gap.' Briefly reunited with his birth mother two decades earlier, this man discovered that his birth parents had also married and that he was the secret eldest of four. But horrified by his reappearance in her life, his birth mother begged that he stay away. Compliant, he has instead scoured social-media websites intent on finding his biological siblings. But his searches have yielded no leads. 'I have now given up,' his email ends, 'as I feel that it is not meant to be.' Another man writes to say that his mother was absent from his life from the age of four until fourteen. His email is short and to the point: 'Many emotional times. I have now been married for 60 years and we hug a lot. Keep well.' An Irish man leaves a private comment on the contact page of my website. There is no salutation or signature. It simply reads, 'I found my Dad thirty-five years ago. I met with him once since then. He always called me about once a month, but I couldn't call him because I was a secret from his family. He didn't call for the longest time, and then I found out he passed away unbeknownst to me. Now I know nothing. It feels very sad and angry at the same time. I just wanted to share that because there is no one else to share it with.' One correspondent writes of the grief of losing a child to adoption. His is the only email I received from a birth father. He thanks me for my honesty, observing, 'Adoption brings a sense of shame and secrecy to all triad members. I have struggled with my daughter's adoption from day one. Reaching out to her and not being able to put adoption behind me has caused pain to my wife (the birth mother), the adoptee, and the children we have raised.'

A man reaches out to me on Facebook from the United States. Born in Ireland and sent for adoption to America – one of Ireland's 'banished babies' – he is desperate to find his mother, still living in Ireland, and to stitch together the missing threads of his early life. 'I do not know what she looks like, her voice, I really know nothing,' he tells me. 'I have to admit I cried quite a bit reading your book and it felt great to cry.' The man tells me that he is soon to travel to Ireland for the first, and possibly the last, time. He has two tasks. 'I have to figure out, a) did she ever get to hold me? Sometimes I think not. And b) who I was named after?' Can I offer some advice, he asks? May we speak by phone? On a humid July afternoon, while my two daughters are at swim-team practice, I dial his number. The man's voice is sonorous, deep, shaded with a southern drawl. An Irish 'search angel' has recently provided him with his mother's address in Dublin, he tells me. Should he knock on her door? I am now in my mid-60, the man says softly, and my mother is 90 years old: 'Time is not on either of our sides.'

I had previously given little thought to the wider familial circle beyond the adoptee and birth parent. Focused on my pain and that of Sarah, in my mind our story did not allow room for others. But just days after publication, after an appearance on a British television chat show, emails touching upon the wider intergenerational effects of adoption on families began to flood in. One was from a woman in London writing to tell me about the decades-long depression her mother had suffered in the wake of losing her first child to adoption:

> What followed was decades of trauma and mental health issues – a tragic time into which my brother and I were born. ... She was too bereft to cope with us. He and I have experienced many bouts of depression because of the attachment problems as a result of our mother's unresolved trauma. ...There really are no winners in the adoption process, so many layered and complex sad tales that ripple through the generations.

Many more write to share stories of family lines poisoned by the legacy of secrecy and shame. A secret adoptee emails from the United States to report that 'like your birth mother, mine keeps me locked in a box in the dark recesses of her brain and thinks her children wouldn't understand or love her if she revealed her secret. I am absolutely convinced it has affected her relationship with the children she raised, but that is not something she is willing to consider.' Another woman, raised in Ireland but now living in Denmark, writes to me about her mother's lifelong dislocation. 'She never found her [birth] mother, and the pain was enormous for us children too.' Regret flows freely. 'My mother had two children that she had to give up,' reports another woman from North America:

> One of these children, my sister, made contact with me when I was twenty-two years old. I am so grateful that she did. She became one of the most important people in my life. We were separated by the Atlantic Ocean, she in the United Kingdom, and me in the United States. We visited as often as possible. Unfortunately, she died five years ago from cancer. Twenty-four years with her was not enough time.

Among the constellation of stories that fill my in-box, the longer, darker arc of adoption becomes apparent: abuse, addiction, attachment disorders, trauma and depression. These emails are both intimate and insistent. They catch my heart off guard. A woman, sent from Asia to Canada as a baby, writes to tell me of her abusive adoptive mother. '[She] always throws things back in my face, starting with my biological mother who "dumped me in the trash",' she writes:

> When I played with the safety pins on my comforter, she would hold my hands out and prick them with the pins. ...Since the very beginning she's used some sort of mind manipulation that made me think I was a terrible child. And to some degree I think I was.

Another adoptee writes to describe the effect that adoption has had on her mental health. Unlike so many others, this woman's birth mother existed on the peripheries of her life while growing up, a secret known to this woman's wider adoptive family but not to the child given away:

> I could go on and on and on about the exhaustingly complicated duality of my life. I don't want to get too personal, but I dislike intimate relationships and I would call myself a loner. I have had mental illness for the better half of twenty years. ...If I can be completely honest, at times I wish I had never been born. ... I know that sounds harsh, but I was often not given the gift of honesty growing up.

Another woman from Ireland writes to tell me how adoption has coloured her life in a way that few can understand: 'I am not in a relationship. I live alone and know that I will never have children of my own. I am sorry if this is really grim, but it's honestly how I feel. ...I have spent my life looking for acceptance, and I believe that my biggest lesson now is to love and accept myself. Which is something I struggle with on a daily, sometimes hourly basis.'

For some the shadow cast by adoption proves too much. An Irish man, Jim, writes to share a letter he wrote and published years before in an Irish newspaper. It tells the story of his aunt Kate who gave birth to a son in Sean Ross Abbey in 1951. The child lived at Sean Ross until he was sent to America at the age of four. Decades later, in an attempt to help his aunt, Jim decided, with Kate's permission, to look for her son. After six months he located a record for the young man in America:

> I wasn't prepared for what came next. I had to tell Kate that her son had died four years earlier in very sad circumstances. His adopted family, still grieving, were lovely and did everything to lessen my aunt's grief. On his first night in his new home his older adopted brother told me that when they were putting him to bed, he pleaded with them not to take his booties. I suppose in his little mind he was thinking, they have taken everything else off me, at least let me keep my shoes. In his twenties depression took over and it was all downhill from there. Sadly, Kate died two years later, a broken woman. ...Two people who once separated lived shattered lives to the day they left this earth.

***

It is late in the afternoon, Christmas Day, December 2014, when my cell phone beeps with an incoming text message. I am in the kitchen of my home in Washington, DC, with my husband Dan, preparing dinner. Through the doorway I can hear the chatter of my three children playing in the living room. My elderly father-in-law is snoozing on the couch. The mood is light, festive. I wipe my hands on my apron and swipe my phone to read the message. It is from Sarah, my birth mother: 'Happy Christmas to u all. Hope ur enjoying ur Christmas dinner and that Santa brought lots of toys. A very happy new year too. Lots of love, Sarah xxxxx.' I glance at the clock. It is late in the evening in Dublin where Sarah lives. I feel a pang of guilt for not reaching out earlier in the day. I type quickly a response: 'Happy Christmas back! Hope you had a lovely day. Santa came and was very generous. …Much love to you all. Sending hugs. Xxxxx.' Dan approaches and hands me a glass of wine. I show him Sarah's message and he smiles. I place my phone back on the kitchen counter and return to the culinary task at hand.

I have not heard from Sarah since that December day. This is the twist in my story. Although I obtained Sarah's enthusiastic permission to write the book – on the condition that her identity remain anonymous, a pledge that my editors at Penguin Random House honoured – silence descended after Sarah sent that cheery Christmas text. There was no argument, no harsh words exchanged; Sarah chose to just simply vanish from my life. At that time I had not yet begun to write the memoir, but in January 2016, three months prior to publication and against the advice of my editor, I sent an electronic copy of the book to Sarah and my two known birth siblings. In the accompanying email I offered to change any inaccuracies or to delete passages that Sarah found painful. Neither Sarah nor my birth siblings responded.

In the intervening five years I have attempted to fill the silence with twice-yearly texts, sent on Sarah's birthday and Mother's Day. I keep these digital missives short and loving, updating her with small victories in the lives of my children – Caoimhe's delight at mastering how to ride a bike, Liam's pride at entering middle school, Neasa's joy at learning to read. In these messages I ask nothing of Sarah. I tell her that I am thinking of her and that I love her. There is never a response. The occasional email to my birth siblings yields the same silence. Just in case, I keep my social-media accounts – containing updates and pictures of my children – available for public viewing. Every few months I enter Sarah's name into the digital Irish death notices. It is only when the search page reveals a 'nothing found' response that I realise I am holding my breath.

'Do you think you've lost her all over again now, Caitríona?' a prominent Irish radio talk-show host asked me live on-air in early 2017.

'Were you in hindsight a little tough on her?' This interview came a week after a celebrity panel of Irish commentators – in a tense, live discussion – reviewed my memoir for a radio book club on the same program. During that thirty-minute segment some of the panellists labelled my search for Sarah as obsessive and predatory, likening the questions I posed to my parents Liam and Mary about their decision to adopt and our first days as a family to the 'Spanish Inquisition.' Far worse, Sarah, who I prayed was not within earshot of a radio at that moment, was portrayed as ruthless and manipulative. At this stage, nearly one year after publication, I was used to being vilified for searching for Sarah, for my alleged betrayal of Liam and Mary, and for the perception that the book alone had led to the estrangement between Sarah and me. (I would never, ever become accustomed to the cruelty in the media directed toward Sarah.) As the first Irish adoptee of my generation to write a memoir about adoption, I knew I would be fair game for criticism; this was my price to pay for telling the truth. Adoption is widely viewed in Ireland as an act of rescue, not of forced trauma, and there remains an astonishing lack of awareness about the lifelong distress to the adoptee. Although I lost not just my mother but my name, my identity and my entire biological family when I was just two days old, I was expected to express nothing but gratitude for my good fortune in finding a loving adoptive family. 'Sure, didn't it all work out?' people often say to me, with just the slightest undercurrent of irritation, unable – or perhaps unwilling – to acknowledge the giant, jagged hole in my heart that persists to this day.

I can be dismissed and disparaged by critics, judged as too needy or too self-absorbed, but the emails and social-media messages that arrived following the publication of *An Affair with My Mother,* a small portion of which I outline in this essay, do not lie. These voices and stories weave a heart-breaking tapestry of pain. They may tell stories from an Ireland of another time, but they are proof that the past does not remain in the past – it becomes the present. Grateful to be heard, they bring Ireland's legacy of forced adoption sharply into focus, shaping an argument that is incontrovertible: that the collusion between the Irish church, state and society toward unmarried mothers – and the continuing legacy of secrecy and silence that persists – ruined lives and continues to do so today.

The American academic Brené Brown, whose work on vulnerability has gained global attention, says that in order to survive, shame needs three ingredients: secrecy, silence, and judgment.[4] In Ireland, shackled to a legacy of misogyny and morality toward the stigmatised 'fallen' mother and her illegitimate child, the country remains awash in secrecy, silence and judgment. Shame has stoked a pervasive sense of cultural silence across Ireland. It has governed and stymied relationships for generations, exposing a hinterland of grief, regret and memories lost and stolen. Ireland may have recently undergone a transformative cultural shift amid a weakening of the church's influence, leading to referendums legalising equal marriage and abortion, yet for Sarah and me – and for those who reached out following the publication of the memoir – very little has changed. I am 47 years old and a proud citizen of Ireland, and yet I still cannot access my birth records, a human right afforded to all other citizens. In the Irish parliament a proposed adoption bill is at odds with adoption legislation in Northern Ireland and the United Kingdom, blocking Irish adoptees from their rights to basic information such as a birth certificate and early life files. The bill as it stands demonises adoptees as a threat to their natural parents' well-being and keeps them, in the interests of Catholic 'respectability,' shut out from the facts of their own life. Thousands of Irish adoptees simply want to know their own story, and yet they are infantilised, pathologised and ostracised, excluded from a closed bureaucratic system that insists on silence and remains indifferent to human suffering. Thousands of innocent women like Sarah, whose children were forcibly taken from them, have no clear way of accessing their files. A dedicated independent archive of institutional and care-related records must be established to give explicit rights of access to personal files for all those who were institutionalised in any setting, all adopted people and others put in informal care, and all parents whose children were taken from them.

Shame corrodes the very part of us that believes we are capable of change, says Brené Brown, but if you douse shame with empathy, it cannot survive. For 15 years I tried to extinguish Sarah's shame with more empathy and compassion than I ever thought possible, but to no avail. But Brown believes that there is also another way to eradicate shame: by telling our stories. Shame cannot survive if it is spoken aloud. Truth-telling and honesty strip away its power. For every email or social-media message written in response to my book, for every story shared, a little shame – I like to believe – was chipped away.

My beloved father Liam, the great love of my life, prays a special intention every Saturday that Sarah and I will be reunited. He has been doing so now every week for the five years since we drifted apart. Twice or three times a year, usually during my trips home to Dublin, Liam will ask – with an abundance of gentleness – how Sarah is, and whether I have had 'any word.' It breaks my heart every time to tell him no. In reality I fear that Sarah has vanished from my life for good, but my father's faith that she will one day return keeps me grounded, as do those who wrote to me to share their own stories. I may have lost Sarah but I have found humanity – and family – in the correspondence that arrived after *An Affair with My Mother* made its way into the world. In the cathedral of silence and shame that has settled over Ireland following generations of historical abuse, this correspondence proves that there is redemption to be found in a shared – and open – grief. The late Irish poet Seamus Heaney wrote in his poem 'Crossings' that 'It steadies me to tell these things,' and I found a grounding – and liberation – in painting a truthful account of growing up adopted and of the intense, furtive 'affair' that Sarah and I conducted.[5] So too did those who courageously wrote to me – a stranger – to share their own stories. These people were not seeking justice nor closure, but simply a desire to bring their truth into the light.

If I were ever to see Sarah again, even if it were just for five minutes, I would read aloud to her the last paragraph from the email sent by the young Irish birth mother that I carry still in my wallet. I have long since committed it to memory. It would be proof that despite all the tragedy that Sarah has endured, her courage in allowing me to share our story, and to shed light on the legacy of forced adoption in Ireland, has brought some healing to others:

> The things 'Sarah' said to you resonated with me, made me face things, and hopefully will help me to heal. So, if and when you are in contact with her again, please thank her too. Indirectly, you both may have saved my life.

CHILDREN IN STATE CARE

SEVENTEEN

Transitional Justice, Trauma and Healing: Indigenous Residential Schools in Canada[1]

Rosemary Nagy

Introduction

Canada's 'Indian' residential school system ran from the late 1800s until 1996. Funded by the federal government and operated by the Catholic, Methodist, Presbyterian, Anglican and United churches, the residential school system affected over 150,000 Indigenous children, their families and communities. Residential schools were a central element in the broader colonial project of 'cultural genocide' of Canada's Indigenous peoples.[2] Designed to 'kill the Indian in the child,'[3] residential schools aimed to disrupt the transmission of Indigenous language, culture and identity from one generation to the next. The logic of settler colonialism dictates the removal of Indigenous peoples because they are obstacles to taking possession of the land: this is the overarching motivation behind cultural genocide.[4] Children as young as four years old were removed, often forcibly, from their families and communities in order to be assimilated into settler society that was in reality unwilling to accept them. Alongside the everyday suffering of loneliness, hunger, illness, racism and neglect, there was pervasive and systemic sexual, physical and psychological abuse.

Genocidal intent marks a clear difference between the Canadian and Irish cases of family separation and institutionalised child abuse. Nonetheless, there are striking parallels between the two systems, perhaps not surprisingly given the global popularity of the industrial/boarding school model, especially across Christian, European empires.[5] In both the

Canadian and Irish situations, there were similar patterns of discipline and abuse, as well as collusion between state and churches in avoiding accountability. Furthermore, individual experiences of sexual, physical and psychological abuse occurred within, indeed were made possible by, broader structures of violence. As Paul Farmer writes, 'Human rights violations are not accidents; they are not random in distribution or effect. Rights violations are, rather, symptoms of deeper pathologies of power and are linked intimately to the social conditions that so often determine who will suffer abuse and who will be shielded from harm.'[6] Neither Canada nor Ireland has sufficiently acknowledged or redressed the structures of violence that precipitated the establishment of residential institutions and comprise part of their ongoing and intergenerational legacies.

To paraphrase the Chair of Canada's Truth and Reconciliation Commission (TRC), Justice Murray Sinclair, residential schools wrought damage for seven generations, and it will take seven generations to heal.[7] The enduring impacts of Ireland's carceral institutions will similarly require long-term reparative measures that redress the stigmatisation and marginalisation of those who were detained, their families and similarly located social groups who continue to experience discrimination – and some also punitive confinement – in Irish society. This chapter is concerned with the ways that struggles for redress and recovery are mediated by discourses of trauma and healing. Indigenous healing paradigms and 'social suffering' frameworks are infused with demands for structural justice in the face of ongoing violence, yet trauma discourse can be taken up in narrowly therapeutic ways that individualise harm and pathologise victims. With regard to redressing structural violence, I argue that we should not overpromise what transitional justice can deliver. Rather, we are well advised to follow Balint, Evans and McMillan's conceptualisation of transitional justice as a set of tools for placing intersecting structural inequalities within a broader 'justice agenda' that will extend beyond the life of transitional justice mechanisms.[8] However, in so doing, we need to pay attention to how articulations of suffering are produced and received.

In the following, I first expand on the proposed role of transitional justice and the importance of attending to the collective interpretive resources or hermeneutical frameworks of the dominant majority. Second, I sketch the relationship between structural violence and intergenerational impacts in Canada and Ireland and point toward frameworks of 'social suffering' and 'Indigenous healing.' I then turn to the doubled-edged impacts of trauma discourse in survivors' struggles for redress. While trauma talk may authenticate victimhood and claims for justice, it is also conjoined with the biopolitical management of marginalised groups. In the last section, I analyse the work of the Canadian TRC, which operated from 2010 until 2015. I argue, one the one hand, that the aesthetic framing and predominance of healing talk during the TRC hearings served to facilitate the colonial pathologisation of Indigenous peoples as unfit for self-determination. On the other hand, the TRC did much to disrupt colonial narratives of 'education policy gone wrong'[9] and 'sad chapter in our history.'[10] This occurred through the centring of Indigenous culture in the TRC process, the TRC's finding of cultural genocide, and recommendations pertaining to the reform and dismantling of contemporary colonial laws and institutions. In these regards, the TRC was able to 'place responses to indigenous injustice within a broader "justice agenda".'[11] The chapter concludes with brief reflections on what Irish readers might draw from the Canadian case.

I write as a white settler Canadian who lives in the traditional territory of the Anishinabek Nation. I do my best to draw from Indigenous scholars, and I approach my work from the perspective of encouraging settler accountability. I attended five of the TRC's seven national events and thus draw on my participant-observations in this chapter.[12] While the chapter describes the psychosocial fallout of institutionalised violence, my aim is to do so as a call for justice, not pathologisation. I acknowledge here the resistance of children in these institutions, as well as the resilience and self-empowerment of victim-survivors and their communities.[13] There are three main groups of Indigenous peoples in Canada: First Nations, Métis and Inuit. There is much diversity amongst these groups; for example, there are 634 First Nations communities in Canada (i.e. 'bands' that are usually based on land reservations), and over seventy reported Indigenous languages. Indigenous peoples comprise 5 per cent of the total population in Canada, and 52 per cent of Indigenous peoples live in metropolitan areas.[14] I generally use the term Indigenous unless specifying the identity of an author's nation (sometimes in parentheses). 'Aboriginal' is a colonial term and has generally fallen out of use, although the term is present in older works, especially state documents.

Transitional Justice and Epistemic Frameworks

Multiple chapters in this volume attest to the need for a transitional justice framework in Ireland in order to develop a holistic, meaningful and legitimate response to human rights abuses perpetrated by the Church and State.[15] At the same time, authors caution against 'overconfidence' in what transitional justice might achieve due to its limited ability to address structural violence and root causes of conflict.[16] Balint, Evans and McMillan argue for a reconceptualisation of transitional justice whereby the conventional focus on individual injury is supplanted by the idea of 'structural harm.' Colonialism, gender inequality and other unjust societal arrangements comprise the 'more routine and hence "invisible" damage' that 'endures beyond the moment of [exceptional] violation, shaping and constraining the conditions of life experienced by both the dominant population and particular groups.'[17] As stable liberal democracies, neither Ireland nor Canada are in transition in the manner of a post-conflict or post-authoritarian rupture between past and future. In this context, the continuities of structural violence rise to the fore, and a transitional justice framework must reject misleading claims of 'historic' injustice.

Rather, as Balint et al. argue, in a stable democracy we should design redress measures that 'facilitate a process of transition' from 'unjust relations to just relations.'[18] They write:

> Rather than pursuing redress for past injustice as a singular goal, transitional justice may be directed towards ensuring substantive justice through prompting societal, political and economic change that addresses the structural underpinnings of harm and injustice in societies.[19]

Articulating structural harm within a transitional justice framework enables us to imagine a shared future that is justice-based, rather than welfare-based.[20] While transitional justice mechanisms might instigate longer-term transformations, it is important to remember that discursive frameworks justify and embed structural harms. Consequently, discriminatory discourses and practices continue to be 'available for appropriation' and must also be addressed.[21]

Miranda Fricker identifies two forms of discriminatory 'epistemic injustice.' 'Testimonial injustice' occurs when speakers are denied credibility and their claims are dismissed due to prejudice on the part of the listener. 'Hermeneutical injustice' refers to the denial of an appropriate conceptual framework in which to articulate harm.[22] I am especially interested in hermeneutical injustice and how a strongly victim-centred truth telling body like Canada's TRC must work within and against the interpretive frameworks of the dominant majority. The production and circulation of knowledge in a society is linked to relations of power. This is amply evident in the epistemological violence of residential schools, which sought to eradicate Indigenous ways of knowing and being. Further, settler colonial ways of knowing the 'Indian problem' affect how testimony of trauma is heard and understood. As Koggel writes, we cannot simply assume that when truth is told, a healing will happen and we can put the past behind us. Rather, we must attend to and transform the ongoing Canada-Indigenous relationship 'as it is shaped by and emerge[s] from the collective interpretative resources of colonisers.'[23]

A transitional justice framework, with its emphasis on the right to truth, accountability and remedy, would arguably address some of the many instances of testimonial injustice that are embedded in Ireland's current redress schemes. Testimonial injustice includes the denial of access to adoption and other records; the existence of a 'gagging order' on survivors of industrial schools in exchange for compensation; the exclusion, side-lining and even destruction of survivor testimony (as has just occurred with the Mother and Baby Homes Commission).[24] To redress testimonial injustice, centring on the experiential knowledge of victim-survivors will be key, as will be providing access to records and archives so that state narratives can be challenged.[25] But, as Enright and Ring note in this volume, victim-survivor truths may be 'rendered unintelligible by inadequate legal and social-hermeneutical resources,' particularly when the state seeks to maintain the status quo.[26] In Ireland, dominant interpretive frameworks pathologise the survivors of Ireland's carceral institutions and refuse to acknowledge or tackle Ireland's treatment of 'women, children, and others marginalised by poverty, sexism, racism, ageism, and ableism both in the past and in the present.' Thus, transitional justice mechanisms or processes in Ireland will also have to confront hermeneutical injustice.[27]

Intergenerational Effects, Social Suffering, and Indigenous Healing

This section demonstrates how the intergenerational effects of state oppression and childhood abuse are intertwined with the continuation of structures of violence that precipitated the establishment of residential institutions and comprise part of their ongoing legacies. To borrow Johann Galtung's wording, acute violence and structural violence are 'two sides of the same coin.'[28] Within the Irish and Canadian schools, there were familiar patterns of discipline and abuse, such as humiliating punishment for children who wet the bed, assigning numbers to children rather than calling them by name, and institutional actors ignoring or denying children's complaints of physical and sexual abuse.[29] These individual instances of abuse are embedded within broader systems of oppression. Ireland's carceral institutions systematically targeted persons deemed morally, socially, and/ or racially inferior, women and their children in particular.[30] Similarly, the settler colonial objective of land dispossession interlocked with racist, sexist narratives of 'civilising the savage.'[31] These structural features are inseparable from the infliction of individual and collective injuries, their ongoing effects and the persistence of discriminatory or colonial attitudes, practices and institutions that undermine guarantees of non-repetition in the present and future. Thus, it is erroneous to characterise either situation as a case of 'historical abuse.'

In Canada, it is quite common to speak of 'intergenerational survivors' due to the impact of the schools over 'seven generations.' Certainly not everyone experiences these impacts, but the intergenerational effects of residential schools include loss of language, culture and identity, family violence and dysfunction, alcohol and substance use, mental health issues and high suicide rates.[32] Despite the ostensible purpose of residential schools, the substandard education and half-day manual labour system did not prepare students for a place in the new economy beyond 'jobs that the white man don't want to do.'[33] The TRC reports that poor educational attainment has contributed to 'chronic unemployment or underemployment, poor housing, substance abuse, family violence, and ill health.'[34] The children of residential school survivors often have more difficulty in school – a system that remains largely closed to Indigenous history, knowledge, and ways of knowing.[35] Today, 70 per cent of Canada's Indigenous languages are endangered.[36] Yet, studies show that having conversational knowledge of an Indigenous language is related to fewer difficulties in school and lower suicide rates for Indigenous youth.[37] While not everyone who attended the schools experienced sexual or physical abuse, many children were deprived of love and affection and the opportunity to learn how to be a parent. Cycles of abuse, dysfunctional parenting and compromised family systems are not uncommon.

The intergenerational effects of residential school additionally combine with ongoing colonial violence in a vicious circle. Examples of ongoing colonial violence include the over-policing, under-protection and over-incarceration of Indigenous peoples, disproportionate rates of child welfare apprehension, resource extraction on Indigenous land and the crisis of thousands of missing and murdered Indigenous women, girls and Two-Spirit persons (MMIWG2S) over the last 40 years – which itself has also been named genocide by a recent National Inquiry.[38] As a result of the cumulative impacts of colonialism, including residential schools, Indigenous peoples in Canada experience disproportionately lower educational, employment and quality of life measures in comparison to non-Indigenous citizens, as well as disproportionately higher rates of suicide, premature mortality, and gender-based violence.[39]

In the Irish institutions, conditions were similar to those in Canada, including 'forced confinement, hunger, illness, forced religiosity, physical and emotional abuse, economic exploitation, isolation, and indignity.'[40] The largest study of victim-survivors found that almost one third experience regular illness and another third regularly experience physical illness requiring hospitalisation.[41] Institutional child abuse can have long-term adverse effects in terms of relationships and life outcomes, physical and mental health problems, premature mortality, alcohol and substance use and suicidal behaviour.[42] In terms of the socioeconomic fall-out, 'over half of Irish residing survivors live in the 20 per cent most disadvantaged areas of the country.[43] This is partly because children were expected to work and received substandard education, much like in the Canadian system. Consequently, there are high rates of illiteracy among Irish victim-survivors.[44]

The intergenerational effects of Ireland's carceral institutions are less recognised than in Canada. In a report submitted by 'Reclaiming Self' to the UN Committee against Torture in 2017, survivors and advocates argue that 'the State has not properly explored and addressed the effect of institutional child abuse that exists in and between many victim families, and also to fully acknowledge the cycle of institutionalism that exists in and between some victim families.'[45] The children of Ireland's institutions suffer marginalisation and stigmatisation 'both during incarceration and post release.'[46] Terri Harrison remarks on her incarceration in a Mother and Baby Home, 'Our adult children inherit the ripple effects of their pariah mother.'[47] On the perpetrator side, Zappone notes the persistence of 'intergenerational institutionalised discrimination' and the need to transform the 'punitive, paternalistic, and misogynistic underpinnings of our institutions of criminal justice, education, medicine, and welfare.'[48]

The (largely anthropological) literature on 'social suffering' focuses on the 'lived experience of distress and injustice' and the 'often close linkage of personal problems with societal problems.'[49] While therapeutic and other sorts of individualised responses to personal distress may offer some remedy, these approaches insufficiently address the social determinants of health and well-being. This is an explicitly *political* claim within the social suffering literature.[50] The argument is not only that poverty, sexism, racism, etc. are instrumental in the unequal distribution of poor health; it is furthermore that structural violence is itself a source of pain and distress and that 'all too regularly bureaucratic responses to social violence intensify suffering.'[51] While the concept of 'social suffering' is most often deployed as tool of critique and analysis, 'solutions' to the problem are linked with social change, ethical transformation, 'positive peace,' and the fulfilment of economic, social and cultural rights.[52] The applicability of these approaches in Ireland seems self-evident given Zappone's quote above, as well as the ways in which survivors experience sometimes degrading or silencing treatment at the hands of the Irish state in its 'redress' efforts.[53]

In the Indigenous context, the fitting response to social suffering is explicitly linked to ideas of Indigenous healing and Indigenous resurgence. These Indigenous-led approaches, which vary across nations and communities, generally focus on revitalising Indigenous knowledges, connections to land, spirit and community and living in balance in one's relations with the human and non-human world.[54] Healing practices include spiritual ceremonies such as sweat lodges, fasting, vision quests, healing circles, 'bush' healing camps, smudging, cedar baths, potlatches, communal meals, powwows and the use of traditional medicines to help detoxify.[55] Intergenerational knowledge transfer through Elders' teachings and (re)learning language also responds to loss of identity and provides 'strength for coping in the mainstream environment.'[56] Indigenous healing and especially Indigenous resurgence movements are also explicitly political responses to a history of genocidal assimilation because they centre on land, culture, and knowledge. Further, these approaches insist on structural transformation within settler society and the return of stolen land; it is colonialism, and not Indigenous peoples, that is in need of a 'cure.'[57]

Trauma Talk: A Double-Edged Sword

In their analysis of the global rise of trauma talk, Fassin and Rechtman note that trauma has become a 'tool used in the demand for justice' because it is conjoined with moral recognition of authentic suffering and victimhood.[58] Athabaskan scholar Dian Million documents how the concept of *anomie* (alienation, lack of social and moral rules) enabled settler Canadians in the post-WWII era to diagnose the 'Indian problem' (i.e. maladaptation to settler society) 'without attributing it specifically to their Indian policy, the Indians' loss of land and the destruction of traditional economies, or their residential schooling.'[59] Disciplinary management of the *deviant* Indian thus included disproportionate rates of policing, imprisonment, child welfare apprehension and further efforts at assimilation. However, the rise of victimology in the 1980s, particularly from feminist analyses of incest and rape, opened space for arguing that colonisation, especially residential schools, was a traumatic experience.[60] Indigenous scholars drew on Holocaust studies and developed the concept of *historical trauma* in order to capture the *cumulative, collective* and *intergenerational* effects of 'deliberate conquest, colonisation, or genocide.'[61] They proposed addressing unresolved grief from historical trauma through individual, group and family therapy, spiritual development and traditional practices and ceremony.[62]

Today, 'historical trauma' and 'intergenerational trauma' are omnipresent in the residential schools context, both as a clinical term and in its popular meaning as an 'an open wound in the collective memory.'[63] While the move toward trauma theory valorised Indigenous peoples as *victims* of colonisation, the shift was a double-edged sword. Maxwell notes that although Indigenous healing practices pre-date the trauma paradigm, the increasing 'bureaucratisation and institutionalisation of Aboriginal mental health' has sometimes resulted in trauma being invoked in ways that are inconsistent with broader narratives of Indigenous healing.[64] She notes that health and child development literatures identify residential school attendance as a 'risk factor' in the context of intergenerational trauma. This thereby perpetuates settler-colonial assumptions about the inherent dysfunction of Indigenous parents and facilitates the disproportionate removal of Indigenous children from their families.[65] Some critics suggest that 'historical trauma' may be a general 'idiom of distress' rather than a psychological disorder.[66] Mental health specialists acknowledge the possibility that 'the more popular the trauma concept becomes the more likely individuals are to think about their problems in this way and to produce narratives and attributions that confirm the model.'[67] The result is a fairly totalising discourse, which leaves little space for those who eschew frameworks of victimhood.

As a social construct, historical trauma also has problematic political ramifications. Within the field of mental health, Kirmayer et al propose rethinking the term 'historical' because 'the persistent suffering of Native peoples in North America reflects *not so much past trauma as ongoing structural violence*' [emphasis supplied].[68] The concept of 'historical' trauma feeds into settler colonial myths that residential schools were a 'sad chapter in our history,' as the Prime Minister termed it in his 2008 apology. It also leads to exaggerated claims that (homogenised) culture is 'inherently' healing. Both of these perceptions undermine the call by Kirmayer et al. for not only cultural competence but also *structural* competence in response to racialised poverty, discrimination, unemployment, the undermining of community autonomy, and the expropriation of land and resources.[69] Furthermore, when settler society takes up trauma talk in pathologising or narrowly therapeutic ways, this creates or reinforces profoundly problematic assumptions about Indigenous self-determination. To paraphrase Million, if all Indigenous peoples are victims of colonisation and/or residential schools, wherein lies their resilience or capacity for self-determination? She writes, 'the space of our medicalised diagnosis as victims of trauma is not a site wherein self-determination is practiced or defined.'[70]

The global rise of trauma discourse has had similarly double-edged impacts in Ireland. In the 1990s, Ring writes, increased recognition of the trauma of childhood sexual abuse resulted in Irish courts accepting historic cases that ordinarily would have been denied due to lengthy delays in reporting that create procedural unfairness. Where delays in reporting are deemed a 'reasonable' response to trauma, the courts will extend temporal jurisdiction as an exception to common law authority. Through trauma, the victim of childhood sexual abuse is shifted from a 'liminal figure [in society], into a member of a defined category of victims' and the courts will 'hear matters that might otherwise have remained buried in the past.'[71] The downside, however, is that lawyers challenge the credibility of witnesses who display symptoms of trauma, while those who do not display trauma are deemed inauthentic victims and the trial is halted.[72]

The (re)traumatising nature of cross-examination is well documented, and in this way, trauma may function as a barometer of fairness through the implementation of trauma-informed responses. Trauma as a barometer of fairness is evident in AnneMarie Crean's concern that sealing of the Ryan Commission and other records of industrial and reformatory school-related abuse for 75 years will create undue emotional stress and, for some, a 'continued process of trauma.'[73] Yet, the risk of relying on trauma is that victims are seen as frozen in time, without agency, and pathologised as broken. For instance, the CEO of Caranua, Ireland's Residential Institutions Statutory Fund, referred to industrial school survivors as 'damaged people' and alluded to the criminality of 'these people.'[74] Witnesses or the state may appropriate victims' pain as 'national shame' or 'therapeutic history' that is cleansed by superficial talk of reconciliation and healing the nation.[75] Representations of social suffering may be appropriated, distorted, decontextualised or consumed as spectacle.

McGettrick documents how Ireland's adoption-information rights movement emerged in the 1990s 'against an international backdrop focusing on the psychological damage of adoption and the need for healing and support.' Thus, adoptees framed their demand for access to information in terms of psychological needs rather than civil rights. This strategy ran the risk of 'backfiring' because it could reinforce perceptions of adoptees as potentially dangerous, promiscuous, or delinquent.[76] McGettrick challenges the pathologisation of Irish adoptees, arguing that the offer of counselling and well-being supports without state accountability 'renders invisible and impenetrable the very system that is under investigation in the first place.'[77] In short, we are seeing a welfare-based response on the part of a state that is unwilling to shift to a justice-based response. A similar unwillingness to respect and fulfil basic human rights is evident in Ireland's refusal to provide the survivors of the Magdalen laundries with access to educational and housing support via a promised but undelivered Dedicated Unit, or access to adequate healthcare, or to the administrative records of the Magdalen system – all of which constitutes ongoing structural harm.[78]

Case Study: The Truth and Reconciliation Commission of Canada

In contrast to the 'fragmented, compartmentalised approach'[79] in Ireland, the transitional justice framework is visibly evident in Canada, both as a familiar discourse in Canadian academic and policy circles, and in the structure of the 2007 Indian Residential Schools Settlement Agreement (IRSSA). The largest out-of-court settlement agreement in Canadian history, the $5.1 billion (CAD) IRSSA resolved over 15,000 individual civil suits, 5,000 Alternate Dispute Resolution cases, and 11 class-action suits. The IRSSA provides compensation, funds for commemoration and healing, and a Truth and Reconciliation Commission. The deliberate establishment of a truth commission rather than a national inquiry was due in part to the influence of the growing field of transitional justice, the South African TRC in particular.[80]

The settlement agreement is not perfect. Notably, the IRSSA excludes Métis peoples who went to a different set of residential schools, as well as people who attended day-schools, which operated separately but with the same assimilative objectives.[81] All former students of 'Indian' residential schools receive a Common Experience Payment (CEP) in recognition of loss of culture and systemic neglect, while an Individual Assessment Process (IAP) provides compensation for physical, sexual or psychological abuse.[82] The Common Experience Payment is symbolically important because it recognises the everyday harm of the schools, regardless of whether someone experienced individualised abuse. Notably, the CEP overcomes a previous hermeneutical injustice whereby Canadian tort law did not recognise loss of culture and language (or genocide) as an actionable tort.[83] However, former students not on record are ineligible for compensation, or at least not without significant effort to prove school attendance. Some survivors applying for compensation found the IAP process to be retraumatising and with inconsistent adjudication.

The Assembly of First Nations, as the lead plaintiff for Indigenous claimants, initially wanted the truth commission to have strong investigative powers. But in the face of intractable government opposition to the idea, they soon realised that such powers would hold up the truth and reconciliation process and lead to more litigation. Chief Negotiator Kathleen Mahoney notes in particular how Ireland's Commission to Inquire into Child Abuse had been held up for two years by the Catholic Church contesting subpoenas in court. Some Canadian Catholic entities indicated that they would take the same approach as their Irish counterparts.[84] Consequently, survivors and the TRC were not allowed to 'name names' of individual abusers, and the TRC had no powers of search and seizure. However, Mahoney indicates, 'there wasn't a huge desire to name names in the community that we could discern... "We want to heal." That was the main message we kept hearing over and over again.'[85]

Thus, the TRC was very much a 'victim-centred' truth commission. It focused on the voices and truths of residential school survivors, and prioritised survivors' demand for public education in the face of Canadian indifference and evolving forms of state and church denial.[86] In my participant-observation, the Commissioners frequently noted that the truth commission belonged to residential school survivors because it was 'their settlement.' The mandate also established a Survivor Committee for consultation, participation, and engagement in the TRC process. Commissioner Chief Wilton Littlechild (Cree) is a residential school survivor, while the parents and grandparents of Commissioner Justice Murray Sinclair (Anishinaabe) attended the schools. Commissioner Marie Wilson (settler Canadian), a former journalist, is married to a residential school survivor from Slavey First Nation (her spouse, Peter Kwafki, is also a former premier of the Northwest Territories, where 50 per cent of the population is Indigenous).

The intertwining of truth, healing and reconciliation is present throughout the TRC process. The preamble to the TRC's mandate, written by survivor Chief Robert Joseph (Gwawaenuk First Nation), states:

> There is an emerging and compelling desire to put the events of the past behind us so that we can work towards a stronger and healthier future. The truth telling and reconciliation process as part of an overall holistic and comprehensive response to the Indian Residential School legacy is a sincere indication and acknowledgement of the injustices and harms experienced by Aboriginal people and the need for continued healing. This is a profound commitment to establishing new relationships embedded in mutual recognition and respect that will forge a brighter future. The truth of our common experiences will help set our spirits free and pave the way to reconciliation.[87]

The Commissioners made clear that healing and reconciliation would require work long after the life of the truth commission. The TRC report insists that 'Without truth, justice, and healing, there can be no genuine reconciliation. Reconciliation is not about 'closing a sad chapter of Canada's past,' but about opening new healing pathways of reconciliation that are forged in truth and justice.'[88]

Just before the TRC set to work, then Prime Minister Stephen Harper offered an apology for residential schools in Parliament in 2008. In an unprecedented step, leaders from the five national Indigenous organisations responded to the apology from the floor of the House of Commons. The symbolic reparation of the Prime Minister's apology was important to many survivors because it was the first time the state fully acknowledged that residential schools were wrong. Compared to the 1998 'statement of regret' delivered by the Minister of Indian Affairs from a meeting room, the 2008 apology was significantly more concrete and meaningful. In 1998 the Minister apologised for individual acts of abuse in a manner that isolated abuse from broader structures and failed to acknowledge loss of language and culture. The 2008 apology clearly acknowledges loss of language, culture, parenting skills, separation of families and communities, as well as experiences of abuse. But for some the apology still rang hollow because it failed to acknowledge genocide or even use the word colonialism, and it positioned the schools as a thing of the past.

From 2010 to 2015, the TRC hosted seven national events and 17 community hearing across the country for truth-telling and public education. National events lasted several days and were usually held in large hotels with multiple conference rooms. These events included truth-sharing panels, 'expressions of reconciliation,' archival and artistic displays, churches' listening areas, academic-style panels on broad issues of (de)colonisation, speeches from 'honorary witnesses,' quiet places for smudging or other forms of support, meals and gathering places for survivors, and nightly celebrations of Indigenous culture. Survivors could publicly share their experiences in the hotel ballroom, which was so large that testimony was broadcast on large television screens placed around the room (and they were also livestreamed). Truth-sharing also occurred in smaller public sharing circles that were not videotaped or streamed, or with private statement takers. The TRC collected more than 6,200 survivor statements. In its final event in Ottawa in December 2015, the TRC released its six-volume report. The National Center for Truth and Reconciliation, established as part of the IRSSA, now houses all TRC-related archives, including online recordings of truth-sharing panels and other events held by the TRC.[89]

The centrality of Indigenous cultures and languages during the national events signalled an empowering and affirmative response to the epistemological and ontological violence of the schools. Sharing sessions opened with a prayer, lighting a *qulliq* (an Inuit oil lamp), the burning of sweetgrass, and sometimes a drum song, while a sacred fire burned outside throughout the three or four days of the event. The Bentwood Box, a traditional medicine box carved by Coast Salish artist Luc Marston, sat on the stage with survivors at the Commissioner's Sharing Panel. Depicting the residential school experience, and the strength and resilience of survivors, the front panel shows the face of Marston's grandmother, with tears running down her cheeks and holding up her hands, fingers crooked from being pushed down the stairs by a nun as a child.[90] The Bentwood Box served as a sacred repository for material offerings and 'expressions of reconciliation' such as archival photos, handwritten notes, artistic gifts or books.

The TRC's mandated emphasis on survivors' knowledges resulted, not surprisingly, in the predominance of narrations of individual experiences of loss and abuse, rather than structural harm and societal complicity.[91]

Part of this is due to the fact that for over 20 years in the court system, survivors were sometimes traumatised and even more often challenged and disbelieved when they spoke of abuse. Another reason is the already established prevalence of the trauma and healing framework. And still another influence was what Niezen calls the 'template' created by the TRC. The TRC leaned on the trauma framework, spoke of 'intergenerational survivors' and 'created conditions that encouraged the narration of [unspeakable] traumatic experience, in part by situating it in the context of sacred acts and objects.'[92] Robinson (Stó:lō) notes that this orientation created 'certain expectations of performing victimry for a settler public.'[93] In particular, critics flag the symbolic cleansing of grief through the TRC's collection of tear-soaked tissues for the sacred fire whereas, in contrast, anger and shame were not similarly ceremonialised.[94] Reynaud writes: 'By constantly reminding the audience that it is a "survivor initiative", the TRC implicitly de-legitimises emotions related to injustice (like anger) felt by some of its participants... It throws back the responsibility of "healing and reconciliation" to survivors, by grouping them together as "the survivors".'[95]

There is no doubt that these aesthetic framings were present. They fed into dominant hermeneutic resources, where racism, stereotypes and the trope of the 'Indian problem' lend themselves to viewing Indigenous peoples as hopeless and broken. A significant amount of media coverage fixated on heart-wrenching descriptions of abuse and advanced the truism that talking is healing.[96] In the public eye, this frames truth-telling as therapeutic, providing survivors with catharsis and settlers with the ability to 'feel good about feeling bad.'[97] Consequently, reconciliation has little to do with settler Canadians acknowledging ongoing colonialism and addressing quality of life gaps experienced by Indigenous peoples. Rather, therapeutic closure is an exercise for survivors and settlers alike, 'one that is grounded in survivors' capacity to tell their stories and to confirm their recovery in a performative separation of past and future.'[98]

Despite the 'trend toward narrations of horror,' as Niezen puts it, the TRC created space for other narratives.[99] As I have argued elsewhere, survivors could and did 'disrupt colonial narratives by speaking in their own language; naming their abusers; using their time slot to challenge government policy and structures of colonialism; and expressing anger, resilience, strength and vibrancy.'[100] The TRC final report also highlights how survivors spoke of healing in broad terms. For example, Alma Mann Scott spoke of 'making changes to laws and education systems'; Reverend Stan McKay challenged 'paternalistic assumptions that only Aboriginal peoples are in need of healing'; and former Lieutenant Governor Stephen Point raised issues of land, poverty, and MMIWG2S.[101] The TRC issued a hefty set of 'Calls to Justice' in the areas of justice, treaty rights, education, child welfare, health, MMIWG2S and language and culture. Finally, it made a determination that residential schools were a 'central element' in the Canadian policy of cultural genocide. In these ways, the TRC succeeded in putting Indigenous justice on a broader 'justice agenda.'

While the majority of survivors may not consider criminal accountability to be important or necessary, there was certainly a desire for state accountability. At the TRC hearings, I witnessed many survivors articulating their experiences as (the crime of) genocide. The TRC's mandate prevented it from making a finding of outright genocide as per the Genocide Convention definition. Thus, its use of 'cultural genocide' works around the culpability limitation while honouring the voices of survivors.[102] The substantive vision of reconciliation as articulated in the 94 Calls to Action turns the public focus toward addressing the problem of colonialism and not Indigenous peoples. However, the *implementation* of substantive changes moving forward will depend in part on a sense of 'social accountability,' which refers to the public demand for answers and the generation of political will to ensure that injustice is not repeated.[103]

Transformative political will is not strongly forthcoming at either the state or societal levels. Canada has yet to acknowledge the finding of cultural genocide. While Canada officially recognises seven genocides around the world, it commemorates its own past with a 'National Indigenous People's Day' and a **'National Day for Truth and Reconciliation'** rather than a genocide memorial day.[104] The National Museum for Human Rights has also faced controversy for distancing itself from the TRC's finding of cultural genocide, which McDonald contends is 'an elision… that is hardly unique in settler society.'[105] Indeed, a 2016 survey indicated that 42 per cent of Canadians did not accept the TRC's finding of cultural genocide, while 11 per cent had no opinion.[106] While the Liberal government under Justin Trudeau has committed to following all 94 of the TRC's Calls to Action, at time of writing it has thus far implemented only eleven. Most of these we might call 'easy fixes' such as increased funding for Indigenous art, culture, language and sports. In comparison, Canada's progress with regard to recommendations around structural racism has been 'minimal and cosmetic' at best.[107] This lack of progress impedes justice and healing.

Concluding Reflections

A basic observation underlying this chapter is that, taken together, the Irish case highlights the need for a meaningful state response that fulfils the pillars of transitional justice, while the Canadian case demonstrates the importance of additionally working outside of and beyond the framework of transitional justice. Discriminatory attitudes embedded in 'common sense' knowledges are slow to change. The remedying of structural injustices that shape and inform the long-term impacts of colonialism, sexism, poverty and childhood abuse will not happen overnight. Transitional justice mechanisms are typically short-lived institutions. At best, they can place structural violence within a broader justice agenda that is taken up after their work is done. Alongside recommendations for substantive change, part this task will be contesting the dominant interpretive resources that exist in a society. Namely, key messaging ought to include the ways that individual injury is linked to structural harm, that harm is ongoing not historic and that justice-based responses are required over the long term.

A constant shortfall of the Irish state's response to industrial and reformatory schools, secret adoptions, and Mother and Baby Homes is the denial of an appropriate framework in which to articulate injustice, as well as pathologisation of victim-survivors due to a lack of shared understanding of their experiences of harm and their calls for justice. Redressing the long-term effects of Ireland's carceral institutions, which in some cases may extend intergenerationally, requires a broad social justice agenda that will shift Ireland toward more just relations amongst all citizens. The dominance of particular interpretive frameworks and conceptual resources is a form and effect of structural violence and inequality. Consequently, as we see in the Canadian case, the public reception of survivor testimony in an official forum may nonetheless be filtered through these dominant frameworks. There is thus far a limited sense of social accountability on the part of many settler Canadians. Indigenous resurgence movements and settler allies continue to call for settler reckoning. Some of these people will draw on the work of the TRC as a resource, while others in the Indigenous resurgence movement have rejected the truth and reconciliation enterprise almost entirely because they feel it is so contaminated with colonial hermeneutics.

I suggest, however, that the experiential knowledge of victim-survivors in an official and public forum does serve to widen the hermeneutical framework. But it is also helpful to be attuned to the 'sociology of knowledge' behind the ways in which articulations of harm and suffering have been expressed and constrained in the past. As Matt James astutely observes in the Canadian context, we need to situate the 'TRC's particular approach to truth and reconciliation as the product of dispersed processes of political interaction and social governance.'[108] While the TRC explicitly identified Indigenous knowledges and cultures as an epistemic resource, the aesthetic framings around healing were insufficiently attuned to the potential for pathologising settler responses to testimony to trauma. The TRC's finding of cultural genocide significantly challenged the dominant interpretations of residential schools as 'benign colonialism.' Unfortunately, however, the finding of cultural genocide came only in the final stages of the TRC's operation; Commissioners officially shied away from it until at least 2012, using instead the term 'assault' on Indigenous children, families and culture.[109] A clearer position on genocide and structural harms from the outset would have better framed survivors' testimony for the settler audience. Nonetheless, the TRC's substantive recommendations have helped place Indigenous justice on the longer-term agenda and hold the state to account for structural transformations that might pave the way toward more just relations.

Eighteen

'I Just Want Justice': The Impact of Historical Institutional Child-Abuse Inquiries from the Survivor's Perspective[1]

Patricia Lundy

What do survivors of institutional abuse need in order to feel that justice has been realised? How can a sense of redress – of justice achieved – be measured? This essay explores such questions by describing the results of an empirical research study investigating Northern Ireland's Historical Institutional Abuse Inquiry (HIAI), which focused on physical, sexual and emotional neglect in children's residential institutions between 1922 and 1995. The research study, carried out primarily in Northern Ireland, provided detailed analysis of survivors' interaction with the inquiry and sought to gauge victims' needs and expectations revealed by their participation in the HIAI. Building on the limited research already done in the field, the study's conclusions suggest that a survivor's sense of justice and redress is affected not just by the original crime but also by her or his involvement in the criminal-justice systems set up to investigate such offenses. This study explored survivors' justice needs constituting redress – including, for example, acknowledgment of abuse, attitudes toward apology, accountability, opportunities to tell their stories and symbolic and financial reparation – as well as their assessment of the inquiry's legal processes.

In November 2009 the Northern Ireland Assembly voted to establish an inquiry to investigate the scale of child abuse in institutions run by the Catholic church and the state.[2] The agreed terms of reference for the inquiry were announced on 31 May 2012. Unlike current UK investigations that focus on sexual abuse, the HIAI covered physical and emotional abuse, neglect and unacceptable practices between 1922 and 1995 in children's residential institutions.[3] The HIAI had two components: a confidential acknowledgment forum offering survivors an opportunity to tell their stories, and a statutory inquiry in which evidence was given in public.[4] In 223 days of hearings conducted between January 2014 and July 2016, almost all of which were held in public, the inquiry investigated twenty-two institutions. The inquiry published its report in January 2017 documenting evidence of systemic failings in residential institutions run by the state, local authorities, churches and charities. Its conclusion noted 'sexual, physical, and emotional abuse, neglect and unacceptable practices across the institutions and homes examined.'[5]

Methods and Analytical Tools of the Research Study

The research study of Northern Ireland's HIAI informing this article was carried out between October 2014 and July 2017.[6] Five focus groups met in Belfast and Derry, with over 75 participants invited to explore their views on redressing historical abuse, express what survivors wanted to see happen and explain why their goals were important.[7] The focus group discussions informed interview themes, and the author subsequently carried out 43 face-to-face interviews with survivors who had attended the HIAI.[8] These interviews reflect the views of a broad cross-section of survivors who were residents in the range of institutions within the inquiry's remit: 25 men and 18 women ranging in age from their late 30s to their 70s, with a mean age of 55 to 65. For the most part interviewees lived in Northern Ireland, but two resided in the Republic of Ireland and four in England. The study's primary aim was to give survivors an opportunity to express what was important to them – to say what they wanted to say in their own ways. Survivors were asked in interviews to assess their experiences of the HIAI and to indicate what was needed in order to feel that justice has been realised.[9] The interviews were recorded, transcribed and thematically analysed. The justice needs expressed by survivors provided the benchmarks to assess the inquiry. Anonymised transcripts of survivors' evidence available on the HIAI website were also analysed. In the statutory inquiry in which evidence was given in public, survivors were asked to explore and comment on the question of redress, apology and memorialisation in anticipation of its own recommendations to the Northern Ireland Executive in those areas. Of the 246 survivors who gave evidence, 177 had responded to HIAI counsel's questions about redress recommendations.[10] This article explores those responses and assesses the inquiry from the perspective of survivors; it therefore considers two different points in time and context of questioning – both testimony to the inquiry and private interviews with the author of this article.

Conceptualising Justice Needs

A key challenge in researching responses to historical institutional abuse involves clarifying what survivors require to achieve justice – that is, conceptualising what justice means from their perspective. Because only limited studies examining what constitutes justice for survivors of historical abuse exist, this aspect of the study's research was central.[11] Although survivors clearly have rights, they often have diverse expectations as well as multiple goals. Additionally, their priorities may evolve over time at different stages in the process of seeking justice.[12]

Justice, as Robyn Holder aptly puts it, is essentially a social, legal and political value embedded in individual thinking as well as institutional design.[13] Anne-Marie McAlinden and Bronwyn Naylor view procedural justice as the 'optimal mode of redress for victims of historical institutional abuse.'[14] Procedural-justice theorists emphasise that process matters as much as outcome, and that survivors are satisfied with the justice system when they perceive its actions as respectful and fair.[15] Participation, control and the right to have a voice are components singled out as important in the process.[16] Significantly, procedural-justice theory makes clear that survivors are affected not just by the original crime, but also by their involvement in the subsequent criminal-justice process.

Procedural-justice scholarship about survivors of sexual violence who seek redress through the criminal-justice system reveals telling patterns.[17] Because survivors often feel dissatisfied and even damaged by their interactions with the justice system, its processes can compound the trauma of the original crime, causing additional psychological harm.[18] Such research also reveals that how survivors experience the justice system has profound implications for their recovery from the initial crime.[19] Using many different terms – for example, 'justice needs,' 'justice interests,' 'victims' rightful entitlement' and a 'sense of justice' – researchers concur that a range of needs must be met in order for survivors to achieve a sense of justice.[20] Although prosecuting perpetrators remains integral to the process of coming to terms with sexual violence, on its own such prosecution is an inadequate response to the survivor's desire for justice and repair.

Acknowledgment is often the first stage in the healing process, for it restores a sense of identity and self-worth to survivors. They want society to acknowledge the suffering that they and others experienced, the nature of the abuse, and its impact on their lives; in other words, they want to have what happened to them recognised as wrong and so documented by authorities.[21] Survivors are powerfully motivated by their desire to break a culture of denial, secrecy, and silence that minimised their victimisation.[22] Judith Lewis Herman reports that their most important objective is to receive validation – 'requiring an admission of the basic facts of the crime and an acknowledgment of harm.'[23] Haley Clark further defines validation as an expression that the victim is believed.[24] The admission of harm perpetrated against victims indicates widespread support of them without any implication that they somehow deserved what happened.[25] Daly recognises two forms of achieving vindication, both elements of the survivor's justice needs: through law and through vindication that the perpetrators' acts were both morally and legally wrong.[26] Survivors, in other words, need to know not only that wrongs are recognised but also that wrongdoers are held accountable for their actions – and for the consequences of them. Daly phrases this as 'calling alleged wrongdoers to account and holding them to account.'[27] Connected with this element of justice is the need for truth exposure, whereby perpetrators are asked and expected to answer questions and 'receive consequences.'[28]

A further aspect of justice that survivors identified involves both symbolic and material reparation – a term used to describe a range of measures seeking to rectify the harm caused and, as far as possible, to restore victims to their positions before the acts in question occurred. Taking responsibility for the wrongful acts might be demonstrated through a sincere apology and expression of remorse, but in Herman's study the participants were divided as to an apology's desirability or value.[29] Although some 'expressed a fervent wish for a sincere apology' as a form of justice, others were wary of the potential for manipulative motives behind this act; still others doubted the capability of wrongdoers to provide a 'meaningful' apology, claiming that 'offenders are empathetically disabled.'[30] However, if some survivors view an apology – when underpinned by some form of reparation – as showing respect, it may represent an important justice need for them. Reparations constitute a form of vindication and recognition of the harms suffered that may have therapeutic value and signify a form of punishment. As Nicola Godden says, survivors want the wrongdoer to pay – literally and symbolically – for their actions. But victims of abuse seek more than simply compensation for purely instrumental purposes; that the wrongdoer pays the compensation remains central to their needs.[31]

Additionally, many survivors desire to tell their stories about what happened in their own words – and to be heard in a meaningful way and in a significant setting.[32] The acquisition of voice in justice proceedings that will convey the survivor's value as an individual is also frequently identified as an important need.[33] But David Backer points to 'the apparent division between participants' attitudes about voice in the abstract (usually desirable) and their reflections upon voice in practice (not always rewarding).'[34] Thus, giving survivors the opportunity to tell their stories does not necessarily bring catharsis, for it may even retraumatise and on occasion hinder recovery. Research indicates that the psychological benefits of testimony are generally realised only when societal issues are addressed: uncovering truth, delivering justice and making reparations.[35] Participation involves agency and empowerment, including the survivor's active participation from an early stage in the development, design and implementation of justice responses and involvement in the negotiation of settlements.[36] Because a priority for many survivors is that they and others will be safe from further abuse by the wrongdoers, procedural-justice literature emphasises prevention and public awareness as well.[37] But although the literature on sexual violence provides important insights, it fails to offer any clear consensus about what survivors want in their search for justice. Studies are usually small-scale and generally do not apply identified-justice needs to interrogate justice mechanisms and what they deliver from the standpoint of survivors.[38]

The Empirical Research Findings

This study's analysis of the public-inquiry model sought to understand survivors' justice needs and what participants themselves had to say about how their needs were met by Northern Ireland's HIAI. Survivors are not homogenous, and their needs are diverse, but it was nevertheless possible to identify recurring themes. Drawing on original empirical research via focus groups and interviews, as well as on the scholarly literature examined above, this article identifies eleven primary justice needs articulated by survivors: voice, acknowledgment, vindication (including validation), apology, redress (monetary and symbolic), rehabilitation measures, intergenerational needs, access to records, authoritative historical records, offender accountability and taking responsibility, and prosecution.[39] These form the basis of the study's analytical framework or measurement tool.

Survivors' Self-identified Justice Needs

Most survivors before their participation in the HIAI had never spoken publicly about their traumatic experiences and the effects of abuse on their lives. Of the 43 survivors interviewed, many stated that the motivation to participate in the inquiry was to 'have a voice.' Some said that they wanted to 'tell their story' or 'set the record straight.' They expressed a desire to break the silence, reassign blame and vanquish their shame. A common theme was the moral imperative to testify before the HIAI 'on behalf of the dead' and 'to speak for those unable to testify.' But their desire to testify arose not simply from a sense of obligation to other survivors. It was, rather, perceived as a duty challenging the culture of denial – to inform wider society, raise awareness and insert what had been previously hidden into the public record: 'Some people wanted the world to know. For me it was about actually being able to challenge history and challenge the authority that had been responsible for the condition of our guys.'[40] Survivors, then, wanted their voices to be heard and the abuse to be publicly acknowledged. They longed to be believed and to restore their self-worth.

Many, but far from all, perceived apologies as vindication and validation. Out of the 43 interviews, 63 per cent said that they wanted an apology, whereas 29 per cent believed an apology had no benefit.[41] Analysis of inquiry transcripts and 177 survivors who responded to HIAI counsel's question about whether there should be an apology shows that 22 per cent favoured an apology and 11 per cent said that such acts had no benefit; others simply did not comment. In interview discussions a more nuanced view on apologies emerged. Survivors said that acceptance of an apology was conditional on prerequisites. Apologies had to have consequences and evidence commitment to other justice needs: 'what good is an apology without action?'[42] 'They do owe us an apology. Now an apology in words is one thing... [T]he apology on its own isn't enough, you have to put something on the table. You have to say this is our way of saying this apology.'[43] Respondents thus linked apologies to acts of contrition, public shaming and acknowledgment and acceptance of responsibility. In the absence of these additional criteria the apology meant nothing or lost its value.

Other survivors, however, were cynical and considered apologies pointless, insincere and strategic: 'They're not sincere, they're not heartfelt; it's like this is what we are saying because we've been found out. We're not apologising because it's wrong, we're apologising because it's a media thing and that is what we need to do.'[44] For some survivors, therefore, an apology as a stand-alone gesture is insufficient in meeting victims' justice needs. On the other hand, if perceived as satisfactory, apologies can be an important form of symbolic redress for past wrongs, a finding consistent with research in other settings.[45] Compensation was the most frequently cited justice need in interviews. Almost 80 per cent of the responses, and participants in all five focus groups, prioritised compensation. But the analysis of inquiry transcripts revealed that only approximately 33 per cent had stated that compensation should be recommended. We presume that this lower percentage is contextual, related to the official and public nature of the inquiry. Survivors were reluctant to talk publicly about financial compensation; some were concerned about being seen as 'in it for the money.' During interviews survivors continually stressed that 'it wasn't about the money,' and some found it difficult and offensive to 'put a price' on their suffering: 'I never started this process looking for compensation. I never, 'cause what price is a childhood, what price is my sister's childhood, what price is my mummy's parenting skills, you know. You can't put a price on all of that.'[46]

'Repair' or rehabilitation measures constantly arose as themes in interviews and were discussed at length in focus groups.[47] Survivors emphasised measures to help rebuild shattered lives – by means of healthcare services, long-term counselling, education and training, intergenerational needs and reunion with family. They understood such rehabilitation measures as justice needs, and many felt entitled to ask for redress for their children. Loss of opportunity was also frequently cited as a prime injury. But despite the prominence of themes of rehabilitation in interviews and focus groups, only two per cent had mentioned family compensation and/or intergenerational needs at the inquiry – underscoring not only the role of context but also of a reticence to raise compensation in any official public arena.

The importance for survivors of accessing personal records cannot be overstated; in most of the study's interviews and all five focus groups access to such records emerged as a key justice need: 'Our lives are in a file somewhere and we can't find out who we are.'[48] Most survivors living with the repercussions of historical abuse every day view that abuse as existential. They view the lack of access to their own historical files and their struggles to attain meaningful information as key sources of distress and frustration. They shared accounts of their disappointment when retrieved records were inadequate and/ or heavily redacted: 'an A4 sheet with four to five lines' representing many years spent in residential care.[49] Family medical histories were largely inaccessible to many survivors, leading to a lack of knowledge about their own hereditary traits. Many felt an acute disconnection from the sources of their own personal identities: from parents, birthplace, medical history, origins, home and childhood experiences.

A key motivation for participating in the inquiry was to get 'the truth,' with 23 per cent of respondents specifically mentioning the word 'truth' as a justice need. However, in interviews and focus groups many survivors alluded to truth in different ways. Some clearly sought to find out *why* the abuse happened, questioning why they had suffered and how perpetrators could justify what they had done: 'the biggest thing is why. Why did they do that? Why? Was it in them to... physically and mentally abuse people? Who gave them the right? Who?'[50] For some, as noted above, justice involved gaining access to new information about personal questions and direct access to files: 'I was trying to understand my childhood. I thought I would get to understand me as a person.'[51] But others maintained that they already knew the truth; all they wanted was acceptance of responsibility and accountability.

Analysis of the inquiry transcripts, however, shows that only two per cent of survivors cited access to files as a recommendation. A likely explanation for this discrepancy involves the inquiry's counsel offering only limited options to survivors at the conclusion of their testimony. They were informed that the HIAI had to make recommendations to the Northern Ireland Executive in three areas – some form of apology, memorial and other means of redress – and asked whether there was anything that they wanted to say about these areas. As disclosed in interviews with the author, the question was put to survivors at the end of their testimony when many were tired and overwhelmed by the experience. In addition, the specific questions put by counsel were perceived by some as setting the boundaries to what could and could not be recommended, limiting consideration of a wider range of options.

Redress can also be symbolic. The HIAI specifically asked survivors about their views on a form of memorial paying tribute to victims of historic institutional abuse, but differing views emerged on this issue. In interviews and focus groups some welcomed the suggestion as a form of acknowledgment and remembrance, whereas others strongly opposed such memorialisation as a reminder that might bring yet more pain. Only 13 per cent were in favour, whereas 26 per cent were not; others did not comment. Inquiry transcripts show that 11 per cent were not and 12 per cent were in favour. What is difficult to untangle is whether symbolic redress would have emerged as it did had the inquiry not posed the question of a material memorial – frequently describing it as a statue.

In the study's interviews a significant number of survivors (71 per cent) expressed a strong desire for the criminal prosecution or punishment of their abusers through the courts:

> Absolutely – very clearly – I want to prosecute my abuser. Because I think they should be held accountable. I do think they should be made to see the damage that they caused. Forget the compensation, there's no better feeling for myself than seeing that person who abused me being found guilty. Justice – money couldn't buy that.[52]

For these respondents criminal prosecution was a necessary part of the healing process – indeed, the motivating factor justifying the trauma of giving oral evidence to the inquiry. 'That's a big thing to me; if people are going and giving evidence at an inquiry and naming individuals who have done such horrific crimes on them, there should be prosecutions.'[53] But in sharp contrast analysis of inquiry transcripts shows that only six per cent (11 survivors) stated then that they wanted prosecutions. We again assume that this significant discrepancy relates to the survivor's understanding of permissible boundaries in regard to the inquiry counsel's redress questions. During interviews the importance of accountability as a justice goal was underscored by many survivors (39 per cent), although they did not necessarily mean that they sought criminal prosecution. They wanted individual perpetrators – as well as those who engaged in cover-ups, turned a blind eye, or failed to exercise oversight – to be held accountable. Accountability was thus linked to acceptance of responsibility, vindication and validation: 'When people stand up and say, what we did was wrong – we shouldn't have done that, ...then you get to think, you know what, maybe I'm not scum – maybe I didn't deserve this.'[54]

Did the Inquiry Meet Survivors' Justice Needs?

The study's work led to an analysis of both the potential and the limits of Northern Ireland's HIAI in meeting justice needs from the perspective of survivors who engaged in the inquiry.[55]

Giving Voice: The Trauma of Testifying

The effects of historical childhood abuse are unlikely to be repaired in any one-off process, but the minimum standard should be to do no harm. Ideally, participation in the inquiry would help to make amends for the silencing of childhood victims; yet many were most vulnerable when discussing abuse that they suffered as children. Over half (55 per cent) of those interviewed stated that giving evidence to the inquiry was an 'emotional experience.' Almost half (47 per cent) described that experience as 'traumatising' or 'abusive' – or said that they 'felt vulnerable' (42 per cent). A smaller number reported that participation was an 'intimidating experience' (18 per cent), and others felt 'victimised' (18 per cent). Existing research on the psychological effects of giving testimony to tribunals, commissions, and similar bodies questions the therapeutic effects of such experience; indeed, giving testimony just as often can prove retraumatising as therapeutic.[56] The 'glow quickly fades' once survivors return home, leaving many with a traumatic sense of abandonment:[57]

> This is our life; this is our feelings and emotions. Some people will be able to let it run off them; some people will go home and think I shouldn't have done that and they'll freak.[58]

> I think I took 28 tablets, a full week's medication in the one night... I just
> kept thinking because of the way I was feeling, I have to take my tablets... I
> looked in the mirror, I scared myself... So this went on for about two weeks
> and I tried to get some type of help.[59]

Public inquiries largely require a binary response of yes or no answers
– specific answers to precise questions that Herman views as restricting
'any personal attempt to construct a coherent and meaningful narrative.'[60]
Survivors' disappointment was compounded because they felt that their
voices were not listened to, and they struggled to be heard (37 per cent).
The inquiry processes thus constricted voice – a factor identified as a key
justice need:

> I felt this sense of being cheated. I didn't know why. Until I realised... we
> only got to answer counsel questions. So I felt that I'd been silenced. Now I
> was shaking at the end of it, do not be fooled... I'd come to give my evidence
> and then you're not allowed to give your evidence – you're only allowed to
> answer the questions. The only way you can add on a wee bit is if you run
> on with that question a wee bit, which she kept trying to close me down.[61]

Providing adequate information and managing expectations are crucial
to ensure that participants understand what the inquiry process involves
and make informed choices about how they wish to deal with their needs
for justice. Of the 43 survivors interviewed, 42 per cent said that they
had 'insufficient information and understanding' of the public-hearing
procedures. Just five per cent said that they were well informed. Clearly,
many found themselves in a process that they did not fully understand –
and over which they felt little control:

> I sat there and listened and people were unprepared for it coming. I certainly
> got a very decent briefing from the solicitors of the inquiry. But I think the
> difficulty was that maybe they were giving everybody the same briefing. But
> the understanding that everybody had of what was required of them, ... most
> of our guys didn't understand.[62]

This falls far short of a victim-centred approach. Even for those describing
the process as positive, some felt that they could have been better prepared:

> I found the court thing intimidating... That court was packed – then you've
> got that panel and all of the electronics and the TV up on the wall – and all
> the people sitting in the background – and you're not sure who they are – and
> what they're doing – why they are there – and I'm thinking are these press or
> social workers. I just didn't know Maybe a little bit more information about
> who everybody is and what their role is.[63]

That an inquiry is usually public and open rather than private and confidential increases discomfort. Some said that the HIAI was not a conducive environment to talk about their trauma – despite their motivating search to have their voices heard and to be acknowledged by the public. The inquiry acknowledged how upsetting testifying could be and made witness-support officers and a representative from Contact Northern Ireland counselling services available to provide assistance. Throughout the inquiry participants who found their experience stressful or distressing were referred to appropriate agencies. Yet half of those interviewed said that 'more victim support was needed'; some strong criticism was also expressed about the adequacy of the available support.

The HIAI Process: Inquisitorial or Adversarial?

Northern Ireland's Statutory Inquiry sought to ascertain facts and evaluate evidence; formality and legality characterised its proceedings. The inquisitorial approach adopted by the inquiry counsel, however, was tempered by the expressed aspiration that questioning be conducted sympathetically. The HIAI reports that counsel 'probed in an appropriate fashion' evidence of both victims and core participants (institutions and organisations) 'without the witness being subjected to inappropriate or unnecessary cross examination.'[64] But many survivors did not share the above perception of how proceedings were conducted. Analyses of interviews show that for some survivors, participating in the public hearing was a taxing experience – a formal legalistic process with complex rules and procedures:

> I'm going to call it a court 'cause it ain't an inquiry... We were told we were going to give our experience. Now this is a court, and there's a man being ripped apart... It's the first time I realised we are on our own. His solicitor would never have allowed this to have happened to him. And the poor fella is being ripped to shreds; and I thought, this is bad.[65]

The inquiry stated that public hearings would 'not be conducted like a trial,' there would be 'no cross-examination of witnesses' and all questions would be directed to 'ascertaining facts.'[66] Despite such assertions, a significant number of survivors regarded the process as adversarial (39 per cent):

> They started bringing up stuff, 'would it be correct that you,' as if you were on trial. And this was their non-adversarial way! It was very adversarial what they were bringing up. What had that got to do with anything? We were getting pulled apart so much it was doing damage.[67]

Some survivors reported feeling as if they were the 'ones on trial' or being 'held to account' (39 percent): 'It actually felt as if you were on trial. We were specifically told it would never have felt like that – but it did, it did – it was terrible... It was an experience I wouldn't want to do again... Honestly, I wouldn't want to put myself through that again.'[68]

Many participants reported that they should have been better prepared in advance. Only 29 per cent said that counsel explained the public hearing's procedures 'clearly.' What might be considered as 'sympathetic' and 'polite' questioning by counsel was perceived by some survivors as deeply intrusive and unnecessarily hostile to their integrity:

> He just started bringing up my past, about my brothers and about my dad going to jail, ...how many times the police was at our door when we were kids. Nothing about the institution; it was all about my home life ...All this stuff was really just wearing me right down. It's as if he was blaming me for this. He's meant to be on my side. But I felt as if, you know, I'm the one here doing the wrong thing.[69]

Some survivors strongly objected to what they viewed as irrelevant details about their past lives being raised during sessions or at the public hearing (37 per cent). Such discussions made some feel as if they 'were offenders' and created defensive attitudes:

> I think it's set too much as a court system, like you're a criminal and that's what's wrong. It should be in a room with a cup of coffee, private. It shouldn't be in front of all those people.[70]

> You see the problem is now that we're starting to feel like we're the guilty party, did we do something wrong, why are we getting this stuff thrown at us when it was us that was babies and it was happening to us.[71]

The study demonstrates that giving oral testimony was emotional and stressful for participants. Some believed that they had not been treated compassionately, which had an impact on their sense of self-worth and their perception of the inquiry's tone toward them:

We were not there to be intimidated. He was treating us the way the nuns treated us, he was intimidating. It should have been a different person with a bit more compassion. Because he acted like how we [have come to] believe how we should be treated, how we've grown up to believe that we're worth nothing. And so we just have to take that because that's what we deserve.[72]

Timely Disclosure of Sensitive and Personal Material

Complaints about the personal nature, extent, and timing of disclosure of sensitive information during the inquiry emerged as a significant factor. As one survivor put it, 'Why are we finding out about ourselves in front of everyone in the dock?'[73] Some complained that they were given personal and sensitive information only in the briefing session immediately prior to testifying. The inquiry's counsel usually prepared survivors on the day they gave evidence, one to two hours in advance. The actual documents providing background information about them gathered by the inquiry were not made available – either in advance of the consultation or for the oral hearings. Such ill-timed disclosure that 'surprised' and 'shocked' survivors had a destabilising effect:

> It was a really hard day because I had to find things out about my mother, and stuff that I had never known in my life. I didn't know that my younger sister was born with [named disease]. I didn't know my mother was in such a hospital... And then I discovered there was a letter... [Counsel] said, 'I know you won't have seen this before but we're going in now; and by the way did you know your mother had syphilis...' And you are supposed to just deal with that and then answer questions.[74]

Despite the HIAI's rationale for failing to offer advance warning of material (i.e. that it could be 'difficult or hurtful'),[75] the survivor on the stand without prior knowledge or control over the content and timing of such disclosures felt disempowered – sometimes traumatised at hearing casual introductions of often-unknown personal episodes from the past. For example, after finding his birth mother but being rejected as an 'Irish bastard' by her partner, one witness returned to the abusive institution he had fled. But he learned about his mother's loving efforts to reach him only when her letter was presented as evidence at the inquiry. Of the 43 survivors interviewed in the study, almost 40 per cent said that 'disclosure was distressing' and should have been 'communicated in advance' of public hearings. After having requested and been refused copies of the disclosed documents, survivors were advised by the inquiry's counsel during briefing sessions that they could obtain these documents from various government bodies. Since many survivors had spent decades looking for snippets of information about their childhood, such a procedure seemed particularly harsh. Not unexpectedly, then, nearly half of those interviewed described their participation in oral hearings as 'traumatising' (47 per cent). Advance disclosure, as discussed below, appears to have been provided only to those participants with legal representation, usually institutions and organisations.

The task of the inquiry was difficult on many levels: the time constraints in which to undertake its work, the volume of material, and the often-harrowing accounts of abuse being investigated. However, in expediting its work, the HIAI's stated principle of 'do no further harm' appears to have been undermined, exposing many survivors to retraumatisation.[76]

Presentation of Evidence

Inquiries are bound by legal rules of procedural fairness in which both accused institutions and individuals must be afforded an opportunity to respond to allegations of misconduct against them. But as this article has previously indicated, important personal evidence relevant to witnesses routinely failed, except in discussions held a few hours before testimony, to be furnished in advance of the public hearing date. In contrast, at least 20 working days before that date, institutions and organisations against which allegations were being made were provided with evidence that the inquiry considered relevant.[77] If participating institutions and organisations wished any questions to be put to a witness, they could submit a request in writing to the inquiry not less than three working days before the witness was scheduled to give evidence.[78] Thus the inquiry provided evidence to alleged perpetrators but not to survivors, who were not furnished with the statements of these alleged perpetrators or information from the relevant institution or authority:

> I said to him [counsel], where did you get that ['letter' disputing victim's evidence]. And he says, it came in this morning. I said 'how come we didn't get this?' I agree that there are two sides of the story, ... they [the institutions] should have their say too. But if they got from us, then we should have got what they said.[79]

Documentation provided to survivors in advance of the hearing was restricted to their draft statements, which were returned to the inquiry after signing. Evidence or questions from the institutions were communicated to survivors in briefing sessions immediately before they testified. Such procedures, in addition to creating a two-tier system, with some better informed and treated than others, added distress to already nervous survivors, many of whom felt underprepared.

Legal Representation and Equality of Arms

Regarding the inquiry's role as balancing the rights of the survivors (the complainants) and the accused, the chairman of the HIAI asserted that its legal team would 'gather the relevant evidence and interview each applicant to ascertain what that person can say about the matters that have to be investigated by the inquiry.' Survivors were therefore discouraged from having their own legal representation: 'It is unnecessary for an individual applicant to have his/her own lawyer present and paid for at the public expense during the public hearings.'[80] Some expressed disappointment with this denial (34 per cent), believing that only those against whom allegations were made (alleged perpetrators and institutions) had 'a right to legal representation' – and if needed 'to have their legal representation paid out of public funds.'[81]

Inequalities between the treatment of complainants and alleged perpetrators existed in other procedures as well. Some members of religious orders accused of abuse were dead, and others were not called to give evidence because they were 'very elderly and too physically frail to give evidence in person, or their mental health or memory had failed to such a degree that they were not able to give reliable evidence.'[82] In those circumstances, their statement was admitted without giving evidence in person, they were excused from giving evidence to the inquiry, or spokespersons for the responding religious orders, without personal experience of the events under consideration, gave generic evidence derived from written records. Survivors were not afforded the same opportunity to present their 'collective account' of an institution. In addition to the oral and written evidence, the inquiry panel considered detailed closing submissions by the institutions (but not by survivors). Alleged perpetrators, having had all the evidence in advance, appeared better prepared for oral hearings and far less dependent on memory than survivors, who had no advance access to documents. They were nevertheless expected to testify at short notice – under pressure to recall specific details of events that had taken place 30 or 40 years earlier. This reliance on memory alone created difficulties for some survivors, leading to further questioning by counsel. Compared to powerful institutions, with access to resources and evidence and independent legal advice, survivors often appeared less assured.[83] As the Law Commission of Canada (LCC) has noted, processes focused on the past must be scrutinised to determine whether current practices are unduly prejudicial to survivors – with little gain in protecting the rights of alleged abusers.[84] Within the specific context of historical child abuse this balance may indeed need to be rethought.

Accountability and Prosecutions

Criminal prosecutions were clearly a justice goal for many of the survivors interviewed in the study. But of the 177 who gave evidence to the inquiry in person, only six per cent (11 persons) stated that they wanted prosecutions. This statistical discrepancy between the evidence of inquiry transcripts and the study's interviews, as already suggested above, might be explained by the perceived parameters set by counsel's questions on redress recommendations. During interviews with the author many survivors maintained that they had been overwhelmed by the whole inquiry experience and lacked confidence in speaking publicly about complex concepts. Significantly, nearly 20 per cent opted to 'leave recommendations to the inquiry' or 'had no recommendations.'

Writing in the *Journal of Human Rights*, Brandon Hamber and Richard A. Wilson note that revenge and retribution may be regarded as low and unworthy emotions.[85] But during interviews survivors did indeed express rage, concern, and frustration about the absence of prosecutions and the ongoing impunity of alleged perpetrators:

> We were told by the police that it's unlikely *they* would ever go to jail, ... and the same day you open the paper and there's an 85-year-old man going to jail in handcuffs for not paying his car tax. Yet they told me that Sister – at the age of 75 – will not be going to jail because she's old... I don't feel like I've got justice in any way. I've been left to worry about my future and my children; and *they* are sheltered and fed by the Catholic church, who's still looking after them.[86]

The HIAI's terms of reference state that the panel 'must not rule on, and has no power to determine, any person's civil or criminal liability.'[87] Inquiries can, however, offer a form of immunity to incentivise alleged perpetrators to cooperate with the search for truth. A form of immunity – termed 'use immunity' – was thus offered by the HIAI. A letter from the director of public prosecutions specifically stated that 'no evidence a person may give before the inquiry will be used in evidence against that person in any criminal proceedings or relied upon for the purpose of deciding whether to bring such proceedings against that person.'[88] Although such an undertaking does not prevent prosecution if other evidence exists or becomes available from other sources, there is nonetheless a fine line between immunity and impunity. The HIAI did refer 190 complainants to the Police Service of Northern Ireland (PSNI) to address any potential for criminal prosecution, from which 77 matters relating to the complaints were reported to the Public Prosecution Service (PPS) for consideration.[89] But, to date, in Northern Ireland no prosecutions have emanated from the cases referred to the PSNI by the inquiry.[90] Most of the survivors interviewed in the study were unaware of the 'use immunity' provision – despite the publication on HIAI's website of letters from the director of public prosecutions and the attorney general confirming the immunity provision. The victim information documents and transcripts of the public-information meetings held by the inquiry, however, show that the subject of immunity was never broached – raising significant questions of informed consent.

Apology, Memorials, and Compensation

Sixty-three per cent of interviewees in the study identified apologies as important, and HIAI's report had recommended that the Northern Irish Executive and those responsible for each institution where systemic failings were found should make a public apology – a whole-hearted and unconditional recognition of a failure to protect children from abuse, undertaken at a suitable venue and on a single occasion. Although survivors failed to identify a memorial as a justice need, the report also recommended that a memorial be erected to remind legislators and others of what many children have experienced in residential homes. The commission chairman endorsed a physical memorial in parliament buildings or on the Stormont Estate, paid for by the Northern Irish Executive. Nearly 80 per cent of interviewees identified compensation as a key justice need; however, academic research shows that the HIAI recommendations fell far short of meeting survivors' justice needs in terms of, among other issues, a low standard payment and overall cap on compensation, restricted eligibility, loss of lifetime opportunity and limited awards to families of deceased survivors.[91]

Most recently, survivors managed to achieve 'significant changes' to the historical-abuse redress legislation reflecting better their needs.[92] In collaboration with academics survivors set up a panel of experts on redress made up of individual survivors, survivor groups, members of human-rights organisations, local and international academics and members of the legal profession.[93] As a survivor-driven process,[94] the panel published a 2017 position paper that set out a detailed critique of the inquiry's redress recommendations and offered proposals to improve redress to meet survivors' needs.[95] Launched at a well-attended public event in Stormont, the document subsequently was used as a lobbying and campaign tool that empowered and gave voice to survivors, leading to better redress.

Future Directions for Redress

This article analyses the potential and limitations of the public-inquiry model to align with justice needs as expressed by survivors – and to deal with the ongoing consequences of historical child abuse. The inquiry model has commendable features, including providing acknowledgment, vindication and validation for survivors. It can satisfy their perceived sense of duty to testify and bear witness in order to provide an authoritative record. Although inquiries do not make final determinations of liability for wrongdoing, their findings can adversely affect reputation. They can be effective at publicising the facts and raising awareness of the extent of wrongdoing – therefore providing a form of public accountability. Such inquiries can lead to apologies, individual and collective.

On the other hand, the inquiry, and particularly its redress recommendations, fell short in meeting key justice needs identified by survivors. Initial high hopes and expectations were often replaced by frustration, disappointment, confusion and even anger. Many wanted individualised answers to questions and personal accountability of perpetrators. The goal of the HIAI was to identify systemic failings and institutional accountability and responsibility, a concept not fully understood and not in accordance with what many survivors giving evidence wanted. Most were unaware of the provision of immunity for alleged perpetrators, a provision that they regarded as clearly favouring their abusers. Compensation was also considered an important aspect of satisfactory redress, but again survivors' needs and wishes were largely unmet in the inquiry's recommendations. Only persistent campaigning by survivors and collaborative participatory action led to the overturning of many of the HIAI's compensation recommendations. Access to records was another critical key justice need, but the HIAI made no specific recommendations in this regard save to refer to access 'to enable survivors to apply for compensation.'[96]And although voice was a clearly articulated justice need, survivors' voices appeared weak compared to those of well-prepared, resourced and legally represented institutions. This discrepancy resulted in more favourable treatment for alleged perpetrators in a process that purported to be survivor-centred. In contrast to that goal the survivors' experienced feelings of disempowerment. The ill-timed disclosure of personal, often highly sensitive information and new evidence caused great distress, undermining the inquiry's potential to restore dignity and self-worth.

In the context of a survivor-centric process the limitations of public inquiries appear to outweigh their perceived benefits, for that form's processes are too limited to address the full range of justice needs identified by survivors. Participating in the HIAI was a bruising experience for many; indeed, the potential risk to mental health through re-traumatisation and re-victimisation raises important questions about the appropriateness of such a model to deal with child abuse. Policy-makers should explore less intrusive – and more humane, inclusive and empowering – forms through which to acknowledge and establish macro-level truth about historical institutional child abuse.

Although this article does not flesh out a model that could embrace survivors' justice needs, it offers some initial suggestions.[97] The starting point should be a determination of what survivors' want – their justice needs. Thereafter, addressing those needs must drive approaches to deal with historical child abuse. The fundamental principle in developing a model is the full participation of survivors from an early stage in the development, design and implementation of justice responses and their involvement in the negotiation of settlements. But a single mechanism is unlikely to address all needs. Most crucial is that harmful aspects of existing processes are not repeated. The Northern Ireland collaborative participatory-panel model discussed above could provide the process for survivor dialogue and potential input into policy. However, for survivor groups to undertake these roles they need to be resourced and have adequate capacities to enable meaningful engagement. The development of a strategy that could embrace survivors' justice needs and empower genuine participation (beyond giving testimony) would require political will, resources and a paradigm shift toward a victim-led approach to historical institutional abuse.

NINETEEN

Visualising the Transfers of Abusers in the 2009 Ryan Report[1]

Emilie Pine, Susan Leavy and Mark T. Keane

The 2009 publication of the Report of the Commission to Inquire into Child Abuse (*Ryan Report*) marked the conclusion of a nine-year, state-funded, licensed investigation into residential care for Irish children at institutions managed by the Catholic church.[2] It comprises five volumes, totalling more than 2,600 pages, including testimony from 1,712 witnesses. As Mary Raftery put it, the *Ryan Report* 'painstakingly charted the vast scale of abuse of tens of thousands of children within institutions.' It established once and for all the systemic nature of abuse in Irish institutions, 'giv[ing] us a compelling vision of the hell to which so many children were consigned.'[3] The presentation of these conditions includes analysis of the Catholic congregations' repeated response to allegations of abuse. For example, the report states in regard to the Christian Brothers: 'The records of the congregation show that on a number of occasions individuals who were accused of sexual abuse were transferred to other residential or day schools.'[4] Transferring an abuser became one way to protect the reputation of the institution and the order by minimising conflict and the potential for public awareness and scandal:

> In some cases brothers who had been sexually abusing children were, in their later careers, appointed to senior positions within the province. When asked at the phase I hearing for Letterfrack how this had happened, Br Gibson explained that because the leadership in the congregation changed every twelve years, there was no memory within the organisation of offences committed before that. He acknowledged that there was a personal file for each brother and concluded that these files were not consulted in making appointments.[5]

Gibson blamed an amnesiac system for the promotion of abusers; the cause, however, was not amnesia. As Marie Keenan argues, 'an unusually consistent pattern has emerged in the handling of abuse complaints by Catholic church leaders.'[6] This pattern includes denial, cover-up and, in the case of staff employed at residential institutions, the transfer of abusers from one institution to another in the wake of allegations of abuse.

The congregational response to abuse – to transfer, to pretend to forget, to avoid public knowledge – was not limited to a few occasions or solely to the Christian Brothers. The report notes the repeated transfer of one priest, Father Santino of the Rosminian Order:

> With the knowledge that the order possessed about his past history and attitudes, they must have been aware of the likelihood that he would sexually abuse boys in this institution. It follows that the order was prepared to put boys at risk in order to find a place for somebody who might cause public scandal if he were to be located elsewhere.[7]

Again, the report contends that 'transferring abusers to other institutions where they would be in contact with children put those children at risk.'[8] It also notes the transfer of problematic nuns in and out of the Sisters of Mercy institution at Cappoquin. The *Ryan Report's* authors conclude, 'When confronted with evidence of sexual abuse, the response of the religious authorities was to transfer the offender to another location where in many instances he was free to abuse again. The safety of children in general was not a consideration.'[9]

Despite this evidence, no consistent analysis of transfers as a system-wide pattern of response to abuse is offered, for the *Ryan Report* is structured as an in-depth narrative focusing on one institution at a time. This organisation generates a thorough story about each institution and certain individuals singled out for analysis; however, it also means that if readers seek to understand systemic congregational responses to allegations of abuse in more than one institution at a time, they must be familiar with the entirety of the document. Missing in the report is a section that specifically analyses the series of events that lead to and follow the transfer of staff *between* institutions. Such an analysis of organisational responses to abuse would not only indicate how congregations responded in its aftermath; it could also illustrate a link between behaviour and response. As Donald Palmer and Valerie Feldman argue, organisational 'structures... shape member attitudes and behaviour.'[10] In other words, organisational responses are not only reactive but also influential; how an organisation responds shapes the behaviour of abusers, so that transferring abusers or ignoring their abuse not only enables but encourages abuse to occur.

The Industrial Memories project at University College Dublin – led by the authors – has digitised the *Ryan Report*, seeking to make it more accessible by creating a new database version that is fully searchable (https://industrialmemories.ucd.ie).[11] This database enabled the team to run searches for keywords that would indicate transfer (keywords included 'transfer,' 'move,' 'removal,' 'reassign,' 'dismiss,' 'dispense,' 'resign') in order to identify individual staff members who had been transferred within the system as a result of allegations or evidence of abuse. These results were filtered to ensure reliability – for example, to remove references to the transfer of children between institutions. Using the above search terms and filters enabled the identification of 462 moves made by abusers within the system, including transfer to another school or order house, and dispensation or dismissal.[12] Performing further textual analysis of each of these 462 moves identified 86 individuals whom the report documents as moving within the system.[13] Combining such quantitative analysis with close reading of the case histories of those 86 individuals allowed the Industrial Memories project to map their trajectories within the system (see Fig. 1).

In Figure 1 each circle represents one of the following: an institution, an alleged abuser who was moved or an outcome. The larger the circle, the more activity is represented by that node – i.e. the more moves by an individual in or out of an institution. The circles are grouped together and color-coded to represent the different religious orders. Perhaps most striking are the crisscrossing lines. These lines indicate *multiple* transfers of abusers, showing how abuse spread unchecked across the system. The graphic representation of this information, in contrast to the written report, immediately communicates the movement of abusers within the system and between different institutions. Viewers can see that based on the evidence in the report, the Christian Brothers' institutions were most likely to have staff members transferred into and out of an institution, with the Artane school having the highest number of transfers. Indeed, the transfer record for the other orders is significantly less – partly a reflection of the smaller scale of these institutions – suggesting that transferring abusers was a more prevalent organisational norm for the Christian Brothers than for other orders. Additionally, looking at the trajectories of abusers in different orders makes clear that the Rosminians were more likely to transfer abusers to the order house where they would have no contact with children, whereas the Christian Brothers were more likely to transfer an abuser to a day school where abuse might again take place. The transfer graph thus immediately and impactfully conveys through a visual medium the scale of transfers of abusers across the system.

There are limitations to this form of visual representation, not least because it is not based on the primary-research material – the records of the commission are unavailable to researchers.[14] As a result, researchers do not have access to the records to recover the full range of transfers, including evidence of decision-making; nor do they have access to information about transfers or abuse available in the records of the Department of Education or captured in victim testimony. The graph also cannot express the stories behind each of the individual staff members, or the scale of the damage they inflicted on children. What the graph achieves, however, is the instant communication of the systemic nature of transfer. The 86 named staff members, the lines connecting institutions, and the crisscrossing lines of multiple transfers illustrate how abuse happened not in isolation, but across the system. The graph thus conveys to an audience unfamiliar with the report's 2,600 pages, or with the full story of the institutions, the operation of a transfer system – a strategy that protected serial abusers. More than preventing 'scandal,' this system enabled the chronic abuse of children by Ireland's Catholic congregations. This single aspect of the Industrial Memories project thus demonstrates how digital humanities methodologies can add to our 'reading' of texts, especially large-scale texts, such as inquiry reports; graphics may additionally be welcome to readers at saturation point regarding inquiries about past institutional abuse. Though these reports are accompanied by 'Executive Summaries,' their findings are embedded within (and necessarily so) in-depth and detailed linear narratives. Visualising data, in contrast, can effectively and accessibly illustrate overarching patterns – adding value to the linear narrative. This is a major benefit, especially for stakeholders with experience of institutions, for whom being seen is vitally important.

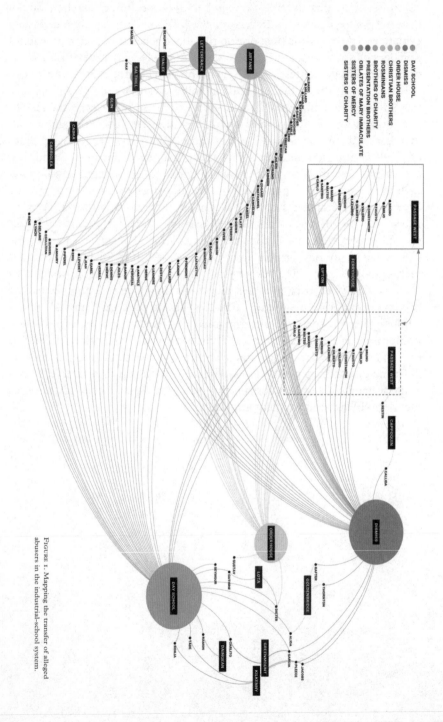

FIGURE 1. Mapping the transfer of alleged abusers in the industrial-school system.

KNOWLEDGE, MEMORY AND
THE MAGDALENE LAUNDRIES

TWENTY

Official Ireland's Response to the Magdalene Laundries: An Epistemology of Ignorance

Katherine O'Donnell

This essay addresses the Irish government's response to the atrocity and the legacy of the Magdalene laundries. Using the lens of 'an epistemology of ignorance' through which to examine a key report drawn up by civil servants, *The Inter-Departmental Committee Report into State Involvement in the Magdalen Laundries* (*IDC Report*), published in February 2013, we examine how this report creates a 'substantive ignorance' that allows the Irish State to systematically not know the traumas endured by the former Magdalene women. The Irish State's internal inquiry into its involvement with the Magdalene institutions has been one of a number of state-commissioned investigations relating to the abuses suffered by those who were coercively confined across a range of residential institutions in twentieth-century Ireland.[1] The lessons learned in examining the *IDC Report* are also, unfortunately, salient in approaching the final report of the Commission to Inquire into Mother and Baby Homes, which is the most recent of the Irish State's commissioned inquiry into residential institutional abuse.[2] This 'architecture of containment' (to quote James M. Smith) included industrial and reformatory schools, Mother and Baby Homes, Magdalene laundries, County Homes and psychiatric institutions.[3] John Banville, writing after the final report of the Commission to Inquire into Child Abuse (CICA) in 2009, described the culture that had enabled the endemic sexual, physical abuse and systemic neglect of children in Irish State-licensed/religious-run residential institutions thus:

Never tell, never acknowledge, that was the unspoken watchword. Everyone knew, but no one said.

Amid all the reaction to these terrible revelations, I have heard no one address the question of what it means, in this context, to know. Human beings – human beings everywhere, not just in Ireland – have a remarkable ability to entertain simultaneously any number of contradictory propositions. Perfectly decent people can know a thing and at the same time not know it.[4]

This essay proposes that practice of constructing an officially sanctioned ignorance might explain, at least in part, how people can both know and not know the atrocities that systematically occur in their society.

we have, obviously, erred totally on the side of believing the women concerned in the first instance

Following a state apology to the Magdalene women issued in February 2013, Mr Justice John Quirke (President of the Irish Law Reform Commission and former High Court judge) published his report in May 2013 recommending an 'ex gratia Restorative Justice Scheme' for the women held in Magdalene institutions and acknowledging that forced unpaid labour, involuntary detention, degradation and denial of education were systemic features of the Magdalene Laundries.[5] A month later, in June 2013, the Irish Human Rights Commission (IHRC) produced a provisional human rights analysis of the *IDC Report's* contents '[i]n the absence of a more thorough investigation, as recommended by the IHRC and the United Nations Committee Against Torture.'[6] This was to be one of the last reports of the independent IHRC before it was severely reduced in numbers and amalgamated with the Equality Authority. The report concluded that:

- 'Magdalen Laundries clearly operated as a *discriminatory regime* in respect of girls and women in the state. The State itself had knowledge of the regime and actively engaged with it, indeed financially benefitting from it in some cases. Society at large accepted the regime, and also supported it by placing sisters, daughters and mothers behind the walls of the laundries... *the State appears to have taken no cognisance of the women's right to equality* when it engaged with, and permitted the laundries to operate';[7]
- '[W]omen were *deprived of their liberty* while in the laundries. The *lawfulness of such detention is questionable* in a number of respects';[8]
- 'The placement of children in Magdalen Laundries, either by the State or others, may have given rise to a *breach of the right*

    to education under the Constitution and the right of access to education under the ECHR [European Convention on Human Rights]';[9]

- 'The *State's culpability in regard to forced or compulsory labour and/ or servitude appears to be threefold...* it failed to outlaw and police against such practices... the State or its agents placed girls and women in the laundries knowing that such girls and women would be obliged to provide their labour in those institutions... the State further supported these practices by benefitting from commercial contracts with the laundries';[10]
- 'from the testimonies of survivors it appears that a certain level of *ill-treatment occurred*';[11] and
- inadequate recording of the identities and burial sites of deceased Magdalene women 'could potentially have impacted on the *Article 8 [ECHR] rights of living relatives* of the deceased women to information about their origins.'[12]

However, since 2013, Irish politicians and civil servants have consistently issued statements in the Dáil (Irish parliament) and at various UN human rights fora, to declare that there is no need for an independent investigation into the Magdalene institutions.[13] Without embarrassment for the lack of logic, the Irish State argues that if criminality had occurred in the Irish Magdalenes, then the Irish State would investigate, but they will not investigate for potential illegalities and criminal wrongdoing because there is nothing to investigate.[14]

By January 2015, nearly two years after the Magdalene Restorative Redress Scheme was established, one of the most crucial aspects of the scheme, the proposed Healthcare package, had not been delivered to the women. During Dáil debates on the Bill to provide healthcare, opposition TDs continued to highlight the harmful impacts that the Department of Justice methods of assessing 'duration of stay' was having on some women.[15] In the Seanad two months later, the Minister for Justice claimed that '[w]e have, obviously, erred totally on the side of believing the women concerned in the first instance.'[16] However, litigation by a number of survivors prompted the Ombudsman in December 2016 to investigate the Scheme's administration, leading to a substantial and scathing report published in November 2017 which found that the Department had 'maladministered' the Scheme, largely because officials refused to treat survivors' own testimony as having evidentiary value while relying heavily on documents and testimony from the nuns in order to establish the women's duration of stay. As the Ombudsman described it: 'There was an over reliance on the records of the congregations and it is not apparent what weight if any was afforded to the testimony of the women and/or their relatives.'[17] The Ombudsman found that officials had accorded 'supremacy' to the religious orders' accounts even, remarkably, where the nuns could not produce supporting contemporaneous documentation.[18] After the Ombudsman's report was published, the Joint Oireachtas Committee on Justice and Equality invited both the Ombudsman and the relevant senior civil servant from the Department of Justice to appear before it early in 2018. The Ombudsman was clearly emotional as he told the Committee that in his ten years in the role: 'I have never reached the point where a Department has, prior to the publication of a report, absolutely and categorically refused to engage with the process around accepting and implementing the recommendations.'[19]

Despite formal apologies and a 'Restorative Justice' scheme we can see that the Irish State also formally insists on not acknowledging the abuses experienced by girls and women in the Magdalene Laundries, despite the women's testimony and despite the vast amount of corroborating evidence and supporting legal and ethical arguments generated over more than a decade of campaigning. It is instructive in this regard, to read the report of an internal enquiry conducted by a number of departments of the civil service and chaired by Senator Martin McAleese into the Irish State's involvement into the Magdalene institutions which was published immediately prior to the state apology in 2013. The *IDC Report* revealed that the state was implicated in a number of key respects, not least in sending countless women and girls into the Magdalene institutions. The *IDC Report* is 1,212 pages long, and while it could not fail to find that the Irish State was deeply implicated in the functioning and flourishing of the Magdalenes, the report managed to deny the extent of the suffering of the women and girls held in the Magdalenes and any wrongdoing on the part of the Irish establishment (that is, the symbiotic governing dyad of the hierarchy of the Catholic Church and senior officials and public representatives of the Irish State). The *IDC Report* is presumed by civil servants and politicians of the Irish State to provide sufficient rationale for its lack of truth-telling in relation to the Magdalene institutions, for its protest at being held accountable, for its inconsistency in how it understands redress and restorative justice, and the worrying implications of the failure to properly reflect on what lessons need to be learned in order to guarantee the non-reoccurrence of such coercive confinement and forced labour in the future.[20]

The Ignorance of Ignoring: Privileged Knowledge

Philosophers have traditionally understood ignorance as being systematically related to knowledge and beliefs. The standard definition of ignorance is that it is founded on either false, unjustified or absent knowledge or beliefs.[21] The philosophical study of knowledge (epistemology) is generally concerned to offer normative accounts of how knowledge ought to be acquired, that is: robustly supported, unbiased, transparently made, communal, testable. The knowledge production they describe is integral to democracy, which requires that citizens operate with a strong sense of a shared reality needed to give collective deliberation sufficient stability and coherence. Epistemologists have tended to worry about the virtues needed by the knowers and, more recently, have been addressing the vices, those culpable character traits, attitudes or thinking styles that systematically get in the way of producing knowledge and lead to ignorance.[22] Often motivated by insights and concerns of feminist, anti-racist, anti-colonial and workers' movements, social epistemologists examine the power dynamics within which knowledge is acquired, disseminated and contested. They have developed the epistemological methodologies to include a focus on the 'unsettling knowledge' that comes from the standpoint of those whose social identities are subordinate to the economically, culturally and politically dominant.[23] They suggest that acquiring knowledge through the perspectives of those who experience social marginalisation can lead to more robust and insightful public knowledge.[24] Yet including those perspectives also has the threatening potential to destabilise the ideology, those hegemonic dominant ideas, that underpin and form the social order and the privileged positions of those in power.[25]

As the *IDC Report* is the key citation offered by the Irish State as a bulwark in its failure to be truthful about the Magdalene institutions, it presents an opportunity to apply an epistemological lens to consider how forms of ignorance can be understood as a suppression of knowledge that has the potential to unsettle the status quo. Linda Martín Alcoff points to how social epistemologists have begun to understand forms of ignorance promulgated by powerful vested interests not simply as '*neglectful* epistemic practice' but as 'a *substantive* epistemic practice in itself.'[26] This type of ignorance is one that resists and fights back, or as Charles W. Mills describes it, is 'active and dynamic.'[27] José Medina, describes it further as 'an ignorance that is not easy to undo and correct, for this requires retraining – the reconfiguration of epistemic attitudes and habits – as well as social change.'[28] In standard philosophical conceptualisations, ignorance results from a deficit of information – the absence of evidence, or convincing argument – and so can be eradicated by the presentation of new information. However, what I term 'belligerent ignorance' is an active substantive epistemic practice resistant to being defeated by the presentation of countervailing information, evidence, argument or even appeals to legal or moral norms. By using the phrase 'belligerent ignorance'

I mean to convey the battling strategies used in the *IDC Report* and by the Irish establishment to combat the 'unsettling knowledge' of the Magdalene institutions: the kind of knowledge that has the challenging potential to disrupt the bases of respectability, hierarchy and control of knowledge, the modes by which those who rule assume and enact their superior power.

The *IDC Report* allows us to examine how governing classes exert power through active strategies of belligerent ignorance in its attempt to remain ignorant about the harms visited on the Magdalene women and hence render a call for justice as unimaginable and therefore unattainable. By considering the *IDC Report* to be a substantive epistemic practice of ignorance we can understand that its primary function is to produce an ignorance in the service of Ireland's official establishment. This cultivated ignorance affirms the production and reproduction of class, gender, ableist and racist hierarchies that informed the establishment and continuance of the Magdalene institutions.[29] Truth is sacrificed in service of the continuation of established ideas of supremacy. The officially sanctioned conception of reality requires, among other things, the patterned insistence on particular narratives, facts, understanding of historical time, methodologies, conceptual frameworks and norms, with an attending patterned rejection, obfuscation, erasure or ignoring of alternatives. The systematic promulgation by key agents of the Irish State that constitute official ignorance of Magdalene institutions is pernicious in a number of respects, not least in its potential to cause confusion, doubt and lack of knowledge among 'perfectly decent people.'

In recent years as the media story of the apology to the Irish Magdalenes fades from memory it is now commonplace that Irish undergraduates (who are overwhelmingly middle class) are surprised to learn that one per cent of the Irish population in the mid-twentieth century were coercively confined in industrial and reformatory schools, Mother and Baby Homes, Magdalene laundries, County Homes and psychiatric institutions.[30] Given that well over 90 per cent of the primary national schools in the Republic of Ireland are Catholic-run and that some 60 per cent of second level schools are run according to a Catholic-religious ethos, it is perhaps not surprising to hear that learning about the recent history of coercive confinement does not feature anywhere on the national curriculum. The era of knowing and not-knowing can quickly become re-established.

The kind of ignorance that functions to produce and reproduce class, gender and racial hierarchies is often referred to in the literature of social epistemology as 'wilful ignorance.' The wilfully ignorant are not simply oblivious to the truth, or disbelieving it, in fact they are aware of fundamental truths such as, in this case, that Magdalene women were denied basic rights under the Irish Constitution. However, those agents

of the Irish State who compiled the *IDC Report* and continue to refer to
it as a factual document, refuse to acquire the knowledge that these girls
and women were coercively confined and forced to hard labour. Kevin
Lynch's analysis points out that the wilfully ignorant are motivated to not
acknowledge facts which they *should* know.[31] The 'should' here points to
the moral claim that we can regard the wilfully ignorant as blameworthy.[32]
The social contract of a democracy such as the Republic of Ireland
requires that at a minimum we should expect that civil servants and public
representatives would acknowledge the facts and affirm the rights of all
citizens, regardless of whether they were women or girls from a Traveller
family; victims of rape and incest; juvenile offenders; unwed mothers; born
'illegitimate'; prostitutes; living with intellectual disabilities; or otherwise
suffering from social and economic marginalisation; in short the 'kinds' of
girls and women who found themselves taken to and held in Magdalene
laundries.

Ignoring and Ignorance

The IDC inquiry is repeatedly described by the Irish State as an independent
commission that produced a comprehensive and factual report rather than
as an intra-departmental civil service internal inquiry that was chaired by
Senator Dr Martin McAleese who was appointed to the Seanad directly
by the Taoiseach. Reading the *IDC Report* is an object lesson in the wilful
practice of substantive ignorance and allows us to consider the rhetorical
strategies by which those in power can control knowledge dissemination
to an extent that things that are known become 'unknown' and truths 'are
treated as if they are outlandish fictions.' [33]

Undoubtedly the most egregious aspect of the IDC inquiry and its report
is its utter failure to engage with the testimony of Magdalene survivors. The
IDC Report is a testament to *the ignorance of ignoring*, both words entwined
by virtue of their shared etymology.[34] The report refuses to contemplate
whether torture and ill treatment of a criminal nature occurred in the
Magdalene Laundries. It fails to question whether breaches of domestic law
or constitutional rights or international human rights treaties took place. By
ignoring these matters, by ignoring the experiences of the girls and women
confined therein, the authors of the Report remain ignorant of them.
The *IDC Report* starts out with five pages of acknowledgements thanking
Bishops, Archbishops, accountants, doctors, historians, academics, state
agencies, civil servants, advocacy and representative groups. At the bottom
of page five, the last line of the acknowledgements reads: 'And finally
a special thanks to all the women who shared the story of their time in
the Magdalen Laundries with the Committee.' The Report describes the

women's testimony of the abuses they suffered as 'the story of their time in the Magdalen Laundries.' They are thanked for 'sharing.' At no point did the IDC issue a public call for survivors to come forward and/or submit their testimony. The IDC fostered the impression among the advocacy group Justice for Magdalenes (JFM) that it would consider the testimony of Magdalene survivors that the group gathered, recorded and transcribed. Responding to a specific inquiry from JFM, the IDC welcomed 'former residents' who wished 'to share their stories,' but added:

> There is no need for input submitted in this way to be sworn or witnessed – this is not a legal forum and the Committee does not have a mandate to consider individual complaints. We would not like any excessive formality in the process to risk altering this perception among the women.[35]

Ultimately the IDC ignored the 800 pages of evidence from these survivors and not once refers to their testimony. Yet the Report says that 118 women 'came forward and engaged with the Committee.' This total includes 58 women still in the institutional setting under the nuns' control.[36] It is unclear under what conditions these 58 survivors, just one of whom is quoted, gave their 'stories.'[37] The remaining 60 women were introduced by JFM, the Irish Women's Survivors' Support Network (IWSSN) and the group Magdalenes Survivors Together but there are scarcely any references to what these women say before Chapter Nineteen (entitled 'Living and Working Conditions'), the second last chapter of the report. Moreover, even in this chapter, Anne Enright notes that the voices of the former Magdalenes are relegated here and throughout the *IDC Report* to the form of a 'chorus'; their voices are disembodied, not related to any name or discreet identity (such as through a pseudonym). The women of the Magdalenes are recorded merely as fragmentary refrains on the fringes of the Report's pages.[38]

The IDC's failure to consider the testimony submitted by JFM is a classic example of what Miranda Fricker terms 'epistemic injustice,' whereby those who suffer from socially stigmatised identities are not considered to be expert or even credible witnesses, even when they offer accounts of their own experiences. This epistemic injustice discounts already marginalised citizens from informing public knowledge, even (or perhaps particularly) when that public knowledge concerns their own lives. By not hearing from the Magdalene survivors, or having their voices validated and affirmed, the public suffers from a lack of available information and interpretative frameworks to begin to make sense of those institutions, a deficit that Fricker calls hermeneutic injustice.[39] Gail Poulhaus Jr uses the term 'wilful hermeneutical ignorance' to describe what happens when 'dominantly situated knowers,' that is those who hold cultural, social, economic and political power, refuse to countenance the knowledge and ways of knowing developed from the 'experienced world of those situated marginally.' Poulhaus argues that 'such refusals allow dominantly situated knowers to misunderstand, misinterpret and/or ignore whole parts of the world.'[40] In other words, the dominant situation of those in power means that they are not interdependent in creating consensus or shared understandings of the social world with those situated on the social and economic margins of a polity. Those who have been on the losing or weaker sides of social and historical struggles suffer from a lack of respectful cultural recognition and social esteem and find themselves ignored or disbarred from being recognised as knowledgeable or capable of contributing to the accumulation of knowledge. Political power is evident in 'the wilful hermeneutical ignorance' where dominantly situated knowers nonetheless 'continue to misunderstand and misinterpret the world' by ignoring the testimony of the marginalised. Because they are ignored, these marginalised members of society fail to gain a popular forum or medium for their knowledge to be shared and 'perfectly decent people' do not know (enough) and injustices and harms continue.[41]

While survivors remain nameless in Chapter Nineteen, other individuals are identified: the directors of the IWSSN and many identified professional men, including doctors, priests and laundry managers.[42] These people's perspectives are recorded and reproduced in detail, through their interviews and letters to the IDC. In contrast, survivors' testimonies are routinely referred to as 'stories' – the trope recurs, like a refrain, throughout the Report. 'Stories' first appears on page one:

> ...the Committee was conscious that the operation of the Magdalen Laundries since the foundation of the State has, prior to this process, not been fully understood, as many State records were neither readily available nor easily accessible and the records of the Religious Congregations were not available for inspection or analysis. It is understandable that – fuelled by this absence of information – stories grew to fill these gaps.[43]

The *IDC Report* claims to give 'information' to counter and dispel 'stories,' while simultaneously the women are almost invariably described as 'sharing their stories.'[44] Among the women's 'stories' recounted in Chapter Nineteen are the following: being made to wear the bed sheets one had wet during the night, being forced to wear a cup one had broken around one's neck, being made to stand on a stool while stripped naked and beaten by auxiliaries. It also includes accounts of the isolation punishment cells where girls and women were kept and denied food for breaches of discipline such as refusing to work, trying to escape, or breaking the many rules around prayer and silence. There are allusions to the humiliation punishment of lying on the ground and kissing the floor, or kneeling on the floor for hours as a spectacle before the nuns and other girls and women. Chapter Nineteen also describes women's hair being cut and kept short which many found humiliating, and relates that haircutting was used as a specific punishment, yet the *IDC Report* characterises these punishments as 'non-physical.'

Without any supporting evidence, and in direct contradiction to the ignored survivor testimony submitted by JFM, the *IDC Report* insists that survivors expressed a 'clear distinction between some of the practices in industrial and reformatory schools and the Magdalen Laundries, in particular in relation to practices of physical punishment and abuse,' which 'enabled' the IDC to clarify the 'confusion in public analysis.'[45] What is meant by the phrase 'confusion in public analysis' remains unclear. Does there have to be a hierarchy between the ill-treatment, physical punishment and abuse associated with being locked up indefinitely and without reason, to slave at hard labour, and be denied one's identity and the horrific physical, sexual and psychological abuse suffered by children in the industrial schools? The *IDC Report* invests significant effort in this pursuit of ranking one form of torture over another. It reproduces extracts from a letter submitted by two directors of the IWSSN in London, Ms Mulready and Ms Morgan, who self-identify as survivors of industrial schools. Their letter acknowledges that girls and women in Magdalene institutions were imprisoned behind iron bars without being told if or when their detention might end, and forced to work at heavy labour constantly with the use of solitary confinement as punishment. However, the letter also argues that: 'As both authors of this submission spent our childhoods and young adulthood in institutions, we are both fully aware from personal experience and observations that violence of all kinds was common place in children's institutions. However, we do not believe such violence took place in the laundries.'[46] Yet, the letter continues: 'Women have often described getting a "thump in the back" or their hair pulled in retaliation for answering back but physical violence from the nuns does not seem to have gone beyond this in most cases.' The IDC states that the summary of the letter from Ms Mulready and Ms Morgan 'suggests that instead of physical punishment, the laundries were places of hard labour and "psychological cruelty and isolation".'[47]

It is unclear what motivated the letter writers and whether they expressly were invited to comment on the IDC's hypothesis that survivors of the Magdalene Laundries were 'confused' about 'abuse.' The chair of the IDC Committee, Senator McAleese had requested an urgent follow-up meeting with women he had met via JFM and had pursued a line of enquiry with them to that effect.[48] What is clear in the morass of obfuscation that is Chapter Nineteen is that the IDC wants us to 'unknow' what constitutes physical punishment. We are directed to conclude that being incarcerated, subjected to forced hard labour, being thumped, having hair pulled, poor food and hygiene facilities, enduring haircutting and solitary confinement without meals and rituals of public humiliation for infractions of the rules, cannot be understood as physical punishment. We are to doubt that 'psychological cruelty and isolation' is enacted on bodies and felt by bodies.

Linda Alcoff and Laura Gray, in writing about female survivors of sexual violence, remind us that:

> The speech of survivors involving reports of their assaults has been excluded speech, constrained by rules more often implicit than explicit but nonetheless powerful. At various times and in different locations survivor speech has been absolutely prohibited, categorized as mad or untrue, or rendered inconceivable: presuming objects (such as a rapist father) that were not statable and therefore could not exist within the dominant discourses.[49]

Judging by oral histories gathered with Magdalene survivors, many of those incarcerated in the Laundry institutions as young girls were victims of rape and incest and their testimonies recount that the perpetrators were never charged.[50] I have argued elsewhere that the incarceration of girls and women in Irish Magdalenes is best understood within the context of the general patriarchal state oppression of female citizens and the stringent denial of reproductive justice.[51] Under this regime those held in the Magdalene Laundries were denied equal status as moral, political or intellectual persons; they were denied their citizenship. The social contract was *de facto* one of domination.[52] Social epistemologists have pointed out that the epistemological requirements for membership of the polity will be determined by the standards – and interests – of the dominant. What is taken to objectively represent the world is a picture of the world that accommodates the convergences of particular viewpoints within it. The section of Chapter Nineteen that purports to represent survivor testimony is immediately followed by a new section entitled 'Comments by the Religious Congregations in response.'[53] The *IDC Report* privileges the perspective of the Religious Congregations and presents the views of the nuns without comment or analysis, leaving them with the final word on the living and working conditions of the Magdalenes: 'In the words of one Sister, "There were a lot of things you would do differently if you had it again. But sure, we were institutionalised too".'[54]

Assertive Obfuscation

On the level of grammar and syntax the *IDC Report* is replete with assertions that are often confusing to understand. For example, the 'Introduction' asserts that '...the majority of the small number of women who engaged with the Committee had been admitted to the laundries either by a non-state route of referral or, most common of all, following time in an Industrial school.' Leaving aside the difficulty of parsing the 'majority of the small number' (*how many?*) this sentence is unfortunately typical of the Report in that it creates obfuscations rather than clarity or certainty. Did the majority of the small number of women who engaged with the Committee enter Magdalene Laundries from Industrial schools – which surely was a 'State route' – or did the majority of the small number of women who engaged with the Committee enter by 'non-State routes?' The 'Introduction' continues with the observation that: 'The vast majority told the Committee that the ill-treatment, physical punishment and abuse that was prevalent in the Industrial School system was not something that they experienced in the Magdalen Laundries.'[55] Does this 'vast majority' relate to the total of 'the small number of women who engaged with the Committee' or does this 'vast majority' number relate to the women who came to the Magdalenes from Industrial Schools? Does the IDC mean to suggest that the physical punishment and abuse prevalent in the Industrial Schools was different to the kind of physical abuse they experienced in the Magdalene institutions or that there was no physical punishment and abuse in the laundries? This unclear statement is followed by other assertions that seem to suggest that the punishment and abuse of Magdalene women was merely different: we are told that the women who talked to the chair of the IDC, Senator McAleese, spoke of an 'uncompromising regime of physically demanding work and prayer,' of the 'deep hurt they felt' arising from 'their loss of freedom, the fact that they were not informed why they were there, lack of information on when they would be allowed to leave, and denial of contact with the outside world, particularly family and friends.'[56] We are not provided information as to what questions were asked, how survivors' answers were recorded, what mechanisms were used to ensure informed consent by the 'small number' of women who engaged with the Committee, or even how they were invited or selected to participate. We are expected to take the IDC's pronouncements as authoritative without any evidence that robust protocols were put in place to ensure that the efficacy of the data on which they base their statements. We are expected to take the IDC's pronouncements as authoritative even when what they announce is unclear and confusing.

There are also instances of where the report's authors find themselves resorting to wilfully dismissing expert evidence and asserting an unsubstantiated counter-claim. Chapter Eighteen, entitled 'Non-State Routes of Entry to the Magdalen Laundries' provides an outstanding example. In this chapter the report attempts to summarise academic work that is unrelentingly critical of the Magdalene regime and the pervasive culture of 'coercive confinement' endemic in twentieth-century Ireland. Amidst detailed descriptions of the brutal social oppression enacted through mass institutionalisation of Ireland's most vulnerable populations, the *IDC Report* insists that: 'such institutions could legitimately claim to be a charitable outreach to the marginalised.'[57]

McAleese and the Modh Coinníollach

The conditional mood (*An Modh Coinníollach*) in the Irish language is synthetically incorporated into verb endings rather than being introduced (as in English) by the equivalent of words 'would,' 'could' or 'should.' The *Modh Coinníollach* is also used much more frequently and diversely than the conditional tense is used by speakers of English. It is not merely used to discuss events that might or might not happen (depending on variable factors or conditions), but in describing events that may not or even did not happen.[58] In the Irish language the *Modh Coinníollach* is used to denote regular occurrences in the past that we might expect to have taken place, but did not, in fact, come to pass. This curious temporal sense is conveyed in Hiberno-English by the phrase 'I did used to be + gerund.' The *IDC Report* is saturated in the conditional mood, ghosted by the *Modh Coinníollach*. Would; would have; should; should have; could; could have; wouldn't; shouldn't and couldn't appear a total of 1,200 times in the 1,212-page document. A significant bulk of the *IDC Report* is comprised of extraneous research notes, irrelevant histories of policy and legal changes, archival material and maps being indiscriminately presented, so the effect of the conditional mood in those sections that do focus more directly on the issues we might expect to see addressed is even more pronounced. Overall, the tone of the report creates a register of uncertainty, instead of categorial statements that something did or did not happen the reader is left with not being able to be sure of clear facts.

Chapter Fifteen, entitled 'Financial (C): Taxation, Commercial Rates and Social Insurance,' provides us with a good case study to explore the use and effect of the conditional tense. After some tangential discussion the Chapter moves to assert that on the one hand, all of the profits of the Magdalene institutions that were the result of unpaid labour were deemed tax exempt – 'any profits earned by the Magdalen Laundries *would not in general have had* an impact on the application of the charitable tax exemption' – and on the other hand, that any work done by paid workers for the same orders was not exempt from tax – *'[th]his would not have been the case* for every trade or activity carried out by Religious Congregations' [emphasis supplied].[59] These sentences are followed by a discussion, replete with conditional qualifications, on whether or not Magdalene Laundries paid commercial rates to local authorities and the assiduous efforts made by Religious Orders operating Magdalene Laundries to legally challenge having to pay such rates.[60] It is not until page 762 of the Report that we come to the question of whether the girls and women held in the Magdalene Laundries were forced to work without pay, and the level of connivance or knowledge by the state of that fact. The *IDC Report* approaches the matter obliquely, through a discussion of whether or not social insurance was paid by the 'employers' [sic], the Religious Orders.[61] This section of the Chapter considers the 'employment status' of the women and girls: 'The application of these tests to the women who worked in the Magdalen Laundries *would establish* whether or not they were in insurable employment. If they were in such employment, *there would have been* a requirement for the Congregations to make insurance contributions on their behalf [emphasis supplied].'[62] The IDC decided that it might be largely held that those put to work in a Laundry would be assumed to be engaged in insurable employment.[63] Yet according to the IDC, a file once existed (that is now presumed to have been destroyed) in the Department of Social Welfare detailing a decision issued that stated that a girl or woman working in a Magdalene Laundry was not engaged in insurable employment.[64] In spite of, or indeed inspired by, the conditional non-existence of this file, the *IDC Report* constructs possible 'legislative bases' for the Department of Social Welfare's supposed decision. The IDC offered these suppositions to current departmental officials who in turn accepted this rationale rather than admit the department's role in depriving Magdalene girls and women of their rights and colluding with extracting their unpaid, forced and hard labour.[65] The *IDC Report* finally asserts that 'after 1979, *it is likely that* the women working in the Magdalen Laundries did not qualify as being in insurable employment, as *they would not have been* in receipt of payment of greater than the threshold amount of £6 per week' [emphasis supplied].[66] So the IDC ultimately, yet conditionally, suggests that girls and women were forced to work without pay but uses this suggestion as a means by which we might exonerate the nuns for not paying social insurance. The second and final reference in the Report to a lack of wages occurs in the penultimate Chapter Nineteen, where a lone unnamed former Magdalene is noted as saying that she received no pay. Otherwise forced labour is simply not addressed.

Confirmation Bias and Motivated Reasoning

The substantive epistemic practice of ignorance evident in the *IDC Report* occasionally offers a veneer of 'reasoning' understood by epistemologists as confirmation bias. Confirmation bias is the tendency to seek and favourably interpret information in a way that confirms or supports one's prior beliefs or values. The authors of the *IDC Report* only consider evidence that provides information and interpretations that reveals the agents of the Irish State in the best possible light. Confirmation bias in the Report is supplemented by motivated reasoning. Motivated reasoning describes the tendency where our emotional biases lead us to produce justifications for the conclusions we desire rather than consider explanations that accurately reflect the evidence. The *IDC Report* does not ostensibly investigate the Magdalene institutions bur rather proceeds with the conclusion that the Magdalene institutions were benign. The *IDC Report* is motivated by prejudice and bias, perhaps unconsciously held, but still deployed defensively by agents of the Irish State, resisting any process whereby the beliefs they promulgate might be falsified. Chapter Nine, entitled 'Routes of Entry to the Magdalen Laundries (A) Criminal Justice System' offers a pithy example of how the *IDC Report* deploys confirmation bias and motivated reasoning to create 'unknowing' – that is, a sense of doubt about what we know to be correct and a confusion about how to assess information presented to us. This part of the *IDC Report* focuses on the Garda practice of arresting girls and women who had escaped from the Magdalene institutions and returning them to their places of imprisonment. The IDC tells us that there was a standing order in the 1923 Garda Handbook that read: 'persons in institution [sic] uniform – if persons are noticed to be wandering about in the uniform of institutions, e.g. workhouse inmates, they should be questioned and if they cannot give a satisfactory account of themselves they should be arrested.'[67] Having asked Garda headquarters what the legal basis for this instruction and its implementation was, the IDC did not question nor comment on the response that: '[it] may refer to the power of arrest at common law for the larceny of the uniform. This was a regular incident that Gardaí had to deal with and indeed some Garda records show that people have received convictions for "larceny of apparel".'[68] We are supposed to accept as unremarkable that the girls and women who were arrested while trying to escape from the Magdalenes were guilty of the crime of wearing the uniform assigned to them. As Simon McGarr puts it, the 'Garda Síochána are arguing that the women were being lawfully arrested for stealing the clothes on their back.'[69]

Later in the same chapter there is an astonishing interpretation offered for the much-reprinted photograph of the women from Sean McDermott

Street Magdalene Laundry walking in a religious procession with a line of Gardaí filed on either side of them. The photograph dates from the mid-1960s. The Committee managed to identify and communicate with the priest and a Garda depicted in the photograph and accepts that it was merely coincidental that the two lines of Gardaí on either side of the Magdalene women just happened to be marching, at the same time in the same procession, 'in veneration of Our Lady and for no other reason.'[70] The IDC does not appear to have made any attempt to find any of the women pictured and ask them whether they thought they were under police surveillance.

'Modern Confusions'

Chapter Five of the *IDC Report* presents what it refers to as the 'large range of legislation underpinning state involvement with the Magdalen Laundries.'[71] The Report asserts that: 'It is possible that a lack of modern awareness of these Acts may have contributed to confusion or a mistaken sense that the Magdalen Laundries were unregulated or that state referrals of girls and women to the laundries occurred in all cases without any legal basis.'[72] A steady parsing of the awkward clauses of this sentence offers us an opportunity to attend to how 'unknowing' is created, that is uncertainty about what we thought we knew and confusion on how to proceed in creating reliable facts. 'It is possible… may have' promises a possible explanation. What will be rectified is a 'confusion or a mistaken sense' (that may or may not be the same thing), namely 'that the Magdalen Laundries were unregulated or that state referrals of girls and women to the laundries occurred in all cases without any legal basis.' So, are we to assume that state referrals of girls and women to the laundries occurred in *some* cases without any legal basis? (How were these Laundries 'regulated?') The reason offered for this 'confusion or a mistaken sense' is presented at the start of the sentence: 'It is possible that a lack of modern awareness of these Acts may have contributed to confusion or a mistaken sense.' What are we to understand by a 'lack of modern awareness of these Acts?' Should the sentence be corrected to state that a modern lack of awareness (or simply a lack of awareness) of some forgotten legislation has meant that we do not realise that the Laundries were regulated and that not all state referrals of girls and women had no legal basis?

What the *IDC Report* dismisses as 'modern confusions' (that the state did not apply proper legal oversight to the Laundries) are in fact accurate assessments both in specific cases and in general terms as attested by many instances given in the report.[73] For example, Chapter Five lists statutory provisions that permitted criminal justice detention in approved institutions for a defined period; permitted the 'recall' of a young person released from Industrial Schools for up to three months' further detention in the Industrial School – only if 'necessary' for their 'protection' and only with authorisation of the Minister for Education if aged older than 18; and empowered the state to pay grants under the Health and Public Assistance Acts for the maintenance of individuals in need of care. However, at no point does the IDC analyse or indicate whether these statutes were complied with. At no point, either, does the IDC mention the relevance or contents of that overarching and overriding piece of Irish legislation, the Irish Constitution, which defends and vindicates the personal rights of the citizen.[74]

Chapter Twelve, entitled 'The Factories Acts and Regulation of the Workplace,' claims to demonstrate that the laundries were under careful monitoring by the state's designated inspectorate of workplaces with the implication that the institutions were therefore compliant with their legal obligations: 'Records of inspections carried out indicate that on many occasions, no contraventions of the standards then in force were identified during these inspections of the Magdalen Laundries.'[75] The IDC fails to question what the content of its report as a whole – including the finding that girls as young as nine worked in Magdalene Laundries – suggests about the quality of the inspections that occurred. The Chapter incorporates evidence from the Department of Industry and Commerce, the Religious Orders, retired Inspectors and, in one case, a man who was the paid Manager of the Limerick Magdalene Laundry. Two former Magdalene women (who refer to the Factory inspectors as 'the suits') also give an account of the process for inspections. They report all work in the laundry coming to a halt, with the girls and women lining up outside the factory area while the Inspectors carried out their duties of checking the workplace and the machines.[76] In other words, no state official enquired about the welfare of those locked inside these 'factories' and forced to compulsory labour in the laundry. In this regard, the Report relays without comment: 'All of these retired Inspectors also confirmed that inspections of institutional laundries (including Magdalen Laundries) were conducted in precisely the same way as inspections of commercial or non-institutional laundries.'[77] A former Manager of the Limerick Magdalene Laundry said that he knew of three bad industrial accidents in the institution, and the Report records his anecdote that: 'The one in which the lady lost her forearm in the callender (large roller iron), I am reliably told by a Resident, was completely her own fault.'[78]

Miscounting and Not Counting, Countless Lives[79]

The Executive Summary of the *IDC Report* claims that '10,012 or fewer women are known to have entered the Magdalen Laundries between 1922 and 1996.'[80] The startling assertion that there may be *fewer* than the 10,012 incarcerated revealed in the religious records remains unexplained. Moreover, this figure is a significant under-estimate given that it excludes women who spent time in the Mercy Order's Magdalene Laundries in Galway and Dun Laoghaire, due to 'the absence of records.'[81] The IDC's claim that '10,012 or fewer *women* entered the Magdalen Laundries' does not give due significance to its own admission that girls as young as nine were held in those institutions, and its use of the word 'entered' is typical of how the Irish State continues to foster the impression that these institutions were somehow destinations of choice for Irish girls and women, who entered 'voluntarily.'[82] Furthermore, this official figure of 10,012 is manifestly unsupported in that the religious records relied upon were returned to the nuns and are unavailable for corroboration: an arrangement put in place prior to the nuns agreeing to cooperate with the IDC's inquiry.[83] The figure of 10,012 girls and women excludes those who entered before 1922 and remained thereafter – the state occludes these girls and women who total at least 762, nominating them as 'legacy' cases.[84] Neither does it include girls detained in 'voluntary' (unregulated but funded by the state) residential children's and teenage institutions known as 'Training Centres,' sometimes on the same grounds as Magdalene Laundries, who were forced by the nuns to enter and work in the laundries for some or all of their days.

The IDC asserts that the state placed 26.5 per cent of the women and girls affected into Magdalene Laundries by way of the courts, the Gardaí, local authority health and social services, Industrial and Reformatory Schools and Mother and Baby Homes.[85] However, this figure of 26.5 per cent is based on only 55 per cent of the already partial records available to the IDC since the remaining 45 per cent did not state a route of entry.[86] Other women and girls were placed in Magdalene Laundries by priests, family members and NGOs that received state support (and often acted on behalf of the state) such as the National Society for the Prevention of Cruelty to Children (NSPCC) or the Legion of Mary (accounting for 7.1 per cent of known entry routes). Most tellingly, the authors of the *IDC Report* do not know whether to count these organisations as 'State or non-State actors' and the Report admits that these organisations were working both in the capacity of agents of the state and as charitable concerns 'in unknown proportions.'[87] The practice of the state funding 'voluntary' denominational organisations rather than developing full state welfare and probation services is underscored in this admission.[88]

Perhaps the most egregious figures asserted by the IDC are those on the length of time women and girls spent incarcerated in the Magdalene institutions. The *IDC Report* claims that women's and girls' 'duration of stay' was on average 3.22 years, and the median was 27.6 weeks.[89] The average and median durations of stay figures are arrived at by treating transfers between Laundries and repeat entries as beginning a new period of detention.[90] It is also unclear if girls and women held in the Sean McDermott Street Magdalene on remand for a few hours or days while awaiting a court trial are also included in the computations. The IDC calculations also disregard the women who had entered Magdalene Laundries before 1922, many of whom died behind the convent walls having lived almost all their lives confined.[91] In calculating 'duration of stay,' the IDC also fails to count the women who remained institutionalised after the laundries closed down. At the time of the *IDC Report's* publication at least 117 former Magdalene women were still living at a number of nursing home locations around Ireland operated by the religious congregations.[92]

The *IDC Report's* presentation of its statistics on 'duration of stay' features prominently in the Executive Summary and the purported median stay of 27.6 weeks made news headlines on the day that the Report was released. The Executive Summary makes no reference to the fact that its figures are arrived at only by dismissing 58 per cent of the 14,607 available entry records on the basis that they do not disclose a duration of stay.[93] This information only becomes clear by an attentive reading to Chapter Eight. The IDC does not acknowledge that the absence of an exit date in a record might denote that a woman never left the institution. In fact, the *IDC Report* asserts that 'because the distribution of length of stay is skewed by the small number of women who remained in the Magdalen Laundries for life, the average length of stay is a biased estimate of central tendency.'[94] The unsupported claim by the IDC that only a 'small number of women remained in the Magdalen Laundries for life' is contradicted in the Magdalene Names Project (MNP) research, which indicates that for at least two institutions (High Park and Donnybrook in Dublin), over half of the girls and women who were registered in the electoral roll for these laundries between 1954 and 1964 died behind convent walls. In the case of the Limerick Magdalene, an average of 60.4 per cent of women on the electoral register between 1961 and 1983 died at the institution.[95]

In the Public Interest

The *IDC Report* closes with Chapter Twenty ('Financial Viability of the Magdalen Laundries'). The Committee claims that in examining the records of the four Magdalene orders it was 'aware' of the 'significant public interest in relation to the question of the profitability of the Magdalen Laundries during their years of operation. A common perception has been that the laundries were highly profitable.'[96] The *Report* goes on to say that 'Although the Committee was not required to do so, it decided, in the public interest, to conduct an analysis of the available financial records of the Magdalen Laundries in order to more accurately assess their financial viability.'[97] On the basis of scant one-page financial statements prepared by the religious orders' accountants, and in the absence of independent verification or a forensic audit of relevant accounts, the IDC concluded that 'in general, the Magdalen Laundries operated on a subsistence or close to break-even basis, rather than on a commercial or highly profitable basis and would have found it difficult to survive financially without other sources of income – donations, bequests and financial support from the state.'[98] The closing lines of the *IDC Report* provides an exculpatory explanation for the Irish State's involvement with the Magdalene institutions: if the state had not given financial support, the nuns would have found it difficult to have their institutions 'survive.' The explanation entirely ignores that the Magdalene Laundries were an abusive regime and the state should not merely have *not* colluded in perpetuating abuses but should have protected the girls and women held in these institutions from the manifold harms they suffered. Moreover, even the figures compiled by the nuns' accountants challenge the blithe assertion by the IDC that they operated 'on a subsistence or close to break-even basis' (it is unclear what the difference is supposed to between these two terms). Taking the account presented for the Limerick institution as an example, the laundry expenditure (excluding capital items) seems very high, given that the figure must represent power, fuel and detergent, yet it is over ten times the amount spent on capital items. Furthermore, the IDC attributes the living costs of the nuns in the Convent as Laundry expenses since 'to ignore their work contribution would distort the laundry costs.'[99] The copious amounts of oral histories, witness statements and journalistic accounts cohere on the view that only a few nuns were involved in running the Magdalene institutions, typically as supervisors and enforcers of discipline. Even assuming that the nuns did significant work (and this contradicts survivor and other eye-witness accounts) the nuns were not specifically recruited to supervise the Laundry. They were there because of a religious calling, a vocation. To offset the cost of the nuns' expenses, which their order would have had to absorb anyway, against the Laundry profits and hence to declare that the laundries were not profitable is hardly justifiable. Finally, the costs of maintaining the girls and women in the Magdalenes were also deducted from the Laundry profits. As Raymond Hill has pointed out, 'To deduct for the expense of imprisoning them amounts to a suggestion that the women should be forced to work to pay for their own imprisonment.'[100]

The state and religious orders deny access to the archives and documents on which their knowledge claims are (apparently) based and so their wilful practice of substantive ignorance is more difficult to challenge and falsify. The Department of the Taoiseach (DoT) currently holds the archive with copies of all state records gathered by the IDC. Although the IDC decided that 'maintenance of these copies together in a single location will be a concrete outcome to the Committee's work and may be a resource for future research,' the DoT has repeatedly rejected requests under the FOI Act 2014 for access to material in the archive.[101] The DoT asserts that: 'these records are stored in this Department for the purpose of safe keeping in a central location and are not held nor within the control of the Department for the purposes of the FOI Act. They cannot therefore be released by this Department.'[102] It seems that the state understands 'safe keeping' to mean denying access to survivors, family members, researchers or members of the public. The Department will not even release the archive's index.[103] The religious orders also refuse to open their Magdalene Laundry records for examination.[104]

Conclusion

Agents of the Irish State in their statements about former Magdalene women and in the production of the *IDC Report* uphold the social and cultural ascendancy of the status quo. The dominant religious and state ideology decided that the girls and women who were incarcerated in the Magdalenes were 'at risk' or guilty of contravening conventional norms of femininity that is a sexuality devoted to married motherhood as enshrined in the Irish Constitution.[105] Irish civil servants and politicians are not unique in seeking to maintain the hegemonic dominance of the cultural scripts and concepts by which they have ruled, so it is not perhaps that surprising that they do not want to know anything other than who and what they already know and recognise in the power systems they enact. This belligerent ignorance is a form of irresponsibility: an ethical and a political failure and an egregious lack of epistemic responsibility, in sustaining injustices that require contestation. Knowledge acquisition is integral to democracy: we need our knowledge to be robustly supported, unbiased, transparently acquired, communal and testable. Democracy requires that its citizens operate with a sense of a shared reality which must have some stability and coherence as the lynchpin of collective deliberation. Enacting democracy involves a literal articulation of how each step of the process of legislating, prosecuting, regulating or investigating adheres to fair processes and attests to the value of these practices. Enacting democracy will often involve changing which facts are brought into consideration. Jacques Derrida encourages us to consider that thinking ought to be a practice that never finds itself at a certain and definite end.[106] Derrida offers us this 'deconstructive' approach to acquiring knowledge as an attempt to render justice; as a relentless pursuit of justice that always remains on the horizon of the future to come. He argues that it is impossible to fully realise justice as ever being absolutely enacted in our present moment.[107] Derrida reminds us that like knowledge, where there is always more to know, so we should consider that there is never any such thing as sufficient justice and that it is necessary work to make justice possible in countless ways. In thinking about how the four principles of transitional justice might guide us in a collective dismantling of the substantive epistemic practice of ignorance promulgated by the Irish State in relation to the harms suffered by the girls and women of the Magdalene Laundries, I am guided by Derrida's example that our thinking practices must never confuse adherence to laws and regulations with justice. The transitional justice epistemic practices of truth-telling, accountability, recognition, redress and efforts to ensure non-recurrence of harms, must entail an on-going, never-ending attention to realising how we fail as we commit ourselves to justice. The practice of wilful ignorance, so evident in the *IDC Report* ignores engaging with factual evidence and belligerently resists legal reasoning and moral obligations including a respectful attention to the perspectives and experiences of former Magdalenes. The substantive epistemic practice of ignorance by the authors of the *IDC Report* seeks to shroud the (in)actions of agents of the state with the cover of adhering to the forms of law and regulations and shirks the work of justice. This ignorance is culpable not merely in being unjust but in risking that the recent traumatic history of the Magdalene laundries and the lessons that might be learned will continue to be something that perfectly decent people will both know and not know.

Acknowledgments: The author would like to thank participants in UCD School of Philosophy's Work-in-Progress seminar and Paul Lodge (Mansfield College, Oxford) and Joan McCarthy (University College Cork) for their generous comment on earlier drafts.

TWENTY-ONE

Materials and Memory: Archaeology and Heritage as Tools of Transitional Justice at a Former Magdalene Laundry[1]

Laura McAtackney

This article argues that refocusing the current emphasis on archaeology in planning laws, and its potential in creating cultural heritage, can play an important role in applying the principles of transitional justice to the legacy of Irish institutional abuse. Whereas transitional justice is frequently invoked in the immediate aftermath of conflict or as part of a decolonialising process, its principles can be applied to major societal traumas. In the context of South Africa, Lucas Lixinski has argued that cultural heritage has real potential in advancing transitional societies' need for social justice. Yet despite its formative role in creating and maintaining narratives of belonging, heritage is frequently overlooked in the transitional-justice process. Lixinski suggests that the significance of heritage lies in its ability 'to write and rewrite history,' an argument that has resonances in contemporary Ireland as we reconsider what we think constitutes 'heritage' and how it reflects the changing understandings of the nation.[2]

With Irish society at a transitional moment in the aftermath of decades of institutional abuse, we should reconsider the place of heritage in our understandings of nation and identity. This article explores how cultural heritage might be created from the material remnants of institutions and inserted into the national memory; it offers a case study based in contemporary archaeological practices and heritage approaches. Initially, it presents the role of archaeology in the planning process – a form of planning consultancy that locates, investigates and mitigates archaeological remains – and will argue for the potential to expand its remit in exceptional cases such as this. The article will present ways to rethink how we *do* this type of archaeology to include the voices of survivors and facilitate the transition of selected materials as cultural heritage and tools of transitional justice.

The Donnybrook Magdalene Laundry (1837–1992)

A traditional archaeological approach to the site of the former Magdalene laundry in Donnybrook is based on the concept of the 'polluter pays,' which places a legal obligation on the owner or developer to mitigate the impacts of construction on the 'environment' (within the Irish planning process, this includes archaeology). This principle governs much archaeological work in the Global North and is embedded in the legal frameworks regulating Irish planning by which archaeologists focus on locating, excavating and recording historic subterranean material and standing structures. Owing to an unsuccessful planning application to redevelop the site of the laundry in 2016–17, I was introduced to the material remains of that institution and advocated a more people-based approach to its 'archaeological' recording.[3]

The laundry has been long associated with its current location. Transferred to the Religious Sisters of Charity in 1833, it was subsequently relocated to its present site in 1837. Given the archaeological and historical evidence of late medieval buildings in the vicinity, Dublin City Council rejected the initial planning application and recommended ascertaining the age of the oldest parts of structure. Furthermore, the social history of the site as a Magdalene laundry led the city archaeologist to note the 'potential for burials being uncovered.'[4] (Undoubtedly, this decision was influenced by the number of recent scandals regarding un-consecrated burials of institutionalised women and children, including the infamous case of the Bon Secours Mother and Baby Home at Tuam, Co. Galway.)[5] In the aftermath of the failed 2017 Donnybrook planning application, the developers took two routes to deal with archaeological issues in the planning process. First, they commissioned geophysical specialists to locate disturbances below ground that might signify potential burials. Subsequently, all noted disturbances were excavated, but no burials were located.[6] They also contracted architectural historians to produce a report confirming the age of the standing structures abutting the road.[7] While these reports were being completed, I was contacted by the advocacy group Justice for Magdalene es Research (JFMR) to consult with the current owners regarding contemporary archaeology's best practices for the site. I was eager to advise on how to meaningfully interpret the legal obligations placed on the owners to archaeologically assess the Donnybrook site as I have a background in investigating recent historical institutions, which is unusual in the Irish context.[8] In interpreting the owners' legal obligations to provide an archaeological assessment of their Donnybrook property, I viewed the remit as exploring the location not just as a collection of functional, industrial buildings with associated contents, but as a place of trauma associated with institutional abuse.

My participation initially involved examining a pre-existing architectural report that used Ordnance Survey (OS) maps and on-site visits to assess when the buildings were constructed and how they evolved. These indicate gaps in the building's biography as the Religious Sisters of Charity, owners of the institution from the 1830s until 1992, had failed to provide specific documentation relating to the early development of the site. After protracted correspondence with colleagues aligned with JFMR, the Order had allowed limited access to records missing at the sale of the site – and hence unavailable to architects. The OS maps, although far from ideal sources because of gaps in the record, nevertheless provided a basic chronology. Although no purpose-built laundry facilities showed up on the maps of 1865, the basic structure of the current buildings was in place by the next OS map of 1907. Analysing the standing structures to ascertain that the building phases lasted from the 1870s to the 1970s, architects confirmed the absence of medieval remains *in situ* and detailed seven attached structures that constitute the former laundry. The three earliest buildings were erected between 1865 and 1907 and were joined by three more during the site's life as a Magdalene laundry. A boiler house was added in the 1930s, an associated building by 1968, and a large, open-plan, one-story structure between the mid-1970s and mid-1980s. The only part of the current structure formally protected is a chimney stack associated with the fourth building phase – the1930s construction is included on the Dublin City Council Record of Protected Structures (reference number 8713).

The architectural report confirms what one sees visiting this site: it is small, not particularly old, architecturally unexceptional, and grew organically as the needs of the laundry changed. All twentieth-century additions expanded the enterprise's industrial capacity, suggesting an increased demand for services and associated profits. The post-Magdalene laundry additions included a new toilet block, indicating the requirement of comfort facilities after the building was cut off from its previously adjoining domestic convent buildings. Representative industrial buildings of the period remain at the site, none with any qualities that would suggest a need to mitigate for them in the planning processes were it not for their social history. Although such history is not explicitly part of an archaeological remit in the planning process, it was, as already noted, the reason for the city archaeologist's request for further studies in response to the 2017 planning application. The architectural report makes clear that the degree and level of preservation of the structure's interior offered potential access to those social histories through the materials at the site:

> The property today has the appearance of a building which was simply locked and abandoned. Many of the presses, irons, industrial washing machines, and other equipment remain fully intact and in their previous positions. Crucifixes and other religious icons remain throughout, denoting the ecclesiastical affiliation of the building. Although there is debris, dirt, and bird droppings throughout, the previous history of the building is fully legible.[9]

Contemporary archaeology and critical-heritage approaches offer the means of engaging with this 'locked and abandoned' laundry in ways that interpret the legal statutes enshrined in Ireland's Planning and Development Act (2000).[10] Furthermore, following Lixinski's work in South Africa, as an act of transitional justice this article advocates that selected remains from this former Magdalene laundry become elevated to the status of national heritage.

A Contemporary Archaeological and Critical-Heritage Approach

The phrase 'contemporary archaeology' can appear oxymoronic to those working outside of a field assumed to be preoccupied with the past; this subdiscipline, however, plays an increasingly important role in the discipline. Although aware of its position in the present, its temporal focus continually shifts as it examines a moving moment unfixed to a bounded period.[11] Such archaeology conceives of the physical traces of the past in the present as palimpsests – assemblages of layered, overlapping histories imbued with the potential to reveal 'material memory.'[12] Although contemporary archaeological studies have existed since at least the early 1980s,[13] the current wave of interest in the field has been influenced by studies of the everyday, marginalised and forgotten, inspired by Victor Buchli and Gavin Lucas's *Archaeologies of the Contemporary Past* (2001).[14] Buchli and Lucas gather an eclectic collection of essays interrogating how and why archaeologists engage with the material world, but with a new emphasis on contemporary social relevance. They elucidate themes that remain touchstones for contemporary archaeologists today, such as the 'absent present' and 'presencing absence.' These concepts can most simply be understood as using archaeological methodologies to understand the interplay between what remains and what does not in order to 'materialise the material in the sense of making it matter.'[15] These concepts have had enduring importance in how we understand and explore our world in terms of seeking out materials that have been discarded, unconsidered or deliberately forgotten.

Following Buchli and Lucas, archaeologies of the present can be more intimately and actively engaged than other more traditional approaches. In James Dixon's words, 'we have a different responsibility to the world we study when the world we study is our own.'[16] However, the methodologies I advocate diverge from Buchli and Lucas's view that contemporary archaeology is by its very nature a distancing discipline. Instead I suggest that archaeologists can shape their methods to reflect the positionality of the researcher and the social-justice imperative inherent in their material. Whereas Buchli and Lucas emphasise the processes of alienation and distancing embedded in their approach to studying a recently abandoned council house, I deliberately offer a different perspective.[17] Rather than being guided by the 'proper' way to do archaeology – emphasising the objective and scientific processes of locating, recording and classifying – I conceived of the Donnybrook archaeological project as an attempt to bring us closer to understanding the people intimately connected with the site. The survivors of Magdalene laundries were therefore explicitly included in the post-closure recording of the site in order to compensate for their former erasure as forced occupants of it. Considering the survivors, their experiences and their wishes for the site inspired the methods used to record the place. Room was made to complete the more traditional role of archaeology in the planning process; Franc Myles took charge of documenting the extant industrial and social artifacts to allow 'preservation by record' of relevant materials from the former site.[18] But the study also offered space for survivors' perspectives to become embedded in the processes.

Considering how we conduct archaeology at the site has led naturally to exploring the implications for heritage, a loosely defined term meriting unpacking. There is a growing consensus that heritage is important: it is implicit in (national) power relations (i.e. whose past 'becomes' heritage and whose does not), and it is not simply a material thing but rather a process of production.[19] Critical-heritage scholars have moved away from focusing on the materials that one might call 'cultural heritage' and instead have dissected the meanings placed on these materials and the processes involved in 'valuing' them as heritage.[20] Laurajane Smith has been particularly influential in articulating the hidden power of the 'authorised heritage discourse' (AHD) of the nation – i.e. those things accepted as national heritage, considered part of our identities, collected by museums and utilised as focal points of memory and commemoration.[21] She has convincingly argued that AHD maintains the status quo and existing unequal power relations so that the things naturalised under the term, our heritage, are in reality solidly mainstream and middle-class. In practice our heritage often excludes those who are marginalised, othered or do not associate their values and experiences with those who are dominant in the mainstream of society.

By combining contemporary archaeology and critical heritage, the Donnybrook Magdalene Laundry project was framed as a form of transitional justice. Rather than allowing archaeological methodologies to distance the subject of the study from the researcher, the artifacts and structures would be used to include or 'presence' survivors. This approach meant that methodologies were selected and modified with the aim of not inadvertently replicating the narratives of power by simply fixating on the intended meanings of what remained in the former Magdalene laundry. From the study's inception we sought to do more than simply create a list of archaeological objects and then allow for disposal of these industrial remnants after they had been recorded. Instead we have aimed to work with heritage institutions to incorporate material remains of the laundry into the nation's authorised heritage discourse.

Site-Responsive Oral Testimonies with Survivors

Site-responsive oral testimonies at the former Donnybrook Magdalene laundry were designed to allow the material world of the former laundry to prompt memories of survivors. This process had three aims: to retrieve narratives personalising and supplementing what the material remains of the site revealed, to comprehend how the site shaped and directed the experiences of survivors, and to assist in the selection of remnants of the laundry that might be transitioned from functional artifacts to heritage. Although contemporary archaeology focuses on how material remains can inform us about the societies that use them, it is still rare to bring living people and places together (almost absent in archaeology undertaken within the planning process). At Donnybrook, however, we sought to make survivors connected to the recording processes.

This intervention was inspired by the work of the Ruin Memories Project (2010–13; http://ruinmemories.org), which has been extremely influential in contemporary archaeology in focusing on modern ruins and processes of ruination as revealing narratives uncollected elsewhere. The project's explorations of 'unwanted, outmoded or discarded' modern ruins, such as a fish-processing plant in Iceland, has obvious synergies with our work with an abandoned Magdalene laundry in contemporary Ireland. However, the emphasis on 'non-human interactions'[22] has inspired many studies of modern ruins being conceptualised as places *apart* from humans. Recording at the former laundry serves as a corrective to such ruin studies by offering an alternative, people-centred practice – not just for archaeology's role in the planning process but for the subdiscipline itself.

Assessing the Donnybrook site in 2018 cannot be divorced from the highly political context of these remains in contemporary Ireland, especially since many former Magdalene laundries have already been redeveloped or demolished without any consideration as to why and how they might be retained.[23] The context of why some places are abandoned, why this abandonment persists and why it is used to justify destruction (or major renovation) is important to consider when conducting such an archaeology project. The reasons why we were undertaking archaeological interventions at this place and time had as much to do with the contemporary as the past. I have previously argued – in the context of post-conflict Northern Ireland – that not all 'ruins' are the same.[24] While the patina of ruination can have the same aesthetic, can take the same material form, create the same patterns and contain the same biological components, the reasons for otherwise functional structures to become ruined can vary greatly. In terms of this former Magdalene laundry there was an imperative to engage with the politics of survival and destruction, ruin and maintenance. To frame this archaeological intervention of an abandoned laundry as a form of transitional justice we needed to be explicit about what the material remains – as they stand now – might reveal about the experiences of the survivors of these institutions. This goal necessitated including the reality of ruin as a point of departure.

Conducting site-responsive oral testimonies made clear that this was more than another defunct industrial site, abandoned and forgotten as a result of a failure of late modern capitalism – the cause that contemporary archaeology commonly attributes to the creation of modern ruins.[25] The abandonment, destruction and/or ruin of Magdalene laundries reveal a pervasive discomfort in contemporary Ireland in dealing with a past that many would rather forget.[26] The material worlds of former laundries can play a central role in remaking the Irish nation. They can add to our reflexive national identity by retaining the 'material memory' of a time when we institutionalised poor and vulnerable women and their children en masse owing to moralistic judgments of 'feminine transgressions.'[27] They presence what we should not be allowed to forget, but from an archaeological point of view they also provoke questions as to how faithful they are as material evidence.

During the process we decided to move beyond faithfully recording the contemporary site's artifacts as if they themselves provided an objective narration of the past. We took into account that there were many absences from its time as a Magdalene laundry that no longer survive, as well as more recent intrusions – objects that have been introduced to the site since it became a private laundry or after its abandonment. But most importantly, we did not want to relegate the Magdalene laundry's many survivors to the side lines. After liaising with JFMR we worked with a small number of them to add their stories as part of the process of archaeological recording. Only two oral testimonies were completed – a very partial representation of the potential to include the memories of a wide group of survivors. These recordings aimed to act as a small pilot project with a more methodological role, investigating the potential for site-responsive oral testimonies to be included in the archaeological process. The two testimonies will become part of a larger deposit, alongside selected material remains, that will be placed in a heritage institution. They are supplemented by pre-existing recordings of survivors' testimonies made by JFMR for a more extensive oral-history project (available on its website at http://jfmresearch.com/home/oralhistoryproject).

The study's site-responsive archaeological methodology included pre-designed guiding principles, with some openness to ad-hoc adjustments as the oral testimonies occurred. The basic methodology was derived from my previous work at both Long Kesh/Maze prison and Cahal McLaughlin's *Prisons Memory Archive* (PMA), projects that emphasised the importance of the individual engaging with the site in the present.[28] Pierre Nora's assertion that 'memory attaches itself to sites' inspired such a methodology of site-responsive interactions between people and material places.[29] The recording sessions were undertaken as a small-scale pilot project conducted over the summer of 2018 (the site has no electricity or heating and so was not suitable for winter recordings), with a significant degree of secrecy surrounding it. Following the advice of JFMR and the developers' wishes to avoid any unnecessary publicity, the site-responsive oral testimonies were not advertised to the general public.[30] In working with survivors we guarded against pressure to participate and also sought to minimise the potential trauma of re-entering the former Magdalene laundry. The oral testimonies, still in the process of being studied, include findings that were expected but also in some ways surprising.

The Impact of Ruination

In the conduct of the site-responsive oral testimonies the contemporary condition of the structure greatly impacted how the survivors were able to remember the former Magdalene laundry (Fig. 1). While both survivors were prepared to revisit the site by being provided with recent photographs, factual details about the site and its current state of dereliction, they were noticeably shocked at the condition of the building. Their experience was disorienting as the structure was fundamentally the same, the large machines were often in the same places, but the site had undergone many significant changes after several years of abandonment. In comparison to the orderly and highly controlled appearance of this site when it functioned, the current site was an uncanny proposition. Its features included large holes (and associated piles of concrete and earth) deposited across the floor of the former packing room, material indicators of where archaeologists had excavated the indicators of disturbance (Fig. 2). There were accumulations of post-functional debris (including cardboard boxes with polystyrene added to the site since its closure). Many portable artifacts had been moved from their original locations and placed in the packing area in preparation for an archaeological watching brief (to allow for the disposal of the post-functional debris).[31] Some of the walls had a liberal coating of recently added graffiti (Fig. 3).

Following Olsen and Pétursdóttir's observations of contemporary ruins, what appeared to be unnerving for the survivors was the site not being a 'clean, fossilised and terminated' ruin of the distant past.[32] As it was involved in the ongoing processes of ruination – 'this transient state, their being in-between and not belonging'[33] – it was shocking to witness. The lack of human activity at the derelict site was also a notable rupture for survivors to process. The feeling that this place should be peopled – that it retained the latent energy and the material evidence of previous activities – made entering it eerie. One of the first comments made by one of the survivors was the feeling that while it was empty, it was not empty: 'you get that feeling that they are just behind you, that they are watching you.' The 'they' whom she referenced were the nuns who previously would have instructed, watched and punished this woman. While the survivor was in a ruin in the present, at points she was simultaneously transported back to the past. The impact of ruination on survivors was real, powerful and potentially significant. Not only did it disrupt how they felt they would react to the place, but it disorientated their memories.

Figure 1. Interior of the industrial laundry at the former Donnybrook Magdalene laundry, summer 2018. Photograph by author.

Figure 2. Evidence of archaeological excavations in the former packing room, summer 2018. Photograph by author.

Figure 3. Graffiti located on the wall of the former packing room, summer 2018. It appears to read 'ABUSE.' Photograph by author.

Memories Evoked

As the survivors were recording oral testimonies in the moving moment of 'now,' the process involved a delicate interplay between walking through the site as it *is* in the contemporary, how it *was* in the past, and how it related in direct and indirect ways to their lives in between. Thus, their memories were often multi-layered owing to their refracting through other experiences occurring throughout their lives. Some memories articulated through site-responsive oral testimonies were not directly related to the survivors' time at the laundry, but rather provided contextual information as to how they were introduced to the laundry, how they left, how they felt about returning – as well as about the impact that the experience had both directly and indirectly on their life and their relationship with themselves and others. These insights were important to record and retain in order to connect the now-silent machines with past trauma.

Many of the comments, elaborations and asides made by survivors during their visit to the site revealed that, in James Deetz's phrase, the 'small things forgotten' of the past were as often remarked upon as were major traumatic events.[34] In listening to the women trying to make sense of the place, I was struck by the 'soft violence' of this now-derelict laundry.[35] Both survivors acknowledged that the return to the laundry provoked negative memories, but they also spoke about how they had actively tried to exorcise, make sense of and subvert the power of the place in the intervening years. Yet the impact of the forced incarceration of vulnerable girls and women during their formative years had left enduring scars. Their testimonies revealed the cruel and mundane nature of their experiences. They recalled the monotony and physicality of work, the harsh names they were called, the attacks on their femininity through cutting their hair as punishment – in short, how they were constantly indoctrinated with a sense of shame and worthlessness. The psychological and emotional abuse they endured was evident throughout their testimonies, as when one survivor involuntarily wept as she recalled having her hair cut to her scalp upon entering the laundry as a teenager.

Illuminating the Objects

Specific comments made by survivors offered information about the functioning of the site and suggested the efficacy of conducting oral histories alongside conventional material-focused archaeological approaches. Such information emerged either through survivors providing an anecdote about an object or space as we walked around the site, or when they were asked to elaborate on how the now-disrupted space had once functioned. In one telling example, one of the women, who was small, responding to queries about the operation of an industrial machine, pointed to a wooden crate on the floor and stated it was used as a makeshift step to help a petite worker like herself reach into large machines and remove laundry (Fig. 4). This anecdote provided an otherwise unknown (and unintended) use for the crate and indirectly revealed conditions that women endured working machines constructed for more physically robust operators.

Figure 4. A blue crate that had previously been used as a step to allow smaller women to access the inside of the industrial laundry machines, summer 2018. Photograph by author.

A discussion with a survivor about a large, modified table in the corner of the room initially offered useful information about how workers would use the various slots on its surface to sort the laundry (Fig. 5). But under questioning the discussion moved on to reveal the limited opportunities that these women had to communicate with each other. The survivor recalled how a nun reciting the Rosary sat on a now-absent rostrum and surveilled the women working beneath her. Only in providing prompted responses to the Rosary could these women break their silence. She revealed that if a Magdalene woman was observed not repeating the responses at the expected time 'one of the nuns would come down and give you a big tap on the head or something and she would say "answer your prayers, please!".' Without material evidence to indicate or 'presence' such information by the study's witnesses, the various regimes of control within the Magdalene institution are often overlooked in traditional archaeological studies.[36] But through working with survivors' memories, now accessed through their exposure to material objects, the study revealed details about the institution's controlling religious ethos. The building's many strategically placed plinths, for example, presenced the now-absent religious statues once displayed on them, and despite the building's derelict state, many religious objects were located throughout (Fig. 6).

Figure 5. A modified table located in the corner of the former packing room, which had been used to sort laundry prior to return to the customers, summer 2018. Photograph by author.

A survivor's memory triggered by a small, nondescript cabinet among rows of modified furniture, trolleys filled with building debris, bags of garbage, and assorted ephemera along one side of the packing room provided a rare insight into the domestic spaces once occupied by the laundry's workers (Fig. 7). Prior to the study this cabinet in the packing room was assumed to date from the time of the former Magdalene laundry, but although archaeologists intended to record and retain it, they lacked any information about its specific former use. Speaking after the conclusion of her formal testimony, one survivor identified that piece of furniture as a bedside table provided to each dormitory resident. She noted the rusted ring in the top corner of the cabinet, which indicated a now-absent water bowl provided for personal hygiene (Fig. 8). Since most domestic objects belonging to the laundry were retained by the neighbouring convent when the industrial parts of the laundry were sold in 1992, our ability to connect this nondescript cabinet with the former residents' domestic lives was significant. As far as we were aware, no other domestic furniture connected with the Magdalene laundry had survived on site by 2018.

Figure 6. A large statue of the Sacred Heart of Jesus alongside a fan placed on a large plinth above two ironing machines, summer 2018. Photograph by author.

Figure 7. Bedside table identified by a survivor located in the former packing room, summer 2018. Photograph by author.

Figure 8. Top of the bedside table in Fig. 7 with a rusted ring from a previous water bowl in the top right-hand corner, summer 2018. Photograph by author.

The Material World of a Magdalene Laundry and 'Authorised Heritage Discourse'

Archaeology's role in the planning process of the construction industry significantly determines what materials are to be recorded or preserved as heritage. In the Irish context official planning documents indicate the need to 'set out any measures to be taken to avoid or moderate any adverse environmental effects.'[37] To date, archaeologists have focused on excavating, recording and preserving old material culture. Less precedent exists for dealing with the materially mundane – if socially important – remains of a derelict industrial site. Indeed, the former Donnybrook Magdalene laundry suffers from a typical problem encountered with recently abandoned institutional sites: the repetitive and banal nature of the mass-manufactured, depersonalised and largely imposed material culture that they leave behind. On first encountering such a material world, we can easily dismiss it as unimportant. But Daniel Miller observes that the ordinary 'stuff' that surrounds us is notable not because of its exceptional nature but because of its seeming lack of importance: 'Stuff achieves its mastery of us precisely because we constantly fail to notice what it does.'[38]

We were fortunate that the redevelopment of Donnybrook's former

Magdalene laundry allowed archaeologists to assess its contents during a time when the National Museum of Ireland (NMI) was publicly reconsidering its traditional role.[39] That institution's increased openness to collecting contemporary material culture reflects a recent change in perspectives about what objects have social significance today.[40] Our group, working with curator Brenda Malone at the NMI, was driven by the shared conviction of archaeologists, JFMR, the developers and the survivors that 'preservation by record' would not be the sole fate of the laundry's contents. The creation of a new NMI collection from the Donnybrook site has not been an easy or straight-forward process. It has involved commitment, primarily on the part of the NMI, resulting in multiple site inspections, ongoing contact between the various stakeholders, updates from the site-responsive oral testimonies (which will eventually be deposited with the NMI) and most importantly the creation of new policies that allow for such contemporary collections to be acquired for the nation.[41] This change in status – from discarded contents of an abandoned industrial site to an official collection at NMI – will guarantee its ongoing survival at Ireland's major institutional definer of national heritage.

Selection for the collection included a range of artifacts from the site: large laundry-related machines; material infrastructure involved with transporting, arranging and receiving laundry around the building; religious statues and parts of the plinths to display now-absent holy figures; the bedside table identified by a survivor; suitcases and hampers stamped with the name of the Magdalene laundry and inscribed with the name and address of the recipients of cleaned goods (including Áras an Uachtaráin, the house of the president of Ireland, Fig. 9); and other large and small items associated with the running of the laundry and with the lives of its occupants. The scale of the site and its ongoing ruination meant that selection became an important part of the interpretative process. As archaeologists and curators, we knew that we could not keep everything; indeed, the repetitive nature of the material world of any institution in many ways simplifies the process of choosing items. Many were replicated into the dozens (for example, laundry carts), making selection imperative. But in the process we agreed about the importance of retaining not only obvious large objects such as the industrial washing machines but also the more mundane and easily overlooked items. The sacred was represented alongside the profane and the personal alongside the industrial, since all were associated with the biography of this site. We thus accessioned the office's fountain pen with accessories that were used to write labels and the cufflinks and rosaries found on the floor in an upstairs room (Fig. 10).

Figure 9. Laundry case with the owner noted on the side, 'Aras an Uachtaráin,' summer 2018.
Photograph by author.

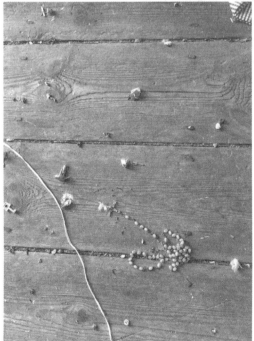

Figure 10.
An assemblage of cufflinks and rosary beads located in an upstairs room in the industrial-laundry buildings, summer 2018.
Photograph by author.

Efforts by all stakeholders to create a nuanced and accessible collection of objects from this former Magdalene laundry were on occasion frustrated by the disappearance of significant artifacts from the site. For example, the last *in situ* religious statue – a Sacred Heart statue above a set of pressing machines (Fig. 6), a modified bell (Fig. 11) and all the original sinks (Fig. 12) disappeared after we noted and photographed them in earlier visits. Illicit entry into the site through a number of access points ended only after more security was put in place, but now some important artifacts exist only in photographs that have been passed to the NMI.

Figure 11. A modified bell located on a shelf in the former packing room, summer 2018. This bell disappeared from the site between June and July 2018.
Photograph by author.

Figure 12. Two original sinks (one damaged) that were located within the industrial laundry, summer 2018. The sinks disappeared from the site between June and August 2018. Photograph by author.

The Way Forward

Formal legal mechanisms have provided some limited recourse to the survivors of the Donnybrook Magdalene laundry and other institutions with histories of abuse. But as various articles in this volume make clear, the state's response to extensive evidence of its collusion with abuse of vulnerable citizens has been unsatisfactory to victims. There have been no prosecutions, and to date no religious body running a Magdalene laundry has paid into the government's restorative-justice ex-gratia scheme. Clearly the routes to 'justice' through traditional legal mechanisms need to be expanded, and meanwhile survivors' calls for redress intensify the need to consider transitional-justice solutions as well as traditional legal ones.

These sites and their contents can hold the key to instrumentalising heritage as a tool of transitional justice in not merely ensuring remembrance of the past but also of inserting into the national narrative the state's failure to protect the most vulnerable. This acknowledgment might sensitise citizens to be cognisant of how little has changed. Marginalised populations continue to be institutionalised in the present, including refugees and undocumented migrants in direct-provision centres.[42] Following Nora's definition of *lieux de memoire*, the former laundries and their contents can act as our 'material memory' of past wrongs.[43] Selection and interpretation as people-centred approaches are crucial. Working in tandem, contemporary archaeologists and national-heritage institutions like the NMI can provide the nation with the means of more fully understanding its past. Other heritage institutions can create policies that encourage collections formed from the remnants of once-repressive institutions. These collections can transform the nation's authorised heritage discourse and in doing so encourage citizens to acknowledge recent church and state wrongs as worth remembering in order to ensure that past abuse is not repeated in the future.

TRUTH-TELLING AND
THE ARCHIVE

TWENTY-TWO

'Finding the me who I truly never quite knew': Lessons from Australia's Find & Connect Project in Facilitating Records Access

Shurlee Swain

Over a 20-year period the Australian Government has commissioned five inquiries into different elements of historical institutional abuse. Distinguished from earlier investigations by their focus on survivor testimony, they constitute a classic example of what Johanna Sköld has characterised as 'national chains of inquiries,' with survivor activism and media pressure using the disclosures of one inquiry to draw attention to similar abuses in other institutional contexts.[1] In Australia the chain began with the inquiry into the removal of Indigenous children from their families primarily during the twentieth century (an inquiry that had its origins in an earlier Royal Commission into Aboriginal Deaths in Custody),[2] then moved on to an investigation of the child migration program, predominantly in the post-war era.[3] Children who had grown up in out-of-home care over a similar period (now known as Forgotten Australians) used this inquiry to draw attention to similar abuses in their situation, earning their own inquiry three years later.[4] Women and their adult children who had been separated by adoption, again primarily in the post-war years, were then successful in having their experiences become the focus of inquiry.[5] The prevalence, although not dominance, of sexual abuse in evidence before each of these inquiries, combined with parallel survivor and media activism around clerical sexual abuse led finally to the establishment of the recent Royal Commission, a five-year investigation that took a broad view of institutions to investigate sexual (but not other forms of) abuse in a wide range of welfare institutions, churches and community organisations.[6] Responding to its findings the Commonwealth Government, for the first time, has added a national redress scheme to the previous response of offering an apology combined with the establishment of support services for survivors.

There are obvious parallels between the Australian and Irish experiences of out-of-home care and the subsequent government and scholarly inquiries into the abuse that it facilitated.[7] However, there has been considerable divergence in each government's response to the issues that the inquiries exposed. That divergence is particularly marked in relation to records access with the Australian state and federal governments showing a willingness to review archival and privacy procedures in order to increase victim/survivor access to information about their past while the Irish Government is slow to embrace calls for change.[8] The Australian willingness to move towards a greater openness is the result of a long period of engagement with survivor support groups, the two most important of which are Care Leavers of Australasia Network (CLAN) founded by Joanna Penglase and Leonie Sheedy in 2000, and the Alliance for Forgotten Australians founded in 2006.[9] This chapter explores the debates around records access in Australia, and the shifts that have occurred through a commitment to working with victim/survivors to bring about change. There is still more to do, as the barriers facing people currently applying for redress make clear, but the Find and Connect web resource does provide a model that Ireland could consider as it navigates competing claims around privacy and confidentiality while maximising access for survivors of institutional abuse and their families.[10]

Each of the Australian inquiries raised the issue of records, making recommendations focused on the preservation and organisation of records, and the need to remove barriers to access for survivors. The Find & Connect web resource was established as a key part of the Commonwealth Government's reparation package which followed the combined apology to former child migrants and Forgotten Australians.[11] Designed as an access point and information resource for the Find & Connect support services established in each of the states and territories, it was constructed by an interdisciplinary team of archivists, historians and social workers, working in collaboration with survivor groups, records holders, government departments and support services, and tasked with providing a comprehensive guide to organisations that had offered out-of-home care in Australia.[12] Although the Commonwealth Government was interested primarily in the period 1920–70, reflecting the experiences of the Forgotten Australians, the research team argued that such a focus was unnecessarily restrictive and set out to document every institution it could find, beginning in colonial times.[13]

The project began by uploading existing directories compiled by state governments, churches and Indigenous organisations in response to earlier inquiries, all of which had argued for improving access for care leavers to their records. The Royal Commission into Institutional Responses to Child Sexual Abuses accelerated this process as churches and other non-government organisations revisited their policies in anticipation of being called before the Commission. In order to speak with one voice Catholic bishops and the heads of religious orders established the Truth Justice and Healing Council which helped to standardise records-access policies and practices across the sector. The Council provided a space in which organisations that were leaders in the field could be used as an example to the more recalcitrant.[14]

Find and Connect then set out to augment the information from existing directories through further research and in response to updates from former care providers and public comments submitted to the website. The site is searchable by name, location and type of institution, and now via a map, and provides a history of each institution, details of its records, their location and access details as well as links to other relevant printed, online or visual material.[15] At the end of three years of active construction the web resource contained more than 15,000 entries, documenting almost 2,000 separate institutions, and 1,900 separate sets of records. Although the Federal Government now provides funding for continuing maintenance only, the team still has the capacity to update or add entries when new information becomes available. The project team also administers a small grants program aimed at assisting record holders to improve access to their archives. In the process of constructing the web resource, the team has learnt a lot about records, much of which is summarised in the fact sheet, *What to Expect*, that can be downloaded from the website.[16] This paper addresses four elements of this learning: the nature of the record, debates around content, issues around ownership and access, and best practice in records release. Such a discussion is particularly pertinent in the light of the recent promise of the Irish Prime Minister (Taoiseach) to establish a national repository for institutional care records.[17]

The nature of the record

As the final report of the Royal Commission observed:

> what constitutes a 'record' can vary depending on the context in which it is created, and who may have an interest in it. In the context of child sexual

abuse, what victims, survivors, law enforcement officials and others might consider a 'record' may be very different from what might be considered a 'record' in other contexts.[18]

Care leavers, Suellen Murray has argued, look to case records to provide the personal identifying documents that are generally held within families.[19] In applying for their records they may expect a single, coherent document that brings together all the key personal material but what they generally receive is neither coherent nor comprehensive. While best practice in records release involves bringing together fragments from a range of sources in an attempt to construct a coherent narrative, the nature and distribution of what has survived mean that the result is partial at best. In Australia, child welfare was a colonial and later state responsibility, with most of the eight jurisdictions maintaining parallel government and charitable or church-based systems. Children moved between systems, the records-keeping standards and practices of which varied very widely. The disorder of the records they left behind, Cate O'Neill and her colleagues have observed, 'mirrors the situations of the families that these children came from, families struggling to cope with hardship resulting from poverty, unemployment, family violence, bereavement, alcohol or mental illness.'[20]

The disorder of the records means that many care leavers struggle to locate the basic documents needed to access full citizenship in Australia.[21] However, by expanding the definition of what constitutes a record, it is possible to fill many gaps in a life story and point to alternative places in which the information needed to do so can be found.[22] This expansion, archivists Jennifer Douglas and Allison Mills have argued, dissolves the distinction between personal and organisational records, recognising that institutional records can function as personal records, and personal records have been used to fulfil institutional aims. A record is rendered personal in the reaction of the reader rather than by its inherent quality.[23] Only by understanding this broader notion of the nature of the record can care leavers and those who are working with them know what to ask for from the records holders they approach.[24]

While admission and discharge registers, and case files where they exist, provide the backbone of the record, that basic information can be augmented through a range of what are too often dismissed as 'administrative' documents. Evidence of a child's presence and experiences within an institution can be recorded in minute books, staff reports and superintendent, matron or cottage mothers' diaries, incident reports and punishment books, internal publications and annual reports. Medical and financial records, school reports, religious registers and staff and holiday host documentation can serve a similar purpose. Visitors' books, correspondence files and maintenance payment documentation can contain traces of parents and other family members otherwise erased from the official record, while death and burial registers can answer questions about missing siblings and friends. Photographic archives, promotional material, policy and procedure manuals and ephemera such as signs, toys and equipment can also be used to provide valuable contextual information to help care leavers reconstruct the lived environment of their childhood.[25] The Forgotten Australians inquiry was the first to recognise the cost of indexing these complex and sometimes fragile records in order to make them accessible, an issue that Find and Connect has been able to address through the small grants program it has been funded to administer over recent years.[26]

Rarely will all these records be found in the one location. Rather the typical search will take a care leaver through a series of archives, institutional, governmental and community, in order to find the '(me) who I truly never quite knew.'[27] For some Indigenous people the search begins with records held by the private landowners on whose stations they were born, their birth, and the deaths of other people in their communities, having been recorded in the pastoral property journals.[28] Publicly, and increasingly digitally, available archives such as births, deaths and marriages records, electoral rolls, telephone directories, courts and police records, military archives, genealogical websites, and newspaper and magazines can also augment the record.[29] Find and Connect entries provide a foundation on which care leavers and workers in support services can draw in attempting to navigate this wider records landscape. As individual records holders index their administrative records, the information can be added to the case file that is going to be released to the care leaver.[30] The best of the support services brings all this material together into something approaching a coherent narrative of a childhood, similar to that which an intact family is able to provide for their child. They also draw on information on the Find and Connect website to help the care leaver 'decode' the information they are receiving, explaining the structure and meaning of terms in the case record, and the historical concepts embedded in much of the contextual material.[31]

Debates around content

Find and Connect was constructed through a series of workshops that brought together care leavers, records holders, policy makers and academic researchers. During that process many of the problems associated with records release were debated. One of the major issues identified was the failure of the records to provide the content that was being sought. Care leavers initially approached their records with high expectations.[32] As one woman who made a submission to the Forgotten Australians Inquiry recalled:

> I dreamt about the answers I might find: why I could not read or write properly until high school; what screening process the homes had for the people who were allowed to take us out on weekends and holidays. More importantly, did they record and monitor the uncontrollable behavior problem I'd been afflicted with, and what was that medication they forced into me on a daily basis? I got to the State Library early and paced the foyer. The head librarian led me to the desk where a large book lay all by itself. My heart was thumping as he opened it. So there was the three-page history of our childhood. Mine was a whole two lines: M.S. Born Dec 1957. Sister of H.[33]

In part this sparsity resulted from a belief that children would be better off if the details of their past were erased, enabling them to make a fresh start away from the family that was seen as having failed.[34] In order to facilitate a clean break, letters were withheld and names and birth dates were changed.[35] However, it also needs to be acknowledged that the records were never designed to meet the purposes for which they are now being sought. As bureaucratic documents, they may have been written about children, but they were not written for them.[36] Even when they are expansive, their content reflects the priority of the organisation rather than the individual. As such they encode the views of the care giver, leaving no space for the voice of the child, giving primacy to negative incidents rather than individual milestones or personal achievements, creating a partial image that, through unquestioned repetition, sets the tone for the file as a whole.[37] As respondents to a survey of care leavers noted: 'Everything written about me was by other people.' 'I had no say in anything.' 'Never asked.'[38]

While care leavers are frustrated by the silences in such records, 'the places where we know there is more to the story, but for the purposes of the record in question, those pieces of the story were not relevant,' often the details that are included are more offensive.[39] Never imagining that the subject of the records would be able to read them, the authors of the case files were free to commit to paper their own moral views, distorted by prejudices around race, gender, class and intellectual disability.[40] As one witness before the Forgotten Australians inquiry commented: 'My parents may not have been the most admirable couple, but it is evident that the authorities took action on the basis of their own value judgements and personal preferences.'[41] Care leaver academics Jacqueline Wilson and Frank Golding see the negative focus of the files as further evidence of the relentless surveillance that marked their lives in care.[42] Historical documents retain, through their biased and inaccurate contents, a continuing capacity to traumatise.[43] The negative evaluations that shaped the lives of children also serve as barriers to achieving justice today, as the Royal Commission concluded, 'effectively concealing the extent and seriousness of sexual abuse that perpetrators committed and the extent of institutional knowledge about those perpetrators' abuse of children.'[44]

The care leaver activism that gave rise to the various inquiries has also redefined good archival practice, emphasising the responsibility of the records holder to explain the context in which the records were created and, more radically, arguing for the right of the person who is the subject of the file to challenge and amend the record.[45] The *Charter of Rights to Childhood Records* developed by CLAN provides the basis for the best practice guidelines released by the Federal Government. The guidelines recognise the right of the care leaver to incorporate their own story into the official record. Where they choose to do so 'the words and expression of the annotation or addition provided by the Care Leaver should be incorporated as provided, with no organisational editing, or changes, made by the Records Holder.'[46] Rather than being static artefacts, records in this conception are shown to acquire new meanings in different contexts, and hence need to be open to reinterpretation.[47] Archival theorists have argued that this process should be understood as a re-purposing of the record. By including the voice of the care leaver, the archive not only better serves those who use it to reconstitute their individual story, but also reshapes the way in which the history of child welfare is written in Australia.[48] 'Instead of being evidence that the organisations did their jobs well, the records show that the welfare agencies did not look after the children who were entrusted to them as they should have done.'[49]

Ownership and access

A second area for debate in the Find and Connect workshops concerned policies around access and ownership. In the past, records holders argued that access needed to be limited in order to protect the care leavers and others in their immediate family. In the process however, it is clear that they were protecting the interests of the organisation as well.[50] Once they became aware that such records existed, care leavers grew increasingly resentful of the restrictions imposed upon them, particularly when they discovered that bureaucrats and selected researchers were not subject to similar bars.[51] The situation was further complicated by the fact that access policies differed between affected groups. Unlike in Ireland, for example, the access provided for adopted people when their files were opened from the mid-1980s was more liberal than that provided for care leavers under later Freedom of Information legislation.[52]

Many care leavers remain profoundly suspicious of the organisations that treated them so badly in the past. Attempts to place conditions on access to records, or to explain their gaps and absences on fire, flood or other misadventure, are met with profound suspicion. As one submission to the Forgotten Australians inquiry concluded: 'The Department has numerous files, reports and information but choose to release only minor non-damning propaganda.'[53] Find and Connect seeks to counter some of such suspicion by providing corroboration, when available, for the events claimed to have led to the destruction of the files. Given the poor relationships, it is also not surprising that care leavers resented having to return to their former institutions to access their records.[54] They also resented restrictions that applied to them but not to scholars and officials who had unlimited access to intimate details of their family life.[55] In the aftermath of the inquiries, attitudes to records release have begun to change. Arguing that the records exist to help their subjects make sense of their childhoods, care leaver organisations believe that records holders are obliged to make access as simple as possible.[56] Identities do need to be verified but the process should be simplified and standardised so that it does not need to be repeated for every new organisation.[57]

Implicit in this shift in emphasis is a debate about the ownership of the materials that former care providers and government archives hold. Many care leaver organisations argue that the records holders should understand themselves as custodians only, with ownership being vested in the individual who should have the right to determine who can see the record, and indeed to remove it if they see fit.[58] Records holders, particularly government archival repositories, do not share this view, arguing that they have a responsibility to all Australians to keep their holdings intact. The Lost Innocents report sought to find a compromise between these two positions, arguing for the need to distinguish between what they called 'documents of identity,' the type of materials that families would normally hold for their children, and the official archives, suggesting that the former should be returned to affected individuals with copies retained in the files, a recommendation incorporated in the latest Commonwealth Government guidelines.[59] These shifts are evidence of what Joanne Evans describes as a move towards archival autonomy, with the individuals and communities whose pasts are the subject of official records becoming participatory agents in determining the conditions under which those records are preserved and made accessible.[60]

The Commonwealth guidelines also endorse the right of care leavers to control access to their records 'as far as possible during their lifetime.'The qualification is important as it applies primarily to family members seeking to access information and is carefully designed not to impede organisational access.[61] At the same time the guidelines aim to maximise the amount of information to which care leavers themselves should have access, seeking to navigate around a defensiveness amongst records holders privileging privacy over freedom of information concerns. The issue of redaction was frequently raised at Find and Connect workshops. In some cases redaction occurred where the records holder believed that the care leaver could be hurt by the information that the record contained, a practice that clearly exceeded the requirements of privacy legislation.[62] More often privacy concerns have led to the redaction of what was described as 'third-party information,' a major problem for a system in which the records for a family were commonly consolidated on the file of the oldest or youngest sibling, and in which the third party is most commonly a family member. Care leavers shared stories about repeated approaches to records holders that produced widely different responses, noting that, ironically, the more they knew from independent research, the more information they were deemed eligible to see.[63] By facilitating discussions between records holders and privacy commissioners Find and Connect contributed to a process of change that has seen care leaver concerns recognised in the national guidelines, which now recommend that they should receive:

> all personal identifying information about themselves, including information which is necessary to establish the identity of close family members, except where this would result in the release of sensitive personal information about others. This includes details of parents, grandparents, siblings – including half siblings, aunts, uncles and first cousins. Such details should, at minimum, include name, community of origin and date of birth where these are available.[64]

Where redaction has to occur, the Royal Commission report recommended that 'specific, not generic, explanations should be provided' to justify the action.[65] This approach redefines the notion of the third party, arguing 'that personal information may belong to more than one person simultaneously' particularly within families where a parent's information is also the child's personal information and hence should be accessible to them.[66] This response answers the frustration of one witness before the Forgotten Australians inquiry who declared: 'I am an adoptee, my birth mother is dead, my grandparents are dead and so is my natural father. Who may I ask are the bureaucracy protecting?'[67]

Best Practice in Supporting Care Leavers

The tensions that arise in discussions about refocusing the archive to meet the needs of survivors and care leavers have been the impetus for the development of best practice guidelines for records release and support services. Funding for support services has been integral to the Commonwealth Government's response to each of the recent inquiries, shared between existing survivor groups, pre-existing services for specific groups, and new services that can work across the sector. There are also records release and survivor support services funded by state governments and former care providers. This array of services reflects the widely held belief that care leavers need specialised support in accessing their records, and that for some, having to return to the organisations associated with their time in care can be a barrier to access.[68] However, it has also come to be recognised, initially in relation to adoption information, but increasingly in relation to care leavers as well, that, in line with the principles of archival autonomy, access to information is a right rather than a therapeutic service. There are people who are more than capable of navigating their records on their own, and they should not be compelled to engage with a protective service in order to do so.[69]

The Find and Connect web resource stands at the intersection of these two contrasting approaches. For people who work with survivors and their family members seeking access to records it provides access to the information they will need to both locate and provide context for the records being requested and includes material that agencies can use in training new staff in the requirements and expectations of the role. For the care leaver who decides to go it alone it provides the core information they need about the institutions in which they were confined in the past, and a guide to what to expect as they go about locating their records. Consolidating knowledge gained through the series of inquiries, and the experiences of survivors, records holders and professionals involved in records release, the Find and Connect web resource defines best practice in records release in a way that is accessible to all.[70]

Twenty-Three

Transitional Justice, Non-Recent Child Abuse and Archival Research: Lessons from the Case of the UK Child Migration Programmes[1]

Gordon Lynch

Between 1869 and 1970, around 100,000 children were sent from the United Kingdom to other parts of the British Empire and Commonwealth. Unaccompanied by their parents, these children travelled through migration programmes delivered by leading churches and charities, often with financial support from the UK and overseas Governments.[2] Inspired, in part, by internal child migration programmes in the United States – which later became known as the 'orphan trains'[3] – late Victorian philanthropists began to use the mass migration of children to Canada as a way both of addressing the material and perceived moral threats to their welfare posed by poverty, family breakdown or future unemployment and of meeting the demand for population growth in Britain's 'white dominions.'[4] By the 1880s a number of leading charities were involved in this work, including Dr Barnardo's Homes, the Church of England Waifs and Strays Society, Quarriers Orphan Homes of Scotland and the Methodist National Children's Home – later joined by the Catholic Church (through the Catholic Emigration Association) and the Salvation Army.[5] These schemes are estimated to have sent around 90,000 children to Canada until their suspension and then widespread closure in the mid-1920s.

This essay is less concerned with this earlier history than with the migration of approximately 4,000 children through child migration programmes operating from the UK in the post-war period. Most of these children went to Australia but several hundreds were also sent to New Zealand, Canada and the former Southern Rhodesia. Whilst the earlier schemes to Canada arguably drew on practices of 'boarding out' children used more widely at that time by voluntary societies and local Poor Law Unions (albeit with an expanded geographical reach underpinned by the imperial imaginary of a 'Greater Britain'), many post-war child migration programmes operated in greater tension with accepted child-care standards of the day. Since the late 1980s growing public attention has been paid to post-war British child migrants' accounts of abuse and neglect in the residential institutions to which they were sent, with the most commonly reported accounts relating to life in Australia. Allegations grew of the migration of children without proper parental consent to geographically isolated and emotionally impersonal residential institutions in which many suffered from physical and/or sexual abuse, a lack of adequate education and the exploitation of their labour, or were inaccurately told that they were orphans who had no surviving family members back in Britain.[6] This has, over time, led to the treatment of post-war British child migrants to Australia becoming the whole or partial focus of nine different inquiries and reports, as well as formal national apologies by the Australian and UK Prime Ministers in 2009 and 2010.[7]

In some respects, the history of post-war British child migration and the critical re-evaluation of its effects on those children caught up in it, does not fit models of transitional justice well. Stephen Winter has, for example, argued that transitional justice in established democracies can be understood in terms of making amends for forms of authorised wrongdoing by the state that were underpinned by historical frameworks of legitimation from which that society has turned.[8] Such a model fits well the critical re-evaluation of harm caused by the culture of Catholic nationalism in post-independence Ireland which fused the moral meanings and institutional structures of Church and nation-state.

Winter's model works less well for the involvement of the UK Government in post-war child migration schemes, however. Far from representing accepted practice within a historical framework of legitimation, the post-war child migration schemes ran counter to an increasingly influential understanding of children's care in that period, shaped in part by ideas from psychoanalytically-informed approaches to child psychology that emphasised the importance of attention to children's inner emotional worlds and their emotional bonds with their parents, as well as interest in the significance of creativity and play for children's social and psychological development.[9] Child migration was viewed with caution in the 1946 *Curtis Report* (which was instrumental in setting the framework for the out-of-home care of children in the emergent post-war British welfare state),[10] which recommended that it only be allowed to resume if children received standards of care overseas at a comparable level to what the report recommended be implemented in England and Wales. More outright concern was expressed by some professional and voluntary bodies involved in social work and mental health. Local authority children's officers, often operating on the basis of Curtis principles which emphasised maintaining family bonds where possible and placing children in 'family-like' environments, were also unenthusiastic about child migration programmes with little more than 10 per cent of post-war child migrants being sent from the care of local authorities.[11] Even within voluntary organisations involved in this work, support for child migration work was not universal.[12]

Post-war child migration resumed not because it was universally assumed to be an appropriate form of child-care, but because it operated in a complex juncture of public policy on childcare and assisted migration in which the post-war politics of Commonwealth migration encouraged gradual reform of this work rather than an outright ban. Conscious of the importance of maintaining good working relationships with Commonwealth partners in an unstable geopolitical context, United Kingdom officials were acutely aware of the desire of the Australian Commonwealth Government to increase Australia's population through immigration as well as varying institutional motivations of the different voluntary societies involved. Continued policy and funding support from the United Kingdom Government was premised less on political enthusiasm than on a willingness to accept an imperfect and administratively fragmented system of assisted child migration in the context of other policy priorities. Far from reflecting a past political consensus now recognised as wrong, post-war child migration operated through failures of systems, judgement, resolve and knowledge particularly amongst civil servants working within the United Kingdom Government.

Some of these organisational and cultural causes of policy failure may well also have shaped government policy and systems in Ireland that are implicated in the various forms of abuse discussed in this book. There are also interesting questions to be explored about the extent to which the growing post-war consensus about children's care in the United Kingdom, exemplified in the *Curtis Report*, were comparable to or different from notions of the best interests of the child amongst professional and voluntary organisations in Ireland. The aim of this chapter is, however, not to consider these historical questions, but to examine potential lessons from the critical re-examination of UK child migration schemes for practices and debates about transitional justice in Ireland. More specifically, this chapter draws on the experience of the numerous public inquiries and investigations – particularly into post-war child migration to Australia – to consider how archival research may contribute to transitional justice processes of truth-telling and accountability.

I write as someone with direct experience of some of these inquiries. In 2016 and 2017 I worked with another colleague, Stephen Constantine, as an expert witness on the UK child migration schemes under instruction to the Independent Inquiry into Child Sexual Abuse. This process involved us co-authoring a substantial report reviewing the legal and policy context of child migration schemes, their operational systems and historic and more recent knowledge about the sexual abuse of British child migrants. This was supplemented by 21 substantial addenda that we co-authored about the work of specific governmental and voluntary organisations involved in these schemes based on primary archival research that utilised material held both in national archives and the archives of specific voluntary organisations, including material to which academic researchers would not normally have access. This material consisted both of archival material that we ourselves identified to the Inquiry team and material that they made available to us following s.21 notices submitted by the Inquiry to relevant governmental and voluntary organisations that legally required respondents to provide various forms of evidence. We were able to analyse this material both to provide broad overviews of the policy context and organisational systems for post-war child migration and to investigate in more detail how these systems operated in practice, how organisational practices adhered to reasonable standards of the day and organisational knowledge and responses to specific incidents of abuse.

Our written and oral evidence was widely used in the Inquiry's final investigation report on the child migration programmes and underpinned its primary recommendation that the United Kingdom Government should urgently establish a redress scheme for all surviving British child migrants given its systemic safeguarding failures. The United Kingdom Government agreed to implement this recommendation in December 2018, and has since made individual payments of £20,000 to over 1,600 former British child migrants, totalling in excess of £32 million. In 2019 and 2020, along with Stephen Constantine and Marjory Harper, I undertook similar work for the Scottish Child Abuse Inquiry's investigation into the emigration of Scottish children, and also produced a complementary report examining the nature and extent of allegations of sexual abuse against staff and visitors at four residential institutions for children run by the Christian Brothers in Western Australia.[13] Through this historical work for public inquiries I have been able to reflect on the different methodologies used by Inquiries, including their uses of archival material, as well as to reflect on and refine my own approach to such research. The reflections presented in this chapter emerge from this experience and are offered in the hope that they may have some relevance to ongoing approaches and debates in relation to the critical re-evaluation of human rights abuses in the post-independence Irish state.

The Nature and Value of Archival Material for National Truth-Telling and Accountability

There is extensive archival material relating to post-war UK child migration to Australia alone. Given the range of governmental departments as well different voluntary societies involved in the United Kingdom and Australia, material relating to these schemes is held in over 30 archives in both countries. These include national archives, state archives in Australia and archives relating to, and often managed by, individual voluntary organisations. Access to this material for researchers varies considerably. Whilst the public archives generally allow greater access and provide clearer cataloguing of holdings, the private archives of voluntary societies can prove far harder to access. Some voluntary society archives that are held at universities – or have been held and catalogued at universities in the past – do have more transparent terms of access and provide better information about the material held. In other cases, however, archives that are entirely managed by voluntary organisations can provide far less information or access for external users, to the extent that there is little or no information about the archive's existence, location or manager in the public domain. Research exemptions within the General Data Protection Regulation allow researchers to use archival material that relates to specific individuals as long as these individuals are not identified and the material is not used in any way to guide decisions affecting them. Despite this, in practice, some voluntary societies place considerable restrictions on access to their archives, either denying access completely or exercising their gatekeeping powers in such a way that researchers cannot easily establish what material they hold and/or have to work with very limited material that the organisation chooses to make available to them. In this regard public inquiries such as the Australian Royal Commission or the Independent Inquiry into Child Sexual Abuse have represented important moments in which voluntary organisations can be compelled to make archival material available for independent scrutiny. Even in these cases, though, inquiries' powers are limited to the national jurisdictions within which they operate, and recent investigations of child migration programmes by inquiries in the United Kingdom have been unable to get some organisations in Australia, including the Christian Brothers in Western Australia, to make their archives available.

The type of material held in archives also varies considerably.

Policy and operational files of government departments include public-facing documents (including copies of reports, regulations and public memoranda), inter-organisational communication (including correspondence and memoranda between government departments and with voluntary societies), and intra-departmental communication (including hand-written notes and memoranda that can often be particularly valuable in understanding the relationship between views held within a department and its external communication and decisions). In the case of voluntary societies' archives, material held includes annual reports, minutes and documents of organisational meetings, internal and external correspondence and case files relating to individual child migrants. Digitisation has transformed the analysis of this material. In the wake of governmental inquiries in Australia in the early 2000s on child migration programmes and the treatment of Australian-born children in out-of-home care,[14] a more sustained effort was made both to create online resources to help former child migrants and care leavers access their records and other historical resources and to make the contents of relevant archive files in the National Archives of Australia available online.[15] The ability to create digital copies of files in public archives has also made it possible for researchers to re-analyse documents over an extended period of time rather than relying on notes they made from single readings of that material whilst visiting the archive itself.

In the case of the UK child migration schemes this has meant that inquiries undertaken in the past five years have had much greater capacity to support close analysis of archival material than the first wave of inquiries undertaken from the mid-1990s. This has made possible a shift in methodology of these later inquiries away from reliance only on witness statements from former child migrants' and organisational self-reports about their historic practices to include independent scrutiny of archival material that might inform an understanding both of individuals' experiences and the institutional cultures and systems of these schemes. In the case of inquiries into the child migration schemes, the relationship between survivor testimony and archival evidence has become further blurred by the fact that survivor accounts of abuse have been collated since the early 1990s. My most recent work for the Scottish Child Abuse Inquiry therefore included analysis of archived letters and other documents generated by the VOICES campaign in Western Australia in which former residents of Christian Brothers' institutions in that state, several of whom are now deceased, described their experiences.

The relationship and balance between survivor testimony and archival evidence remains a complex and sensitive one for inquiries.[16] In contexts in which survivors of abuse have often, for various reasons, found it difficult to find restitution through the criminal justice system or civil litigation, inquiries have sometimes come to stand as an alternative form of symbolic restitution which claim to give greater public recognition to survivors' experiences.[17] Belief of the survivor's account thus acquires particular public and moral significance in the absence of legal redress. It is evident, however, that both survivor testimony and archival analysis can serve as complementary sources of knowledge, without one necessarily needing to be privileged over the other. Survivor testimony provides crucial insights into lived experiences of abuse, the inter-personal dynamics that facilitated abuse and the ways in which institutional practices failed to adhere to expected or claimed standards of the day. Equally, archival sources provide insights into policy contexts, organisational systems and the knowledge and decision-making of key organisational figures of which survivors were unlikely to have been aware at the time. In this respect, it is clear that Inquiries into historic abuse are best served by making use both of survivor testimony and archival analysis in ways that allow each to inform understanding of the other.

More difficult questions arise when evidence from survivor testimony and archival materials appears to contradict each other. In some cases this may be because an individual survivor does not necessarily recall clearly the chronology or individuals involved in their abuse or may have come to interpret the wider institutional context for their abuse in ways that are not supported by wider data. In other cases such apparent contradictions can also lead to more nuanced interrogation of archival data. For example at the Christian Brothers' residential training institution at Bindoon in Western Australia, former British child migrants recalled sexual abuse by a Brother whom registers indicated was never on the staff at that time. Their recollections have helped to raise questions about informal visits between institutions that Brothers undertook for various reasons, which were not easily identified from initial archival analysis. As these informal visits have become a greater focus for investigation, stronger grounds have emerged for believing that the recollections of these child migrants reflected a wider network of relationships between abusers that spread across a number of the Brothers' institutions in Western Australia.

Whilst questions about the use of different kinds of sources of knowledge require careful reflection in the design and operation of public inquiries, the numerous investigations of the UK child migration programmes over a 25-year period have demonstrated why independent analysis of archives has an important role to play in this process. Archival analysis can provide a stronger evidence-base on which to think critically about organisational self-reports about their historic practices. For example the multi-agency nature of the UK child migration programmes has meant that, in a number of instances, organisations have sought to minimise their involvement or sought to shift responsibility onto other organisations involved (a process that can also, on occasion, be observed whilst these programmes were operating). In a meeting with the Western Australian Select Committee into Child Migration in 1996, the then Parliamentary Undersecretary of State for the UK Government's Department of Health 'was at pains to emphasise that the UK Government had not delivered the service and did not play a central part in it.'[18] In its interim report the Select Committee expressed scepticism about this assertion having located a copy of the Report of the 1956 UK Fact-Finding Mission which made clear both the degree of financial support given to these programmes by the UK Government at the time as well as the extent to which the programmes were subject to Government regulation and ongoing policy discussions. In its evidence to the 1997/98 House of Commons Health Committee on the welfare of former British child migrants, the Royal Overseas League claimed that it had been involved in recruiting child migrants for New Zealand only at the invitation of the New Zealand Government, with the latter taking primary responsibility for the operation of that scheme. In its final report the Health Committee challenged this claim, noting archival material provided by the New Zealand Government that indicated that this particular child migration programme had been actively proposed to it by the Royal Overseas League.[19]

Other instances have occurred in which witnesses representing organisations have made inaccurate claims to investigations about organisational knowledge of abuse which have only been successfully challenged by subsequent investigations based on independent archival research. In evidence to the UK Health Committee Inquiry, the then Director of the Fairbridge Society, David Haynes, suggested that claims about the abuse of children at Fairbridge farm schools in Australia had been led by what he regarded as sensationalised media coverage of the schemes. Whilst criticising his view as 'complacent' in their final report, the Select Committee was not aware that Fairbridge archives contained historical documents concerning the physical and sexual abuse of children at Molong.[20] The Independent Inquiry into Child Sexual Abuse subsequently established that, in 2007, Mr Haynes had authorised a briefing document for journalists enquiring about cases of abuse at Fairbridge farm schools which inaccurately stated that the Fairbridge archives contained no evidence of any cases of abuse – a claim shown to be demonstrably false by independent inspection of those archives undertaken for the Inquiry.[21] Similarly, Br Shanahan, a Christian Brother, was Convenor of the Catholic Church's Joint Liaison Group into Child Migration that made a submission to the Senate Community Affairs Committee Inquiry in Australia in 2001.

This submission stated that the standard of care within Catholic institutions was generally within the bounds of what was safe, proper and lawful and that any instances of sexual abuse did not seem to have come to the notice of congregational, diocesan, federal or state supervising authorities. Later, in his evidence to the Royal Commission into Institutional Responses to Sexual Abuse in Australia in 2014, Br Shanahan said that he was now embarrassed by that claim given that the Commission had received documentary evidence drawn from the Provincial archives of the Christian Brothers that demonstrated that the sexual abuse of children in their care was known to the leadership of the Christian Brothers in Australia in every decade from the 1920s to the 1960s.[22]

These examples make the, perhaps obvious, point that organisations' self-reports about their involvement in work in relation to which concerns about historic abuse have been raised is not a reliable source of evidence, without corroboration from independent scrutiny of those organisations' archival records. Such scrutiny can be difficult to achieve, however, for investigations undertaken with limited resources of staff, time and expertise. The lack of such scrutiny can inevitably impose limits on the evidence base from which investigations draw their findings, with this effecting both the investigation's role as an exercise in 'truth-telling' and its precise conclusions about organisational responsibility. In Northern Ireland the Historical Institutional Abuse Inquiry was able to identify systemic failings in post-war child migration from Sisters of Nazareth institutions in Australia drawing on some primary archival sources and secondary literature. However, the limited analysis that it was able to undertake of archival sources meant that its findings were presented without an understanding of the awareness of problems amongst some leading Catholic administrators with receiving institutions in Australia, the possible implications of children's direct recruitment by Australian Catholic officials for the legality of their emigration, and of the wider policy context in which Catholic child migration ended in December 1956.[23]

Analysis of archival materials can therefore support more nuanced understandings of organisations' historic policy decisions and practices than can be relied on simply through organisational self-reports. Such nuance is important as contemporary understandings of the organisational contexts of non-recent abuse can sometimes be shaped by the assumption that the past represents a darker and less enlightened time, in which standards of care that might be expected in contemporary society were not understood. Whilst such assumptions can sit easily within a view of society as progressively moving towards ever-higher standards of care and respect for human rights, they are often challenged by historical research. Historical analysis of policy debates and safeguarding regulations – such as the relevance of the 1946 *Curtis Report* in framing the policy context for post-war child migration – can demonstrate how governmental and voluntary organisations may simultaneously have understood the needs of children and vulnerable adults whilst failing to protect them in practice. Archival analysis – including of the kinds to be described in the next section of this chapter – can also produce more nuanced understandings of the causes of safeguarding failures within specific institutions. Whilst public understanding of non-recent abuse can be informed by broad narratives about historic institutional failures, sharper understandings of the ways in which the specific cultures and structures of different organisations contributed to this can help both to clarify the nature of organisational responsibility for past harm and also raise questions about whether problematic aspects of these organisations continue in some form in contemporary society.

Approaches to analysing archival material

Drawing on my experience of work on the history of the UK child migration schemes, this chapter will now explore different approaches to the analysis of archival material. One of the major advantages of undertaking this work using digital technologies is that it was far easier to make use of material from geographically dispersed archives than it had been for any of the inquiries on the child migration programmes undertaken before 2014. Whilst previous inquiries had made use of some archival material this tended to be limited in volume and with inquiries usually only using material from archives in the country in which they were based. By contrast, the work for the Independent Inquiry into Child Sexual Abuse and the Scottish Child Abuse Inquiry was able to utilise material from archives in both the United Kingdom and Australia in ways that generated valuable new insights into this history.

A central observation to be made here is that the quality of insight produced from archival analysis is often increased by access to multiple organisational archives which both support richer understandings of how common issues and events were understood from different perspectives and also indicate the dynamics of communication between organisations. Such source material, inevitably, has its limitations as historians and archivists have noted more generally in relation to the processes through which archives are produced and interpreted.[24] The preservation of written records of interactions, views and decisions in archives do not necessarily capture complex inter-personal relationships between historical actors. Personal conversations, which often provided an important context for these organisational processes, are often lost or appear only as traces in written documents. Historical decisions about what was worth recording in organisational documents do not always fit the questions that contemporary researchers wish to ask. Some material is also often lost to archives over time either through periodic sifting of material judged not to be worth retaining by archivists or more systematic decisions to dispose of material judged irrelevant or unhelpful to the organisation's interests. Whilst gaps in archival records can, in some cases, provide useful insights into patterns of communication between organisations or omissions in organisational practices, in other cases these gaps mean that some historical questions cannot easily be answered. What is found in archives has to be understood as what was perceived within organisations as being worth recording at the time, reflecting institutional practices, power structures and often competing interests, rather than any complete record of the past.

Reliance on a single archive can have significant limitations. In some earlier inquiries, organisations involved in the operation of UK child migration programmes have presented accounts of their past work solely on the basis of an analysis of their own archival holdings. This can, at times, be a consequence of inquiry methodologies that invite organisations to provide statements purely on the basis of their own institutional archives, although some inquiries do invite organisations to comment on any other archival material they are aware of that has a bearing on their work. When commenting on the contents of their own archives, organisations can on occasion provide inaccurate accounts or, more often, the most benign interpretations of this material. Failure to situate the contents of these institutional archives in the context of other material, for example material that is publicly available at national archives, can sometimes lead organisations to fail to recognise the policy context and standards in which they were operating, to miss evidence of systemic failures of which they should have been aware at the time, or even to make basic factual errors. These problems are often compounded by the fact that organisations implicated in non-recent abuse have not often taken a pro-active approach to develop a critical understanding of their historic practices informed by wider historical research.

By contrast comparative analysis of material from multiple archives can generate far more complex accounts of inter- and intra-organisational processes. Four different types of analysis will be briefly discussed here: first, the development of chronologies of events from multiple archives; second, the analysis of material to establish the process and basis of policy decisions that shaped the contexts in which non-recent abuse took place; third, the use of comparative analysis to establish gaps or failures in organisational systems; and fourth, the comparative analysis of different types of data from multiple archives to clarify specific organisational processes.

First, then, the development of a chronology of events from multiple archival sources is an obvious element of more complete historical narratives about past organisational knowledge, decisions and activities. Broad narratives charting key moments in national policy development or major changes in the organisational knowledge, resources and practices are of obvious value in providing a framework within which closer analysis of individual organisations can be undertaken. Producing such narratives in a way that is attentive to wider, relevant political, economic and socio-cultural changes is also important for ensuring that historical events are understood in context. Through the process of undertaking archival research on the UK child migration programmes it also became clear, however, that there was considerable value in producing more detailed chronologies of events focused on more specific periods, events or organisations.

One example of this was the analysis of the early post-war child migration work of the Overseas League.[25] In this case, the League had been unable to offer much detailed insight into its child migration work to Australia from its own records as its archival holdings in relation to its child migration activities appear to have been substantially disposed of at some point since the mid-1950s. A file from the UK National Archives recorded correspondence in 1948 between child-care officials in London County Council and the Children's Department of the Home Office in which concerns were discussed about the rigour of the League's selection processes for its child migration work to Australia. Within this correspondence, it was noted that Cyril Bavin, the League's migration secretary, had claimed that the League had already sent 130 child migrants to Australia between the end of the war and February 1948.

Analysis of archives held in Australia, however, showed that the League only formally approached Australian Commonwealth and state immigration officials for approval of this scheme in August 1948. Despite this approval being refused by Australian authorities that summer, the League continued to send some children to private households in Australia after this date.

It was later claimed by Bavin that all of these children were returning to Australia having previously been evacuated there from Britain during the war through the Children's Overseas Reception Board (CORB) scheme. Again, material held in other archive files in the United Kingdom and Australia raise doubts about this claim. A specific case discussed between London Country Council and the Home Office concerned two boys whom the League were proposing to send to Australia who had no prior contact with the CORB. Similarly, an archive file in Australia contained a query in June 1949 from a State Department of Immigration official in New South Wales to the Chief Migration Officer at Australia House in London asking why some children had arrived in Australia under a 'CORB' designation when in fact they were not returning CORB evacuees. The reply from the Chief Migration Officer implied that it was best not to challenge this arrangement as it was helpful to have the League's involvement in supporting child migration. A few months later the most senior civil servant in the Australian Commonwealth Department of Immigration wrote to the Chief Migration Officer in London explicitly telling him to discontinue his practice of designating some child and juvenile migrants as returning CORB evacuees when this was not the case.

The significance of the use of the CORB designation in relation to children emigrated by the League was that the Australian Commonwealth Government was prepared to accept returning CORB evacuees but not the League's proposal to send other children directly to private Australian households. In response to the Commonwealth Government's refusal to approve the League's wider scheme, it appears that Bavin and immigration officials at Australia House in London had operated a system for the migration of children in which some were inaccurately designated as returning CORB evacuees in order to circumvent the government restrictions. In this instance, a closer chronology of the League's post-war child migration activities suggested that Bavin may not always have been careful or honest in his administration and presentation of this work, and that there may have been some collusion by immigration officials at Australia House, who were, themselves, under pressure to try to keep a regular flow of children and other immigrants arriving in Australia.

A second form of analysis that proved valuable in relation to the UK child migration schemes focused on the systems and basis on which policy decisions were made. Despite the shift towards more coherent administration of children's out-of-home care in the United Kingdom after the 1946 *Curtis Report*, post-war child migration to Australia operated on the basis of complicated lines of communication involving different departments in State Governments in Australia, the Australian Commonwealth Department of Immigration, the UK High Commission in Canberra (which acted as the go-between in most governmental communication between the UK and Australia), and the Commonwealth Relations Office, Home Office and Scottish Office within the UK Government. There were substantial archival holdings in Australia and the United Kingdom that documented communication between these different governmental bodies, the different policy priorities that departments had in relation to child migration work and the basis on which specific policy decisions were made. Archival holdings such as internal memoranda and correspondence and public reports, and press and parliamentary statements, gave a clear indication of the different policy imperatives underpinning child migration. For the Australian Commonwealth Government, key policy drivers were the wish to increase the Australian population through immigration – ideally 'good (white) British stock' from the United Kingdom – as well as a belief that child migration was an attractive policy because child immigrants would not immediately be competing for limited housing resources or job opportunities, and a recognition that this policy would only be cost effective if delivered through voluntary societies. For the United Kingdom Government, there were more complex tensions between the wish to maintain standards of child-care set out in the *Curtis Report* and the perception that ending support for child migration would be politically difficult in terms of Anglo-Australian relations. Recognition of the limited powers that British authorities could exert once child migrants were in care in Australia also led to a policy of encouraging gradual reform of child migration programmes through moral persuasion rather than regulation.[26]

Alongside these more overt policy motivations, however, observation of how these policy discussions evolved over time also made it possible to note other, more implicit, aspects of the organisational cultures of government that shaped them. For example, civil servants, who were responsible for the operational oversight and policy recommendations for these programmes were often reluctant to press their views on colleagues in other departments if they felt this might involve transgressing the boundaries of departmental policy briefs.[27] The principle of precedence was also commonly assumed in policy discussions amongst civil servants, with precedence helping both to delimit the issues on which civil servants felt they needed to make policy decisions and to provide a means of managing demands for resources and special treatment made by voluntary societies and other stakeholders. Deference to the principle of precedence meant, for example, that despite having learned about problems with standards of care, training and accommodation at receiving institutions in Australia during the war, British civil servants agreed to resume financial support for child migration in 1946 because it followed funding agreements under the terms of the Empire Settlement Act which had already become well-established in the inter-war period. The safety of the child migration programmes was further compromised by poor policy decisions made on the basis of inadequate knowledge of receiving institutions in Australia, knowledge which was itself compromised by the complex inter-departmental systems and interests through which these programmes were managed. Analysis of the content of inspection reports produced by state officials in Australia, and the pathways through which these were shared between Australian and UK Government departments, showed for example that the views of state officials were sometimes coloured by their desire to promote immigration and support local voluntary societies, that the Australian Commonwealth Government did not always pass on critical reports to UK authorities, that there was no agreed standards between UK Government departments on how the content of reports should be judged, and that the Home Office generally failed to press its concerns on particular institutions into any decisive policy changes. This evidence of systemic failures of oversight by the United Kingdom Government was to become a key basis of the recommendation by the Independent Inquiry into Child Sexual Abuse that the United Kingdom Government establish its redress scheme for former child migrants.[28]

A third form of archival analysis that proved productive was the examination of how specific organisational systems operated. One example of this was the system through which residential institutions in Australia were approved by Australian and British government officials to receive UK child migrants. Reviewing a trail of inspection reports, related correspondence and shipping lists in national archives made it possible to identify some points in which significant failures occurred in these systems.[29] For example, in the autumn of 1947, 334 children were sent to Catholic residential institutions in Western Australia. Initial inspection reports produced in May 1947, indicated that the nominating body in Western Australia, the Catholic Episcopal Migration and Welfare Association (CEMWA), had proposed a number of institutions that were not in a fit state to receive the numbers or ages of children being requested. Negotiations in Western Australia between Catholic and state officials led to promises of some improvements at these institutions and on that basis, the UK High Commission in Canberra agreed to revised numbers and age ranges for children to be sent to all but one of these homes. No thought appeared to be given as to whether the unsuitable nominations originally made by CEMWA raised questions about its fitness as an organisation for overseeing child migrants' welfare.

Analysis of shipping lists of children sent to these institutions the following autumn demonstrated, however, that there was no effective oversight of whether agreements about the numbers and ages of children being sent to specific institutions were being adhered to. In the case of the Castledare Junior Orphanage run by the Christian Brothers, nearly double the number of boys approved were sent there with more than half of the children under the agreed age of seven. This most likely occurred because the Australian administrator recruiting children from the United Kingdom, Br Conlon, had obtained a much larger proportion of younger children than officials had originally agreed to. Overcrowding of boys at Castledare remained a significant problem in the post-war period, and with very few Brothers running the institution, boys were at increased risk of abuse from a specific staff member, Br Murphy, who is now recognised as one of the most serious sexual offenders in that order in Western Australia in the post-war period.[30] Some boys were also sent under the agreed age limit to Bindoon, another institution run by the Christian Brothers, with one witness to the Scottish Child Abuse Inquiry describing how he became vulnerable to sustained sexual abuse from several Brothers after being placed there.[31] One of the most striking failures of oversight was the fact that 52 girls were sent to Nazareth House, Geraldton despite this being the one institution to which UK officials had not given their approval. It was not until 1949 that UK authorities realised this error, with the institution receiving hurried approval from the Commonwealth Relations Office without consultation with child-care specialists in the Home Office. One of the specific concerns that had led to this Nazareth House not being approved was the fact that children would be living in the same institution as elderly residents. This issue was never addressed, however, even when the Commonwealth Relations Office did give its belated approval and some former child migrants have recalled being removed from full-time education at that institution whilst still under school-leaving age to act as auxiliary carers on the elderly wards.

A fourth, and related form of analysis concerns the comparative use of complementary data from different archives to understand particular events or processes.[32] The majority of the 334 children sent to Catholic institutions in Western Australia in the autumn of 1947 had been recruited from residential institutions across the United Kingdom run by the Sisters of Nazareth. A small number of these children were sent from Homes in Northern Ireland having previously been transferred across the border from institutions in Éire. Earlier inquiries had raised concerns about the comparatively low rate of children whose emigration from Sisters of Nazareth institutions had been approved by parents or guardians, with consent for the majority of children being given by the Mother Superior in charge of a particular institution. Previous analyses of rates of consent had focused on the total percentage of cases in which approval by parents and guardians had been given.[33] For the IICSA investigation, however, the digitisation of archives in Australia made it possible for the first time to compare what was known about the chronology of arrangements for the emigration of these children with a sample of immigration forms ('LEM3's) which were used for the approval of each child by Australian immigration officials and which contained the signature of the person consenting to each child's emigration.[34] By comparing consent for individual children against this chronology, it became clear that rates of parental consent fell significantly for children whose immigration applications were approved from the start of 1947 compared to those approved the previous autumn (see Table 1).

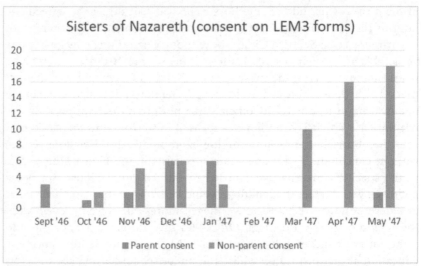

Table 1: Analysis of parental consent for child's migration from digitised LEM3 forms available from the National Archives of Australia

The decline in levels of parental consent coincided with Br Conlon's belief early in the spring of 1947 that shipping arrangements for these children were about to be made imminently, suggesting that applications for children recruited from Sisters of Nazareth institutions were potentially being processed more quickly and without parental consent being sought. This practice would be consistent with other evidence of this religious order supporting child migration for particular organisational reasons rather than the needs of the individual child. This example suggests that more general statistical data of total rates of parental consent for children sent from the Sisters of Nazareth are usefully supplemented by more fine-grained consideration of these statistics in relation to particular periods of organisational activity. More detailed analysis of this kind has the potential to give greater insight into organisations' working practices than may always be provided by broader overviews of organisational data.

From these examples, it is possible to summarise more broadly the following different types of historical analysis in relation to institutional abuse:

Type of analysis	Type of source material	Potential benefit
Broad historical narratives of key policy and organisational changes	Primary and secondary sources	Provides over-arching structure for understanding organisational histories and placing these in their wider social and political context.

Chronologies of more specific periods/events	Primary sources (e.g. correspondence, memoranda and minutes, internal notes)	Provides closer understanding of organisational practices, which may not always accord with organisations' accounts of their histories or wider historical overviews, and which may have fallen below expected standards of the day.
Analysis of policy-making processes	Primary sources (e.g. correspondence, memoranda and minutes, internal notes, public reports, press and parliamentary statements)	Provides better understanding of how policy decisions were shaped not only by explicit motivations but more implicit organisational cultures, as well as the role of flaws in organisational systems for policy-making.
Analysis of operation of specific systems	Primary sources providing multiple points of evidence about the stated, approved and actual operation of specific systems	Provides greater understanding of whether systems operated in practice according to agreed guidelines.
Analysis of complementary data to understand particular processes or events	Primary sources providing multiple points of evidence about how processes or events occurred	Provides more nuanced understanding of how organisational practices may have varied under different circumstances, potentially giving greater insight into policy and operational decisions within those organisations.

Table 2: Different types of archival analysis for understanding organisational contexts of non-recent abuse

Whilst these different types of archival research are far from novel in terms of the range of approaches used by historians in their research more broadly, they have generally been utilised to a lesser extent in public inquiries into non-recent abuse. Indeed, inquiries have, when commissioning or using historical research, often tended to confine such research to broader historical narratives of organisational practices and policy contexts, rather than more detailed archival analysis of particular events, operational systems or processes described above. As I have argued so far in this chapter, more fine-grained analysis of this kind has the potential to generate far more nuanced understandings of organisational practices, cultures and systems that can clarify how policy and organisational contexts contributed to environments in which individuals were subjected to different kinds of abuse. Moving beyond broad organisational apologies for their involvement in a darker and less enlightened past, such analysis can provide clearer understandings of specific organisational failings that can add to the evidence base on which contemporary views can be taken about appropriate forms of apology, redress and memorialisation. Furthermore, by heightening understanding of how policy-making processes and organisational practices can fail children and vulnerable adults, it may be easier to identify ways in which specific failures continue to occur in contemporary contexts rather than assuming that the traumatic events of non-recent abuse are located in a hermetically sealed, distant past.

Truth-telling, accountability and access to archives

Truth-telling about past wrongs is a common principle in transitional justice. Without rigorous interrogation of the past, effective accountability or reparation for institutional abuses cannot be fully achieved. This chapter has indicated ways in which such truth-telling, understood as richer and more strongly evidenced narratives about the past, relies on access to as wide a range as possible of relevant archival material. It is also important to recognise – as historians understand in relation to their research more generally – that such truth-telling can never be a one-off event, just as no single historical narrative can provide a final and definitive account of the past. Our understanding of the past is continually evolving, and effective historical research rests on the willingness continually to revise and amend our interpretations of the past based on new evidence and insights. Historical understanding is therefore best promoted through ongoing cycles of investigation and multiple analyses and interpretations.

Understanding truth-telling as an unfolding process clearly raises challenges in relation to archival research on non-recent abuse. As noted above, inquiries usually have powers to compel the release of material from organisations, which researchers may not normally have access to. As a consequence, archival analysis undertaken by inquiries can sometimes offer unique opportunities for reviewing material that cannot easily be studied if voluntary organisations refuse access to it otherwise. Inquiries can even exacerbate such restrictions with some voluntary organisations arguing that temporary access to their archives given for that purpose constitutes sufficient independent scrutiny and that no further access is needed once this investigation has concluded. Particular difficulties have also arisen in

Ireland in relation to its particularly restrictive legal constraints around public access to archival material gathered through the work of inquiries and committees of investigation.[35] Such challenges place great pressure on expert witnesses commissioned by inquiries, who may have to review considerable amounts of archival material at speed, knowing that they may enjoy access to material at levels that will not be replicated for potentially several decades. In cases where inquiries adopt approaches to analysing archival material that do not command wider confidence and operate in ways that make subsequent access to that material even harder to achieve in the future, an inquiry can reasonably be seen as impeding rather than supporting transitional justice.

Important implications arise for inquiries and for public policy on archival access more generally if truth-telling is understood as an ongoing process. Whilst inquiries have typically had their terms of reference set on the basis of informing public understanding and policy decisions in relation to non-recent abuse, there is also value in inquiry teams understanding their work as constituting a form of public history that has an ongoing value after the inquiry has presented its final findings and recommendations.[36] Thinking of inquiries as forms of public history, and as constituting a form of archive in their own right, might encourage inquiries to make digital copies of primary source material used in their work available in easily searchable forms, to include more detailed discussion of archival sources and methods of archival analysis as appendices to their reports and to cite archival material in their publications in forms that make it easier to trace the original primary material. More widely, though, the experience of archival research on histories of non-recent abuse suggest that it is not appropriate that those organisations whose past work requires critical, independent scrutiny should have the power to foreclose access to that material. The GDPR already contains clear guidelines on how researchers should use sensitive archival material and powers within the GDPR to enable archival access have also been demonstrated through the recent work of the Unseal the Archive campaign in the autumn of 2020.[37] More thought, and quite possibly primary legislation, is also needed to ensure that organisations cannot refuse access to their archives when there is a clear public interest for such access to be allowed, credible analysis is to be undertaken and researchers agree to operate within reasonable guidelines. Given Ireland's complex history of non-recent abuse across a range of organisational contexts, and its more recent experience of inquiries and truth-telling in relation to this, there remains a pressing need for archival analysis of the kind described in this chapter and for inquiry processes and public policy to ensure that such research can be supported.

TWENTY-FOUR

Knowing and Unknowing Tuam: State Practice, the Archive and Transitional Justice[1]

James M. Smith

'Everyone knew, but no one said. Perfectly decent people can know a thing and at the same time not know it. We knew, and did not know. That is our shame today.'
John Banville, 'A Century of Looking the Other Way,' *The New York Times*, 22 May 2009.

'The Irish added another category: unknown knowns, things that were understood to be the case and yet remained unreal.'
Fintan O'Toole, *Ship of Fools: How Stupidity and Corruption Sank the Celtic Tiger* (Faber and Faber, 2009), pp 180–1.

This essay proposes to document what the Irish State *did* know about the Tuam Baby Home, where 798 children died between 1925 and 1961. What did the state know about the health of the children there, when did it know it and, most troubling of all, what did the state do with its knowledge? Part of the answer lies in documents housed in the Department of Health that detail the substantial administrative apparatus whose appointed duty was to gather knowledge about the women and children in these institutions, the conditions in which they lived and died, and the pathways that those lucky enough to survive could find back to society. As a state practice, however, compiling data has rarely resulted in meaningful intervention to alleviate deficits in the provision of care. The information – like the infants entombed at Tuam – was and remains buried. And as with the punitive carceral response to female sexuality and so-called 'illegitimacy,' the state's readiness to unknow what it knew about institutional abuse was at bottom an act of self-preservation.[2]

The essay's archival research also suggests that very little has changed in the Irish State's current posture. When confronted with evidence of historical abuse in the present, the state again cultivates unknowingness by way of a routine set of responses: first, it establishes an investigation; second, it draws from the National Archives to support the investigation; and third, upon publication of a final report, it then denies access to all the evidence by asserting a statutory obligation to protect the privacy and confidentiality of testimony taken from survivors, other witnesses and alleged perpetrators. With this final step the Irish State once again impedes truth-telling about its own involvement. To detail this coupling of historical amnesia and the contemporary erasure of witness testimony, I will move from an analysis of four sample archival documents to the state's responses to demands for greater transparency. A transitional-justice approach to historical abuse should always view truth-telling and guarantees of nonrecurrence as intrinsically linked: there cannot be one without the other.[3]

InSight/Site: Knowing Tuam

Ireland knows about St Mary's Home for Unmarried Mothers and its so-called illegitimate children, managed by the Bon Secours Sisters in Tuam, Co. Galway, because of the work of historian Catherine Corless.[4] Corless's findings – summarised by Alison O'Reilly in her May 2014 feature article 'A Mass Grave of 800 Babies' – were first published in 2012 but received with silence.[5] Corless's research led her to acquire, at significant personal expense, the death registration records for 798 children officially documented by the state as having died at the public-assistance-authority institution operated by Galway County Council. Securing those records led Corless to ask the decisive question: where were these babies buried? She identified graves for two children at the local public cemetery, but there was no public record of graves for the other 796.[6]

Shortly after the story broke in 2014, the names of all 796 children appeared in newsprint, on a plethora of websites and in an incessant scroll on numerous Twitter feeds.[7] Each child now possessed a name, and details regarding his or her age and cause of death. The Tuam babies story quickly became an international media event, and Irish politicians had little choice but to respond. They did so – initially with exclamations of shock and horror – by asserting the 'need to know what happened' at places like Tuam.[8] Simultaneously, politicians disclaimed knowledge of Ireland's past.[9] This rhetorical outpouring reached its apogee with Taoiseach Enda Kenny's so-called 'chamber of horrors' speech in 2017:

> Tuam is not just a burial ground, it is a social and cultural sepulchre. That is what it is. As a society in the so-called 'good old days,' we did not just hide away the dead bodies of tiny human beings, we dug deep and deeper still to bury our compassion, our mercy, and our humanity itself. No nuns broke into our homes to kidnap our children. We gave them up to what we convinced ourselves was the nuns' care...

We had better deal with this now because if we do not, some other Taoiseach will be standing here in twenty years saying, 'If only we knew then, if only we had done then.' What will be his or her then is our now. Now, we do know. Now, we have to do.[10]

Despite his apparent outrage, Kenny – like many of his colleagues – elicited political consensus in the present only by a double displacement of the past. First, he effectively separated Ireland's present from its past, positioning his government as having 'to deal with' a legacy – as if some accidental inheritance – from failed political administrations decades earlier in 'the so-called "good old days"'.[11] And second, he simultaneously redirected culpability away from the state and back onto families ('no nuns broke into our homes to kidnap our children') and the religious orders ('we gave them up to what we convinced ourselves was the nuns' care').[12] Legislation, however, had long made clear from 1923 forward that the Irish State had been obliged to license, inspect and regulate these institutions.[13] Kenny effaced these state responsibilities, the state's duty of care, by passing them off on the past – and on those outside the government.[14]

Under intense scrutiny at home and abroad, Kenny's government ultimately did act in response to the Tuam revelations. Minister for Children and Youth Affairs James Reilly revealed that the government agreed to establish a Commission of Investigation into Mother and Baby Homes in July 2014.[15] Publication of its terms of reference came in February 2015, and a series of interim reports followed in turn.[16]

On 3 March 2017 then Minister for Children and Youth Affairs Katherine Zappone announced that scientific testing confirmed the presence of significant human remains at the former Mother and Baby Home site consistent with very young children between 35 foetal weeks and two to three years of age, and dating from the 1920s to the 1960s.[17] Days later, speaking in Dáil Éireann, she embraced a broader transitional-justice response to the legacies of Ireland's historic and institutional abuses:

> Transitional justice puts survivors and victims at the heart of the process. It commits to pursuing justice through truth. It aims to achieve not only individual justice but a wider societal transition from more repressive times in order to move from one era to another. Taking a transitional-justice approach means that we will find out and record the truth, ensure accountability, make reparation, undertake institutional reform and achieve reconciliation.[18]

In October 2018 Zappone further announced the government's commitment to a comprehensive human-rights-focused plan that included full forensic exhumation on the Tuam site, DNA testing to effect individualisation and identification of human remains where possible, respectful reburial and memorialisation of remains, and preservation of the site.[19]

A complete picture of the Tuam institution and a detailed accounting of the number of children buried there eludes survivors and family members despite the publication of the Commission's final report in January 2021. The government plans to publish the 'Certain Institutional Burials (Authorised Interventions) Bill' in 2022, but legal experts continue to raise concerns about the disapplication of the role of the coroner and the possible exclusion of related institutions in the current draft. And it took a massive social media campaign in October/November 2020 to ensure that the State acknowledge survivors' rights to access personal information, held as part of the Commission's archive, in accordance with the EU's General Data Protection Regulation (GDPR). Meanwhile, the Commission's archive remains sealed to public and scholarly scrutiny. The Mother and Baby Homes Commission of Investigation was governed by the Commissions of Investigation Act (2004), which embargoes archives and impedes truth-telling.[20] Access to information – to individual records, records of loved ones who died in these institutions, and the administrative and bureaucratic records that shed light on how these institutions operated – remains the primary form of redress demanded by many survivors. Reparation without access to information constitutes a continuing violation of human rights.

The Archive: What the State Knew about Tuam

Cultural critics, historians and social scientists have demonstrated that for five decades after political independence children deemed illegitimate by Irish society were three to five times less likely to survive to their first birthday.[21] Although Maria Luddy asserts that illegitimacy rates remained 'fairly constant' across this period, Lindsey Earner-Byrne contends that official statistics for nonmarital births are 'distorted' as a result of 'an under-registration' owing to 'social pressure.'[22] Paul Michael Garrett highlights reports that the 'abnormal death rate' among 'illegitimate infants' was a matter of 'grave concern.'[23] And yet numerous governments failed to offer a concrete policy – 'there was no vision or long-term strategy' – to address vulnerable women and children's needs, which, as Earner-Byrne argues, effectively enabled the state to avoid dealing with the 'problem':

> The central problem was that there was no service that dealt specifically with the unmarried mother and her child. The inspectors of boarded-out children,

in theory in charge of illegitimate or orphaned children, were in reality the only ones who consistently highlighted the connection between the treatment of the unmarried mother and the welfare of illegitimate children. The case of the unmarried mother lay outside the domain of child welfare services; in fact, there was no specific service for the unmarried mother... Segregation and institutionalisation were seen as the most appropriate response.[24]

Contemporary scholarship continues to reckon with the costs – human, political, social and financial – associated with this response whereby the state abdicated responsibility for disadvantaged women and children primarily to Catholic religious orders that managed Mother and Baby Homes and county homes. Scholars, myself included, have relied on statistics produced by the state to benchmark rates of nonmarital births and infant mortality in these institutions: i.e. the Department of Local Government and Public Health's *Annual Report of the Registrar-General* and the Central Statistics Office's *Reports on Vital Statistics*. However, statistics tell only part of the story. They are compiled from on high, focus on abstractions and rarely convey the conditions experienced by individuals in the system. Archival evidence thus complements what official statistics admit – precisely because the archive has the potential to reveal the processes of monitoring and regulation, the array of state practices emanating from within the institutions, and the on-the-ground manifestation of state involvement. The archive betrays what the state knew about its provision (and failures within that provision) of services in real time. Hence the importance of affording access to state archives in effecting truth-telling about the past.

This essay turns to four documents from the Department of Health's archives that signal state knowledge of conditions at the Tuam Baby Home, especially in the 1940s and 1950s when high infant mortality rates occurred.[25] Each marks the ways in which Tuam was part of a state infrastructure that surveilled, documented and recorded vulnerable women and children under the administration of the public-assistance authority.[26] Each document evinces inspection, regulation and funding of this specific institution. They constitute knowledge that the Irish State had to disavow over time in order to claim in 2014 that it did not know about Tuam.

Circular P.24/48, Department of Health

This circular, entitled 'Births and Deaths of Illegitimate Children in Local Government Institutions for Year Ended 31.3.1947,' is dated 22 March 1948, the day it was issued to Ireland's local authorities.[27] The institutions in question include county hospitals and homes, the two Mother and Baby institutions operated directly by specific public-assistance authorities

– St Patrick's on the Navan Road in Dublin and the Tuam Baby Home established by Galway County Council – and presumably, although unspecified, the three private Mother and Baby Homes operated by the Sisters of the Sacred Heart of Jesus and Mary at Bessborough, Co. Cork, Sean Ross Abbey in Roscrea, Co. Tipperary, and Castlepollard, Co. Westmeath. The three Sacred Heart institutions also provided for mothers and children whose maintenance was charged to various local governments under the Public Assistance Act (1939) in addition to accepting private, fee-paying clients. Circular P.24/48, however, seeks information from the local authority only for those children paid for by the public purse.[28]

	I No. of Births of Illegit. Children in P.A. Institutions	II No. of Still-Births of Illegitimate Children in P.A. Institutions	III No. of Illegitimates under 1 year admitted into P.A. Institutions excluding "Transfers" included in Column I	IV No. of Deaths of Illegitimate Children under 1 year in P.A. Institutions
Balrothery				
Dublin				
Rathdown	Nil	Nil	4	Nil
Carlow	15	Nil	1	2
Cavan	16	1	3	4
Clare	22	Nil	Nil	1
Cork, North	40	1	4	7
Cork, South	45	1	20	21
Cork, West	18	Nil	1	2
Donegal	45	1	7	15
Galway { Tuam	44	nil	30	25
Galway { Cnt. Hosp.	17	2	1	2 (Tuam)
Kerry	50	1	2	13
Kildare	29	Nil	6	6
Kilkenny	23	Nil	5	7
Laoighis	17	Nil	3	5
Leitrim	5	Nil	1	Nil
Limerick	95	7	27	8
Limerick Co. Boro	23	Nil	3	6
Longford	9	Nil	3	2
Louth	34	Nil	13	8
Mayo				
Meath	20	1	1	4
Monaghan	23	Nil	1	1
O'Failghe	11	1	4	3
Roscommon	19	Nil	5	6
Sligo	23	Nil	9	7

Figure 1. Survey tabulating responses to Department of Local Government and Public Health Circular P.24/48 (File A124/18, DOH).

The circular requested information in four areas: the number of births of illegitimate children in public assistance (PA) institutions, the number of stillbirths of illegitimate children in PA institutions, the number of illegitimate children under one year admitted to PA institutions and the number of deaths of illegitimate children under one year in PA institutions. The circular also sought details on the cause of death for each child. Each authority submitted written responses to the department, and the information was then complied into a table (Fig. 1).

Circular P.24/48 documents a total of 1,426 Irish children under one year of age whose maintenance was chargeable to local authorities. Of this number, 1,038 children were born in the institutions in which they were resident, whereas an additional 388 were admitted after birth but under one year of age (in some cases accompanied by the unmarried mother). In addition, there were a total of 32 stillbirths, or three per cent of all births over that year. Finally, there were 249 infant deaths recorded, which represents just under 17.5 per cent, or 175 per 1000 births, for the 1,426 children.

Circular P.24/48 is noteworthy on a number of levels. First, it firmly establishes that not all nonmarital infants in Ireland were resident in PA institutions.[29] Official statistics state that there were 2,642 such births in 1946 and 2,348 in 1947. But according to the survey, only 1,426 of that number found their way onto the maintenance roles of local authorities.[30] These figures suggest that many infants were provided for outside of the PA administration – some of whom were likely in the very same institutions but in a private fee-paying capacity. Others were cared for in any number of smaller private nursing homes or hostels where better-off families might also finance a daughter's confinement, and some remained in the care of their extended families.[31]

Circular P.24/48 offers a snapshot of a distinct population of children at a specific moment in history. All of these children were deemed 'illegitimate'; they were born, lived at and in some cases died in an institutional setting regulated by the state; they were all under one year of age and local authorities (i.e. public ratepayers) funded their care. Dedicated 'special institutions' were not superior to local county homes or hospitals. Children died at high rates at both; the location and size of the institution was likely more determinative. There was, however, often a gap between how local authorities reported the cause of death for these children and how the state reflected that information in its annual statistical reports. But there is no mistaking that the state was indeed adept at gathering precise data on vulnerable children: who they were, where they were, who was caring for them and more. Most crucially, the state also knew how many children were dying and why.

The information returned by Galway and Mayo County Councils (Table 1) reveals how the Tuam Baby Home differed from other publicly funded alternatives and the dire consequences that this difference would have for mortality.

Table 1.

Deaths and Stillbirths as Reported by Galway and Mayo Returns[32]

INSTITUTION AND LOCAL AUTHORITY	NUMBER OF BIRTHS	NUMBER OF ADMISSIONS UNDER AGE 1	TOTAL INFANTS UNDER AGE 1	NUMBER OF DEATHS UNDER AGE 1	INFANT DEATHS AS PERCENT OF TOTAL	NUMBER OF STILLBIRTHS
Tuam Baby Home (Galway)	49	30	79	25	31.6%	0
Central Hospital (Galway)	17	1	18	2	11.1%	2
TOTAL, GALWAY	**66**	**31**	**97**	**27**	**27.8%**	**2**
Tuam Baby Home (Mayo)	22	7	29	12	41.4%	0
County Home (Mayo)	2	1	3	1	33.3%	0
TOTAL, MAYO	**24**	**8**	**32**	**13**	**40.6%**	**0**
Total, Galway and Mayo	90	39	129	40	31%	2
TOTAL, TUAM BABY HOME ONLY	**71**	**37**	**108**	**37**	**34.25%**	**0**

That both local authorities utilised the same institution for a majority of children in their care enables two-way comparison between children from both authorities sent to the Tuam home, and between children sent to the Tuam home as compared to the in-county alternative institutional setting.

Of the 129 infants maintained by Galway and Mayo over the 12-month period, 40 children (31 per cent) died before their first birthday. This compares with 17.5 per cent for all 1,426 children reported on in the circular. To turn to each authority separately, 27.8 per cent of the Galway infants died during the 12-month period, whereas 40.6 per cent of Mayo children did not live to their first birthday. To look at the distinct institutions utilised by both local authorities, 31.6 per cent of the Galway infants at the Tuam Baby Home and 11.1 per cent of the infants at Galway's Central Hospital died in the same period, whereas 41.4 per cent of the Mayo children in the Tuam Baby Home and a third of the children at Mayo's County Home died. All told, over a third (34.3 per cent) of the 108 infants at the Tuam

Baby Home died in the 12-month period. These figures suggest that an infant being maintained by a local authority in 1946–47 was twice as likely to die if resident at the Tuam Baby Home than in any other publicly funded care setting. Infant mortality figures for the Tuam home, and in particular the figures for children chargeable to County Mayo, exceeded all other local authorities in the national survey. These figures are all the more disturbing given that nationally, mortality rates for such children were already high. The ratio of illegitimate to legitimate infant mortality rates for 1946 and 1947 in Ireland was 3.38 and 3.49 respectively.[33] The state was aware of these disturbing disparities in 1948. And yet Tuam remained a state-licensed, state-regulated and partially state-funded institution for an additional 13 years before closing in 1961.

The circular also records the various causes of death for all 249 children under one year of age who died in the 12 months covered, as well as contributing causes that official state publications could overlook. In many cases these causes mirror those for infant mortality recorded in the *Annual Report of the Registrar General* for both 1946 and 1947. For example, the Registrar-General points to 'congenital debility' (i.e. 'weakness existing at or before birth'), 'premature birth' and 'diarrhoea and enteritis' as among the leading causes of infant mortality.[34] Unlike the *Registrar General* reports, however, the cause of death information for the 249 children in the circular points to multiple and overlapping medical conditions (Fig. 2). Thus, while 'gastro enteritis' is reported as the cause of death in 16 cases, iterations of the same disease, signalled by references to 'diarrhoea' and/or 'diarrhoea/vomiting,' and at times combined with other medical conditions such as 'infective gastro enteritis,' appear in an additional 13 cases. Likewise, 'congenital debility' and 'general debility' are listed as the cause of death for 29 infants but are combined with other conditions in an additional 39 cases (Table 2).

The *Annual Report of the Registrar General* for 1946 and 1947 never once refers to 'marasmus,' otherwise known as acute malnutrition. Yet this condition is identified repeatedly in replies to the circular and is given as the cause of death for seven infants under one year of age.

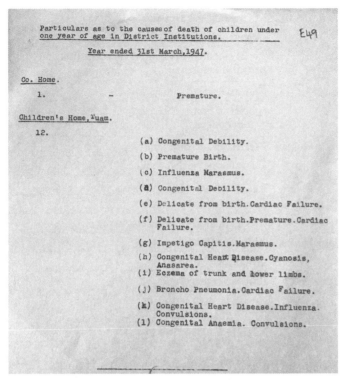

Figure 2. Mayo cause-of-death returns to Circular P.24/48 (File A124/18, DOH).

Table 2.

Partial Cause-of-Death Information for Infants under 1 Year of Age Maintained by Local Authorities in Public-Assistance Institutions, 1 April 1946–31 March 1947[35]

LOCAL AUTHORITY	STATED CAUSE OF DEATH	CASES
Dublin Board of Assistance	marasmus, debility and cardiac failure	2
	marasmus, sepsis neonatorum	1
	sepsis neonatorum, prematurity	1
	enteritis, marasmus	1
	general debility and cardiac failure	3

South Cork Board of Assistance	marasmus gastritis	2
	congenital syphilis	2
	congenital talipes and debility, asthenia and cardiac failure	1
	infective gastro enteritis	3
	infective gastro enteritis, peritonitis (tuberculosis)	1
Tuam Baby Home (Galway)	laryngitis, cardiac failure	1
	bronchitis, cardiac failure	1
	disseminated tuberculosis	1
	congenital debility	5
	congenital debility, scleroedema	1
Tuam Baby Home (Mayo)	congenital debility	2
	premature birth	1
	influenza marasmus	1
	delicate from birth, cardiac failure	1
	delicate from birth, premature, cardiac failure	1

Malnutrition is given as the cause of death for an additional three infants. And marasmus is listed as a secondary cause of death in a further 11 cases. In other words, malnutrition was a significant cause of death for 21 infants (8.4 per cent of the total of 249 infants). If marasmus had been named publicly at the time – if the registrar general's annual report had noted that condition for the official record – questions might well have been asked in Dáil Éireann via a parliamentary question or an oversight committee as to the problematic levels of care or the failure to make medical interventions to prevent such deaths. Instead information that children were dying of hunger remained unknown outside the compilers and readers of the circular in the Department of Health.

Responses to the circular, including those from County Galway and County Mayo, named the infants who died in the 12 months surveyed (Fig. 3). This correspondence demonstrates that the state possessed knowledge of these children's identities and their age, date and cause of death some six decades prior to Corless compiling information based on death-registration certificates. Moreover, Galway's General Assistance Department informed the Department of Health that it had 'received' the information detailing the identities and cause of death directly from 'Mother H–, Superioress of the Children's Home, Tuam.'[36] Significant actors in the Irish State knew these details in real time and chose to elide and ignore them for decades to come.

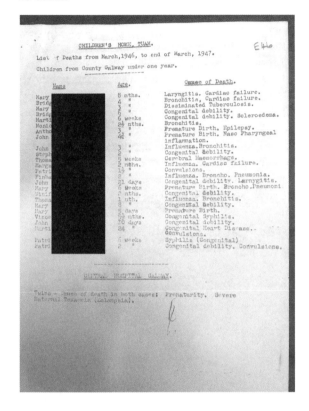

Figure 3. Tuam List of Deaths, Galway Returns to Circular P.24/48 (File A124/18, DOH).[37]

Biannual Returns, 1948–57

Circular P.24/48 was a one-off event capturing data from a fixed window of time. It is by no means the only trace of the Tuam home in the national archive. Indeed, the state documented each woman and child at Tuam through a comprehensive bureaucratic process of biannual returns. A Department of Health Circular P.99/42, dated 26 August 1942, required local authorities to submit half-yearly returns recording detailed information for all children boarded out by PA authorities, children placed at service or in a trade, children in institutions maintained by a PA authority, unmarried mothers in institutions maintained by a PA authority, and children registered as at nurse under the Children's Acts (1908–34).[38] Much of this trove of documentation survives and has been incorporated into the AIRR digitisation project.

The original paper versions of the biannual returns for children in institutions maintained by a PA authority are detailed. They include columns capturing the following information for each child: number, name, date of birth, date of admission, whether 'legitimate or illegitimate,' age, sex, state of health, whereabouts of parents, observations of matron, observations of medical officer and orders of county manager (Fig. 4). The institution's matron completed and signed the form and submitted it to the local authority, where the county manager also signed it before it was forwarded to the Department of Health, where it was signed by the department secretary. The three signatures, together with information from the resident medical officer, make clear that each child in the system was known, monitored, and recorded at least twice a year, on 31 March and 30 September. Additionally, the forms were officially stamped by the county council and the Department of Health – confirming that someone there handled them upon arrival.

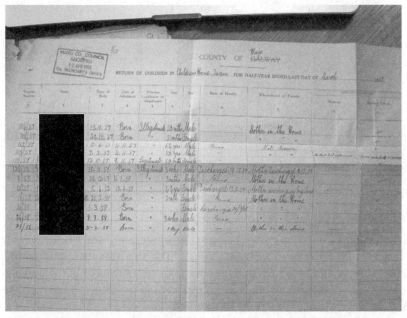

Figure 4. County of Mayo, Return of Children in Children's Home, Tuam, for Half-Year Ended Last Day of March 1957.[39]

In early 2012, while the McAleese inquiry was ongoing, I surveyed select half-yearly returns for Counties Galway and Mayo for 1948–57 when researching the transfer of women between Mother and Baby Homes and Magdalen laundries.[40] This archival work identified 24 children at the Tuam Baby Home for whom the 'whereabouts of parents' column had been recorded as 'mother in Magdalen home' – in one instance specifically stating 'mother in Galway Magdalen home'[41] and one additional case reporting, 'sent to the Good Shepherds.'[42] These children reappear on the semi-annual forms, enabling me to follow their progress across four to six years, noting changes relating to health, whereabouts of parents and discharge information. The forms include two survivors, John P. Rodgers and Peter Mulryan, who have been prominent in the media coverage of Tuam since 2014. Their mothers were transferred from the Bon Secours Mother and Baby Home to the Sisters of Mercy Galway Magdalene asylum where they lived, worked and, in one case, died behind convent walls 40-plus years later.[43]

For many other children the 'whereabouts of the parents' column states 'mother in the home,' signalling that she remained working in the Tuam institution after the birth of her child, without pay, to satisfy the expectation of the religious congregation and the state that she contribute to her child's upkeep.[44] Other mothers are listed as discharged, others still as 'gone to England,' 'gone to USA,' or simply 'not known.' The nuns were aware that some mothers left Ireland soon after leaving the institution and reported that fact to the state.[45] Furthermore, the biannual returns betray that some of Tuam's infants were placed for adoption domestically via state-licensed agencies, including St Patrick's Guild and the Catholic Protection and Rescue Society, as well as sent overseas to the United States. Notations to this effect appear occasionally, written onto the form's right-hand margins. Notably, every child listed on the forms examined was registered as nonmarital; not a single instance of a father's identity or location was recorded. The fate of the unmarried mother and her child did not involve the putative father, and neither the state nor the county council, nor the religious order made it its business to collect that particular information.

The forms evince a lack of attention to detail. The medical information conveyed in the columns labelled 'state of health,' 'observations of matron' and 'observations of medical officer' is superficial at best, with references to 'normal' and 'good' as indicative of the level of expert opinion provided. And if the matron was sparse in her remarks, the medical office was positively meagre in fulfilling his responsibilities. In many instances, this column was simply left blank. Nowhere under the observations of medical officer column is there a mention of debility, congenital malformation, gastroenteritis, or any of the other medical conditions listed on the Department of Health survey discussed above. And the terms 'marasmus' and 'malnutrition' do not appear. Why there is such disparity between this information and the circular remains open to speculation. Likewise, we may never know whether the Department of Health ever challenged Galway County Council or the Bon Secours Sisters for additional or more complete information. But the biannual returns manifest the state's obligation to monitor and regulate the

Tuam institution. They reveal, just as surely, that regulation stopped short of actually intervening to save children and instead operated in a fashion that satisfied a monitory onus in a perfunctory manner.

Inspector's Report, 1947[46]

Because the Tuam home was licensed and regulated by the state, it was also inspected on an ongoing basis. These inspections resulted in detailed reports that were returned to the Department of Health and survive in its archives.[47] The 1947 inspector's report for the Tuam home was shared by a surviving family member, a redacted copy of which was released to her because it references a relative.[48] The copy obscures identifying information for all the other children named in the report. Like the documents above, however, this three-page, single-spaced report evinces once more the rich vein of information in the state's possession, in real time, related to vulnerable children living and dying in its care.

The report details the inspector's visit to the Tuam home on 16 and 17 April 1947, when 333 people were in residence. Three years earlier, the inspector recommended a maximum capacity of 243. In an era of communicable illnesses and given the institution's remit to serve women giving birth at the institution and admit those who gave birth outside, overcrowding was hardly conducive to disease control. The inspector reported on the home's seven nurseries, listing the number of infants, toddlers and older children in each. Additionally, she commented on the conditions therein, stating, for example, that babies 'are healthy in appearance,' 'mainly healthy and normal,' or 'all seem healthy or mostly normal.' She provided details for 'exceptions' in each of the dormitories, listing the child by name and age and commenting on the child's health. These comments betray medical conditions reminiscent of the cause-of-death information revealed in Circular P.24/48 discussed above: 'a miserable, emaciated child with voracious appetite and no control over bodily functions,' 'wizened limbs,' 'delicate and wasted,' 'pot-bellied, emaciated, epileptic,' and 'emaciated, flesh hanging on limbs.' Some children were described as disabled: 'deaf and dumb, ...awaiting entry to institute for deaf and dumb'; others were deemed a 'mental defective, ... refused entry at Cabra owing to lack of accommodation'; others still were described as in need of 'surgical treatment,' but 'accommodation cannot be obtained... in central hospital Galway.' The report betrays both class and ethnic prejudice, asserting, 'mother poor,' 'from poor family' or 'described child of itinerants.' The inspector recommended certain interventions, including securing placement in an industrial school and prioritising the transfer of four 'mentally defective' children for whom 'continued efforts must be made to obtain vacancies at the home in Cabra.' Ultimately, of the 255 children reported on, some 39 (or 15.3 per cent) were noted as exceptions to the general normalcy in the health of the institution's charges.

Table 3.
Mortality Information Taken from Inspector's Report,
Tuam Children's Home, 28 April 1947

YEAR ENDED	NUMBER OF BIRTHS AND ADMISSIONS	NUMBER OF DEATHS	APPROXIMATE RATE
31 March 1943	159	54	34%
31 March 1944	169	42	25%
31 March 1945	153	36	23%
31 March 1946	143	39	27%

The report also addresses mortality at the Tuam institution over a four-year period, which makes for disturbing reading (Table 3). It reveals, simply stated, that 'the death rate among infants is high.' The inspector's ensuing analysis asserted that after a downward trend, the most recent half-yearly figures prior to September 1946 – when 21 deaths had occurred among the 66 births or admissions – signal that the 'rate... has begun to rise again.'[49] In accounting for where the fault lay, her report pointed to the lack of an 'isolation unit,' something that 'Dr. D – drew attention to... in July 1945,' but evidently to no avail.[50] Mingling between populations and cross-infection played its part, especially for children from families of 'itinerants, destitutes, evicted persons' who enhanced the 'risk of infection brought in from outside.'[51] The inspector bemoaned the lack of 'routine examination' or testing for 'venereal disease,' but did not clarify whether this was something the Bon Secours nuns objected to.

The report identifies the age of the resident medical officer as 'over 80 years old' and wonders whether the 'advice and assistance' of a younger doctor with 'more up-to-date knowledge and methods' might make a difference in the levels of care. These remarks suggest that medical service had become residual and likely second-rate – reflecting how the state perceived the residents of this institution. Finally, the report queries Galway County Council's decision not to admit or pay for the care of expectant mothers prior to their seventh month of pregnancy, which placed additional hardship on the 'girls' seeking to 'conceal their condition' and avoid its becoming 'common knowledge.' This too, the inspector pointed out, 'must have a bad effect on the health of their infants.' The state's inspector identified poverty, sexual immorality, outdated expertise and a punitive withholding of funds as contributing causes for high infant mortality at the Tuam home.

The report refuses, however, to lay the blame for infant mortality upon the Bon Secours Sisters, who managed the institution from its opening in 1925. Indeed, it affirms that the 'care given to infants in the home is good, the sisters are careful and attentive, diets are excellent.' The challenge remains how best to square this assertion with the same document signalling children who are 'emaciated,' 'pot-bellied' and 'wizened'; the final report of the Mother and Baby Homes Commission of Investigation fails to account for such contradictions.[52] Ultimately, the inspector's report exculpates the nuns from all responsibility: 'it is not here [the sisters] that we must look for the cause of the death rate.' In light of countervailing evidence, we might surmise that this conclusion betrayed the Department of Health's undue deference toward the religious congregation. Such deference in turn masked the state's near-total dependence on Catholic religious orders for the provision of services for which it paid – yet for which it otherwise willingly abdicated responsibility.[53]

Annual Statistical Returns

In addition to the biannual returns discussed above, the Department of Health also required public-assistance maternity homes to submit annual statistical returns for mothers and children in their care. I conclude this section by looking briefly at Tuam's annual statistical returns for a number of years in the 1950s, a decade that witnessed improvements in the delivery of health services and a concurrent decline in infant mortality across the maternity-home sector (Fig. 5).

Unfortunately, Tuam's annual statistical returns for certain years are missing or illegible as a result of deterioration of the original documents on file.[54] Those that survive capture information for the 12-month period ending on 31 March each year. The form comprises distinct sections requesting separate information for mothers and children. For mothers, it queries the number in the institution, the number discharged, the number of deaths, numbers pre- and post-confinement, and the number on discharge sent to 'situations' (i.e. a job), sent to parents or relatives, married, sent to other homes, or otherwise discharged. The ensuing section asks for the number of children resident, the numbers born and admitted after birth, the number of deaths and the numbers and circumstances surrounding those discharged: via boarding-out by local authorities, placed at nurse by

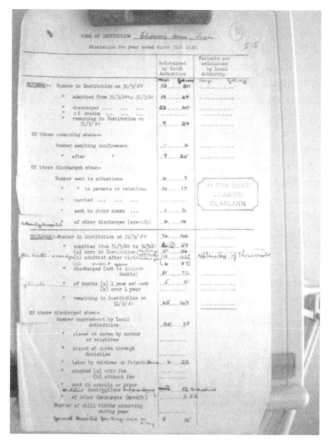

Figure 5. Annual Return, Tuam 1951 (File A 124/34, National Archives of Ireland, Dublin)

mother or relatives, placed at nurse by societies, taken by relatives and friends, adopted with and without fee, sent to schools and other institutions, and other discharges. Finally, the form solicits information on the number of stillbirths occurring during the year. A full analysis of these forms may yet be provided by the Commission of Investigation's final report, but certainly, a forensic comparison between this data (e.g. information on deaths and on transfer of mothers and children to other institutions) and that contained in inspection reports and biannual returns discussed above will assist in facilitating an understanding of state failures in the oversight of institutions providing services to Ireland's most vulnerable women and children.

Some infant mortality remained a feature of the Tuam institution in its final years of operation, even as the population declined in anticipation of the home's closure in 1961 (see Table 4). And while infants also died at Ireland's other maternity institutions in the 1950s, one might surmise that many of them also experienced significant drops in infant-mortality rates from the late 1940s onward. Collectively, these forms underscore that despite the accumulation of knowledge – data actively collected by the state at national and local levels – throughout the 1940s that signalled disturbing rates of infant mortality, the state allowed the Tuam home to continue operating. No evidence demonstrates any attempt to intervene, effect change or respond to the recommendations of its own inspectors. This essay stops short of suggesting that there was anything anomalous in the management of the Tuam institution beyond the manner in which the Bon Secours Sisters buried children who died in their care. Rather, it argues that the evidence in the state's own archives reveals that the high infant-mortality rate at the Tuam home was known and that the state played an active and ongoing role in inspecting and overseeing its operation without a desire to intervene. It is not that the state did not know about Tuam. Rather, the archive suggests that it chose to unknow what it knew about this particular institution.

Table 4.
Tuam Annual Statistic Returns[55]

YEAR	CHILDREN BORN OR ADMITTED AFTER BIRTH	DEATHS OF CHILDREN UNDER 1 YEAR FROM GALWAY	DEATHS OF CHILDREN UNDER 1 YEAR FROM MAYO	DEATHS OF CHILDREN OVER 1 YEAR	MORTALITY RATE
1951	77	10	5	0	19.4%
1952	86	7	1	1	10.4%
1955	70	4	0	2	8.6%
1957	77	3	2	4	11.7%
1958	64	1	0	0	1.6%
1959	53	0	1	0	1.9%
1960	55	2	1	0	5.5%
Total	482	27	10	7	9.1%

Out of Sight, Out of Mind: Impeding Access to the Archive

In February 2019 Ireland's Minister for Education and Skills Joe McHugh announced the publication of the Retention of Records Bill (2019), which would transfer to the National Archives and seal for 75 years the historically significant archive – estimated at some two million documents – related to the Commission to Inquire into Child Abuse (CICA), the Residential Institutions Redress Board (RIRB) and the Residential Institutions Redress

Review Committee (RIRRC).[56] In announcing the bill, Minister McHugh recognised that:

> retention of the records is essential to ensure that we never forget the abuse that was perpetrated against innocent children in institutions, and that future generations can be made aware of and understand what took place. *We must learn from the past.* We want to ensure records of such huge historical importance are preserved while at the same time respecting the real-life stories and deeply personal testimony of all of the individuals who engaged with the redress bodies.

> ...Seventy-five years is a very long period of time to restrict access to records, but it is essential given the sensitivity of the material. Leaving the documents sealed for a shorter period is not possible given *the issue of confidentiality around witness testimony and other sensitive records.* [emphasis supplied][57]

McHugh here interprets the Commission to Inquire into Child Abuse Act (2000) – the original legislation governing the three redress bodies – as stipulating the destruction of records. The state heretofore seized upon the provision calling for commissions' records to be safeguarded or disposed of in accordance with the National Archives Act (1986) to insist on their destruction.[58] Following this interpretation, Minister McHugh now endorses the new bill as providing a statutory guarantee preserving these materials for posterity, thereby enabling future generations to 'understand' and 'never forget' the nation's history of abuse. Speaking before the Oireachtas Joint Committee on Education and Skills, survivor Mary Harney characterised the 75-year delay as detrimental to survivors' interests and demanded access to all records immediately: 'If this bill passes, it would make survivors of the industrial schools invisible once more... Our memories were wiped from us and now we are asking, "Can we have them back please?".'[59] The minister's explanation exposes a fundamental contradiction: how does denying access to this archive for 75 years enable society today to 'learn from the past?'

To unravel the state's agenda it is necessary to uncouple the minister's inferred equivalence between 'witness testimony,' for which a guarantee of confidentiality was granted at the time,[60] and the 'other sensitive records,' which I read as indicating state and religious archives, including administrative and financial records as well as material from the judiciary, the medical profession, social workers and other vested social agents involved in the provision of child-residential care in the past and the present. The Retention of Records Bill would deny access to this archive of state papers, material in some cases recalled from the National Archives to assist the work of the CICA, and now to be sealed from further inspection for at least three generations. Crucially, these administrative files would shed light on state failures in the past, which in turn would enable lessons to be learned that might influence treatment of vulnerable children in various care settings today. Barely a decade has passed since the Irish State struggled to provide accurate information on the number of children known to social services (i.e. in state care) who died between 2000 and 2010. The figure escalated over six months from 20, to 23, to 37, to 188, to 199, with the last number later shown to be an erroneous undercount.[61] Children living today in the flawed foster-care system, caught up in the direct provision service for asylum seekers, leaving state-care homes, and placed by agents of the state in B&B accommodation on a nightly basis for lack of a more permanent care setting would be best served by the state learning from past failures and effecting reforms to ensure nonrecurrence.[62] Denying access to state administrative records – literally locking them away – impedes rather than enables prevention of abuse in the present.

Catríona Crowe, the former head of special projects at the National Archives, concurs.[63] She sees the Retention of Records Bill as an attempt to 'bypass' the 1986 National Archives Act in that it denies the right to appeal or have recourse to the Freedom of Information Act (2014): 'The precedent set by this bill, in disregarding and disabling the main piece of legislation dealing with Irish archives, is ill-considered and dangerous.'[64] When she appeared before the Oireachtas Joint Committee on Education, Crowe foregrounded its implications for other archival material that 'the state would prefer its citizens not to have access':

> Administrative records that are currently held in the archives of the Ryan commission, the McAleese committee, and the Murphy Mother and Baby Homes commission should be available when they are more than 30 (soon to be 20) years old. There are no privacy issues with these records, and it would set an extraordinary precedent if this bill made it possible for the state to wrongly close important archives when it so chooses, without recourse to the National Archives Act.[65]

Nine years after the Inter-departmental Committee to Establish the Facts of State Involvement with the Magdalen Laundries (the McAleese committee) concluded its work, its archive is still being held by the Department of the Taoiseach. We know with some certainty that it is comprised primarily of state papers: documents formerly held by the nine government departments represented on the committee and materials recalled from the National Archives related to its work. We also know that the McAleese archive includes little or no material related to individual survivors, for those records are held by the four religious congregations that operated the ten Magdalen institutions under investigation. In June 2011 the government entered into an agreement with the orders whereby the nuns voluntarily made their records available for inspection on the understanding that 'all such records will be destroyed and/or returned to the relevant religious order upon conclusion of the committee's work and publication of its report.' As the committee's interim report explains, this approach was necessitated 'in light of sensitive personal data contained in those records and the legal obligations of the orders in their role as data controllers.'[66]

Suffice it to say that a pattern is evident in the Irish State's handling of such matters: impede access to archival material implicating the state in historic abuse and justify doing so by asserting statutory obligations to secure testamentary evidence, including the confidentiality and privacy of alleged perpetrators and survivors.[67] Consequently, access to the McAleese archive, as with the material governed by the Retention of Records Bill, is prohibited absolutely. These archives are also not subject to data requests under the Freedom of Information (FOI) Act (2014).[68] Indeed an FOI request refusal, issued to the Justice for Magdalenes Research (JFMR) group in 2016, stipulated that the Department of the Taoiseach was holding the McAleese archive for 'safe keeping' and 'not... for the purposes of the FOI Act.'[69] The department added that the Commissions of Investigation Act (2004) informed the decision to deposit the archive in the department, but also pointed out that the act 'does not apply to the work of the interdepartmental [McAleese] committee or bind it in any way.'[70] In other words, the state's archive of Magdalen-related material is quarantined, literally placed 'out of sight, out of mind.' The inability to access any of this material – including documents previously released under the National Archives Act's 30-year rule – impedes greater understanding and truth-telling. The state knows what the McAleese committee archive contains; however, it does not want survivors, family members, academics or members of the public to know.

Published in October 2018, the *CLANN Report: Ireland's Unmarried Mothers and their Children: Gathering the Data* identifies the denial of access to information as constituting an ongoing form of harm to victims and survivors of historic and institutional abuse.[71] Indeed, CLANN's primary recommendation calls for 'a new form of investigation that makes access to information its primary goal' and for the establishment of 'an independent repository where all privately and publicly held records [would be] deposited' and made accessible in an appropriate format.[72] The report identifies the commission-of-investigation model and its underpinning legislation as fuelling the compartmentalisation and lack of transparency characteristic of the state's response to historical abuses to date.[73] According to CLANN, such a model imposes secrecy: investigators conduct their work in private, and witnesses have neither access to a transcript of their interview nor to evidence related to their abuse. Moreover, the archives gathered by commissions are immune to FOI requests, and their evidence is inadmissible in both criminal and civil proceedings. And because the legislation entitles commissions to embargo their archives, it thwarts additional inspection, analysis and transparency.[74] Ireland's Commissions of Investigation Act inhibits truth-telling about state practice in the past and in the present – and it does so in the service of consolidating state power.[75]

Conclusion: Unknowing Tuam Today

The evidence examined above suggests very little has changed in the state's response to knowledge of institutional abuses in the past. In February 2012, slightly more than two years before the Tuam story became international headline news, I wrote to the independent chairperson of the McAleese committee and shared information about Tuam's biannual returns analysed above.[76] I provided the committee with the location and archive-file information for the original documents and attached sample photographs. Finally, I submitted an Excel spreadsheet with information for the 24 Tuam infants whose mothers were listed as 'in the Magdalen,' referred to above (see Fig. 6). Abiding by my understanding of data protection legislation at the time, I opted to use initials rather than reveal the identities of the children involved, and I redacted the copies of the original documents that I submitted for the same reason. But the spreadsheet indicated the file reference number and each child's registration number, enabling the committee to conduct additional investigations. Or so I assumed.

The McAleese report, published in 2013 and now routinely described by the government as the official narrative on the Magdalene laundries, mischaracterises its receipt of these submissions and minimises the significance of the information:

A11/342, Vo. II, Galway, Children and Unmarried Mothers in Institutions, Returns, 1952-1957. NATA RCH/ ARC/ 0/ 411768

Date	Ref	DOB	Date/Born	Status	Age	Sex	Health	Remarks
31.3.52	998 B, JG	4.3.47	18.3.49	Illegitimate	5 yrs	Male	Good	Mother in M... Normal
31.3.52	437 E, MA	20.7.46	Born	Illegitimate	5 1/2 yrs	Female	Good	Mother in M... Normal
31.3.52	452 K, M	26.7.46	9.8.46	Illegitimate	5 1/2 yrs	Female	Good	Mother in M... Normal
31.3.52	617 R, JP	5.5.47	Born	Illegitimate	4 3/4 yrs	Male	Good	Mother in M... Normal
30.9.52	998 B, JG	4.3.47	18.3.49	Illegitimate	5 1/2 yrs	Male	Good	Mother in M... Good
30.9.52	452 K, M	9.8.46	27.8.52	Illegitimate	6 yrs	Female	Good	Mother in M... Good
30.9.52	437 E, MA	20.7.46	Born	Illegitimate	6 yrs	Female	Good	Mother in M... Good
30.9.52	452 K, M	27.7.46	9.8.46	Illegitimate	6 yrs	Female	Discharged,	Mother in Magdalen Home
30.9.52	617 R, JP	5.5.47	Born	Illegitimate	5 yrs	Male	Discharged,	Mother in Magdalen Home
30.9.52	963 H, MA	25.1.49	Born	Illegitimate	3 3/4 yrs	Female	Good	Mother in M... Good
31.3.53	998 B, JG	4.3.47	18.3.49	Illegitimate	6 yrs	Male	Not very str...	Mother in M... Under treatm... Bronchitis under treatment
30.9.53	660 K, M	9.8.46	27.8.52	Illegitimate	7 yrs	Female	Normal	Mother in M... Normal ... Normal
30.9.53	998 B, JG	18.3.47	18.3.49	Illegitimate	5 yrs	Male	Discharged,	Mother in M... Galway Magdalen Home
31.3.54	660 K, M	26.7.46	27.8.52	Illegitimate	7 3/4 yrs	Female	Good	Mother in M... Normal
31.3.54	789 C, PJ	6.9.53	6.9.53	Illegitimate	1 yr	Male	Good	Mother in M... Reccomended for Adoption
30.9.54	660 K, M	27.7.46	27.8.52	Illegitimate	8 yrs	Female	Good	Mother in M... For Adoption in America, good
30.9.54	219 C, TJ	7.5.50	16.5.50	Illegitimate	4 yrs	Male	Discharged	Mother in Magdalen Home
31.3.55	789 C, PJ	6.9.53	6.9.53	Illegitimate	1 1/3 yrs	Male	Discharged,	Mother in Magdalen Home
30.9.55	916/54 G, J	13.7.54	Born	Illegitimate	10 mths.	Male	Died, 24.5.5...	Mother in Magdalen Home
30.9.55	864/54 H, MC	26.2.54	Born	Illegitimate	1 1/2 yrs	Female		Mother in Magdalen Home
31.3.65	864/54 H, MC	26.2.54	Born	Illegitimate	2 yrs	Female	Good	Mother in M... Normal
30.9.56	864/54 H, MC	26.2.54	Born	Illegitimate	2 1/2 yrs	Female	Good	Mother in Magdalen Home
31.3.57	864/54 H, MC	26.2.54	Born	Illegitimate	3 yrs	Female		Mother in M... Healthy	OK?

Figure 6. Partial copy of Excel spreadsheet compiled by author and submitted to the McAleese committee, 21 February 2012

Information was also identified in the annual returns of the Tuam home to the Department of Health. The information recorded in those cases differs, as it is focused primarily on the children in the home. Nonetheless, between 1950 and 1965 the returns calculating the number of and providing information on children in Tuam identified that the mothers of twenty-four of these children were in a Magdalen laundry ('mother in Magdalen home'). As some of these children remained in the Tuam home for a number of years, certain cases are reported more than once. The files in question identify the women and children by initials only, with the result that the committee was unable to track these cases in the records of the religious congregations to determine what subsequently became of the women in question.[77]

The problem, it would appear, was that the committee was 'unable to track' these cases in the records of the religious orders. Yet the committee had unimpeded access to all departmental files and staff of the various departments at its disposal. The report fails to note that the committee could have identified these children by checking the original document on file in the state's own archive – the state was also capturing biannual returns for all unmarried mothers in PA institutions from at least 1942, as indicated by Circular P.99/42 – and cross-referencing the mothers' and children's information to identify the women in the nuns' records. To do so, of course, might have taken additional resources, which the government was ill-disposed to commit in an era of economic austerity.[78] And yet the McAleese report, which was instituted as the alternative to a 'prompt, independent, and thorough' investigation called for by the UN Committee Against Torture, remains the official history of state involvement with the laundries.[79] According to Maeve O'Rourke government officials routinely reference it precisely because it does 'not support the allegations that women were systematically detained unlawfully in these institutions or kept for long periods against their will.'[80] Crucially, there is no route to challenge the McAleese report's professed authority because the committee's archive is now sitting in a legal limbo in the Department of the Taoiseach, not subject to freedom-of-information requests and likely to remain inaccessible for decades to come. Indeed, there is nothing to suggest that the ongoing Mother and Baby Homes Commission of Investigation has been provided with access to the McAleese archive even though both sets of institutions operated hand in glove.[81]

If evidence of transfers between Mother and Baby Homes and Magdalene laundries signifies one form of state disavowal in the present, then evading evidence of significant infant mortality at Mother and Baby Homes constitutes another variety of contemporary unknowing. In my February 2012 letter I directed the attention of the McAleese committee to the excessively high infant mortality at the Tuam Baby Home:

I know from other archival research (D/Health A124/18 Replies to Circular P.24/48...) that the government conducted a survey in 1948... of all local government and public-assistance authorities recording the number of illegitimate children born in 'the year ending 31st March 1947' in both county homes and mother and baby homes. The same survey requested information for the numbers of illegitimate children who died in the same period. According to the returns submitted to the government, 12 of the 22 'illegitimate' children from County Mayo born at the baby home, Tuam, died within the year. Likewise, 25 of the 49 'illegitimate' children from County Galway born at the baby home, Tuam, for the same period also died. This information reveals how dangerous an environment the baby home, Tuam, could be for illegitimate children in residence. Such disturbing statistics certainly beg the question as to whether these children would have been better off remaining in their mother's care?[82]

At the time my intent was to signal how these transfers – the forcible removal of mothers from caring for their vulnerable children – might have been a contributing factor to the infants' deaths. Unlike earlier correspondence, which was routinely acknowledged and occasionally queried, the McAleese committee never contacted me in response. Neither was this information alluded to in its published final report – infant mortality (even when it involved children of women transferred to a Magdalene institution) fell outside the committee's purview; its terms of reference remained obscure because they were never made public.

But the matter did not end there. Conall Ó Fathárta, writing in *The Irish Examiner*, utilised FOI to access previously withheld government memoranda, reports and letters from 2012, which shed light on how various state agencies responded behind the scenes after being confronted with information about high infant-mortality rates at the Tuam Baby Home:

By 2012 the HSE was expressing stark concerns about the mother and baby home records it had uncovered. The McAleese committee had requested records relating to the ten Magdalen laundries be examined by the HSE. Permission was granted to include two mother and baby homes in this trawl – Bessborough in Cork and Tuam in Galway. This decision was 'based on potential pathways references by the advocacy group Justice for Magdalenes (JFM).' Prof. Jim Smith of Boston College and JFM group had written to the chairperson of the inquiry, then-senator Martin McAleese on February 21, 2012, outlining a circular he had discovered relating to a 1948 government survey which revealed 'disturbing' infant death rates in excess of fifty percent at the Tuam Mother and Baby Home. Within eight months HSE staff in Cork and Galway had turned up enough shocking material that concerns were being expressed about whether or not these issues warranted a state inquiry in and of themselves. By October 2012 such was the level of consternation the material was causing, an internal memo was prepared... [I]t notes there were letters from the Tuam Mother and Baby Home to parents asking for money for the upkeep of their children, and notes that duration of stay for children may have been prolonged by the order for financial reasons. It

> also uncovered letters to parents asking for money for the upkeep of some children that had already been discharged or had died ...[and] a list of 'up to 1,000 names' ...relate[ed] to the adoption of children by parents, possibly in the USA.
>
> [The report concludes that] 'this may prove to be a scandal that dwarfs other, more recent issues with the church and state... A concern is that if there is evidence of trafficking babies, that it must have been facilitated by doctors, social workers, etc.'...The report ends with a recommendation that an 'early warning' letter be written [that]... goes all the way up to the minister.[83]

The October 2012 memorandum, marked 'strictly confidential,' details explosive allegations about both Tuam and Bessborough. Indeed, the memorandum concludes with a recommendation that the information be brought to the minister's attention immediately. But nothing happened. No investigation ensued. The Department of Children and Youth Affairs contends that the minister was never informed in 2012.[84]

A full two years before Catherine Corless made the story known to Irish society for a second time, the state still failed to act, keeping Tuam an 'unknown known' and making 'unreal' what it knew to be 'real.' The state understood the ramifications of the knowledge in its possession. It chose not to make that knowledge public. Yet again it prioritised limiting the state's liability and attempted to consolidate its own power rather than to empower survivors and family members to understand what happened to their loved ones. It remains to be seen how and whether the Mother and Baby Homes Commission of Investigation and its archive will correct state practice in the past and encourage truth-telling in the present. Doing so hinges on the Irish state facilitating access to information – on a statutory basis – as the fundamental building block of reparation for historic abuses. Confronting this imperative represents the first step toward instituting structural reforms in the nation's political order. Only with such reforms will the contemporary nation, in its treatment of vulnerable Irish women and children, guarantee the nonrecurrence of historic abuse.

Notes

EDITORS' INTRODUCTION

1. An earlier version of this introduction appeared in *Éire-Ireland: An Interdisciplinary Journal of Irish Studies* 55.1 (Spring/Summer 2020), pp 9–16, DOI: 610.1353/ eir.2020.0000.

2. Mary Lodato, *Redress: Breaking the Silence*, Prod. Mick Peelo, RTÉ, 2 & 3 Mar. 2020.

3. Carmel McDonnell Byrne, Submission to the Joint Education Committee regarding the Retention of Records Bill 2019, 8 Nov. 2019, http://jfmresearch.com/ wp-content/uploads/2019/10/Carmel-McDonnell-Byrne-Submission.pdf

4. Tom Cronin, Submission to the Joint Education Committee regarding the Retention of Records Bill 2019, 8 Nov. 2019, http://jfmresearch.com/wp-content/ uploads/2019/10/Tom-Cronin-Submission.pdf

5. Elizabeth Coppin, Witness Statement to the UN Committee Against Torture in the case of *Elizabeth Coppin v Ireland*, Communication No 879/2018, para 107, on file with the authors.

6. James M. Smith, *Ireland's Magdalen Laundries and the Nation's Architecture of Containment* (Southbend, IN, 2007).

7. Magdalene Laundries were neither specifically Irish nor exclusively Catholic institutions, but the majority of such institutions operating in Ireland in the twentieth century were run by Catholic religious orders. See Smith, *Ireland's Magdalen Laundries*, xiv–xvi. Consistent with the survivor-centred focus required of a Transitional Justice approach, we spell Magdalene using the form more frequently used by survivors. Most academic and official texts drop the final 'e'.

8. In addition to Smith above, see Maria Luddy, *Prostitution and Irish Society, 1800–1940* (New York, 2007) and Maria Luddy, *Women and Philanthropy in Nineteenth Century Ireland* (New York, 1995); Jacinta Prunty, *The Monasteries, Magdalen Asylums and Reformatory Schools of Our Lady of Charity in Ireland 1853–1973* (Dublin, 2017); Frances Finnegan, *Do Penance or Perish: Magdalen Asylums in Ireland* (Piltown, Co. Kilkenny, 2001); Lindsey Earner-Byrne, *Mother and Child: Maternity and Child Welfare in Dublin, 1920s–1960s* (Manchester, 2007); Jennifer Redmond, *Moving Histories: Irish Women's Emigration to Britain from Independence to Republic* (Liverpool, 2018); Leanne McCormick, *Regulating Sexuality: Women in Twentieth-century Northern Ireland* (Manchester, 2010); Sarah-Anne Buckley, *The Cruelty Man: Child Welfare, The NSPCC and the State in Ireland, 1889–1956* (Manchester, 2013), and Donnacha Lucey, *The End of the Irish Poor Law? Welfare and Healthcare Reform in Revolutionary and Independent Ireland* (Manchester, 2015).

9. Seamus Heaney, *The Redress of Poetry* (New York, 1995), p. 15.

10. Ibid.

11. See Boston College, The Institute for the Liberal Arts, *Towards Transitional Justice:*

Recognition, Truth-telling and Institutional Abuse in Ireland, 1–2 Nov. 2018, https://www.bc.edu/bc-web/academics/sites/ila/events/towards-transitional-justice.html.

12. See *Justice for Magdalenes Research: A Resource for People Affected by and Interested in Ireland's Magdalene Institutions*, n.d., jfmrearch.com.

13. The Final Report of the Mother and Baby Homes Commission of Investigation is available online at: https://www.gov.ie/en/publication/d4b3d-final-report-of-the-commission-of-investigation-into-mother-and-baby-homes/. See 'Executive Summary', p. 2 (para.1), p. 4 (para. 12), [Hereafter MBHCOI Final Report].

14. See Sarah-Anne Buckley, Vicky Conway, Máiréad Enright *et al.*, 'Joint Submission to Oireachtas Committee on Children, Equality, Disability and Integration RE: General Scheme of a Certain Institutional Burials (Authorised Interventions) Bill (Justice for Magdalenes Research, 26 Feb. 2021), http://jfmresearch.com/wp-content/uploads/2021/03/Institutional-Burials-Bill_Joint-Submission-26.2.21.pdf, pp 23–6.

15. The MBHCOI Final Report, Ch. 36, 'Human Rights', p. 29 (paras 36.80–36.81).

16. The MBHCOI Final Report, 'Executive Summary', p. 3 (para. 8) and 'Recommendations', p. 9 (para. 34).

17. See for example Claire McGettrick and Maeve O'Rourke on behalf of the CLANN Project, 'Clann Project Submission to Oak Consulting RE: Consultation Process on the Development of an *Ex-Gratia* "Restorative Recognition Scheme"', (Clann Project, 31 Mar. 2021), http://clannproject.org/wp-content/uploads/Clann-Project-Submission-to-Oak-Consulting_31.3.21.pdf, pp 38–9.

18. See, for example, Noelle Brown, email campaign, 'Adopted people and Mother and Baby Homes survivors need your help!', Feb. 2021, http://noellebrown.com/survivors/.

19. See CLANN Project, 'Transcript of Oxford University Seminar with Professor Mary Daly', available online at http://clannproject.org/commission-report/oxfordtranscript/, esp. p. 12, p. 22, p. 26, p. 27; also see Elaine Loughlin, 'Mother and Baby Homes Inquiry Discounted Hundreds of Survivors' Testimonies', *The Irish Examiner*, 2 June 2021; Jennifer Bray, 'Mother and Baby Homes: What did Prof Mary Daly Tell the Oxford Seminar?', *The Irish Times*, 3 June 2021.

20. See CLANN Project, 'Clann Publishes Findings of Three-Year Project on Adoption and Mother and Baby Homes', 15 Oct. 2018, http://clannproject.org/2018/10/15/clann-publishes-findings-of-three-year-project-on-adoption-and-mother-and-baby-homes/.

21. Department of Children, Equality, Disability, Integration and Youth, 'Mother and Baby Institutions Payment Scheme: Government Proposals', 16 Nov. 2021, https://www.gov.ie/pdf/?file=https://assets.gov.ie/204595/b3a52e17-ae0c-4897-8a3e-9ae7a6e59d08.pdf#page=null.

22. Department of Children, 'Settlement of applications for judicial review of Final Report of Commission of Investigation into Mother and Baby Homes', 17 Dec. 2021. Available at: https://www.gov.ie/en/press-release/b981a-settlement-of-applications-for-judicial-review-of-final-report-of-commission-of-investigation-into-mother-and-baby-homes/.

23. Also see, Clair Wills, 'Architectures of Containment', *London Review of Books* 43, 10, 20 May 2021, https://www.lrb.co.uk/the-paper/v43/n10/clair-wills/architectures-of-containment; Catriona Crowe, 'The Commission and the Survivors', *The Dublin Review* (Summer, 2021), https://thedublinreview.com/article/the-commission-and-the-survivors/; Fintan O'Toole, 'Mother and Baby Report Cannot be Left to Stand', *The Irish Times*, 8 June 2021; and Máiréad Enright, Aoife O'Donoghue, et al, *Mother and Baby Homes Commission of Investigation Report Draft Alternative Executive*

Summary (2021), https://www.tudublin.ie/media/website/news/2021/main-news/Draft-Report-July-15-2021.pdf

24. UN Committee Against Torture, 'Information received from Ireland on the implementation of the Committee's concluding observations', UN Doc CAT/C/IRL/CO/1/Add.1, 25 Apr. 2013, paras 13–14, https://tbinternet.ohchr.org/_layouts/15/treatybodyexternal/Download.aspx?symbolno=CAT%2fC%2fIRL%2fCO%2f1%2fAdd.1&Lang=en; UN Committee Against Torture, 'Second periodic reports of States parties due in 2015: Ireland', UN Doc CAT/C/IRL/2, 20 Jan. 2016, para 224, https://tbinternet.ohchr.org/_layouts/15/treatybodyexternal/Download.aspx?symbolno=CAT%2fC%2fIRL%2f2&Lang=en

25. See Claire McGettrick, Katherine O'Donnell, Maeve O'Rourke, James M. Smith and Mari Steed, *Ireland and the Magdalene Laundries: A Campaign for Justice* (London, 2021), pp 127–62.

26. Leanne McCormick and Sean O'Connell, with Olivia Dee and John Privilege, *Mother and Baby Homes and Magdalene Laundries in Northern Ireland, 1922–1990: A Report for the Inter Departmental Working Group on Mother and Baby Homes, Magdalene Laundries and Historical Clerical Child Abuse* (Belfast, 2021).

27. See www.truthrecoverystrategy.com; Northern Ireland, Department of Health, 'Mother and Baby and Magdalene Laundry Institutions—Truth Recovery Design Team Announced', 4 Mar. 2021, https://www.health-ni.gov.uk/news/mother-and-baby-and-magdalene-laundry-institutions-truth-recovery-design-team-announced; for the final report of the Truth Recovery Design Panel, see Deirdre Mahon, Maeve O'Rourke and Phil Scraton, Truth Recovery Design Panel, 'Report for the Northern Ireland Executive: Mother and Baby Institutions, Magdalene Laundries and Workhouses in Northern Ireland: Truth, Acknowledgement and Accountability' (Oct. 2021), https://truthrecoverystrategy.com/panel-launch-truth-recovery-report/.

28. See Northern Ireland Executive Office, Press Release, 'Executive announces major steps forward on mother and baby institutions and Magdalene Laundries', 15 Nov. 2021, https://www.executiveoffice-ni.gov.uk/news/executive-announces-major-steps-forward-mother-and-baby-institutions-and-magdalene-laundries.

29. McCormick and O'Connell, *Mother and Baby Homes and Magdalene Laundries*, pp 76–8.

30. UN Secretary General, *The Rule of Law and Transitional Justice in Conflict and Post-Conflict Societies: Report of the Secretary-General*, 23 Aug. 2004, S/2004/616, p. 4. Also see Office of the United Nations High Commissioner for Human Rights, *Transitional Justice and Economic, Social and Cultural Rights* (Geneva: Office of the United Nations High Commissioner for Human Rights, 2014).

31. There is an extensive scholarly literature addressing Transitional Justice: see e.g.; Ruti G. Teitel, *Transitional Justice* (Oxford, 2000); Pablo De Greiff, 'A Normative Conception of Transitional Justice', *politorbis* 50.3 (2010), pp 17–30; Juan E. Méndez and Catherine Cone, 'Transitional Justice', in Scott Sheeran and Nigel Rodley (eds.), *The Routledge Handbook of International Human Rights Law* (London, 2013), p. 761.

32. Méndes and Cone, 'Transitional Justice', p. 761.

33. Transitional justice approaches have been utilised in South Africa, Chile, Argentina and Guatemala, for example.

34. See for example the array of articles addressing Northern Ireland in the *International Journal of Transitional Justice* (Oxford), https://academic.oup.com/ijtj/search-results?page=1&q=Northern%20Ireland&fl_SiteID=5176&SearchSourceType=1&allJournals=1

35. See Nicola Henry, 'From Reconciliation to Transitional Justice: The Contours of Redress Politics in Established Democracies', *International Journal of Transitional Justice* 9.2 (2015), pp 199–218; Rosemary Nagy, 'The Truth and Reconciliation

Commission of Canada: Genesis and Design', *Canadian Journal of Law and Society* 29.2 (2014), pp 199–217; Kathleen Daly, 'Conceptualizing Responses to Institutional Abuse of Children', *Current Issues in Criminal Justice* 26.1 (2014), pp 5–29; Katie Wright, Shurlee Swain, Kathleen McPhillips, 'The Australian Royal Commission Into Institutional Responses to Child Sexual Abuse', *Child Abuse & Neglect* 74 (Dec. 2017), pp 1–114.

36. See Eoin O'Sullivan and Ian O'Donnell (eds.), *Coercive Confinement in Ireland: Patients, Prisoners, and Penitents* (Manchester, 2012), p. 7.

37. See Department of Culture, Heritage and the Gaeltacht, *Decade of Centenaries*, 2012–2022, https://www.decadeofcentenaries.com/.

38. Katherine O'Donnell, 'Let's Listen Attentively to Survivors of Magdalene Laundries', *The Irish Times*, 5 June 2018.

39. During a 'Listening Exercise' conducted with survivors during the Dublin Honours Magdalenes event in June 2018, the women repeatedly asked that their abuse be recorded in the history books and taught in schools trusting that younger generations of Irish would never forget nor stand idly by in the face of recurring injustice. See, Katherine O'Donnell and Claire McGettrick et. al., *Dublin Honours Magdalenes Listening Exercise Report Vol 1: Report on Key Findings* (Dublin, 2020), pp 33–6, http://jfmresearch.com/wp-content/uploads/2020/04/DHM-Listening-Exercise-Report_Vol-1.pdf

40. In the fall semester 2018, James Smith offered an undergraduate elective at Boston College entitled 'Outcast Ireland: Paupers, Penitents, Patients', in which the students researched and designed poster-boards for presentation at the 'Towards Transitional Justice' conference in Nov., see Mary Cobble, Liza Frost, Isabelle Morford, Haley Walker, and Oliver Whitters, *How do I know who I am?: An Analysis of the Ramifications of Ireland's Adoption Policies*, 2018. http://hdl.handle.net/2345/bc-ir:108343; Tara Coffey, Meg Dolan, Isabel Rivera, and Daniel Walsh, *Narrating Neglect at Artane Industrial School*, 2018. http handle.net/2345/bc-ir:108345://hdl.; Meghan Dougherty, Sophia Fox, Megan Kelly, and Sydney Walters. *Making Visible the Truth of the Galway Magdalen Laundry*, 2018. http://hdl.handle.net/2345/bc-ir:108346; Audrey Ballard, Kathleen Flaherty, Taylor Puccini, and Jessica Rowe, *Confronting Compartmentalization: Bessboro Mother & Baby Home*, 2018, http://hdl.handle.net/2345/bc-ir:108348; Emily Lyons, *House of the Good Shepherd Boston MA*, 2018. http://hdl.handle.net/2345/bc-ir:108344.

41. Heaney, *The Redress of Poetry*, pp 3–4.

42. Ibid., p. 4.

CHAPTER 1 – TESTIMONY

1. This essay was previously published in *Éire-Ireland: An Interdisciplinary Journal of Irish Studies* 55.1 (Spring/Summer 2020), pp 17–34, DOI: 10.1353/eir.2020.000.
2. See 'Towards Transitional Justice: Recognition, Truth-Telling, and Institutional Abuse in Ireland', Boston College Institute for the Liberal Arts, 1–2 Nov. 2018, https://www.bc.edu/bc-web/academics/sites/ila/events/towards-transitional-justice.html, archived at https://perma.cc/8QY4-KR8E.

CHAPTER 2 – ANTIGONE IN GALWAY: ANNE ENRIGHT ON THE DISHONOURED DEAD

1. This essay was previously published in the *London Review of Books*, 37.24, 17 Dec. 2015, pp 11–14, and is reprinted here with permission of the author.

Chapter 3 – The Lost Children of Tuam

1. This essay was previously published in *The New York Times*, 27 Oct. 2017 and is reprinted here with permission.

Chapter 4 – Family Secrets

1. This essay was previously published in *The New York Review of Books*, 16 Aug. 2018 and is reprinted here with permission.

Chapter 5 – The Mother of Us All

1. This essay is developed from a shorter piece entitled, 'I Wish Ann Lovett Were Out Buying a Swimsuit for Lanzarote', originally commissioned by EVA international, Ireland's Biennial of Contemporary Art, 2017.

2. These efforts were successful, and in 1983 Ireland added the 8th amendment to its constitution, giving an embryo or foetus the same right to life as the woman carrying it.

3. In the summer of 1985, Ireland underwent a phenomenon whereby statues of the Virgin Mary were witnessed to move, bleed, shimmer, smile, and even speak at grottos throughout the country. While the Catholic Church was careful to withhold any official sanction for the moving statues, the faithful were undeterred. For example, at Ballinspittle, Co. Cork, where one of the first sightings took place, up to a quarter of a million people made the pilgrimage in the hope that they, too, would see Our Lady move. For more information, see Colm Tóibín (ed.), *Seeing is Believing: Moving Statues in Ireland* (Mountrath, 1985).

4. Paula Meehan, 'The Statue of the Virgin at Granard Speaks', in *Mysteries of the Home* (Dublin, 2013), p. 26.

5. Eavan Boland, 'Being an Irish Poet: The Communal Art of Paula Meehan', in *A Journey With Two Maps: Becoming a Woman Poet* (London, 2012), p. 228.

6. To read more about the Kerry Babies case, see: Nell McCafferty, *A Woman to Blame: The Kerry Babies Case* (Cork, 1985.)

7. In Jan. 2018 Hayes finally received an apology from the Irish state for its role in her treatment.

8. *Cillíní* are burial grounds for un-baptised and stillborn babies.

9. James M. Smith, *Ireland's Magdalen Laundries and the Nation's Architecture of Containment* (Southbend, IN, 2007).

10. The term *Bean an Tí* (direct translation: Woman of the House) refers to a woman living in a *Gaeltacht* or Irish speaking region who takes language students as borders in her home.

11. Fidelma Farley, 'Interrogating Myths of Maternity in Irish Cinema: Margo Harkin's' *Hush-a-Bye Baby*', *Irish University Review* 29.2 (1999), pp 219–37.

12. Cited in Diana Taylor, *The Archive and the Repertoire: Performing Cultural Memory in the Americas* (Durham, 2003), p. 44.

13. Ibid., p. 46.

14. Ibid., p. 50.

15. The 7th century Irish writer Cogitosus's *Vita Sanctae Brigitae* describes a miracle in which Brigit makes excellent ale for thirsty lepers out of some nearby bathwater as well as one in which she aborts the pregnancy of a nun. The abortion miracle is worth citing, I think: 'With a strength of faith most powerful and ineffable she blessed a woman who, after a vow of virginity, had lapsed through weakness into youthful

concupiscence, as a result of which her womb had begun to swell with pregnancy. In consequence, what had been conceived in the womb disappeared and she restored her to health and penitence without childbirth or pain.' I find it particularly cool that the beneficiary of this miracle is not a victim of rape or abandonment, but rather just a young woman who did the tempting things that young women often do. And I love that the abortion Brigit provided was painless. Later Christian accounts of the life of Brigit excise the abortion story. But you can read Cogitosus in English translation here: Sean Connolly and J. M. Picard, 'Cogitosus's "Life of St Brigit" Content and Value', *The Journal of the Royal Society of Antiquaries of Ireland* 117 (1987), pp 5–27.
16. When Éiru, the goddess who gives her name to Ireland, is insulted by Donn Mac Míled, a leader of the invading Milesians (or Gaels), she tells him that neither he nor his children will ever enjoy her beautiful country, and he soon drowns, bad cess to him. James McKillop, *A Dictionary of Celtic Mythology* (Oxford, 2004).
17. For example, Badb could turn into a crow, screaming to distract her enemies on the battlefield. The Morrigan could transform into a fish, bird, or animal, and from a beautiful young woman to an old hag. McKillop, *A Dictionary of Celtic Mythology*.
18. The Morrigan prophesised Cúchulainn's death, and Badb prophesised the end of days. McKillop, *A Dictionary of Celtic Mythology*.
19. Macha famously outran the fastest horses of the Kings of Ulster while heavily pregnant to win a bet for her husband. She then cursed the men of Ulster through seven generations to suffer the pains of childbirth in the moment of their greatest need. McKillop, *A Dictionary of Celtic Mythology*.
20. The teenage girl at the Centre of the X case is known as Miss X.
21. In 1997, Miss C, a suicidal 13-year-old who had survived a brutal rape had to go to the high court to obtain the right to travel for an abortion. You can read the court decision here: A. and B. v. Eastern Health Board [1997] IEHC 176; [1998] 1 IR 464; [1998] 1 ILRM 460 (28 Nov 1997) http://www.bailii.org/ie/cases/IEHC/1997/176.html
22. Amy Dunne, known during her high court case as Miss D, was a 16-year-old whose pregnancy was diagnosed with a fatal foetal abnormality in 2007. The Health Service Executive (HSE) used lies and threats to prevent her from travelling to the UK for an abortion. See: *The Irish Times*, 'Court rules 'Miss D' can travel to UK for abortion', *The Irish Times*, 10 May 2007. https://www.irishtimes.com/news/court-rules-miss-d-can-travel-to-uk-for-abortion-1.1205100
23. In 2010, Miss A, B, and C took a case to the European Court of Human Rights to argue that Ireland's abortion laws contravened their privacy rights. The cases of A and B did not succeed while the case of C did. You can read the judgment here: Case of A, B and C v. Ireland ECHR 25579/05 (16 Dec 2010), http://hudoc.echr.coe.int/eng?i=001-102332
24. Ms. Y was a pregnant, suicidal teenage asylum seeker, pregnant through rape, who, in 2014, was forced by the HSE to carry her pregnancy until 26 weeks, then forcible c-sectioned. You can read a timeline of her case here: Kitty Holland, 'Timeline of Ms. Y Case', *The Irish Times*, 4 Oct 2014. https://www.irishtimes.com/news/social-affairs/timeline-of-ms-y-case-1.1951699
25. Amanda Mellet made a submission to the United Nation Human Rights Committee (UNHRC) arguing that her treatment on finding that her pregnancy had a fatal foetal abnormality was cruel, inhuman, and degrading. In 2016, the Committee agreed and also found that Ireland had violated Ms. Mellet's privacy rights. See: Irish Council for Civil Liberties, 'Case in Focus: Amanda Mellet', n.d., https://www.iccl.ie/her-rights/privacy/case-focus-amanda-mellet/.
26. Siobhán Whelan challenged the state's abortion laws before the UNHRC a second time, and, in 2017, was also successful in demonstrating that her treatment by the

state was cruel, inhuman, and degrading. See: Irish Council for Civil Liberties, 'Case in Focus: Siobhán Whelan', n.d., https://www.iccl.ie/her-rights/siobhan-whelan/.

27. In 2014, a braindead woman was kept alive and physically deteriorating for 4 weeks in the name of the 8th amendment, even though the second trimester foetus she was carrying had no chance of survival. Her family had to go to the High Court to fight for the right to turn off her life support and bury her with dignity. 'The unborn' had its own legal representation. See: 'Doctors Told They Can Withdraw Life Support for Clinically Dead Pregnant Woman', *thejournal.ie*, 26 Dec 2014, https://www.thejournal.ie/life-support-clinically-dead-woman-judgement-1852228-Dec2014/.

28. Amnesty International. *She is Not a Criminal: The Impact of Ireland's Abortion Law* (London 2015), p. 5.

29. Rosita Sweetman, @rositasweetman; Ann O'Gorman is a Mother and Baby Home Survivor', Instagram Post, 13 Nov 2020, https://www.instagram.com/p/CHhyHYpH4L3

30. Savita Halappanavar was an Indian dentist who died of sepsis when she was denied a medical abortion during a partial miscarriage on the grounds that it would be against Irish law. To learn more about her life, her family, and the circumstances of her death you might read: Kitty Holland, *Savita: The Tragedy that Shook a Nation* (Dublin, 2013).

31. Paula Meehan, 'The Statue of the Virgin at Granard Speaks', in *Mysteries of the Home* (Dublin, 2013), p. 26.

32. Tara Flynn, 'Not a Funny Word', Unpublished Script, 2018.

33. Ibid.

34. Eavan Boland, *A Journey with Two Maps: Becoming a Woman Poet* (London, 2012), p. 229.

CHAPTER 6 – STATE RESPONSES TO HISTORICAL ABUSES IN
IRELAND: 'VULNERABILITY' AND THE DENIAL OF RIGHTS

1. An earlier version of this essay appeared in *Human Rights Quarterly* 43.3 (Aug. 2021), pp 435–59. Declaration of Interest: In this article I refer to testimony published by the 'Clann Project' (www.clannproject.org), a voluntary evidence-gathering and advocacy initiative of which I am co-director with Claire McGettrick. I refer also to the work of the Justice for Magdalenes Research group of which I am a voluntary member, and to the ongoing individual complaint of *Elizabeth Coppin v. Ireland* before the United Nations Committee Against Torture in which I am acting as one of Mrs Coppin's legal team. I gratefully acknowledge Mrs. Coppin's wish to place her experiences on the public record. Her address to the Oxford Union in 2019 is available on www.youtube.com.

2. Martha Fineman, 'Vulnerability and Inevitable Inequality', *Oslo Law Review* 4.3 (2017), pp 133, 147.

3. Ibid., p. 143.

4. Catriona MacKenzie, Wendy Rogers and Susan Dodds, 'Introduction', in Mackenzie C, Rogers W and Dodds S (eds), *Vulnerability: New Essays in Ethics and Feminist Philosophy* (Oxford, 2014), pp 1, 6–7.

5. Ibid., pp 5–9.

6. Ibid., p. 7.

7. Fineman, 'Vulnerability and Inevitable Inequality', (n. 2), p. 147.

8. Ibid., p. 134.

9. Fineman states that her theory 'does not dictate the form responses should take, only that they reflect the reality of human vulnerability'. Ibid., p. 134 (n. 2).

10. Ibid., pp 144–5.

11. See, for example, Kate Brown, 'The Governance of Vulnerability: Regulation, Support and Social Divisions in Action', *International Journal of Sociology and Social Policy* 37, 11/12 (2017), p. 667; MacKenzie et al, 'Introduction', pp 1, 6 (n. 4).

12. Martha Albertson Fineman, 'The Vulnerable Subject and the Responsive State', *Emory Law Journal* 60.2 (2010), pp 251, 255.

13. I use this terminology throughout the Ch. to reference those affected by the human rights violations I describe, but it is important to acknowledge that these terms are not preferred by all so affected.

14. See for an example of the Irish Government's use of this adjective, the State apology to survivors of Ireland's Magdalene Laundries: *Dáil Éireann Debates*, 'Magdalen Laundries Report: Statements', 19 Feb. 2013, https://www.kildarestreet.com/debates/?id=2013-02-19a.387.

15. See for example Fine Gael, Press Release, 'Government agreed details of implementation of Quirke Scheme for women in Magdalen laundries', 7 Nov. 2013, https://www.finegael.ie/government-agreed-details-of-implementation-of-quirke-scheme-for-women-in-magdalen-laundries/; CEDAW, Introductory statement by Ms Carol Baxter, Assistant Secretary General, Department of Justice and Equality, 15 Feb. 2017, p. 9 (regarding the Mother and Baby Homes).

16. *Magdalen Laundries Report: Statements*, (n. 14).

17. '"Ireland failed you": President Higgins apologises to Magdalene Laundries survivors at Aras an Uachtarain event', *The Irish Examiner*, 5 June 2018, https://www.irishexaminer.com/breakingnews/ireland/ireland-failed-you-president-higgins-apologises-to-magdalene-laundries-survivors-at-aras-an-uachtarain-event-846951.html.

18. Juno McEnroe, 'Magdalene Redress: Official Ireland took its time with apology, admits Charlie Flanagan', *The Irish Examiner*, 6 June 2018, https://www.irishexaminer.com/ireland/magdalene-redress-official-ireland-took-its-time-with-apology-admits-charlie-flanagan-471525.html

19. See for a summary of publicly available evidence and official reports, Maeve O'Rourke, 'Justice for Magdalenes Research, NGO Submission to the UN Committee against Torture' (Justice for Magdalenes Research, 2017), pp 7–15, https://tbinternet.ohchr.org/_layouts/15/treatybodyexternal/Download.aspx?symbolno=INT%2fCAT%2fCSS%2fIRL%2f27974&Lang=en; See also Maeve O'Rourke and James M Smith, 'Ireland's Magdalene Laundries: Confronting a History Not Yet in the Past', in Alan Hayes and Maire Meagher (eds), *A Century of Progress? Irish Women Reflect* (Dublin, 2016).

20. See for the most recent example: Ireland, *Information on follow-up to the concluding observations of the Committee against Torture on the second periodic report of Ireland*, UN Doc CAT/C/IRL/CO/2/Add.1, 28 Aug. 2018, para 15.

21. See for one example of this repeated statement: Ireland, *Replies to the Human Rights Committee's List of Issues*, UN Doc CCPR/C/IRL/Q/4/Add.1, 5 May 2014, para 54.

22. Ireland, *Replies to the List of Issues Prior to Submission of the Second Report of Ireland*, UN Doc CAT/C/IRL/2, 20 Jan. 2016, para 237.

23. Comm. Against Torture (CAT), *Elizabeth Coppin v. Ireland*, Communication No 879/2018, *Submission of the Government of Ireland on the Merits of the Communication to the Committee Against Torture Made by Elizabeth Coppin*, 31 July 2020, para 115 (on file with author).

24. Most recently, Irish Human Rights and Equality Commission, *Submission to*

the United Nations Committee against Torture on Ireland's Second Periodic Report, July 2017, pp 53–8.

25. Committee Against Torture (CAT), Concluding Observations on the First Periodic Report of Ireland, UN Doc CAT/C/IRL/CO/1, 17 June 2011, para 20; CAT, Concluding Observations on the Second Periodic Report of Ireland, UN Doc CAT/C/IRL/CO/2, 31 Aug. 2017, para 25; Human Rights Committee (HRC), Concluding Observations on the Fourth Periodic Report of Ireland, UN Doc CCPR/C/IRL/CO/4, 19 Aug. 2014, para 10; Committee on the Elimination of Discrimination Against Women (CEDAW), Concluding Observations on the Combined Sixth and Seventh Periodic Reports of Ireland, UN Doc CEDAW/C/IRL/CO/6–7, 3 Mar. 2017, paras 14–15; Committee on Economic, Social and Cultural Rights (CESCR), Concluding observations on the third periodic report of Ireland, UN Doc E/C.12/IRL/CO/3, 19 June 2015, para 18; Report of the Special Rapporteur on the sale and sexual exploitation of children, UN Doc A/HRC/40/51/Add.2, 1 Mar. 2019, paras 16–19, 78.

26. See for example Maeve O'Rourke, Claire McGettrick, Rod Baker, Raymond Hill et al., *CLANN: Ireland's Unmarried Mothers and their Children: Gathering the Data: Principal Submission to the Commission of Investigation into Mother and Baby Homes*, 15 Oct. 2018 (hereafter *CLANN* Report), http://clannproject.org/wp-content/uploads/Clann-Submissions_Redacted-Public-Version-Oct.-2018.pdf

27. Ibid.

28. CAT (2017), paras 27–28 (n. 25); CEDAW (2017), above para 15 (n. 25); HRC (2014) above para 10 (n. 25).

29. *CLANN* Report, para 1.37 (n. 26).

30. See Child and Family Agency, *St Patrick's Guild Adoption Records*, https://www.tusla.ie/services/alternative-care/adoption-services/tracing-service/st-patricks-guild-adoption-records/; Department of Children, *Draft Heads and General Scheme of Birth Information and Tracing Bill*, 11 May 2021, https://www.gov.ie/en/press-release/14c5c-minister-ogorman-publishes-proposed-birth-information-and-tracing-legislation/.

31. See Aoife Hegarty, 'Who am I? The Story of Ireland's Illegal Adoptions' *RTÉ Investigates*, 5 Mar. 2021, https://www.rte.ie/news/investigations-unit/2021/0302/1200520-who-am-i-the-story-of-irelands-illegal-adoptions/; Marion Reynolds, *A Shadow Cast Long: Independent Review Report into Incorrect Birth Registrations: Commissioned by the Minister for Children and Youth Affairs*, May 2019, https://www.gov.ie/pdf/?file=https://assets.gov.ie/126409/d06b2647-6f8e-44bf-846a-a2954de815a6.pdf#page=null.

32. Conall Ó Fátharta, 'Special Report: Women Forced to Give up Babies for Adoption Still Failed by State bodies', *The Irish Examiner*, 3 Dec. 2018.

33. *CLANN* Report, para 1.47 (n. 26).

34. Ibid., para 1.49.

35. Ibid., para 1.42.

36. Ibid., para 1.91.

37. Ibid., para 1.159.

38. Ibid., para 1.84.

39. Ibid., para 1.54–1.55.

40. Ibid., para 1.172–1.173.

41. Ibid., para 1.208.

42. Ibid., para 1.224.

43. Ibid., para 1.225.

44. Mother and Baby Homes Commission of Investigation [hereafter MBHCOI], *Final Report*, 2020, https://assets.gov.ie/118565/107bab7e-45aa-4124-95fd-1460893dbb43.pdf [hereinafter MBHCOI *Final Report*].

45. Ibid., Exec. Summary para 8.
46. Ibid., Recommendations para 27.
47. Ibid., Recommendations para 30.
48. Ibid., Recommendations para 34.
49. Ibid., Exec. Summary para 248.
50. Ibid., Ch. 36 para 248.
51. Ibid. pt. 4. (Confidential Committee Report), p. 12. Ibid., 10, the MBHCOI explains that only nineteen people gave evidence to the investigative arm of the Commission (which had powers to make adverse findings against institutions or individuals) whereas 550 met the Confidential Committee (which had the power only to make a report of a general nature). In Aug. 2016 Hogan Lovells International LLP wrote to the MBHCOI on behalf of the Clann Project noting with concern that 'the Commission's rules and procedures, which identify the two ways to give evidence, are not shown on the website and there is no mention of being able to give direct evidence in person to the Commission other than via the Confidential Committee': see Rod Baker, Hogan Lovells International LLP, 'Letter to Maeve Doherty, Mother & Baby Homes—Commission of Investigation', 9 Aug. 2016, http://clannproject. org/wp-content/uploads/Letter-from-Hogan-Lovells-to-MBHCOI_09-08-2016.pdf
52. MBHCOI *Final Report*, Part 4, Confidential Committee Report, p. 12.
53. Committee Against Torture, *Concluding Observations on the Second Periodic Report of Ireland*, U.N. Doc. CAT/C/IRL/CO/2, 31 Aug. 2017, para 26–28.
54. See the numerous *Concluding Observations* at n. 25.
55. O'Rourke, 'NGO Submission', para 3.1 (n. 19).
56. See Ireland, *Information on Follow-up to the Concluding Observations of the Committee against Torture on the Second Periodic Report of Ireland*, para 19 (n. 20); Committee Against Torture, *Information received from Ireland on the implementation of the Committee's concluding observations*, U.N. Doc. CAT/C/IRL/CO/1/Add.1, 22, 31 July 2012; Ireland, *Replies to the Human Rights Committee's List of Issues*, para 57 (n. 21); Ireland, *Follow-Up Material to the Concluding Observations of the UN Human Rights Committee on the Fourth Periodic Review of Ireland under the International Covenant on Civil and Political Rights*, 17 July 2015, p. 3, https://tbinternet.ohchr. org/_layouts/15/treatybodyexternal/Download.aspx?symbolno=INT%2fCCPR%2f AFR%2fIRL%2f21460&Lang=en; Ireland, *Second Periodic Report to the Committee Against Torture*, UN Doc CAT/C/IRL/2, 20 Jan. 2016, para 241, https://tbinternet. ohchr.org/_layouts/15/treatybodyexternal/Download.aspx?symbolno=CAT%2 fC%2fIRL%2f2&Lang=en; Ireland, *Combined sixth and seventh periodic reports to the United Nations Committee on the Elimination of All Forms of Discrimination Against Women*, U.N. Doc. CEDAW/C/IRL/6–7, 30 Sept. 2016, para 43; Ireland, *Information on follow-up to the concluding observations of the Human Rights Committee on the fourth periodic report of Ireland*, UN Doc CCPR/C/IRL/CO/4/Add.1, 15 Aug. 2017, para 6.
57. *Information on Follow-up to the Concluding Observations of the Committee Against Torture on the Second Periodic Report of Ireland*, para 18 (n. 20).
58. According to the Adoption Rights Alliance group and Mike Milotte, the only known prosecution of an adoption agency is in 1965 at the Dublin District Court, where the manager of a private nursing home, Mary Keating, was convicted for registering births falsely; Keating continued her operations for more than a decade afterwards. See *CLANN* Report, para 1.117 (n. 26), citing Mike Milotte, *Banished Babies: The Secret History of Ireland's Baby Export Business* (Dublin, 2012), p. 126.
59. Ibid., para 2.19 (the testimony of a witness).
60. See Kevin Doyle, 'Charges are "not Likely" After Garda Probe Into Adoptions', *The Irish Independent*, 1 June 2018.

61. Conall Ó Fátharta, 'Bessborough Report Referred to Gardaí', *The Irish Examiner*, 24 Apr. 2019; MBHCOI, *Fifth Interim Report*, 2019, para 8.38, https://www.gov. ie/en/press-release/169f8f-commission-of-investigation-into-mother-and-baby-homes-fifth-interim/ [hereinafter MBHCOI *Fifth Interim Report*].

62. Oireachtas Joint Committee on Children, Disability, Equality and Integration, General Scheme of a Certain Institutional Burials (Authorised Interventions) Bill: Discussion, Evidence of Anna Corrigan, 14 Apr. 2021, https://www.oireachtas. ie/en/debates/debate/joint_committee_on_children_disability_equality_and_integration/2021-04-14/3/.

63. 'Appeal for Information About Crimes at Mother-and-Baby Homes', *RTÉ News*, 29 Apr. 2021, https://www.rte.ie/news/mother-and-baby-homes/2021/0429/1212798-mother-baby-appeal/.

64. An Garda Síochána, Press Release, 'Garda Appeal re Mother and Baby Homes', 29 Apr. 2021, https://www.garda.ie/en/about-us/our-departments/office-of-corporate-communications/press-releases/2021/Apr./garda-appeal-re-mother-and-baby-homes.html.

65. See Commissions of Investigation Act 2004, section 19, http://www. irishstatutebook.ie/eli/2004/act/23/section/19/enacted/en/html#sec19. This legislation underpinned the MBHCOI and specifies that no 'statement or admission' made to the MBHCOI, nor 'document given or sent to [the MBHCOI] pursuant to a direction or request', nor 'document specified in an affidavit' is admissible as evidence against a person in any criminal or other proceedings.

66. Oireachtas Joint Committee on Children, Disability, Equality and Integration, General Scheme of a Certain Institutional Burials (Authorised Interventions) Bill, Discussion, Evidence of Anna Corrigan, (n. 62).

67. Ibid.

68. James Gallen, *Historical Abuse and the Statute of Limitations* 39 Statute L. Rev., 2016, p. 104.

69. Ibid. p. 109. The 'disability' exception to the running of the limitation period applies only if (a) the person is 'of unsound mind', or (b) the person's court action is based on sexual abuse suffered in childhood, which caused a 'psychological injury' of 'such significance that his or her will, or his or her ability to make a reasoned decision, to bring such action [was] substantially impaired Statute of Limitations Act 1957 (as amended by Statute of Limitations (Amendment) Act 2000), section 48A.

70. *O'Dwyer v. The Daughters of Charity of St Vincent de Paul & Ors* [2015] IECA 226 (Court of Appeal) para 45. See also *EAO v. Daughters of Charity of St. Vincent de Paul & Ors* [2015] IEHC 68 (High Court); *Elizabeth Anne O'Dwyer v. The Daughters of Charity of St. Vincent de Paul, the Sisters of Our Lady of Charity of Refuge, and the Health Service Executive* [2016] IESCDET 12 (unreported), 22 Jan. 2016, (Supreme Court).

71. *O'Keeffe v. Ireland* (2014) 59 EHRR 15.

72. Mary Carolan, 'State Awarded Costs in School Abuse Case', *The Irish Times*, 24 Mar. 2006; *O'Keeffe v. Ireland*, paras 27, 47 (n. 70).

73. Colin Smith and Apr. Duff, chapter 8 in this volume..

74. Ibid.

75. O'Rourke, *NGO Submission*, p. 16 (n. 19)

76. MBHCOI *Final Report*, Index, p. 39 (n. 44)

77. Ibid. Exec. Summary, para 229, 243. See also Ibid., Ch. 33A, p. 6, observing that '[m]ortality rates in each of the institutions were very high in the period compared to the overall national rate of infant mortality'. The higher-than-average rate of mortality continued into the 1980s, Ibid., ch 33A, p. 11.

78. Sarah-Anne Buckley, Vicky Conway, Máiréad Enright, Fionna Fox, James

Gallen, Erika Hayes, Mary Harney, Darragh Mackin, Claire McGettrick, Conall Ó Fátharta, Maeve O'Rourke & Phil Scraton, *Joint Submission to Oireachtas Committee on Children, Equality, Disability and Integration RE: General Scheme of a Certain Institutional Burials (Authorised Interventions) Bill* 26 Feb. 2021, pp 23–26, http://jfmresearch.com/wp-content/uploads/2021/03/Institutional-Burials-Bill_Joint-Submission-26.2.21.pdf

79. Coroners Act 1962 (as amended), § 17, https://revisedacts.lawreform.ie/eli/1962/act/9/front/revised/en/html.

80. Ibid., section 24(1).

81. Buckley, et al, *Joint Submission*, p. 7 (n. 78).

82. MBHCOI, Fifth Interim Report, p. 65 (n. 61).

83. See National Archives Act 1986 (as amended), sections 1, 2, 13, which establish that 'public service organisations' (a local authority, health board, or body established by or under statute and financed wholly or partly by the state) *may* but are not required to deposit records with the National Archives. The National Archives Act 1986 says nothing about the records of non-state bodies which provide state-funded services.

84. Reynolds, *Shadow Cast Long*, paras 1.11, 2.1, 4.13 (n. 31).

85. They are subject to the Local Government Act 2001 section 80(2), which simply states that 'it is a function of a local authority to make arrangements for the proper management, custody, care and conservation of local records and local archives and for inspection by the public of local archives'.

86. These bodies are not listed in the Schedule to the National Archives Act 1986. The Adoption Authority of Ireland holds approximately 30,000 adoption records including those created by four former adoption agencies or societies: Reynolds, *Shadow Cast Long*, para 3.3 (n. 31).

87. Creative Cultures and Associates, *National Archives, Ireland: A Comparative Management Survey for Fórsa, Archivists' Branch*, 2019, p. 22, https://www.forsa.ie/wp-content/uploads/2019/12/Forsa-NAI-final-2.pdf

88. Ibid., p. 35.

89. *See* Freedom of Information Act 2014, sections 2, 11. The exception is where disclosure of older records is necessary or expedient to understand the more recent records or where the older records 'relate to personal information about the person seeking access to them'. Freedom of Information Act 2014, section 11.

90. Ibid., Schedule 1.

91. Conall Ó Fátharta, Tony Groves & Martin McMahon, 'Illegal Adoptions', *Echo Chamber Podcast*, Episode 163, 31 May 2019.

92. Ireland, *Information on follow-up to the Concluding Observations of the Committee against Torture*, U.N. Doc. CAT/C/IRL/CO/2/Add.1, para 28 (n. 20).

93. *Dáil Éireann Debates*, 'Magdalen Laundries', Written Answer by Minister for Justice and Equality, Alan Shatter TD, 6 Mar. 2013, https://www.oireachtas.ie/en/debates/question/2013-03-06/170/.

94. Irish Government News Service, Government Statement on Mother and Baby Homes, 28 Oct. 2020, https://merrionstreet.ie/en/news-room/news/government_statement_on_mother_and_baby_homes.html.

95. Justice for Magdalenes Research, *Campaigns, Retention of Records Bill 2019*, http://jfmresearch.com/retention-of-records-bill-2019/. This campaign was in response to the Retention of Records Bill 2019 (as initiated), https://data.oireachtas.ie/ie/oireachtas/bill/2019/16/eng/initiated/b1619d.pdf

96. Justice for Magdalenes Research, *Campaigns, Mother and Baby Homes Commission Archive*, http://jfmresearch.com/commission-archive/. This campaign followed Press Release, Ireland, Department of Children, Equality, Disability, Integration and

Youth, Minister O'Gorman to Introduce Legislation to Safeguard the Commission on Mother and Baby Homes General Archive of Records and Database, 15 Sept. 2020, https://www.gov.ie/en/press-release/96a99-minister-ogorman-to-introduce-legislation-to-safeguard-the-commission-on-mother-and-baby-homes-general-archive-of-records-and-database/.

97. Ireland, Report of the Inter-departmental Committee to Establish the Facts of State Involvement with the Magdalen Laundries (hereafter *IDC Report*), 2013, http://www.justice.ie/en/jelr/pages/magdalenrpt2013.

98. O'Rourke, 'NGO Submission', para 15–16 (n. 19).

99. Ms P and Department of the Taoiseach, Office of the Information Commissioner, Case Number: OIC-53487-S3Q7X3, 24 Jan. 2020, https://www.oic.ie/decisions/ms-p-and-department-of-th/.

100. Committee Against Torture, *Elizabeth Coppin v Ireland, Communication No 879/2018, Submission of the Government of Ireland*, para 156 (n. 23).

101. MBHCOI *Final Report*, Archives Ch. (n. 44).

102. Maeve O'Rourke, Loughlin O'Nolan & Claire McGettrick, *Joint Submission to the Oireachtas Joint Committee on Justice regarding the General Data Protection Regulation*, 26 Mar. 2021, http://jfmresearch.com/wp-content/uploads/2021/03/Submission-to-Oireachtas-Justice-Committee-Re-GDPR-MOR-CMG-LON-26.3.21.pdf

103. See *CLANN* Report, para 3.45, 3.58 (n. 26)

104. Padraig O'Morain, 'Adoption Society Admits Supplying False Information to Shield Mothers' Identities', *The Irish Times*, 7 Apr. 1997.

105. Conall Ó Fátharta, 'Tusla Considers Damage Release of Personal Information Can Cause', *The Irish Examiner*, 16 July 2019.

106. Ibid.

107. Ibid.

108. Regarding mixed personal data, see *Dr B v. The General Medical Council* [2016] EWHC 2331 (QB).

109. Conall Ó Fátharta, 'Adoption Body Reported Illegal Record in 2002', *The Irish Examiner*, 18 June 2018.

110. See Sean Murray, 'Adoption Scandal: Officials Questioned Whether Telling Those Affected Would "Do More Harm Than Good"', *thejournal.ie*, 6 July 2018.

111. Ibid.

112. See Press Release, Fine Gael, Government Agreed Details of Implementation of Quirke Scheme for Women in Magdalen Laundries, 7 Nov. 2013, https://www.finegael.ie/government-agreed-details-of-implementation-of-quirke-scheme-for-women-in-magdalen-laundries/; *Dáil Éireann Debates*, 'Redress for Women Resident in Certain Institutions (Amendment) Bill 2019 [Seanad]: Second and Subsequent Stages', Statement by Fiona O'Loughlin, TD, 10 July 2019.

113. CEDAW, Introductory Statement by Ms. Carol Baxter, para 9 (n. 14).

114. *Dáil Éireann Debates*, 'Commission of Investigation into Mother and Baby Homes: Motion' [Private Members], Statement by Noel Grealish, TD, 24 Feb. 2021.

115. *Seanad Éireann Debates*, 'Report of the Mother and Baby Homes Commission of Investigation: Statements (Resumed)', Statement by Sen. Sharon Keogan, 19 Feb. 2021.

116. Oireachtas Joint Committee on Children and Youth Affairs, *Report of the Commission of Investigation into Mother and Baby Homes: Engagement with the Minister for Children, Disability, Equality, Integration and Youth*, Statement by Jennifer Murnane O'Connor, TD, 16 Feb. 2021.

117. *Dáil Éireann Debates*, 'Report of the Commission of Investigation into Mother and Baby Homes: Statements (Resumed)', Statement by Cormac Devlin, TD, 20 Jan. 2021.

118. Ibid. Statement by Robert Troy, TD.

119. Ibid. Statement by Mary Butler, TD.

120. *Seanad Éireann Debates*, 'Report of the Mother and Baby Homes Commission of Investigation: Statements', Statement by Minister for Children, Disability, Equality, Integration and Youth, Roderic O'Gorman, TD, 19 Jan. 2021.

121. Ireland, *Replies to the List of Issues Prior To Submission of the Second Periodic Report of Ireland*, U.N. Doc. CAT/C/IRL/2, para 248 (n. 22).

122. Letter from Jimmy (James) Martin (Assistant Secretary, Department of Justice and Equality) to Tom Morgan (Senior Investigator, Office of the Ombudsman), 3 Aug. 2016 (on file with author).

123. MBHCOI *Final Report*, recommendations para 3 (n. 44).

124. Ibid.

125. See O'Rourke et al, *Joint Submission to the Oireachtas Joint Committee*, n. 102.

126. Ibid. at 6, citing Habte v Minister for Justice and Equality [2020] IECA 22.

127. MBHCOI *Final Report*, Recommendations para 4 (n. 44).

128. Ibid., para 52.

129. Ireland, Department of Justice, *Draft Memorandum for the Government, Magdalen Laundries*, Mar. 2011 (on file with author), referenced in Conall O'Fatharta, 'Government "Conscious of Redress" for Magdalene Survivors', *The Irish Examiner*, 18 Nov. 2014 (on file with author).

130. *Dáil Éireann Debates*, 'Mother and Baby Homes: Motion, Statement by Minister for Children and Youth Affairs', Katherine Zappone TD, 15 May 2019, https://www.kildarestreet.com/debates/?id=2019-05-15a.288#g292.

131. Ibid.

132. See Rosemary Adaser, Noelle Brown & Máiréad Enright, 'The Commission of Investigation into Mother and Baby Homes', *The Irish Times Women's Podcast*, Episode 466, 15 Jan. 2021, https://www.irishtimes.com/life-and-style/people/the-women-s-podcast/the-irish-times-women-s-podcast-ep-466-the-commission-of-investigation-into-mother-and-baby-homes-1.4458448?mode=amp; Jude Hughes & Philomena Mullen, 'Mother and Baby Homes Discrimination', *RTÉ Radio 1: Drivetime*, 18 Jan. 2021, https://www.rte.ie/radio/radioplayer/html5/#/radio1/21894770; Noelle Brown, 'Mother and Baby Homes', *RTÉ Radio 1: Today with Claire Byrne*, 13 Jan. 2021, https://www.rte.ie/radio/radioplayer/html5/#/radio1/21892875.

133. Oireachtas Joint Committee on Children and Youth Affairs, *Report of the Commission of Investigation into Mother and Baby Homes*, Statement by Jennifer Murnane O'Connor, TD, 16 Feb. 2021. For an alternative view, that the MBHCOI was not sufficiently legalistic, see Maeve O'Rourke, 'Survivors Appeal for Garda Specialised Investigations', *RTÉ Radio 1: Morning Ireland*, 13 Jan. 2021, https://www.rte.ie/radio1/morning-ireland/programmes/2021/0113/1189425-morning-ireland-wednesday-13-Jan.-2021/.

134. General Scheme of a Certain Institutional Burials (Authorised Interventions) Bill, 10 Dec. 2019, https://www.gov.ie/en/publication/51a535-general-scheme-of-a-certain-institutional-burials-authorised-interve/.

135. See Buckley, et al, *Joint Submission*, p. 7, (n. 78).

136. Commission of Investigation (Mother and Baby Homes and Certain Related Matters) Order 2015, S.I. No. 57 of 2015.

137. MBHCOI, Fifth Interim Report, Ch. 7 (n. 61)

138. Ibid., para 7.4.

139. Ibid., para 11.

140. MBHCOI *Final Report*, Ch. 36, para 36.2 (n. 44).

141. European Convention on Human Rights Act 2003, section 3.

142. For a description of the 'effective investigation' requirements of Articles 2 and

3 of the European Convention on Human Rights, see *CLANN* Report paras 4.63–4.69 (n. 26).

143. See Ibid., section 5. See also Maeve O'Rourke, '10 Ways Institutional Abuse Details Are Still Being Kept Secret', *RTÉ Brainstorm*, 8 May 2019, https://www.rte.ie/brainstorm/2019/0503/1047282-10-ways-institutional-abuse-details-are-still-being-kept-secret/.

144. Conall Ó Fátharta, 'Baby Home Survivors Denied Public Hearings', *The Irish Examiner*, 7 Apr. 2018.

145. *IDC Report*, Ch. 19 (n. 97).

146. Irish Human Rights Commission, *Follow-Up Report on State Involvement with Magdalen Laundries*, 2013, paras 261, 292, https://www.ihrec.ie/app/uploads/download/pdf/20130618164449.pdf

147. See O'Rourke, 'NGO Submission', para 3.3 (n. 19).

148. Department of Justice, *The Magdalen Restorative Justice Ex-Gratia Scheme* (n.d.), http://www.justice.ie/en/JELR/Pages/WP15000111.

149. Ombudsman, *Opportunity Lost: An investigation by the Ombudsman into the administration of the Magdalen Restorative Justice Scheme*, 2017.

150. Ibid., p. 8.

151. Ibid., p. 40.

152. Human Rights Commission, *Examination of the Fourth Periodic Report of Ireland*, 14 and 15 July 2014, Statement by Sir Nigel Rodley, 0.00–1.08; 4.33–5.55 mins <www.youtube.com/watch?v=v0NCIB3uHns> accessed 5 Sept. 2019:

    a. The state's response has been one of seeking to find material responses to the needs of the victims, and I don't want to pour cold water on that. However, there remains the problem of accountability—the accountability for assault and worse. In all of these cases, the issue that remains for the state party is to consider what it is going to do about accountability. Accountability for its own responsibilities, accountability for its failures to monitor what others have been doing, and the accountability of others for committing abuses that the State might well be able to think of as crimes. The accountability that I mention is missing in everything that we've heard so far.

153. 'State Apology: Taoiesach's Full Statement on Mother and Baby Homes', *The Irish Times*, 13 Jan. 2021, https://www.irishtimes.com/news/social-affairs/state-apology-taoiseach-s-full-statement-on-mother-and-baby-homes-1.4457328.

CHAPTER 7 – STATE RESPONSES TO HISTORICAL ABUSES IN IRELAND: SHAME, SOVEREIGNTY, AND EPISTEMIC INJUSTICE

1. In writing this paper, we benefitted from constructive and generous comments from the editors of this volume and the anonymous reviewers. We thank them and the attendees of the Boston College conference in Nov. 2018 for their invaluable insights. An earlier version of this essay appeared in *Éire-Ireland: An Interdisciplinary Journal of Irish Studies* 55.1 (Spring/Summer 2020), pp 68–99, DOI: 10.1353/eir.2020.000

2. Clara Fischer, 'Gender, Nation, and the Politics of Shame: Magdalen Laundries and the Institutionalization of Feminine Transgression in Modern Ireland', *Signs: Journal of Women in Culture and Society* 41.4 (2016), pp 821–43; Eoin O'Sullivan and Ian O'Donnell (eds.), *Coercive Confinement in Ireland: Patients, Prisoners, and Penitents* (Manchester, 2012); James Smith, *Ireland's Magdalen Laundries and the Nation's Architecture of Containment* (Manchester, 2008); Sarah-Anne Buckley, *The Cruelty Man: Child Welfare, the NSPCC, and the State in Ireland, 1889–1956* (Manchester,

2013); Miryam Clough, *Shame, the Church, and the Regulation of Female Sexuality* (London, 2017).

3. Bruce Arnold, *The Irish Gulag: How the State Betrayed Its Innocent Children* (Dublin, 2009); Karen Coleman, *Haunting Cries: Stories of Child Abuse from Industrial Schools* (Dublin, 2010), p. 121; Commission to Inquire into Child Abuse (hereafter CICA), *Report of the Commission to Inquire into Child Abuse, Volumes I–V* (Dublin, 2009), vol. 1, ch.8.

4. O'Sullivan and O'Donnell, *Coercive Confinement*, p. 257.

5. James Gallen and Kate Gleeson, 'Unpaid Wages: The Experiences of Irish Magdalene Laundries and Indigenous Australians', *International Journal of Law in Context* 14.1 (2018), pp 43–60; Maeve O'Rourke, 'The Justice for Magdalenes Campaign', in Suzanne Egan (ed.), *International Human Rights: Perspectives from Ireland* (London, 2015), pp 153–65; Sinéad Ring, 'The Victim of Historical Child Sexual Abuse in the Irish Courts, 1999–2006', *Social and Legal* Studies 26.5 (2017), pp 562–80.

6. We do not consider other ways in which law has responded to the demands for justice of historical institutional-abuse survivors, such as the jurisprudence emanating from the High Court and Supreme Court on the impact of the passage of time on the fair-trial rights of those charged with sexual crimes. Law's role has allowed such prosecutions to take place, albeit at the cost of creating hierarchies of victimhood and silencing stories of children's resistance to a culture of disbelief. Ring, 'Victim of Historical Abuse.' See also chapter 8 by Colin Smith and April Duff in this volume.

7. Mahmood Mamdani, 'A Diminished Truth', in Wilmot James and Linda van de Vijver (eds), *After the TRC: Reflections on Truth and Reconciliation in South Africa* (Athens, 2000), pp 58–61; Karin Van Marle, 'Holding Out for Other Ways of Knowing and Being', *feminists@law*, 7.2 (2017), pp 1–14; Christine M. Koggel, 'Epistemic Injustice in a Settler Nation: Canada's History of Erasing, Silencing, Marginalizing', *Journal of Global Ethics*, 14.2 (2018), pp 240–51.

8. Ian James Kidd, et al, *The Routledge Handbook of Epistemic Injustice* (Abingdon, 2017), p. 1.

9. Miranda Fricker, *Epistemic Injustice: Power and the Ethics of Knowing* (Oxford, 2007), p. 1.

10. Giorgio Agamben, *Remnants of Auschwitz: The Witness and the Archive* (New York, 1999), pp 104–5.

11. Ibid., p. 106, 128.

12. Lisa Guenther, 'Resisting Agamben: The Biopolitics of Shame and Humiliation', *Philosophy & Social Criticism* 38.1 (2012), pp 59–79.

13. Agamben, *Remnants*, p. 106.

14. Bruce Janz, 'Shame and Silence', *South African Journal of Philosophy*, 30.4 (2011), p. 465.

15. Catherine Mills, *The Philosophy of Agamben* (London, 2014), p. 104.

16. Brian Cowen, 'Ryan Report on the Commission to Inquire into Child Abuse: Motion', *Dáil Debates*, 11 June 2009, <https://www.oireachtas.ie/en/debates/debate/dail/2009-06-11/5>. Emphasis added.

17. Fintan O'Toole, 'Enough Shame About the Past: What We Need Is Guilt', *The Irish Times*, 23 Apr. 2019.

18. Clara Fischer, 'Revealing Ireland's "Proper" Heart: Apology, Shame, Nation', *Hypatia: A Journal of Feminist Philosophy* 32.4 (2017), pp 751–67.

19. Povinelli, Elizabeth, *The Cunning of Recognition: Indigenous Alterities and the Making of Australian Multiculturalism* (Durham, 2002), p. 18.

20. Timothy Bewes, *The Event of Postcolonial Shame* (Princeton, 2011), p. 38; Máiréad Enright, '"No. I Won't Go Back": National Time, Trauma, and Legacies of

Symphysiotomy in Ireland', in Siân Beynon-Jones and Emily Grabham (eds), *Law and Time* (London, 2019), pp 46–74.

21. Sara Ahmed, *The Cultural Politics of Emotion* (London, 2004), p. 102.

22. Enda Kenny, 'Magdalene Laundries Report: Statements', *Dáil Debates*, 19 Feb. 2013, <https://www.oireachtas.ie/en/debates/debate/dail/2013-02-19/29>.

23. O'Sullivan and O'Donnell, *Coercive Confinement*, p. 8, figure 1.2.

24. According to the *Reformatory and Industrial Schools Systems Report* (1970) completed by the Committee on Reformatory and Industrial Schools, better known as the Kennedy report, nineteen percent of children in industrial schools were 'known to be illegitimate.' Committee on Reformatory and Industrial Schools, *Reformatory and Industrial Schools Systems Report* (Dublin, 1970), p. 9.

25. CICA 1:234

26. CICA 2:275.

27. Seán Bourke, 'Daingean Days', *The Limerick Post*, 6 June 2009. Rpt. from *Limerick Socialist* 1982.

28. H. Kletter, C. Weems, and V. Carrion, 'Guilt and Posttraumatic Stress Symptoms in Child Victims of Interpersonal Violence', *Clinical Child Psychology and Psychiatry* 14.1 (2009), pp 71–83.

29. CICA 4:455; Ring, 'Victim of Historical Abuse'.

30. Smyth was a Catholic priest who pleaded guilty to seventy-four charges of indecent and sexual assault involving the sexual abuse of twenty young people over a period of thirty-six years. He had previously served four years in a Northern Ireland prison for similar offences. The case became notorious when it emerged that the attorney general delayed processing requests for Smyth's extradition to Northern Ireland, where he faced more abuse charges. Taoiseach Albert Reynolds was forced to resign as a result of the political fallout. Smyth's abuse formed the basis of a module of the Historical Institutional Abuse Inquiry, which investigated the period from 1922 to 1995 in Northern Ireland. Anthony Hart, Geraldine Doherty, and David Lane, *Report of the Historical Institutional Abuse Inquiry* (Belfast, 2017), Ch. 10.

31. Joe Little, 'Apology for Institutional Child Abuse, RTÉ News Report, 11 May 1999', *RTÉ News Archive*, <https://www.rte.ie/archives/2019/0430/1046590-apology-to-victims-of-institutionalchild-abuse>. The implication in the apology that the state had been ignorant of abuse until relatively recently ignored the fact that successive governments had overlooked evidence of institutional abuse uncovered as early as the 1970 Kennedy report. See also James Smith, 'Remembering Ireland's Architecture of Containment: "Telling" Stories in *The Butcher Boy* and *States of Fear*', *Éire-Ireland: An Interdisciplinary Journal of Irish Studies* 36: 3&4 (2001), pp 111–30.

32. Other state legal responses were the extension of the statute of limitations for civil suits in which the claimant had suffered sexual abuse and the creation of a sex-offenders register. See Sex Offenders Act (2001), Acts of the Oireachtas, *Electronic Irish Statute Book*, http://www.irishstatutebook.ie/eli/2001/act/18/enacted/en/html.

33. For a full list of objectives of both committees, see sections 12(1) and 15 of the Commission to Inquire into Child Abuse Act (2000), available at Acts of the Oireachtas, *Electronic Irish Statute Book*, http://www.irishstatutebook.ie/eli/2000/act/7/enacted/en/html.

34. CICA 4:453.

35. Anne-Marie McAlinden, 'An Inconvenient Truth: Barriers to Truth Recovery in the Aftermath of Institutional Child Abuse in Ireland', *Legal Studies* 33.2 (2013), pp 189–214; Emilie Pine, Susan Leavy, and Mark T. Keane, 'Re-reading the Ryan Report. Witnessing Via Close and Distant Reading', *Éire-Ireland: An Interdisciplinary Journal of Irish Studies*, 52.1&2 (2017), pp 198–215.

36. See the challenge brought by the Christian Brothers in Murray v. Commission to Inquire into Child Abuse [2004] IEHC 102. The Christian Brothers dropped their legal actions after the chairperson announced that the commission no longer intended to name anyone. See Carol Brennan.

37. Sinead Pembroke, 'Historical Institutional Child Abuse in Ireland: Survivor Perspectives on Taking Part in the Commission to Inquire into Child Abuse (CICA) and the Redress Scheme', *Contemporary Justice Review* 22.1 (2019), p. 55.

38. The agreement was not subjected to public scrutiny in the Oireachtas.

39. €4.21 million has yet to be paid under this agreement. See Patsy McGarry, 'Religious Congregations Indemnity Deal Was "A Blank Cheque," Says Michael McDowell', *The Irish Times* 5 Apr. 2019.

40. CICA 1:14.

41. Comptroller and Auditor General, *Special Report 96—Cost of Child Abuse Inquiry and Redress* (Dublin, 2017); Mary Raftery, 'Piling Insult upon Injury', *The Irish Times*, 3 Mar. 2005; Mary Raftery, 'Cheating Abuse Victims', *The Irish Times*, 26 Apr. 2007.

42. Dec. 2002–15 Dec. 2005, Karen Coleman, *Haunting Cries: Stories of Child Abuse from Industrial Schools* (Dublin, 2010), Ch. 14; Late applications were accepted in exceptional circumstances until 16 Sept. 2011. Residential Institutions Redress Board, *Annual Report, 2012* (Dublin, 2013).

43. Pembroke, 'Historical Institutional'; Jeff Moore, Christine Thornton, and Mary Hughes, 'On the Road to Resilience: The Help-Seeking Experiences of Irish Emigrant Survivors of Institutional Abuse' *Child Abuse Review* 26 (2017), pp 375–87.

44. Reclaiming Self, *Ryan Report Follow-Up: Submission to the United Nations Committee against Torture, Session 61*, June 2017, <https://tbinternet.ohchr.org/Treaties/CAT/Shared%20Documents/IRL/INT_CAT_CSS_IRL_27959_E.pdf>. p. 26.

45. Coleman, *Haunting Cries*, p. 237.

46. Reclaiming Self, *Ryan Report Follow-Up*, appendix IV(c).

47. Patsy McGarry, 'Brothers Denied Abuse Days before Report', *The Irish Times*, 3 June 2009.

48. Michael Corry, 'Residential Institutions Redress Board', *The Irish Times*, 19 May 2005.

49. See sec. 28 of the Residential Institutions Redress Act (2002). Hereafter cited as RIRA.

50. RIRA secs. 28(6) and (9).

51. RIRA sec. 34.

52. There is no legislation requiring religious organisations to make their archives accessible to victim-survivors and their families, researchers, the child protection services, or the gardaí.

53. Caranua, *Applying for Services Booklet* (Dublin, 2016).

54. Reclaiming Self, *Ryan Report Follow-Up*.

55. Kitty Holland, 'Survivors Tell of Re-abuse by State Redress Group Caranua', *The Irish Times*, 20 Mar. 2017.

56. Bruton, Richard, 'Residential Institutions Statutory Fund: Motion (Resumed) [Private Members]', *Dáil Debates*, 24 May 2017, <https://www.oireachtas.ie/en/debates/debate/dail/2017-05-24/29>.

57. P. McGarry, 'Redress for Abuse in Religious Institutions Falls Short of 2009 Commitments', *The Irish Times*, 8 Sept. 2021.

58. Comptroller and Auditor General, *Special Report*.

59. Comptroller and Auditor General, *Annual Report, 2002* (Dublin, 2003), p. 83.

60. Michael O'Regan, 'Religious Have "Moral Responsibility" for Half Cost of Redress Scheme', *The Irish Times*, 9 Mar. 2017.

61. Kate Gleeson, 'A Woman's Work Is . . . Unfinished Business: Justice for the Disappeared Magdalen Women of Modern Ireland', *Feminist Legal Studies* 25.3 (Nov. 2017), p. 294; Brian Titley, 'Magdalen Asylums and Moral Regulation in Ireland', in A. Potts and T. O'Donoghue (eds), *Schools as Dangerous Places: A Historical Perspective* (Youngstown, NY, 2007), pp 132–3.

62. Kylie Jarrett, 'Laundering Women's History: A Feminist Critique of the Social Factory', *First Monday*, 23.3 (2018), <https://doi.org/10.5210/fm.v23i3.8280>.

63. Alexiadora Pérez Vides, 'Disciplined Bodies: The Magdalene Spectacle in Contemporary Irish Cultural Texts', *Revista Canaria de Estudios Ingleses* 73 (2016), pp 15–30; Maria Luddy, 'Moral Rescue and Unmarried Mothers in Ireland in the 1920s', *Women's Studies* 30.6 (2001), pp 797–817; Sheila Killian, 'For Lack of Accountability: The Logic of the Price in Ireland's Magdalene Laundries', *Accounting, Organisations, and Society*, 43 (2015), p. 18.

64. Louise Ryan, *Gender, Identity, and the Irish Press, 1922–1937: Embodying the Nation* (London, 2002), p. 275; Smith, *Ireland's Magdalen Laundries*; A. V. Simpson, S. R. Clegg, et al, 'Doing Compassion or Doing Discipline? Power Relations and the Magdalene Laundries', *Journal of Political Power*, 7.2 (2014), pp 253–74; Katherine O'Donnell, 'Academics Becoming Activists: Reflections on Some Ethical Issues of the Justice for Magdalenes Campaign', Pilar Villar-Argáiz (ed), *Irishness on the Margins: Minority and Dissident Identities* (London, 2018), p. 82.

65. S. E. Wilmer, *Performing Statelessness in Europe* (London, 2018), p. 105.

66. Karen Brennan, 'Punishing Infanticide in the Irish Free State', *Irish Journal of Legal Studies* 3.1 (2013), pp 12–13. The exception was Seán McDermott Street Laundry in Dublin, which was a remand home for female offenders under the Criminal Justice Act (1960).

67. Gleeson, 'A Woman's Work', p. 296; Maeve O'Rourke and James M. Smith, 'Ireland's Magdalene Laundries: Confronting a History Not Yet in the Past' in Alan Hayes and Máire Meaghar (eds), *A Century of Progress? Irish Women Reflect* (Dublin, 2016), pp 107–34.

68. O'Donnell, 'Academics Becoming Activists', pp 82–3.

69. Maeve O'Rourke, Claire McGettrick, Rod Baker, Raymond Hill, et al. *CLANN: Ireland's Unmarried Mothers and Their Children: Gathering the Data: Principal Submission to the Commission of Investigation into Mother and Baby Homes* (Dublin, 15 Oct. 2018), <http://clannproject.org/wp-content/uploads/Clann-Submissions_Redacted-Public-Version-Oct.-2018.pdf>. Archived at <https://perma.cc/38CR-YLT2>, p. 18.

70. Gleeson 'A Woman's Work', p. 307; Claire McGettrick, *Death, Institutionalisation, and Duration of Stay: A Critique of Ch. 16 of the Report of the Inter-departmental Committee to Establish the Facts of State Involvement with the Magdalen Laundries and Related Issues*, 19 Feb. 2015, <http:// jfmresearch.com/wp-content/uploads/2017/03/JFMR_Critique_190215.pdf>.

71. O'Rourke et al. *CLANN*, p. 19; O'Donnell, 'Academics Becoming Activists', p. 83.

72. Fischer, 'Gender', p. 836; Maeve O'Rourke, 'Prolonged Impunity as a Continuing Situation of Torture or Ill-Treatment? Applying a Dignity Lens to So-Called "Historical" Cases', *Netherlands International Law Review* 66.1 (2019), p. 134, 137.

73. Colin Gleeson, 'I Never Spoke to Anybody Like This. Our Voices Are Heard Today', *The Irish Times*, 5 June 2018.

74. , Ellen Coyne, 'Magdalene Compensation Rule Is Fair, Says Taoiseach', *The Sunday Times* [London], 24 Oct. 2018.

75. O'Donnell, 'Academics Becoming Activists', pp 84–94.

76. Martin McAleese, *Report of the Inter-departmental Committee to Establish the Facts of State Involvement with the Magdalen Laundries* (Dublin, 2013); O'Rourke and Smith, 'Ireland's Magdalene Laundries'; O'Rourke et al., *CLANN*, pp 20–22.

77. Enda Kenny, 'Magdalene Laundries Report: Statements', *Dáil Debates*, 19 Feb. 2013, <https://www.oireachtas.ie/en/debates/debate/dail/2013-02-19/29>; O'Rourke, 'Prolonged Impunity', p. 131 (See n. 72 above for full citation).

78. John Quirke, *The Magdalen Commission Report* (Dublin, 2013); Elain Edwards, 'Women from Magdalene Laundries Invited to Apply to Redress Scheme', *The Irish Times*, 7 July 2018.

79. UN Committee Against Torture (CAT), *Consideration of Reports Submitted by States Parties under Article 19 of the Convention—Ireland*, 17 June 2011, UN Doc. CAT/C/IRL/CO/1, <https://tbinternet.ohchr.org/_layouts/treatybodyexternal/Download.aspx?symbolno=CAT%2fC%2fIRL%2fCO%2f1&Lang=en>; UN Committee Against Torture (CAT), *Concluding Observations on the Second Periodic Report of Ireland*, 31 Aug. 2017, UN Doc. CAT/C/IRL/CO/2, <https://tbinternet.ohchr.org/_layouts/15/treaty bodyexternal/Download.aspx?symbolno=CAT%2fC%2fIRL%2f CO%2f2&Lang=en>.

80. Justice for Magdalenes' principal submission, *State Involvement in the Magdalene Laundries*, ran to 175 pages in length and was supported by 796 pages of survivor testimony and an additional 3,200 pages of archival documentation. None of the testimony appears in the McAleese report.

81. Gallen and Gleeson, 'Unpaid Wages', p. 53.

82. Claire O'Sullivan, 'Interviews Lacked Transparency, Say Victims' Groups', *The Irish Examiner*, 7 Feb. 2013.

83. Quirke, *Magdalen Commission Report*, p. 5.

84. The High Court has heard just three reported cases involving Magdalen women since 2013. One of these was brought to the Court of Appeal. One concerned the exclusion of a woman from the Quirke redress scheme. See MKL v. Minister for Justice and Equality [2017] IEHC 389.

85. O'Rourke, 'Prolonged Impunity', p. 132.

86. Maeve O'Rourke, 'The Justice for Magdalenes Campaign', in Suzanne Egan (ed), *International Human Rights: Perspectives from Ireland* (London: Bloomsbury Professional, 2015), p. 155.

87. Evelyn Glynn, 'Magdalene Matters', in Rebecca Anne Barr, Sarah-Anne Buckley, and Laura Kelly (eds), *Engendering Ireland* (Newcastle-upon-Tyne, 2015), p. 45.

88. McAleese, *Report of Inter-departmental*, p. 263.

89. Justice for Magdalenes Research, 'Sean McDermott Street', *Justice for Magdalenes Research*, 2018, <http://jfmresearch.com/home/preserving-magdalene-history/sean-mcdermott-street>.

90. Quirke, *Magdalen Commission Report*, p. 25.

91. Peter Tyndall, *Opportunity Lost: An Investigation by the Ombudsman into the Administration of the Magdalen Restorative Justice Scheme* (Dublin 2017), pp 39–42.

92. Quirke, *Magdalen Commission Report*, p. 25.

93. Conall Ó Fátharta, '32 Magdalene Laundry Survivors Get Increased Redress Payment', *The Irish Examiner*, 7 Sept. 2019.

94. BBC, 'Magdalene Laundries Victim Mary Cavner to Get Compensation', *BBC.com*, 21 Aug. 2019, <https://www.bbc.co.uk/news/uk-england-hampshire-49393418>.

95. Ellen Coyne, 'Magdalene Compensation Rule Is Fair, Says Taoiseach', *Sunday Times* [London], 24 Oct. 2018.

96. Quoted in O'Rourke, 'Prolonged Impunity', p. 136.

97. We use 'testimony' to mean victim-survivors' accounts of the wrongs that they

suffered and the meanings that those wrongs should hold for the state and for Irish society.

98. Agamben, *Remnants*, p. 39.

99. Fricker summarises her two forms of epistemic injustice as follows: 'We might say that testimonial injustice is caused by prejudice in the economy of credibility, and that hermeneutical injustice is caused by structural prejudice in the economy of collective hermeneutical resources'. Fricker, *Epistemic Injustice*, p. 1.

100. Reclaiming Self, *Ryan Report Follow-Up*, pp 26–7.

101. Sorcha Pollak, 'Magdalene Survivor: "They're Ignoring My Basic Human Rights"', *The Irish Times*, 19 Jan. 2015.

102. Fricker, *Epistemic Injustice*, p. 5. This is an intrinsic injustice, although where such harm goes deep in the psychology of the subject, it can limit self-development.

103. O'Rourke, 'Prolonged Impunity', p. 136.

104. Reclaiming Self, *Ryan Report Follow-Up*, p. 26

105. CICA 4:461.

106. Fricker, *Epistemic Injustice*, p. 1; Miranda Fricker, 'Evolving Concepts of Epistemic Injustice' in Ian James Kidd, José Medina, and Gaile Pohlhaus, Jr. (eds), *The Routledge Handbook of Epistemic Injustice* (Abingdon, 2017), p. 53.

107. Dotson, Kristie. 'A Cautionary Tale: On Limiting Epistemic Oppres*sion*', *Frontiers: A Journal of Women's Studies* 33.1 (2012), p. 31.

108. Patrick Bolger and Maria Quinlan, *I Am One in Four: Exhibition at CHQ Building, 17 May, and Accompanying Report* (Dublin, 2019); Nancy Costello, Kathleen Legg, Diane Croghan, Marie Slattery, and Marina Gambold, *Whispering Hope: The True Story of the Magdalene Women* (London, 2015); Paddy Doyle, *The God Squad* (London, 1988); Gerard Mannix Flynn, *Nothing to Say*, 1983, second edn (Dublin, 2003).

109. O'Rourke et al., *CLANN*.

110. See chapter 8 by Duff and Smith in this volume.

111. Or as Gaile Pohlhaus, Jr., might say, state actors are engaging in wilful hermeneutical ignorance: '*Wilful hermeneutical ignorance* describes instances where marginally situated knowers actively resist epistemic domination through interaction with other resistant knowers, while dominantly situated knowers nonetheless continue to misunderstand and misinterpret the world.' Gaile Pohlhaus, Jr., 'Relational Knowing and Epistemic Injustice: Toward a Theory of Willful Hermeneutical Ignorance', *Hypatia: A Journal of Feminist Philosophy*, 27.4 (2012), p. 716.

112. For Agamben shame is not only present in moments of indignity: 'Shame is what is produced in the absolute concomitance of subjectification and desubjectification, self-loss and self-possession, servitude and sovereignty'. Agamben, *Remnants*, p. 107). It would be possible for state actors to be shamed, for example, by their own strength and power in the face of witness testimony.

113. Enright, 'No. I Won't Go Back.'

114. Emilios Christodoulidis, '"Truth and Reconciliation" as Risks', *Social and Legal Studies* 9.2 (2000), p. 189.

115. Andrew Schaap, 'Assuming Responsibility in the Hope of Reconciliation', *Borderland E-Journal*, 3.1, 2004, <http://www.borderlands.net.au/vol3no1_2004/schaap_hope.htm>, p. 19.

116. 'State Apology: Taoiseach's Full Statement on Mother and Baby Homes', *The Irish Times*, 13 Jan. 2021.

117. Ibid.

118. This issue was compounded by the fact that many witnesses had expected that the Commission had retained transcripts of their evidence. This was not done. The Commission instead had retained completed questionnaires and notes of interviews.

The Commission insisted that, although witness interviews had been recorded, these audio recordings had been destroyed. Eventually backup recordings were retrieved, but this was done in the face of strong resistance from the Commission; Órla Ryan, 'Varadkar Says He Was "quite Surprised" That Mother and Baby Home Testimony Was Destroyed', *thejournal.ie*, 4 Feb. 2021; 'Irish Mother and Baby Homes: Inquiry "backup Tapes" Discovered', *BBC News*, 20 Feb. 2021; Elaine Loughlin, 'Data Protection Commission Seeks Answers on Destruction of Mother and Baby Homes Recordings', *The Irish Examiner*, 2 Feb. 2021.

119. Órla Ryan, 'Mother and Baby Homes: Three Test Cases Could Be Used as Survivors Seek Judicial Review', *thejournal.ie*, 13 July 2021.

120. See s. 34, Commissions of Investigation Act, 2004.

121. Department of Children, 'Settlement of applications for judicial review of Final Report of Commission of Investigation into Mother and Baby Homes', December 17 2021. Available at: https://www.gov.ie/en/press-release/b981a-settlement-of-applications-for-judicial-review-of-final-report-of-commission-of-investigation-into-mother-and-baby-homes/.

122. Lucy O'Toole, 'Clann Project: "The Injustices Are Compounded by the State's Ongoing Inaction"', *Hotpress*, 18 May, 2021.

123. 'Transcript of Oxford University Seminar with Professor Mary Daly', The Clann Project, http://clannproject.org/commission-report/oxfordtranscript/.

124. See further, 'Full Letter Sent to Oireachtas by Former Members of Mother and Baby Homes Commission', *The Irish Times*, 11 June 2021.

125. Gabija Gateveckaite, 'Mother and Baby Homes Commission Chair Declines Invitation to Appear before Oireachtas Children's Committee', *The Irish Independent*, 5 Feb. 2021; Patsy McGarry and Jennifer Bray, 'Refusal of Mother and Baby Home Report Authors to Face Oireachtas "Deeply Regrettable" – Varadkar', *The Irish Times*, 11 June, 2021.

126. See, for example, Noelle Browne's production *Home: Part One*, broadcast on St. Patrick's Day, 17 Mar. 2021, https://www.abbeytheatre.ie/whats-on/home-part-one/.

127. Our account of epistemic justice differs from that in Fricker's work, which focuses on the (ethical) epistemic virtues of individuals. See Fricker, *Epistemic Injustice*, pp 176–77.

128. Guenther, 'Shame', p. 35.

129. Thanos Zartaloudis, *Agamben and Law* (London, 2016), p. 335.

130. Leo Bersani and Adam Phillips, *Intimacies* (Chicago, 2008), p. 116.

131. Agamben, *Remnants*, p. 130.

132. Schaap, 'Assuming Responsibility', pp 27, 4.

133. Gillian Rose, *Mourning Becomes the Law: Philosophy and Representation* (Cambridge, 1996), p. 62.

CHAPTER 8 – ACCESS TO JUSTICE FOR VICTIMS OF HISTORIC INSTITUTIONAL ABUSE

1. This essay was previously published in *Éire-Ireland: An Interdisciplinary Journal of Irish Studies* 55.1 (Spring/Summer 2020), pp 100–19, DOI: 10.1353/eir.2020.0004.

2. Some of the institutions, such as Bethany Home, which was operated by the Church of Ireland, were affiliated with other religious denominations. See chapter 14 by Mary Burke in this volume.

3. Eoin O'Sullivan and Ian O'Donnell (eds), *Coercive Confinement in Ireland: Patients, Prisoners, and Penitents* (Manchester, 2012), parts 1 and 3; James M. Smith, *Ireland's Magdalen Laundries and the Nation's Architecture of Containment* (Manchester, 2008), pp 23–84.

4. Gerard Hogan, Gerry Whyte, David Kenny, and Rachael Walsh, *Kelly: The Irish Constitution*, 5th edn (Bloomsbury Professional, 2018), Ch. 7.3.I. See, for example, Ryan v. Attorney General [1965] IR294; G. v. An Bord Uchtála [1980] IR 32; and State (C) v. Frawley [1976] IR 365.

5. Brian McMahon and William Binchy, *Law of Torts*, 4th edn (Dublin, 2013), Ch. 22.

6. Meskell v. Córas Iompair Éireann [1973] IR 121, and Hanrahan v. Merck Sharpe & Dohme (Ireland) Ltd. [1988] ILRM 629.

7. Law Reform Commission, *Consultation Paper on the Law of Limitation of Actions Arising from the Non-Sexual Abuse of Children* (LRC-CP16–2000; Dublin, Law Reform Commission), 3.

8. Department of Health, *Report on the Inquiry into the Operation of Madonna House* (Dublin, 1996).

9. Law Reform Commission, *Consultation Paper*, 3.

10. Residential Institutions Redress Act (2002), s. 13(6); Order 134A RSC, as inserted by Rules of the Superior Courts (Residential Institutions Redress Act2002) (S.I. No. 529/2008), *Electronic Irish Statute Book*, http://www.irishstatutebook.ie/eli/2008/si/529/made/en/print. Rules of the Superior Courts hereafter cited as RSC.

11. John Quirke, *The Magdalen Commission Report* (Dublin, May 2013); Department of Justice, *Report of the Inter-Departmental Committee to Establish the Facts of State Involvement with the Magdalen Laundries* (Dublin, 2013); Department of Justice and Equality, *Terms of an Ex Gratia Scheme for Women Who Were Admitted to and Worked in Magdalen Laundries, St. Mary's Training Centre Stanhope Street, and House of Mercy Training School, Summerhill, Wexford* (May 2013, updated Nov. 2018).

12. Martin Canny, *Limitation of Actions* (Dublin, 2010), p. 166.

13. Statute of Limitations (1957), s. 11(2).

14. Statute of Limitations (Amendment) Act (1991), ss.2 and 3, and Civil Liability and Courts Act (2004), s. 7.

15. Statute of Limitations (1957), s. 48A, as inserted by the Statute of Limitations (Amendment) Act (2000), s.2.

16. James Gallen, 'Historical Abuse and the Statute of Limitations', *Statute Law Review* 39:2 (2018), pp 116–17.

17. See, for example, Mary McAleese, 'Remarks by President McAleese at an Event at Áras an Uachtaráin for Survivors of Institutional Abuse' (Dublin, 28 June 2009); Enda Kenny, 'Magdalen Laundries Report: Statements', *Dáil Éireann Debates*, 793, 19 Feb. 2013, p. 1; Michael D. Higgins, 'Speech to Representatives of the Christine Buckley Centre for Education and Support' (Dublin, 10 May 2019).

18. Ó Dómhnaill v. Merrick [1984] IR 151.

19. McNamee v. Boyce [2016] IECA 19. The judgment of the Court of Appeal was upheld by the Supreme Court: [2017] 1 ILRM 168.

20. O'Keeffe v. Ireland [2014] ECHR 2014-I 155. Vicarious liability refers to the liability of one person for wrongs committed by another.

21. LO'K v. LH and Others [2006] IEHC 13. The judgment of the High Court was affirmed by the Supreme Court, save that the order for costs made against Ms. O'Keeffe was set aside on the basis that her case, which was a test case, raised an issue of exceptional public importance. See O'Keeffe v. Hickey and Others [2009] 2 IR 302.

22. O'Keeffe v. Ireland [2014] ECHR 2014-I, §169.

23. Eoin English, 'State Accused of Reneging on Payment to Abuse Victims', *The Irish Examiner*, 13 May 2019.

24. Gerry Whyte, *Social Inclusion and the Legal System: Public Interest Law in Ireland*, 2nd edn (Dublin, 2015), pp 184–5.

25. Ibid., 186 n319.

26. Cahill v. Sutton [1980] IR 269, 285. Although Henchy J. observed that this general rule of practice 'must, like all such rules, be subject to expansion, exception, or qualification when the justice of the case requires', in the actual expansions and exceptions recognised to date remain few. In Society for the Protection of Unborn Children (SPUC) v. Coogan [1989] IR 734, SPUC's standing to challenge the provision of information about abortion by the University College Dublin students' union was acknowledged on the basis that the unborn could not litigate in their own protection. In Irish Penal Reform Trust Limited (IPRT) v. The Governor of Mountjoy Prison [2005] IEHC 305, Gilligan J., relying on the remarks of Henchy J. in *Cahill v. Sutton*, held that the IPRT was entitled to represent mentally ill prisoners in legal proceedings against the state. The court noted that although theoretically these prisoners might be capable of asserting their constitutional rights, they were unlikely to be in a position to do so. Although the judgment of Gilligan J. was set aside by the Supreme Court in 2008, the appeal succeeded on the narrow ground that standing should have been dealt with in the substantive action rather than as a preliminary issue. The remitted case was subsequently discontinued. In Digital Rights Ireland, Ltd. v. Minister for Communication [2010] 3 IR 251, 293, the High Court held that the plaintiff company had standing to assert not only its own rights but also to bring an *action popularis* (a case on behalf of the general public) in circumstances where the impugned legislation, which required telecommunications service providers to retain traffic and location data relating to the use of fixed-line and mobile phones, could have a possible effect on virtually the entire population.

27. Construction Industry Federation v. Dublin City Council [2005] 2 ILRM 256, and Garda Representative Association v. Minister for Public Expenditure and Reform [2014] IEHC 237.

28. National Maternity Hospital v. Information Commissioner [2007] 3 IR 643.

29. Civil Legal Aid Act (1995), s. 28.

30. Persona Digital Telephony v. Minister for Public Enterprise and Others [2017] IESC 27.

31. RSC Order 99 Rule 1(4).

32. Friends of the Curragh Environment Ltd. v. An Bord Pleanála [2009] 4 IR 451, 461.

33. RSC Order 99, Rule 2.

34. See, for example, Marie O'Halloran, 'Kenny Urged to Step in in Row over Letters to Child Sex Abuse Victims', *The Irish Times*, 23 July 2016; Fintan O'Toole, 'Letter Shows State Saw Bridget McCole Not as the Victim but as the Enemy', *The Irish Times*, 2 Aug. 1997.

35. Civil Liability Act (1961), ss. 34 and 35.

36. Hickey v. McGowan [2017] 2 IR 196, p. 210.

37. Ibid., p. 229.

38. Ibid., p. 236.

39. Ibid., p. 209.

40. Ibid., p. 235.

41. Ibid., p. 210.

42. RSC Orders 1 and 1A.

43. RSC Order 1A.

44. RSC Order 20. The defendant to the proceedings is required to enter an appearance within eight days in response to the summons. This merely indicates that the defendant intends to defend the action and does not contain any substantive reply. See RSC Order 12 Rule 2.

45. RSC Order 19 Rule 7.

46. A formal document setting out the defendant's response to the statement of claim or personal injuries summons, specifying which elements of the claim are accepted and which denied.

47. RSC Order 1A Rule 8 and Order 21 Rule 1.

48. RSC Order 27 Rule 9.

49. RSC Order 27 Rule 9(1).

50. RSC Order 27 Rule 9(3).

51. See, for example, Moloney v. Kelleher [2014] IEHC 358, and Cassidy v. Provincialate [2015] IECA 74.

52. Martin Canny, *Limitation of Actions* (Dublin, 2010), p. 32.

53. O'Connor v. John Player and Sons, Ltd. [2004] 2 ILRM 321; C. v. McG and Others [2009] IEHC 438.

54. RSC Order 31 Rule 12.

55. Hilary Biehler et al., *Delany and McGrath on Civil Procedure*, 4th edn (Dublin, 2018), pp 217–33.

56. Armstrong v. Moffatt [2013] 1 IR 417, 429.

57. Ibid., p. 423.

58. Irish Nationwide Society v. Charlton [1997] 3 JIC 0502.

59. Peter Charleton and Saoirse Molloy, 'Case Management: Fairness for the Litigants, Justice for the Parties', *The Bar Review* 20:3 (2015), p. 59.

60. McFarlane v. Ireland, App No. 31333/06 (10 Sept. 2010).

61. Chancery and Non-Jury Actions: Pre-trial Procedures, RSC S.I. 255/2016.

62. A notice posted on the website of the Courts Service on 22 Sept. 2016 states that 'pending the provision of appropriate necessary resources, the president does not intend to appoint either a list judge or registrar.' See Notice by Kevin O'Neill, Principal Registrar of the High Court, 22 Sept. 2016, *An tSéirbhis Chúirteanna/Courts Service Ireland*, http://www.courts.ie/Courts.ie/Library3.nsf/pagecurrent/3E33803598D813AF8025803700520F83?opendocument, archived at https:// perma.cc/L2BA-R66Y.

63. Limitation Act (1980), s. 33.

64. Council of the Bar of Ireland, *Submission by Council of the Bar of Ireland to the Review Group on the Administration of Civil Justice* (Feb. 2018), pp 12–13, ss. 7.4, 7.6.

65. Commission Recommendation of 11 June 2013 on Common Principles for Injunctive and Compensatory Collective Redress Mechanisms in the Member States Concerning Violations of Rights Granted under Union Law [2013] OJ, L201/60.

66. Ibid., recital 9.

67. Ibid., articles 4–7.

68. Ibid., articles 14–16.

69. Law Reform Commission, *Report: Charitable Trusts and Legal Structures for Charities* (LRC 80/2006; Dublin, Law Reform Commission).

CHAPTER 9 – STATE'S REACTION IS TO DENY, DELAY AND TO BUY SILENCE

1. Editors' Note: As underlined by the many citations of his work across this edited collection, Conall Ó Fátharta's investigative reporting in *The Irish Examiner* has contributed significantly, for well over a decade, to truth-telling about the State's responses to revelations of historic institutional abuse and forced and illegal adoption. An earlier version of this essay appeared as a long-form Opinion-Commentary in *The Irish Examiner* on 10 Dec. 2018 and is reprinted here with permission. It offers a retrospective overview of state practices linking Ireland's Magdalene Laundries, Mother and Baby Homes, and illegal adoptions to suggest that they are all part of a

single story. Ó Fátharta's journalism is searchable at https://www.irishexaminer.com/. The Editors have made silent edits to adapt the writing to this different context, and have inserted footnotes to direct readers to supporting materials.

2. Conall Ó Fátharta, 'Government Must Put Money Where its Mouth is to Cleanse "Stains on Our State"', *The Irish Examiner*, 28 Aug. 2018.

3. 'Zappone to Pope Francis: Church should contribute substantially to Tuam reparations', *The Irish Examiner*, 27 Aug., 2018.

4. Conall Ó Fátharta, 'Minister Raised Fears of Magdalene redress cost in 2011', *The Irish Examiner*, 27 Mar. 2017.

5. Daniel McConnell and Fiachra Ó Cionnaith, 'Grace Inquiry to Probe Cover-up by HSE', *The Irish Examiner*, 9 Mar. 2017.

6. Health Service Executive, 'Irish State health authorities' intervention in the Magdalene laundries: A narrative analysis', 18 Oct. 2012 [Confidential Draft version 11.3]. (Copy in possession of the author).

7. Health Service Executive File Note, 'OCT. MAC BRIEFCASE/OCT12 MGD Bessboro and Tuam Mother and Baby Homes Teleconference with Davida De La Harpe and Phil Garland', 12 Oct. 2012. (Copy in possession of the author).

8. Ibid.

9. Conall Ó Fátharta, 'SPECIAL INVESTIGATION: Fears over "Trafficking" of Children to the US', *The Irish Examiner*, 3 June 2015.

10. Appendix 4.3.12 Bessboro Mother and Baby Home, 'Sacred Heart/Bessboro Mother and Baby Home (Aug 2012)', in 'Irish State Health Authorities' Intervention in the Magdalene Laundries: A Narrative analysis', 18 Oct. 2012 [Confidential Draft version 11.3]. (Copy in possession of the author).

11. Ibid.

12. Declan McKeown, 'Preliminary Briefing Paper re: Tuam and Bessboro Mother and Baby Homes', 19 Oct. 2012. (Copy in possession of the author).

13. Declan McKeown, 'Draft Briefing Paper re: Tuam and Bessboro Mother and Baby Homes', 18 Oct. 2012. (Copy in possession of the author).

14. Ibid.

15. Letter from Dr Declan McKeown to Denis O'Sullivan, 'Irish State health authorities' intervention in the Magdalene laundries', 1 November 2012.

16. Email from Denis O'Sullivan to Gordon Jeyes, 'Re: FW: Magdalene', 7 Nov. 2012. (Copy in possession of the author).

17. See https://www.gov.ie/en/press-release/33202b-incorrect-registrations-of-birth-new-evidence-in-st-patrick-guild-re/.

18. See for example Shane Phelan, 'Illegal adoption scandal to spark a raft of lawsuits as clamour for answers grows', *The Irish Independent*, 8 June 2019.

19. See for example, Padraig O'Morain, 'Adoption Society Admits Supplying False Information to Shield Mothers' Identities', *The Irish Times*, 7 Apr. 1997.

20. Also see, https://www.kildarestreet.com/wrans/?id=2018-06-13a.53.

21. See Conall Ó Fátharta, 'Long Fight Over Illegal Adoption Finally Ends', *The Irish Examiner*, 13 July 2018.

22. See Conall Ó Fátharta, 'In Search of a Long-Lost Boy' and 'Tortured Journey', *The Irish Examiner*, 19 Apr. 2010.

23. Conall Ó Fátharta, 'Adoption Authorities to Audit Tracing Records', *The Irish Examiner*, 11 June 2010.

24. AAI Audit Report, June 2011 (Released under FOI).

25. Department of Children and Youth Affairs, 'Note of Meeting re Illegal Registrations', 5 June 2013 (Released under FOI).

26. Ibid.

27. Ibid.

28. Press statement issued to the author by the Department of Children and Youth Affairs, 31 Aug. 2018.

29. Ibid.

30. Frances Fitzgerald, 'Written Answers: Adoption Records Issues', *Dáil Éireann Debates*, 28 Nov. 2013, https://www.kildarestreet.com/wrans/?id=2013-11-28a.409& s=Fitzgerald+Adoption+Audit#g411.r.

31. Frances Fitzgerald, 'Priority Questions: Adoption Records Provision', *Dáil Éireann Debates*, 17 Dec. 2013, https://www.kildarestreet.com/debates/?id=2013-12-17a.66&s=Fitzgerald+adoption+subsequent#g74.

32. Press statement issued to the author by the AAI, 10 Aug. 2018.

33. Conall Ó Fátharta, 'Special Report: Women Forced to Give up Babies for Adoption Still Failed by State Bodies', *The Irish Examiner*, 3 Dec. 2018.

34. Conall Ó Fátharta, 'Excluded agency "aware of illegal birth registrations"', *The Irish Examiner*, 13 Apr. 2015.

35. Conall Ó Fátharta, 'Mother and Baby Homes: Plenty of Information About Adoption Records to be Found if State Wishes to Look', *The Irish Examiner*, 3 Dec. 2015.

36. Katherine Zappone, 'Incorrect Birth Registrations: Statements', *Dáil Éireann Debates*, 14 June 2018, https://www.kildarestreet.com/debates/?id=2018-06-14a.26 4&s=Zappone+validation+adoption#g265.

37. Conall Ó Fátharta, 'Calls to Widen Scope of Adoption Probe', *The Irish Examiner*, 2 June 2018.

38. The final report of the independent review into illegal birth registrations was published on 9 Mar. 2021. For further information see: https://www.gov.ie/en/press-release/bba2b-minister-ogorman-publishes-independent-review-report-into-illegal-birth-registration-requests-special-rapporteur-on-child-protection-examine-issue-and-propose-next-steps/. Also see: Conall Ó Fátharta, 'Illegal birth registrations: Reynolds Review only repeated what we already knew', *The Irish Examiner*, 13 Mar. 2021.

39. Conall Ó Fátharta, 'Report on Scoping Exercise Into Illegal Birth Registrations Delayed for Second Time', *The Irish Examiner*, 18 Dec. 2018.

40. Conall Ó Fátharta, 'Department Refuses to Reveal How Many Records Will Be Examined in Illegal Adoptions Audit', *The Irish Examiner*, 9 Aug., 2018.

41. Michael Woods, 'Written Answers: Child Abuse', *Dáil Éireann Debates*, 12 Feb., 2002.

42. Batt O'Keeffe, 'Written Answers: Residential Institutions Redress Scheme', *Dáil Éireann Debates*, 6 Oct. 2009.

43. 'Ombudsman Investigation Finds Women Wrongfully Excluded from Magdalene Scheme', in *The Irish Examiner*, 23 Nov. 2017.

44. Conall Ó Fátharta, 'Magdalene Laundry Survivors Still Waiting For Medical Benefits Promised To Them', *The Irish Examiner*, 25 June 2020.

45. Conall Ó Fátharta, 'Campaigners Frustrated as State Won't Open Up Magdalene Archives', *The Irish Examiner*, 16 Aug., 2018.

46. Conall Ó Fátharta, '"No Plans" to Open Committee Archive on Magdalene Laundries', *The Irish Examiner*, 8 Sept. 2018.

CHAPTER 10 – REPARATIONS FOR HISTORIC INSTITUTIONAL GENDER VIOLENCE IN IRELAND: LEARNING FROM TRANSITIONAL JUSTICE

1. Editors' note: Professor Rubio Marín's key-note lecture has been silently edited to adapt it for essay format. Boston College Institute for the Liberal Arts, 'Towards

Transitional Justice: Recognition, Truth-Telling and Institutional Abuse in Ireland', *Boston College Institute for the Liberal Arts*, 1–2 Nov. 2018, https://www.bc.edu/bc-web/academics/sites/ila/events/towards-transitional-justice.html. My deepest gratitude to Maeve O'Rourke for opening my eyes to the plights of women in Ireland's Madgalene Laundries; for her incessant commitment to the fight for justice for survivors of Ireland's historic institutional violence and last, but not least, for her generous help in editing the lecture into a written form for the purpose of this publication.

2. Dinah Shelton, 'The World of Atonement: Reparations for Historical Injustices', *Netherlands International Law Review* 50 (2003), p. 289, 291.

3. Maeve O'Rourke, Claire McGettrick, Rod Baker, Raymond Hill et al., *CLANN: Ireland's Unmarried Mothers and their Children: Gathering the Data: Principal Submission to the Commission of Investigation into Mother and Baby Homes*. Dublin: Justice For Magdalenes Research, Adoption Rights Alliance, Hogan Lovells, 15 Oct. 2018; Paul Michael Garrett, '"Unmarried Mothers" in the Republic of Ireland', *Journal of Social Work* 16.6 (2016), pp 708–25; Maria Luddy, 'Unmarried Mothers in Ireland, 1880–1973', *Women's History Review* 20:1 (2011), pp 109–26; Lindsey Earner-Byrne, *Mother and Child: Maternity and Child Welfare in Dublin 1922–60* (Manchester, 2007); James M. Smith, 'The Politics of Sexual Knowledge: The Origins of Ireland's Containment Culture and the Carrigan Report (1931)', *Journal of the History of Sexuality* 13.2 (2004), pp 208–33.

4. Máiréad Enright, '"No. I Won't Go Back": National Time, Trauma, and Legacies of Symphysiotomy in Ireland', in Siân Beynon-Jones and Emily Grabham (eds.), *Law and Time* (Abingdon, 2019), pp 46–74.

5. *LF v Ireland*, App no 62007/17 (ECtHR, 10 Nov. 2020), paras 54–5.

6. Survivors of Symphysiotomy, Submission to the 61st Session of the United Nations Committee Against Torture on the Second Periodic Report of Ireland (ohchr.org 2017), p. 5, https://tbinternet.ohchr.org/Treaties/CAT/Shared%20Documents/IRL/INT_CAT_CSS_IRL_27972_E.pdf

7. Ibid, p. 6.

8. The most up-to-date estimations are contained in Commission of Investigation into Mother and Baby Homes, *Final Report*, 12 Jan. 2021, 'Executive Summary', 2, https://www.gov.ie/en/publication/d4b3d-final-report-of-the-commission-of-investigation-into-mother-and-baby-homes/.

9. O'Rourke, McGettrick et al, *CLANN*.

10. Commission to Inquire into Child Abuse, Statement of Chairperson, 25 Nov. 2019, http://www.childabusecommission.ie.

11. Commission to Inquire into Child Abuse, *Final Report*, http://www.childabusecommission.ie/rpt/.

12. Maeve O'Rourke, 'The Justice for Magdalenes Campaign' in Suzanne Egan (ed), *International Human Rights: Perspectives from Ireland* (London, 2015), p. 145.

13. Dáil Éireann, Tuam Mother and Baby Home: Statements, 25 Oct. 2018, https://www.oireachtas.ie/en/debates/debate/dail/2018-10-25/34/. Dr Katherine Zappone served as Minister for Children and Youth Affairs from May 2016 until June 2020. As of the time of going to production in 2021, the Government's promised exhumations have not taken place. A General Scheme of a Certain Institutional Burials (Authorised Interventions) Bill was published on 10 Dec. 2019 but the legislation has not yet been introduced into the Oireachtas. The General Scheme, which proposes to disapply the existing powers of the Coroner wherever a new specialised Agency is established for the purpose of exhuming, identifying and re-interring remains buried at institutional sites, is currently undergoing pre-legislative consultation and scrutiny: see Department of Children, Equality, Disability, Integration and Youth, 'General Scheme of a Certain Institutional Burials (Authorised Interventions)

Bill, 13 Jan. 2021, https://www.gov.ie/en/publication/51a535-general-scheme-of-a-certain-institutional-burials-authorised-interve/.

14. James M Smith, *Ireland's Magdalen Laundries and the Nation's Architecture of Containment* (South Bend, IN, 2007), pp 1–20.

15. Ibid. Also, see Eoin O'Sullivan and Ian O'Donnell, eds., *Coercive Confinement in Post-Independent Ireland: Patients, Prisoners and Penitents* (Manchester, 2012).

16. Anne-Marie McAlinden, 'An Inconvenient Truth: Barriers to Truth Recovery in the Aftermath of Institutional Child Abuse in Ireland', *Legal Studies* 33 (2013), p. 189, 205.

17. Human Rights Committee, Concluding Observations on the fourth periodic report of Ireland, UN Doc CCPR/C/IRL/CO/4, 19 Aug. 2014, https://tbinternet.ohchr.org/_layouts/15/treatybodyexternal/Download.aspx?symbolno=CCPR%2fC%2fIRL%2fCO%2f4&Lang=en.

18. Committee on Economic, Social and Cultural Rights, Concluding observations on the third periodic report of Ireland, UN Doc E/C.12/IRL/CO/3, 8 July 2015, https://documents-dds-ny.un.org/doc/UNDOC/GEN/G15/150/67/PDF/G1515067.pdf?OpenElement.

19. Committee on the Elimination of Discrimination against Women, Concluding observations on the combined sixth and seventh periodic reports of Ireland, UN Doc CEDAW/C/IRL/CO/6–7, 9 Mar. 2017, https://tbinternet.ohchr.org/_layouts/15/treatybodyexternal/Download.aspx?symbolno=CEDAW%2fC%2fIRL%2fCO%2f6-7&Lang=en.

20. Committee against Torture, Concluding Observations on the second periodic report of Ireland, UN Doc CAT/C/IRL/CO/2, 31 Aug. 2017, https://tbinternet.ohchr.org/_layouts/15/treatybodyexternal/Download.aspx?symbolno=CAT%2fC%2fIRL%2fCO%2f2&Lang=en.

21. Irish Human Rights Commission, Follow-up Report on State Involvement with Magdalen Laundries (June 2013), https://www.ihrec.ie/documents/ihrc-follow-up-report-on-state-involvement-with-magdalen-laundries-june-2013/; Irish Human Rights and Equality Commission, Submission to the United Nations Committee on the Elimination of Discrimination Against Women on Ireland's combined sixth and seventh periodic reports (Jan. 2017), https://tbinternet.ohchr.org/Treaties/CEDAW/Shared%20Documents/IRL/INT_CEDAW_NHS_IRL_26596_E.pdf; Irish Human Rights and Equality Commission, Submission to the United Nations Committee against Torture on Ireland's Second Periodic Report, July 2017, https://tbinternet.ohchr.org/Treaties/CAT/Shared%20Documents/IRL/INT_CAT_CSS_IRL_27975_E.pdf

22. Ireland, Second Periodic Report to the Committee Against Torture, UN Doc CAT/C/IRL/2, 20 Jan. 2016, para 241, https://tbinternet.ohchr.org/_layouts/15/treatybodyexternal/Download.aspx?symbolno=CAT%2fC%2fIRL%2f2&Lang=en; Ireland, *Information on follow-up to the concluding observations of the Human Rights Committee on the fourth periodic report of Ireland*, UN Doc CCPR/C/IRL/CO/4/Add.1, 15 Aug. 2017, para 5 https://tbinternet.ohchr.org/_layouts/15/treatybodyexternal/Download.aspx?symbolno=CCPR%2fC%2fIRL%2fCO%2f4%2fAdd.1&Lang=en.

23. Council of Europe, *Council of Europe Convention on preventing and combating violence against women and domestic violence*, 11 May 2011 (Istanbul Convention). Article 3a provides: '"violence against women" is understood as a violation of human rights and a form of discrimination against women and shall mean all acts of gender-based violence that result in, or are likely to result in, physical, sexual, psychological or economic harm or suffering to women, including threats of such acts, coercion or arbitrary deprivation of liberty, whether occurring in public or in private life'.

24. *Dáil Éireann Debates*, Leaders' Questions, Tuesday 5 Feb. 2013, Statement by the

Taoiseach Enda Kenny TD, https://www.oireachtas.ie/en/debates/debate/dail/2013-02-05/14/; also *IDC Report* Ch. 19.

25. Relatedly, Maeve O'Rourke has argued that many individuals and families are experiencing continuing degrading treatment at the hands of the State and indeed non-State individuals and institutions, due to their powerlessness to bring about an accounting from those who were involved in the abuse of unmarried mothers and their children during the 20th century and the suffering that is caused by that fact: Maeve O'Rourke, 'Prolonged Impunity as a Continuing Situation of Torture or Ill-Treatment? Applying a Dignity Lens to So-Called "Historical" Cases', *Netherlands International Law Review* 66(1) (2019), p. 101.

26. Organization of American States (OAS), *Inter-American Convention on the Prevention, Punishment and Eradication of Violence against Women ('Convention of Belem do Para')*, 9 June 1994, Article 7.

27. African Union, *Protocol to the African Charter on Human and People's Rights on the Rights of Women in Africa*, 11 July 2003, Article 4.

28. Council of Europe, *Council of Europe Convention on preventing and combating violence against women and domestic violence*, 11 May 2011, Article 5.

29. UN General Assembly, *Basic Principles and Guidelines on the Right to a Remedy and Reparation for Victims of Gross Violations of International Human Rights Law and Serious Violations of International Humanitarian Law: resolution / adopted by the General Assembly*, 21 Mar. 2006, A/RES/60/147.

30. Notably, the submissions of Justice for Magdalenes / JFM Research to numerous human rights bodies and the Irish Government since 2011 have drawn considerably on the *Principles*: see, for example, Maeve O'Rourke, James M Smith, Raymond Hill, Claire McGettrick and Katherine O'Donnell, 'Follow-up Report to the UN Committee Against Torture on behalf of Justice for Magdalenes' (May 2012), https://tbinternet.ohchr.org/Treaties/CAT/Shared%20Documents/IRL/INT_CAT_NGS_IRL_12078_E.pdf

31. See Ruti Teitel, *Transitional Justice* (Oxford, 2000); and Paige Arthur, 'How "Transitions" Reshaped Human Rights: A Conceptual History of Transitional Justice', *Human Rights Quarterly* 31.2 (2009), pp 321–67.

32. See Report of the Special Rapporteur on the promotion of truth, justice, reparation and guarantees of non-recurrence, Pablo de Greiff, A/HRC/21/46, 2012.

33. For the potential of transitional justice measures to address the historical abuse resulting in mass sexual violence in settled democracies see also James Gallen, 'Jesus Wept: The Roman Catholic Church, Child Sexual Abuse and Transitional Justice', *International Journal of Transitional Justice* 10(2) (2016), pp 332–349.

34. Bruce Ackerman, *We the People, Volume 1: Foundations* (HUP 1993).

35. For example, Fionnuala Ní Aoláin and Colm Campbell, 'The Paradox of Transition in Conflicted Democracies', *Human Rights Quarterly* 27.1 (2005), p. 172; Fionnuala Ní Aoláin and Naomi Cahn, 'Hirsch Lecture: Gender, Masculinities, and Transition in Conflicted Societies', *New England Law Review* 44 (2010), p. 101.

36. Pablo de Greiff, 'Justice and Reparations' in Pablo de Greiff (ed.), *Handbook of Reparations* (Oxford, 2006), pp 451–77, p. 458.

37. The reports of the United Nations treaty bodies and Irish Human Rights Commission and Irish Human Rights and Equality Commission above at (n. 19) to (n. 23) address this point. See further the essays of O'Rourke (chapter 6), and Enright and Ring (chapter 7), in this volume. Most recently, numerous survivors of Mother and Baby Homes have expressed their concern over what they contend to have been the non-consensual destruction of their witness testimony by the Mother and Baby Homes Commission of Investigation prior to the Commission's delivery of its Final Report to Government: see Elaine Loughlin, 'Data Protection Commission

seeks answers on destruction of mother and baby homes recordings', *The Irish Examiner,* 2 Feb. 2021, https://www.irishexaminer.com/news/arid-40218473.html.

CHAPTER 11 – THE INNER AND OUTER LIMITS OF GENDERED TRANSITIONAL JUSTICE

1. This essay was previously published in *Éire-Ireland: An Interdisciplinary Journal of Irish Studies* 55, 1 (Spring/Summer 2020), pp 279–298, DOI: 10.1353/eir.2020.0012. My deep and abiding thanks to Dr Katherine Zappone, Professor Fiona de Londras, and Professor Ruth Rubio-Marín, whose friendship and intellectual probing have shaped my thinking on transitional justice in Ireland. My thanks as well to Scott May for research assistance.
2. Jorge Luis Borges, 'Limits', in R. G. Barnes and Robert Mezey (trans.), *Poetry* 162:3 (1993), pp 157–58.
3. Ruti G. Teitel, *Transitional Justice* (Oxford, 2002).
4. Fionnuala Ní Aoláin and Colm Campbell, 'The Paradox of Transition in Conflicted Democracies', *Human Rights Quarterly* 27:1 (2005), pp 172–213.
5. Here I note that gender harms include violations experienced by women and men as well as by LGBTQI+ persons. I am conscious that the tendency—even in my own work—has been to elide gender harms with a focus on violations of women's rights. While acknowledging the need to continue to press the scope and scale of harms to women, I affirm the importance of seeing the broad spectrum of gendered violations, as this wide angle may ultimately provide the most significant means to transform gender ordering and the gender hierarchies that produce violence and exclusion in the first place.
6. Fionnuala Ní Aoláin, 'Transformative Gender Justice?' in Paul Gready and Simon Robins (eds), *From Transitional to Transformative Justice* (Cambridge, 2019), pp 150–71.
7. See, for example, Poland's Act on the Institute of National Remembrance (IPN), a controversial law concerning the Holocaust that criminalised references to Polish guilt in Nazi atrocities and even prescribed jail sentences, and Guatemalan legislation in the form of Bill 5377, which would grant amnesty to perpetrators of crimes against humanity. The latter would free more than thirty convicts, mostly former military officers, and invalidate current and future trials for crimes linked to the 1960–96 war.
8. Fionnuala Ní Aoláin, 'Gutting the Substance of a Security Council Resolution on Sexual Violence', *Just Security*, 24 Apr. 2019, https://www.justsecurity.org/63750/gutting-the-substance-of-a-security-council-resolution-on-sexual-violence.
9. Notably, the scholarly and activist group identified as central to the emergence of a transitional-justice field includes prominent women scholars—most significantly Ruti Teitel and Diane Orentlicher—but the identified groups of leader/ activists are predominantly men (José Zalaquett, Neil Kritz, Aryeh Neier, Carlos Nino, Thomas Buergenthal, Theo van Boven, Philippe Schmitter, Samuel Huntington, Juan Linz, and John Hertz).
10. See Neil J. Kritz (ed.), *Transitional Justice: How Emerging Democracies Reckon with Former Regimes* (Washington, DC, 1995). I note that this phrase was coined in the study produced by the United States Institute of Peace for the foundation.
11. Fionnuala Ní Aoláin, Dina Francesca Haynes, and Naomi R. Cahn, *On the Frontlines: Gender, War, and the Post-Conflict Process* (Oxford, 2011); Cynthia Cockburn, *The Space Between Us: Negotiating Gender and National Identities in Conflict* (New York, 1998).
12. Christine Bell and Catherine O'Rourke, 'Does Feminism Need a Theory of

Transitional Justice? An Introductory Essay', *International Journal of Transitional Justice* 1:1 (2007), p. 23.

13. Kelly Dawn Askin, *War Crimes Against Women: Prosecution in International War Crimes Tribunals* (Cambridge, MA, 1997); Françoise Krill, 'The Protection of Women in International Humanitarian Law', *International Review of the Red Cross* 25:249 (1985), p. 337; Beth Goldblatt and Sheila Meintjes, 'South African Women Demand the Truth', in Meredeth Turshen and Clotilde Twagiramariya (eds), *What Women Do in Wartime: Gender and Conflict in Africa* (New York, 1998), pp 27–61; Louise Mallinder, *Amnesty, Human Rights, and Political Transitions: Bridging the Peace and Justice Divide* (Oxford, 2008); Swen Dornig and Nils Goede, *Ten Years of Women, Peace, and Security: Gaps and Challenges in Implementing Resolution 1325* (n.p.: Institute for Development and Peace Policy Brief, July 2010).

14. Ruth Rubio-Marín, 'The Gender of Reparations in Transitional Societies', in Ruth Rubio-Marín (ed.), *The Gender of Reparations: Unsettling Sexual Hierarchies While Redressing Human Rights Violations* (New York, 2009), p. 63. See also Georgina Waylen, *Engendering Transitions: Women's Mobilization, Institutions, and Gender Outcomes* (Oxford, 2007); Colleen Duggan, Claudia Paz y Paz Bailey, and Julie Guillerot, 'Reparations for Sexual and Reproductive Violence: Prospects for Achieving Gender Justice in Guatemala and Peru', *International Journal of Transitional Justice* 2:2 (2008), pp 192, 200–1.

15. Catherine O'Rourke, 'The Shifting Signifier of "Community" in Transitional Justice: A Feminist Analysis', *Wisconsin Journal of Law, Gender & Society* 23:2 (2008), pp 269–91.

16. Fionnuala Ní Aoláin and Eilish Rooney, 'Underenforcement and Intersectionality: Gendered Aspects of Transition for Women', *International Journal of Transitional Justice* 1:3 (2007), pp 338–54.

17. Sherene H. Razack, 'Stealing the Pain of Others: Reflections on Canadian Humanitarian Responses', *Review of Education, Pedagogy, and Cultural Studies* 29:4 (2007), p. 375.

18. Maria Elander argues that victim expression in international legal processes 'relies on simplified representations of victimhood that do not adequately address victims.' See 'The Victim's Address: Expressivism and the Victim at the Extraordinary Chambers in the Courts of Cambodia', *International Journal of Transitional Justice* 7:1 (2013), pp 95–115. Mariana Pena and Gaelle Carayon argue, *inter alia*, that the process through which victims must apply to participate in International Criminal Court proceedings is not suited for victims' needs. See 'Is the ICC Making the Most of Victim Participation?' *International Journal of Transitional Justice* 7:3 (2013), pp 518–35.

19. United Nations Secretary-General, *Report of the Secretary-General on the Implementation of Security Council Resolutions 1820 (2008) and 1888 (2009)* (UN Doc. A/65/592-S/2010/604, 24 Nov. 2010), par. 5. This report defines 'conflict-related sexual violence . . . [as] sexual violence occurring in a conflict or post-conflict setting that has a direct or indirect causal link with the conflict itself.'

20. Notably, the United Kingdom has maintained that the Northern Ireland Troubles do not constitute a 'conflict' for the purposes of United Nations Security Council Resolution 1325—a matter that is subject to substantial contestation by feminist scholars and activists. See Aisling Swaine, *Conflict-Related Violence Against Women: Transforming Transition* (Cambridge, 2018).

21. United Nations Secretary-General, *Conflict-Related Sexual Violence: Report of the Secretary-General* (UN Doc. A/66/657-S/2012/33, 13 Jan. 2012).

22. Elizabeth D. Heineman (ed.), *Sexual Violence in Conflict Zones: From the Ancient World to the Era of Human Rights* (Philadelphia, PA, 2011).

23. See Ruth Seifert, 'The Second Front: The Logic of Sexual Violence in Wars', *Women's Studies International Forum* 19:1–2 (1996), pp 35–36; Deborah Blatt, 'Recognizing Rape as a Method of Torture', *New York University Review of Law and Social Change* 19:4 (1991–92), pp 821–65.

24. Compare, for example, Kimberly Theidon, 'First Do No Harm: Enforced Sterilizations and Gender Justice in Peru', *Open Democracy*, 29 Apr. 2015, https://www.opendemocracy.net/en/opensecurity/first-do-no-harm-enforced-sterilizations-and-gender-justice-in-peru.

25. Note Karen Engle's exhortation to feminists to 'question the assumption that women who have been raped in wartime are destroyed.' See Karen Engle, 'Judging Sex in War', *Michigan Law Review* 106:6 (2008), p. 942. Managing these two divergent approaches has no easy middle path, though the work of Louise du Toit offers a start. Du Toit has argued that 'in highlighting and interpreting the political dimension and meanings of rape, we should take great care to simultaneously acknowledge the meaning and damage of rape to the victims (do epistemic justice to them . . .).' See Louise du Toit, 'How Not to Give Rape Political Significance', in Debra Bergoffen, Paula Ruth Gilbert, Tamara Harvey, and Connie L. McNeely (eds), *Confronting Global Gender Justice: Women's Lives, Human Rights* (New York, 2011), pp 85–86. Du Toit goes on to state that 'feminists should simultaneously investigate the ways in which rape fulfills a variety of political functions *and* should insist on bringing rape into the public domain as an always politically significant phenomenon.' She explores the contradictory tensions that a focus on rape's political significance may create for feminist theorists who 'epistemologically prioritize the plight of rape victims' (p. 85).

26. See Lara Stemple, 'Human Rights, Sex, and Gender: Limits in Theory and Practice', *Pace Law Review* 31:3 (2011), p. 826. Stemple questions in a broader context 'how movements for transformative gender change can ever describe inequality ('women are victims') without re-inscribing sex-based stereotypes ('women are victims').'

27. *Actus reus* denotes the action or conduct that is a constituent element of a criminal act. *Mens rea* refers to the intention or knowledge of wrongdoing that constitutes the mental aspect of proof to a criminal offence. Andrew Ashworth and Jeremy Horder, *Principles of Criminal Law*, 7th edn (Oxford, 2013).

28. Louise Chappell, *The Politics of Gender Justice at the International Criminal Court: Legacies and Legitimacy* (New York, 2016).

29. Note that the governments of many countries maintain national sexual-assault statistics. See, for example, *4510.0—Recorded Crime—Victims, Australia, 2010* (Canberra Australian Bureau of Statistics, 23 June 2011); Tina Hotton Mahony, 'Women and the Criminal Justice System', *Women in Canada: A Gender-Based Statistical Report*, 6th edn (Ottawa, Apr. 2011); Home Office, *Crime in England and Wales 2010/11: Findings from the British Crime Survey and Police Recorded Crime*, 2nd edn, Rupert Chaplin, John Flatley, and Kevin Smith (eds) (London, July 2011).

30. Kwong-Leung Tang, 'Rape Law Reform in Canada: The Success and Limits of Legislation', *International Journal of Offender Therapy and Comparative Criminology* 42:3 (1998), pp 258–70.

31. See 'National Statistics', *Rape Crisis Network Ireland*, https://www.rcni.ie/national-statistics; see also Ed O'Loughlin, 'Acquittal in Irish Rugby Rape Case Deepens Debate on Sexual Consent', *The New York Times*, 15 Apr. 2018; Valeriya Safronova, 'Lawyer in Rape Trial Links Thong with Consent, and Ireland Erupts', *The New York Times*, 15 Nov. 2018.

32. These doctrines have been historical barriers to successful prosecution. 'Fresh complaint' is an evidentiary rule that allows the testimony of an individual to whom

a victim has told about a sexual assault to corroborate the victim's testimony. Failure to 'tell' another person of the harm has, in parallel, functioned to make the victim less credible. 'Mistake of fact' in sexual assault/rape cases enables a defendant to argue as a defence that he believed consent was forthcoming from the victim, even in cases that stretch the credulity of such a belief. Passivity, or a failure to 'fight' back physically, has historically functioned to divest the victim of consent, based on the patriarchal assumption that a woman would physically fight back to prevent being raped or sexually harmed.

33. Goldblatt and Meintjes, 'South African Women', pp 27–61.

34. Truth and Reconciliation Commission of South Africa, *Truth and Reconciliation Commission of South Africa Report, Volume Four* (n.p.: 29 Oct. 1998).

35. Fiona C. Ross, *Bearing Witness: Women and the Truth and Reconciliation Commission in South Africa* (Sterling, VA, 2003); Fionnuala Ní Aoláin and Catherine Turner, 'Gender, Truth, and Transition', *UCLA Women's Law Journal* 16.2 (2007), pp 229–79.

36. Legacy Gender Integration Group, *Gender Principles for Dealing with the Legacy of the Past* (Belfast, Sept. 2015).

37. Louise Mallinder, Kieran McEvoy, Luke Moffett, and Gordon Anthony, 'The Historical Use of Amnesties, Immunities, and Sentence Reductions in Northern Ireland', *Transitional Justice Institute Research Paper No. 16–12,* 28 June 2016. President Trump's use of presidential pardons for soldiers who have committed war crimes in Iraq sets a highly worrying precedent for the application of the laws of war in a consistent and rule-of-law-focused manner. See Gabor Rona, 'Can a Pardon Be a War Crime? When Pardons Themselves Violate the Laws of War', *Just Security,* 25 May 2019, https://www.justsecurity.org/64288/can-a-pardon-be-a-war-crime-when-pardons-themselves-violate-the-laws-of-war.

38. Note that the Philippines departed from the International Criminal Court on the basis of an executive decision by President Duterte. See Jason Gutierrez, 'Philippines Officially Leaves the International Criminal Court', *The New York Times,* 17 Mar. 2019.

39. The source of this contemporary challenge has a long antecedent in the efforts of the Roman Catholic church to undermine and delegitimise the use of the terminology of gender in international legal instruments including, but not limited to, the Rome Statute of the International Criminal Court. See Mary Anne Case, 'After Gender the Destruction of Man? The Vatican's Nightmare Vision of the 'Gender Agenda' for Law', *Pace Law Review* 31.3 (2011), 802. See also, more generally, Dario C˘epo, review of Roman Kuhar and David Paternotte (eds), *Anti-Gender Campaigns in Europe: Mobilizing against Equality, Revija Za Sociologiju* 47:3 (2017), pp 361–64.

40. UN Security Council, *Security Council Resolution 2467* (UN Doc. S/RES/2467, 23 Apr. 2019).

41. Loretta J. Ross et al. (eds), *Radical Reproductive Justice: Foundations, Theory, Practice, Critique* (New York, 2017).

42. Daniela Grunow, Katia Begall, and Sandra Buchler, 'Gender Ideologies in Europe: A Multidimensional Framework', *Journal of Marriage and Family* 80:1 (Feb. 2018), pp 42–60; Gillian Kane, 'Right-Wing Europe's War on "Gender Ideology,"' *The Public Eye* (Spring 2018).

43. Ní Aoláin and Campbell, 'The Paradox of Transition.'

44. On the continued international legal responsibilities of Ireland to provide appropriate remedy for serious and systematic violations of human rights, see 'Draft Articles on Responsibility of States for Internationally Wrongful Acts', *Report of the International Law Commission on the Work of Its Fifty-Third Session (23 Apr.–1 June and 2 July–10 Aug. 2001)* (UN Doc. A/56/10, 2001), Ch. 4, sect. E, art. 1 and 31:

32–33, 91–93; *Basic Principles and Guidelines on the Right to a Remedy and Reparation for Victims of Gross Violations of International Human Rights Law and Serious Violations of International Humanitarian Law* (G.A. Res. 60/147, UN Doc. A/RES/60/147, 16 Dec. 2005).

45. See the other contributions to this volume. See also Maeve O'Rourke, Claire McGettrick, Rod Baker, Raymond Hill, et al., *CLANN: Ireland's Unmarried Mothers and Their Children: Gathering the Data: Principal Submission to the Commission of Investigation into Mother and Baby Homes* (Dublin, 15 Oct. 2018), sect. 4–5; Maeve O'Rourke, '10 Ways Institutional Abuse Details Are Still Being Kept Secret', *RTÉ Brainstorm*, 5 Sept. 2019, https://www.rte.ie/brainstorm/2019/0503/1047282-10-ways-institutional-abuse-details-are-still-being-kept-secret.

46. Rosemary L. Nagy, 'The Scope and Bounds of Transitional Justice and the Canadian Truth and Reconciliation Commission', *International Journal of Transitional Justice* 7:1 (2013), pp 52–73.

47. Commissions of Investigation Act (23/2004).

48. Retention of Records Bill (16/2019).

49. James M. Smith, 'Commission of Investigations Act Inhibits Truth-Telling about Past and Present', *The Irish Times*, 30 Oct. 2018; Conall Ó Fátharta, '"No Plans" to Open Committee Archive on Magdalene Laundries', *The Irish Examiner*, 8 Sept. 2018.

50. See, for example, the assessment of South Africa's transitional-justice process (often viewed as one of the archetypal best-practice examples) in Mahmood Mamdani, 'Amnesty or Impunity? A Preliminary Critique of the Report of the Truth and Reconciliation Commission of South Africa (TRC)', *Diacritics* 32:3/4 (2002), pp 33–59.

51. See, for example, Kirsten Ainley, 'Evaluating the Success of Transitional Justice in Sierra Leone and Beyond', in Kirsten Ainley, Rebekka Friedman, and Chris Mahony (eds), *Evaluating Transitional Justice: Accountability and Peacebuilding in Post-Conflict Sierra Leone* (London, 2015), pp 241–63.

52. See the well-documented limitations of transitional-justice processes as articulated by the United Nations Special Rapporteur on the promotion of truth, justice, reparation, and guarantees of nonrecurrence found in the *Report of the Special Rapporteur on the Promotion of Truth, Justice, Reparation, and Guarantees of Non-recurrence* (A/HRC/42/45, 11 July 2019), https://ap.ohchr.org/documents/dpage_e.aspx?si=A/HRC/42/45.

CHAPTER 12 – TRANSITIONAL JUSTICE AND IRELAND'S LEGACY OF HISTORICAL ABUSE

1. An earlier version of this essay appeared in *Éire-Ireland: An Interdisciplinary Journal of Irish Studies* 55.1 (Spring/Summer 2020), pp 35–67, DOI: 10.1353/eir.2020.0002.

2. A consolidated democracy can be defined as one where 'no significant political groups seriously attempt to overthrow the democratic regime or secede from the state.' See Juan J. Linz and Alfred Stepan, *Problems of Democratic Transition and Consolidation: Southern Europe, South America, and Post-Communist Europe* (Baltimore, 1996), p. 5. This article will address the Republic of Ireland only and will exclude consideration of transitional justice related to the Troubles on the island of Ireland.

3. This article will predominantly examine abuse involving the Irish state and the dioceses and religious orders of the Roman Catholic church. However, this is not the full extent of Irish historical abuses, which also involved other denominations.

Mary Burke's essay, chapter 14, in this volume address the ways in which abuse in Protestant institutions is rendered invisible in the contemporary moment.

4. Georges Balandier, A. M. Sheridan Smith (trans.), *Political Anthropology* (New York, 1970), p. 41.

5. Elaine Loughlin, 'Katherine Zappone: "We Will Find the Truth and Achieve Reconciliation"', *The Irish Examiner*, 10 Mar. 2017.

6. Paige Arthur, 'How "Transitions" Reshaped Human Rights: A Conceptual History of Transitional Justice', *Human Rights Quarterly* 31.2 (2009), p.321–67; Ruti F. Teitel, *Transitional Justice* (Oxford, 2000), p. 215; Ruti G. Teitel, 'Transitional Justice Genealogy', *Harvard Human Rights Journal* 16 (2003), pp 69–94.

7. UN Secretary General, *The Rule of Law and Transitional Justice in Conflict and Post-Conflict Societies: Report of the Secretary-General* (UN Doc. S/2004/616, 23 Aug. 2004), https://undocs.org/S/2004/616.

8. Paul Gready and Simon Robins, 'From Transitional to Transformative Justice: A New Agenda for Practice', *International Journal of Transitional Justice* 8.3 (2014), pp 339–61.

9. Kieran McEvoy, 'Beyond Legalism: Towards a Thicker Understanding of Transitional Justice', *Journal of Law and Society* 34:4 (2007), pp 411–40.

10. Alexander L. Boraine, 'Transitional Justice: A Holistic Interpretation', *Journal of International Affairs* 60.1 (2006), pp 17–27; Pablo de Greiff, *Report of the Special Rapporteur on the Promotion of Truth, Justice, Reparation and Guarantees of Non-Recurrence* (UN Doc. A/HRC/21/46, 27 Aug. 2017), par. 22–7, https://undocs.org/A/HRC/21/46.

11. Kai Ambos, 'The Legal Framework of Transitional Justice: A Systematic Study with a Special Focus on the Role of the ICC', in Kai Ambos, Judith Large, and Marieke Wierda (eds.), *Building a Future on Peace and Justice* (Berlin and Heidelberg, 2009), pp 19–103.

12. Oskar Thoms, James Ron, and Roland Paris, 'State-Level Effects of Transitional Justice: What Do We Know?', *International Journal of Transitional Justice* 4.3 (2010), p. 329; Hugo van der Merwe, Victoria Baxter, and Audrey R. Chapman (eds), *Assessing the Impact of Transitional Justice: Challenges for Empirical Research* (Washington D.C., 2009).

13. Gready and Robins, 'From Transitional to Transformative Justice', p. 339.

14. Kirsten Campbell, 'The Gender of Transitional Justice: Law, Sexual Violence, and the International Criminal Tribunal for the Former Yugoslavia', *International Journal of Transitional Justice* 1:3 (2007), p. 411.

15. Catherine Turner, *Violence, Law, and the Impossibility of Transitional Justice* (Abingdon, UK, 2017).

16. Gready and Robins, 'From Transitional to Transformative Justice', p. 340.

17. Dáire McGill, 'Different Violence, Different Justice? Taking Structural Violence Seriously in Post-Conflict and Transitional Justice Processes', *State Crime Journal* 6.1 (2017), p. 80.

18. Dustin N. Sharp, 'Emancipating Transitional Justice from the Bonds of the Paradigmatic Transition', *International Journal of Transitional Justice* 9.1 (2015), pp 150–69; Rosemary L. Nagy, 'The Scope and Bounds of Transitional Justice and the Canadian Truth and Reconciliation Commission', *International Journal of Transitional Justice* 7.1 (2013), pp 52–73; Kim Stanton, 'Canada's Truth and Reconciliation Commission: Settling the Past?', *International Indigenous Policy Journal* 2.3 (2011), pp 1–18; Mark McMillan and Sophie Rigney 'Race, Reconciliation, and Justice in Australia: From Denial to Acknowledgment', *Ethnic and Racial Studies* 41.4 (2018), pp 759–77.

19. Stephen Winter, 'Towards a Unified Theory of Transitional Justice', *International Journal of Transitional Justice* 7.2 (2013), pp 224–44.

20. Nicola Henry, 'From Reconciliation to Transitional Justice: The Contours of Redress Politics in Established Democracies', *International Journal of Transitional Justice* 9.2 (2015), p.199–218.

21. James Gallen, 'Jesus Wept: The Roman Catholic Church, Child Sexual Abuse, and Transitional Justice', *International Journal of Transitional Justice* 10.2 (2016), pp 332–49.

22. Turner, *Violence, Law*.

23. Paul Michael Garrett, 'Excavating the Past: Mother and Baby Homes in the Republic of Ireland', *British Journal of Social Work* 47.2 (2017), pp 358–74.

24. Anne-Marie McAlinden, 'An Inconvenient Truth: Barriers to Truth Recovery in the Aftermath of Institutional Child Abuse in Ireland', *Legal Studies* 33.2 (2013), p. 213.

25. Jennifer Balint, Julie Evans, and Nesam McMillan, 'Rethinking Transitional Justice, Redressing Indigenous Harm: A New Conceptual Approach', *International Journal of Transitional Justice* 8.2 (2014), pp 194–216.

26. Ratna Kapur, 'Normalising Violence: Transitional Justice and the Gujarat Riots', *Columbia Journal of Gender and Law* 15.3 (2006), p. 889.

27. Paul Gready, *The Era of Transitional Justice: The Aftermath of the Truth and Reconciliation Commission in South Africa and Beyond* (Abingdon, UK, 2011), p. 15.

28. Residential Institutions Redress Board, Annual Report of the Residential Institutions Redress Board (2017) n.p.

29. Commission to Inquire into Child Abuse, *Report of the Commission to Inquire into Child Abuse Report* (Dublin, 2009), hereafter cited as *Ryan Report*.

30. Francis D. Murphy, Helen Buckley, and Laraine Joyce, *The Ferns Report: Presented to the Minister for Health and Children, Oct. 2005* (Dublin, 2005), hereafter cited as *Ferns Report*; Commission of Investigation into the Catholic Archdiocese of Dublin, *Report of the Commission of Investigation into the Catholic Archdiocese of Dublin* (Dublin, 29 Nov. 2009), hereafter cited as *Murphy Report*; Commission of Investigation into Catholic Diocese of Cloyne, *Report into the Catholic Diocese of Cloyne, Dec. 2010* (Dublin, 2010), hereafter cited as *Cloyne Report*.

31. Figures compiled from annual reports available from the National Board for Safeguarding Children in the Catholic Church in Ireland, available at National Board for Safeguarding Children in the Catholic Church in Ireland (NBSCCCI), 'Publications', *safeguarding.ie*, 20 Apr. 2020, https://www.safeguarding.ie/publications.

32. Maeve O'Rourke and James M. Smith, 'Ireland's Magdalene Laundries: Confronting a History Not Yet in the Past', in Alan Hayes and Máire Meagher (eds), *A Century of Progress? Irish Women Reflect* (Dublin, 2016), pp 107–34.

33. Lindsey Earner-Byrne, *Mother and Child: Maternity and Child Welfare in Dublin, 1922–60* (Manchester, 2013), p. 189.

34. Commission of Investigation into Mother and Baby Homes, *Final Report, Executive Summary* (Dublin, 2021), p.2.

35. Donogh O'Malley, 'Written Answer—County Homes', *Dáil Éireann Debates*, 220, 17 Feb. 1966.

36. Mike Milotte, *Banished Babies: The Secret History of Ireland's Baby Export Business* (Dublin, 2012).

37. Marie O'Connor, *Bodily Harm: Symphysiotomy and Pubiotomy in Ireland, 1944–92* (Dublin, 2011).

38. Maeve O'Rourke, *Justice for Magdalenes (JFM) Ireland: Submission to the United Nations Committee against Torture 46th Session* (Cavan, 2011); Adoption

Rights Alliance Ireland, *NGO Submission to the UN Committee for the Convention against Torture and Other Cruel, Inhuman, or Degrading Treatment or Punishment, in Respect of Ireland* (Malahide, 2017); AnneMarie Crean and Fionna Fox on behalf of Reclaiming Self, CLG, *Ryan Report Follow-Up: Submission to the United Nations Committee against Torture, Session 61* (Dublin, 2017); Marie O'Connor, Ruadhán Mac Aodháin, and Michael Lynn, *Submission of Survivors of Symphysiotomy to the United Nations Human Rights Committee* (Dublin, 2014).

39. Maeve O'Rourke, *Justice for Magdalenes Research: NGO Submission to the UN Committee on the Elimination of Discrimination against Women in Respect of Ireland* (Cavan, 2017); UN Committee on the Elimination of Discrimination against Women, *Concluding Observations on the Combined Sixth and Seventh Periodic Reports of Ireland* (UN Doc. CEDAW/C/IRL/CO/6–7, 9 Mar. 2017), p. 4, https://undocs.org/CEDAW/C/IRL/CO/6–7.

40. Kathleen Daly, 'Conceptualising Responses to Institutional Abuse of Children', *Current Issues in Criminal Justice* 26.1 (2014), p. 18.

41. Shurlee Swain, Katie Wright, and Johanna Sköld, 'Conceptualising and Categorising Child Abuse Inquiries: From Damage Control to Foregrounding Survivor Testimony', *Journal of Historical Sociology* 31.3 (2018), pp 282–96.

42. Anne Marie McAlinden and Bronwyn Naylor, 'Reframing Public Inquiries as 'Procedural Justice' for Victims of Institutional Child Abuse: Towards a Hybrid Model of Justice', *Sydney Law Review* 38.3 (2016), p. 291.

43. Department of Justice, *Report of the Inter-departmental Committee to Establish the Facts of State Involvement with the Magdalene Laundries* (hereafter *McAleese Report*) (Dublin, 2013)

44. Commission of Investigation into Mother and Baby Homes, *Final Report* (Dublin, 2020).

45. James M. Smith, Maeve O'Rourke, Raymond Hill, and Claire McGettrick, *State Involvement in the Magdalene Laundries: JFM's Principal Submissions to the Inter-departmental Committee to Establish the Facts of State Involvement with the Magdalene Laundries* (Cavan, 2013); Maeve O'Rourke, Claire McGettrick, Rod Baker, Raymond Hill, et al., *CLANN: Ireland's Unmarried Mothers and Their Children: Gathering the Data: Principal Submission to the Commission of Investigation into Mother and Baby Homes* (Dublin, 15 Oct. 2018), pp 14–105. Hereafter cited as *CLANN Report*.

46. Máiréad Enright, Aoife O'Donoghue, et al, *Mother and Baby Homes Commission of Investigation Report Draft Alternative Executive Summary*, 2021, https://www.tudublin.ie/media/website/news/2021/main-news/Draft-Report-July-15-2021.pdf

47. Eoin O'Sullivan and Ian O'Donnell, *Coercive Confinement in Ireland: Patients, Prisoners, and Penitents* (Manchester, 2012).

48. Priscilla B. Hayner, *Unspeakable Truths: Transitional Justice and the Challenge of Truth Commissions*, 2nd edn (New York, 2011).

49. UN Secretary General, *The Rule of Law and Transitional Justice in Conflict and Post-Conflict Societies: Report of the Secretary-General* (UN Doc. S/2004/616, 23 Aug. 2004), p. 17, section XIV, par. 50, https://undocs.org/S/2004/616.

50. Adam Ashforth, 'Reckoning Schemes of Legitimation: On Commissions of Inquiry as Power/Knowledge Forms', *Journal of Historical Sociology* 3.1 (1990), p. 9.

51. Simon Robins, 'Towards Victim-Centred Transitional Justice: Understanding the Needs of Families of the Disappeared in Postconflict Nepal', *International Journal of Transitional Justice* 5.1 (2011), pp 75–98.

52. UN Office of the High Commissioner for Human Rights (OHCHR), *Rule of Law Tools for Post-Conflict States: National Consultations on Transitional Justice* (UN Doc. HR/PUB/09/2, 2009).

53. *Ferns Report*, pp 3–5; *Ryan Report*, vol. 1, par. 1.26.

54. Maureen Harding Clark, *The Surgical Symphysiotomy Ex Gratia Payment Scheme: Report to Minister for Health Simon Harris TD* (Dublin, 2016), pp 96–7.

55. Department of Children and Youth Affairs, 'Mother and Baby Homes Collabourative Forum Meetings', *Rialtas na hÉireann/Government of Ireland*, 1 Sept. 2019, https://www.gov.ie/en/collection/346782-mother-and-baby-homes-collabourative-forum-meetings.

56. Conall Ó Fátharta, 'Forum Members Dismayed by Refusal to Publish Mother and Baby Homes Report in Full', *The Irish Examiner*, 16 Apr. 2019. See the essay by Claire McGettrick, chapter 15, and the contributors to the testimony section, chapter 1, of this volume.

57. UN OHCHR, *Rule of Law Tools*, p. 14.

58. Bruce Arnold, *The Irish Gulag: How the State Betrayed Its Innocent Children* (Dublin, 2009), pp 249–56.

59. *Murphy Report*, par. 11.9; *Cloyne Report*, par. 1.6.

60. *Ferns Report*, p. 2.

61. Commission of Investigation (Mother and Baby Homes and Certain Related Matters) Order 2015 (SI 57/2015), *Electronic Irish Statute Book*, http://www.irishstatutebook.ie/eli/2015/si/57/made/en/print.

62. Ibid.

63. *CLANN Report.*, pp 14–64.

64. Commission of Investigation into Mother and Baby Homes, *Final Report, Recommendations* (Dublin, 2021), p. 9.

65. Committee of Public Accounts, *Third Interim Report on the Procurement of Legal Services by Public Bodies* (Dublin, 2011), p. 25.

66. Seamus McCarty, Comptroller and Auditor General, *Special Report 96: Cost of Child Abuse Inquiry and Redress* (Dublin, 2016), https://www.audit.gov.ie/en/Find-Report/Publications/2017/Special-Report-96-Cost-of-Child-Abuse-Inquiry-and-Redress.pdf, archived at https://perma.cc/2T2F-WG35.

67. Taoiseach Enda Kenny, TD, 'Leaders Questions', *Dáil Éireann Debates*, p. 791, 6 Feb. 2013.

68. Commission of Investigation into Mother and Baby Homes, *Final Report, Introduction* (Dublin, 2021), p. 15.

69. Yvonne Murphy, *Independent Review of Issues Relating to Symphysiotomy* (Dublin, 2014), 31; *Report of the Inter-departmental Group on Mother and Baby Homes*, pp 28–31.

70. Katie Wright, 'Remaking Collective Knowledge: An Analysis of the Complex and Multiple Effects of Inquiries into Historical Institutional Child Abuse', *Child Abuse and Neglect* 74 (2017), p. 16.

71. Matthew Colton, Maurice Vanstone, and Christine Walby, 'Victimisation, Care, and Justice: Reflections on the Experiences of Victims/Survivors Involved in Large-Scale Historical Investigations of Child Sexual Abuse in Residential Institutions', *British Journal of Social Work* 32.5 (2002), pp 541–51.

72. Carol Brennan, 'Trials and Contestations: Ireland's Ryan Commission', in Johanna Sköld and Shurlee Swain (eds), *Apologies and the Legacy of Abuse of Children in 'Care': International Perspectives* (London, 2015), p. 64.

73. Carol Brennan, 'Facing What Cannot Be Changed: The Irish Experience of Confronting Institutional Child Abuse', *Journal of Social Welfare and Family Law* 29.3–4 (2007), p. 250.

74. But see Sinead Pembroke, 'Historical Institutional Child Abuse in Ireland: Survivor Perspectives on Taking Part in the Commission to Inquire into Child Abuse (CICA) and the Redress Scheme', *Contemporary Justice Review* 22.1 (2019), pp 43–59, and Crean and Fox, *Ryan Report Follow-Up*, pp 18–21.

75. Brennan, 'Trials and Contestations', p. 56.

76. Ibid., p. 64.

77. 'Living and Working Conditions', *McAleese Report*, Ch. 19, par. 7.

78. Claire O'Sullivan, 'Interviews Lacked Transparency, Say Victims Groups', *The Irish Examiner*, 7 Feb. 2013.

79. Letter from Rod Baker, Hogan Lovells to Commission of Investigation into Mother and Baby Homes, 9 Aug. 2016, http://clannproject.org/wp-content/uploads/Letter-from-Hogan-Lovells-to-MBHCOI_09-08-2016.pdf

80. Transcript of Oxford University Seminar with Professor Mary Daly, available at Claire McGettrick Transcript of Oxford University Seminar with Professor Mary Daly, 2021, http://clannproject.org/commission-report/oxfordtranscript/.

81. Conall Ó Fátharta, 'Commission Says They Are Prohibited from Telling Surviving Family Members about Burial Locations', *The Irish Examiner*, 19 Apr. 2019; *CLANN Report*, p.131.

82. Justice for Magdalenes Research, *CLANN: Ireland's Unmarried Mothers and Their Children: Gathering the Data, Ethical Protocols* (Dublin: Justice for Magdalenes Research and Adoption Rights Alliance, n.d.), http://clannproject.org/wp-content/uploads/Clann-Ethical-Protocols.pdf

83. Commission of Investigation into Mother and Baby Homes, *Final Report, Ch. 36 Human Rights* (Dublin, 2021), p. 24.

84. Mark Freeman, *Truth Commissions and Procedural Fairness* (Cambridge, 2006), pp 222–6.

85. UN High Commissioner for Human Rights, *Promotion and Protection of Human Rights: Study on the Right to the Truth* (UN Doc. E/CN.4/2006/91, 8 Feb. 2006), https://undocs.org/E/CN.4/2006/91.

86. Johanna Sköld, 'The Truth about Abuse? A Comparative Approach to Inquiry Narratives on Historical Institutional Child Abuse', *History of Education* 45.4 (2016), p. 501.

87. Murray v. Commission to Inquire into Child Abuse [2004] 2 IR 222.

88. McAlinden and Naylor, 'Reframing Public Inquiries', p. 287.

89. 'Establishment, Membership, and Mandate of the Committee', *McAleese Report*, Ch. 2, par. 27.

90. 'Living and Working Conditions', *McAleese Report*, Ch. 19, par. 15, 34, 35.

91. Katherine O'Donnell, Sinead Pembroke, and Claire McGettrick, 'Magdalene Institutions: Recording an Oral and Archival History', Justice for Magdalenes Research, n.d., http://jfmresearch.com/home/oralhistoryproject, archived at https://perma.cc/2DA7-PXUC; Jennifer Yeagar, 'The Oral History Recordings', *The Waterford Memories Project*, 2015, https://www.waterfordmemories.com/recordings, archived at https://perma.cc/4JUV-CSEN.

92. Maeve O'Rourke, 'Ireland's Magdalene Laundries and the State's Duty to Protect', *Hibernian Law Journal* 10 (2011), pp 200–37; James M. Smith, *Justice for Magdalenes: State Complicity and Constitutional Rights* (Cavan, 2010); Maeve O'Rourke, *Submission to the United Nations CAT*.

93. Maeve O'Rourke, *Submission to the United Nations CAT*, par. 3.1–4.14.

94. UN Committee Against Torture (CAT), *Consideration of Reports Submitted by States Parties Under Article 19 of the Convention—Ireland* (UN Doc. CAT/C/IRL/CO/1, 17 June 2011), par. 21, https://undocs.org/CAT/C/IRL/CO/1.

95. UN CAT, *Concluding Observations on the Second Periodic Report of Ireland* (UN Doc. CAT/C/IRL/CO/2, 31 Aug. 2017), par. 6, https://undocs.org/CAT/C/IRL/CO/2.

96. Commission of Investigation into Mother and Baby Homes, *Final Report, Ch. 36 Human Rights* (Dublin, 2021).

97. Máiréad Enright, Aoife O'Donoghue, et al, *Mother and Baby Homes Commission of Investigation Report Draft Alternative Executive Summary*, 2021, https://www. tudublin.ie/media/website/news/2021/main-news/Draft-Report-July-15-2021.pdf

98. Commission of Investigation into Mother and Baby Homes, *Executive Summary* (Dublin, 2021), p. 2.

99. Robert Nathaniel Kraft, *Violent Accounts: Understanding the Psychology of Perpetrators through South Africa's Truth and Reconciliation Commission* (New York University Press, 2014). For the potential of restorative justice to address sexual abuse in the Irish context, see Marie Keenan, *Sexual Trauma and Abuse: Restorative and Transformative Possibilities?* (Dublin, 2014).

100. See submissions in Nov. 2019 on the Retention of Records Bill 2019 from survivors and academic experts, available at Claire McGettrick, 'Retention of Records Bill 2019', *Justice for Magdalenes Research*, 2019, http://jfmresearch.com/ retention-of-records-bill-2019, archived at https://perma.cc/A4XF-YCHS.

101. Patsy McGarry, 'Over Two Million Documents from Redress Bodies to Be Sealed in National Archives', *The Irish Times*, 28 Feb. 2019.

102. Barbara Walshe and Catherine O'Connell, *Consultations with Survivors of Institutional Abuse on Themes and Issues to Be Addressed by a Survivor-Led Consultation Group* (n.p.: July 2019), p. 16, https://www.education.ie/en/Publications/Education-Reports/consultations-with-survivors-of-institutional-abuse-on-themes-and-issues-to-be-addressed-by-a-survivor-led-consultation-group.pdf, archived at https:// perma.cc/8LP9-SQW6.

103. Conall Ó Fátharta, 'Abuse Survivors' Concern over Plan to Seal Records', *The Irish Examiner*, 16 Aug. 2019.

104. Justine McCarthy, 'Bill to seal Ryan commission abuse testimonies put on ice after survivors' campaign', *The Sunday Times*, 2 Aug. 2020.

105. Conall Ó Fátharta, '"No Plans" to Open Committee Archive on Magdalene Laundries', *The Irish Examiner*, 8 Sept. 2018.

106. Department of Children, Equality, Disability, Integration and Youth, *Minister O'Gorman publishes proposed Birth Information and Tracing Legislation*, 2021, https:// www.gov.ie/en/press-release/14c5c-minister-ogorman-publishes-proposed-birth-information-and-tracing-legislation/.

107. Claire McGettrick, Maeve O'Rourke, Katherine O'Donnell, and Loughlin O'Nolan, *Clann Project Submission to the Committee on Children, Disability, Equality and Integration on the General Scheme of the Birth Information and Tracing Bill 2021*, 2021, http://clannproject.org/wp-content/uploads/Clann-Project-Submission-to-Oireachtas-Childrens-Committee.pdf, pp 22–30.

108. Steven R. Ratner, Jason S. Abrams, and James L. Bischoff, *Accountability for Human Rights Atrocities in International Law: Beyond the Nuremberg Legacy* (Oxford University Press, 2009).

109. Clare McGlynn and Vanessa Munro, *Rethinking Rape Law: International and Comparative Perspectives* (Abingdon, UK, 2011).

110. Miriam J. Aukerman, 'Extraordinary Evil, Ordinary Crime: A Framework for Understanding Transitional Justice', *Harvard Human Rights Journal* 15 (2002), pp 39–97.

111. William A. Schabas, 'The Rwanda Case: Sometimes It's Impossible', in M. Cherif Bassiouni (ed.), *Post*-Conflict Justice (Ardsley, New York, 2002), pp 499–522.

112. Daniel W. Shuman and Alexander McCall Smith, *Justice and the Prosecution of Old Crimes: Balancing Legal, Psychological, and Moral Concerns* (Washington DC, 2000), pp 27–8.

113. UN General Assembly, *Basic Principles and Guidelines on the Right to a Remedy and Reparation for Victims of Gross Violations of International Human Rights Law and*

Serious Violations of International Humanitarian Law (UN Doc. A/RES/60/147, 21 Mar. 2006), https://undocs.org/A/RES/60/147. Note, however, that evidence in support of the therapeutic role played by criminal prosecution and conviction for victim-survivors remains extremely limited and may be undermined by the additional trauma imposed on those victims who testify as part of the prosecution process. See Judith Lewis Herman, 'The Mental Health of Crime Victims: Impact of Legal Intervention', *Journal of Traumatic Stress* 16.2 (2003), pp 159–66.

114. *Murphy Report*, par. 5.43.

115. UN CAT, *Consideration of Reports*, par. 20.

116. Mike Milotte, 'Adoption Controversy: Only One Person Was Ever Charged Over Bogus Birth Certificates', *The Irish Times*, 1 June 2018.

117. Katie Wright, Shurlee Swain, and Kathleen McPhillips, 'The Australian Royal Commission into Institutional Responses to Child Sexual Abuse', *Child Abuse and Neglect* 74 (2017), p. 4.

118. O'Keeffe v. Ireland [2014] ECHR 2014-I 155.

119. Conor O'Mahony, 'Stop Treating Abuse Victims with Contempt', *The Irish Examiner*, 10 July 2019.

120. Iarfhlaith O'Neill, *Decision of the Independent Assessor Iarfhlaith O'Neill* (Athlone, Department of Education and Skills, 2019), par. 46, 52.

121. See essay in this volume by Smith and Duff, chapter 8.

122. UN Human Rights Committee (HRC), *General Comment No. 31 [80]: The Nature of the General Legal Obligation Imposed on States Parties to the Covenant* (UN Doc. CCPR/C/21/Rev.1/Add.13, 26 May 2004), par. 16, https://undocs.org/CCPR/C/21/Rev.1/Add.13.

123. Pablo De Greiff, *Report of the Special Rapporteur on the Promotion of Truth, Justice, Reparation, and Guarantees of Non-recurrence* (UN Doc. A/69/518, 14 Oct. 2014), par. 11, https://undocs.org/A/69/518.

124. Residential Institutions Redress Act (2002), *Electronic Irish Statutes Book*, http://www.irishstatutebook.ie/eli/2002/act/13/enacted/en/html.

125. Peter Tyndall, *Opportunity Lost: An Investigation by the Ombudsman into the Administration of the Magdalen Restorative Justice Scheme* (Dublin, 2017), p. 32, https://www.ombudsman.ie/publications/reports/opportunity-lost/Magdalen-Scheme.pdf, archived at https://perma.cc/CJ7U-ZBEC.

126. Evidence of Michael Woods, Former Minister for Education, 24 June 2004, to the Commission to Inquire into Child Abuse, *Commission to Inquire into Child Abuse Held at 145–151 Church Street, Dublin, on Thursday, 24th June 2004, Day 3* (n.p.: Gwen Malone Stenography Services, n.d.), 15, http://www.childabusecommission.ie/public_hearings/documents/04/Transcript-24June2004.pdf

127. But see Pembroke, 'Historical Institutional Child Abuse.'

128. Patsy McGarry, 'Religious Congregations Indemnity Deal Was "A Blank Cheque," Says Michael McDowell', *The Irish Times*, 5 Apr. 2019.

129. An Oblate of Mary Immaculate, 'The Moral Challenge Posed to Religious about the Cost of Redress', *The Oblates*, 21 Mar. 2017, p. 9, https://oblates.ie/wp-content/uploads/2017/03/The-moral-challenge-posed-to-religious-about-the-cost-of-redress-updated.pdf, archived at https://perma.cc/JL8D-7URL.

130. Caranua, 'Caranua Annual Report 2016', *Caranua.ie*, p. 6, http://caranua.ie/wp-content/uploads/2018/01/Annual_Report_2016.pdf; Christina Finn, 'Caranua Boss Withdraws Comments in Which She Said Abuse Survivors Were "Damaged,"' *thejournal.ie*, 14 Apr. 2017. See Connie Roberts's poem 'My People' in the testimony section, chapter 1, of this volume.

131. *Murphy Report*, par. 8.3.

132. Charities of the Roman Catholic Archdiocese of Dublin, *Annual Financial*

Report, Financial Year Ended 31 Dec. 2017 (Dublin, 2018), p. 7, https://www.dublindiocese.ie/wp-content/uploads/2018/11/Charities-of-the-Roman-Catholic-Archdiocese-of-Dublin-Financial-Report-2017.pdf

133. John Quirke, *The Magdalen Commission Report* (Dublin, May 2013), p. 9, http://www.justice.ie/en/JELR/THE%20 Quirke%20report.pdf/Files/THE%20Quirke%20 report.pdf

134. Ibid., 40.

135. Maeve O'Rourke, *Justice for Magdalenes Research: NGO Submission to the UN Committee against Torture in Respect of Ireland (for the Session) July 2017* (Cavan, 2017), para. 4.12.

136. Ibid., par. 4.8.

137. Tyndall, *Opportunity Lost*, pp 24–25.

138. MKL v. Minister for Justice and Equality [2017] IEHC 389.

139. Ibid., par. 38.

140. Tyndall, *Opportunity Lost*, p. 31.

141. Ibid., p. 4.

142. Pablo de Greiff (ed.), *The Handbook of Reparations* (New York, 2006), p. 11.

143. UN Committee on the Rights of the Child (CRC), *Concluding Observations on the Combined Third and Fourth Periodic Reports of Ireland* (UN Doc. CRC/C/IRL/CO/3–4, 29 Jan. 2016), https://undocs.org/CRC/C/IRL/CO/3-4; UN Committee on Economic Social and Cultural Rights (CESCR), *Concluding Observation on the Third Periodic Report of Ireland* (UN Doc. E/C.12/IRL/CO/3, 8 July 2015), https://undocs.org/E/C.12/IRL/CO/3; UN Human Rights Committee, *Concluding Observations on the Fourth Periodic Report of Ireland* (UN Doc. CCPR/C/IRL/CO/4, 19 Aug. 2014), https://undocs.org/CCPR/C/IRL/CO/4; UN CAT, *Consideration of Reports*.

144. Crean and Fox, *Ryan Report Follow-Up*, 1.

145. Pablo de Greiff, 'Justice and Reparations', in de Greiff, *Handbook of Reparations*, pp 451–77.

146. Anne-Marie McAlinden, *Apologies and Institutional Child Abuse* (Belfast, 2018), https://apologies-abuses-past.org.uk/assets/uploads/Apologies-Institutional-Abuse-Report_Sept-2018.pdf, archived at https://perma.cc/Y2SR-SBP4; *thejournal.ie* 'Here's what religious orders have said in response to the mother and baby homes report', 2021, https://www.thejournal.ie/mother-and-baby-homes-4-5324151-Jan2021/.

Chapter 13 – Creating 'Common Sense' Responses to the 'Unmarried Mother' in the Irish Free State

1. This essay was previously published in *Éire-Ireland: An Interdisciplinary Journal of Irish Studies* 55.1 (Spring/Summer 2020), pp 120–41, DOI: 10.1353/eir.2020.0005. I am very grateful for the work of Valeria Ballarotti, the editors, and the two anonymous peer reviewers who offered invaluable suggestions on various aspects of the article. Staff at the Oireachtas Library in Dublin also kindly aided my research activity. Any errors contained in this article are entirely my own responsibility.

2. Henceforth I will not encase the phrase unmarried mother in quotation marks, but readers are welcome to infer them given my critical exploration of this construction.

3. With a focus on Britain in the years from the end of World War II until the late 1970s, the social potency of 'primary definers' is articulated by Stuart Hall, Chas Critcher, Tony Jefferson, John Clarke, and Brian Roberts, *Policing the Crisis: Mugging, the State, and Law and Order* (Macmillan Education, 1978).

4. Commission on the Relief of the Sick and Destitute Poor, Including the Insane

Poor (Dublin, Stationery Office, 1927), appendix 1, pp 145–9. Hereafter cited as *CRSDP*.

5. Aidan Beatty, 'The Strange Career of R. S. Devane' (conference paper, American Conference for Irish Studies National Meeting, Kansas City, MO, 2017), https://aidanbeatty.com/2017/03/29/the-strange-career-of-r-s-devane, archived at https://perma.cc/UA4N-VCK2. See also Martin Walsh, *Richard Devane SJ: Social Commentator and Advocate, 1876–1951* (Messenger, 2019).

6. Finola Kennedy, 'The Suppression of the Carrigan Report: A Historical Perspective on Child Abuse', *Studies* 89.356 (2000), pp 354–63; Anthony Keating, 'Sexual Crime in the Irish Free State, 1922–33: Its Nature, Extent, and Reporting', *Irish Studies Review* 20:2 (2012), pp 135–55. See also James M. Smith, 'The Politics of Sexual Knowledge: The Origins of Ireland's Containment Culture and the Carrigan Report (1931)', *Journal of the History of Sexuality* 13.2 (Apr. 2004), pp 208–33. Producing a careful reading of Devane's testimony to the Carrigan committee, Smith observes that the Jesuit articulated critical concerns that would remain prominent in sociological debates for decades to come in Ireland.

7. R. S. Devane, 'The Unmarried Mother and the Poor Law Commission: Illegitimacy and Allied Problems 110 Years Ago', *Irish Ecclesiastical Record*, 5th ser., 31 (1928), p. 572.

8. R. S. Devane, 'The Unmarried Mother: Some Legal Aspects of the Problem, Part 2', *Irish Ecclesiastical Record*, 5th ser., 23 (1924), p. 186.

9. Karl Marx, *Capital: Volume One* (London, 1990), p. 769.

10. Ibid., p. 493.

11. Kate Crehan, 'Gramsci's Concept of Common Sense: A Useful Concept for Anthropologists?', *Journal of Modern Italian Studies* 16:2 (2011), pp 273–87; Kate Crehan, *Gramsci's Common Sense: Inequality and Its Narratives* (Durham, NC, 2016).

12. Jonathan Joseph, *Marxism and Social Theory* (Houndsmill, UK, 2006), p. 52.

13. Stuart Hall and Doreen Massey, 'Interpreting the Crisis', *Soundings* 44 (2010), p. 59. See also Juha Koivisto and Mikko Lahtinen, 'Conjuncture, Politico-Historical', *Historical Materialism* 20:1 (2012), pp 267–77.

14. Michel Foucault, *Discipline and Punish: The Birth of the Prison* (Harmondsworth, 1977), p. 182.

15. John Regan, *The Irish Counter-Revolution, 1921–36: Treatyite Politics and Settlement in Independent Ireland* (Dublin, 1999); Aidan Beatty, 'An Irish Revolution without a Revolution', *Journal of World-Systems Research* 22.1 (2016), pp 54–76.

16. Ciara Breathnach and Eunun O'Halpin, 'Scripting Blame: Irish Coroners' Courts and Unnamed Dead, 1916–32', *Social History* 39:2 (May 2014), p. 223.

17. James Connolly, *Selected Writings* (New York, 1973), p. 275.

18. Beatty, 'Irish Revolution', p. 59.

19. Marx, *Capital*, p. 860.

20. David Lloyd, *Ireland after History* (Cork, 1999), p. 103. See also Franz Fanon, *Wretched of the Earth*, Richard Philcox (trans) (1961; New York, 2004). Fanon was preoccupied by the situation of the 'Third World', in and he was of course writing during a different period. Nonetheless, his coruscating perceptions on the role played by the postcolonial bourgeoisie in Africa might inform our understanding of the role of economic elites and intellectuals in Ireland post-1922.

21. Maryann Gialanella Valiulis, 'Free Women in a Free Nation: Nationalist Feminist Expectations for Independence', in *The Creation of the Dáil*, Brian Farrell (ed.) (Dublin, 1994), pp 84–5.

22. Liam O'Dowd, 'Church State and Women: The Aftermath of Partition' in Chris Curtin, Pauline Jackson, and Barbara O'Connor (eds), *Gender in Irish Society* (Galway, 1987), p. 4.

23. See also Nancy Fraser, *Fortunes of Feminism: From State-Managed Capitalism to Neoliberal Crisis* (London, 2016).

24. John Henry Whyte, *Church and State in Modern Ireland* (Dublin 1971), Ch. 2.

25. Mary Clancy, 'Aspects of Women's Contribution to the Oireachtas Debate in the Irish Free State, 1922–1937', in Maria Luddy and Cliona Murphy (eds), *Women Surviving* (Dublin, 1990), p. 211. See also Una Crowley and Rob Kitchin, 'Producing "Decent Girls": Governmentality and the Moral Geographies of Sexual Conduct in Ireland (1922–1937)', *Gender, Place, and Culture* 15:4 (2008), pp 355–72.

26. Betty Hilliard, 'The Catholic Church and Married Women's Sexuality: Habitus Change in Late 20th-Century Ireland', *Irish Journal of Sociology* 12.2 (2003), pp 28–49.

27. Diarmaid Ferriter, *The Transformation of Ireland, 1900–2000* (London, 2005); Diarmaid Ferriter, *Occasions of Sin: Sex and Society in Modern Ireland* (London, 2009).

28. Eoin Sullivan and Ian O'Donnell, *Coercive Confinement: Patients, Prisoners, Penitents* (Manchester, 2012).

29. Commission to Inquire into Child Abuse, *Report of the Commission to Inquire into Child Abuse Report* (Dublin, Stationery Office, 2009); James M. Smith, *Ireland's Magdalen Laundries and the Nation's Architecture of Containment* (South Bend, IN, 2007). See also Paul Michael Garrett, 'A "Catastrophic, Inept, Self-Serving" Church?: Re-examining Three Reports on Child Abuse in the Republic of Ireland', *Journal of Progressive Human Services* 24:1 (2013), pp 43–65.

30. Zygmunt Bauman, *Liquid Modernity* (Cambridge, 2000).

31. Joseph Robins, *The Lost Children: A Study of Charity Children in Ireland, 1700–1900* (Dublin, 1980). See also Mary Raftery and Eoin O'Sullivan, *Suffer the Little Children: The Inside Story of Ireland's Industrial Schools* (Dublin, 1999).

32. Eoin O'Sullivan and Ian O'Donnell, 'Coercive Confinement in the Republic of Ireland: The Waning of the Culture of Control', *Punishment & Society* 9.1 (Jan. 2007), p. 35. In 1951, for example, there were just 443 people held in prison, yet there were 5,844 children in industrial schools, 1,983 in homes for unmarried mothers and Magdalen homes, and 18,343 in district and auxiliary mental hospitals.

33. Peter Ives, *Language and Hegemony in Gramsci* (London, 2004), p. 74.

34. Antonio Gramsci, *Antonio Gramsci: Selections from Prison Notebooks*, repr. ed., Quentin Hoare and Geoffrey Nowell-Smith (eds) (London, 2005), p. 423.

35. Antonio Gramsci, *A Gramsci Reader: Selected Writings, 1916–1935*, David Forgacs (ed.) (London, 1998), p. 300.

36. Ibid., p. 321.

37. Joe Lee, 'The Irish Constitution of 1937', in Sean Hutton and Paul Stewart (eds), *Ireland's Histories* (London, 1991), p. 82.

38. See also Tom Inglis, *Moral Monopoly: The Rise and Fall of the Catholic Church in Modern Ireland* (Dublin, 1998).

39. R. S. Devane, 'Indecent Literature', *Irish Ecclesiastical Record*, 5th ser., 25 (1925), pp 182–205; Beatty, 'Strange Career.'

40. Beatty, 'Strange Career.' Perhaps, as Beatty suggests, there are also conceptual risks apparent in perceiving the church as a 'singular, coherent entity.'

41. Albeit not always in agreement on the granular aspects of policy, specific individuals performed vital 'definitional labour' in relation to the unmarried mother. Significantly, the notion of 'labour' illuminates the systematic *work* undertaken to instill a particular mood, emotional tonality, and 'structure of feeling' facilitating the introduction of social policies bolstering specific material interests. See Irving Goffman, *The Presentation of Self in Everyday Life* (1959; Harmondsworth, 1971); Raymond Williams, *Marxism and Literature* (Oxford, 1977), Ch. 9.

42. Maria Luddy, 'Prostitution and Rescue Work in Nineteenth-Century Ireland', in Maria Luddy and Cliona Murphy (eds), *Women Surviving* (Dublin, 1990). Many of these refuges, reflecting the influence of religious symbolism, used the title 'Magdalen asylum.' The earliest refuge was the Magdalen asylum in Leeson Street, Dublin, established in 1766. This was a lay asylum, based on one founded in London a few years previously, yet a number of others established later were run by female religious orders and were attached to convents. See also Linda Mahood, *The Magdalenes: Prostitution in the Nineteenth Century* (London, 1990); Maria Luddy, *Women and Philanthropy in Nineteenth-Century Ireland* (Cambridge, 1995).

43. A good deal of retrospective attention afforded to institutions for unmarried mothers erroneously links the regimes found in Magdalen asylums and mother-and-baby homes solely to aspects of Roman Catholic spirituality. Thus, explicitly or implicitly, discourses centred on Catholicism and repressed sexuality are conflated in a somewhat simplistic way, and not infrequently, the oppression encountered by those detained is viewed as being entirely attributable to Roman Catholicism in Ireland— see, for example, the Steve Humphries-produced documentary, *Witness: Sex in a Cold Climate* (Channel 4, 16 Mar. 1998). Such an approach fails to recognise and explain these institutions by placing them in a more encompassing conceptual framework that takes account of other emerging contemporary structures that were similarly seeking to incarcerate, demarcate, contain, and classify troublesome populations. In this context, see also Lara Marks, 'The Luckless Waifs and Strays of Humanity: Irish and Jewish Immigrant Unwed Mothers in London, 1870–1939', *Twentieth-Century British History* 3:2 (1992), pp 113–37.

44. Beatty, 'Strange Career.'

45. Devane, 'Indecent Literature', p. 202.

46. Beatty, 'Strange Career.'

47. Smith, *Ireland's Magdalen Laundries.*

48. Pierre Bourdieu, *Language and Symbolic Power* (Cambridge, 1991), p. 202.

49. Foucault, *Discipline and Punish*, p. 156.

50. R. S. Devane, 'The Unmarried Mother: Some Legal Aspects of the Problem, Part 1', *Irish Ecclesiastical Record*, 5th ser., 23 (1924), pp 55–68. See also M. H. MacInerny, 'A Postscript on the Souper Problem', *Irish Ecclesiastical Record*, 5th ser., 19 (1922), pp 246–61; Joseph Glynn, 'The Unmarried Mother', *Irish Ecclesiastical Record*, 5th ser., 18 (1921), 461–67; Sagart, 'How to Deal with the Unmarried Mother', *Irish Ecclesiastical Record*, 5th ser., 20 (1922), pp 145–54.

51. Devane, 'Unmarried Mother, Part 1', p. 64.

52. Ibid., p. 60.

53. Devane, 'Unmarried Mother, Part 2', p. 173. Perhaps Devane's protestations on this question contributed to the passing of the Illegitimate Children (Affiliation Orders) Act (1930). I am grateful to one of the peer reviewer's observations on this point. See also Maria Luddy, 'Moral Rescue and Unmarried Mothers in Ireland in the 1920s', *Women's Studies* 30.6 (2001), pp 809–13.

54. Devane, 'Unmarried Mother, Part 2', p. 174.

55. Ibid., p. 179. Across decades to come, his view remained key in interventions by other influential clerical figures. Monsignor Barrett, the primary definer of child adoption and unmarried mothers in the 1950s and 1960s, criticised 'non-Catholic social workers' in 'other countries' for becoming 'purely humanitarian.' According to Barrett, the 'emphasis is laid on her social and economic difficulties to the disregard of her moral problems. No cognisance is taken of the gravity of sin or the beauty of the virtue of purity.' See Cecil Barrett, *Adoption: The Parent, the Child, the Home* (Dublin, 1952), p. 23.

56. Devane, 'Unmarried Mother, Part 2', pp 180–1, p. 183.

57. The chairman of the commission, Charles H. O'Conor, was previously a member of the Local Government Board. He was joined by nine other commission members. Dr Thomas Hennessy was a medical practitioner and member of the governing party. He had been elected to Dáil Éireann at a by-election in the Dublin South constituency on 11 Mar. 1925, a few days prior to the appointment of the commission. Knighted in 1915, Sir Joseph Glynn (1869–1943), born in Gort, Co. Galway, had served as the chairman of the Galway County Council from 1902 to 1912. Glynn also served as chairman of the Natural Insurance Commissioners from 1911 to 1933 and appeared as a witness before the Carrigan committee. Now rarely registering in historical accounts, he was a significant figure whose funeral was attended by a range of dignitaries from Ireland's elite strata. Sir John Keane, a senator and barrister, was supportive of the government's austerity policies and an opponent of facets of censorship. Major James Myles was an independent TD for Donegal. He was elected in 1923 and again on a further six occasions. Serving in the British Army during the First World War, he had been awarded the Military Cross for bravery. The Right Reverend Monsignor Dunne and the Reverend M. E. Murphy were the religious personnel on the commission. Pádraig Ó Siochfhradha was the eighth member of the commission. Richard Corish was a TD who may have been appointed to symbolically incorporate Labour's reformist interests. A former blue-collar worker from Wexford, he had been blacklisted by employers because of his involvement in the 1913 Dublin Lockout. He had become a trade-union official and, as a Labour Party candidate, was also elected mayor of Wexford in 1920. The tenth commissioner was Jennie Wyse Power. A feminist, independent senator, and successful business entrepreneur, she was the only female member of the commission. Her report was tabled on 11 Oct. 1927. See also Donnacha Sean Lucey, *The End of the Irish Poor Law* (Manchester, 2015).

58. The minutes of evidence for the commission, bound in five volumes, are held by the Oireachtas Library in Dublin: volume 1 (27 May 1925–14 July 1925); volume 2 (15 July 1925–22 Oct. 1925); volume 3 (3 Nov. 1925–19 Jan. 1926); volume 4 (20 Jan. 1926–11 Feb. 1926); volume 5 (10 Mar. 1926–17 Dec. 1926). Additional material relating to miscellaneous documents and correspondence is held by the Oireachtas Library. All evidence was provided in 1925.

59. Fitzgerald-Kenney, in her final year as a lady inspector for boarded-out children, had initially undertaken that role under the British administration in 1902. She was the sister of James Fitzgerald-Kenney, the Mayo TD appointed as the minister for justice after the assassination of Kevin O'Higgins. He served in this capacity in two cabinets of W. T. Cosgrave (1927–30 and 1930–32). This sibling relationship illuminates the network of familial and kinship ties that helped to forge an insular classed-based power elite within the new state.

60. Mary Cruice Witness Testimony, 16 July 1925 (Minutes of Evidence of the Commission on the Relief of the Sick and Destitute Poor, Oireachtas Library, Dublin [herafter cited as MEC]).

61. Seamas MacLysaght Witness Testimony, 11 June 1925 (MEC).

62. Lucy Desmond Witness Testimony, 16 Sept. 1925 (MEC).

63. Mary Cruice Witness Testimony, 16 July 1925 (MEC).

64. R. S. Devane Witness Testimony, 5 Nov. 1925 (MEC).

65. Jane Power Witness Testimony, 14 July 1925 (MEC).

66. Seamas MacLysaght Witness Testimony, 11 June 1925 (MEC). The Pelletstown Institution, on the Navan Road in Dublin, was later known as 'St. Patrick's Home.' See also James M. Smith, *Ireland's Magdalen Laundries*, 48–49. Smith's research reveals that the idea of enhanced classificatory practices had been mooted in early 1922 in correspondence passing between the Rev. Edward Byrne, Dublin's Roman

Catholic archbishop, and the Department of Local Government. Rev. Monsignor Dunne (one of the members of the 1927 commission) was also involved in these exchanges. As Smith observes, one of the main concerns of the church centred on its demand to be adequately reimbursed by the state for any relief to unmarried mothers provided by its charities.

67. Jane Power Witness Testimony, 14 July 1925 (MEC).
68. Seamas MacLysaght Witness Testimony, 11 June 1925 (MEC).
69. Jane Power Witness Testimony, 14 July 1925 (MEC).
70. Ibid.
71. R. S. Devane Witness Testimony, 5 Nov. 1925 (MEC).
72. Anneenee Fitzgerald-Kenney Witness Testimony, 15 July 1925 (MEC).
73. Jane Power Witness Testimony, 14 July 1925 (MEC).
74. Anneenee Fitzgerald-Kenney Witness Testimony, 15 July 1925 (MEC).
75. Ibid.
76. See also Noel Parry, Michel Rustin, and Carole Satyamurti, eds., *Social Work, Welfare, and the State* (London, 1979).
77. Anneenee Fitzgerald-Kenney Witness Testimony, 15 July 1925 (MEC).
78. Ibid.
79. Ibid. This was not to occur until eighty-six years later when in 2011 the Department of Children and Youth Affairs was established. In 2013 the Child and Family Agency, also referred to as Tusla, was created. It is answerable to the minister for children and youth affairs.
80. Mary Cruice Witness Testimony, 16 July 1925 (MEC).
81. Jane Power Witness Testimony, 14 July 1925 (MEC).
82. Mary Cruice Witness Testimony, 16 July 1925 (MEC).
83. Anneenee Fitzgerald-Kenney Witness Testimony, 15 July 1925 (MEC).
84. Ibid.
85. Jane Power Witness Testimony, 14 July 1925 (MEC).
86. Anneenee Fitzgerald-Kenney Witness Testimony, 15 July 1925 (MEC).
87. Ibid. Emphasis added.
88. Karl Marx, *Capital*, 799.
89. Mary Cruice Witness Testimony, 16 July 1925 (MEC).
90. Marx, *Capital*, 794.
91. Foucault, *Discipline and Punish*, p. 148.
92. *CRSDP*, 68. Emphasis added.
93. Lindsay Earner-Byrne, 'The Boat to England: An Analysis of the Official Reactions to the Emigration of Single Expectant Irishwomen to Britain, 1922–1972', *Irish Economic and Social History* 30 (2003), p. 57. See also Lindsay Earner-Byrne, *Mother and Child: Maternity and Child Welfare in Dublin, 1922–1960* (Manchester, 2007).
94. Paul Michael Garrett, 'The Abnormal Flight: The Migration and Repatriation of Irish Unmarried Mothers', *Social History* 25.3 (Oct. 2000), pp 330–43; Paul Michael Garrett, 'The Hidden History of the PFIs: The Repatriation of Unmarried Mothers and Their Children from England to Ireland in the 1950s and 1960s', *Immigrants and Minorities* 19.3 (2000), pp 25–44; Louise Ryan, 'Sexualising Emigration: Discourses of Irish Female Emigration in the 1930s', *Women's Studies International Forum* 25.1 (2002), pp 51–65; Jennifer Redmond, 'In the Family Way and Away from the Family: Examining the Evidence for Irish Unmarried Mothers in Britain, 1920s– 40s', in Elaine Farrell (ed.), *'She Said She Was in the Family Way': Pregnancy and Infancy in Modern Ireland* (London, Institute of Historical Research, 2012), pp 163–85.
95. See Williams, *Marxism and Literature*, Ch. 8. Here Williams usefully articulates

the 'dominant', in the 'residual', in and the 'emergent.' In any cultural formation these are always in dynamic interaction.

96. This is not to deny the continuing harm caused to many women, still alive, who were labeled and treated as unmarried mothers in Ireland's past.

97. Kathy Weeks, *The Problem of Work: Feminism, Marxism, Antiwork Politics, and Postwork Imaginaries* (Durham and London, 2011).

CHAPTER 14 – 'DISREMEMBRANCE': JOYCE AND IRISH PROTESTANT INSTITUTIONS

1. Previously published in *Éire-Ireland:An Interdisciplinary Journal of Irish Studies* 55, 1 (Spring/Summer 2020), pp 201–222, DOI: 10.1353/eir.2020.0008.

2. James Joyce to Stanislaus Joyce, Nov. 1906, *Letters*, Stuart Gilbert (ed.) (New York, 1966), vol. 2, p. 192. Joyce himself was familiar with Dublin's brothel scene from a relatively young age. We cannot presume, however, as Joyce does, that all those incarcerated in Dublin by Lamplight were prostitutes. As James Smith has noted in our conversations, Magdalen survivors have generally considered such an assumption a pejorative stereotype.

3. Marian Eide, 'James Joyce's Magdalenes', *College Literature* 38.4 (2011), pp 57–75; Margot Norris, 'Narration under a Blindfold: Reading Joyce's "Clay,"' in Margot Norris (ed.), *Suspicious Readings of Joyce's Dubliners* (Philadelphia, 2003), pp 140–57.

4. Mary Burke, 'Forgotten Remembrances: The 6 Jan. "Women's Christmas" and the 6 Jan. 1839 "Night of the Big Wind" in "The Dead,"' *James Joyce Quarterly* 54.3–4 (2017), notes 104, 110, 111. Furthermore, Bethesda is embedded in a discussion on pages 258–60 of the article, which I draw upon here.

5. Philip Hardy, *The New Picture of Dublin: Or, Stranger's Guide through the Irish Metropolis* (Dublin, 1831), pp 165–66.

6. Thomas P. Power, *A Flight of Parsons: The Divinity Diaspora of Trinity College Dublin* (Eugene, OR, 2018), p. 18.

7. Ibid., p. 18–19.

8. 'Dreadful Hurricane', *The Dublin Evening Mail*, 7 Jan. 1839, p. 2.

9. 'Hurricane in Dublin—Destructive Fire: From Our Own Correspondent', *The Times* [London], 10 Jan. 1839, p. 5.

10. M. D., 'The Poet and the Painter', *The Irish Monthly* 19 (1891), p. 432; 'The Late Awful Hurricane', *The Dublin Evening Mail*, 9 Jan. 1839, p. 3.

11. 'Hurricane in Dublin', p. 5.

12. James Joyce, 'The Dead', in *Dubliners* (New York, 1993), p. 214. All subsequent citations refer to this edition.

13. 'Hurricane in Dublin', p. 5.

14. 'Late Awful Hurricane', p. 3.

15. See Justice for Magdalenes Research, http://jfmresearch.com; James Smith, *Ireland's Magdalen Laundries and the Nation's Architecture of Containment* (Notre Dame, IN, 2007).

16. Joyce, 'Clay', in *Dubliners*, p. 96.

17. Maria Luddy, Foreword to Margaret Preston, in *Charitable Words: Women, Philanthropy, and the Language of Charity in Nineteenth-Century Dublin* (Westport, CT, 2004), pp x, xi.

18. Joseph Robins, *The Lost Children: A Study of Charity Children in Ireland, 1700–1900* (Dublin, 1980), pp 118–19, 122, 118.

19. Quoted ibid., p. 122.

20. Ibid., p. 294.

21. Rosa Barrett, *Guide to Dublin Charities* (Dublin, 1884), p. 78. Factors other than sectarian difference led to the abuse of vulnerable children in disordered colonial Ireland, but sectarianism links the experiences of such children across centuries.

22. In response to estimates that eighty percent of children living in the world's orphanages at present have at least one living parent and are placed therein because of the economic benefits of 'voluntourism', in Australia became the first country in the world to recognise so-called 'orphanage trafficking' as a form of modern-day slavery in the Modern Slavery Act (No.153, 2018).

23. 'When adoption is pitched, the needs of the paying customer (i.e. the prospective adoptive parent) get elevated. If the parents are the clients, this means that the child . . . becomes the object of exchange, . . . tak[ing] on an objectified role because to be chosen, it inevitably means that another child gets passed over Thus the process of choosing and being chosen is one of consumption.' See Elizabeth Raleigh, *Selling Transracial Adoption: Families, Markets, and the Color Line* (Philadelphia, 2017), p. 2.

24. See the reference to the adoptee's 'wonderful Irish blue eyes' in 'Puts a Word in for Pal; Brings Luck o' the Irish', *The Chicago Daily Tribune*, 5 Dec. 1949, p. 1. Repeated references to adoptees' 'fair' hair and blue eyes in the period is a dog whistle revealed more directly in the words of a nun interviewed about the trade: 'Irish children are pure-blooded.' See 'Irish Police Say 50 Babies Sold to U.S. Couples', *The Boston Sunday Globe*, 2 Jan. 1955, p. 34.

25. See Mary Burke, 'The Cottage, the Castle, and the *Couture* Cloak: "Traditional" Irish Fabrics and "Modern" Irish Fashions in America, c. 1952–1969', *Journal of Design History* 31.4 (2018), pp 364, 365, 369–70, 372–73.

26. Swift's speaker, who suggests fattening up Irish toddlers and feeding them to native landlords, concedes with seeming regret that 'this kind of commodity will not bear exportation.' Jonathan Swift, 'A Modest Proposal' (1729), *Prose Works of Jonathan Swift*, 2 vols. (London, 1841), vol. 2, p. 102.

27. Anne Phelan call to *Gay Byrne Show*, RTÉ Radio 1, 4 Mar. 1996, quoted in Mike Milotte, *Banished Babies* (Dublin, 1997), p. 68.

28. Sr. Elizabeth to Fr. Mangan, 4 June 1951 (McQuaid Papers, American Adoptions, File 1950–57, Dublin Archdiocesan Archives, Dublin [hereafter cited as DAA]). Sr. Frances Elizabeth headed St. Patrick's Guild, founded in 1910 to care for illegitimate Catholic babies.

29. This organised kidnapping of children for transportation to the British crown's American colonies was to feed its demand for indentured servants. See James Kelly, '"This Iniquitous Traffic": The Kidnapping of Children for the American Colonies in Eighteenth-Century Ireland', *Journal of the History of Childhood and Youth* 9.2 (2016), pp 236, 234.

30. 'Irish Orphans Fly in, Meet New Parents', *The New York Times*, 18 Mar. 1950, p. 30.

31. 'Enterprise in Old Erin', *Life*, 10 Aug. 1953, p. 47.

32. Milotte, *Banished Babies*, pp 11–12.

33. 'Woman Turns Tables on Husband Bringing 2 Orphans as "Surprise,"' *The New York Times*, 29 July 1949, p. 23.

34. 'Irish Tot Arrives for Adoption', *The Chicago Daily Tribune*, 21 Sept. 1958, p. 11.

35. One article notes without comment that an Irish toddler was being adopted by a single adult male, another child had never had orange juice, and a third had never seen a dog. See Ruth Moss, 'Bachelor "Dad" Whisks 2 Boys to Wonderland: Kids from Ireland Learn about Toys—and Dog', *The Chicago Daily Tribune*, 7 May 1951, p. 17.

36. Milotte, *Banished Babies*, pp 199–201, p. 186.

37. 'American Adoptions Criticised in Ireland', *The Washington Post and Times Herald*, 20 July 1956, p.16.

38. Milotte, *Banished Babies*, p. 22, 26.

39. Ibid., pp 15–16.

40. See the relevant census records and the obituary of McDowell's Irish-born grandfather, which lists his funeral at a Methodist church: J. Allen Crider, 'Crider-McDowell Family Tree: McDowell, Rollie William', in and 'Crider-McDowell Family Tree: McDowell, Adolphus Linn', in *Crider and McDowell Families Genealogy*, 2014, http://www.cridermcdowellfamily.com/genealogy/ppl/2/9/ce970d0347567c-537c28ae79292.html, archived at https://perma.cc/657R-A624, http://www.cridermcdowellfamily.com/genealogy/ppl/a/8/ce970d028797092dc389bd7918a.html, archived at https://perma.cc/LR63-SLG4; Ed and Sandy Mackley, 'Obituaries: A. L. McDowell', in *Mackley Genealogy*, 2009, http://mackleygenealogy.com/~mackley/Obit_ Display.php?pid=MC_000768.jpg, archived at https://perma.cc/5AMU-PFVW.

41. Although Braemar House 'was not formally linked to the Church of Ireland', in 2015 Church of Ireland bishop Dr Paul Colton referred to it as a 'pan-Protestant' institution when calling on Judge Murphy and Minister James Reilly to widen the scope of the mother-and-baby home inquiry to include Protestant institutions. See Conall Ó Fátharta, 'Scrutinise Protestant Mother and Baby Home', *The Irish Examiner*, 13 Oct. 2015.

42. Document Titled 'Some Reasons against Sending Children to America for Adoption', 14 Mar. 1950 (McQuaid Papers, American Adoptions, File 1950–57, DAA).

43. Fr. Barrett to Fr. Mangan (McQuaid's Secretary), 29 May 1951 (ibid.).

44. Paul Michael Garrett, '"Unmarried Mothers" in the Republic of Ireland', *Journal of Social Work* 16.6 (2016), pp 718–20. Founded in 1913, CPRSI is currently known as Cúnamh (http://www.cunamh.com)

45. Milotte, *Banished Babies*, p. 44, 58.

46. Hugh Curran, 'Irish Restrict Baby Adopters to Catholics', *The Chicago Sunday Tribune*, 22 Apr. 1951, p. 27.

47. Ireland's ostensibly secular authorities genuflected to the archbishop, as in this letter regarding McQuaid's initial opposition to legal adoption: 'Please accept our thanks for your Grace's most helpful and prompt advice about the scripts on legal adoption which you were so good as to read and consider in relation to our status as a state institution.' See Francis MacManus, Radio Éireann, to Archbishop McQuaid, 22 July 1948 (Adoption Legislation, File 1948–52, Department of Justice and Equality Archive, Dublin, Ireland [hereafter cited as DJA]).

48. Document Headed 'The following are the conditions required by his Grace the Archbishop before he allows the adoption of a Catholic child from the diocese of Dublin by an American or other family', n.d. (McQuaid Papers, American Adoptions, File 1950–57, DAA).

49. Memo of Telephone Message to Archbishop McQuaid from Mr Coyne of the Department of Justice, 13 Mar. 1953 (Adoption Legislation, 1948–52, DJA).

50. Milotte, *Banished Babies*, p. 62.

51. 'Irish Police Say 50 Babies Sold to U.S. Couples', p. 34.

52. 'Baby Kidnappings in Ireland Linked to U.S. Officers', *The Boston Daily Globe*, 21 Dec. 1954, 11; Milotte, *Banished Babies*, pp 66–8, p. 113.

53. Eudora Welty, "The Bride of The Innisfallen," in *The Bride of The Innisfallen and Other Stories* (New York, 1955), pp 47–83, p. 54.

54. Marianne Elliott, *Hearthlands: A Memoir of the White City Housing Estate in Belfast* (Belfast, 2017), pp 90–7.

55. In the photo of the children taken on their arrival and captioned 'Youngsters Here from Irish Orphanage', in an anxious Michael James clutches the unsmiling four-month-old Patricia Frances, who has a 'Hold [checked-in] TWA' label attached to her wrist. See 'Woman Turns Tables on Husband Bringing 2 Orphans as "Surprise,"' *The New York Times*, 29 July 1949.

56. Derek Leinster, *Hannah's Shame* (Long Preston: Magna, 2011), p. 30.

57. Of a total of 219 dead children for the period 1922–49, 54 died from convulsions, 41 from heart failure, and 26 from marasmus (malnutrition). Well over one-third of Bethany's child deaths in those years occurred in 1935–39, and nearly two-thirds, or 132, died in the 1935–44 period. See Niall Meehan, 'Church and State and the Bethany Home', supplement to *History Ireland* 18.5 (2010), p. 2, https://www.history ireland.com/wp-content/uploads/2013/05/Bethany_HI_expanded__plus_mag_ver_ Sep-Oct2010_.pdf, archived at https://perma.cc/5PGV-3B7G.

58. James Joyce, *Ulysses*, Hans Walter Gabler (ed.) (New York, 1993), 6, p. 512, 514.

59. Meehan, 'Church and State', p. 7.

60. Carol Coulter, 'Claim of Abuse at Children's Home Being Investigated by Health Board', *The Irish Times*, 9 Feb. 2001, p. 4.

61. Carol Coulter, 'Not Just One Protestant People', *The Irish Times*, 16 Jan. 2003, p. 14.

62. Daragh Brophy, 'The Protestant Orphanage Where Children Were Whipped, Beaten—and Everyone Had the Same Name', *thejournal.ie* (July 2014), https://www. thejournal.ie/westbank-protestant-orphanage-1551863-Jul2014, archived at https:// perma.cc/8GD8-MB5V.

63. 'Claims of Abuse Shatter Image of Devout Auntie's Big, Happy Family', *The Sunday Independent*, 5 June 2011.

64. Leinster, *Hannah's Shame*, p. 8.

65. Coulter, 'Not Just One', p. 14.

66. Meehan, 'Church and State', p. 6.

67. Derek Leinster, 'Protestant Abuse Victims Must Also Be Heard', *The Irish Times*, 1 July 2009, p. 12.

68. Ibid.

69. Joyce, 'Clay', p. 96.

70. J. O. Siy and S. Cheryan, 'Prejudice Masquerading as Praise: The Negative Echo of Positive Stereotypes', *Personality and Social Psychology Bulletin* 42 (2016), pp 941–54.

71. Breda O'Brien, 'State Must Apologise for Dire Conditions of Bethany Home', *The Irish Times*, 23 Feb. 2013, p. 14.

72. Meehan, 'Church and State', p. 7.

73. Both Meehan and Leinster contributed a media package during the height of the Justice for Magdalenes campaign in 2014. Although Bethany was not a Magdalen institution in the strict sense, it functioned as what Smith called an institutional 'catch-all-catch-can for Protestant women in trouble.' Personal communication, James Smith to author, 2 July 2018.

74. Leinster explicitly blames both his church and the state, concluding that he was 'totally abandoned by all authority.' Leinster, *Hannah's Shame*, p. 7.

75. In response to eighteenth-century authorities' failure to make child kidnapping a felony, mobs sometimes attacked the (often female) snatchers. Although the numbers involved can only be surmised, in one day alone in 1781, credible press accounts recorded that fifty-two kidnapped children who were being forcibly held for deportation were rescued by members of the public. See Kelly, 'This Iniquitous Traffice', p. 233, 239.

76. 'Ireland', *The Times* [London], 28 Mar. 1892, p. 10.

77. Rev. Samuel Cotton, 'The Foundling', *The Three Whispers and Other Tales* (Dublin, 1870), pp 149–218.
78. 'A Reverend Brute Convicted', *The New York Times*, 30 Mar. 1892, p. 9.
79. Robins, *Lost Children*, p. 309.
80. Joyce, *Finnegans Wake* (New York, 1999), I. 5.108, lines 19, 24–5.
81. Cathy Caruth, *Unclaimed Experience: Trauma, Narrative, and History* (Baltimore, 1996), p. 4.
82. McAleer and Rushe, the UK architectural firm in charge of the 2006–7 Maldron Hotel renovation, has not responded to my July 2019 inquiry regarding the wall fragment.

CHAPTER 15 – 'ILLEGITIMATE' KNOWLEDGE:
TRANSITIONAL JUSTICE AND ADOPTED PEOPLE

1. This essay was previously published in *Éire-Ireland: An Interdisciplinary Journal of Irish Studies* 55.1 (Spring/Summer 2020), pp 181–200, DOI: 10.1353/eir.2020.0007.
2. See, for example, 'The Gathering Ireland', *Discover Ireland*, 2020, https://www.discoverireland.ie/The-Gathering-Ireland.
3. Such a closed, secret adoption system was not unique to Ireland.
4. Adoption Act (25/1952), *Electronic Irish Statute Book* (hereafter cited as *EISB*), http://www.irishstatutebook.ie/eli/1952/act/25/enacted/en/html.
5. Ibid. An example of the preoccupation with interference from natural mothers can be found in Cecil J. Barrett, *Adoption: The Parent, the Child, the Home* (Dublin, 1952), pp 51–2.
6. Registration of Births and Deaths (Ireland) Act (1863), 26 & 27 Vict. c.11; Department of Employment Affairs and Social Protection, 'Search Room at the General Register Office (GRO)', *Rialtas na hÉireann/Government of Ireland*, 9 June 2020, https://www.welfare.ie/en/Pages/GRO_Research.aspx.
7. Through its website the Adoption Rights Alliance (http://adoption.ie) provides information to adopted people on how to obtain their birth certificates by a process of elimination using the civil-registration system and other data, such as nonidentifying information provided by adoption agencies, personal data obtained through subject-access requests under data protection legislation and, more recently, information acquired through DNA testing.
8. Maeve O'Rourke, Claire McGettrick, Rod Baker, Raymond Hill, et al., *CLANN: Ireland's Unmarried Mothers and Their Children: Gathering the Data: Principal Submission to the Commission of Investigation into Mother and Baby Homes* (Dublin, Oct. 2018), pp 88–9, p. 96, 105, http://clannproject.org/wp-content/uploads/Clann-Submissions_Redacted-Public-Version-Oct.-2018.pdf, archived at https://perma.cc/38CR-YLT2. The CLANN project testimonies informed a submission made by Justice for Magdalenes Research (JFMR) and Adoption Rights Alliance (ARA) to the Commission of Investigation into Mother and Baby Homes.
9. Department of Health and Children, 'Hanafin Announces New Draft Legislation on Adoption Information', *An Roinn Sláinte/Department of Health*, 24 May 2001, https://health.gov.ie/blog/press-release/hanafin-announces-new-draft-legislation-on-adoption-information, archived at https://perma.cc/D3M5-KB7T.
10. Department of Health and Children, *Heads of Proposed Adoption Information, Post-Adoption Contact, and Associated Issues Bill* (Dublin, Stationery Office, 2001).
11. Department of Health and Children, 'Hanafin Announces New Draft Legislation.'
12. Department of Health and Children, *Adoption Legislation Consultation Discussion Paper* (Dublin Stationery Office, 2003).

13. Michael Brennan, 'Laws Could "Criminalise" Adopted Children', *The Irish Examiner*, 23 July 2003, 10; Evelyn Ring, 'Adopted Seeking Parents Not Criminal', *The Irish Examiner*, 18 Oct. 2003, p. 4.

14. Department of Health and Children, 'Minister Brian Lenihan Launches the Adoption Board's National Adoption Contact Preference Register', *An Roinn Sláinte/Department of Health*, 30 Mar. 2005, https://health.gov.ie/blog/press-release/minister-brian-lenihan-launches-the-adoption-boards-national-adoption-contact-preference-register, archived at https://perma.cc/4CMA-NBGG.

15. Department of Health and Children, *Adoption Legislation*, p. 2.

16. Adoption Act (21/2010), *EISB*, http://www.irishstatutebook.ie/eli/2010/act/21/enacted/en/print.html; The Hague Conference on Private International Law, *Hague Convention on Protection of Children and Co-operation in Respect of Intercountry Adoption* (The Hague Conference on Private International Law, 1993).

17. Conall Ó Fátharta, 'A Hidden Heritage', *The Irish Examiner*, 20 Apr. 2010, 8–9; O'Rourke et al., *CLANN*, 85–105.

18. Dan Barry, 'The Lost Children of Tuam', *The New York Times*, 28 Oct. 2017.

19. Department of Children and Youth Affairs, 'Minister Reilly Publishes Adoption Information and Tracing Legislation', Press Release, 27 July 2015.

20. Department of Children and Youth Affairs, *Heads and General Scheme of the Adoption (Information and Tracing) Bill, 2015* (Dublin Stationery Office, 2015).

21. Ibid., 55. Emphasis added. Minister Reilly referred the heads of bill to the Oireachtas Joint Committee on Health and Children for prelegislative scrutiny. When its work was completed, the committee said that 'based on the weight of evidence and the legal submissions received from witnesses, the committee [could] find no convincing reason for the inclusion of a statutory declaration in the bill.' See Oireachtas Joint Committee on Health and Children, *Report on the Pre-legislative Scrutiny of the General Scheme and Heads of the Adoption (Information and Tracing) Bill* (Dublin Stationery Office, 2015), p. 12.

22. Adoption (Information and Tracing) Seanad Bill (100/2016), *Tithe an Oireachtais/Houses of the Oireachtas*, https://www.oireachtas.ie/en/bills/bill/2016/100.

23. Adoption Rights Alliance, *Briefing Note and Amendments to Adoption Information and Tracing Bill, 2016* (Dublin, 2019).

24. Conall Ó Fátharta and Elaine Loughlin, 'Thousands May Have Been Illegally Adopted', *The Irish Examiner*, 30 May 2018.

25. Claire McGettrick, '"Old Ireland" Still Exists for Adoptees', *The Irish Examiner*, 2 June 2018; Conall Ó Fátharta, 'Adoption Bill's Privacy Provisions to Be Revised', *The Irish Examiner*, 27 Feb. 2019.

26. 'Adoption (Information and Tracing) Bill, 2016: Committee Stage', *Seanad Debates*, 266, 12 June 2019, 2. This bill was initiated in the Seanad. It has yet to be debated in the Dáil.

27. Ibid., 2.

28. Adoption Rights Alliance, 'Adoption Rights Alliance Incredulous at Progression of Deeply Discriminatory Bill', *Adoption Rights Alliance*, 8 June 2019, http://adoption.ie/wp-content/uploads/2019/06/ARA-press-release-08-06-19.pdf, archived at https://perma.cc/76J5-8ZNH. See also Caitríona Palmer, 'The State Demonises Adoptees as a Threat to Their Natural Parents', *The Irish Times*, 28 June 2019, and Claire McGettrick, 'Zappone's Haste Risks Further Offending Adopted People', *The Irish Examiner*, 14 June 2019.

29. See, for example, Claire McGettrick, Susan Lohan, Mari Steed, and Angela Murphy, *Letter to TDs and Senators* (Dublin, 2019).

30. Adoption Rights Alliance, 'Adoption Bill: Previous News', *Adoption Rights*

Alliance, 2019, http://adoption.ie/adoption-bill-previous-news, archived at https:// perma.cc/9ET6-FWCQ.

31. Conall Ó Fátharta, 'Adoptees Write to Zappone to Express Disgust', *The Irish Examiner*, 17 Aug. 2019; 'Adoption, Information and Tracing: Statements', (266 No. 5), *Seanad Debates*, 19 June 2019, *EISB*, https://www.oireachtas.ie/en/debates/debate/seanad/2019-06-19/12.

32. Joint Committee on Children, Equality, Disability, Integration and Youth Report on pre-legislative scrutiny of the General Scheme of the Birth Information and Tracing Bill, December 2021. https://data.oireachtas.ie/ie/oireachtas/committee/dail/33/joint_committee_on_children_equality_disability_integration_and_youth/reports/2021/2021-12-14_report-on-pre-legislative-scrutiny-of-the-birth-information-and-tracing-bill_en.pdf

33. Orla Ryan, 'Adopted people to get access to their birth certs and other records under new legislation', *thejournal.ie*, 12 Jan. 2022. https://www.thejournal.ie/birth-information-and-tracing-bill-adopted-people-ireland-5651940-Jan2022/.

34. For example, Ivana Bacik TD, Birth Information and Tracing Bill 2022: Second Stage https://www.oireachtas.ie/en/debates/debate/dail/2022-01-19/speech/199/.

35. Erica Haimes and Noel Timms, *Adoption, Identity, and Social Policy: The Search for Distant Relatives* (Aldershot, UK, 1985), pp 19–21, p. 27.

36. Ibid., p. 80. 36.

37. Ibid., pp 80–1.

38. John Triseliotis, 'Obtaining Birth Certificates', in Philip Bean (ed.), *Adoption: Essays in Social Policy, Law, and Sociology* (London and New York, 1984), p. 46.

39. Ibid.

40. Ibid.

41. Ibid., p. 51.

42. Unless they were illegally adopted and registered as the natural child of their adoptive parents.

43. The Department of Justice had responsibility for adoption until 1983; however, at that point it was transferred to the Department of Health (which subsequently became the Department of Health and Children). See Justice (Transfer of Departmental Administration and Ministerial Functions) Order (S.I1982/327), *EISB*, http://www.irishstatutebook.ie/eli/1982/si/327/made/en/print?q=S.I.+No.+327+of+1982.

44. Prior to the introduction of the GDPR, these requests were made under the Data Protection Acts (1988–2018). Adoption records are exempt from freedom-of-information requests in Ireland.

45. For further information on adoption myths and facts, see Adoption Rights Alliance, *Briefing Note*, 4–6.

46. O'Rourke et al., *CLANN*, 92.

47. Triseliotis, 'Obtaining Birth Certificates', p. 51.

48. Haimes and Timms, *Adoption*, 50.

49. Ibid., p. 51. Emphasis in original.

50. Ibid.

51. See, for example, Caitríona Palmer, *An Affair with My Mother: A Story of Adoption, Secrecy, and Love* (Dublin, 2016), and *Secrets and Lies*, directed by Mike Leigh (London: Oct. Films, 1996), DVD.

52. Jo Woodiwiss, 'What's Wrong with Me? A Cautionary Tale of Using Contemporary "Damage Narratives" in Autobiographical Life Writing', in Kerstin W. Shands, Giulia Grillo Mikrut, Dipti R. Pattanaik, and Karen Ferreira-Meyers (eds), *Writing the Self: Essays on Autobiography and Autofiction* (Huddinge, SE, 2015), p. 184.

53. See, for example, Betty Jean Lifton, *Lost and Found: The Adoption Experience*

(New York, 1979); Nancy Newton Verrier, *The Primal Wound: Understanding the Adopted Child* (Baltimore, 1993).

54. Verrier, *Primal Wound*, 1; Betty Jean Lifton, *Journey of the Adopted Self: A Quest for Wholeness* (New York, 1994), p. 7, pp 92–3.

55. Woodiwiss, 'What's Wrong', p. 185. Also see Heidi Marie Rimke, 'Governing Citizens through Self-Help Literature', *Cultural Studies* 14.1 (2000), pp 70–1.

56. Rimke, 'Governing Citizens', p. 62, 72.

57. Jennifer Bray and Mark Hilliard, 'Identifying People Adopted Illegally Is "Slow Work", Says Tusla', *The Irish Times*, 25 Apr. 2019; Conall Ó Fátharta, 'No Date for Report on Scoping Exercise', *The Irish Examiner*, 16 Sept. 2019.

58. Joe Little, 'Package of Supports for Mother and Baby Home Survivors Announced', *RTÉ News*, 16 Apr. 2019, https://www.rte.ie/news/2019/0416/1043016-mother-and-baby-homes-zappone; Conall Ó Fátharta, 'Forum Members Dismayed by Refusal to Publish Mother and Baby Homes Report in Full', *The Irish Examiner*, 16 Apr. 2019. The Collaborative Forum is a government-appointed group comprised of adopted people, natural mothers, and relatives of children who died in mother-and-baby homes.

59. Haimes and Timms, *Adoption*, pp 56–7.

60. Anselm L. Strauss, *Mirrors and Masks: The Search for Identity* (New Brunswick, NJ, 1997), p. 17.

61. Anecdotal evidence suggests that some adoptive parents were brought to nurseries in institutions such as Temple Hill in Blackrock, Co. Dublin, and allowed to choose a child.

62. O'Rourke et al., *CLANN*, pp 85–105.

63. Haimes and Timms, *Adoption*, p. 51.

64. Miranda Fricker, *Epistemic Injustice: Power and the Ethics of Knowing* (Oxford, 2007), p. 155, pp 158–9.

65. See, for example, Verrier, *Primal Wound*, pp 150–65; David M. Brodzinsky, Marshall D. Schechter, and Robin Marantz Henig, *Being Adopted: The Lifelong Search for Self* (New York, 1993), pp 128–29; Marshall D. Schechter and Doris Bertocci, 'The Meaning of the Search', in David M. Brodzinsky and Marshall D. Schechter (eds), *The Psychology of Adoption* (New York, 1990), pp 71–85; Haimes and Timms, *Adoption*, p. 76.

66. Ibid.

67. See, for example, E. Wayne Carp, *Adoption Politics: Bastard Nation and Ballot Initiative 58* (Lawrence, 2004), pp 13–24.

68. Personal communication from early AAA member. See also Adopted People's Association, 'The Adult Adoptee's Association', *adoptionreland.com*, May 2000, http://www.connect.ie/~apa/apa/contacts/aaa.htm, archived at https://perma.cc/4PNU-7HJ3.

69. Ibid.

70. 'Adoption Action', *The Irish Times*, 10 Nov. 1992, p. 29; Mairéad Nally, 'Call for Free Information for Adopted Children and Both Sets of Their Parents', *The Limerick Chronicle*, 13 Dec. 1994, p. 3.

71. Eileen Ryan, 'Secret Adoption', *The Irish Press*, 25 Aug. 1992, p. 25. The AAA also reproduced Betty Jean Lifton's charter, *Rights and Responsibilities for Everyone in the Adoption Circle*, in handouts provided to attendees at support meetings. See Lifton, *Lost and Found*, pp 274–79.

72. Eileen Ryan, 'Secret Adoption', p. 25.

73. Haimes and Timms, *Adoption*, p. 53.

74. Ibid., p. 50. This paradigm also presumes that any approach made by an adopted person to his or her natural mother or family members will be unwanted.

75. See, for example, Verrier, *Primal Wound*, pp 150–65; Brodzinsky, Schechter, and Henig, *Being Adopted*, pp 128–29; Schechter and Bertocci, 'Meaning of the Search', pp 71–85.
76. See also Eleana J. Kim, *Adopted Territory: Transnational Korean Adoptees and the Politics of Belonging* (Durham, 2010), p. 9.
77. Myrna L. Friedlander, 'Adoption: Misunderstood, Mythologized, Marginalized', *The Counseling Psychologist* 31.6 (2003), pp 745–52.
78. For example, in Jan. 2010 the Irish government suspended intercountry adoptions from Vietnam because of two damning reports highlighting serious issues in that country's adoption practices in which the principles of the Hague Convention had been flouted in favour of the demands of prospective adopters seeking 'available' children. See Hervé Boéchat, Nigel Cantwell, and Mia Dambach, *Adoption from Viet Nam: Findings and Recommendations of an Assessment* (Geneva, 2009); Ministry of Labour, Invalids, and Social Affairs, *Creating a Protective Environment for Children in Vietnam: An Assessment of Child Protection Laws and Policies, Especially Children in Special Circumstances in Vietnam* (Hanoi, 2009); Department of Health and Children, 'Minister Barry Andrews T.D. Announces Government Decision to Suspend Bilateral Inter-country Adoption Negotiations with Vietnam', Press Release, 14 Jan. 2010.
79. Since the 1990s historians, literary scholars, and others writing about the treatment of unmarried mothers and their children in Ireland have made an invaluable contribution to our understanding of the historical, social, and cultural contexts of adoption. For example, see Sandra L. McAvoy, 'The Regulation of Sexuality in the Irish Free-State, 1929–35', in Greta Jones and Elizabeth Malcolm (eds), *Medicine, Disease, and the State in Ireland, 1650–1940* (Cork, 1999), 253–66; Maria Luddy, 'Sex and the Single Girl in 1920s and 1930s Ireland', *Irish Review* 35 (Summer 2007), pp 79–91; James M. Smith, *Ireland's Magdalen Laundries and the Nation's Architecture of Containment* (Notre Dame, IN, 2007); Lindsey Earner-Byrne, *Mother and Child: Maternity and Child Welfare in Dublin, 1922–60* (Manchester, 2007); Jennifer Redmond, '"Sinful Singleness"? Exploring the Discourses on Irish Single Women's Emigration to England, 1922–1948', *Women's History Review* 17.3 (2008), pp 455–76; Donnacha Seán Lucey, *The End of the Irish Poor Law? Welfare and Healthcare Reform in Revolutionary and Independent Ireland* (Manchester, 2015), pp 82–118; Paul Michael Garrett, '"Unmarried Mothers" in the Republic of Ireland', *Journal of Social Work* 16.6 (2016), pp 708–25.
80. Haimes and Timms, *Adoption*, p. 12, 63, 76.
81. Ibid., pp 76–7.
82. Ibid., p. 77.
83. In 1999 taoiseach Bertie Ahern apologised to people who had been abused in residential institutions as children. Following the apology the state set up the Commission to Inquire into Child Abuse and the Residential Institutions Redress Board. In 2011 the government established the Inter-departmental Committee to Establish the Facts of State Involvement with the Magdalen Laundries; however, an official state apology to Magdalen survivors would not come until 2013. In 2015 the government established a Commission of Investigation into Mother and Baby Homes.
84. Vivienne Darling, 'Social Work in Adoption: Vignette', in Noreen Kearney and Caroline Skehill (eds), *Social Work in Ireland: Historical Perspectives* (Dublin, 2005), p. 187; O'Rourke et al., *CLANN*, p. 80.
85. Harold J. Abramson, *Issues in Adoption in Ireland* (Dublin, 1984), p. 53.
86. UN Office of the High Commissioner for Human Rights, *Transitional Justice and Economic, Social, and Cultural Rights* (UN Doc. HR/PUB/13/5, 11 Apr. 2014), p. 5.

87. The same is true of people raised in informal-care settings and others affected by historical abuse.

88. Precise figures for the number of adoptions from mother-and-baby homes, public hospitals, private hospitals, private nursing homes, etc., are not currently available. Commission of Investigation (Mother and Baby Homes and Certain Related Matters) (SI 2015/57), *EISB*, http://www.irishstatutebook.ie/eli/2015/si/57/made/en/html. ARA and JFMR are aware of over 180 agencies, institutions, and individuals that were involved with unmarried mothers and their children. For a critique of the Commission of Investigation and its processes and operation, see O'Rourke et al., *CLANN*, pp 129–34.

89. O'Rourke et al., *CLANN*, pp 134–7.

90. See ibid., pp 85–105. Donor-conceived children in Ireland have few identity rights, and although plans exist to outlaw anonymous egg and sperm donations, the relevant parts of the Children and Family Relationships Act (2015) have not been enacted.

91. Adoption Act (21/2010), *EISB*, http://www.irishstatutebook.ie/eli/2010/act/21/enacted/en/html.

92. See, for example, Rosita Boland, 'Changes to Adoption Law Have Shattered My Hopes of Becoming a Parent', *The Irish Times*, 8 Mar. 2014.

Chapter 16 – 'It Steadies Me to Tell These Things': Memoir and the Redemptive Power of Truth-Telling

1. This essay was previously published in *Éire-Ireland: An Interdisciplinary Journal of Irish Studies* 55.1 (Spring/Summer 2020), pp 299–314, DOI: 10.1353/eir.2020.0013.

2. Caitríona Palmer, *An Affair with My Mother: A Story of Adoption, Secrecy, and Love* (Dublin, 2016).

3. A. M. Homes, *The Mistress's Daughter. A Memoir* (New York, 2007).

4. Brené Brown, 'Listening to Shame', TED, Mar. 2012,<https://www.ted.com/talks/brene_brown_listening_to_shame?language=en>.

5. Seamus Heaney, *Open Ground: Selected Poems, 1966–1996* (New York, 1998).

Chapter 17 – Transitional Justice, Trauma and Healing: Indigenous Residential Schools in Canada

1. I am very grateful to James Smith and Maeve O'Rourke for their generous support and guidance in the writing of this chapter.

2. TRC, 'Honouring the Truth, Reconciling for the Future: Summary of the Final Report of the Truth and Reconciliation Commission of Canada', (Ottawa, 2015).

3. This saying is attributed to Colonel Richard Henry Pratt, the founder of Carlisle Indian Boarding School in Pennsylvania, US. Pratt favoured a policy of 'aggressive assimilation', in stating 'All the Indian there is in the race should be dead. Kill the Indian in him, and save the man.' TRC of Canada, *Final Report of the Truth and Reconciliation Commission of Canada* (Canada, 2015), 1, p. 80.

4. Patrick Wolfe, 'Settler Colonialism and the Elimination of the Native', *Journal of Genocide Research* 8.4 (2006), pp 387–409.

5. Britain conquered New France in 1763 and Canada gained statehood with the 1867 British North America Act. French Catholic and British Protestant missionaries laid the foundations for the eventual 1883 residential school system that was operated by the churches in partnership with the federal government. This system drew on the industrial school model operating in Europe, as well as the Indian boarding schools

in the United States. Notably, Nicholas Flood Davin, an Irish immigrant to Canada, penned the influential 'Davin Report' in 1879 that pointed favourably to the Carlisle Indian Boarding School in Pennsylvania, US as a model. TRC of Canada, *Final Report of the Truth and Reconciliation Commission of Canada* (Canada, 2015), volume 1, p. 80. On the use of boarding schools for Indigenous peoples in the Americas, Australia, New Zealand, Russia, Asia, Africa and Scandinavia, see Andrea Smith, *Indigenous Peoples and Boarding Schools: A Comparative Study* (Prepared for the United Nations Permanent Forum for Indigenous Issues, 2010) E/C.19/2010/11. On the colonial origins of the Irish industrial schools, see Jane Barnes, *Irish Industrial Schools, 1868–1908: Origins and Development* (Dublin, 1989); Joseph Robins, *The Lost Children: A Study of Charity Children in Ireland, 1700–1900* (Dublin, 1980).

6. Paul Farmer, *Pathologies of Power: Health, Human Rights and the New War on the Poor* (Berkely and Los Angeles, 2003), p. 7.

7. 'Seven generations' is highly significant for a number of Indigenous peoples. The 'Seven Generations' principle is enshrined in the 1142 Great Law of the Haudenosaunee Confederacy. This principle states that the decisions we make today should result in a sustainable world seven generations into the future.

8. Jennifer Balint, Julie Evans, and Nesam McMillan, 'Rethinking Transitional Justice, Redressing Indigenous Harm: A New Conceptual Approach', *International Journal of Transitional Justice* 8.2 (2014), p. 212.

9. As claimed by then Minister of Aboriginal Affairs, John Duncan, in 2011. Taryn Della, 'Residential School Survivors Outraged over Duncan's Residential School Statement', *APTN news* 28 Oct. 2011.

10. This is the opening line in the Canadian Prime Minister's 2008 apology for residential schools (available at https://www.rcaanc-cirnac.gc.ca/eng/110010001564 4/1571589171655).

11. Balint, Evans, and McMillan, 'Rethinking Transitional Justice', p. 212.

12. For extensive reflections on my role as a settler, see Rosemary Nagy, 'Settler Witnessing at the Canadian Truth and Reconciliation Commission', *Human Rights Review* 21.3 (2020), pp 219–41.

13. For example, Sinead Pembroke, 'Exploring the Post-Release Experience of Former Irish Industrial School "Inmates"', *Irish Studies Review* (2017) 25.4, 454–71; Madeleine Dion Stout and Gregory D. Kipling, *Aboriginal People, Resilience and the Residential School Legacy* (Ottawa, 2014).

14. Statistics Canada, 'Aboriginal Peoples in Canada: Key Results from the 2016 Census', (Ottawa: Statistics Canada, 2016). Accessed 12 June 2020.

15. In this volume, see O'Donnell, O'Rourke and Smith, 'Introduction'; Claire McGettrick, chapter 15; James Gallen, chapter 12; and see Katherine Zappone, 'Love's Pursuit: An Approach to Transitional Justice in Ireland', *Éire-Ireland: An Interdisciplinary Journal of Irish Studies* 55, 1&2 (Spring/Summer 2020), pp 315-32.

16. In this volume, see Fionnuala Ní Aoláin, chapter 11; James Gallen, chapter 12; and James M. Smith, chapter 24, f. 17. For a summary of the 'structural critique' within the field as a whole, see Dustin N. Sharp, 'Interrogating the Peripheries: The Preoccupations of Fourth Generation Transitional Justice', *Harvard Human Rights Journal* 26 (2013), 149–78.

17. Balint, Evans, and McMillan, 'Rethinking Transitional Justice', p. 199.

18. Ibid., p. 214.

19. Ibid.

20. Ibid., p. 213.

21. Ibid., p. 206.

22. Miranda Fricker, 'Epistemic Justice as a Condition of Political Freedom?', *Synthese* 190.7 (2013), pp 1317–32.

23. Christine M. Koggel, 'Epistemic Injustice in a Settler Nation: Canada's History of Erasing, Silencing, Marginalizing', *Journal of Global Ethics* 14.2 (2018), p. 244.

24. Enright and Ring, chapter 7 in this volume; Claire McGettrick, chapter 15 in this volume; Maeve O'Rourke, chapter 6, in this volume; AnneMarie Crean and Fionna Fox, 'Ryan Report Follow-Up: Submission to the United Nations Committee against Torture', (Ireland: Reclaiming Self, 2017). Hereafter 'Reclaiming Self report'; Elaine Loughlin, 'Data Protection Commission seeks answers on destruction of mother and baby homes recordings', *The Irish Examiner,* 2 Feb. 2021, https://www.irishexaminer.com/news/arid-40218473.html.

25. Enright and Ring, chapter 7, in this volume, p. 8, p. 15.

26. See Máiréad Enright and Sinéad Ring, 'State Legal Responses to Historical Institutional Abuse: Shame, Sovereignty, and Epistemic Injustice', *Éire-Ireland: An Interdisciplinary Journal of Irish Studies* 55.1 (Spring/Summer 2020), p. 88.

27. O'Donnell, O'Rourke and Smith, in this volume.

28. Johan Galtung, 'Violence, Peace, and Peace Research', *Journal of Peace Research* 6.3 (1969), pp 167–91. Acute violence refers to direct, interpersonal violence.

29. On child abuse in Irish industrial schools, see *Report of the Commission to Inquire into Child Abuse ['The Ryan Report']* (Dublin: The Stationery Office, 2009); Mary Rafferty and Eoin O'Sullivan, *Suffer the Little Children: The Inside Story of Ireland's Industrial Schools* (New York, 2001).

30. On the double stigmatisation of mixed-race children in Irish industrial and reformatory schools, see the testimony of Rosemary Adaser and Conrad Bryan, chapter 1, in this volume.

31. On colonialism's 'civilizing mission', see TRC, *Summary Final Report*, p.46. On the gendered nature of settler colonialism, see Andrea Smith, *Conquest: Sexual Violence and American Indian Genocide* (Cambridge, MA, 2005).

32. Amy Bombay, Kimberly Matheson, and Hymie Anisman, 'The Intergenerational Effects of Indian Residential Schools: Implications for the Concept of Historical Trauma', *Transcultural Psychiatry* 51, 3 (2014), 320–38; Laurence J. Kirmayer, Joseph P. Gone, and Joshua Moses, 'Rethinking Historical Trauma', ibid.299–319.

33. Survivor of Port Alberni residential school, Walter Russell Jones, quoted in TRC, 'The Final Report of the Truth and Reconciliation Commission of Canada', (Ottawa: Truth and Reconciliation Commission of Canada, 2015), 5, p. 72.

34. Ibid., p. 5.

35. Ibid., p. 69.

36. Ibid., p. 6.

37. Ibid., p. 69, 174.

38. NIMMIWG, 'Reclaiming Power and Place: The Final Report of the National Inquiry in Missing and Murdered Indigenous Women and Girls', (Ottawa: National Inquiry on Missing and Murdered Indigenous Women and Girls, 2019).

39. See TRC, *Final Report*, vol. 5; NIMMIWG, *Reclaiming Power and Place*.

40. See Katherine Zappone, 'Love's Pursuit: An Approach to Transitional Justice in Ireland', pp 315–332, p. 326.

41. Crean and Fox, 'Reclaiming Self Report', 28, citing Carr, A. (2009) The psychological adjustment of adult survivors of institutional abuse in Ireland. Report submitted to the Commission to Inquire into Child Abuse, as cited in Ryan Report, Vol 5, pp 78–350.

42. Ibid.; Alan Carr, Barbara Dooley, Mark Fitzpatrick, Edel Flanagan, et al, 'Adult Adjustment of Survivors of Institutional Child Abuse in Ireland', *Child Abuse & Neglect* 34.7 (2010), pp 477–89.

43. Ibid., pp 28–9.

44. Ibid., p. 31.

45. Ibid., p. 28.

46. Ibid., pp 28–9.

47. 'Testimony', in this volume, p. 9.

48. Zappone, 'Love's Pursuit: An Approach to Transitional Justice in Ireland', p. 327.

49. Barbara Rylko-Bauer and Paul Farmer, 'Structural Violence, Poverty, and Social Suffering', in David Brady and Linda M. Burton, eds, *The Oxfood Handbook of the Social Science of Poverty* (Oxford, 2016), p. 47; see also Arthur Kleinman, Veena Das, and Margaret Lock, 'Introduction', in Arthur Kleinman, Veena Das, and Margaret Lock, eds, *Social Suffering* (Berkeley and Los Angeles, 1997), p. ix.

50. Clare Herrick and Kirsten Bell, 'Concepts, Disciplines and Politics: On "Structural Violence" and the "Social Determinants of Health,"' *Critical Public Health* (2020), pp 1–14.

51. Kleinman, Das, and Lock, 'Introduction', p. x.

52. Rylko-Bauer and Farmer, 'Structural Violence, Poverty, and Social Suffering.'; Galtung, 'Violence, Peace, and Peace Research.'

53. See 'Reclaiming Self report'; Justice for Magdalenes, Submission to the United Nations Committee Against Torture, 46th session, 2011 at http://jfmresearch. com/wp-content/uploads/2017/03/jfm_comm_on_torture_210411.pdf; Maeve O'Rourke, Claire McGettrick, Rod Baker, Raymond Hill et al., *CLANN: Ireland's Unmarried Mothers and their Children: Gathering the Data: Principal Submission to the Commission of Investigation into Mother and Baby Homes.* Dublin: Justice For Magdalenes Research, Adoption Rights Alliance, Hogan Lovells, 15 Oct. 2018.

54. Krista Maxwell, 'Historicizing Historical Trauma Theory: Troubling the Trans-Generational Transmission Paradigm', *Transcultural Psychiatry* 51.3 (2014), 407–35.

55. TRC, 'Final Report', vol. 5, p. 171; Joseph Gone, 'Redressing First Nations Historical Trauma: Theorizing Mechanisms for Indigenous Culture as Mental Health Treatment', *Transcultural Psychiatry* 50, 5 (2013), 683–706; Yvonne M. Boyer, 'Guidebook Supporting the Use of Natural Medicines in Culturally-Based Healing Practices for Nnadap/Nysap Counsellors', *Culturally Based Healing Practices Series* (Thunderbird Partnership Foundation, n.d.).

56. Rod McCormick, 'Aboriginal Approaches to Counselling', in *Healing Traditions: The Mental Health of Aboriginal Peoples in Canada*, ed. Laurence J. Kirmayer and Gail Guthrie Valaskis (Vancouver, 2009), p. 341.

57. Jo-Ann Episkenew, *Taking Back Our Spirits: Indigenous Literature, Public Policy and Healing* (Manitoba, 2009), p. 11.

58. Didier Fassin and Richard Rechtman, *The Empire of Trauma: An Inquiry into the Condition of Victimhood*, trans. Rachel Gomme (Princeton and Oxford, 2009), p. 279.

59. Dian Million, *Therapeutic Nations: Healing in an Age of Indigenous Human Rights* (Tucson, 2013), p. 84.

60. Ibid.

61. Gone, 'Redressing First Nations Historical Trauma', p. 687.

62. Maria Yellow Horse Braveheart and Lemyra M DeBruyn, 'The American Indian Holocaust: Healing Historical Unresolved Grief', *American Indian and Alaska Native Mental Health Research* 8, 2 (1998), pp 56–78.

63. Fassin and Rechtman, *Empire of Trauma*, p. 2.

64. Maxwell, 'Historicizing Historical Trauma Theory', pp 416–17.

65. Ibid.

66. James Waldram, 'Healing History? Aboriginal Healing, Historical Trauma, and Personal Responsibility', ibid., pp 370–86.

67. Kirmáyer, Gone, and Moses, 'Rethinking Historical Trauma', p. 307.

68. Ibid., p. 301. Emphasis added.

69. Ibid., p. 312.

70. Million, *Therapeutic Nations*, p. 150.

71. Sinéad Ring, 'Trauma and the Construction of Suffering in Irish Historical Child Sexual Abuse Prosecutions', *International Journal for Crime, Justice and Social Democracy* 6, 2 (2016), 88–103, pp 91–2.

72. Ibid., p. 93.

73. AnneMarie Crean, 'Survivor Advocate Submission', submission to the Oireachtas Joint Committee on Education and Skills regarding the Retention of Records Bill (Ireland, 2019), p. 2 at http://jfmresearch.com/wp-content/uploads/2019/10/Annemarie-Crean-Submission.pdf

74. See survivor Connie Roberts' poem, 'My People' in 'Testimony', chapter 1, in this volume.

75. Sara Ahmed, 'The Contingency of Pain', *Parallax* 8, 1 (2002), pp 17–34; Simon Robins, 'Failing Victims? The Limits of Transitional Justice in Addressing the Needs of Victims of Violations', *Human Rights and International Legal Discourse* 11, 1 (2017), pp 41–58. Enright and Ring, 'State Legal Responses', chapter 7, in this volume.

76. McGettrick, 'Illegitimate Knowledge', chapter 15, in this volume.

77. Ibid.

78. Maeve O'Rourke, 'Justice for Magdalenes Research, NGO Submission to the United Nations Committee Against Torture' (July 2017), https://tbinternet.ohchr.org/_layouts/15/treatybodyexternal/Download.aspx?symbolno=INT%2fCAT%2fCSS%2fIRL%2f27974&Lang=en.

79. Maeve O'Rourke, Claire McGettrick, Rod Baker, Raymond Hill et al., *CLANN: Ireland's Unmarried Mothers and their Children: Gathering the Data: Principal Submission to the Commission of Investigation into Mother and Baby Homes.* (Dublin, 2018), p. 134.

80. Rosemary Nagy, 'The Truth and Reconciliation Commission of Canada: Genesis and Design', *Canadian Journal of Law and Society* 29.2 (2014), pp 199–217.

81. Roughly 200,000 Indigenous children attended the day schools, with many enduring trauma, loss of language and culture, and physical and sexual abuse. Class action lawsuits for the day schools were settled in 2019 with a compensation package, but no avenue for truth-telling. Jessica Deer, 'What you need to know about filing an Indian day schools settlement claim', *CBC News*, 13 Jan. 2020, https://www.cbc.ca/news/indigenous/indian-day-schools-settlement-claims-1.5425226, accessed 26 May 2020.

82. The CEP payments are CAD $10,000 for the first year and an additional CAD $3,000 for each subsequent year spent in residential school. The IAP payments go to a maximum of $275,000. Of an estimated living 80,000 survivors living at the time of the IRSSA, 38,275 people applied with an 89% success rate. The average payment was $91,000 for a total of $3.232 billion. Indian Residential Schools Adjudication Secretariat, 'IAP Statistics: From Sept. 19, 2007 to Apr. 30, 2020', (2020) at http://www.iap-pei.ca/stats-eng.php.

83. On Ireland's legal constraints on the framing of justice demands, see Smith and Duff, chapter 8, in this volume.

84. Kathleen Mahoney, 'The Settlement Process: A Personal Reflection', *University of Toronto Law Journal* 64.4 (2014), pp 505–28.

85. Cited in Nagy, 'The Truth and Reconciliation Commission of Canada: Genesis and Design', p.13.

86. Matt James, 'A Carnival of Truth? Knowledge, Ignorance and the Canadian Truth and Reconciliation Commission', *International Journal of Transitional Justice* (2012), pp 1–23.

87. Indian Residential Schools Settlement Agreement, Schedule N, preamble.

88. TRC, 'What We Have Learned: Principles of Truth and Reconciliation', (Ottawa: Truth and Reconciliation Commission of Canada, 2015), p. 117.

89. Notably, by order of the courts, Independent Assessment Process records will be destroyed unless survivors indicate that they want them preserved in the NCTR archives.

90. See Elizabeth Kalbfleisch, 'Gesture of Reconciliation: The TRC *Medicine Box* as Communicative Thing', in Robinson D, Martin K (eds), *Arts of Engagement: Taking Aesthetic Action In and Beyond the Truth and Reconciliation Commission of Canada.* (Waterloo, ON, 2016).

91. James, 'A Carnival of Truth?.'

92. Ronald Niezen, 'Templates and Exclusions: Victim Centrism in Canada's Truth and Reconciliation Commission on Indian Residential Schools', *Journal of the Royal Anthropological Institute*, 4 (2016), p. 920, 932.

93. Dylan Robinson, 'Intergenerational Sense, Intergenerational Memeory', in *Arts of Engagement: Taking Aesthetic Action in and Beyond the Truth and Reconciliation Commission of Canada*, ed. Dylan Robinson and Keavy Martin (Waterloo, ON, 2016), p. 44.

94. Niezen, 'Templates and Exclusions.'; Robinson, 'Intergenerational Sense.'

95. Anne-Marie Reynaud, 'Dealing with Difficult Emotions: Anger at the Truth and Reconciliation Commission of Canada', *Anthropologica* 56.2 (2014), p. 377.

96. Rosemary Nagy and Emily Gillespie, 'Representing Reconciliation: A News Frame Analysis of Print Media Coverage of Indian Residential Schools', *Transitional Justice Review* 1, 3 (2015), 2, p. 17.

97. Sara Ahmed, 'The Politics of Bad Feeling', *Australian Critical Race and Whiteness Studies Association Journal* 1 (2005), pp 72–85.

98. Nagy and Gillespie, 'Representing Reconciliation', p. 19.

99. Niezen, 'Templates and Exclusions', p. 922.

100. Nagy, 'Settler Witnessing', p. 234.

101. TRC, 'Summary Final Report', pp 8–9, p. 14.

102. David B. MacDonald, *The Sleeping Giant Awakens: Genocide, Indian Residential Schools, and the Challenge of Conciliation* (Toronto, 2019), p. 126.

103. Kim Stanton, 'Looking Forward, Looking Back: The Canadian Truth and Reconciliation Commission on the Indian Residential Schools Legacy and the Mackenzie Valley Pipeline Inquiry', *Canadian Journal of Law and Society* 27.1 (2012), pp 81–99.

104. The governing Liberal party chose not to sponsor Indigenous Member of Parliament (Liberal) Robert-Falcon Ouelette's 2016 private member's genocide bill. MacDonald, *The Sleeping Giant Awakens*, p. 165.

105. Ibid., p. 169.

106. Environics Institute for Survey Research, 'Public Opinion About Aboriginal Issues in Canada 2016', (2016), p. 31.

107. Eva Jewell and Ian Mosby, 'Calls to Action Accountability: A Status Update on Reconciliation', (Toronto: Yellowhead Institute, 2019); Eva Jewel and Ian Mosby, 'Calls to Action Accountability: A 2021 Status Update on Reconciliation' (Toronto, Yellowhead Institute, 2021). To be fair, some recommendations will take longer to implement and there is a significant number of projects proposed or underway.

108. James, 'A Carnival of Truth?', p. 18.

109. TRC, 'Interim Report', (Ottawa: Truth and Reconciliation Commission of Canada, 2012).

CHAPTER 18 – 'I JUST WANT JUSTICE': THE IMPACT OF HISTORICAL
INSTITUTIONAL CHILD-ABUSE INQUIRIES FROM THE SURVIVOR'S PERSPECTIVE

1. This essay was previously published in *Éire-Ireland: An Interdisciplinary Journal of Irish Studies* 55.1 (Spring/Summer 2020), pp 252–78, DOI: 10.1353/eir.2020.0011. The author gives acknowledgment and thanks to the Leverhulme Trust for a Major Research Fellowship Grant (MRF-2015–124) that enabled the research for this article.

2. BBC, 'MLAs Vote for a Child Abuse Inquiry', *BBC News*, 2 Nov. 2009, http://news.bbc.co.uk/1/hi/northern_ireland/8338850.stm.

3. The narrow focus on residential institutions meant that survivors of clerical child abuse perpetrated outside residential care in churches, church halls, schools, and other locations were excluded; those in foster care and former residents of mother-and-baby homes were also omitted.

4. In this article the term survivor rather than victim is used whenever possible to describe those who suffered abuse and harm as children in residential institutions. It is acknowledged that the term victim may be appropriate in addition to, or instead of, survivor in some situations.

5. Anthony Hart, David Lane, and Geraldine Doherty, *Report of the Historical Institutional Abuse Inquiry (Vol. 1)*, *The Inquiry into Historical Institutional Abuse, 1922 to 1995* (Northern Ireland Executive Office, 2017), pp 8–42.

6. This research was approved by Ulster University's Ethics Committee.

7. Survivor groups facilitated access to participants through informal discussions enabled by individuals experienced in working with victims of historical human-rights abuse. The author attended the sessions. The format/research instrument was designed in collaboration with survivors, and the focus groups were recorded and transcribed with the permission of participants. See Patricia Lundy, *Historical Institutional Abuse: What Survivors Want from Redress* (research report, Ulster University, Mar. 2016).

8. survivors gave evidence in person to the inquiry. A further 87 submitted evidence through written witness statements only. The inquiry also heard from 194 witnesses who were not former residents (staff, police, and public officials), making a total of 527 people who gave evidence.

9. For example, were survivors able to say what they wanted to say to the inquiry? Were there adequate support services, information, preparation, and representation? Was the process helpful or challenging, and why?

10. Reasons for the lower response rate of 177 out of 246 giving oral evidence include the significant number of survivors who gave oral-evidence statements but did not show up to the statutory-inquiry public hearings; several were no longer alive. In these circumstances counsel summarized and read aloud previously given evidence/statements. On a few occasions the inquiry chairman had to adjourn proceedings because the survivor was too upset, and typically, these individuals did not return. Some survivors were simply not asked to comment on recommendations. Although the HIAI figure (246 persons) includes all of the above circumstances, percentages used in this article are based on the 177 who responded to counsel's questions.

11. Kathleen Daly, *Redressing Institutional Abuse of Children* (London, 2014), pp 163–7; Rhonda Claes and Deborah Clifton, *Needs and Expectations for Redress of Victims of Abuse at Residential Schools* (Ottawa Law Commission of Canada, 1998); Law Commission of Canada (LCC) (ed.), *Restoring Dignity: Responding to Child Abuse in Canadian Institutions* (Ottawa Law Commission of Canada, 2000), pp 249–60.

12. David A. Backer, 'The Human Face of Justice: Victims' Responses to South

Africa's Truth and Reconciliation Commission Process' (Ph.D. diss., University of Michigan, 2004); Robyn Holder and Kathleen Daly, 'Sequencing Justice: A Longitudinal Study of Justice Goals of Domestic Violence Victims', *British Journal of Criminology* 58.4 (2017), pp 778–80.

13. Robyn Holder, 'Untangling the Meanings of Justice: A Longitudinal Mixed Methods Study', *Journal of Mixed Methods Research* 12.2 (2018), p. 1.

14. Anne-Marie McAlinden and Bronwyn Naylor, 'Reframing Public Inquiries as "Procedural Justice" for Victims of Institutional Child Abuse: Towards a Hybrid Model of Justice', *Sydney Law Review* 38.3 (2016), p. 285.

15. Daly, *Redressing Institutional Abuse*, p. 117; Robert Folger et al., 'Effects of "Voice" and Peer Opinions on Responses to Inequity', *Journal of Personality and Social Psychology* 37.12 (1979), pp 2253–61; Tom Tyler and E. Allan Lind, 'A Relational Model of Authority in Groups', *Advances in Experimental Social Psychology* 25 (1992), pp 115–91.

16. Jonathan Doak and Louise Taylor, 'Hearing the Voices of Victims and Offenders: The Role of Emotions in Criminal Sentencing', *Northern Ireland Legal Quarterly* 64.1 (2013), pp 25–46; Zachari Duncalf, Moyra Hawthorn, Jennifer Davidson, Jim Goddard, and Will McMahon, *Time for 'Justice': Research to Inform the Development of a Human Rights Framework for the Design and Implementation of an 'Acknowledgment and Accountability Forum' on Historic Abuse of Children in Scotland* (Glasgow and Manchester, 2009), p. 48; Folger et al., 'Effects.'

17. Haley Clark, 'A Fair Way to Go: Justice for Victim-Survivors of Sexual Violence', in Anastasia Powell, Nicola Henry, and Asher Flynn (eds), *Rape Justice: Beyond the Criminal Law* (Basingstoke, UK, 2015), pp 18–35; Kathleen Daly, 'Reconceptualising Sexual Victimisation and Justice', in Inge Vanfraechem, Antony Pemberton, and Felix Mukwiza Ndahinda (eds) *Justice for Victims: Perspectives on Rights, Transition, and Reconciliation* (New York, 2014), pp 378–95; Nicola Godden, 'Seeking Justice for Victim-Survivors: Unconventional Legal Responses to Rape' (M.A. thesis, Durham University, 2013); Judith Lewis Herman, 'Justice from the Victim's Perspective', *Violence Against Women* 11 (2005), pp 571–602; Shirley Jülich, 'Views of Justice among Survivors of Historical Child Sexual Abuse: Implications for Restorative Justice in New Zealand', *Theoretical Criminology* 10 (2006), pp 125–38; Mary P. Koss, 'Restoring Rape Survivors: Justice, Advocacy, and a Call to Action', *Annals of the New York Academy of Sciences* 1087.1 (2006), pp 206–34.

18. Edna Erez and Joanne Belknap, 'In their Own Words: Battered Women's Assessment of the Criminal Proceeding System's Responses', *Violence and Victims* 13 (1998), pp 251–68; Judith Lewis Herman, 'The Mental Health of Crime Victims: Impact of Legal Intervention', *Journal of Traumatic Stress* 16.2 (2003), pp 159–66; Ulrich Orth, 'Secondary Victimization of Crime Victims by Criminal Proceedings', *Social Justice Research* 15.4 (2002), pp 313–25; Jim Parsons and Tiffany Bergin, 'The Impact of Criminal Justice Involvement on Victims' Mental Health', *Journal of Traumatic Stress* 23.2 (2010), pp 182–8.

19. Rebecca Campbell et al., 'Preventing the 'Second Rape': Rape Survivors' Experiences with Community Service Providers', *Journal of Interpersonal Violence* 16.2 (2001), pp 1239–59.

20. For a useful summary of a range of justice needs, see Kathleen Daly, 'Sexual Violence and Victims' Justice Interests', in Estelle Zinsstag and Marie Keenan (eds), *Restorative Responses to Sexual Violence: Legal, Social, and Therapeutic Dimensions* (Oxford. Routledge, 2017), table 6.a2.

21. Backer, 'Human Face', pp 201–2; Clark, 'Fair Way to Go', p. 30; LCC, *Restoring Dignity*; Godden, 'Seeking Justice', pp 53–4; Herman, 'Mental Health', pp 159–66.

22. Backer, 'Human Face', p. 202; Jülich, 'Views of Justice.'

23. Herman, 'Justice from the Victim's Perspective', p. 585.

24. Clark, 'Fair Way to Go'; Haley Clark, 'What Is the Justice System Willing to Offer? Understanding Sexual Assault Victim/Survivors' Criminal Justice Needs', *Family Matters* 85 (2010), pp 28–37.

25. Clark, 'What is the Justice System Willing to Offer?'; Clark, 'Fair Way to Go.'

26. Daly, 'Sequencing Justice.'

27. Ibid., p. 118.

28. Clark, 'What Is the Justice System Willing to Offer?' p. 30.

29. Godden, 'Seeking Justice', 74; Herman, 'Justice from the Victim's Perspective', pp 586–87.

30. Ibid.

31. Godden, 'Seeking Justice', pp 68–71.

32. Herman, 'Mental Health', p. 160.

33. Godden, 'Seeking Justice', pp 60–1.

34. Backer, 'Human Face', p. 206.

35. Edna Erez and Michael Kilchling (eds), *Therapeutic Jurisprudence and Victim Participation in Justice* (Durham, NC, 2011); Brandon Hamber, *Transforming Societies after Political Violence: Truth, Reconciliation, and Mental Health* (New York, 2009).

36. Patricia Lundy and Kathleen Mahoney, 'Representing Survivors. A Critical Analysis of Recommendations to Resolve Northern Ireland's Historical Child Abuse Claims', *Annual Review of Interdisciplinary Justice Research* 7 (2018), pp 258–91.

37. Herman, 'Justice from the Victim's Perspective', p. 594.

38. Daly, 'Sexual Violence and Victims' Justice Interests.' Daly has developed a model that may enable comparative analysis and assessment of a variety of justice mechanisms; she terms this the victimization and justice model (VJM). Its core justice elements are participation, voice, validation, vindication and offender accountability, and taking of responsibility. See also Godden, 'Seeking Justice.' Godden identifies five elements of justice, and these are used to compare the three different legal responses to rape, namely, criminal justice, restorative justice, and tort law.

39. It was considered inappropriate and unethical to determine the nature of the harms and injuries of participants in the research. It is, however, acknowledged that the type of crime (sexual, physical, and emotional) may have an impact on the sense of justice.

40. Interview with M3, Sept. 2016.

41. Percentages are used to compare results as the number of people in the different datasets are not the same (e.g. 43 interviews out of 177 inquiry-transcript responses).

42. Interview with F4, July 2016.

43. Interview with M5, Nov. 2015.

44. Interview with F15, Sept. 2016.

45. Patricia Lundy and Bill Rolston, 'Redress for Past Harms? Official Apologies in Northern Ireland', *International Journal of Human Rights* 20:1 (2016), pp 104–22.

46. Interview with F19, July 2016.

47. Lundy, *Historical Institutional Abuse*; Lundy and Mahoney, 'Representing Survivors.'

48. Male participant, focus group 4.

49. Claire McGettrick's essay in chapter 15 of this volume addresses access to information in the context of closed adoption records in the Republic of Ireland.

50. Interview with F6a, Sept. 2015. This interview contains more than one interviewee.

51. Interview with F2, Jan. 2016.

52. Interview with M7, Nov. 2015. This interview contains more than one interviewee.

53. Interview with F2, Jan. 2016.
54. Interview with M10, Nov. 2016.
55. Most of the interviews were concluded before the HIAI report was published in Jan. 2017.
56. Jonathan Doak, 'Honing the Stone. Refining Restorative Justice as a Vehicle for Emotional Redress', *Contemporary Justice Review* 14:4 (2011), 439–56; Hamber, *Transforming Societies*; Herman, 'Mental Health', 159–66; Eric Stover, 'Witnesses and the Promise of Justice in The Hague', in Eric Stover and Harvey M. Weinstein (eds) *My Neighbor, My Enemy: Justice and Community in the Aftermath of Mass Atrocity* (Cambridge, 2004), pp 104–20.
57. Stover, 'Witnesses', p. 107.
58. Interview with F15, Sept. 1016.
59. Interview with F2, Jan. 2016.
60. Herman, 'Mental Health', 160.
61. Interview with F2, Jan. 2016.
62. Interview with M5, Nov. 2015.
63. Interview with M10, Nov. 2016.
64. Hart et al., *Report of the HIAI*, vol. 1, p. 12.
65. Interview with F2, Jan. 2016.
66. Anthony Hart, 'Remarks at the Third Public Session of the HIAI Inquiry' (speech, Ramada Encore Hotel, St. Anne's Square, Belfast, 4 Sept. 2013), p. 12, https.//www.hiainquiry.org/sites/hiainquiry/files/media-files/chairman_s_address_130904_low_res.pdf, archived at https.//perma.cc/466G-TB3K.
67. Interview with F4, July 2016.
68. Interview with F1b, June 2017; F1a & F1b interviews were conducted at the same time.
69. Interview with F1a, June 2017.
70. Interview with F15, Sept. 2016.
71. Interview with M13, Jan. 2016.
72. Interview with F15, Sept. 2016. ·
73. Interview with M13, Jan. 2016.
74. Interview with F15, Sept. 2016.
75. *In the Matter of a Decision of the Inquiry into Historical Institutional Abuse, 1922 to 1995* [2015] NIQB 3, p. 6, par. 15.
76. Ibid.
77. In addition to the witness statements from the victims, the evidence bundles included material that the inquiry had gathered from core participants, social services, the police, or from its own work in the Public Record Office in Northern Ireland.
78. HIAI, *Procedural Protocols to Be Followed by the Inquiry into Historical Institutional Abuse, 1922 to 1995* (HIAI, 2013), par. 15, 23, 24, 31, https.//www.hiainquiry.org/sites/hiainquiry/files/media-files/hia_inquiry_procedural_protocol_final-2.pdf, archived at https.//perma.cc/2V9G-QY7V.
79. Interview with M12, Jan. 2016.
80. Hart, 'Remarks at the Third Public Session', 16.d.
81. *In the Matter of a Decision of the Inquiry into Historical Institutional Abuse, 1922 to 1995* [2015] NIQB 3, pp 10–11, par. 30.
82. Hart et al., *Report of the HIAI*, vol. 1 p. 15.
83. The HIAI chairman's decision not to allow victims personal representation was judicially reviewed. It was upheld at first but overturned on appeal.
84. LCC, *Restoring Dignity*.
85. Brandon Hamber and Richard A. Wilson, 'Symbolic Closure through Memory,

Reparation, and Revenge in Post-conflict Societies', *Journal of Human Rights* 1:1 (2002), pp 35–53.

86. Interview F15, Sept. 2016.

87. Inquiry into Historical Institutional Abuse Act (Northern Ireland) (2013), par. 1(5).

88. Director of Public Prosecutions, 'Undertaking to Witnesses to the HIAI', 22 Apr. 2013, https://www.hiainquiry.org/sites/hiainquiry/files/media-files/Public%20 Prosecution%20Service%20-%20Undertaking.pdf, archived at https://perma.cc/ KF59-QDW8.

89. Freedom of Information, Historical Institutional Abuse Inquiry, FOI 2017, F-2017–02046. However, a follow-up FOI in 2020 (FIO F-2020–00172) stated that 184 cases had been referred to the PSNI by the HIAI.

90. The UN Commission Against Torture pointed to a similarly low number of prosecutions stemming from the Ryan report when the Republic of Ireland was examined in 2011 and again referenced the matter in 2017.

91. Lundy and Mahoney, 'Representing Survivors.'

92. UK Government, *Report Pursuant to Section 3(14) of the Northern Ireland (Executive Formation, etc.) Act 2019—Historical Institutional Abuse* (London, 2019), p. 5, archived at https://perma.cc/YUL4-R5LQ.

93. The panel was formed after a series of meetings and discussions with survivor groups in early Oct. 2014, initiated by Patricia Lundy and Kathleen Mahoney (University of Calgary, Canada).

94. See Lundy, *Historical Institutional Abuse.*

95. Panel of Experts on Redress, *Response to the Historical Institutional Abuse Inquiry Redress Recommendations: The Panel of Experts on Redress Position Paper and Recommendations* (Ulster University, Apr. 2017). See also Panel of Experts, *Briefing Paper: Proposed Improvements to HIA Inquiry Compensation* (Ulster University, Sept. 2018).

96. Hart et al., *Report of the HIAI*, 1:232, par. 16f.

97. See Brandon Hamber and Patricia Lundy, 'Lessons from Transitional Justice? Toward a New Framing of a Victim-Centred Approach in the Case of Historical Institutional Abuse', *Victims and Offenders* (Apr. 2020), https://doi.org/10.1080/1556 4886.2020.1743803. This article discusses in detail the positives and negatives of transitional justice and makes recommendations for an alternative approach.

CHAPTER 19 – VISUALISING THE TRANSFERS OF ABUSERS IN THE 2009 RYAN REPORT

1. This essay was previously published in *Éire-Ireland: An Interdisciplinary Journal of Irish Studies* 55, 1 (Spring/Summer 2020), pp 247–251, DOI: 10.1353/eir.2020.0010.

2. See the website of the Commission to Inquire into Child Abuse, available at http:// www.childabusecommission.ie. The original report is available on this site. The digitized, searchable version of the report is available on the website of the Industrial Memories project, https://industrialmemories.ucd.ie/ryan-report.

3. Mary Raftery, 'Report a Monument to a Society's Shame', *The Irish Times*, 21 May 2009. The Ryan report is one of several reports into the abuse of children by the Catholic religious orders. See also the Ferns report (2005), the Cloyne report (2010), and the Murphy report (2009). See also Carole Holohan, *In Plain Sight: Responding to the Ferns, Ryan, Murphy, and Cloyne Reports* (Dublin, 2011).

4. Commission to Inquire into Child Abuse, *Report of the Commission to Inquire into Child Abuse* (Dublin Stationery Office, 2009; hereafter cited as *Ryan Report*), vol. 1, Ch. 6, para. 85.

5. Ibid.

6. Marie Keenan, *Child Sexual Abuse and the Catholic Church: Gender, Power, and Organizational Culture* (Oxford, 2012), pp xxiv–xxv.

7. *Ryan Report*, volume 2, Ch. 2, paragraph 148.

8. *Ryan Report*, volume 2, Ch. 2, paragraph 216.

9. 'Executive Summary, Conclusions: 22', *Ryan Report*.

10. Donald Palmer and Valerie Feldman, 'Toward a More Comprehensive Analysis of the Role of Organizational Culture in Child Sexual Abuse in Institutional Contexts', *Child Abuse & Neglect* 74 (2017), p. 23.

11. This research project was funded by the Irish Research Council (2015–19) under the New Horizons scheme.

12. A 'dispensation' granted permission for a nun or brother to leave the religious order.

13. The transfer graph is based solely on the evidence of transferring abusers noted in the Ryan report; the figure of 86 thus reflects the number of staff that the report identifies as having been a result of allegations or evidence of abuse. The number of abusers working within the system was much higher, given that many abusers were never transferred. The number of staff transferred was also probably higher than recorded in the report, given that the Ryan report did not specifically profile transfers. Thus there were likely transfers that the report's authors did not include. Only access to the underlying evidence files—those of the commission and of the religious orders—can give an authoritative picture.

14. The records of the Commission to Inquire into Child Abuse are still held by the commission. At the time of writing, the government proposes to keep the records of the commission sealed, for up to 75 years. See Jack Power, 'Sealing abuse records would make survivors invisible once more', *The Irish Times*, 26 Nov. 2019, available at: www.irishtimes.com/news/social-affairs/sealing-abuse-records-for-75-years-would-make-survivors-invisible-once-more-1.4095847, accessed 11 May 2021. See also Ralph Riegel, 'Survivors outraged at plan to seal abuse records for 75 years', *The Irish Independent*, 23 Mar. 2015, available at: www.independent.ie/irish-news/survivors-outraged-at-plan-to-seal-abuse-reports-for-75-years-31086753.html, accessed 11 May 2021.

CHAPTER 20 – OFFICIAL IRELAND'S RESPONSE TO THE MAGDALENE
LAUNDRIES: AN EPISTEMOLOGY OF IGNORANCE

1. See for example the final reports of the Commission to Inquire into Child Abuse (2009) and the Commission to Inquire into Mother and Baby Homes and Other Related Institutions (2021).

2. The *Final Report* is available to download at https://www.gov.ie/en/collection/mbhcoi/. See also: Fintan O'Toole, 'Mother and Baby Report Cannot be Left to Stand', *The Irish Times*, 8 June 2021.

3. James M. Smith's *Ireland's Magdalen Laundries and the Nation's Architecture of Containment* (South Bend IN, 2007), Eoin O'Sullivan and Ian O'Donnell, eds., *Coercive Confinement in Post-Independent Ireland: Patients, Prisoners and Penitents.* (Manchester, 2012).

4. John Banville, 'A Century of Looking the Other Way,' *The New York Times*, 22 May 2009. A 21.

5. *Magdalen Commission Report*, 8, para 3.03, 5.09, 5.13. See also Claire McGettrick, Katherine O'Donnell, Maeve O'Rourke, James M. Smith and Mari Steed 'Ch. 6:

Never Tell, Never Acknowledge (…everyone knew, but no one said)' *Ireland and the Magdalene Laundries: A Campaign for Justice* (London, 2021).

6. Irish Human Rights Commission, *Follow-up Report on State Involvement with Magdalen Laundries* [hereafter *IHRC Follow-up Report*], June 2013, Executive summary, p. 4.

7. *IHRC Follow-up Report*, para 76.

8. *IHRC Follow-up Report*, para 171.

9. *IHRC Follow-up Report*, para 185.

10. *IHRC Follow-up Report*, para 229.

11. *IHRC Follow-up Report*, para 237.

12. *IHRC Follow-up Report*, para 254.

13. See Mr Gerard Corr, Permanent Representative of Ireland to the United Nations Office at Geneva, letter to Ms Felice D Gaer, Rapporteur, Committee Against Torture, 8 Aug. 2013.

14. United Nations, *Ireland, Second Periodic Report to the Committee Against Torture*, UN Doc CAT/C/IRL/2, 20 Jan. 2016, para 241; United Nations, *Ireland, Information on follow-up to the concluding observations of the Committee against Torture on the second periodic report of Ireland*, UN Doc CAT/C/IRL/CO/2/Add.1, 28 Aug. 2018, para 15; United Nations, Human Rights Committee, *Replies of Ireland to the list of issues*, UN Doc CCPR/C/IRL/Q/4/Add.1, received 27 Feb. 2014, published 5 May 2014; United Nations, *Ireland, Information on follow-up to the concluding observations of the Human Rights Committee on the fourth periodic report of Ireland*, UN Doc CCPR/C/IRL/CO/4/Add.1, 15 Aug. 2017, para 5 (third round); United Nations, *Ireland, Follow-Up Material to the Concluding Observations of the UN Human Rights Committee on the Fourth Periodic Review of Ireland under the International Covenant on Civil and Political Rights*, 17 July 2015, 3 Ireland, *Combined sixth and seventh periodic reports to the United Nations Committee on the Elimination of All Forms of Discrimination Against Women*, 30 Sept. 2016, 8; UN, HRC, *Replies of Ireland to the list of issues*, 5 May 2014; *Follow-Up Material to the Concluding Observations of the UN Human Rights Committee on the Fourth Periodic Review of Ireland*, 17 July 2015, 3; *Submission by Ireland of further information to the UN Human Rights Committee following Ireland's Fourth Periodic Review under the International Covenant on Civil and Political Rights*, 13 June 2016; *Information on follow-up to the concluding observations of the Human Rights Committee on the fourth periodic report of Ireland*, 15 Aug. 2017, para 5 (third round); *Information on follow-up to the concluding observations of the Committee against Torture on the second periodic report of Ireland*, 28 Aug. 2018, para 15.

15. *Dáil Éireann Debates* (hereafter *DED*), Maureen O'Sullivan, Healthcare Bill 2nd stage, 28 Jan. 2015. See also, for example, *DED*, Catherine Murphy, 29 Jan. 2015.

16. *Seanad Éireann Debates* (hereafter *SED*), 'Redress for Women Resident in Certain Institutions Bill 2014: Report and Final Stages', 11 Mar. 2015; See for a related response: *DED*, Written Answers, Department of Justice and Equality: Restorative Justice, 28 Feb. 2017.

17. Peter Tyndall, *Opportunity Lost: An Investigation by the Ombudsman into the Administration of the Magdalen Restorative Justice Scheme* (Dublin, 2017), p. 8.

18. Ibid., 41.

19. *DED*, Joint Oireachtas Justice Committee on Justice, Defence, and Equality, Administration on Magdalen Restorative Justice Scheme: Report of Ombudsman, 31 Jan. 2018.

20. For an example of criticisms levelled at the *IDC Report* on behalf of the JFM Campaign (later Justice for Magdalenes Research) see Maeve O'Rourke, *Submission to the UN Committee against Torture regarding Follow-up to Ireland's most recent State Party Report and List of Issues for Ireland's next State Party Report*. 7 Mar. 2013;

Maeve O'Rourke, *Follow-Up Submission to the UN Human Rights Committee in respect of Ireland*. 111th Session. July 2014; Maeve O'Rourke, *Submission to UN Commission on the Status of Women*. 1 Aug. 2014; Maeve O'Rourke, *Parallel Report to the United Nations Committee on Economic, Social and Cultural Rights for its examination of Ireland*, 55th Session. June 2015; Maeve O'Rourke, *NGO Submission to the UN Committee on the Elimination of Discrimination Against Women in respect of Ireland for List of Issues Prior to Reporting*. 2015; Maeve O'Rourke, *NGO Submission to the UN Committee on the Elimination of Discrimination Against Women in respect of Ireland*. Feb. 2017; Maeve O'Rourke, *NGO Submission to the UN Committee Against Torture in respect of Ireland* (for the session). July 2017. Maeve O'Rourke and Claire McGettrick. *Submission to the Council of Europe Commissioner for Human Rights*. 18 Nov. 2016; Maeve O'Rourke, Submission to the Council of Europe Commissioner for Human Rights. 18 Nov. 2016.

21. See Rik Peels, 'What Is Ignorance?' *Philosophia* 38 (2010), pp 57–67 for an overview of Standard and New View conceptions of ignorance as related to propositions.

22. See Quassim Cassam, *Vices of the Mind: From the Intellectual to the Political* (Oxford, 2019).

23. See for example, Sandra Harding, 'Rethinking Standpoint Epistemology: What is Strong Objectivity?' *Feminist Epistemologies*, Linda Martín Alcoff and Elizabeth Potter eds. (New York, 1993), pp 49–82. and Harding 'Standpoint Theories: Productively Controversial', *Hypatia: A Journal of Feminist Philosophy*, 24(4) (2009), pp 192–200.

24. See for example, Lorraine Code, *What Can She Know? Feminist Theory and Construction of Knowledge* (Ithaca, 1991).

25. See for example, Lorraine Code, *Ecological Thinking: The Politics of Epistemic Location* (Oxford, 2006) and José Medina, *The Epistemology of Resistance: Gender and Race Oppression, Epistemic Injustice, and Resistant Imaginations* (New York, 2013).

26. Linda Martín Alcoff, 'Epistemologies of Ignorance. Three Types', in *Race and Epistemologies of Ignorance*, edited by Sharon Sullivan and Nancy Tuana (Albany, 2007), pp 39–40.

27. Charles W. Mills, 'White Ignorance.' *Race and Epistemologies of Ignorance*, Sharon Sullivan and Nancy Tuana, eds. (New York, 2007), p. 11.

28. José Medina, *The Epistemology of Resistance* (Oxford, 2013), p. 39.

29. Charles W. Mills, *The Racial Contract* (New York, 1997), p. 18.

30. James M. Smith's *Ireland's Magdalen Laundries and the Nation's Architecture of Containment* (South Bend IN, 2007), Eoin O'Sullivan and Ian O'Donnell, eds., *Coercive Confinement in Post-Independent Ireland: Patients, Prisoners and Penitents* (Manchester, 2012).

31. Kevin Lynch, 'Willful Ignorance and Self-deception', *Philosophical Studies: An International Journal for Philosophy in the Analytic Tradition*, 173.2 (2016), pp 512–13.

32. Philosophical discussion of 'culpable ignorance' has tended to follow the paper by Holly Smith published in *The Philosophical Review* 92.4 (1983), pp 543–71, where it is assumed that the ignorant person is *not* motivated to be ignorant but nonetheless is blameworthy because they 'should have known' that is they had a moral duty to know that of which they were ignorant and this ignorance facilitated harm to occur. Hence 'wilful ignorance' is of a different order than how 'culpable ignorance' is generally discussed in moral and legal terms.

33. On the publication of the final report of the CICA, Fintan O'Toole remarked that:

> There is a propensity for Irish culture to have 'unknown knowns' – things that are known to be true but are treated as if they are outlandish fictions. No honest person seriously doubted that the industrial schools were instruments of terror

and torture – why, otherwise, were children threatened with Letterfrack and Daingean, words that induced a numbing chill of fear? Likewise, many of the abusive priests were not secretive but behaved, on the contrary, with a flagrant and swaggering arrogance. Yet, as dramatists have understood since the time of the ancient Greeks, there is often much more power in being forced to confront what you already know than in being amazed by the unexpected. 'Ryan Report', *The Irish Times* 28 Dec. 2009.

34. The *Oxford English Dictionary* defines the verb to Ignore thus: †1. transitive. Not to know, to be ignorant of. Obsolete or rare.

35. Email, Nuala Ní Mhuircheartaigh to James Smith, 'Letter for Senator McAleese', 29 Mar. 2012, 12:13 pm.

36. *IDC Report*, Ch. 19, para 16, 929.

37. *IDC Report*, Ch. 19, para 35, 933.

38. Anne Enright, 'Antigone in Galway', chapter 2, in this volume.

39. Miranda Fricker, *Epistemic Injustice: Power and the Ethics of Knowing* (Oxford, 2007).

40. Gaile Pohlhaus Jr., 'Relational Knowing and Epistemic Injustice: Toward a Theory of "*Willful Hermeneutical Ignorance*"', *Hypatia* 27.4 (2012), p. 715.

41. Poulhaus Jr., 716.

42. *IDC Report* Ch. 19, paras 60-138, 958-986.

43. *IDC Report*, Introduction, para 5–6, I.

44. For example, see *IDC Report*, Introduction, para 10–11, IV; also para 18, VII, and para 23–24, X.

45. *IDC Report* Ch. 19, para 15, 928–9.

46. *IDC Report*, Ch. 19, para 134, 985.

47. *IDC Report*, Ch. 19, para 135, 985.

48. For a full discussion of Dr McAleese's meetings with survivors introduced to him by JFM see 'Ch. 4: Anatomy of a Campaign: Developing a Human Rights and Justice Agenda', in Claire McGettrick, Katherine O'Donnell, Maeve O'Rourke, James M. Smith & Mari Steed, *Ireland and the Magdalene Laundries: A Campaign for Justice* (London, 2021).

49. Linda Alcoff and Laura Gray, 'Survivor Discourse: Transgression or Recuperation?', *Signs*, 18.2 (1993), pp 265–6.

50. Katherine O'Donnell, Sinead Pembroke and Claire McGettrick, *Magdalene Institutions: Recording an Oral and Archival History*, Government of Ireland Collaborative Research Project funded by the Irish Research Council, 2012. See: http://jfmresearch.com/home/oralhistoryproject/. O'Donnell, Pembroke and McGettrick, 'Oral History of Caitríona Hayes'; O'Donnell, Pembroke and McGettrick, 'Oral History of Maisie K.(a)'; O'Donnell, Pembroke and McGettrick, 'Oral History of Evelyn'. See also, *JFM Principal Submission*, pp 76–80.

51. Katherine O'Donnell, 'Academic & Activist: Ethical Issues arising from the Justice for Magdalene Campaign and Oral History', in *Irishness on the Margins: Minority and Dissident Identities*. Pilar Villar-Argáiz ed. (Basingstoke, 2018), pp 77–100.

52. Carole Pateman, *The Sexual Contract* (London, 1988).

53. *IDC Report*, Ch. 19, Section B, 958.

54. *IDC Report* Ch. 19, para 77, 963.

55. *IDC Report*, Introduction, VII

56. *IDC Report*, Introduction, VIII.

57. *IDC Report*, 'Ch. 18: Non-State Routes of Entry to the Magdalen Laundries (Part B)', para 97, 920.

58. An Modh Coinníollach is used: (i) when there's an understood condition and

you wish to enquire what might be expected to happen. (ii) used after dá (if) for conditions that may or may not happen; (iii) after certain words: b'fhéidir (perhaps), ar eagla go (for fear that), níl a fhios ag xxx (xxx doesn't know) cá bhfios do xxx (how does xxx know); (iv) Irish is a language that, compared to English, is quite courtly in making polite requests and An Modh Coinníollach is also used in those instances; (v) to recount a statement that someone has made about their future plans; (vi) it is regularly used instead of the past tense to add to the surprise or effect of a story; and (vii) in rhetorical questions; (viii) traditionally Irish speakers appreciate the use of 'seanfhocail'/proverbs, metaphorical expressions and An Modh Coinníollach is regularly used in these cases; (ix) it is used instead of the past habitual to describe regular occurrences in the past. The conditional being incorporated into verb endings and the diverse and frequent occasions that feature An Modh Coinníollach mean that it has totemic for the difficulties experienced by students of the Irish language see: 'Des Bishop agus An Modh Coinníollach' https://www.youtube.com/watch?v=PfLuFHdUG6k.

59. *IDC Report*, Ch. 15, para 37, 753 and para 38, 754. Emphasis added.

60. *IDC Report*, Ch. 15, para 62–5, 762.

61. *IDC Report*, Ch. 15, paras 66–123, 762–78

62. *IDC Report*, Ch. 15, paras 66–7, 763. Emphasis added.

63. *IDC Report*, Ch. 15, 'Financial (C), Taxation, Commercial Rates and Social Insurance', para 107, 774

64. *IDC Report*, Ch. 15, para 96, 771–2.

65. *IDC Report*, Ch. 15, paras 102–9, 773–4.

66. *IDC Report*, Ch. 15, para 107, 774. Emphasis added.

67. *IDC Report* Ch. 9, para 281, 308.

68. *IDC Report* Ch. 9, para 282, 308.

69. Simon McGarr, 'How to Read the McAleese Report into the Magdalen Laundries', https://www.mcgarrsolicitors.ie/2021/01/14/how-to-read-the-mcaleese-report-into-the-magdalen-laundries/amp/.

70. *IDC Report* Ch. 9, Par. 294, p. 313.

71. *IDC Report*, Ch. 5, summary, 70.

72. *IDC Report* Ch. 5, para 2, 71.

73. Indeed, the State's own Department of Justice as late as June 2010 insisted that the only statutory provision for the State sending a woman to a Laundry was the *1960 Criminal Justice Act*, and that referred specifically to one institution and only for remand cases.

74. Article 40.3 states:
   1. The State guarantees in its laws to respect, and, as far as practicable, by its laws to defend and vindicate the personal rights of the citizen.
   2. The State shall, in particular, by its laws protect as best it may from unjust attack and, in the case of injustice done, vindicate the life, person, good name, and property rights of every citizen.

Article 40.4 states: No citizen shall be deprived of his [sic] personal liberty save in accordance with law.

75. *IDC Report*, Ch. 12, summary, 523.

76. *IDC Report*, Ch. 12, para 152, 575.

77. *IDC Report*, Ch. 12, para 141, 570.

78. *IDC Report*, Ch. 12, para 182, 585.

79. See also McGettrick, O'Donnell, O'Rourke, Smith and Steed 'Ch. 6: Never Tell, Never Acknowledge (…everyone knew, but no one said)', 2021.

80. *IDC Report*, Ch. 7, Par. 34, pp 150–1.

81. *IDC Report*, Ch. 7, Par. 20–23, p. 148.

82. See Mr Seán Aylward's remarks on 24 May 2011, https://www.youtube.com/watch?v=tSrDbeO5wYs; also, UN Committee against Torture, Summary record of the 1005th meeting held at the Palais Wilson, Geneva, on Tuesday, 24 May 2011, at 3pm, UN Doc CAT/C/SR 1005.
83. See S.I. No. 486 of 2011, http://www.irishstatutebook.ie/eli/2011/si/486/made/en/pdf
84. *IDC Report*, Executive Summary, XIII; see also Ch. 7 Par. 27, 30, p. 149, 150. JFM brought numerous examples to the IDC's attention of women listed on the 1901 and 1911 censuses who died in Magdalene Laundries post-1922, some as late as 1961, 1967, and as late as 1985: Maggie M. died in the care of the nuns after the closure of the Limerick institution, having spent seventy-four years there.
85. *IDC Report*, Ch. 8, Par. 19, p.163.
86. *IDC Report*, Executive Summary, XIII.
87. *IDC Report*, Ch. 8, Par. 19, p. 163
88. Gerry Mc Nally, 'Probation in Ireland: A Brief History of the Early Years', *Irish Probation Journal*, 4, no. 1 (Sept. 2007), 12ff.
89. *IDC Report*, Executive Summary, XIII.
90. The *IDC Report*, Ch. 8, Par. 6, p. 159 explains that 14,607 entry records were available to it, not including records of entries prior to 1922 or to the Magdalene Laundries in Dun Laoghaire or Galway. The Executive Summary, XIII explains that the 14,607 entry records relate to 10,012 women. Ch. 8 provides statistics that relate to individual entry records, not individual women. In other words, it does not collate entry records that concern the same woman and present them as a whole.
91. *IDC Report*, Ch. 8, Par. 7, p. 159.
92. *The Magdalen Commission Report*. Dublin: Department of Justice and Equality. May 2013, Par. 4.10, 5. The IDC also disregarded these women in its 'list of deaths': 'Deaths occurring in nursing homes after the closure of the Magdalen Laundries, of women who had in their earlier lives been admitted to a Magdalen Laundry, were not included'. *IDC Report*, Ch. 16, Par. 37, pp 790–1.
93. *IDC Report*, Ch. 8, Par. 29 and table, 168, notes that duration of stay was discernible only for 6,151 'women' which should read 'entries' or 'admissions' because it is acknowledged to be 6,151 from a database of 11,198 entries. The dataset of 11,198 entries is explained in Ch. 8, Par. 7, pp 159–160 to be a subset of the overall database of 14,607 known admissions (not including entries prior to 1922 or entries to the Magdalene Laundries in Galway or Dun Laoghaire).
94. *IDC Report*, above note 8, Ch. 8, Par. 31, p. 169.
95. http://jfmresearch.com/home/magdalene-names-project/.
96. *IDC Report*, Ch. 20, para 2, 994.
97. *IDC Report*, Ch. 20 para 4, 994.
98. *IDC Report*, Ch. 20 para 5, 994.
99. *IDC Report*, Ch. 20 Para 51, 1007.
100. The author is indebted to notes provided by Raymond Hill, incorporated in JFMR's submissions to UN Commission on the Status of Women in Aug. 2014: Maeve O'Rourke, *Justice for Magdalenes Research: Submission to UN Commission on the Status of Women* (JFM Research, 1 Aug. 2014).
101. Department of Justice and Equality, *Report of the Inter-Departmental Committee to establish the facts of State Involvement with the Magdalen Laundries (AKA the McAleese Report)*, 5 Feb. 2013, 137, 140; Letter from Eamonn Molloy, Assistant Secretary General, Department of the Taoiseach, to Maeve O'Rourke, 13 Nov. 2018 (Ref FOI/2018/0351). See JFMR Briefing Note Re: McAleese Archive for further details of our efforts to access these records.
102. Letter from Cillian Doyle, Department of the Taoiseach, to Maeve O'Rourke,

25 Sept. 2018 (Ref FOI/2018/0351). This decision was upheld on appeal by the internal reviewer.

103. Molloy, letter, 13 Nov. 2018.

104. Although recently one scholar, who is a religious sister was allowed access to the archive of the congregation of Our Lady of Charity, see: Jacinta Prunty, *The Monasteries, Magdalen asylums and Reformatory Schools of Our Lady of Charity in Ireland, 1853–1973* (Dublin, 2017).

105. Article 41.1 which declares that the family (historically interpreted as the heteronormative family based in marriage) is the 'natural primary and fundamental unit group of society'. Article 41.2 proceeds to define the circumscribed position of the woman/mother within this moral institution.

> 2.1 In particular, the state recognises that by her life within the home, woman gives to the state a support without which the common good cannot be achieved.
>
> 2.2 The state shall, therefore, endeavour to ensure that mothers shall not be obliged by economic necessity to engage in labour to the neglect of their duties in the home.

106. Jacques Derrida, 'Force of Law,' trans., Mary Quaintance, in *Deconstruction and the Possibility of Justice*, Drucilla Cornell, Michael Rosenfeld, and David Gray Carlson, eds. (New York, 1992), pp 24–6.

107. Derrida, 1992, pp 26–8.

CHAPTER 21 – MATERIALS AND MEMORY: ARCHAEOLOGY AND HERITAGE AS TOOLS OF TRANSITIONAL JUSTICE AT A FORMER MAGDALENE LAUNDRY

1. This essay was previously published in *Éire-Ireland: An Interdisciplinary Journal of Irish Studies* 55.1 (Spring/Summer 2020), pp 223–246, DOI: 10.1353/eir.2020.0009.

2. Lucas Lixinski, 'Cultural Heritage Law and Transitional Justice: Lessons from South Africa', *International Journal of Transitional Justice* 9 (2015), pp 278–9.

3. Olivia Kelly, 'Donnybrook Magdalene Laundry Demolition Proposal Scrapped', *The Irish Times*, 8 Apr. 2017.

4. Ibid.

5. Dan Barry, 'The Lost Children of Tuam', *The New York Times*, 28 Oct. 2017.

6. Irish Archaeological Consultancy Limited (IAC), *Archaeological Assessment at the Crescent, Donnybrook, Dublin 4* (unpublished report, 2018).

7. MESH Architects, *Preliminary Historic Structure Report* (unpublished report, 2018).

8. Laura McAtackney, *An Archaeology of the Troubles: The Dark Heritage of Long Kesh/ Maze Prison* (Oxford, 2014).

9. MESH, *Preliminary*, p. 10.

10. Planning and Development Act (2000), *Electronic Irish Statute Book*, http://www.irishstatutebook.ie/eli/2000/act/30/enacted/en/html.

11. Christopher Witmore, 'The Realities of the Past: Archaeology, Object-Orientations, Pragmatology', in Brent Fortenberry and Laura McAtackney (eds), *Modern Materials: Papers from CHAT Oxford (2009)* (Oxford, 2012), pp 25–36.

12. Rodney Harrison, 'Surface Assemblages: Towards an Archaeology *in* and *of* the Present', *Archaeological Dialogues* 18.2 (2011), pp 141–61; Laurent Olivier, *The Dark Abyss of Time: Archaeology and Memory*, Arthur Greenspan (trans) (London, 2011).

13. See Richard A. Gould and Michael B. Schiffer (eds), *Modern Material Culture: The Archaeology of Us* (New York, 1981).

14. Victor Buchli and Gavin Lucas (eds), *Archaeologies of the Contemporary Past* (London, 2001).

15. Victor Buchli and Gavin Lucas, 'The Absent Present: Archaeologies of the Contemporary Past', ibid., p. 13.

16. James R. Dixon, 'Is the Present Day Post-medieval?', *Post-medieval Archaeology* 45.2 (2011), p. 319.

17. Victor Buchli and Gavin Lucas, 'The Archaeology of Alienation: A Late Twentieth-Century British Council House', in Buchli and Lucas, *Archaeologies*, pp 158–68.

18. For further details, see Jeremy Huggett, 'Preservation by Record', *Introspective Digital Archaeology: Understanding the Computational Turn in Archaeology*, 25 May 2015, http://introspectivedigitalarchaeology.com/2015/05/25/preservation-by-record, archived at https://perma.cc/X5ED-NJDU.

19. See Laurajane Smith, *Uses of Heritage* (Abingdon, UK, 2006).

20. David C. Harvey, 'The History of Heritage', in Brian Graham and Peter Howard (eds), *The Ashgate Research Companion to Heritage and Identity* (Bodmin, UK, 2008), pp 19–36.

21. Smith, *Uses of Heritage*, p. 6.

22. Þóra Pétursdóttir, 'Concrete Matters: Ruins of Modernity and the Things Called Heritage', *Journal of Social Archaeology* 13.1 (2012), p. 37, 41.

23. It is worth noting the fate of the other postindependence Magdalen laundries within the contemporary Irish state: the Galway Laundry building and New Ross convent demolished; Waterford and Limerick repurposed as part of third-level educational facilities (institutes of technology); Sunday's Well (Cork) and Sean McDermott Street (Dublin), sitting derelict and with major degradation and demolition issues, awaiting potential development; High Park, Drumcondra (Dublin), repurposed as part of a social-housing development; and Galway convent repurposed as a homeless shelter for domestic-violence survivors.

24. Laura McAtackney, 'Manifestations of Conflict in a Post-ceasefire State: Material, Memory, and Meaning in Contemporary Northern Ireland', in Þóra Pétursdóttir and Bjørnar Olsen (eds), *Ruin Memories: Materialities, Aesthetics, and the Archaeology of the Recent Past* (Abingdon, UK, 2014), pp 319–34.

25. Laura McAtackney and Krysta Ryzewski (eds), *Contemporary Archaeology and the City: Creativity, Ruination, and Political Action* (Oxford, 2017).

26. Including the derelict Magdalen laundries at Sunday's Well in Cork and on Sean McDermott Street in central Dublin.

27. Olivier, *Dark Abyss*; Clara Fischer, 'Gender, Nation, and the Politics of Shame: Magdalen Laundries and the Institutionalization of Feminine Transgression in Modern Ireland', *Signs: Journal of Women in Culture and Society* 41.4 (2016), pp 821–43.

28. McAtackney, *Archaeology of the Troubles*; Christopher Bannerman and Cahal McLaughlin, 'Collaborative Ethics in Practice-as-Research', in Ludivine Allegue, Simon Jones, Baz Kershaw, and Angela Piccini (eds) *Practice-as-Research in Performance and Screen* (Basingstoke, UK, 2009), pp 64–81.

29. Pierre Nora, 'Between Memory and History: Les Lieux de Mémoire', *Representations* 26 (1989), p. 22.

30. A much larger oral-testimony project was directed by Dr Katherine O'Donnell at University College Dublin and is available online on the JFMR website at http://jfmresearch.com/home/oralhistoryproject.

31. Laura McAtackney, *Monitoring Report* (unpublished report, July 2018), and Laura McAtackney, *Monitoring Report* (unpublished report, Aug. 2018).

32. Bjørnar Olsen and Þora Pétursdóttir (eds), *Ruin Memories: Materialities, Aesthetics, and the Archaeology of the Recent Past* (Abingdon, UK, 2014), p. 7.
33. Ibid.
34. James Deetz, *In Small Things Forgotten: An Archaeology of Early American Life* (1977; New York, 1996), p. 4.
35. See Pierre Bourdieu, *Language and Symbolic Power*, Gino Raymond and Matthew Adamson (trans) (Cambridge, 1991).
36. For some nuanced discussion of these issues, see Barbara Hausmair, Ben Jervis, Ruth Nugent, and Eleanor Williams (eds), *Archaeologies of Rules and Regulation: Between Text and Practice* (Oxford, 2018).
37. *Archaeology in the Planning Process* (Dublin Department of the Environment, Heritage, and Local Government, 2006).
38. Daniel Miller, *Stuff* (Cambridge, 2010), p. 155.
39. For example, in the aftermath of the referendum to repeal the 1983 Eighth Amendment to the Irish Constitution that effectively outlawed any access to abortion, Brenda Malone, a curator of the National Museum of Ireland, created a collection derived from the material culture of the #repealthe8th movement, including banners, leaflets, and other ephemera.
40. Deirdre Falvey, 'What's the National Museum of Ireland Collecting? Repeal Posters, Bees, and a Wedding Dress', *The Irish Times*, 16 Apr. 2019.
41. Brenda Malone to author, 27 Sept. 2018.
42. Zoë O'Reilly, *The In-Between Spaces of Asylum and Migration: A Participatory Visual Approach* (London, 2020).
43. Nora, 'Between Memory and History'; Olivier, *Dark Abyss*.

Chapter 22 – 'Finding the me who I truly never quite knew': Lessons from Australia's Find & Connect Project in Facilitating Records Access

1. Johanna Sköld, 'Apology Politics: Transnational Features', in Johanna Sköld and Shurlee Swain (eds), *Apologies and the Legacy of Abuse of Children in 'Care': International Perspectives* (Houndsmills, 2015), pp 17–20. For a discussion of the sequence of inquiries in Australia see Katie Wright, Shurlee Swain and Kathleen McPhillips, 'The Australian Royal Commission into Institutional Responses to Child Sexual Abuse', *Child Abuse & Neglect* 74 (2017), p. 2.
2. Human Rights and Equal Opportunity Commission, *Bringing Them Home: Report of the National Inquiry into the Separation of Aboriginal and Torres Strait Islander Children from Their Families* (Sydney, 1997).
3. Australian Senate Community Affairs References Committee (ASCARC), *Lost Innocents: Righting the Record Report on Child Migration* (Canberra, 2001).
4. Australian Senate Community Affairs References Committee (ASCARC), *Forgotten Australians: A Report on Australians who Experienced Institutional or Out-of-Home Care as Children* (Canberra, 2004).
5. Australia Senate Community Affairs References Committee (ASCARC), *Commonwealth Contribution to Former Forced Adoption Policies and Practices* (Canberra, 2012).
6. Royal Commission into Institutional Responses to Child Sexual Abuse (RCIRCSA), *Final Report* (Sydney, 2017).
7. See for example: Kate Gleeson, 'Responsibility and Redress: Theorising Gender Justice in the Context of Catholic Clerical Child Sexual Abuse in Ireland and Australia', *University of New South Wales Law Journal*, 39.2 (2016), pp 779–812; and Katie Wright, 'Remaking Collective Knowledge: An Analysis of the Complex and

Multiple Effects of Inquiries into Historical Institutional Child Abuse', *Child Abuse & Neglect* 74 (2017), pp 10–22.

8. For an insight into ongoing debates around this issue see: Maeve O'Rourke, 'Here's a full analysis of the problems with the Government's Mother and Baby Homes Bill', *thejournal.ie*, 21 Oct. 2020, available at: https://www.thejournal.ie/readme/maeve-orourke-analysis-mother-and-baby-homes-5240049-Oct2020/, accessed 23 Dec. 2020; Adoption Rights Research JFM Research, 'Adoption Rights Alliance, Justice for Magdalenes Research and the Clann Project Welcome Government Statement on Mother and Baby Homes', press release 29 Oct. 2020, available at: http://jfmresearch.com/wp-content/uploads/2020/10/ARA-JFMR-Clann-statement-28.10.20.pdf, accessed 23 Dec. 2020.

9. CLAN website: https://clan.org.au/, accessed 24 Dec. 2020; Alliance for Forgotten Australians website: https://forgottenaustralians.org.au/, accessed 24 Dec. 2020.

10. Frank Golding, 'Problems with Records and Recordkeeping Practices are not Confined to the Past: A Challenge from the Royal Commission into Institutional Responses to Child Sexual Abuse', *Archival Science*, 20(1) (2020), pp 1–19.

11. Find and Connect Web Resource, https://www.findandconnect.gov.au/, accessed 12 May 2020.

12. The full range of services included under the Find and Connect umbrella can be found at: https://www.dss.gov.au/families-and-children/programmes-services/family-relationships/find-and-connect-services-and-projects/find-and-connect-support-services-and-representative-organisations, accessed 23 Dec. 2020.

13. Australia came into existence in 1901 as a result of the federation of the six pre-existing British colonies. Child welfare, however, remained the responsibility of the states, creating a continuity which the Irish Government is able to deny by classifying pre-1922 cases as a British responsibility.

14. Truth Justice and Healing Council website: http://www.tjhcouncil.org.au/, accessed 23 Dec. 2020.

15. For an explanation of the relational online archival model underlying the resource see: Gavan McCarthy & Joanne Evans, 'Principles for Archival Information Services in the Public Domain', *Archives and Manuscripts* 40.1 (2012), pp 54–67.

16. *What to Expect when Accessing Records About You*, https://www.findandconnect.gov.au/wp-content/uploads/2013/08/FACPFS-2016-10-17-what-to-expect.pdf, accessed 12 May 2020.

17. Jack Horgan-Jones, 'No Obstacle to Publication of Mother and Babies Home Report, Says Taoiseach', *The Irish Times*, 30 Oct. 2020, available at: https://www.irishtimes.com/news/ireland/irish-news/no-obstacle-to-publication-of-mother-and-baby-homes-report-says-taoiseach-1.4395720, accessed 23 Dec. 2020.

18. RCIRCSA, *Final Report*, vol. 8: Recordkeeping and Information Sharing, p. 40.

19. Shurlee Swain and Nell Musgrove, 'We are the Stories We Tell about Ourselves: Child Welfare Records and the Construction of Identity among Australians who, as Children, Experienced out-of-Home "Care"', *Archives and Manuscripts* 40.1 (2012), p. 6.

20. Cate O'Neill, Vlad Selakovic, and Rachel Tropea, 'Access to Records for People who were in Out-of-Home Care: Moving Beyond "Third Dimension" Archival Practice', *Archives and Manuscripts* 40.1 (2012), p. 37.

21. RCIRCSA, *Final Report*, 8: Recordkeeping and Information Sharing, p.43.

22. Care Leavers Australasia Network [CLAN], *A Charter of Rights to Childhood Records*: https://clan.org.au/wp-content/uploads/2020/02/CLAN-Charter-of-rights-to-childhood-records-6323.pdf, accessed 11 May 2020; Suellen Murray, *Finding Lost Childhoods: Supporting Care-Leavers to Access Personal Records* (Cham, 2017), p. 180.

23. Jennifer Douglas and Allison Mills, 'From the Sidelines to the Center: Reconsidering the Potential of the Personal in Archives', *Journal of Archival Science* 18.3 (2018), p. 258.

24. Murray, *Finding Lost Childhoods*, p. 55.

25. Department of Social Services (DSS), *Access to Records by Forgotten Australians and Former Child Migrants* (Canberra, 2015), p. 48.

26. ASCARC, *Forgotten Australians*, p. 262.

27. Swain and Musgrove, 'We are the Stories We Tell about Ourselves', pp 9–10.

28. HREOC, *Bringing Them Home*, p. 410.

29. Murray, *Finding Lost Childhoods*, p. 181.

30. ASCARC, *Forgotten Australians*, pp 283–4.

31. CLAN, *Charter of Rights to Childhood Records*.

32. Frank Golding, 'The Care Leaver's Perspective', *Archives and Manuscripts* 44.3 (2016), p. 161.

33. Submission 22 quoted in ASCARC, *Forgotten Australians*, p. 268.

34. Submission 71 quoted in ibid., p. 265.

35. ASCARC, *Lost Innocents*, p. 169.

36. Murray, *Finding Lost Childhoods Records*, pp 193–4. RCIRCSA, *Final Report*, 8: Recordkeeping and Information Sharing, p. 47.

37. Swain and Musgrove, 'We are the Stories We Tell About Ourselves', pp 7–8. Viviane Frings-Hessami, 'Care Leavers' Records: A Case for a Repurposed Archive Continuum Model', *Archives and Manuscripts* 46.2 (2018), p. 161. Murray, *Finding Lost Childhoods*, p. 69.

38. Jacqueline Z. Wilson and Frank Golding, 'Contested Memories: Caring About the Past – or Past Caring?', in Sköld and Swain, *Apologies and the Legacy of Abuse of Children in 'Care'*, p. 34.

39. Douglas and Mills, 'From the Sidelines to the Center', p. 272. Murray, *Finding Lost Childhoods*, p. 67.

40. Jacqueline Z. Wilson and Frank Golding, 'Latent Scrutiny: Personal Archives as Perpetual Mementos of the Official Gaze', *Journal of Archival Science* 16.1 (2016), p. 97. Murray, *Finding Lost Childhoods*, pp 63–4. Wilson and Golding, 'Contested Memories', p. 34. Golding, 'The Care Leaver's Perspective', p. 161.

41. Submission 18 quoted in *Forgotten Australians*, p. 269.

42. Wilson and Golding, 'Latent Scrutiny', p. 95.

43. Ibid., p. 96.

44. ASCARC, *Forgotten Australians*, p. 270; RCIRCSA, *Final Report*, 8: Recordkeeping and Information Sharing, p. 49.

45. CLAN, *Charter of Rights to Childhood Records*.

46. DSS, *Access to Records by Forgotten Australians and Former Child Migrants*, p. 33.

47. Swain and Musgrove, 'We are the Stories We Tell About Ourselves', p. 5.

48. Frings-Hessami, 'Care Leavers' Records', pp 162–3.

49. Ibid., p. 164.

50. Murray, *Finding Lost Childhoods*, p. 194. ASCARC, *Lost Innocents: Righting the Record Report on Child Migration*, p. 146.

51. Nell Musgrove, 'The Role and Importance of History', in Sköld and Swain, *Apologies and the Legacy of Abuse of Children in 'Care'*, p. 151.

52. DSS, *Access to Records by Forgotten Australians and Former Child Migrants*, p. 11.

53. O'Neill, Selakovic, and Tropea, 'Access to Records for People who were in Out-of-Home Care', p. 36.

54. ASCARC, *Lost Innocents*, p. 147. Wilson and Golding, 'Contested Memories', p. 36; Submission 211 quoted in ASCARC, *Forgotten Australians Children*, pp 257–8.

55. Douglas and Mills, 'From the Sidelines to the Center', p. 271. Hansard transcript cited in ASCARC, *Forgotten Australians*, p. 274.

56. CLAN, *Charter of Rights to Childhood Records*.

57. DSS, *Access to Records by Forgotten Australians and Former Child Migrants*, p. 40.

58. HREOC, *Bringing Them Home*, p. 413. Frings-Hessami, 'Care Leavers' Records', p. 164; CLAN, *Charter of Rights to Childhood Records*.

59. ASCARC, *Lost Innocents*, p. 157, 72. DSS, *Access to Records by Forgotten Australians and Former Child Migrants*, p. 31.

60. Joanne Evans et al., 'Self-Determination and Archival Autonomy: Advocating Activism', *Journal of Archival Science* 15.4 (2015), p. 347.

61. DSS, *Access to Records by Forgotten Australians and Former Child Migrants*, p. 51.

62. Swain and Musgrove, 'We are the Stories We Tell about Ourselves', p. 9.

63. ASCARC, *Forgotten Australians*, p. 284. Swain and Musgrove, 'We are the Stories We Tell about Ourselves', p. 9. Hansard transcript cited in ASCARC, *Forgotten Australians*, p. 274.

64. DSS, *Access to Records by Forgotten Australians and Former Child Migrants*, p. 7.

65. RCIRCSA, *Final Report*, 8: Recordkeeping and Information Sharing, p. 23.

66. DSS, *Access to Records by Forgotten Australians and Former Child Migrants*, p. 21.

67. Submission 154 cited in ASCARC, *Forgotten Australians*, p. 274.

68. Submission 53 cited in ASCARC, *Forgotten Australians*, p. 279.

69. Murray, *Finding Lost Childhoods*, p. 55. This point is well made by Claire McGettrick, chapter 15, in this volume.

70. For guides to best practice in records release see Murray, *Finding Lost Childhoods*, p. 57. and DSS, *Access to Records by Forgotten Australians and Former Child Migrants*, p. 54.

CHAPTER 23 – TRANSITIONAL JUSTICE, NON-RECENT CHILD ABUSE AND ARCHIVAL RESEARCH: LESSONS FROM THE CASE OF THE UK CHILD MIGRATION PROGRAMMES

1. The term 'non-recent abuse' is used in this paper rather than 'historic abuse' in recognition of the fact that although instances of abuse may have occurred some decades ago their effects are often on-going.

2. See, e.g. Ellen Boucher, *Empire's Children: Child Emigration, Welfare and the Decline of the British World, 1869–1967* (Cambridge, 2014); Gordon Lynch, *Remembering Child Migrants: Faith, Nation-Building and the Wounds of History* (London, 2015).

3. Stephen O'Connor, *The Orphan Trains: The Story of Charles Loring Brace and the Children He Saved and Failed* (Chicago, 2001).

4. Joy Parr, *Labouring Children: British Immigrant Apprentices to Canada, 1869–1924*, 2nd edition (Toronto, 1994).

5. Roy Parker, *Uprooted: The Shipment of Poor Children to Canada, 1867–1917* (Bristol, 2010).

6. See, e.g. Philip Bean & Joy Melville, *Lost Children of the Empire* (London, 1989); Margaret Humphreys, *Empty Cradles* (London, 1994); Alan Gill, *Orphans of the Empire: The Shocking Story of Child Migration to Australia* (Sydney, 1998).

7. See Legislative Assembly, Western Australia, Select Committee into Child Migration, *Interim Report* (Perth 1996); UK Parliament Health Committee, Third Report, *The Welfare of Former British Child Migrants* (London, 1998), 2 Vols.; *Preliminary Report on Neerkol for the Commission of Inquiry into Abuse of Children in Queensland Institutions* (Brisbane, 1998) *Report of the Commission of Inquiry into Abuse of Children in Queensland Institutions* (Brisbane, 1999) also known as the Forde Report; Australian Senate Community Affairs Committee, *Lost Innocents: Righting the*

Record, Report on Child Migration (Canberra, 2001); Historical Institutional Abuse Inquiry, *Report of the Historical Institutional Abuse Inquiry* (Belfast, 2017); Australian Royal Commission, *Case studies 5 (on Salvation Army institutions in Queensland and New South Wales)*, *11 (on Christian Brothers institutions in Western Australia)* and *26 (on St Joseph's Orphanage, Neerkol)* (Canberra, 2014/15); Independent Inquiry into Child Sexual Abuse, *Child Migration Programmes Investigation Report* (London, 2018). The findings of the Scottish Child Abuse Inquiry in relation to its investigation of child migration have not been published at the time this chapter went to press. For a useful summary of the wider context of critical understandings of child migration programmes in Australia, see Andrew Murray & Marilyn Rock, 'Child migration schemes to Australia: a dark and hidden Ch. of Australia's history revealed', *Australian Journal of Social Issues*, 38.2, 2003, pp 149–67.

8. Stephen Winter, *Transitional Justice in Established Democracies: A Political Theory* (Basingstoke, 2014).

9. On this post-war ethos, see, e.g. Mathew Thomson, *Lost Freedom: The Landscape of the Child and the British Post-War Settlement* (Oxford, 2013)

10. Gordon Lynch, 'Pathways to the 1946 Curtis report and the post-war reconstruction of children's out-of-home care', *Contemporary British History*, 34.1 (2020), pp 22–43.

11. Stephen Constantine, 'The British Government, child welfare and child migration to Australia after 1945', *Journal of Imperial and Commonwealth History*, 30.1 (2002), pp 99–132.

12. See, e.g, criticisms within the Church of England of the child migration work undertaken by the Church of England Advisory Council on Empire Settlement (Gordon Lynch, 'The Church of England Advisory Council of Empire Settlement and post-war child migration', *Journal of Ecclesiastical History*, 74.1 (2020), pp 798–826).

13. Gordon Lynch, *Possible Collusion Between Individuals Alleged to Have Sexually Abused Boys at Four Christian Brothers' Institutions in Western Australia: A Secondary Analysis of Material Collated by Historical Abuse Inquiries*, published online 24th Feb., 2020, accessible at https://kar.kent.ac.uk/79274/.

14. Australian Senate Community Affairs Committee, *Lost Innocents*; see also Australian Senate Community Affairs Committee, *Forgotten Australians: A Report on Australians Who Experienced Institutional or Out-of-Home Care as Children* (Canberra, 2004).

15. See the *Find and Connect* service (https://www.findandconnect.gov.au/) and the on-line reading guide for archival resources, *Good British Stock: Child and Youth Migration to Australia* (http://guides.naa.gov.au/good-british-stock/index.aspx).

16. On this see also Gordon Lynch, Pirjo Markkola, Eoin O'Sullivan, Johanna Sköld and Shurlee Swain, *The Uses of Historical Research in Child Abuse Inquiries, History and Policy* paper, first published online 7 May 2020, accessible at www.historyandpolicy. org/policy-papers/the-uses-of-historical-research-in-child-abuse-inquiries.

17. See, e.g. Ronald Niezen, *Truth and Indignation: Canada's Truth and Reconciliation Commission on Indian Residential Schools* (Toronto, 2017). As chapters in this volume indicate, the effectiveness of recent Inquiries in Ireland in enabling such public recognition is highly contested.

18. Select Committee into Child Migration, *Interim Report*, p.10; see also Health Committee, *The Welfare of Former British Child Migrants*, Vol. 1, paras 92–3 in which the UK Government appeared still to be downplaying its role, with one civil servant initially claiming in oral evidence that they were not aware of any on-going financial subsidies being paid for the overseas maintenance of child migrants by

the UK Government; a claim challenged by archival records of UK Government maintenance agreements for such payments.

19. Health Committee, *The Welfare of Former British Child Migrants*, Vol. 1. para 31.

20. Health Committee, The *Welfare of Former British Child Migrants*, Report, Vol. 1, paras 61, 73, and Vol 2, p. 193.

21. See Independent Inquiry into Child Sexual Abuse, *Child Migration Programmes Investigation*, Public Hearings, Day 17, 19 July 2017, pp 9–15.

22. Royal Commission into Institutional Responses to Child Sexual Abuse, *Report of Case Study No. 11*, p. 36.

23. See, e.g. both gaps in knowledge and, in one instance, inaccurate interpretation of source material in Historical Institutional Abuse Inquiry, *Report of the Historical Institutional Abuse Inquiry*, paras 38–40, 108–110. Errors and gaps here include some incorrect historical detail about events in the summer of 1947, a lack of knowledge about criticisms of Christian Brothers' institutions amongst UK civil servants and Catholic authorities during the Second World War and the unfulfilled promise of Catholic authorities to inspect these institutions before sending child migrants to them again after the war, the lack of readiness of some Catholic institutions in Western Australia to receive children sent to them and a failure to understand UK Government responses to its 1956 Fact-Finding Mission to Australia.

24. See, e.g. Michel-Rolph Trouillot, *Silencing the Past: Power and the Production of History* (Boston, 2015).

25. See Independent Inquiry into Child Sexual Abuse, *Child Migration Programmes Investigation*, Public Hearings, Day 13, 13 July 2017. Another similar example is a reconstruction of the post-war chronology of child migration undertaken within the Church of England which showed that concerns raised by the Home Office about its standards in 1958 followed many years in which senior clergy within the Church had been aware that the agency undertaking this work was doing so with minimal resources and over-sight (Lynch, 'The Church of England Advisory Council').

26. For further discussion of these explicit and implicit policy drivers, see Gordon Lynch, *UK Child Migration to Australia: A Study in Policy Failure* (Basingstoke, 2021); also Constantine, 'The British Government'.

27. On this, see also Lynch, *UK Child Migration to Australia*.

28. Independent Inquiry into Child Sexual Abuse, *Child Migration Programmes Investigation Report*.

29. Independent Inquiry into Child Sexual Abuse, *Child Migration Programmes*, Public Hearings, Day 15, 17 July 2017.

30. See Lynch, *Possible Collusion*.

31. See, e.g. Scottish Child Abuse Inquiry, Day 197 Transcript, 7 Oct., 2020

32. An excellent example of such analysis of complementary data in the context of transitional justice in Ireland is the Magdalene Names Project, undertaken by Claire McGettrick, which has compared data from grave sites, electoral registers, census records, exhumation records and newspaper archives to provide a more detailed overview of women incarcerated in Magdalene institutions, their length of stay and their movement between institutions (see http://jfmresearch.com/home/magdalene-names-project/).

33. See Australian Senate Community Affairs Committee, *Lost Innocents*, 3.55; Historical Institutional Abuse Inquiry, *Report of the Historical Institutional Abuse Inquiry*, Vol. 2, paras 122–9.

34. Copies of LEM3 forms for child migrants are available at the National Archives of Australia, series PP93/10.

35. See, e.g. Máiréad Enright and Sinéad Ring, chapter 7 in this volume.

36. On inquiries as a form of public history, see Lynch et al, *The Uses of Historical Research*.
37. See http://clannproject.org/commission-archive/.

CHAPTER 24 – KNOWING AND UNKNOWING TUAM: STATE PRACTICE, THE ARCHIVE AND TRANSITIONAL JUSTICE

1. An earlier version of this essay appeared in *Éire-Ireland: An Interdisciplinary Journal of Irish Studies* 55.1 (Spring/Summer 2020), pp 142–180, DOI: 10.1353/eir.2020.0006. I thank my two coeditors and the peer reviewer for their helpful feedback. I also thank Christopher Wilson, Andrew Sofer, Claire McGettrick, Jane Biondi, and Beatriz Valdés for reading this essay. All errors are my own.
2. No child is illegitimate; rather, society deems it so. This distinction should be kept in mind when encountering subsequent usages of this term in this essay. The focus here is on the Tuam Baby Home, but the state's pattern of unknowing is system-wide and applies with equal force to historic abuse in related institutions and to Ireland's closed and secret adoptions.
3. UN Office of the High Commissioner for Human Rights, *Transitional Justice and Economic, Social, and Cultural Rights* (UN Doc. HR/PUB/13/5, 11 Apr. 2014), 5.
4. At the time much was made of the description of Corless as a 'local' or 'amateur' historian. Questions might be asked as to why this history was not written by professional historians. Irish historiography traditionally privileges the archive, and thus access to material remains foremost to any such discussion. See also Scott Frickel et al., 'Undone Science: Charting Social Movement and Civil Society Challenges to Research Agenda Setting', *Science, Technology, and Human Values* 35.4 (2010), pp 444–73.
5. Alison O'Reilly, 'A Mass Grave of 800 Babies', *The Irish Mail on Sunday*, 25 May 2014, pp 1, 4–5. The media coverage on the Tuam story is voluminous. See Anne Enright, 'Antigone in Galway: Anne Enright on the Dishonored Dead', *London Review of Books* 37.24, 17 Dec. 2015, pp 11–14; Sarah Hampson, 'Ireland's "House of Tears": Why Tuam's Survivors Want Justice for Lost and Abused Children', *The Globe and Mail* (Canada), 29 Sept. 2017; Dan Barry, 'The Lost Children of Tuam', *The New York Times*, 28 Oct. 2017; Catherine Corless, 'The Home', *Journal of the Old Tuam Society* 9 (2012), pp 75–82. See also Declan Tierney, 'Memorial for 788 Babies Buried in Tuam Orphanage', *The Connacht Tribune*, 10 Oct. 2013.
6. Corless has been recognised with numerous awards—accepted reluctantly—for her unwavering perseverance and ethical leadership in demanding justice for the Tuam babies. See Olivia Kelly, 'Galway Historian Catherine Corless Receives Human Rights Award', *The Irish Times*, 26 Oct. 2017; and Sarah Burns, 'NUI Galway Awards Honorary Doctorates to Corless and Shannon', *The Irish Times*, 16 Oct. 2018.
7. See, for example, 'Names of the 800 Babies and Children in Septic Tank', *tuambabies.org*, https://www.tuambabies.org/tuam-baby-names.html, archived at https://perma.cc/256U-N6TE; Sheila Langan, 'Death Records for 796 Children at Tuam Home Published in Full', *Irish Central*, 17 June 2014; and 'These Were the 796 Children Who Died at Tuam Mother and Baby Home', *thejournal.ie*, 4 Mar. 2017, http://www.thejournal.ie/list-names-tuam-babies-children-3270019-Mar2017, archived at https://perma.cc/L9RW-JCYK.
8. Survivors, advocates, and journalists had, for at least two decades, campaigned for investigations of historic abuses at related institutions to no avail. In particular, note the advocacy organisation Adoption Rights Alliance (http://adoption.ie) and

journalist Conall Ó Fátharta in this regard (https://conallofatharta.wordpress.com). See also Claire McGettrick's essay, chapter 15 in this volume.

9. See, for example, Taoiseach Enda Kenny's early assertion, 'I *know* from the part of the country I come from that there are implications in terms of what happened to children. What we need to *know* is what happened', 'Leaders' Questions', *Dáil Éireann Debates*, p. 843, 10 June 2014; Caoimhghín Ó Caoláin, 'We *knew* these homes existed and that they were places of suffering for women and children. We did not *know*, however, the full extent of what occurred in them', 'Death and Burial of Children in Mother and Baby Homes: Motion [Private Members]', *Dáil Éireann Debates*, p. 843, 10 June 2014; Robert Troy, 'We all *know* now, and it was *known* at the time, that there was a much higher mortality rate among children in such homes', 'Interdepartmental Report on the Commission of Investigation into the Mother and Baby Homes: Statements', *Dáil Éireann Debates*, p. 849, 17 July 2014; and Clare Daly, 'It is the case that much of the information in respect of Tuam and what emerged there was *known*', ibid. Emphasis added.

10. Enda Kenny, 'Leaders' Questions', *Dáil Éireann Debates*, 7 Mar. 2017, p. 941.

11. Minister Charlie Flanagan engaged in a similar strategy when addressing the Tuam scandal: 'And Ireland was, at least in some respects, not entirely unique amongst countries in dealing with its most vulnerable citizens in a manner that would not be countenanced in a modern, civilised democracy. But in Ireland today we are confronted by the fact that as a newly established state, we besmirched our lofty ambitions and made hollow our promise to cherish all the children of the nation equally.' See 'Statement by Minister Flanagan', *Merrionstreet.ie*, 5 June 2014, https://merrion street.ie/en/News-Room/Speeches/statement-by-minister-flanagan-topical-issues-debate-thursday-5th-june-2014-the-need-for-an-independent-investigation-into-the-mass-grave-next-to-a-home-for-unmarried-mothers-and-babies.html, archived at https://perma.cc/DZ7V-QGTU.

12. Lindsey Earner-Byrne has pointed out that 'what has not taken place is any real "national conversation" regarding the ways in which Irish society as a whole facilitated "the system" that ultimately violated the rights of poor families and led to the abuse of so many children.' See Lindsey Earner-Byrne, 'Child Sexual Abuse, History, and the Pursuit of Blame in Modern Ireland', in Katie Homes and Stuart Ward (eds), *Exhuming Passions: The Pressure of the Past in Ireland and Australia* (Dublin, 2011), p. 51.

13. The Tuam home, like other mother-and-baby homes and county homes, was always state-licenced, with funding provided by both local and national government. The state's obligations toward the unmarried mother and her child were established within the framework of the Local Government (Temporary Provisions) Act (1923), which was later augmented by the Public Assistance Act (1939) and the Health Act (1953). See Local Government (Temporary Provisions) Act (9/1923), *Electronic Irish Statute Book* (hereafter cited as *EISB*), http://www.irishstatutebook.ie/eli/1923/act/9/enacted/en/print.html; Public Assistance Act (27/1939), *EISB*, http.//www.irish statutebook.ie/eli/1939/act/27/enacted/en/html; and Health Act (26/1953), *EISB*, http://www.irishstatutebook.ie/eli/1953/act/26/enacted/en/html.

14. Like Earner-Byrne, I recognise that the state and the Catholic church were extensions of Irish families and reflect the widely held belief in the decades after political independence that 'poverty was a crime' and was 'self-inflicted.' See Earner-Byrne, 'Child Sexual Abuse', p. 58.

15. James Reilly, 'Mother and Baby Homes Inquiries, Written Answers (Question to Children) No. 327', *Dáil Éireann Debates,* 16 July 2014, https://www.oireachtas.ie/en/debates/question/2014-07-16/327/#pq_327.

16. See Commission of Investigation (Mother and Baby Homes and Certain Related

Matters), SI 57/2015, *EISB*, http://www.irishstatutebook.ie/eli/2015/si/57/made/en/ print. Government announcements related to the Commission of Investigation into Mother and Baby Homes are available at Government of Ireland, 'Commission of Investigation into Mother and Baby Homes and Certain Related Matters', *Rialtas na hÉireann/Government of Ireland*, 22 Aug. 2015, https://www.gov.ie/en/ publication/873470-commission-of-investigation-into-mother-and-baby-homes-and-certain-r.

17. Department of Children and Youth Affairs, 'Minister Zappone Makes Statement on Excavations on Site of Former Mother and Baby Home Site, Tuam', *Rialtas na hÉireann/Government of Ireland*, 3 Mar. 2017, http://www.gov.ie/en/press-release/ e8ad3a-minister-zappone-makes-statement-on-excavations-on-site-of-former-mo, archived at https://perma.cc/JR7U-S6D2.

18. 'Commission of Investigation Announcement on Tuam Mother and Baby Home: Statements', *Dáil Éireann Debates*, p. 942, 9 Mar. 2017. Given my argument on the marked continuities between past and present state practices, I acknowledge the possibility that the government's embrace of transitional justice may yet prove to be another 'screen discourse' that masks ongoing inequalities in contemporary Ireland. See Loïc Wacquant (ed.), *Pierre Bourdieu and Democratic Politics: The Mystery of Ministry* (Malden, MA, 2005).

19. Department of Children and Youth Affairs, 'Government Approves Programme of Action to Respect the Memory and Dignity of Children Who Died in Tuam Mother and Baby Home', *Rialtas na hÉireann/Government of Ireland*, 23 Oct. 2018, https:// www.gov.ie/en/press-release/3a0827-government-approves-programme-of-action-to-respect-the-memory-and-di, archived at https://perma.cc/WMF5-CLR4. In Dec. 2018, Minister Zappone published legislation reflecting her earlier commitment to ensure that dignity and respect are afforded.

20. Commissions of Investigation Act (23/2004), *EISB*, http://www.irishstatutebook. ie/eli/2004/act/23/enacted/en/html. See also Maeve O'Rourke, '10 Ways Institutional Abuse Details Are Still Being Kept Secret', *RTÉ Brainstorm*, 5 Sept. 2019, https:// www.rte.ie/brainstorm/2019/0503/1047282-10-ways-institutional-abuse-details-are-still-being-kept-secret, archived at https://perma.cc/CAL3-DLD2.

21. See James M. Smith, *Ireland's Magdalen Laundries and the Nation's Architecture of Containment* (South Bend, IN, 2007), pp 54–57, 55. See also Maria Luddy, 'Unmarried Mothers in Ireland, 1880–1973', *Women's History Review* 20.1 (2011), pp 109–26; Lindsey Earner-Byrne, *Mother and Child: Maternity and Child Welfare in Dublin, 1922–60* (Manchester, 2007), pp 172–211; Paul Michael Garrett, 'Excavating the Past: Mother and Baby Homes in the Republic of Ireland', *British Journal of Social Work* 47.2 (2017), pp 358–74; Eoin O'Sullivan and Ian O'Donnell (eds) *Coercive Confinement in Ireland: Patients, Prisoners, and Penitents* (Manchester, 2012); Moira Maguire, *Precarious Childhood in Post-Independence Ireland* (Manchester, 2009), pp 86–149; Donnacha Seán Lucey, 'Single Mothers and Institutionalisation' and 'Child Welfare and Local Authorities', in *The End of the Irish Poor Law? Welfare and Healthcare Reform in Revolutionary and Independent Ireland* (Manchester, 2015), pp 82–147; Sarah-Anne Buckley, *The Cruelty Man: Child Welfare, the NSPCC, and the State in Ireland, 1889–1956* (Manchester, 2013).

22. Luddy, 'Unmarried Mothers', p. 113; Earner-Byrne, *Mother and Child*, p. 174. Earner-Byrne quotes the Registrar-General's *Annual Report* for 1932, which states, 'The accuracy of these figures [registrations of illegitimate births], however, is open to some doubt. It is inferred that many births that are really illegitimate are registered as legitimate.' See also Department of Local Government and Public Health, *Annual Report of the Registrar-General, 1932* (Dublin, Stationery Office, 1932), p. xiii.

23. Garrett, 'Excavating the Past', p. 234.

24. Earner-Byrne, *Mother and Child*, pp 180, 182.

25. I accessed the Department of Health archives after writing and seeking permission directly from James Reilly TD on 18 Jan. 2012. I examined the original documents discussed below, but in most instances they were also stamped as captured by the Access to Institutional and Related Records (AIRR) digital-archive project. According to Eneclann, the company that facilitated AIRR, the 'project addressed DoHC [Department of Health and Children] records related to child care services from the 1920s through to the 1990s. The approach was that files were microfilmed/scanned and placed on a server; each file was then assigned a unique ID 'tracker no.' The archivists extracted personal details and recorded all references to children; date(s) of birth, name(s) of carer(s), dates in care and biographical information where possible. The project required the highest level of accuracy and confidentiality. To ensure this, Eneclann developed a methodology for standardisation, accuracy, and accessibility. The project employed a proven validation system where every entry was checked by qualified archivists. The team indexed in excess of 200,000 records to this standard.' See the archived webpage, Eneclann, 'Department of Health and Children', *Eneclann.ie*, Nov. 2017, https://perma.cc/3Z4Z-TSXH.

26. This focus of analysis for this essay is on the 1940s, when many of these institutions were governed in accordance with the Public Assistance Act (1939). The modern Department of Health itself came into existence in Jan. 1947; prior to this it was the Department of Local Government and Public Health.

27. Replies to Circular P.24/48, Children Returns of Births, Deaths, etc. of Illegitimate Children p.A.A. Institutions During Year Ending 31.3.1947 (File A124/18, Department of Health, Records Management Unit, Hawkins House, Dublin [hereafter cited as DOH]).

28. See Letter from Secretary, Dublin Board of Assistance, to Secretary, Department of Health, 28 June 1948 (File A124/18, DOH).

29. See Buckley, *Cruelty Man*, p. 88.

30. The circular covered twelve months but straddled the two calendar years for which we have official statistics.

31. The CLANN project furnished the Commission of Investigation on Mother and Baby Homes with a list of 182 institutions, agencies, and individuals who were involved in Ireland's closed and secret system of adoption from 1922 onward. According to its terms of reference, the commission is investigating fourteen institutions and four sample county homes. See Maeve O'Rourke, Claire McGettrick, Rod Baker, Raymond Hill, et al., *CLANN: Ireland's Unmarried Mothers and Their Children: Gathering the Data: Principal Submission to the Commission of Investigation into Mother and Baby Homes* (Dublin, 15 Oct. 2018), p. 7, 22, http://clannproject. org/wp-content/uploads/Clann-Submissions_Redacted-Public-Version-Oct.-2018. pdf, archived at https://perma.cc/38CR-YLT2.

32. Source: Letter from Secretary, Galway County Council General Assistance Department, to Secretary, Department of Health, 5 Apr. 1948, and Letter from Secretary, Mayo County Council, to Secretary, Department of Health, 6 Apr. 1948 (File A124/18, DOH).

33. See Department of Health, *Annual Report of the Registrar General, 1946* (Dublin, Stationery Office, 1948), p. xxxv; Department of Health, *Annual Report of the Registrar General, 1947* (Dublin. Stationery Office, 1949), p. xxxv.

34. Ibid. Other medical conditions leading to death include 'pneumonia', 'congenital malformations', and 'convulsions.' It should be noted, however, that in the 1940s (unlike earlier and later decades), the Registrar General's annual report fails to separate out cause of death for legitimate and illegitimate-born infants.

35. Source: Circular P.24/48 (File A124/18, DOH).

36. Circular P.24/48 (File A124/18, DOH). I deliberately redact this nun's name (as I have redacted all names in this essay). Doing so adheres to good practice in utilising archival material; it also ensures that critical attention falls equally on both the religious sister and the state agency.

37. See Letter from Secretary, Galway County Council General Assistance Department, to Secretary, Department of Health, 5 Apr. 1948 (File A124/18, DOH).

38. See Letter from Secretary, Department of Health, to Secretary, Public Assistance Authority, 4 Mar. 1949 (File MA 124/12, 'Boarded Out Children, General', DOH). In his letter, circulated to all public-assistance authorities, the secretary signaled his minister's displeasure that 'some local authorities have neglected to submit such returns, and that in some instances the returns admitted contained inaccuracies.' He insisted that 'in future, returns required will be compiled and forwarded promptly to this department.'

39. See, for example, Mayo Returns, Children and Unmarried Mothers (File L112/212, b, DOH). For other examples, see Mayo Returns (File A21/158/v.2 (b), DOH); Children and Unmarried Mothers, Returns (File AL113/21, DOH); Galway, Children and Unmarried Mothers in Institutions, Returns 1952–57 (File A11/342/v.2, DOH); Limerick County, Children and Unmarried Mothers in Institutions, Returns (File L 17/164, DOH). Note that on the archival original, the Mayo County Council reported on forms produced for County Galway but penciled out the latter and inserted the word 'Mayo' instead.

40. Based on information related to exit pathways for 428 women (19.3% of total admissions) from the Tuam Baby Home, the MBHCOI Report suggests that 3% were transferred to Magdalene Laundries. The Commission identified 14 women who were transferred directly from Tuam to Magdalene Laundries between 1942 and 1958, but acknowledges that children's records suggest a further 84 mothers ended up in a Magdalene institution after discharge, and an additional 13 children entered Tuam unaccompanied while their mothers were admitted to a Magdalene Laundry. Records also signal that Galway County Council directed a further 22 women to enter a Magdalene Laundry on their discharge from Tuam, but the Commission failed to establish whether, in fact, they did so. See MBHCOI Report, Ch. 15, 29 (Para. 15.75) and Ch. 15 A, 15.

41. In his 1958 book, and following an interview with the nuns at the Tuam institution, Halliday Sutherland recounts being told by the 'sister-in-charge' that 'girls' who had 'two confinements' were sent 'to the Magdalen home laundry in Galway.' He interviewed the mother superior of the Galway Magdalen Laundry the following day, who asserted that 'seventy percent of the women in that laundry' were sent to them because they were 'unmarried mothers.' See Halliday Sutherland, *Irish Journey* (New York, 1958), pp 77–78.

42. The Good Shepherds operated Magdalen laundries at Limerick, Cork, Waterford, and New Ross. See also James M. Smith et al., *State Involvement in the Magdalene Laundries: JFM's Principal Submissions to the Inter-departmental Committee to Establish the Facts of State Involvement with the Magdalene Laundries* (Dublin, 2013), pp 68–74, esp. 71, http://jfmresearch.com/wp-content/uploads/2017/03/State_Involvement_in_the_Magdalene_Laundries_public.pdf, archived at https://perma.cc/FJT2-YCBB. For the McAleese inquiry, see Department of Justice, *Report of the Inter-departmental Committee to Establish the Facts of State Involvement with Magdalen Laundries* (Dublin, 2013), Ch. 11, pp 498–9, http://www.justice.ie/en/JELR/Pages/MagdalenRpt2013. Hereafter cited as *McAleese Report*.

43. I name Rodgers and Mulryan in this context with their permission. See also Fred Barbash, 'The "Mother and Baby Home" at Tuam, Ireland, Where Friends

Just "Disappeared, One after the Other,'" *The Washington Post*, 13 Mar. 2017; Nick Bramhill, 'Nuns Stopped Mother and Baby Home Survivor Saying Goodbye to Dying Mother', *Irish Central*, 21 Sept. 2018.

44. See Luddy, 'Unmarried Mothers', and Earner-Byrne, *Mother and Child*.

45. This information suggests how emigration worked to remove so-called 'problem women' from Ireland. Kevin Kenny argues that 'above all, emigration acted as a social safety valve by reducing poverty, unemployment, and class conflict. A big untold story in the history of Irish emigration is the benefits it produced for those who stayed behind.' See Kevin Kenny, 'The Irish Diaspora', *Aeon*, 7 Sept. 2017, https://aeon.co/essays/the-irish-experience-and-the-meaning-of-modern-diaspora, archived at https://perma.cc/PT57-HMA7. The state's awareness of this information at the time now obliges the ongoing Commission of Investigation to engage survivors in Ireland's diaspora impacted by this history. See James M. Smith, 'Will Mothers and Baby Homes Commission Advertise to the Hidden Irish Diaspora?' *The Irish Times*, 9 Nov. 2016.

46. The MBHCOI Report also examines the 1947 Inspector's Report, see Ch. 15, pp 35–9 (Paras. 15.94-15-100).

47. See the following files for copies of inspectors' reports from other mother-and-baby homes: St. Patrick's Home, Navan Road, Dublin, Inspectors' Reports (File A121/107, DOH); Manor House, Castlepollard, Inspectors' Reports (File A121/139, DOH); Special Homes Conducted by the Sisters of the Sacred Heart of Jesus and Mary (File A121/181, DOH).

48. I thank Anna Corrigan for sharing the document and granting permission to write about it. The document was also captured as part of the AIRR Project.

49. This upward trend is confirmed by Circular P.24/48.

50. Name redacted.

51. Earner-Byrne's argument regarding the 'class framework' that conceptualised Ireland's 'policy' of sending vulnerable children to industrial schools applies with equal force in this context. See Earner-Byrne, 'Child Sexual Abuse', pp 62–3.

52. See the MBHCOI Report, Ch. 15, 38 (Paras. 15.98).

53. The Ryan report finds similar levels of deference on the part of the Department of Education toward the religious congregations who managed the state's child residential institutions. See Commission to Inquire into Child Abuse, *Report of the Commission to Inquire into Child Abuse* (Dublin, Stationery Office, 2009), vol. 1, 16, available at http://childabusecommission.ie/publications/index.html. Hereafter cited as *Ryan Report*.

54. Annual Statistical Returns, Tuam (File A 124/34, National Archives of Ireland, Dublin); Annual Statistical Returns, Tuam (INACT/INACT/0/426512, DOH). The file includes returns from Bessborough, Castlepollard, Sean Ross Abbey, St. Patrick's Navan Road, Tuam, and, after it opened, Ard Mhuire, Dunboyne.

55. Source: Annual Statistical Returns, Tuam (File A 124/34, National Archives of Ireland, Dublin). The forms vary by year in terms of distinguishing between children admitted after birth under and over 1 year.

56. Retention of Records Dáil Bill (2019), https://www.oireachtas.ie/en/bills/bill/2019/16. Some 1,400 complainants as well as representatives from eighteen religious congregations appeared before the CICA to give evidence. As of 31 Dec. 2016, the RIRB had received 16,650 applications seeking redress and made 12,016 financial awards, the average of which was €62,250, at a total cost to the taxpayer— including administrative and legal fees—of €1.4 billion. See Residential Institutions Redress Board, *Annual Report of the Residential Institutions Redress Board*, 2016, https:// www.rirb.ie/annualReport.asp. See also Patsy McGarry, 'Religious

Congregations Indemnity Deal Was "a Blank Cheque," Says Michael McDowell', *The Irish Times*, 5 Apr. 2019.

57. 'Minister McHugh Announces Publication of the Retention of Records Bill 2019 to Transfer Records Relating to Residential Institutional Child Abuse to the National Archives', *Department of Education and Skills*, 28 Feb. 2019, https://www.education. ie/en/Press-Events/Press-Releases/2019-press-releases/PR19-02-28.html, archived at https://perma.cc/4RBR-2PBV. Emphasis added.

58. Commission to Inquire into Child Abuse Act (7/2000), *EISB*, http://www. irishstatutebook.ie/eli/2000/act/7/enacted/en/html, sec. 7(6) and 27(6). Minister McHugh, at the Dáil report stage for the bill, stated that 'the ultimate protection provided in the acts was for the disposal and destruction of the records of the bodies once they had completed their work and prior to their dissolution, which is also provided for in the legislation enacted by the Oireachtas.' See McHugh, 'Retention of Records Bill 2019: Second Stage', *Dáil Éireann Debates*, p. 981, 2 Apr. 2019, https://www.oireachtas.ie/en/debates/debate/dail/2019-04-02/27. Legal scholars Maeve O'Rourke, Máiréad Enright, and Sinéad Ring challenge this interpretation of the earlier legislation, arguing that the 2000 act envisaged the commission's records being kept in custody or disposed of in accordance with the National Archives Act (1986), and further that '"disposal" does not necessarily mean "destruction"'. Similarly, they underscore how the proposed legislation, if enacted, would make Ireland an outlier when compared to current practice in other jurisdictions, notably Scotland and Australia. For their submission and those of others appearing before Education and Skills Committee on 13 Nov. 2019, see 'Retention of Records Bill 2019', *Justice for Magdalenes Research*, http://jfmresearch.com/retention-of-records-bill-2019, archived at https://perma.cc/WJW8-KRLU.

59. See Jack Power, 'Sealing Abuse Records for 75 Years Would Make Survivors "Invisible Once More"', *The Irish Times*, 26 Nov. 2019. Oireachtas refers to both houses of Ireland's parliament, Dáil Éireann and Seanad Éireann.

60. The state has not adequately consulted survivors to ascertain their views on making testimony, which can be suitably redacted, available via a national repository of institutional records. Witnesses/survivors were not provided with a copy of, nor can they now access, their own testimony provided to the commission, a right provided in other jurisdictions, including Scotland and Australia.

61. See Paul Michael Garrett, '"The Children Not Counted": Reports on the Deaths of Children in the Republic of Ireland', *Critical and Radical Social Work* 2.1 (2014), pp 23–4.

62. See Sorcha Pollak, 'Three Girls Suffered "Grave and Heinous Sexual Abuse" While in Foster Care, Report Finds', *The Irish Times*, 28 May 2019; Emer O'Toole, 'Asylum Seekers in Ireland are Intimidated into Silence over Their Poor Treatment', *The Guardian*, 10 May 2019; Laura Lynott, 'Children in Homeless Accommodation Are Displaying "Suicidal Ideation," says FOCUS Ireland', *Sunday Independent*, 11 June 2019.

63. See National Archives Act (11/1986), *EISB*, http://www.irishstatutebook.ie/eli/1986/act/11/enacted/en/html. Crowe first called for a centralised, independent repository of church and state institutional records that can be accessed by survivors, academics, and genealogists in her 'Guilt, Shame, Acknowledgement, and Redress: Some Reflections on Ireland's Institutional Treatment of Women and Children' (Dean's Lecture, Maynooth University, 19 Oct. 2017). See Conall Ó Fátharta, 'Staying off the Record on Access to Archives', *The Irish Examiner*, 18 Oct. 2017.

64. Daniel McConnell, 'Dangerous Bill Is Anti-Democratic and Should Be Axed', *The Irish Examiner*, 9 Mar. 2019. See also Conall Ó Fátharta, '"A Dangerous

Precedent": 75-Year Seal Put on Child Abuse Testimony', *The Irish Examiner*, 1 Mar. 2019.

65. McConnell, 'Dangerous Bill'; Catríona Crowe, 'Submission to the Joint Committee on Education and Skills on the Provisions of the Retention of Records Bill 2019', 12 Nov. 2019. Copy shared with the author.

66. Inter-departmental Committee to Establish the Facts of State Involvement with the Magdalen Laundries, *Interim Progress Report*, Oct. 2011, p. 7, http://www.justice.ie/en/JELR/MagdelanInterimReport2011Oct.pdf/Files/MagdelanInterim Report2011Oct.pdf, archived at https://perma.cc/Q2SE-HX4M. I would point out that this arrangement was sanctioned at a statutory level; see Data Protection Act 1988 (Section 2B) Regulations (SI 486/2011), *EISB*, http://www.irishstatutebook.ie/eli/2011/si/486/made/en/pdf

67. See essays by Claire McGettrick, James Gallen, and Máiréad Enright and Sinéad Ring, chapters 15, 12, and 7 respectively in this volume, for other iterations of this argument.

68. Freedom of Information Act (2014), *EISB*, http://www.irishstatutebook.ie/eli/2014/act/30/enacted/en/html.

69. See James M. Smith, 'Commissions of Investigations Act Inhibits Truth-Telling about Past and Present', *The Irish Times*, 30 Oct. 2018.

70. See Conall Ó Fátharta, '"No Plans" to Open Committee Archive on Magdalene Laundries', *The Irish Examiner*, 8 Sept. 2018.

71. The CLANN project is a joint initiative between Justice for Magdalenes Research and the Adoption Rights Alliance in association with global law firm Hogan Lovell. Its final report draws on seventy-seven witness statements, extracted from conversations with 164 people separated from their families through Ireland's forced, secret adoption system and related institutional abuses. See O'Rourke et al., *CLANN*.

72. Ibid., p. 10.

73. The failure to preserve and ensure access to archival material related to two earlier state investigations of abuse in Ireland's industrial and reformatory schools, the Cussen committee and report (1936) and the Kennedy committee and report (1970), ensured that lessons went unlearned. According to Mary Raftery and Eoin O'Sullivan, 'every single shred of material' from both investigations disappeared from the Department of Education's archives. See Raftery and O'Sullivan, *Suffer the Little Children: The Inside Story of Ireland's Industrial Schools* (Dublin, 1999), p. 332.

74. O'Rourke et al., *CLANN*, p. 107, pp 129–33, p. 143.

75. See James Gallen's essay, chapter 12 in this volume.

76. James M. Smith to Martin McAleese, 21 Feb. 2012. I also wrote to Senator McAleese a week earlier, on 16 Feb. 2012, and provided a more in-depth analysis of the biannual returns signaling the transfer of unmarried women from the Tuam Baby Home to Magdalen laundries. Over the course of the committee's work, and together with my JFMR colleagues, I met with the committee three times, arranged two meetings in Leinster House with survivors, made over a dozen email submissions, and wrote at least five letters before ultimately JFMR made its principal submission in Aug. 2012. See Smith et al., *State Involvement in the Magdalene Laundries*.

77. *McAleese Report*, Ch. 11, pp 498–9.

78. The taoiseach and members of his party lauded the fact that the Magdalen inquiry cost a mere €11,000. See Enda Kenny, 'Leaders' Questions', *Dáil Éireann Debates*, p. 791, 6 Feb. 2013, https://www.oireachtas.ie/en/debates/debate/dail/2013-02-06/2; Joe O'Reilly, 'Magdalen Laundries Report: Statements (Resumed)', *Dáil Éireann Debates*, p. 794, 26 Feb. 2013, https://www.oireachtas.ie/en/debates/debate/dail/2013-02-26/28.

79. UN Committee Against Torture, *Consideration of Reports Submitted by States Parties under Article 19 of the Convention—Ireland* (UN Doc. CAT/C/IRL/CO/1, 17 June 2011), p. 6. UNCAT reiterated this recommendation in its *Concluding Observations* after Ireland was examined in 2017. See Maeve O'Rourke on behalf of Justice for Magdalenes Research, *NGO Submission to the UN Committee Against Torture in Respect of Ireland (For the Session) July 2017*, pp 7–15, http://jfmresearch.com/wp-content/uploads/2017/07/JFMR-report-to-CAT-for-the-session-2017-Main-Report.pdf, archived at https://perma.cc/PWX6-VJJQ; Maeve O'Rourke and James M. Smith, 'Ireland's Magdalene Laundries: Confronting a History Not Yet in the Past', in Alan Hayes and Máire Meagher (eds) *A Century of Progress? Irish Women Reflect* (Arlen House, 2016), pp 107–33. Also see Sinéad Ring and Máiréad Enright's essay, chapter 7 in this volume, for the various strategies deployed by the state to prop up the McAleese report as the final word on the laundries.
80. See Maeve O'Rourke, chapter 6 in this volume.
81. The MBHCOI Report suggests that the Department of Children and Youth Affairs shared items related to the 'Inter Departmental Committee on the Magdalen Laundries 2011–2013', see Part V, 'Archives', 44–5.
82. James M. Smith to Martin McAleese, 21 Feb. 2012.
83. Conall Ó Fátharta, 'State's Reaction Is to Deny, Delay, and to Buy Silence', *The Irish Examiner*, 10 Dec. 2018.
84. Ibid.

Contributors

ROSEMARY C. ADASER, B.A. (Hons.), M.Sc./Dip. Rosemary spent eighteen years in Irish industrial schools and Mother and Baby Homes. Rosemary is founder and CEO of the Association of Mixed Race Irish (AMRI), a campaign and advocacy NGO. Rosemary is the AMRI lead delegate to the UN Committee for the Elimination of Racial Discrimination (CERD), where her submission to CERD is listed as a key theme. Ireland attended in December 2019. Rosemary is a member of Katherine Zappone's Collaborative Forum and was previously a board member for three years (2014–17) at Caranua.

DAN BARRY is a long-time reporter and columnist for *The New York Times*, having written both the 'This Land' and 'About New York' columns. The author of several books, he writes on myriad topics, including sports, culture, New York City and the nation. His many honours include the 2003 American Society of Newspaper Editors Award for deadline reporting, for his coverage of the first anniversary of 9/11; the 2005 Mike Berger Award, from the Columbia University Graduate School of Journalism; and the 2015 Best American Newspaper Narrative Award. He has also been nominated as a finalist for the Pulitzer Prize twice: once in 2006 for his slice-of-life reports from hurricane-battered New Orleans and New York, and again in 2010 for his coverage of the Great Recession and its effects on the lives and relationships of America.

CONRAD BRYAN is a member of the Collaborative Forum and a trustee of the Association of Mixed Race Irish (AMRI). He currently works as a financial consultant at Viatores Christi, a development and humanitarian aid organisation based in Dublin. He trained as an accountant while working in Ireland and qualified as a chartered certified accountant in 1992; he has worked in several senior finance roles in both Dublin and London. Conrad's main interest is to advocate on behalf of survivors of institutions in Ireland and in particular to seek justice and reparations for the racial discrimination and racism suffered by children incarcerated in Irish institutions, many of whom suffer consequences today as adults.

MARY BURKE, associate professor of English and director of the Irish literature concentration at the University of Connecticut, is author of '*Tinkers*': *Synge and the Cultural History of the Irish Traveller* (Oxford University Press, 2009). Recent articles include a *James Joyce Quarterly* lead article and a *Journal of Design History* cover article (both 2018). She has forthcoming articles on the Tuam babies and Tom Murphy's drama (*Irish University Review*) and on Grace Kelly (*American Journal of Irish Studies*). Recently appointed to Fulbright's National Screening Committee, Burke has held the NEH Keough-Naughton Fellowship at Notre Dame, is former chair of the MLA Irish Literature Committee, and a former New England American Conference for Irish Studies president.

APRIL DUFF is a graduate of University College Dublin (B.C.L., LL.M), where she was an Ad Astra and James Healy Scholar and is currently a tutor. She is a practicing barrister specialising in human rights and related areas. She was formerly the chairperson of Education Equality, an education-rights NGO.

ANNE ENRIGHT has written seven novels, two collections of short stories and a book of essays about motherhood. She was the inaugural Laureate for Irish Fiction (2015–18). Her short stories have appeared in several magazines including *The New Yorker* and *The Paris Review*. Essays, lectures and articles are published by *The London Review of Books*, *The Dublin Review*, *The Guardian*, *The Irish Times* and *The New York Times*. She was editor of *The Granta Book of the Irish Short Story* (2011). Key awards were The Man Booker Prize (2007), which brought her work to global attention, The Andrew Carnegie medal for Excellence in Fiction (2012), and the Irish Novel of the year (2008 and 2016). Her work has been translated into almost 40 languages.

MÁIRÉAD ENRIGHT joined Birmingham Law School, University of Birmingham, in 2016. Her research is in feminist legal studies and law and religion. She is especially interested in how patriarchal legal and religious structures can be resisted and changed. Her research in this respect looks beyond traditional methods of law reform to consider illegality, protest, private litigation and experimental legal drafting. She is co-director of the Northern/Irish Feminist Judgements Project and often consults with and advises groups campaigning around reproductive rights and historical gender-based violence in Ireland.

JAMES GALLEN is a lecturer in the School of Law and Government at Dublin City University. His present research agenda and recent publications concern transitional justice and *jus post bellum*, and a transitional-justice approach to historical abuse in consolidated democracies, especially child sex abuse in the Roman Catholic church. In 2017 he was appointed as an expert advisor on transitional justice by the Department of Children and Youth Affairs to advise on a transitional-justice approach to the issue of Mother and Baby Homes. His research interests include human rights, international law and legal and transitional justice.

PAUL MICHAEL GARRETT works at NUI Galway. He is the author of many internationally peer-reviewed articles and several books, including *Welfare Words* (Sage, 2018) and *Social Work and Social Theory: Second Edition* (Policy Press, 2018). In 2018 he was visiting professor at the City University of New York (CUNY), and he has presented keynote papers at international conferences across Europe and in China. For two decades he has been a member of the editorial collective of Critical Social Policy. Contemporary neoliberalism and historical practices of marginalisation and domination are some of his key concerns.

TERRI HARRISON was imprisoned at the age of eighteen in a Mother and Baby Home institution. Currently, she is a director of the Christine Buckley Centre (CBC) and serves on the Collaborative Forum. The CBC offers help to all who are impacted by institutional and historic abuse. Terri runs support groups for women detained in institutions. She also runs Origins Ireland, a worldwide support group founded in Australia for forced separations of mother and child. She focuses on gender injustice in all areas of her advocacy work.

MARK T. KEANE has been chair of computer science at University College Dublin since 1997. He has a B.A. in psychology from UCD and a PhD in cognitive psychology from Trinity College Dublin (TCD). He was previously a lecturer in TCD and is a onetime fellow (1994); in 2004–7 he was director of information and communications technology, UCD, and director-general of Science Foundation Ireland. He has published fifteen books with several co-authors, including *Analogical Problem Solving* (1988), *Lines of Thinking* (1990), *Advances in the Psychology of Thinking* (1992) and *Cognitive Psychology: A Student's Handbook* (1990–2015, eight editions; six foreign-language editions).

SUSAN LEAVY is an assistant professor at the School of Information and Communication in University College Dublin. Her research concerns the ethics of artificial intelligence and cultural analytics. Her recent work is on the prevention of bias and discrimination in artificial intelligence. Susan earned a PhD in computer science at Trinity College Dublin using AI to detect bias in political news. She holds an M.Phil. in gender and women's studies and an M.Sc. in artificial intelligence from Edinburgh University.

SUSAN LOHAN became involved in campaigning for identity rights for Irish adopted people when seeking information on her natural father. In 2001 she joined Adoption Ireland, which successfully campaigned for the withdrawal of Ireland's draft Adoption Information and Tracing Bill. In 2003 Susan was appointed by the minister for children to represent adopted people on an advisory group to the Irish Adoption Board. In the continued absence of legislation to vindicate Irish adopted people's rights to identity, in 2009 Susan co-founded the Adoption Rights Alliance.

PATRICIA LUNDY is professor of sociology at the University of Ulster. In 2016 she was awarded a Leverhulme Trust Major Research Fellowship, following a British Academy Senior Research Fellowship in 2009. Her research interests deal with the legacy of political conflict, truth recovery and the politics of memory. Her most recent project is an empirical study of the Historical Institutional Abuse Inquiry (HIAI) from the perspective of victim/survivors. Her work has been published in the *International Journal of Transitional Justice*; *Sociology, Law, and Society*; *Law and Social Challenges*; and the *International Journal of Human Rights*.

GORDON LYNCH is Michael Ramsey Professor of Modern Theology at the University of Kent. Whilst interested in wider historic cases of institutional abuse, much of his recent research has focused on the history of post-war UK child migration schemes to Australia, focusing particularly on the policy and institutional context in which these operated. He has served as an expert witness on this history for both the Independent Inquiry into Child Sexual Abuse and the Scottish Child Abuse Inquiry, and has also played a leading role in other public engagement work including co-curating the national exhibition, 'On Their Own: Britain's Child Migrants' and co-producing the musical project, the 'Ballads of Child Migration'.

LAURA MCATACKNEY is associate professor in sustainable-heritage management at Aarhus University, Denmark, and docent in contemporary historical archaeology at Oulu University, Finland. She has worked for over 15 years on exploring the material worlds of prisons, with special focus on Long Kesh/Maze Prison in Northern Ireland and Kilmainham Jail in Dublin. She is the author of *An Archaeology of the Troubles: The Dark Heritage of Long Kesh/Maze Prison* (2014). She is the principal investigator of the Danmarks Frie Forskningsfond-funded *Enduring Materialities of*

Colonialism (EMoC): Temporality, Spatiality, and Memory on St. Croix, USVI (2019–23).

CLAIRE MCGETTRICK is an Irish Research Council postgraduate scholar at the School of Sociology at University College Dublin. Her research interests focus on adoption, so-called historical abuses and related injustices in twentieth-century Ireland. Her PhD research investigates the bodies of expert knowledge on adoption. She is co-founder of Justice for Magdalenes Research (JFMR) and Adoption Rights Alliance. She jointly coordinates the multi-award-winning CLANN project with Dr Maeve O'Rourke, as well as the Magdalene Names Project, which has recorded the details of over 1,900 women who lived and died in Ireland's Magdalen laundries. She is co-author of *Ireland and the Magdalene Laundries: A Campaign for Justice* (Bloomsbury/I.B. Tauris, 2021) and recently published an article in the double special issue of *Éire-Ireland* (Spring/Summer 2020) on Transitional Justice and institutional abuse in Ireland.

ROSEMARY NAGY is Associate Professor of Gender Equality and Social Justice at Nipissing University in North Bay, Canada, in Robinson-Huron treaty territory. She researches and teaches in the field of transitional justice, with work on the cases of South Africa, Rwanda and Canada. She has published in *Third World Quarterly*, *International Journal of Transitional Justice* and *Human Rights*.

FIONNUALA NÍ AOLÁIN is concurrently Regents Professor at the University of Minnesota Law School and professor of law at the Queen's University, Belfast. She is the recipient of numerous academic awards, including the Leverhulme Fellowship, Fulbright Scholarship, ASIL Certificate of Merit for Creative Scholarship, Alon Prize, Robert Schumann Scholarship and Lawlor Fellowship. She has published extensively on issues of gender, conflict regulation, transitional justice and counterterrorism. She has held academic positions at Columbia Law School, Harvard Law School, Princeton University and the Hebrew University of Jerusalem. Ní Aoláin is currently the United Nations Special Rapporteur on Human Rights and Counter-Terrorism.

KATHERINE O'DONNELL is associate professor of the history of ideas, UCD School of Philosophy, and has published widely on the history of sexuality and gender and the intellectual history of eighteenth-century Ireland. She is co-author of *Ireland and the Magdalene Laundries: A Campaign for Justice* (Bloomsbury/I.B. Tauris, 2021) and recently co-edited a double special issue of *Éire-Ireland* (Spring/Summer 2020) on Transitional Justice and institutional abuse in Ireland. She has been principal investigator on a number of funded research projects, including gathering an archival and oral history of the Magdalene institutions funded by the Irish Research Council. Her teaching awards include the UCD President's Gold Medal for Teaching Excellence and the British Universities' Learning On-Screen Award. She has gained academic honours, including a Fulbright Fellowship and the University of California, Berkeley, Chancellor's Prize for Prose. As a member of Justice for Magdalenes Research (JFMR), she has shared in activist honours, including the Irish Labour Party's Thirst for Justice Award.

CONALL Ó FÁTHARTA is an award-winning former journalist who worked as a Senior News Reporter with *The Irish Examiner* newspaper for more than a decade. He currently lectures in Journalism at National University of Ireland, Galway. His work is primarily investigative in nature and focuses on Ireland's treatment of unmarried women and related practices, including forced and illegal adoption, infant trafficking, falsification of identities and records, medical and vaccine trials, infant mortality and the use of infant remains for anatomical research. He has also written extensively about Ireland's Magdalene Laundries and reported on recent advocacy campaigns, government inquiries and redress schemes.

MAEVE O'ROURKE is assistant professor of human rights at the Irish Centre for Human Rights, School of Law, NUI Galway, and a graduate of University College Dublin, Harvard Law School, and Birmingham Law School, University of Birmingham. She is also a barrister (England and Wales) and attorney-at-law (New York). She is co-author of *Ireland and the Magdalene Laundries: A Campaign for Justice* (Bloomsbury/I.B.Tauris, 2021), and recently coedited a double special issue of *Éire-Ireland* (Spring/Summer 2020) on Transitional Justice and institutional abuse in Ireland. In 2021 she was tasked by the Northern Ireland Executive with co-designing the framework for an impending State investigation into Magdalene, Mother and Baby and Workhouse Institutions, as part of a three-person independent Truth Recovery Design Panel working with survivors and relatives. Since 2009 she has provided *pro bono* legal assistance to Justice for Magdalenes Research (JFMR) and is currently co-director of the CLANN project, an evidence-gathering and advocacy collaboration between JFMR, Adoption Rights Alliance, and Hogan Lovells International, LLP. She was named UK Family Law Pro Bono Lawyer of the Year in 2013 and received the NUI Galway President's Award for Teaching Excellence in 2021.

EMER O'TOOLE is Associate Professor of Irish Performance Studies at the School of Irish Studies, Concordia University. Her current research, funded by the Fonds de Recherche de Quebec and by the Social Sciences and Humanities Research Council of Canada, examines the relationship between aesthetics and activism in contemporary Irish theatre. She is the author of the book *Girls Will Be Girls* and co-editor of the collection *Ethical Exchanges in Translation, Adaptation and Dramaturgy*. She is also a contributor to publications including *The Guardian, The Irish Times* and *The Independent*.

CAITRÍONA PALMER is the author of two best-selling books, the memoir *An Affair with My Mother: A Story of Adoption, Secrecy and Love* (Penguin, 2016) and *Climate Justice* (Bloomsbury, 2018), co-written with former president of Ireland Mary Robinson. A writer, journalist and adoptee, Palmer is a frequent commentator on national and international media on the legacy of secrecy and shame generated by Ireland's closed-adoption system. A native of Dublin, Caitríona is a graduate of University College Dublin and Boston College, where she was a Fulbright scholar.

EMILIE PINE is professor in the School of English, Drama, and Film in University College Dublin and editor of the *Irish University Review*. Pine is director of the Irish Memory Studies Network and principal investigator of the major Irish Research Council New Horizons project *Industrial Memories* (2015–19). She is the author of *The Politics of Irish Memory: Performing Remembrance in Contemporary Irish Culture* (Palgrave Macmillan, 2010), *The Memory Marketplace: Witnessing Pain in Contemporary Theatre* (Indiana University Press, 2020) and the multi award-winning *Notes to Self: Essays* (Tramp Press, 2018; Penguin, 2019).

SINÉAD RING is assistant professor of law at Maynooth University. Her publications include 'The Victim of Historical Child Sexual Abuse in the Irish Courts, 1999–2006' (*Social and Legal Studies*, 2017) and 'Due Process and the Admission of Expert Evidence on Recovered Memory in Historic Child Sexual Abuse Cases: Lessons from America' (*International Journal of Evidence and Proof*, 2012). Ring is a former Irish Research Council for the Humanities and Social Sciences Scholar. She has held visiting positions at Osgoode Hall Law School and Harvard Law School. Sinéad is currently writing a monograph, *Legal Responses to Historical Child Sexual Abuse: Critical and Comparative Perspectives* (Routledge, forthcoming), with Kate Gleeson (Macquarie University) and Kim Stevenson (University of Plymouth).

CONNIE ROBERTS, an Irish poet, teaches creative writing at Hofstra

University, New York City. Her collection *Little Witness* (Arlen House, 2015) was inspired by her experiences growing up in an industrial school in the Irish midlands. Her 14 siblings spent their childhoods in various industrial schools throughout Ireland.

RUTH RUBIO MARÍN is Professor of Constitutional Law at the University of Sevilla, Director of the Gender and Governance Programme at the School of Transnational Governance, European University Institute, Florence, and a member of the Faculty of The Hauser Global Law School Program at New York University. Her research represents an attempt to understand how public law creates categories of inclusion and exclusion around different axis including gender, citizenship, nationality and ethnicity. Professor Rubio is the author of over 40 articles and author, editor and co-editor of eight books (plus two in press). She is currently working on the book *The Disestablishment of Gender in the New Millennium Constitutionalism*. As a consultant and activist, Rubio has worked for several national and international institutions and agencies including with the UN and the EU, and has extensive in-country experience in dealing with reparations in post-conflict societies, including in Morocco, Nepal and Colombia. Her image will be included in the Legacy Wall to be installed in the new building of the International Criminal Court in The Hague to honour her lifelong commitment to gender justice.

COLIN SMITH is a barrister practicing in the field of human-rights law. He is an adjunct assistant professor in the School of Law at Trinity College Dublin and a member of the Human Rights Committee of the Bar Council of Ireland. He is a former chairperson of the Irish Society of International Law and has worked as a consultant for the United Nations, the Council of Europe, the Organization for Security and Cooperation in Europe, the International Bar Association and the International Committee of the Red Cross. Before practicing in Dublin, he worked in chambers at the Special Court for Sierra Leone in Freetown and in the War Crimes Division of the Office of the Prosecutor at the State Court of Bosnia and Herzegovina in Sarajevo. He is a graduate of Trinity College Dublin (LL.B., M.Litt.) and the Honourable Society of King's Inns.

JAMES M. SMITH is an associate professor in the English department and the Irish Studies Program at Boston College. He has published articles in *Signs*, *The Journal of the History of Sexuality*, *Éire-Ireland* and *ELH*. He is co-author of *Ireland and the Magdalene Laundries: A Campaign for Justice* (Bloomsbury/I.B. Tauris, 2021). His book, *Ireland's Magdalen Laundries and the Nation's Architecture of Containment* (Notre Dame UP), was published in 2007 and awarded the Donald Murphy Prize for Distinguished First Book by the American Conference for Irish Studies. With Maria Luddy, he co-edited a double special issue of *Éire-Ireland* (Spring/Summer 2009) and the collection *Children, Childhood and Irish Society: 1500 to the Present* (Four Courts Press, 2014). He recently co-edited a double special issue of *Éire-Ireland* (Spring/Summer 2020) on Transitional Justice and institutional abuse in Ireland. He is a member of the advocacy group JFMR.

MARI STEED was one of more than 2,000 children exported from Ireland to the United States. She was born in the Bessborough Mother and Baby Home in Cork, where she also endured being part of the vaccine trials. Mari's mother spent time in a Magdalene laundry. Mari serves as U.S. coordinator with the Adoption Rights Alliance. In 2003 Mari co-founded Justice for Magdalenes Research (JFMR), an advocacy organisation that successfully campaigned for a state apology and restorative justice for survivors of Ireland's Magdalen laundries. She currently serves on the group's executive committee. She also serves as vice-president on the executive committee of U.S. adoptee-rights organisation Bastard Nation. She is co-author of *Ireland and the Magdalene Laundries: A Campaign for Justice* (Bloomsbury/I.B. Tauris, 2021).

SHURLEE SWAIN is an Emeritus Professor at Australian Catholic University and a Fellow of the Academies of both the Humanities and the Social Sciences in Australia. She has published widely in the area of child and family welfare history in Australia and co-edited with Professor Johanna Sköld, *Apologies and the Legacy of Abuse of Children in 'Care'*, (Palgrave Macmillan, 2015). Her research has informed government inquiries into the history of sexual and physical abuse in out-of-home care, and of forced adoptions and the historical component of official post-apology responses.

CLAIR WILLS is the King Edward VII Professor of English Literature in the Faculty of English at Cambridge University. She previously taught at Queen Mary University of London, and at Princeton in the United States. She was elected an Honorary Member of the Royal Irish Academy in 2016. She writes about the social, cultural and literary history of Britain and Ireland in the twentieth century. She is particularly interested in migration in post-war Europe and the ways in which it is represented, by migrants and by others; in literature and culture in Northern Ireland; in contemporary British fiction; in feminism and women's writing; and in the history and experiences of coercive confinement in institutions (including psychiatric institutions) in Britain and Ireland in the twentieth century. She works across the disciplines of literature, history and cultural theory and is keen to explore new genres of academic writing.

Index